The Media in Your Life

An Introduction to Mass Communication

Jean Folkerts *George Washington University*

Stephen Lacy *Michigan State University*

Lucinda Davenport *Michigan State University*

Allyn and Bacon *Boston • London • Toronto • Sydney • Tokyo • Singapore*

Vice President and Editor-in-Chief: Communication and Political Science: Paul Smith
Series Editor: Karon Bowers
Developmental Editor: Allen Workman
Series Editorial Assistant: Leila Scott
Marketing Manager: Kris Farnsworth
Composition and Prepress Buyer: Linda Cox
Manufacturing Buyer: Suzanne Lareau
Cover Administrator: Linda Knowles
Photo Researcher: Laurie Frankenthaler
Production Coordinator: Deborah Brown
Editorial-Production Service: Barbara Gracia
Copyeditor: Barbara Willette
Text and Art Designer: Carol Somberg/Omegatype Typography, Inc.

Copyright © 1998 by Allyn and Bacon
A Viacom Company
160 Gould Street
Needham Heights, MA 02194

Internet: www.abacon.com
America Online: keyword: College Online

Library of Congress Cataloging-in-Publication Data
Folkerts, Jean.
     The media in your life : an introduction to mass communication /
Jean Folkerts, Stephen Lacy, Lucinda Davenport.
         p.   cm.
     Includes bibliographical references and index.
     ISBN 0-205-15414-X (pbk. : alk. paper)
     1. Mass media.   I. Lacy, Stephen, 1948–   .   II. Davenport,
Lucinda.   III. Title.
P90.F628   1998
302.23—DC21   97-31498
                                                             CIP

Printed in the United States of America
10 9 8 7 6 5 4 3 2 1 RRD 01 00 99 98 97

Photo Credits

Chapter 1: pp. xxx-1, 3, AP/Wide World Photos; p. 4, Courtesy of Sony Electronics; p. 7, Porter Gifford/Gamma Liaison; p. 11, UPI/Corbis-Bettmann; p. 12, Bernard Gotfryd/Archive Photos; p. 13, UPI/Corbis-Bettmann. *Chapter 2:* pp. 16–17, 19, Joseph Nettis/Stock, Boston; p. 19, Brian Smith; p. 23, Chris Smith/Archive Photos; pp. 24, 30, AP/Wide World Photos. p. 33, Courtesy of Cablevision Systems Corporation; p. 35, Forrest Anderson/Gamma Liaison; p. 37, Lisa Rudy Hoke/Black Star. *Chapter 3:* pp. 44–45, 47, Hollywood Pictures/Shooting Star; p. 47, North Wind Picture Archives; 49, Colonial Williamsburg Foundation; p. 50, Courtesy of the

Photo credits are continued on page iv and are considered an extension of the copyright page.

Dedication

For Leroy and Jenny Towns and Sean Lange

For Leslie, Katie, and Laurie Lacy

For Fred, Rachael, and Jason Taylor Davenport-Greene

Contents

Contents

Preface

Preface

How should we be looking at the media and media products that we see in our everyday lives? Even children know on some level that entertainment content on television and other media does not depict life in the United States in a realistic fashion. Should we consider these products as simple works of art? Popular culture entertainment? Symbolic representations of power and ideology in society? Are they reflections of media as a corporate institution? Perhaps they can be all of these.

Thinking about these questions as teachers led us to encourage our classes to observe how audiences interpret and incorporate the media into world views and lifestyles. An entertainment product, such as the 1956 film, *Invasion of the Body Snatchers,* can be used to demonstrate the potential of a movie for engaging the popular imagination. The movie is a story about an unknown and unseen force that invades people's minds while they sleep and replaces their bodies with foreign replicas (grown from 4-foot long seed pods). These replicas are emotionless members of a community with an unknown purpose. Looking for clues to the movie's power to resonate with social values of its time, one typical media analyst noted that the United States was emerging from the Korean War when *Invasion of the Body Snatchers* was filmed and claimed that the movie's powerful effect was based on its reception as an overt anti-Communist metaphor for the brainwashing experienced by GIs in Korea. The pod society represented a mechanistic utopia, a metaphor for communism.* Apart from what we may think of this interpretation, the rich range of possible responses to the movie, which was remade several times, shows students how a media event extends its role from an entertainment product to a cultural symbol.

Cultural dimensions of media consumption are highlighted in the text among four features that illustrate key social and technical influences intersecting with the media.

---

*Peter Biskind developed this interpretation in his book *Seeing Is Believing: How Hollywood Taught Us to Stop Worrying and Love the Fifties.* See the description of Biskind's claims in Michael Real, *Super Media: A Cultural Studies Approach* (Newbury Park, CA: Sage, 1989), pp. 172–173.

xxvi

What we came to consider important for students to discover is not how to spin imaginative interpretations, but to see that media products and their impact on audiences have powerful functions in society that interact with and influence the industry that generated them. Media products have social, economic, and potentially political roles that need to be examined along with their immediate role for consumer audiences and producer industries.

A book to help students interpret the media

As teachers of mass communication, we have developed a textbook that guides students on how to view and interpret media messages. This book moves students beyond the "gee-whiz" level of interpretation of the media to evaluating how the media affect each of our personal and professional lives. Organizational and pedagogical aids in the text will help students enjoy the study of media and to understand its influence and relevance day to day. We have, therefore, titled the book: *The Media in Your Life: An Introduction to Mass Communication.*

This book's scope is geared to a broader audience than many introductory texts for the mass media course. It is appropriate for both majors in journalism and mass communication programs and for nonmajors who seek a general education course that provides media literacy. With this wider audience in mind, the book can best be characterized as a liberal arts approach—consistent with the needs of nonmajors but also with accreditation standards of the Accrediting Council in Journalism and Mass Communication. While a large amount of information as to how the media work is provided for professionals, the book is extremely relevant for general communicators, not just journalists.

Chapter introductions conclude with an interactive panel feature, "The Media in Your Life," alerting readers to how their everyday media behavior relates to forthcoming issues in the chapter.

Goals for this book

As we began to see a need for a book showing the media as an economic and cultural segment of American life, we developed the goal of showing the role of media *within* the society. This emphasis enabled us to focus on important social, cultural, and economic issues that affect everyone's lives. It also enabled us to ask students to seek explanations for the way media function within society, rather than limiting them to a microscopic examination of day-to-day operations of media organizations.

Economic Impact

"Economic Impact" boxes in each chapter illustrate key economic influences intersecting with the media.

Unknown Hits the Big Time

Best-selling author Tom Clancy struck it rich on publication of his first novel, *The Hunt for Red October*. Clancy's book was first published by the obscure Naval Institute Press, but Clancy soon moved to Putnam-Berkley Group, Inc. and increased sales with each successive book. Altogether, Putnam-Berkley has shipped more than 31 million copies of his books.

The success of Clancy's book indicated a demand structure that supported the successful development of not only one novel, but of a series of "technological thrillers" in the context of real-life political events. Clancy's work was in demand by larger publishers because they recognized that his work would support a more mainstream "product line" than Clancy had originally imagined.

Clancy wrote *The Hunt for Red October* on an IBM Selectric typewriter in his office during the afternoons and at home on the weekends. When it was finished, he told his wife, Wanda, to lock herself in the bedroom and read the book while he watched the kids. She read it reluctantly, fearing it would be terrible and she'd have to tell him so. "I thought he was crazy when he started writing the book," Wanda told a reporter for the *Saturday*

Evening Post. But once Wanda had read the book, she changed her mind, predicting that it would sell for more than 5,000 copies Clancy hoped for. She anticipated the demand. In 1984, when Clancy was earning $100,000 from his insurance business, *The Hunt for Red October* hit the bookstores, and Clancy's income jumped to a reported $15 million, representing an economic boon to the author and to his publisher.

He received an eight-figure advance for his 1992 thriller, *The Sum of All Fears.* By 1994, the 47-year-old writer was living with his wife and four children in a 16,000 square foot mansion on an estate that used to be a boys' camp. Clancy keeps hitting the big time. After *The Hunt for Red October* came other technological thrillers: *Patriot Games, Red Storm Rising, The Cardinal of the Kremlin, Clear and Present Danger, The Sum of All Fears,* and *Without Remorse.*

The Clancys' lives changed quickly. Invitations arrived daily, including one to dinner at the White House with President Reagan. Clancy's daughter Michele says that some people expect her to be a snob

just because her parents have money. Clancy says it was easier to keep his new-found wealth and popularity in perspective, however, because he was in his thirties before it arrived. But fame did have an impact, and in April 1995, Clancy and his wife separated. By the end of the year, however, they had reunited. Despite some of the complications of a wealthy and more leisurely life, however, nobody in Clancy's family wishes he were still selling insurance.

Clancy continues to turn out novels, CD-ROMs, and recently did a stint as a space reporter. His versatility earns him about $16 million a year.

SOURCES: Dick Victory, "Clancy's Game: How Tom Clancy has Turned the Art of Revenge Into Earning of $16 million a Year," January 1997, *Washingtonian,* p. 49; Tom Reeves, "Corporate America's Most Powerful People," *Forbes,* May 25, 1992, p. 160; and November 9, 1992; *Publisher Weekly,* August 10, 1992, p. 9; and Christopher Phillips, "Red October's Tom Clancy: After the Hunt," *Saturday Evening Post,* September 1991, p. 16.

every passing year. In fact, the total volume of sales increased from $435 million in 1947 to more than $25 billion in 1995. Although only about 10,000 titles were sold annually in the mid-1950s, by the early 1990s, about 50,000 titles were sold each year. Table 4.1 shows the increase in number of titles from 1993 to 1994, broken down by field.

Paperbacks are a significant staple in the book business. In 1995, in an average 24-hour period, 27 percent of Americans aged 30 to 59 reported having read a paperback book, up from 17 percent in 1987. The numbers in younger and older age groups

88

xxvii

We especially believe students will benefit from a text that examines the professional and cultural aspects of media within an economic framework. Only when the media assume their true place as an institution that interacts systematically in the functioning of other institutions, such as churches and schools, can the media be studied. We find that students need a systemwide view of where the media functions on a day-to-day basis rather than a projection of the media's social negative effects.

The commerce of media is discussed, therefore, from the assumption that collectively media organizations form an institution that rank with government and religion in impact on American society. Because of this power, we think the U.S. media system should be understood for what it is—a collection of primarily commercial organizations that affect people and society in both positive and negative ways. A key part of this understanding is a neutral discussion of how the media operate within the U.S. economic system and its member organizations.

Seeing the media as a coherent story

We believe that understanding the media in contemporary society is based on an understanding of the history of media, which means seeing key segments of the media as stories that make sense. Each chapter in this book is built upon a section that outlines the story of a topic or media channel within American society. Too often the economic, political, social, and cultural strands of the media have been seen as individual threads in a tapestry to be examined individually or in small sections. But seeing the full effect of the media tapestry requires that one view all the threads as a whole picture, presented as a coherent story over time. Because many schools no longer require a separate media history course, this complete picture may be unavailable, even to media majors.

History sections conclude with a graphic continuum "Dateline" showing major media events across time so that students can relate events and sequences in the media story with familiar historic events.

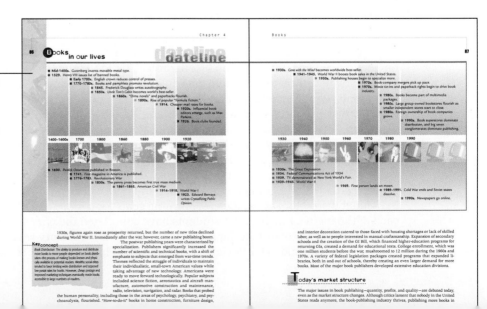

Chapter 4 Books

86

Books in our lives

dateline

87

- Mid-1400s. Gutenberg invents movable metal type.
- 1529. Henry VIII issues list of banned books.
- Early 1700s. English crown reduces control of presses.
- 1770–1790s. Books and pamphlets promote revolution.
- 1845. Frederick Douglass writes autobiography.
- 1850s. *Uncle Tom's Cabin* becomes world's best-seller.
- 1860s. "Dime novels" and paperbacks flourish.
- 1890s. Rise of popular "formula fiction."
- 1914. Cheaper mail rates for books.
- 1920s. Book clubs founded.

- 1930s. *Gone with the Wind* becomes worldwide best-seller.
- 1941–1945. World War II boosts book sales in the United States.
- 1950s. Publishing houses begin to specialize more.
- 1970s. Book-company mergers pick up pace.
- 1970s. Movie tie-ins and paperback rights begin to drive book industry.
- 1980s. Books become part of multimedia packages.
- 1980s. Large group-owned bookstores flourish as smaller independent stores start to close.
- 1980s. Foreign ownership of book companies grows.
- 1990s. Book superstores dominate distribution, and big seven conglomerates dominate publishing.

| 1400-1600s | 1700 | 1800 | 1860 | 1880 | 1900 | 1920 |

| 1930 | 1940 | 1950 | 1960 | 1970 | 1980 | 1990 |

- 1690. *Publick Occurrences* published in Boston.
- 1741. First magazine in America is published.
- 1776–1783. Revolutionary War
- 1830s. The penny press becomes first true mass medium.
- 1861–1865. American Civil War
- 1914–1918. World War I
- 1923. Edward Bernays writes *Crystallizing Public Opinion.*

- 1930s. The Great Depression
- 1934. Federal Communications Act of 1934
- 1939. TV demonstrated at New York World's Fair.
- 1939–1945. World War II
- 1969. First person lands on moon.
- 1989–1991. Cold War ends and Soviet states dissolve.
- 1990s. Newspapers go online.

1930s, figures again rose as prosperity returned, but the number of new titles declined during World War II. Immediately after the war, however, came a new publishing boom.

Key concept

Book Distribution: The ability to produce and distribute more books to more people depended on book distribution—the process of making books known and physically available to potential readers. Wealthy social elites tended to favor limiting wide distribution and opposed low postal rates for books. However, cheap postage and improved marketing techniques eventually made books accessible to large numbers of readers.

The postwar publishing years were characterized by specialization. Publishers significantly increased the number of scientific and technical books, with a shift of emphasis to subjects that emerged from war-time trends. Themes reflected the struggle of individuals to maintain their individualistic, small-town American values while taking advantage of new technology. Americans were ready to move forward technologically. Popular subjects included science fiction, aeronautics and aircraft manufacture, automotive construction and maintenance, radio, television, navigation, and radar. Books that probed the human personality, including those in the areas of psychology, psychiatry, and psychoanalysis, flourished. "How-to-do-it" books in home construction, furniture design,

and interior decoration catered to those faced with housing shortages or lack of skilled labor, as well as to people interested in manual craftsmanship. Expansion of secondary schools and the creation of the GI Bill, which financed higher-education programs for returning GIs, created a demand for educational texts. College enrollment, which was one million students before the war, mushroomed to 12 million during the 1960s and 1970s. A variety of federal legislation packages created programs that expanded libraries, both in and out of schools, thereby creating an even larger demand for more books. Most of the major book publishers developed extensive education divisions.

Today's market structure

The major issues in book publishing—quantity, profits, and quality—are debated today, even as the market structure changes. Although critics lament that nobody in the United States reads anymore, the book-publishing industry thrives, publishing more books in

This book is unique in offering its chapters as complete stories of how a part of the media evolved, what its issues and elements are, and where it seems to be headed.

As part of the ongoing story of media within society, the development of technology is woven into this book to a greater degree than most current texts. In particular, we stress the concept of "Converging Technologies" to highlight important overlaps and blending in media functions as technological changes create new combinations from the traditional channels. Because media technology and the technology industries are constantly changing, we have stressed the effects of evolving technology as part of the media's social, economic, and cultural roles.

The plan of this book

The book is organized for clarity and understanding. Chapters 1–3 are introductory, focusing on media in contemporary society, the elements of the communication process, and the history of mass communication. Chapters 4–11 address individual media: books, newspapers, magazines, movies, radio, television, music, and computers. Chapters 12–16 address issues and related industries: regulation, ethics, public relations, advertising, and research. Because the material for an introduction to mass communication course is vast and can be organized in various ways, individual instructors wishing to customize their presentation will have no difficulty assigning the chapters in a different order. Two additional chapters are also available as part of the supplement program. A chapter on "Visual Communication" is available on this book's Web site (www.abacon.com/folkerts) as a possible download assignment for students, and another chapter on "Power and Ideology" is available for handout as a copy master within the *Instructor's Resource Manual.*

Starting with Chapter 4, each chapter has a similar organization. An introductory vignette leads into a feature titled "Media in Your Life," to help readers become aware of the chapter's ongoing issues that are summarized at the end of the introduction. Each chapter begins with an historical narrative related to its media topic that includes discussions of media impact on American life. The chapter moves on to "Today's Market Structure," thoroughly describing economic and institutional processes that affect each segment of the media, including production. It concludes with a section on "Trends and Innovations" that is strongly focused on new technology.

Guidance for learning
important ideas, concepts and terms

The Media in Your Life's unique learning system is centered on the "Key Concepts" announced at the opening of each chapter. These reappear as definitive statements in chapter sections where they play the leading role. The ideas encapsulated under these "Key Concepts" are central to the media topic in each chapter and are highlighted as guideposts to students when reviewing main ideas. These "Key Concepts," along with the recurring issues posed in the chapter introduction, are designed to help students focus on main ideas and terms to make sense of the media story and follow the thread of each chapter. In addition to these learning guides, distinctive *media terms* within the chapter text are boldface and featured with glossary definitions in marginal panels alongside the text. While these media terms function to ensure that students absorb the unique terminology of the media without confusing their grasp of larger concepts, they can also be used by individual instructors as the focus of learning goals for a more technical understanding of each of the media. Finally, after students have completed the chapter and are ready to review, they will discover that the issues listed in the introductory section have been crystallized with "Questions for Review," and "Issues to Think About" at the end of the chapter.

The ideas encapsulated under the "Key Concept" are central to the story of the media topic in each chapter and are highlighted as guideposts to students when reviewing main ideas and following the thread of the chapter. In addition, media terms are bolded and defined on the page.

Special features to focus interest and learning

A number of special feature pieces are introduced within the text at appropriate intervals to highlight key ideas and serve as a focus of special instructional units.

THE MEDIA IN YOUR LIFE The introductory section of each chapter concludes with an interactive panel feature, "The Media in Your Life," alerting readers to how their everyday media behavior relates to forthcoming issues in the chapter. This feature is not a quiz or learning check, but a chance for readers to take note of their media awareness and become alert to issues in the chapter that will intersect with their own media behavior.

"Profiles" of typical and influential players in each media area are highlighted and are linked to the Allyn & Bacon Interactive Video Program, to the Video User's Guide and to the Web site for this text.

DATELINES A graphic continuum "Dateline" spreads out major media events across time, helping students to relate events and sequences in the media story with historic events that may be familiar to them.

PROFILES A prominent figure is highlighted with a special portrait in each media to focus attention on key roles played by typical and influential players. This feature provides a miniature "case study" of a career that can be analyzed in assignments, especially as supplemented by the *Allyn & Bacon Interactive Video Program*—a series of *video modules* designed for classroom presentation and for critical thinking projects focused on key media personalities. The video modules are linked to critical thinking questions that can be presented to students via handouts from copymasters in the *Video User's Guide* and from the Web site that accompanies *The Media in Your Life* (www.abacon.com/folkerts).

IMPACT FEATURES Four kinds of special-feature boxes present stories throughout the chapters to illustrate key social and technical influences that intersect with the media. To focus attention on key concepts and themes, the text includes these boxes: "Cultural Impact," "Economic Impact," "Converging Technologies" (stressing the continuing overlaps and blending of media functions as technologies develop), and "Global Impact" (calling attention to international influences in key areas) throughout respective media chapters.

GRAPHIC CHARTS, DIAGRAMS, AND PHOTOS An array of graphic material runs alongside the text in each chapter to provide supplementary data, useful charts illustrating key ideas, and historical and current photos that provide visual examples of text concepts.

NAVIGATING THE WEB Each chapter has a special section offering two sets of Web sites that pertain to the material in the chapter. Chapter 4, for example, includes sites that illustrate how books are offered or promoted on the Web, and sites that contain material and data about the book industry. The second set of addresses can be consulted for special projects, collaborative discussions, or term papers.

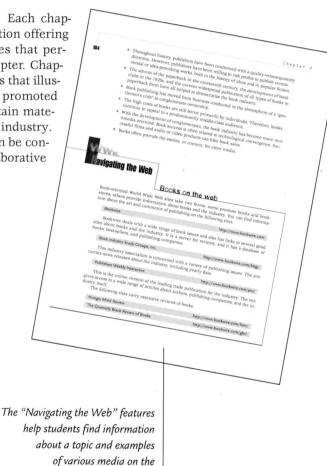

The "Navigating the Web" features help students find information about a topic and examples of various media on the World Wide Web.

"Converging Technologies" and "Global Impact" boxes in each chapter stress the continuing overlap and blending of media functions and call attention to international influences on media.

Supplements for the Instructor and Student

INSTRUCTOR'S RESOURCE MANUAL This manual provides outlines, questions, teaching suggestions, copy masters, and a supplementary chapter on "Power and Ideology" along with material for classroom assignments linked to the video modules in the *Allyn & Bacon Interactive Video Program*.

TEST BANK AND PRACTICE TESTS   The *Test Bank*—over 1000 true/false, multiple-choice, short-answer, and essay questions—is available both in print and computerized formats for instructors only. *Practice Tests* for students, consisting of approximately 15 questions per chapter, are offered to help students gain mastery of chapter material.

THE ALLYN & BACON INTERACTIVE VIDEO PROGRAM   Video modules based on the key media players featured in the text's "Profiles," provide a live "case study" of a media career. Modules are linked to critical thinking questions that can be presented to students via handouts from the *Video User's Guide* and from the Web site accompanying this text.

VIDEO USER'S GUIDE   This separate guide provides instructors with additional information about working with the video modules for use in critical thinking investigations and special class or collaborative projects.

THE MEDIA IN YOUR LIFE WEBSITE   A state of the art Web site is available for students and instructors (www.abacon.com/folkerts) to access in connection with work in this text. It provides an online study guide, links to critical thinking exercises and the video modules, a special survey section linked to "The Media in Your Life" features in the text, Internet-linked versions of the "Dateline" charts, and new "Profiles" features in addition to those in the text.

COLLEGE NEWSLINK   A special subscription rate to College Newslink is available to adopters and students using *The Media in Your Life*. College Newslink (www.ssnewslink.com) is a media-oriented channel that provides news articles, periodical subscriptions, and other media industry data via e-mail and newsgroups.

POWERPOINT PRESENTATION PACKAGE   Slide material combining graphic and text images are offered to instructors in modular units to accompany each chapter. Software is compatible with all platforms, and a PowerPoint viewer is included to access and produce the images on the instructor's local equipment.

THE A&B QUICK GUIDE TO THE INTERNET FOR MASS COMMUNICATION, 1998   This handy reference book acquaints users with efficient ways to use all Web search and communication resources. This guide including the free *Sprint Internet Passport* CD-ROM is available packaged with the text for free. See inside the front cover of the text for ordering information.

THE A&B MASS COMMUNICATION VIDEO LIBRARY AND THE *MOVIE LIBRARY*   Adopters of this text have access to two rich libraries: (1) a set of videos about the media created through Insight Media and Films for the Humanities, and (2) the *Movie Library* featuring ten popular entertainment movies, each related to one of the media (for example, *Radio Days, Network,* etc.). Conditions for adopters' access to these libraries can be obtained by contacting your Allyn & Bacon representative.

MESSAGES 4: THE WASHINGTON POST MEDIA COMPANION   Prepared from columns of the *Washington Post,* these articles on the media can be used concurrently with the text. This collection of articles is available separately for student purchase.

Acknowledgments

This text has evolved over time and through experience in teaching at two major mass media programs at George Washington University and at Michigan State University. We wish to thank our colleagues at these schools who have encouraged us to shape an introductory course in the direction that this book has taken. In particular, we thank Leslie Lacy and Leroy Towns, Barb Miller and DeeDee Johnson of the Michigan State University staff, and Maria George, executive aide in the School of Media and Public Affairs at The George Washington University. We would also like to thank Dwight Teeter, whose advice across the years has been thoughtful and sustaining and whose great joy in being an administrator has been invaluable in helping others along their way. At Allyn and Bacon, many editors and marketing people have helped bring this book to a level that best expresses our approach to the course. In particular, Allen Workman, the developmental editor, motivated us to complete the project and systematically helped conceptualize the pedagogical elements of the text. Barbara Gracia, as gracious as her name indicates, kept us going through the final integration of text, photos, and pedagogical materials.

As we wrote and reworked these chapters, a number of our colleagues have provided helpful manuscript reviews at each stage of development. We hope they feel the book has benefited from their comments and advice. We wish to thank Edward Adams, Angelo State University; Tom Buckner, McClennan Community College; Thomas Draper, University of Nebraska, Kearney; Jack Keever, Evelyn Plummer, Seton Hall University; Marshel Rossow, Mankato State University; Roger Soenksen, James Madison University; Ardyth Sohn, Butler University; Hazel Warlaumont, California State University, Fullerton; and Sandra Wertz, The University of South Carolina.

The Media in Your Life

An Introduction to Mass Communication

We the People and the Mass Media

"Thank you, MTV!" gloated Al Gore, in front of 4,000 of America's most connected at MTV's Inaugural ball in January [1993]. "Thank you for winning this election. You did it."

Even during that week of inflated rhetoric, Gore's 30-second MTV love-in wasn't much of an exaggeration. After all, hadn't MTV's election specials inspired America's jaded youth to unplug their Sony Discmans long enough to tune into campaign '92? Hadn't the music station's funky get-out-the-vote drive prompted nearly a million young voters to register and thousands to volunteer for the campaigns? Hadn't MTV helped make politics hip again? Of course it had. Indeed, the new vice president—in fact, all of America—had much to be thankful for.

—Christopher Georges, *The Washington Monthly*

Politicians must be masters of media in modern election campaigns. In 1996, Bob Dole greeted microphones and cameras from traditional network news correspondents, as well as from the X-Generation's MTV political commentators.

MTV, Phil Donahue's TV show, town hall–style television debates, a saxophone debut—all of those were part of the makings of the 1992 presidential campaign when Bill Clinton triumphed over his predecessor, George Bush, who was from an older generation and a more conservative political party. Popular culture had come to politics. Traditional politics hit the musical stage; news blended with entertainment; technologies blurred. By 1996, however, even the older generation and the more conservative political party had jumped on the bandwagon: The senior senator from Kansas, Robert Dole, was on the MTV stage, and the mainstream press covered his appearance on the youth-oriented music cable channel.

But the writer who commented on the 1992 election for *The Washington Monthly* wasn't convinced that MTV politics was all to the good. Christopher Georges argued that the viewers

1

of MTV—two million weekly—had been shown by mass communication research to be "politically malleable and detached from news sources other than those on TV." He argued that MTV was boldly slanted to the left and that it had "become such a political bigfoot among politicians that President Clinton held his first national interview not with Ted Koppel or Tom Brokaw but with MTV's Tabitha Soren."[1]

In the 1996 presidential campaign, however, Tabitha Soren interviewed Bob Dole and told an Associated Press reporter that 1996 differed from 1992 in that "we don't have to explain why we're there. That'll allow me to redirect a lot of my energy into reporting."[2] Bob Dole learned a lesson from George Bush, who had said that because he wasn't a "teeny-bopper" he had no business on MTV.

Although the power of media has long been recognized, the 1992 and 1996 presidential campaigns dramatized the new forms of media technology and programming. Technologies are converging. Now, for example, telephone lines are being wired to computers and television, thus offering new order-on-demand programming. Traditional forms of news gathering and news coverage not only come under attack but require continued justification in a profit-driven media industry. Will the old forms survive? More importantly, will journalistic values be carried on even if the old media forms change or die? Are the new forms capable of providing the kinds of information necessary to a democratic, participatory society? Are the viewers of MTV, in fact, "politically malleable" and uninformed? Are they only plugged into the Discman? Or are they simply seeking relevant, current information through new technologies and new formats?

Angela Lauria, a student at George Washington University, regularly communicates with her professors, her high school friend Jenny Towns, and a variety of *user groups* through the university's GWIS program, which allows her access to the Internet. Students at Indiana University and other colleges across the country carry on a dialogue with their professors and classmates through electronic mail (e-mail). No longer does access to a professor have to be limited to two class periods a week and a few office hours. Messages can be sent, received, and answered in a matter of minutes. Angela and Jenny can "talk" to each other or play games via the Internet if both of them have their computers turned on. They are on the information highway.

Students are heavy consumers of mass media. They listen to the radio an average of six hours a day, they read textbooks and novels, and they watch television (TV sets are turned on in the average household in the United States for seven and a half hours each day). Many spend hours on the Internet in chat groups or use various forms of e-mail. They also read newspapers and magazines. Music, tell-all talk shows, soap operas, situation comedies, and *infotainment shows* are popular. Some critics argue that this generation spends so much time with entertainment media that they have become a dumbed-down generation. Are the critics correct? Or do high school and college students simply consume media content in a different way than their parents or professors did?

Media in American society are an institution, just as education, religion, and government are institutions. That means that the issues, which include technology, regulation, and content, are complex and cross social, political, and economic boundaries. They also cross geographical boundaries; they are international. The questions below speak to some of the most critical issues:

■ How will the convergence of technology and the introduction of new forms of communication affect daily life?

■ How will mass media, traditionally supported through advertising, react economically to new technologies and new forms of communication?

■ What are the implications of changing media for a democratic society?

■ How do media affect cultural and social change?

■ What are the implications for a new internationalism based on information?

Media in your life

Background Noise and Information

Many students love to listen to the radio. They watch television as well, and they listen to CDs. They use other kinds of media, such as textbooks, but students don't often think of books as being part of their "media mix." What about you? As you read this introductory chapter and the chapters that follow, think about how you use media, when and why, and how often. But also look for information in this book about how media content is constructed. Think about its social and political meaning and its relationship to government. And don't forget to wonder a bit about new forms of media you'd like to encounter.

MEDIA FORM	HOURS PER DAY	TYPE OF USE (INFORMATION, KNOWLEDGE, RELAXATION, ETC.)	NEVER USE
Cable			
Computer information services			
Magazines			
Movies			
Newspapers			
Popular books (excluding textbooks)			
Radio			
Recording industry products			
Television			
Textbooks			

Technology: New and convergent

Technological change has been an enduring factor in the evolution of mass media. Improvements in typesetting and in printing presses changed the nature and form of newspapers. Radio was the result of discovering how technology could be put to use in new ways. At first, it was conceived of as communication from point-to-point or from person-to-person and was used in ship-to-shore messages. Later, it was used to address mass audiences and to broadcast advertising, entertainment, and information. Television added pictures and became one of the technological wonders of the twentieth century.

Today, old media are using new technologies. In the 1990s, one of the first major battles in a new wave of competition among media technologies was the struggle between newspapers and direct providers over delivery of **online information services.** Such strug-

> **online information services:** Companies that provide searchable databases via telephone line and modems for a fee.

3

4

gles over technology do not represent a new phenomenon. During the 1930s, newspapers and radio broadcasters fought over whether radio would have access to information provided by the wire services, such as the Associated Press. In the 1990s, many industry analysts viewed the struggle over control of technology as a mere battle over profit, but the editors of the *Media Studies Journal* wrote that "the more important issues over the long haul have to do with access to information, the quality of news and entertainment, the diversity of media in the marketplace and, most important, freedom of expression itself."[3]

Keyconcept

Technological Convergence: Continual development in media technology causes the forms and functions of the mass media to keep shifting. Technical changes not only create new forms, but also cause formerly distinct media forms such as newspapers to blend or overlap functions with newer media, as has occurred with news on television or the Internet. This process is called *merging* or *converging.*

What does *technological convergence* mean? It means "to blend technologies to deliver a message." And although the word *convergence* is defined as "coming together," convergence doesn't necessarily mean reducing choice. In fact, blending technologies probably will increase the number and types of methods through which individuals can acquire information. Media convergence is already here. For example, newspapers regularly offer a variety of telephone services, including high school sports scores and stock quotations: But media convergence is expected to increase. Consumers will soon have access to a variety of printed publications and audiovisual recordings through their television sets. As computer technology and the television industry become more integrated, we will be able to view and search sophisticated databases for everything from encyclopedia information to movies. Then instead of waiting for a particular movie to be broadcast or traveling to a video store for a tape from a relatively limited selection, the home user—you—will order the movie you want to see when you want to see it.

By 1996, the evolution of technology had created conditions that required major policy changes, for the first time in sixty years. The Telecommunications Act of 1996 (see Chapter 12) changed existing media ownership rules, deregulated cable television, outlawed transmission of sexually explicit material to minors, and required television makers to install a computer chip in new TV sets that allows people to block shows that are electronically labeled for violence and other content.[4]

Traditional media are experimenting with new technologies and new combinations of old technologies. For example, in 1993, the ChicagoLand Television regional cable news channel went on the air. The station operated from a TV ministudio inside the *Chicago Tribune*'s fourth-floor newsroom. In the suburb of Oak Brook, the ChicagoLand TV studios share space with the suburban news bureau. But convergence for the Tribune Company didn't stop with blending television and newspaper technologies. In the same year, the company spent nearly $200 million to buy into the **CD-ROM** business and to purchase two educational publishing companies. It also bought a stake in

Converging technologies provide audiences with access to content through different media. Therefore, newspaper content may be read on line, or a television crew may shoot a story to produce for television or for computer delivery.

CD-ROM:
Compact diskette with read only memory. An electronic storage diskette with enough memory to support multi-media applications.

Economic Impact

I n late 1996, America Online (AOL) was the biggest online service of them all, with 1,500 employees in its main office and six million subscribers. But what was happening at AOL showed that new information technologies faced old issues of determining content, recruiting subscribers, earning a profit, and keeping up with the times. AOL was losing subscribers as fast as it was signing up new ones.

America Online was a trendsetter in the early 1990s, with splashy screen graphics, more speed than its primary competitor, **Prodigy,** and access to services such as encyclopedias that were useful to families. By 1996, however, a number of relatively inexpensive **direct Internet providers** offered fixed monthly prices for access to the Internet for unlimited amounts of time. For those who wanted to spend their evenings playing on the Internet, AOL was an expensive service. AOL subscribers

Technological Convergence: Old Issues in New Form

were paying monthly fees of $9.95 for five hours of use or $19.95 for 20 hours, plus $2.95 for each additional hour. Because direct Internet providers charge about $20 a month, AOL would be hard pressed to raise its prices.

So AOL made a decision to rely more heavily on advertising instead of subscription fees and went to a fixed price system. When they did, their phone lines were flooded with calls. Consequently, customers quickly became frustrated because they couldn't get through the busy signals. Ultimately, attorneys general from 36 states threatened to sue the company for deceptive business practices. America Online reached a settlement with the attorneys, offered some customers refunds, and agreed to quit promoting the service until they could install ad-

equate technology to serve existing customers.

AOL does have some advantages over direct providers. It categorizes material, making it more accessible to people who are not familiar with the technology. Also, its services, such as e-mail, are simple to understand and use and provide almost flawless transfer of documents from one subscriber to another.

The AOL dilemma exemplifies many of the issues that confront those who try to master the new technologies. These are issues of economics, consumer need or desire, content, and delivery.

SOURCE: Steve Lohr, "On Line Service Adds Modems and Posts Quarterly Loss," *New York Times Online,* AOL, February 14, 1997.

America Online (AOL), the country's largest online service provider. The Tribune Company created Chicago Online as an extension of America Online, giving subscribers access to *Chicago Tribune* classifieds and stories, as well as allowing them to shop online. Thus the Tribune Company offers information through old media, newspapers and television, but it also has invested in new media for those who have become computer users.

The Tribune Company's chief executive officer, Charles Brumback, argued that the strategy was to "develop content for our important local markets. We will provide information and entertainment as digitized text, graphics, images, audio and video. We will deliver that content in any manner desired by the consumer—print, broadcast, coaxial (cable used for cable television transmission), fiber (optic) or telephone. Our many initiatives will enable us to give consumers the opportunity to drill down deep to get what they want, when they want it."[5]

Prodigy: An online information service.

direct Internet provider: A company that provides access to the Internet.

America Online (AOL): The online information service with the most subscribers in 1997.

6

Although old media, such as newspapers, are benefiting from new technology, new technologies also create forms of information exchange that were not possible with the old styles of production and distribution. Sophisticated computer users realized early on that they might be able to communicate with others via the computer. In the late 1960s, the U.S. government connected four computers in Utah and California, using what was then a new network technology called **packet switching.** The goal was to develop the framework for an emergency communication system by sending information from computers across special high-speed telephone lines. After the mid-1970s, smaller networks such as that used by the National Science Foundation (NSFnet) decided to work together—to internetwork. Today the **Internet** links thousands of academic, governmental, and commercial sites. It is the Internet that allows Jenny and Angela to talk to each other, that allows students to communicate with professors, and that allows researchers worldwide to exchange ideas. No one owns the Internet. Rather, it is a loose collection of computer networks whose users pass along information and share files.[6] Costs are shared rather informally by a variety of institutions.

Keyconcept

Media Regulation: Governments enforce rules and regulations to promote social stability and mediate social conflicts. Because the media and the public "space" they occupy can affect many members of society, the government has always had a special concern with regulation of the media.

Because students often have greater access to computers than most people do, the development of online services meant great change for them. In May 1994, the *New York Times* signaled the change with a headline, "I wonder what's on the PC tonight."[7] *Times* writer John Markoff predicted that the personal computer would surpass television in interactive capability, a dynamic that students find intriguing. Although some companies argue that television will win over computers because everyone already has a TV set, Markoff wrote, "Sounds like the argument buggy makers made after the Model T was introduced 85 years ago."

Integration of television and computers is on its way. One of the major information companies, Viacom, is developing multimedia games and educational programs that blend CD-ROM interactivity with Nickelodeon or MTV-style programming. In mid-1994, the Intel Corporation introduced a **modem** that hooks a personal computer to cable television lines, allowing users to receive information more than 2,000 times as fast as they can through a conventional modem. Online services also were experimenting with local cable lines. The hookup to cable provides sound and video, as well as text, to computer aficionados. In 1996, *USA Today* and ViewCall, a subsidiary of Colorocs Information Technologies, Inc., joined to provide On-TV, which allows users to read the newspaper on the World Wide Web on television. On-TV is being designed as a subscription-based Internet-access service targeting people who do not have personal computers. Internet access, original content, **chat groups,** and **e-mail** are all being designed for television.

Computer technology also has many implications for university and public libraries. Many universities have reallocated their budget dollars and are spending more on CD-ROM and online services than on printed journals and books. Although the change to electronic services offends some book devotees, it also allows professors and students to access information from their home or university office.

packet switching: Small envelopes, or packets, of information are sent along the Internet. This allows the Internet to send information without actually establishing an extended connection between two computers.

Internet: A linkage of thousands of academic, government, and commercial computer sites created when the U.S. government saw the need for an emergency communication system. Computers are tied together through special high-speed telephone lines.

modem: A device that allows a computer to receive data over telephone lines or cable.

chat groups: People who discuss a specific topic using computers for two-way communication at a specific time.

electronic mail (e-mail): Written communication sent via computer to one or more people. Receivers of mail read it at their leisure.

Economics: Who will pay the piper? And who will the piper be?

Who builds the **information highway** is an economic as well as a political question. Development of new technology requires massive **capital investments** and new regulations to govern new competing systems. Among those most likely to dominate the information highway during the next decade are the seven telephone companies created by a court-ordered breakup of the massive American Telephone & Telegraph (AT&T) apparatus in the mid-1980s. During the next decade, those companies added more high-speed, high-capacity, **fiber-optic cable,** and **digital switching systems.** The telephone companies had an edge over cable. They already had elaborate billing and customer-service systems. Bell Atlantic Corporation, a Philadelphia-based telephone company, planned to invest $11 billion between 1994 and 1998 to upgrade its network; Pacific Telesis Group targeted $16 billion to bring video to five million homes; and Time Warner, Inc., planned to spend $5 billion building a network with Silicon Graphics, Inc.

New media opportunities sometimes result from once-competing forces being formed into new partnerships. The results may bring more media products to consumers, but they also concentrate media resources and may limit the viewpoints expressed in the public arena.

But most analysts believe that the information highway will open immense markets. John Sculley, former Apple Computer Company chief executive, predicted in 1993 that the information highway could become a $3 trillion market by the end of the 1990s.[8]

Whenever a media system is reliant on huge infusions of capital, critics begin to worry about the implications of economic control. Even as new technologies can create new choices for consumers, mergers among companies can constrict who produces content for distribution. Ben Bagdikian, former journalism school dean and *Washington Post* editor, noted in his 1983 book, *The Media Monopoly,* that about fifty corporations controlled the major media in the United States. In a 1993 revision of that book, Bagdikian noted that fewer than twenty corporations had majority control of the newspaper, magazine, book, TV, and movie industries.[9] Some journalists argue that economic control doesn't matter, that reporters and editors make independent decisions that are unrelated to ownership. Nevertheless, when CBS fired 200 employees in a single day in 1987 as part of a $30-million reduction of the news budget, that action had a significant impact on how news was gathered and produced at CBS. That type of **allocative control,** or the allocation of resources,

Key concept

Economic Concentration in the Media: Whenever a few suppliers dominate a large supply of anything, including access to media information, those suppliers can control its price as well as its form, content, and means of delivery. As corporations strive to control larger and larger portions of a particular media market, their concentrated economic power allows them to dominate its messages.

information highway: The international network of cables and computers that support electronic communication through computers.

capital investment: Start-up money. Funds spent for acquisition or improvement of equipment of technology.

fiber optic cable system: A cable company that uses fiber optic cable to transmit programs. Fiber optic cable uses glass fibers and light to carry electronic information.

digital switching system: System that is computer operated and based on quantities represented electronically as digits.

allocative control: Control over how money is spent by an organization.

can sometimes be more significant than the operational control exercised by reporters and editors.

With the development of a high-technology information system, the concern about domination and control increases because of the expense and technological expertise required to enter the information system. Some speculate that fewer individuals will be in positions to control what information gets sent onto the new highway and who will have access to it.

Economic concentration also still characterizes the traditional media, including major newspaper and magazine markets. The top 15 percent of consumer magazines accounts for about two-thirds of all magazine circulation. However, in the mid-1990s, cable channels were rapidly gaining on the four established television networks.

Prices for traditional broadcast television stations slumped during the late 1980s and early 1990s, but in 1994, the price of stations rose significantly. The resurgence in the broadcast television market further indicates that traditional forms of mass media are here to stay, but it does not mean the end of change. One of the reasons for the price increase in the mid-1990s was the opportunity for independent stations to join new networks. During the early 1990s, Fox garnered a number of stations; by 1994, the Tribune Company was also enticing independent stations.[10] Mass and specialized media are big business, and nearly every entity is part of a larger corporation or **conglomerate.**

Keyconcept

Advertising in the Media: To finance their operations, the mass media in the United States depend heavily on the selling of advertising space or time (and hence an audience) to businesses or organizations. This may allow advertisers to shape the content of the media. However, this system also gives consumers access to information at little or no direct cost.

Will mass media continue to rely as heavily as in the past on advertising as their major source of economic support? Media analysts predict that individual pricing will accompany many of the new services. The possibility of shifting additional costs to the consumer and fewer to the advertiser has implications for who will have access to information—and who will be active participants in the society. If individual consumers have to pay for their own information, then only the wealthy and those who are connected to information through institutions such as law firms, universities, and corporate headquarters will have access. In a society that has experienced significant **corporate downsizing** and an increase in **contracted services,** the issue of institutional support is critical. The question of access raises serious questions in the United States; it becomes even more significant when considered as a global issue.

A political revolution

What are the implications of new technologies for politics? Media and political critics grow increasingly concerned about the reliance on popular-culture television for political news. The emergence of new media in the 1992 and 1996 presidential campaigns included new formats as well as new technologies. In 1992, President Clinton appeared on the *Arsenio Hall Show* and on *Donahue,* in addition to responding to journalists on traditional political shows such as *Meet the Press* and the *MacNeil-Lehrer News Hour.* He played his saxophone, trying to establish a link with the ordinary folk. He participated in a new style of debate in Richmond, Virginia, responding to questions from the audience rather than to questions from journalists. By 1996,

conglomerate: A collection of different types of business under one ownership. The term usually means a media company is owned by a corporation with non-media businesses.

corporate downsizing: A term popularized during the 1990s, used when a company laid off employees to lower their business costs.

contracted services: These occur when an organization hires someone outside the organization to perform services instead of putting an employee on the payroll.

this type of media behavior did not seem unusual. However, scholars worry that the emphasis on television image will detract from **issue candidacies.**

Michael Kelly, in a *New York Times Magazine* article, argued that "the conversation of politics now is carried on in the vernacular of advertising. The big sell, the television sell, appears to be the only way to sell. Increasingly, and especially in Washington, how well one does on television has come to determine how well one does in life." Kelly describes Washington as a national capital where increasingly the "distinction between reality and fantasy has been lost. . . . Movie stars show up with their press agents and their bodyguards to 'testify' before Congress. Politicians and reporters make cameo appearances as movie stars, playing themselves in fictional scenes about politics and reporting."[11]

However, the concern about new information technologies and politics goes beyond the business of politics. As Supreme Court Justice Hugo Black noted in 1945, the First Amendment guarantee of a free press "rests upon the assumption that the widest possible dissemination of information from diverse and antagonistic sources is essential to the well-being of the public." The United States was founded on the assumption that a populace could govern if it was well-informed. President James Madison wrote that "knowledge will forever govern ignorance, and a people who mean to be their own governors, must arm themselves with the power knowledge gives. A popular government without popular information or the means of acquiring it is but a prologue to a farce or a tragedy or perhaps both."[12]

Because information available through new technology requires that someone purchase the technology, the possibility exists for a society divided into information-poor and information-rich segments. In such a society, information is the golden key to success, and the information is available only to those with money. Research has consistently shown that those with already high levels of information gain even more information as they begin to use technologies, and even if information-poor consumers become more knowledgeable, they continually fall behind in the socio-information struggle. People who are among the first to adopt innovations are called "early adopters." Early adopters have higher social status, more education, more exposure to mass media, more effective use of interpersonal channels, more social interaction, a more cosmopolitan nature, and a higher level of literacy than later adopters.[13] Therefore, the knowledge gap, the distance between those who use information technologies at the highest levels and those who do not, usually those of lower socio-economic status, increases rather than decreases.[14]

The creation of a knowledge gap is of concern for humanitarian reasons. A 1972 study showed that information distribution inequities in a society could be directly related to inequities in the distribution of other elements of social life, such as education, affluence, and exposure to communication channels. The United States has long succeeded as a democracy at least in part because of its high literacy rates and its emphasis on maintaining a solid middle class; democracies are known to survive longest in countries with a strong middle class. If class begins to be defined not only by education and social status but also by access to and possession of information, the creation of a knowledge gap equals the weakening of the middle class. In a January 16, 1787 letter to Colonel Edward Carrington, Thomas Jefferson wrote, "Were it left to me to decide whether we should have a government without newspapers, or newspapers without government, I should not hesitate a moment to prefer the latter." But his next sentence is less widely quoted: "But I should mean that every [person] should receive those papers and be capable of reading them."[15]

issue candidacies: Campaigns for political office that emphasize public issues rather than the candidates' images.

Power to the People

During the 1930s, communications researchers were convinced that media had tremendous power. In fact, they believed the power of media was so great that it acted like a "magic bullet." Although researchers have altered their view of media impact, almost all researchers, media critics, and philosophers believe that media have the power to shape society at least in some ways.

Critics argue that a small number of gatekeepers—reporters, editors, and producers—determine which information the audience sees or hears. With the advent of the computer information network—the Internet as well as commercial online services—gatekeepers can be avoided. The possibility of avoiding gatekeepers could have a radical impact on the politics of our society. Howard Rheingold wrote in *The Daily Telegraph,* "Philosophers such as John Locke and pamphleteers such as Tom Paine proposed the radical notion that, if people are educated and free enough to discuss issues among themselves, then citizens would be able to govern themselves, not only by electing representatives by secret ballot, but by discussing the issues that affect them. This notion has been called the 'public sphere.' "

Rheingold further argued that television had converted the public sphere into a "commodity that could be bought and sold. Reasoned argument lost ground to riveting images and emotional sound-bites." Rheingold believes that computer technologies can revitalize the public sphere by creating a new "forum for free speech."

SOURCE: Howard Rheingold, "Switching on the World," *The Daily Telegraph,* May 11, 1994, p. 17.

Social and cultural impact

Although critical discussion of media has been going on since the mass production of books, modern media criticism and concerns about the impact of media on society started in the 1920s with the introduction of radio and intensified in the 1930s with the advent of feature-length sound films. Would radio corrupt traditional values? How would adolescents react to watching movies in a dark theater? What would movies do to teenagers' values? Would they encourage behavior that did not conform to traditional standards? How would parents maintain control over their children once the children had seen the movies?

Through the years, researchers have looked at the social and political effects of mass media, particularly at the effects of television, that ubiquitous screen that brightens nearly every living room or family room in America. Many studies have focused on the political process. Does television enhance democracy? Foster voting by image rather than issue? Propel good-looking, smooth-talking candidates ahead of intellectual but less attractive ones?

Keyconcept

Socialization Effects of the Media: Every culture has means of preparing and conditioning its members to adopt expected social roles and activities. In our culture, mass media messages have an important, though often unrecognized, role in this process.

Researchers also have been concerned about the effects of television on individuals and on societal norms. Does heavy exposure to violent television programming increase individual violence? Does it make viewers believe that society as a whole is more violent than it really is? Are individuals exploited by creative advertising? Do they lose their ability to assess the credibility of a source? Does the ability to purchase consumer products become a life goal? Do adolescents choose their role models from the media? Does watching attractive young people having sex on television lead adolescents to believe that all their friends are having sex? Does mass culture replace local subcultures that once defined the regions of the nation?

Researchers are more skeptical of the power of media than they once were. But they are still convinced that media have socialization and cultivation effects.

Many of society's and individuals' images come from the mass media. However, those images are countered by other factors, such as interpersonal communication or conversations. People's access to knowledge gained from experience and education often counter the images they receive from television or other media forms. With the advent of computer-exchanged information, critics and consumers once more are concerned about what kind of information they, their children, and their society will acquire.

These Beatles fans are reacting with immediacy and intensity to a public performance. Media research tries to understand what factors blend to create certain effects and how individual characteristics influence audience reactions to messages.

Keyconcept

Media Cultivation Effect: According to one theory, a person who takes in a steady diet of mass media messages—especially from television—may be conditioned to believe that the world presented by the media is an accurate reflection of reality.

A new internationalism

Angela and Jenny are not the only ones who talk to each other via computers. Professors, students, and all other consumers of online services can communicate. Such communication takes place not only within the United States but across national boundaries—to and from Europe, Australia, Africa, South America, and Asia. Computer-accessible information crosses the boundaries of space, time, and political boundaries in ways that no other technology has been able to do.

During the 1960s, Canadian professor of English literature and media guru Marshall McLuhan popularized the concept that electronic media were key players in public affairs and argued that media power could bring about a better world. McLuhan envisioned a "global village," in which humankind could be liberated from the linear thinking of printing, a vision both "tribal and collective."[16] But critics are more pessimistic and argue that the explosion of information and the economic costs that go with it will continue to divide underdeveloped countries from those that are more advanced.

Internationalism can be looked at by (1) analyzing ownership in terms of how many companies are multinational or by (2) analyzing who produces what content for what audiences. A third level of analysis involves looking at international news and information flow, in terms of volume, direction, and access. Most multinational companies are Western-based and dominate the production of information that is distributed throughout the less-developed world. The flow of information raises concerns about cultural imperialism. Will superior production quality and media economic systems allow the West to dominate the cultures of less developed countries?

Western countries, particularly the United States, have operated under different principles than those adopted in most parts of the world. After World War II, U.S. reporters and editors worked in cooperation with the U.S. government to try to ensure a flow of information across national boundaries through an open system similar to that

[profile]

Marshall McLuhan

Marshall McLuhan argued that the "medium is the message." McLuhan believed that the nature of technology was as important as its content.

His ideas were so controversial for the time and had so much influence on scholars of mass media that the term *McLuhanism* appears in the *Oxford English Dictionary*. The dictionary distills his entire work into a statement that the introduction of mass media deadens the critical faculties of individuals.

Herbert Marshall McLuhan was born in Edmonton, Alberta, Canada on July 21, 1911, to a Protestant family of Scottish-Irish descent. His mother, Elsie, was an actress, and his father, Herbert, was a salesman.

He went to the University of Manitoba to become an engineer but switched his major to English literature. He graduated with a bachelor of arts degree in 1933 and earned a master's degree the following year. He then studied literature at Cambridge University in England, where he obtained a B.A. in 1936 and a doctorate in 1942. McLuhan married Corrine Keller, a Texan who studied drama at the Pasadena Playhouse in California.

McLuhan established his teaching and scholarly career at the University of Toronto, where he was influenced by Harold Innis, a pioneer in communication studies. In 1963, McLuhan was appointed director of the University of Toronto's Marshall McLuhan Center for Culture and Technology, where he worked for fourteen years before retiring.

McLuhan wrote more than fifteen books, including *The Mechanical Bride: Folklore of Industrial Man*, published in 1951. That book was his first attempt to examine the effects of mass culture and "the pressures set up around us today by the mechanical agencies of the press, radio, movies, and advertising." He made a greater impact with his second book, *The Gutenberg Galaxy*, written in 1961, which discusses the effect of movable type on Western European culture in the fifteenth century.

In 1964, McLuhan earned popular acclaim with *Understanding Media: The Extensions of Man*, in which he contends that the introduction of electronic circuitry made behavior less isolated and more conformist than before. He expands on his concept of the "global village," arguing that media bring different cultures closer together. Another popular book, *The Medium Is the Massage,* published in 1967, illustrated McLuhan's ideas of "hot" and "cold" media. His objective was to show that a medium is not neutral but rather it transforms life.

McLuhan earned praise as the media guru of the 1960s, but he also was the target of criticism from scholars. He received many honors, awards, and medals, including citations from the British and Italian governments. McLuhan died on December 31, 1980, at the age of 69.

SOURCES: Alden Whitman, "Marshall McLuhan, Author, Dies," *The New York Times,* January 1, 1981, Sec. 1, p. 1; Alan M. Kriegsman, "Marshall McLuhan Dies," *The Washington Post,* January 1, 1981, Section Metro, p. C16.

of the United States. In the 1970s, UNESCO (United Nations Educational, Scientific, and Cultural Organization) took up the communication controversy. Governments in many underdeveloped countries expressed concern about the Western values that were being beamed into their countries. By 1984, for example, Latin America imported 42 percent of its media programs; the United States imported only 2 percent. Underdeveloped countries expressed concern that Western-dominated news focused on disasters rather than on economic development, that it promoted a massive consumer culture that eroded national identity in many parts of the world, and that it fostered Western domination of the

The televised Vietnam war brought Marshall McLuhan's concept of a "global village" to the forefront. Unlike McLuhan's vision of harmony brought about through the exchange of international media messages, these images were of disharmony and destruction.

world through media imperialism. The United States argued that it had promoted a complex communication system that benefited all parts of the world through improved educational, social, and technological services.[17] The UNESCO debate was never resolved, and the United States ultimately withdrew from the organization.

The evolution of an information highway has new implications for underdeveloped and former Communist countries. For example, in 1994 Russia had 11 to 15 telephone lines for every 100 people; Spain had 35 lines for every 100 people; and the United States had 70 lines for every 100 people. If telephone lines are to be a major carrier of information, improving telephone

Global *Impact*

Lingling Zhu and the Internet

A decade ago, Lingling Zhu, a twenty-one-year-old student from Beijing, would have died, unknown to all but her friends and family. Instead, she is a symbol of what scholar Marshall McLuhan called the global village.

In March 1995, Zhu slipped into a coma, exhibiting symptoms that her doctors could not diagnose. For the second time in a year, her hair fell out, she suffered from dizziness, and she had pain in her hands and feet. The pain turned to paralysis. Two of her friends sent a plea for help via the Internet.

Of the 2,000 responses from eighteen countries, more than one hundred from doctors and pharmacists suggested thallium poisoning. Zhu was tested; the results showed that her body contained one hundred times the normal amount of thallium. Thallium poisoning can occur by eating food with a high content of the heavy metal or by handling it in some manufacturing processes. Her doctors administered an antidote, and her condition improved. However, she remained in a coma because of the length of exposure.

Zhu's case illustrates the emergence of a global communication system. In 1962, Marshall McLuhan said mass communication would make the world into a global village where distance had little meaning. Zhu's story was publicized by Anita Srikameswaran, a writer for the *Chicago Tribune.* But it took the development of personal computers and the Internet before individuals could hook into a global communication system to respond so quickly and easily to a personal request for help.

Even a global village can be a place where people share concerns. Concerns about disease, disasters, and the loss of freedom have long existed throughout the world. Now, village Earth has communication systems that allow people to express those concerns globally.

SOURCE: Anita Srikameswaran, "Internet Weaves Global Web of Aid to Ailing Students," *Chicago Tribune,* September 3, 1995, pp. 1, 8.

14

Keyconcept

Cultural Imperialism: Media products and political and business practices of one culture may have important influences on another culture. These influences may be considered "imperialistic" if they impose patterns and values that ignore or denigrate local customs.

systems in underdeveloped countries will be a prerequisite for creating an equitable system of acquiring information. "It's hard to speak seriously of economic and business development in Russia without the development of modern telecommunications systems," Dmitri B. Garamov, director general of Westelcom, which operates Russia's main international telephone service, told the *New York Times.*[18]

Summary

- New forms of technology, such as the World Wide Web, package politics in different ways than did old media, such as newspapers. Candidates from all political parties are beginning to adapt to the new forms.

- New technologies, alone and in combination with older forms of media, will have an impact on our daily lives, but no one can predict the exact impact of each technology.

- Media companies are experimenting with converging technologies by combining news functions in a single newsroom, but they continue to use various distribution systems, such as newspapers, broadcast, and online delivery.

- Media organizations are trying to determine how to profit from the new forms of technology. If advertising becomes the primary economic base of new media, sales appeals and targeting markets will have to be adapted. Media organizations also may shift the burden of costs to the consumer.

- Deregulation of the telephone industry will allow telephone companies to compete to deliver new forms of information.

- Shifting the burden of the cost of new technologies to the consumer may produce a society that is divided into information-rich and information-poor segments.

- Politicians will find new ways to send their messages, or their images, to the public. Critics are concerned that politicians will increasingly direct messages to the public and that journalists will have less opportunity to place those messages within a critical context.

- No one lives in an isolated nation-state. Everyone is part of an international community.

- In some ways, our world is like the Internet. It has main highways and side roads to communication, and the roads are connected through an international network.

Navigating the Web

Media on the web

Among the tools for navigating the **World Wide Web** are sites called **search engines.** Those sites are enormous indexes of what's on the Web. Try some of the following search engines to find sites that are of interest to you.

AltaVista	http://www.altavista.digital.com/
Magellan	http://www.mckinley.com/
Infoseek	http://guide.infoseek.com/
Yahoo	http://www.yahoo.com/

During the elections of 1996, most candidates for the House of Representatives and the Senate had **home pages,** designed to present their image and message to individuals who use computers to gather information. Once they were elected to office, many of the candidates refashioned their pages to provide services to constituents. To find information about a politician or political candidate, use one of the search engines listed above, enter the name of the person, and wait for the choices of web sites to appear on your screen.

■ Questions for review

1. In what ways are students heavy consumers of mass media?
2. What does *technological convergence* mean?
3. What is the significance of ChicagoLand Television?
4. What does it mean to describe people as information-rich or information-poor?
5. What is a knowledge gap?

■ Issues to think about

1. How will the convergence of technology affect your life?
2. What is the significance of competition between newspapers and computer companies over the delivery of online services?
3. What are some of the problems of applying advertising models to on-line and other computer information services?
4. During the 1992 and the 1996 presidential campaigns, the candidates took their political messages to the younger generation via MTV. How did their appearances signal a shift in political communication?
5. How do television images dominate our views of society at home and abroad?

■ Suggested readings

Bagdikian, Ben H. *The Information Machines: Their Impact on Men and Media* (New York: Harper & Row, 1971).

Bogart, Leo. *Commercial Culture: The Media System and the Public Interest* (New York: Oxford University Press, 1995).

Dizard, Wilson P. *The Coming Information Age: An Overview of Technology, Economics, and Politics* (New York, Longman, 1989).

Schiller, Herbert I. *Culture, Inc.* (New York: Oxford University Press, 1989).

World Wide Web: A network of computers that allows people to move easily from material stored on one computer to material stored on another.

search engine: A computer program that allows a person to search computer networks, such as the World Wide Web, for specific information.

home page: The opening screen, or page, of a location on the World Wide Web.

How People Communicate: Uses and Structure

Key concepts

- Mediated Communication
- Feedback
- Mass Communication
- Interpersonal Communication
- Individual Uses of Information
- Correlating the Parts of Society
- Transmission of Social Heritage
- Mass Consumption Society
- Mass Communication in a Market System
- Mass Communication in a Nonmarket System
- Agenda-Setting in the Media
- The Media as a Consumer Market
- The Media as an Advertising Market
- The Media as a Marketplace of Ideas
- Public Forum
- Media Organizations in a Market System

Amy, a rookie college newspaper reporter, had a ticket to a Smashing Pumpkins concert. The newspaper had bought the ticket and paid for her transportation because she had been assigned to write a review. What a deal!

Crowds gathered in Philadelphia on July 4, 1993, to watch this widescreen simulcast of President Clinton presenting the Medal of Freedom to South African President LeClerk and leader Nelson Mandela.

Getting to attend a concert and then write about it. When she returned to the office after the concert, however, she had difficulty getting started. She wanted to discuss her impressions with someone first, to try out her ideas on a friend or colleague. Sitting next to her was a veteran arts reporter. "Let's go have coffee," he said. "We can talk about what you might want to say in the review."

The process Amy went through in writing her review involved interpersonal as well as mediated communication. Interpersonal communication is the direct exchange of information with another person. Through language, which is a collection of symbols, people attempt to share their experiences and impressions. Mediated communication, on the other hand, uses some mechanism, such as television, to communicate those symbols. The terms *mediated communication* and *mass communication* often are used interchangeably, but mass communication implies that a person is communicating to large audiences.

17

Amy used interpersonal communication when she discussed and analyzed her ideas with the veteran reporter; she used mediated communication when her review was published in the college newspaper. Had she written the review and sent it to a few friends via e-mail, she would have used mediated communication that probably would not be classified as mass communication. Students routinely use a combination of interpersonal and mediated communication as they study for classes, discuss issues with their friends, and adapt to college life.

This chapter introduces you to concepts that will help you understand the economic and theoretical structure of mediated communication. Although these concepts seem difficult to comprehend, they can be divided into a few simple issues.

- How does the communication process work?
- How do people use communication?
- What is the structure of the communication system in the United States?
- How does the U.S. system compare to other systems in the global marketplace?

The communication process

As Amy neared the end of her college newspaper career, she decided to apply for a position as a reporter at the *Los Angeles Times.* She wrote a letter to the editor, noting that she was a Phi Beta Kappa scholar and had held three internships in national news bureaus for statewide newspapers. She sent her letter (the message) through a **channel** (the postal service). The *Times* editor (the receiver) read it. The editor, through the message, formulated an image of Amy. Those activities reflect one description of the communication process, based on a famous communication **model** developed by scholars Claude E. Shannon and Warren Weaver.[1] See Figure 2.1 on page 20.

In Shannon and Weaver's model, the sender has an idea that is translated into symbols, such as words, drawings, or gestures. The symbols make up a message that is communicated across a *channel,* or system used to physically transfer the message from the sender to another person or group of people. A telephone, television set, and the human voice are all channels. The person or people who get the message are receivers. The receiver translates the message from the channel into a mental image. One can assess the accuracy of the process by asking whether the mental image of the receiver corresponds to the idea of the sender. This process can be applied to all human communication.

The process of sending and receiving a message, however, involves more elements. **Channel noise** (technical or physical interference) or **semantic noise** (the interference created by language or interpretation) can disrupt or distort the message. If the postal service had lost Amy's letter, she would have experienced channel noise, just

Keyconcept

Mediated Communication: Individuals may share messages using an intermediate device or mechanism, perhaps to overcome distances or obstacles. By using media, people can also reach a large number of other individuals.

channel: A way of transmitting a message from a person or group of people to a person or group of people, e.g., a telephone line or newspaper.

model: A diagram or picture that attempts to represent how something works. In communication, models are used to try to explain what happens in the creation, sending, and receiving of a message.

18

Communication in your life

Interacting with Others and Using Media

This chapter discusses some of the differences between interpersonal communication and mediated communication. It also explains how mass-media systems work. Think about the role of communication in your life. As you understand the concept of a media system better, your perception of media in your own life may change.

- Describe a recent experience that involved both the use of media and interaction with another person.

- How was the interpersonal interaction different from your experience using a particular mediated communication?

- How was the media product (program, newscast, advertisement) designed to affect you and others?

- How did you use the media product, and how did you share your experience with others?

as if she had been trying to talk to the editor on the telephone and her roommate had turned up the radio volume too loud. However, channel noise is usually solved rather simply—by sending a second letter or by asking a roommate to turn down the volume. Further, technological improvement has solved many problems of channel noise, such as radio static.

Semantic noise, however, is less easily reduced or ended because it involves underlying meaning. For example, Amy might complain to her roommate that the dorm room is a mess. This could be a simple statement of condition, or it might mean "You made the mess. Now you clean it up!" The tone of delivery may be part of the message, and Amy's roommate may or may not interpret the message as Amy hopes she will.

Similar problems arise when a word has more than one meaning. For example, readers don't know whether they're invited to a feeding frenzy or being fed spot news when they read the *Washington Post* headline "H. Robert Heller to Be Fed Nominee."[2] Careful crafting of the message by the sender and the use of feedback reduce semantic noise.

As shown in Figure 2.1, feedback involves signals sent in response to a message. Feedback usually starts from the receiver in response to a message, but a series of messages, sent in a conversation, for example, will generate many feedback messages. The slovenly roommate might ask, "What do you mean by that remark?" The fastidious Amy could reply, "You live like a pig, and I want you to pick up your mess." In this situation, feedback has eliminated the semantic noise, although it may not have improved the relationship between the two women.

In mediated communication, a sender passes a message through a channel to an individual or group. In the process, the message may encounter "channel noise," such as when an e-mail is improperly coded. Noise—either technological or semantic—can result in a misinterpretation of the original message.

channel noise: Interference in a communication channel, e.g., static on a radio.

semantic noise: An interference with communication because of misunderstandings about the meaning of words or symbols.

FIGURE 2.1

The Communication Process
(modified Shannon-Weaver model)

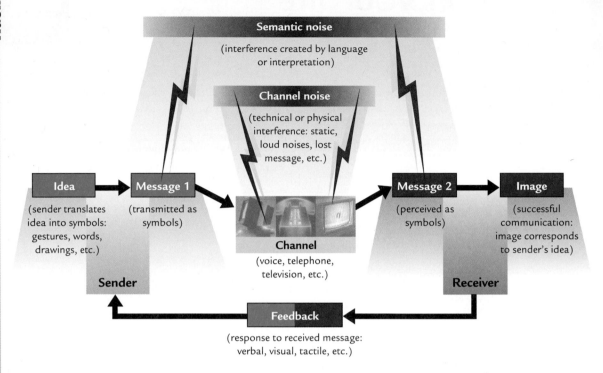

Semantic noise
(interference created by language or interpretation)

Channel noise
(technical or physical interference: static, loud noises, lost message, etc.)

Idea → **Message 1** → **Channel** → **Message 2** → **Image**

Idea
(sender translates idea into symbols: gestures, words, drawings, etc.)

Message 1
(transmitted as symbols)

Channel
(voice, telephone, television, etc.)

Message 2
(perceived as symbols)

Image
(successful communication: image corresponds to sender's idea)

Sender

Receiver

Feedback
(response to received message: verbal, visual, tactile, etc.)

Source: Claude Shannon and Warren Weaver, *The Mathematical Theory of Communication* (Urbana: University of Illinois Press, 1949), p. 98.

Feedback can take many forms: verbal, visual, and tactile. Face-to-face communication provides opportunity for feedback while watching television does not. A simple nod or a quiet "uh-huh" provides feedback that the message is understood. People who have known each other for a long time can give feedback with just a facial expression. Because mediated communication requires a technological channel, it limits feedback and increases the possibility of mistakes in communication. This is particularly true for mass media, which send the same message to large numbers of people.

Keyconcept

Feedback: Receivers of messages often react to them with responding signals, called *feedback*. Interpersonal feedback might take the form of gestures or facial expressions; audience feedback to broadcast media might take the form of phone calls to the station to complain about something or to request something.

Mediated communication and mass media

What is a **mass medium?** A mass medium is a form of communication that is transmitted through a medium and reaches many receivers, but people disagree on what size audience constitutes a "mass." On any given Thursday night, eighteen million U.S. households turn on the television program *Seinfeld.* On the same day, about 5,000 households in Wexford County, Michigan, read the *Cadillac*

mass medium: A form of communication (radio, newspapers, television, etc.) used to reach a large number of people.

News. Both daily newspapers and television programs are considered mass media, but they can vary greatly in absolute number of receivers.

Absolute size tends not to be as important in defining mass media as relative size. The eighteen million households watching *Seinfeld* account for almost 30 percent of all households watching television, and the 5,000 households reading the *Cadillac News* account for more than half the county's households. The percentage of households taking a particular newspaper, listening to a radio program, or watching a television program continually declined in the 1990s because the variety and number of media outlets continually increased. However, mass-media companies try to attract as large a proportion as possible of the audience targeted by the program or publication.

Whether a medium has long-term impact is another determining characteristic of mass media. A television show reaching eighteen million households and a newspaper reaching half the homes in its market obviously fit the definition of mass media. However, some books, movies, and recordings that circulate among smaller audiences may reach many individuals over a period of years. Charles Dickens's books remain a staple of high school English classes even though they were written more than a century ago, and the Bible continues to be one of the most influential books ever. Those media products have had a strong social impact across time and therefore qualify as mass media.

Mass communication thus involves sharing ideas across a large audience either at a given point or through an extended time frame. Most people agree that mass media include newspapers, magazines, books, films, television, radio, and recordings. Today scholars debate whether the Internet is a mass medium. Because it allows people to select from so much information, it differs from traditional, less interactive media. But some World Wide Web home pages receive a great deal of activity. The home page for the comic strip "Dilbert" received more than 1.5 million hits a day during 1996. Web material certainly has the potential to involve "mass" communication; the Internet will be treated in this book as a mass medium. Direct mail, telemarketing, and outdoor advertising may also qualify as mass media even though the particular medium involved may not be considered "mass" by most people.

Keyconcept

Mass Communication: Messages distributed by institutions such as the media have the potential to reach very large and anonymous audiences in a process called *mass communication.*

The mass communication process

The mass communication process, like the general communication process, can be represented by a model. During the preseason of the 1996 presidential campaign, Senator Bob Dole caused a major uproar when he attacked Time Warner and other entertainment companies at a Hollywood fund-raiser. Dole charged that Hollywood was producing movie "nightmares of depravity," along with rap music that contained "gross, violent, offensive, and misogynistic lyrics."[3] The model in Figure 2.2, a modified version of the Westley-MacLean model first published in 1957,[4] shows how information such as Dole's speech flows as a message to an audience through a mass medium. The communicator in the model selects information from sources and processes them for delivery to an audience. News stories about Dole's attack on Hollywood were based on the event. In other words, the event was the primary source of the message. Journalists also interviewed people who work in Hollywood for a response to the speech. These journalists, represented as communicators in the model, prepared stories for their magazines, television networks, or newspapers that would eventually be read by their audience of readers and viewers.

mass communication: Communicating with a high proportion of the designated audience for a message.

FIGURE 2.2

The Mediated Communication Process
(modified Westley-MacLean model)

Unlike the simple communication process, mediation requires a communicator to carry the message from a source or sources to an audience. The source provides information to a communicator, such as a journalist, and the communicator analyzes the information and passes on a version of it to the audience. Both steps are subject to semantic and channel noise.

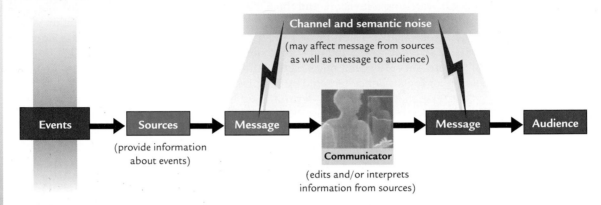

Source: Bruce H. Westley and Malcolm S. MacLean, Jr., "A Conceptual Model for Communication Research," *Journalism Quarterly 34* (1957), pp. 31–38.

Figure 2.2 could represent any mass communication process. It changes only slightly from the simple communication process by adding a communicator between the sender (source) and the receiver (audience). The communicator can drastically alter the communication process because he or she selects what the mass communication message will and will not contain. In addition, the communicator often interprets the meaning of the source and the events.

The impact of a communicator on a message was illustrated by the coverage of the 1996 summer Olympics. The United States women's softball team defeated the Chinese team in a close, tense, gold-medal game. The two teams had developed an intense rivalry that gave every pitch and hit dramatic meaning. The thousands of people watching the game in person experienced the exciting tension, but viewers of NBC saw only the highlights of the game long after it was over. Critics attacked NBC for not providing live coverage of women's team sports, such as softball, basketball, and soccer. A different communicator—ABC, for example—might have broadcast those sports differently and changed viewers' perceptions of the Olympics.

Keyconcept

Interpersonal Communication: In communication, people use language, gestures, and symbols to share meaning and messages. The communication is interpersonal when it occurs directly between one individual and another, as in a face-to-face conversation.

A journalistic issue demonstrated by Figure 2.2 concerns the reporter's dependence on sources. Often journalists cannot experience events themselves and must rely on sources for their information. Sources gain power by influencing how a reporter (communicator) interprets an event, and often politicians try to use such power to get favorable coverage for their point of view. Because journalists are aware of their dependence on sources, they try to seek many different points of view to provide balance to any given story.

The Republican and Democratic conventions in 1996 illustrate how politicians used television coverage to promote their parties. Once the television networks agreed to cover those events, the coverage was determined mostly by the people running the conventions. Few delegates who disagreed with party leaders were heard. One way around

23

This reporter gathers information from a variety of sources in a process that results in a " mediated" message. The reporter speaks to officials, observers, and perhaps checks public documents in order to produce a reasonably accurate story.

source control is to use analysts to interpret the convention events, but the networks also wanted to be careful not to make themselves look biased against the parties.

The mass communication process faces the same problems as the interpersonal communication process. Both channel noise and semantic noise affect how well audience members understand the message they receive. Two steps of interpretation occur during mass communication. The semantic noise that occurs when the communicator interprets the message and when the audience interprets it helps to explain media inaccuracy. Journalists and sources sometimes disagree about the meaning of what the source said, and audience members always interpret the meaning of mediated messages in light of their own experiences. Today college students view the federal government through experiences shaped by the presidencies of Ronald Reagan, George Bush, and Bill Clinton. Their grandparents view federal programs in light of Franklin Delano Roosevelt and the New Deal. Their parents' perceptions of the federal government were shaped by the presidencies of John Kennedy, Lyndon Johnson, and Richard Nixon. Those vastly different experiences affect what the students, their parents, and their grandparents think about federal programs.

When people look at the impact of mass communication, they ask questions such as: How do propaganda and other forms of information bias change political attitudes? Do people depend on mass media for their perceptions of social reality? Do mass media perpetuate the dominant culture at the expense of minority cultures? Can mass media shape people's images of the national economy? As you will see in Chapter 16, mass media—and questions about their effects—permeate the fabric of U.S. society.

Uses of mass communication

Both individuals and groups use mass communication. Individuals use mass communication to satisfy their information needs and wants. When Jerry and Ruth decide to buy a house, they buy the Sunday newspaper for information about house prices, locations, and styles. Sunday morning they watch the real estate channel, which features pictures of homes, along with information about prices and locations. John buys the newspaper to read the box scores of all the major league teams. Jennifer buys *Vogue* to catch the new fashions and read up on women's issues.

Groups use information to promote group interaction among members or to act collectively. A local parent-teacher association may distribute newsletters about the importance of passing a school bond issue. Neighborhood-association newsletters help foster a sense of community and rally people to a variety of causes.

Group information, provided by the PTA newsletter, for example, may also influence individual decisions. Ruth and Jerry may decide to buy in a specific neighborhood because the newsletter indicates that parents are active in the school.

How individuals use information

Individual uses of mass communication have long been a focus of interest in media studies. Media scholars have identified the "uses" involved when people seek information to fulfill their needs and wants. Those uses fall into five types: **surveillance,** decision making, social and cultural interaction, diversion,[5] and self-understanding.[6]

Surveillance means checking out what is happening in the environment. It occurs in two types of situations: everyday surveillance, such as checking baseball scores or stock prices, and extraordinary surveillance, such as keeping up with events during a war or natural disaster. Surveillance keeps people in touch with environmental and other social and political changes that are crucial to their lives. When people watched CNN at the height of the Gulf War, they were surveilling, or monitoring, their environment. Surveillance also helps people decide how to use information for decision making, social and cultural interaction, and diversion.

Decision making involves collecting information to be able to select among options. The decision may be as minor as which TV program to watch or as important as which presidential candidate to vote for. Use of information for decision making is purposeful and specific. Surveillance and decision making overlap because surveillance often determines what types of decisions need to be made.

Social and cultural interaction uses information that defines, identifies, and maintains membership in a group. All groups define themselves with information, which allows individuals to hold and demonstrate membership in the group. The group may be as large as a country or as small as a household. Sometimes people get information formally, for example, through classes for people who want to become U.S. citizens. Other times information passes informally through conversations among group members, for example, in discussions during fraternity and sorority rushes.

Diversion involves using information for entertainment and enjoyment. Watching football on television or reading a short story may make a person feel sad, happy, or even horrified. Individuals seek different types of diversion, which is why some people prefer films by Spike Lee and others prefer films by Steven Spielberg.

Self-understanding means that people use mass media to gain insight into their own behaviors and attitudes. A

Mass media correlate different parts of the society, bringing people together to exchange opinions and ideas. Here fans gather to watch a sports event and compare views on details of the game and players.

surveillance: Identifying important events and issues that affect a person's life.

Interactivity

Four decades ago, families gathered around radio sets to listen over the snap, crackle, and pop of static to comedians such as Jack Benny, George Burns, and Gracie Allen. That audio center for family entertainment eventually faded as television developed. Now, television faces just as radical a change. Equipped with fiber optic cable that carries 500 TV channels and television sets with computer microchips, future homes can become on-ramps to the information superhighway.

A central question shaping the information superhighway is how active the consumer will choose to be in using technology. Will people delight in simply watching movies if they have greater choice over content and viewing times? Or will they use the new superhighway to access video games or communicate with others?

Media involvement requires varying levels of activity. If you are seeing, touching, feeling, smelling, or listening, you are active. Watching an Arnold Schwarzenegger action film may not require as much thought as watching Kenneth Branagh perform Shakespeare on screen, but all media use requires some mental processing.

A second level of activity—**interactivity**—represents two-way communication. A computer game is interactive because you must constantly tell the computer what to do next. You must respond in order for the game to continue.

In the future, people will be able to make choices about the levels of media involvement they want. The evolution of technology, therefore, has not only to do with invention but also with how people express what they want and need. Technology may continue along the lines we anticipate, or different forms may arise somewhat spontaneously.

person feeling alone and isolated might gain solace from hearing REM sing, "Everybody hurts. Everybody cries, sometimes." A college student reading a news story about the causes of binge drinking might better understand why he or she wakes up Saturday mornings on a strange couch with no money and an aching head.

The five distinct individual uses of information often are related. The seemingly simple process of selecting a movie to go to includes checking the newspaper to find out what is showing (surveillance), asking friends about the two or three films you are considering and picking one (decision making), and going to see the movie (diversion).

The same information can be used in more than one way. For example, people may see a movie for entertainment. The next day, they may discuss it with people at work (social and cultural interaction). Then, the following year, they may remember how much they enjoyed a particular actor and decide to see the next movie starring the same person (decision making). The more different uses a person has for a given message, the more utility that message has. (Chapter 16 describes the "uses and gratifications" research that gave rise to these "uses" categories.)

> **interactivity:** Mental and sensory participation. Used as a media term, it means actually having a physical interaction with a medium—ordering a movie via computer or typing in a response to a question.

How groups use information

Although individual members of a group may use mass communication to create social and cultural interaction, communication also may serve a group by correlating actions of its members and by transmitting its social and cultural heritage.[7] Groups vary in size from a small group of friends to a tribe to an entire society, but they all involve member interactions and a common culture and heritage.

Large groups, such as societies, act economically, politically, and socially. *Economic actions* involve the exchange of goods, services, and money. News, as well as advertising, can affect economic actions. If Mary intends to buy an imported car, she may postpone her purchase if she reads a newspaper article that suggests that Congress is about to cut import taxes, which increase the cost of cars from other countries.

> **Key**concept
>
> *Correlating the Parts of Society:* Social groups may use information from mass communication to make sense of the behavior of other groups. Information about others can help a group to bring into perspective, or correlate, the actions of one part of the society with the actions of another part.

Mass media correlate *political actions* by providing information about politicians and the political process. John and Catherine may watch the television coverage of presidential debates either to make up their minds about a candidate or to reinforce their closely held beliefs. An irate property owner may write a letter to the newspaper editor complaining about the actions of a city council member. In countries where citizens have a great deal of political power, the media gain importance because of their role in the political process. The need to correlate political activities forms the basis for the First Amendment to the Constitution. Without a free flow of information, people in a democracy cannot decide who should run their country.

Mass media correlate social activities and actions. The correlation may be as simple as helping a community to coordinate and attend a Memorial Day parade, local club activities, or school events. Or media may help correlate a national march in support of integration—an act that is both political and social. The media's coverage of the 1963 March on Washington helped convince Congress and the population that Civil Rights legislation was needed to promote equality in the United States.

In addition to correlating a society's activity, fostering the transmission of social heritage is another important function of mass communication. Societies are defined by their common heritage. Although education plays the most important role in this transmission, mass media often contribute to the common understanding of social and cultural heritage. When people say they are Americans, they recognize a common history with others who claim the same label. History can be shared at a local, regional, national, or international level. The 1996 Olympic Games in Atlanta gave the South an opportunity to transmit its social heritage to the world. The closing ceremonies included a concert that featured jazz, blues, Hispanic music, and country music—all part of the Southern and American heritage.

> **Key**concept
>
> *Transmission of Social Heritage:* One important use of mass communication is to carry a society's cultural messages. The heritage of traditional societies is often transmitted through stories and legends passed from one generation to the next; in technologically sophisticated societies, the mass media can be a means to connect the generations.

Just as one message can serve more than one purpose for individuals, so one message can serve more than one purpose for society. Social and economic activities often are connected. The 1994 Rolling Stones tour was a commercial enterprise composed of a series of carefully designed social events. Each generation shares music and culture that provide self-identity for that generation. Those who make and communicate that music and culture also make considerable profit.

The U.S. mass communication system

It is hard to imagine life in the United States without a mass communication system. Those who wrote the Constitution believed an informed populace was necessary to maintain a democracy. In a nation with no mass communication system, people would not have access to diverse information and political opinions. Democracy might wither and die if voters had access only to a narrow band of political information packaged by the government. In addition, without information about the availability of goods and services, a "mass-consumption" economy could not function. The country's standard of living would plummet. Moreover, social and cultural interaction would focus on local relationships. The cultural community that transcends geographic boundaries would no longer exist. A day without radio, television, newspapers, magazines, compact discs, movies, and books would be difficult for most of us or at least very different from what we're used to.

Keyconcept

Mass Consumption Society: Technologically sophisticated societies tend to have an economy based on the purchase of ever increasing amounts of goods by larger and larger numbers of consumers.

As the United States has become a vast social system, a mass communication system has evolved that creates and supplies information to those who demand it. The system is circular because those who demand information also supply information. Journalists and movie producers not only produce content in the system but use it as well. Several types of mass media organizations participate in the system, and within each type, thousands of organizations supply information to audiences. Mass communication must be viewed as more than a collection of individual entities, but rather as a system. Understanding how media organizations function within a larger system of supplying and receiving information enables us to understand the significance of mass communication within a nation or, indeed, the world. Mass media systems have enormous economic, social, and political impact.

A global context

The United States is not unique. Every country has a mass communication system that coordinates its activities. Highly industrialized countries have complex systems and depend on sophisticated computer technology. Oral tradition, print media, and radio dominate the communication systems of less industrialized countries. Most mass media systems can be defined as market or nonmarket systems. In market systems, consumers demand information and media companies supply it. Media companies in market systems supply the types and amounts of information that people will pay for. Nonmarket systems supply information based on what some institution, usually a government, decides that people should have.

Keyconcept

Mass Communication in a Market System: In a free-market society, mass communication can be described as a system that produces information on the basis of the interaction between two forces: audience demand and the ability of media companies to supply content. Media companies produce what someone will pay for.

Mass Communication in a Nonmarket System: In a highly structured nonmarket or authoritarian society, mass communication may function as a system in which content is decided by an institution, usually a government. In such societies the media produce not what the public will pay for, but what the authorities want the public to know.

The messages produced in the two communication systems differ greatly. Elements of both market and nonmarket systems often exist in a single society, but one approach tends to dominate. As the world becomes a global village and as satellite delivery crosses national boundaries, the line between the two systems becomes less defined.

■ U.S. mass media as a market system

U.S. mass communication is a market system. Figure 2.3 explains how it works. The center of the diagram shows the individuals and groups who participate in the mass communication system. They include almost all people in the United States—anyone who sees a movie, reads a newspaper, listens to the radio, or watches a television show. People have different information needs and wants, which come from their psychological states and from their interactions in groups. Those needs and wants translate into a demand for information and ideas.

> **Key**concept
>
> *Agenda-Setting in the Media:* Many observers believe that a strong mass media system has power to set the agenda for discussion of public issues or control the public's sense of the importance of certain issues.

Not only do individuals and groups fulfill wants and needs though the mass communication system, they also act as sources for that system. When a newspaper runs a story about a fire, sources of information may include a neighbor who called the fire department or firefighters who fought the blaze.

Because people are both information sources and information consumers, they make the mass communication system an important part of the political and social process. Mass media serve as agenda setters: the content of media helps determine the topics and issues that society considers important. Who gets to comment affects the information we all receive, so if only one political party were permitted to comment, content presented by the media would not reflect the social and political world we all must deal with. Similarly, if social issues were presented from only one point of view, such as that of the businessperson, the social context of those on welfare, of working single parents, or of educators would be excluded from the picture.

■ Three communication markets

Looking at mass communication as a market system, we can say that people seek information, and businesses either sell or give information through communication markets. People can use the information for any of the purposes mentioned above, but as in all markets, an exchange takes place. A consumer may buy a book or a recording, thus exchanging money for information or entertainment. In another instance, a business may buy an advertisement, thus exchanging money for access to people's attention. Further, people may share and debate ideas in another type of exchange—the marketplace of ideas. Thus, three markets emerge in this view of the U.S. system: the *consumer market,* the *advertising market,* and the *marketplace of ideas.*

People use the two commercial markets—consumer and advertising—to satisfy their individual needs (surveillance, decision making, social and cultural interaction, self-understanding, and diversion). Communities use the marketplace of ideas to find ways to satisfy their information needs (correlating group actions and transmitting heritage).

CONSUMER AND ADVERTISING MARKETS People use the consumer market most often. This market involves delivering information to readers, viewers, and listeners. In this market, the purpose of the information varies from entertainment to persuasion to education. Those who acquire information pay with either money or the attention they give to advertisements. People buy newspapers, watch television, and listen to recordings in this market. The consumer, not the originator, of the information determines how a particular bit of information is used.

> **Key**concept
>
> *The Media as a Consumer Market:* The mass media can be described as operating in a market that sells useful information to readers, viewers, and listeners.

FIGURE 2.3 The Mass Media Market System

The U.S. mass media market system is cyclical with people at the center. People have needs and wants which they take to the three types of markets in the system (consumer, advertising, and the marketplace of ideas). These wants and needs become demand for information, advertising space and time, and ideas to help society function properly. The media companies observe the demand and supply content to the three markets to satisfy the wants and needs. At the same time people are exercising their demand, they also act as sources of information for the media organizations. This mass media system is not isolated from the rest of the world. It serves the demand from other countries by sending content to them. At the same time, other countries supply content to the U.S. system based on demand from that system.

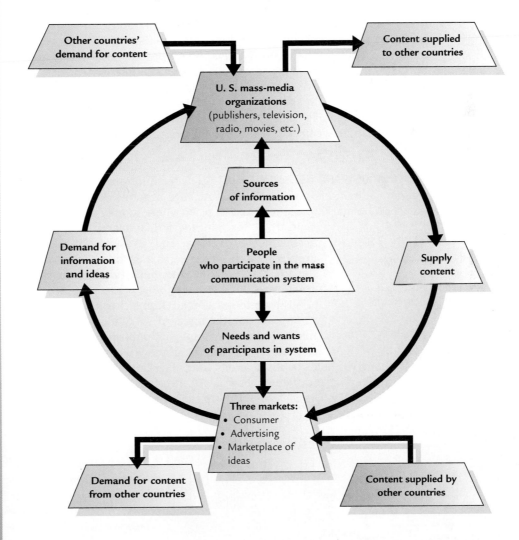

30

The advertising market involves selling the attention of readers, viewers, and listeners to advertisers. Businesses and other groups buy time or space in this market to influence what people buy or believe. An organization that advertises wants people to buy some good or service. "You've come a long way, baby" entices women to buy Virginia Slims cigarettes by identifying with women's advancements. Guys would go a long way for a Camel cigarette. And, just maybe, one more cosmetic product might attract that elusive man!

Assigning transactions to one of the two commercial markets is easier from the media company's perspective than from the consumer's perspective. Media organizations have different departments that serve the advertising and consumer markets. Often, an ad is labeled as advertising to separate it from news and editorial content. On the other hand, readers, listeners, and viewers do not necessarily make the distinction between markets. When people want to buy a car, they may consult *Consumer Reports'* guide to cars on America Online, check local prices in newspaper advertisements, and watch the Neon's lights peek over the hill in a television advertisement. Just how much each of these influences a particular buyer depends on the individual. Because people seek information from both advertising and news and often don't distinguish between the two, some advertisers deliberately create ads that look like news.

> **Key**concept
>
> *The Media as an Advertising Market:* The mass media can be described as operating in a market that sells the attention of readers, viewers, and listeners to product advertisers.

THE MARKETPLACE OF IDEAS AND THE PUBLIC FORUM The consumer and advertising markets are both commercial markets. An identifiable exchange of money takes place between supplier and user. The marketplace of ideas is a place where money and media space or time are not exchanged. In this market, ideas compete for acceptance by society and its subgroups. People and groups seek to influence this exchange of ideas because the arguments made in the marketplace of ideas may help create laws and norms for behavior.

> **Key**concept
>
> *The Media as a Marketplace of Ideas:* The mass media can be described as operating in a market in which ideas interact and compete for acceptance. Traditionally, a free exchange of ideas in the marketplace has been considered necessary for a democracy.

Efforts to develop a national health-care policy is an example of how the marketplace of ideas works. Politicians make speeches, newspapers publish editorials, and radio stations have listeners call in with comments about health care. Eventually, Congress holds public hearings, drafts legislation, and votes on a health-care bill. The president signs or vetoes the bill. All the steps include communication, much of it via mass media. The ideas compete in the marketplace of ideas for final acceptance as official policy.

Ideas are exchanged within the public arena through entertainment and talk shows, as well as through serious newscasts. First lady Hillary Clinton and Oscar appear here on the Rosie O'Donnell Show.

The effectiveness of the marketplace of ideas in different societies varies with the type of government and with the extent of commercialism in each country. In authoritarian countries, the government often limits access to the public forum. In a country where ordinary citizens participate in governance, extensive participation in the marketplace of ideas is crucial for effective government. In the United States, media critics recently have become concerned about the quality of political participation because of the commercialization of the political process through television advertisements and the sensationalism of quasi-entertainment political talk shows. Some argue that television has corrupted the marketplace of ideas into a showplace for images rather than a forum for issues and that it has destroyed any possibility for rational political discourse. Others argue that popularization of politics through television and other avenues has brought—and will continue to bring—more individuals into the political process.

Keyconcept

Public Forum: As in ancient Rome or on any street corner, a forum is a public space in which ideas can be expressed and debated. With modern mass media the public forum is rarely in one physical location; instead, it relies on intermediate mechanisms that create opportunity or space for people to interact, such as the Internet.

Although the three markets can be distinct, information produced for one can be used in another. Political candidates try to influence the marketplace of ideas through their purchase of advertisements. When Walt Disney portrayed Donald Duck rushing to the mailbox to pay his taxes on time during World War II, he used his Hollywood reputation to influence the marketplace of ideas by building patriotic spirit. In the same period, movies provided diversion in the consumer market by entertaining viewers through stories that emphasized cultural stereotypes of the enemy. Advertisers such as Benetton often use cultural ideas in the consumer market to promote their products in the advertising market.

■ Media organizations

The needs and wants that people take to the three communication markets result in a demand for information and ideas. Mass-media organizations supply that demand with media content, which flows into the three markets. Some needs and wants are fulfilled, and the cycle starts again. In that circular process, mass-media organizations must (1) evaluate the demand for information and ideas in the three markets, (2) draw on people as sources in the system, and (3) supply content to fulfill the demand. The steps involve difficult decisions, and many mass-media companies fail to make those decisions successfully.

Media organizations are varied entities. Individual television stations, newspapers, or magazine and book companies are media organizations. But the term also can be applied to corporations that own and/or manage several newspapers, television stations, or magazines. Most media organizations are part of larger conglomerates, or groups, that own varied types of media. Table 2.1 on page 32 shows some of these multimedia groups and their holdings. In 1996, Gannett owned eighty-four daily newspapers, ten television stations, and eleven radio stations.

Keyconcept

Media Organizations in a Market System: In a market society, media companies are organized to produce an efficient and competitive supply of information for the demands of consumption, advertising, and idea exchange.

The groups, or conglomerates, can be owned either publicly or privately. Under public ownership, the corporation sells stock to the public. Anyone who has enough money to buy stock can become part owner of the public corporation. Under private ownership, a person or group of people owns all the company stock. Ownership type has a significant impact on organizations. For example, the higher percentage of stock owned by the public, the less likely the company is to reinvest its profit in the company. This happens because the profit is returned to investors to keep the stock prices high.[8] The danger in this policy is that it can lower the quality of content produced by the organization.

TABLE 2.1 Types of Media Outlets by Multimedia Groups

GROUP	DAILY NEWSPAPERS	TELEVISION STATIONS	RADIO STATIONS
Freedom Newspapers	25	5	0
Gannett	84	10	11
Lee Enterprises	19	8	0
New York Times Co.	24	6	2
Park Communication	32	9	17
Scripps Howard	12	9	0

Source: Business Reports, America Online, February 1996.

Demand for information and ideas

Demand in the U.S. mass communication system reflects social and economic changes. During the twentieth century, technological development and the growth of mass media interacted with an increase in disposable income and leisure time to create and fill an increasing demand for diversion, reflecting a significant social and economic change. The film, radio, and television industries grew substantially. The movement of political power during the middle of the century from local and state authorities to the federal government also increased the demand for national and international news, again representing social—as well as political—change.

Demand for information and ideas derives from individual needs and wants. However, mass-media organizations must aggregate individual demand or address it at a macro level, because they supply audiences at a market level. Demand cannot be met by addressing individuals, but must be met by addressing commonality. *Demand structure* determines the nature of the aggregate demand and involves three characteristics: audience similarity, the geographic nature of the market, and the available technology.

Audience similarity can be charted on a continuum from everyone being exactly alike to everyone being entirely different. Members of any audience share characteristics, but those members also differ in many ways. However, members of some mass-media audiences share more similarities than do others. In Michigan, the readers of the *Tuscola County Advertiser* share more similarities than do readers of the *Detroit Free Press.* Tuscola County is an agricultural area populated primarily by people who were born and raised in the county. Detroit is a giant metropolis populated by people from all over the world. The more varied the audience, the more difficult it is to serve that audience in a given amount of media space and time. A diverse audience requires diversity of content, which is expensive to create.

In addition to audience similarity, geography also defines demand structure. Information helps define communities, sometimes through audience similarity, as in the women's suffrage movement of the early twentieth century, and other times through geography. The success of *USA Today*'s state blurbs capitalizes on people's identification with their home states. Geography also affects demand because geographic features, such as lakes, rivers, and mountains, determine the history, economy, and culture of people in a given market. Those factors in turn affect the type of information and advertising the audience demands. While Kansas farmers may pay attention to fertilizer ads on television, such ads would be wasted on a New York City audience.

[profile]

Charles Dolan

Today's mass media world is filled with flurries of conglomerate competition, megamergers, and takeovers. Industries that once regarded each other as competitors are teaming up. Behemoths such as Disney and ABC and Time Warner and Turner Network are combining their resources. Companies are also raising the stakes in high-speed technology: Internet connections, satellite transmissions, and wireless television operations.

One cable company, however, is still managing to go it alone: Cablevision Systems Corp., based in Long Island, New York, the sixth-largest multisystem cable television company. Cablevision, which is twenty-three years old, is still run by its founder, Charles Dolan. Dolan was also founder of HBO (Home Box Office) and one of the earliest believers in cable sports programming and twenty-four-hour news channels. In addition, he professes to being one of the first few people who believed that cable was more than another way to receive broadcast programs in isolated areas. He has always believed in the unique and local content of cable broadcasting.

Dolan grew up in Cleveland, where he worked his way through high school at a radio station. Later, he and his wife, Helen, operated a small business from their apartment, putting together footage of sports events and selling fifteen-minute reels to television stations. In the early 1960s, he helped start a New York cable company that became Cablevision. After wiring some Manhattan hotels for news and visitor information, his company won the franchise for lower Manhattan. From there, Dolan concentrated on unique programming content.

Cablevision now has 2.8 million subscribers concentrated in nineteen states. In 1995, Cablevision became half owner of Madison Square Garden, with rights to broadcast Knicks, Rangers, and Yankees games. Its programming entity, Rainbow Programming Holdings, Inc., includes American Movie Classics, Bravo, SportsChannel New York, News 12, and three new channels, MuchMusic, NewSport, and the Independent Film Channel. The company is expanding its operations to include local news channels—electronic neighborhoods—called Neighborhood Network and Extra Help. Cablevision's new fiber optic upgrades will give subscribers two hundred digital channels. It will also allow for high-speed Internet connections, interactive television, and an expansion of its telephone subsidiary, Cablevision Lightpath.

Charles Dolan is a man of firsts: he started Home Box Office as a nationwide pay-television service; Cablevision's News 12 was the nation's first local twenty-four-hour cable news operation; and Cablevision's Rainbow Advertising Sales was the first cable advertising sales division in the nation. At the end of 1994, Dolan was worth $715 million.

SOURCES: Alice Lipowicz, "Channel Surfer Boys: The Dolans Ride Rising Tide of Mergers with Cablevision Steering a Solo Course," *Crains New York Business,* Section News, July 1, 1996, p. 1; "Cablevision Systems Names James L. Dolan Chief Executive Officer; Charles Dolan to Remain Chairman of the Board," *Business Wire,* October 16, 1995; Kathryn Harris, "Cable Ready: Maverick CEO Charles Dolan's Vision Makes Cablevision a Powerhouse," *Los Angeles Times,* Section Business, December 11, 1994, p. 1.

The final determinant of demand structure is technology, a factor that can make geography less important. Just as the telegraph expanded mass-media audiences in the mid-nineteenth century, now cable and satellite technology have expanded the political, social, and economic range of those who have access to television. In addition, satellites transmit newspaper content to printing plants across the United States, making a local or regional daily newspaper available throughout the country. The expansion of national and international media distribution reduces the distinctions of separate cultures. In the process, cultures may either come together as they share common ideas, or local or minority cultures may be overwhelmed.

The convergence of technology will continue to give consumers more choice, opening up new avenues of distribution for print media and fostering interactive communication in television and other electronic media.

DEMAND IN THE CONSUMER MARKET Consumer demand for media content varies considerably depending partly on household decisions about **media mixes.** For example, one person might mix media by watching an hour of television a day and reading a couple of newspapers. Another person might watch television and not read newspapers or magazines.

Consumers also choose content based on **packaging.** To buy one specific channel, such as MTV, people might have to buy a package that also offers TNT or TNN.

The way that media products are bundled or mixed reflects the wants and needs of consumers. Those wants and needs reflect life style, social-group memberships, and personality. However, other factors such as price and accessibility also affect demand. Generally, as the price of a media commodity increases, some consumers will substitute different content or media. The ability to read or to use a computer also will affect media choices.

A student in a family with a computer can complete a high school report using a CD-ROM encyclopedia, online databases, and the Internet, in addition to books and magazines. A student in a family without a computer may be limited to books and magazines. Either student can produce a good report, but which sources of information students use affects the way future information is supplied. Increasing demand for CD-ROMs will likely move some demand away from books.

DEMAND IN THE ADVERTISING MARKET Demand in the advertising market is straightforward compared to demand in the consumer market. Advertisers want to pay the lowest possible price to send their message to the highest possible percentage of potential customers. To do this, the advertiser must identify the location of potential customers and the best medium for reaching those customers. In most cases, advertisers use a combination of media to target the media mixes used by their audience.

Advertisers choose between mass and **targeted advertising,** depending on the size and type of audience they want to reach. A local department store uses mass advertising aimed at a diverse group because individuals with different levels of income or different interests will all buy products from their store. However, a Mercedes Benz dealership targets only those with a large enough income to buy its cars.

Technology—computer databases, narrowly focused channels, and online services—can be used to define advertising markets and allow for segmented advertising.

DEMAND IN THE MARKETPLACE OF IDEAS Demand in the marketplace of ideas is more complex than transactions in the two commercial communication markets. Transactions in this market involve no money, space, or time. The demand is for ideas, information, and reinforcement of cultural values that allow society to maintain and improve it-

media mix: Consumer's use of a variety of types of media, such as newspapers, television, and World Wide Web.

packaging: Selling of content in a bundle. For example, cable systems sell channel packages; newspapers bundle sections targeted to certain socio-economic groups through zip code sorting.

targeted advertising: Trying to sell a product or service to a particular group of people, such as women between the ages of 25 and 39.

As media products cross geographical borders, questions arise about their impact on local societies and cultures. Will international films destroy traditional value systems? Will they promote international recognition of legitimate differences? Both?

self. The demand is diffuse and difficult to quantify because not all members of society agree on how to maintain and improve the society.

In the United States, society uses the marketplace of ideas to form majority views about government and social norms. People and groups compete—often through media—to get their ideas adopted. Media coverage of an issue can help it gain political attention, but the U.S. system of government ensures, for better or worse, that political change is evolutionary, rather than rapid. The right of a woman to choose whether to have an abortion has been a political and social issue for many decades. Abortion continues to gain media attention as a political and social issue because people are divided. *Roe v. Wade* established the right of women to choose and maintained that right for nearly twenty years, but subsequent legislation and court decisions have chipped away at that position. Recent social developments indicate that many individuals support a more conservative social agenda in general, a trend that could affect the abortion issue. The marketplace of ideas continues to entertain varying points of view.

Access to the marketplace of ideas varies according to country. A dictatorship allows very little access because a dictator wants to retain power, which becomes difficult to hold if people have open access to information and ideas. When a dictator is able to control the marketplace of ideas, the country may suffer economic and social harm. For example, Fidel Castro's dictatorship of Cuba has succeeded in controlling the marketplace of ideas since 1959, but the country's economy has crumbled, and most people live in poverty. However, it is not always government that controls access to ideas. In some countries, public opinion excludes groups such as women or minorities from the public forum.

As national economies become more international through growing exports and imports, a global marketplace of ideas will increase in importance. This marketplace raises issues about how much access countries should have to one another's markets and how much mass communication will move across national borders. Beginning in 1996, the British Broadcasting Corporation broadcast directly into Germany, trying to attract German viewers with a twenty-four-hour English news service. Although BBC broadcasts had been available over cable and satellite, that marked the first commercial over-the-air television signal aimed at attracting viewers in another country. International television is likely to continue its growth, with remarkable implications. How extensively will the cultures of different countries affect one another once "free" television is available across boundaries? What control should and can a government exercise over the broadcasts into its nation? These and other questions will be debated in the global marketplace of ideas.

■ Supply of content

As shown in Figure 2.3, mass-media organizations supply content to the three communication markets to meet demand. In order to do this, every mass-media organization must go through six processes:

1. Media organizations must *generate content.* Sometimes organizations create original content, and sometimes they buy content from other sources.

2. Once the organization generates content, it must *produce and reproduce content in quantity.* That is how media become mass media. Content must be replicated

many times over to serve large audiences. The replication can come because a press prints thousands of copies or because a million television sets change electronic pulses into pictures and sound.

3. Content must be *delivered to users*. Once it has been reproduced, the content must somehow reach users. A delivery person might throw a newspaper onto a porch, or a cable may carry electronic pulses into living rooms.

4. Mass media must *generate financial support*. Most mass-media organizations either sell information to users or sell space and time to advertisers. However, other forms of financing are available. The selling of information and advertisements reflects the commercial nature of U.S. economic, social, and political systems. Some media organizations, such as public television and radio, are supported with grants, donations, and even government support.

5. The products of the organization must be *promoted*. Because so many media options are available today, an organization cannot assume that potential users will even know its product exists. Advertising and public-relations activities inform and persuade people to buy or use their products.

6. The first five processes must be *managed*. The generation, reproduction, delivery, financing, and promotion of mass media must be coordinated so that certain activities are accomplished in specific periods of time.

Effective strategies for carrying out these processes differ according to the size and complexity of each organization. At a weekly newspaper with a circulation of 5,000, the editor and one or two reporters write stories, take pictures, and compose headlines. A computer printer produces the text, which is pasted on paper the size of the newspaper pages. The "paste-up" goes to a printing shop that someone else owns, where it is photographed and turned into metal plates that go on a printing press. After the newspaper copies are printed, someone, often the editor, picks up the copies and returns to the newspaper office. After address labels are placed on subscribers' copies, most of the newspapers are delivered by mail. Promotion at the weekly might include annually delivering a paper containing a subscription flier to every household in town. Advertising salespeople collect money from advertisers; subscription fees are paid by mail. The editor and publisher manage the newspaper processes. A weekly can often survive with four to six full-time employees and three to six part-time employees.

In contrast, a metropolitan daily with a circulation of 350,000 has a department for each process. The newsroom and advertising department create the content. A metropolitan daily owns its own presses. Its composing room uses computers to create entire pages of text and graphics, and turns them into plates for the presses. The circulation department places copies in news racks and delivers newspapers to customers' doorsteps. The promotion department buys advertising on radio, television, and billboards, as well as running telemarketing campaigns. The accounting office bills advertisers and collects subscription money. The publisher, department heads, and dozens of assistant managers coordinate the activities, which might involve 500 or more people.

SUPPLY IN THE CONSUMER MARKET In supplying the consumer market, mass-media organizations either charge consumers, rely exclusively on advertising, or seek alternative funding sources. Most of those who charge consumers also carry advertising. Only a small proportion of media organizations, such as *Consumer Reports* magazine and Public Broadcasting System television stations, exist without advertising.

SUPPLY IN THE ADVERTISING MARKET Media organizations sell space and time to advertisers. With that space and time, they potentially attract readers, viewers, and listeners. The price of advertising increases with the number of potential customers an organization can provide to the advertiser and with the similarity of fit between the socioeconomic profile of the audience and the customers of the advertiser's business.

Advertising content can be classified by medium, such as television, radio, newspapers, magazines, yellow pages, billboards, and direct mail. In the 1970s and 1980s, movies began to increase advertising through **product placement,** charging a fee to place a particular product so that it attracts attention during the movie.

The advertising and consumer markets overlap to a degree because audience members use advertising content as information. Some people buy newspapers, for example, because of grocery-store advertisements.

After the bombing of the federal building in Oklahoma City, media provided a forum for people to express ideas. Here a mother of a child killed in the bombing was interviewed after the Timothy McVeigh verdict of guilty was handed down.

SUPPLY IN THE MARKETPLACE OF IDEAS The marketplace of ideas assumes that all ideas should be discussed in the open. The more ideas, the better. Only when ideas—even those thought radical—gain access to the public forum can social change occur. Women fought for almost a century before gaining the right to vote through a constitutional amendment adopted in 1920. Their ideas were considered radical by many men—and women.

The marketplace of ideas involves social discourse, and social discourse can lead to policy formation. All of this occurs because there is access in the United States to a marketplace of ideas that can filter into the political system. For example, the state of Oregon adopted strict recycling standards for its population by the early 1970s, ten to twenty years before most other states did the same. Oregon's marketplace of ideas considered the recycling issue important, and the discussion in that marketplace led to policy changes that other states eventually copied.

The supply for the marketplace of ideas comes from all sources of information, including individuals, newspapers, movies, television, recordings, and radio. Consumers, journalists, lobbyists, public-relations personnel, and government officials determine, both as individuals and as groups, what content has use in the marketplace of ideas.

▪ Interaction of supply and demand

Interaction between supply and demand in the consumer and advertising markets determines the amount and nature of media products and how financial resources are distributed among media companies. Consumers demand information to help them live. Mass media companies provide the content to make money. Ideally, consumers will get useful information, advertisers will get effective advertisements, and media companies will make a reasonable profit. However, market interactions often fail to achieve this ideal.

Three important factors create interaction problems: the level of competition for consumers, an organization's understanding of its customers, and the organization's goals. All three affect the responsiveness of media organizations to consumer and advertiser demand.

Competition moves power from producers to consumers. If some readers do not like *Time,* they can subscribe to *Newsweek.* Competition means choice, and choice forces companies to respond to consumer

product placement: Showing products in movies as a way of advertising the product without viewers thinking of the presentation as advertising.

Politically Correct in the Marketplace

In 1993, the University of Pennsylvania charged a student with verbal racial harassment, an action subject to expulsion from the university. The incident started when five members of an African American sorority held a founder's day celebration outside a dormitory. The women reported hearing someone say, "Shut up, you black water buffalo. Go back to the zoo where you belong." A white male student reported saying, "Shut up, you water buffalo. If you're looking for a party, there's a zoo a mile away." He denied the comments were intended to be racial.

The incident was widely publicized, although the university eventually dropped the charge when the women withdrew their complaint. The university claimed the student had undermined the judicial process by going to national media with the incident.

The incident and the subsequent media attention were part of a politically correct speech controversy that began in the early 1990s. The debate about PC defines a basic conflict between freedom of expression and infringement on others' rights. In a democratic society, the flow of ideas and opinions that constitutes the marketplace of ideas depends on how society answers two questions: (1) Does the exercise of an individual's freedom of speech harm someone else? (2) If harm occurs, at what point is individual freedom sacrificed to prevent that harm?

Western democracies assume that free speech should be protected unless serious harm can be shown. The traditional marketplace-of-ideas concept requires that even wrong information and hateful ideas be allowed into the market.

As the media report on those issues and describe racial incidents and other culturally loaded topics, they inevitably become involved in controversies over the choice of words and of description. As builders of a cultural narrative, media are involved in the debate over politically correct language, whether they choose to be or not.

SOURCE: Richard Bernstein, "Cap, Gown and Gag: The Struggle for Control," *The New York Times,* May 30, 1993, Sec. 4, p. 3; Nancy E. Row, "Penn's delay of trial for 'slur' called political, but not correct," *The Washington Times,* April 27, 1993, A1.

demand. Typically, media companies respond to competition for consumers by keeping the price of their product low, by increasing spending on content, and by trying to improve the usefulness of the information to the consumer. The goal of these responses is to provide a better product at a lower price than the competition.

A similar effect results from competition in the advertising market. If an advertiser does not like the price that one television station charges for advertising time, it can buy time from another. Competition holds down advertising prices and improves service to advertisers.

Although competition serves the consumer and the advertiser, it costs the media company. It is more expensive to produce and deliver information in competitive markets than in monopoly markets. The result of higher cost is lower profit. If given a choice, most media managers would pick a less competitive market.

Even though competition forces media companies to respond to consumer demand, it does not guarantee that the company's response will fulfill the customer's needs. The increased spending and lower price that results from competition will benefit the consumer only if companies produce more useful information or more attractive content.

The managers of media organizations must guess, through intuition, experience, and research, what type of information would be more useful to the consumer.

The final factor affecting the outcome of market interaction is organizational goals. Most mass-media organizations seek profits, but some aspire to higher profits than others. To increase profits, media organizations must either lower their expenses or raise their revenues. Efforts to increase revenues are risky, but cutting costs is not, at least in the short run. As a result, the local daily newspaper, which is usually the only one in town and thus has little direct competition, may get by with fewer reporters than it should have to cover news well. Similarly, organizations with higher profit goals will keep a closer watch on advertising prices to make sure they are getting the highest price possible. Over time, however, efforts to cut costs and hike prices often result in lower quality and fewer customers.

The profit goal is basic to the market system, but the impact of that goal differs depending on whether managers take a short-term or long-term approach. Profit goals motivate some media businesses to invest in long-term quality, which usually increases long-term profits because many consumers are attracted to quality information. Profit goals motivate others to cut costs to the bone for short-term profits. Over time, new technology usually allows more companies to enter a market, and the effect of more companies is to reduce the ability of individual companies to squeeze profit from consumers and advertisers during the short run.

TECHNOLOGY AND THE INTERACTION OF SUPPLY AND DEMAND The positive impact of technology does not always occur in the short run. For example, cable technology increased content options, but the high cost of running a cable to every house in the market required a government-sanctioned monopoly. Many cable companies took advantage of that monopoly to hike prices. Now, telecommunication companies and satellite distribution threaten the cable monopoly. The result will be even more choice and eventually lower prices for consumers.

Technology does not develop in a vacuum. It reflects investment by companies and regulation by governments. Despite the First Amendment to the Constitution, which prohibits Congress from restricting freedom of expression, many media organizations are regulated at the local and federal levels. Such regulation often attempts to promote competition or reduce the impact of monopoly. Those goals are not always accomplished, as demonstrated when the Federal Communications Commission (FCC) regulated cable prices in 1993. The FCC's effort to reduce monopoly pricing ended up increasing prices in a third of the cable markets. Because of rapidly changing communication technology, regulation also will increasingly affect the market interactions of supply and demand. Those interactions, in turn, affect technology convergence trends.

Market interactions are dynamic. Over time, consumer and advertiser demands change, and media companies must alter their practices and content accordingly. Ultimately, the success or failure of a market system rests on competition, which in turn depends on technology and government regulation.

CYCLICAL SYSTEMS Mass-media systems are cyclical. Each cycle allows media organizations to adjust to changing demands of consumers, advertisers, and society itself. The nature of the cycles varies, but some are consistent. The broadcast television industry in the United States has a yearly cycle. Every fall, networks drop programs and add new ones to attract more viewers. The more successful a network was the previous year, the fewer changes it makes. CBS provides a good example of how a network reacts.

During the 1995–96 television season, CBS found itself behind both ABC and NBC in attracting viewers. It seemed that the relative newcomer Fox Network was snapping at CBS's heels. As a result, CBS was losing money on its network operations. Advertisers

"There's no free lunch," an old saying goes. Someone always pays the bill. Historically, most of the bills for mass media have been paid by advertisers, with a smaller portion paid directly by consumers.

Advertising and consumer payment each have advantages and costs. People who pay directly for media get a content vote, but high costs to the consumer mean that people with lower incomes are excluded. That exclusion has implications for the marketplace of ideas because people with more money have access to more in-

Who Pays the Bills?

formation than those with less money. For example, most local cable systems carry public meetings. People who cannot afford cable have less access to information about political activity in the community than those who buy cable. If computer-based television grows, the results could magnify the problem. Many families may not be able to buy a TV set with a built-in

computer or pay the rates needed for a one hundred–channel cable system.

The long-term impact of new technology will be shaped by who pays for the traffic on the information highway. If advertisers pay, we will see more electronic billboards and less information. If advertisers don't pay, fewer people will be able to get the information that will be available.

won't buy time unless a network can deliver enough viewers to make their expenditure worthwhile. CBS's programming no longer met the entertainment wants of a large number of people in the consumer market. The company conducted research to identify consumer demands and designed programs to try to meet those demands.

CBS's strategy in supplying programming was to use formerly popular television stars in new programs. Ted Danson and Bill Cosby appeared in new shows, and CBS promoted those programs heavily. The competing networks did not remain unchanged, even though they had fewer changes. ABC returned Michael J. Fox to television in a move similar to CBS's.

The cycle of adjusting content to the demands of consumers to make a profit allows consumers to influence content. The amount of that influence depends on how attractive particular types of consumers are to advertisers. Young viewers have more influence over content than elderly viewers because young people spend more money on the goods that advertisers want to sell.

The test of a mass-media system's ability to serve its society is the variety of content that is available for all people in that society. If content serves minority groups as well as the majority, the system will more likely energize the marketplace of ideas that society depends upon for survival. Openness to a variety of ideas and information is the hallmark of a democracy.

The U.S. mass media system and the world

The U.S. mass media system does not exist independently. Although Figure 2.3 concentrates on the U.S. system, it also shows that people in other countries demand products from U.S. mass media organizations, and people in the United States demand information from other parts of the world. Media organizations supply that information and aggressively market it across national boundaries.

The international trade in information and ideas undoubtedly will grow. The U.S. economy has become an international economy, and international sources of news and information will grow in importance, especially in the marketplace of ideas. A well-informed person can no longer pay attention just to what happens in the United States.

If one were to diagram the world mass media system, the depiction would be a series of circular systems, such as the one in Figure 2.3, with lines showing the interconnections of supply, demand, and sources among all the systems. The three communication markets exist to some degree in all countries, but the advertising market remains much less developed in most other societies. Major world changes in the late 1980s and early 1990s, particularly the decline of communist-supported autocracies, created the potential for widespread development of mass media systems.

Most countries seem to be moving toward a market system like the U.S. system, although many hope to modify that model to suit their own countries.

Summary

- Communication is central to human beings, both as individuals and as group members.

- The communication process involves transmitting information and ideas to one person or to a large group of people.

- Typically, mass media are newspapers, magazines, television, radio, books, recordings, and movies.

- Individuals use mass communication for decision making, diversion, surveillance, social and cultural interaction, and self-understanding.

- Groups use mass communication to coordinate the political, economic, and social activities of their members and to transmit their social and cultural heritage.

- Successful communication of information from a sender to a receiver depends on eliminating semantic noise and channel noise.

- The U.S. mass media system is a circular process through which people and groups turn their information wants and needs into demand for content.

- Demand occurs in the consumer market, advertising market, and the marketplace of ideas.

- Demand for information reflects the personality and socioeconomic environment of those seeking information.

- Mass media organizations meet demands for information by supplying content in different media forms.

- Individuals and groups act as sources of information, as well as consumers.

- As suppliers of content, all mass media organizations must carry out six processes. Content must be generated, reproduced, and delivered. Those three processes must be financed, promoted, and managed.

- Supplying the advertising market means selling space and time primarily to businesses and other organizations so they can transmit messages that influence the behavior of their audience.

- Supplying the consumer market involves selling or giving information to people in exchange for their potential attention to advertising.

42

- Supplying the marketplace of ideas means contributing ideas and information to political leaders and other citizens.
- The long-term existence of a mass media organization depends on how useful its product is to the people who pay for it.
- No mass media system can be isolated from other systems in the world. The U.S. system supplies and demands information and ideas from systems in other countries.

Navigating the Web

Communication on the web

Media institutions and industries use World Wide Web sites to generate interest in their activities and to provide information about business ventures. At the other end of the spectrum are research sites that provide critical information about media as institutions. The sites that provide critical information tend to be produced by academics.

Veronis, Suhler & Associates	www.vsacomm.com

This site contains financial and economic data about all types of media, such as television, newspapers, and books. VS&A is a communication investment banking organization that also provides yearly industry-level data about communication data. More detailed information is made available through books published yearly.

Resources in Communication Economics	www.fullerton.edu/titan/commecon/homepage.html

Professor Robert G. Picard at the University of California, Fullerton, started this site to provide information about the economic nature of communication media. The site contains bibliographies for academic research in a variety of media, lists of texts, and a few syllabi from courses. It also has an extensive list of links.

Media Communications Studies page on media institutions	www.aber.ac.uk/~dgc/gen.html#D

The Media Communication Studies site was established by Daniel Chandler at the University of Wales, Aberystwyth. Included among its numerous pages is one about media institutions. It also provides other links and material by Ben Bagdikian and Noam Chomsky about media institutions and society.

▓ Questions for review

1. What is channel noise? Semantic noise?
2. Explain the difference between interpersonal, mediated, and mass communication.
3. What are the five individual uses of mass media?
4. How do groups use mass media?
5. What are the differences between market and nonmarket communications systems?
6. What are the three communication markets as described in this chapter?
7. What is demand structure?
8. What processes must media organizations carry out to supply content to the three communication markets?

▓ Issues to think about

1. How can an individual have an impact on the content of mass media?
2. What are the positive and negative impacts on society of market and nonmarket systems of communication?
3. How important is interactivity in a media system to the development of individuals and of society?
4. If you were the president of a developing country and you wanted to create a market system of communication, what modifications in the U.S. system would you seek to make?

▓ Suggested readings

Alexander, Alison, and Hanson, Jarice, eds. *Taking Sides: Clashing Views on Controversial Issues in Mass Media and Society,* 3rd ed. (Guilford, CT.: The Dushkin Publishing Group, Inc., 1995).

Altschull, J. Herbert. *Agents of Power: The Media and Public Policy,* 2nd ed. (White Plains, NY: Longman, 1995).

Blumler, Jay, and Katz, Elihu, eds. *The Uses of Mass Communication* (Beverly Hills, CA: Sage, 1974).

Lasswell, Harold D. "The Structure and Function of Communication in Society," in *The Communication of Ideas,* ed. Lyman Bryson (New York: Institute for Religious and Social Studies, 1948).

Lazarsfeld, Paul F., and Merton, Robert K. "Mass Communication, Popular Taste, and Organized Social Action," in *The Communication of Ideas,* ed. Lyman Bryson (New York: Institute for Religious and Social Studies, 1948).

McManus, John H. *Market-Driven Journalism: Let the Citizen Beware* (Thousand Oaks, CA: Sage, 1994).

McQuail, Denis. *Mass Communication Theory: An Introduction,* 2nd ed. (Newbury Park, CA: Sage, 1987).

Tunstall, Jeremy. *The Media Are American* (London: Constable, 1977).

Historical Development of Mass Communication

Keyconcepts

- Gatekeeping Roles in the Media
- The Enlightenment and a Free Democratic Press
- Subcultures in the Media
- Buyer-Beware Advertising
- Public Relations and the Media
- Wartime Press Controls and the Committee on Public Information
- Radio and the News Wire Services
- Oligopoly in Media Industries
- Consumer Culture and the Media
- Cold War Controls and the Media
- Popular Culture as Media Creation
- New and Old Media

In 1733, a poor printer named John Peter Zenger criticized the royal governor of New York for acquiring property by illegal means. The governor was determined to improve his own financial situation at the expense of the citizens of New York, and a group of prominent citizens had hired Zenger to put their complaints into print.

Zenger was arrested and charged with seditious libel. Andrew Hamilton, a famous Philadelphia lawyer, traveled to New York to defend the hapless printer. In doing so, he made an eloquent plea to the jury, asking it to act for the benefit not of the printer alone but for every "freeman that lives under a British government on the Main of America." Hamilton argued his case:

> It is the best cause. It is the cause of liberty; and I make no doubt but your up-right conduct this day will not only entitle you to the love and esteem of your fellow citizens; but every man who prefers freedom to a life of slavery will bless and honor you as men who have baffled the attempt of tyranny, and, by an impartial and uncor-rupt verdict, have laid a noble foundation for securing to ourselves, our posterity, and our neighbors that to which nature and the laws of our country have given us as a right—the liberty both of exposing and opposing arbitrary power (in these parts of the world, at least) by speaking and writing truth.

When Andrew Hamilton argued in 1733 for the cause of liberty, he never realized that media eventually would become targets of investigation for deceptive practices such as those that flourished in 1950s quiz shows.

45

Although scholars debate whether the Zenger case established a legal precedent in creating a truth defense in libel cases, its powerful call for freedom of expression in the United States has never been questioned. Hamilton argued that colonists who wanted to escape the tyranny of European authority and oppression must establish the right to express and discuss political issues and to oppose arbitrary power. Among the many factors that contributed to the American Revolution, opposing the arbitrary power of British rule provided the emotional incentive for patriots to fight zealously for a new type of government. When the Bill of Rights was passed, all citizens theoretically were given the right to freedom of expression. Despite that guarantee, over the years both government and the strong arm of public opinion have battered that right in both the political and social arenas. The history of freedom of expression is not a history of triumph but a history of continuing struggle.

The study of history includes learning dates, places, and names. But history is more about events and their meaning in the context of their time. Studying history can help us understand conflict and change. By watching how issues have been resolved in the past, we are more able and willing to deal with current problems and ideas. As media have developed in their many forms, issues surface and resurface in American society. Some of those include the following:

- The relationship of media to government. Do the media serve as a useful watchdog over government activity and the possible exercise of arbitrary power?

- The relationship of media to business. How does consumer capitalism affect media development?

- The role of media industries in a democratic society. What is the role of industries such as public relations and advertising in the development and maintenance of a free society?

Printing and mass production: A technological revolution

Men and women have always sought ways to communicate not only with each other individually but with groups of people as well. Through the lectures of Socrates in ancient Greece to the beating of drums in Africa, individuals have conveyed messages to inform and challenge people. Such messages were critical to survival as well as to the development of various types of civilizations.

As long ago as 1,700 years before the birth of Christ, in the Mediterranean, those trying to preserve information created a system of movable type by pressing signs into clay. Other carvings in stone and on **papyrus** sheets or scrolls are historical remnants of an attempt to communicate and to preserve ideas in various forms of writing. In 1041, the Chinese printer Pi Sheng used movable type made of hundreds of clay blocks bearing Chinese ideograms to print books. That printing technique was introduced to Europe when Marco Polo returned from his travels in China in 1295.

In medieval Europe, religious elites controlled information sources and channels. The Catholic Church acted as an early gatekeeper of information by dominating the dis-

Keyconcept

Gatekeeping Roles in the Media: Any person or institution that controls what is published and what is kept away from the public eye has a gatekeeping role. In modern times the term *gatekeeper* describes an editor or anyone who selects information to be published, broadcast, or distributed in the media.

papyrus: A Mediterranean plant whose stem was used to make paper and other products, such as twine.

Did You Know?

One of the goals of freedom of the press was to allow opposition to arbitrary power. In many ways, that is still a goal today. In many historical situations, people used media—at first print and then broadcast—to create tension between ideas and to challenge, as well as maintain, the status quo. As you read subsequent chapters, think about times when the tension between ideas seems to increase or decrease.

- Did you know that Andrew Hamilton, the first American lawyer to exhort fellow citizens to prefer "freedom over slavery," "battle tyranny," and "oppose arbitrary power," made his speech forty years before the American Revolution began?

- Did you know that in the 1830s the American Bible Society adapted new technology more quickly than most newspaper companies or book publishers did? And that the conservative social movement of the mid-1990s uses advanced computer technologies to communicate with its members and with Congress?

- Did you know that the *Ladies' Home Journal* in 1906 spearheaded a reform movement to teach the dangers of venereal disease to adolescents during a time when such diseases were not discussed in polite company?

- Did you know that from 1962 to 1981 people trusted CBS news anchorman Walter Cronkite more than almost any other person in America?

---

semination of official notices. Even then, informal networks spread alternative messages and challenged ideas, transmitting a social heritage with a greater dimension than that conveyed by official proclamations. Books were printed through the laborious copying of manuscripts, usually within the confines of a monastery. Official notices also were hand copied and carried as letters or posted where those who could read could pass on the information to those who could not.

Although Eastern cultures had experimented with various printing techniques, the development of movable type in the Western world by Johannes Gutenberg in the fifteenth century paved the way for the expansion of a print culture. Gutenberg carved wood so that letters stood in relief on tiny blocks that could be rearranged as different words and then inked so that multiple copies of documents could be made. The wood blocks made fuzzy letters, but Gutenberg's assistant, Peter Schoeffer, soon recognized that metal could be used instead of wood to produce a cleaner type. He used this method to print the English Bible in 1455.[1]

As always, the invention of technology had major ramifications. The marketplace of ideas became a commodity market. The mass production of books not only loosened the church's grip on information, but it also created new relationships between the church and the entrepreneur or merchant. Soon merchants began to produce and sell books, providing an outlet

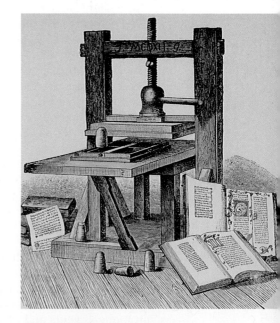

A flatbed press from the Gutenberg era.

for ideas and values that had been kept out of print and confined to oral transmission. The public eagerly sought the histories, religious books, travelogues, and romances that were traded on the open market. Some books that offended the official gatekeepers were prohibited by the church, but they still were sold on the black market. Once printing was available, it was not easily controlled, despite the best efforts of kings and church officials.[2]

Communication networks in colonial North America

When the first English settlers arrived on North American shores in the 1600s, they set up communities with strong ties to their mother country. The bonds between the church and government in England were also present in English America. The government did not trust the popular printing press and maintained firm control over it. The colonies were relatively isolated from one another, and until the 1750s, official communication in small communities was oral. Settlers arrived from a variety of European countries, but communication ties existed between the colonies and a country of origin, rather than among the colonies. Until the late 1600s, transportation across the continent that was to become the United States was practically nonexistent. Therefore, ships from Europe brought letters, newspapers, and books that kept elite colonists in touch with their home government and church. Those who did not read had less contact with the home country and relied more strongly on oral communication.

In the absence of widely distributed printed forms of information, ministers held a good deal of power as the educated elite who could convey information—and persuade—from the pulpit. Ministers, especially in New England, passed along official information as well as moral instruction in their sermons. Such communication was only supplemented, not replaced, by the first printing press, established by Elizabeth Glover in 1638 in Cambridge, Massachusetts. Mrs. Glover's press issued *The Freeman's Oath,* a formal contract of behavioral rules that citizens in the colony were required to sign, and the *Bay Psalm Book.* Those books and documents were not intended for casual reading but for creating standards for the public life of the community. Religious elites used information channels to promote prosocial values, such as keeping one's word, keeping the faith in public worship, and advancing literacy. In the South, where life revolved around property owners, books and magazines imported from England were regarded as essential for improving one's conversational ability and therefore promoted the concept of a gentleman planter elite.[3]

Formal communication systems in the colonies did not develop until postal systems were established in the late 1600s. Once postal routes operated alongside trade routes, information became a commercial as well as a political and social commodity. Communication was always closely allied with transportation. Information could travel no faster than a man or woman could walk, or a horse could gallop. Therefore, newspapers tended to serve local communities and then to circulate along some of the more popular trade routes, which also served as the delivery system for books.

Challenges to elite authority

During the early colonial period, books were primarily imported. Colonists bought histories, religious books, professional books, and some romances. Newspapers focused first on foreign events and then on local events. They both challenged and cooperated with the royal government. Benjamin Harris in 1690 published the newspaper *Publick Occurrences, Both Foreign and Domestick,* but the royal government was not ready to tolerate

Colonial printshops were often distribution points for information from Europe as well as for political dissent. The colonial newspaper rarely made enough money to support the printing business, but it supplemented income made from selling books and stationery items.

critical comment on local affairs and prohibited Harris from publishing a second issue. By 1701, postmaster John Campbell circulated a handwritten *News-Letter,* published "with authority," or approval of the governor. By 1704, the newspaper circulated in printed form from Boston. Competing newspapers developed in the city with the *Gazette* in 1719 and the *Courant* in 1721. William Brooker succeeded Campbell as postmaster and started a competing paper because Campbell would not relinquish his own editorship.

Newspapers were moving rapidly into the marketplace and began to target a wider audience. Reprints from English newspapers introduced middle-class wit and humor, and in 1721, the *New England Courant* began to discuss public controversies and to emphasize local news, clear challenges to elite authority. The newspaper, started by James Franklin, Benjamin Franklin's brother, was radical by colonial standards. James Franklin soon found himself jailed by colonial elites who resisted the challenge while his brother Ben secretly carried on as editor. The newspaper industry spread to New York and Philadelphia, and by 1740, thirteen newspapers had been established along the coast of the British colonies.

Other editors found themselves in situations similar to that of James Franklin. In 1733, John Peter Zenger, printing the *New York Journal* for a radical attorney named James Alexander, was charged with **seditious libel**. At that time, the law allowed a jury to determine only whether a printer had actually published specific material, not whether it was true or was, indeed, seditious. After a highly publicized trial and the eloquent defense by Andrew Hamilton presented at the beginning of this chapter, Zenger was acquitted, thereby establishing a political, although not legal, **precedent** for the right to criticize government. Hamilton argued that truth should be a defense in any seditious libel trial and that a jury should be able to judge not only whether an accused printer actually printed the material but whether it was seditious. He appealed to the colonists' dislike of arbitrary power, an aversion that would become even stronger as colonists began to move toward considering independence.[4]

■ Independence and the marketplace of ideas

Newspapers and pamphlets played an important role during the late eighteenth-century struggle for independence. They not only recounted events but presented competing ideologies for discussion in the marketplace of ideas. During the mid-eighteenth century—especially after the French and Indian War, which required colonists to contribute to what they considered a British cause—colonists began to entertain the idea of increased independence from Britain. Most of the books they read were still imported, with the exception of religious books and some quasipolitical tracts written by Puritan ministers. Nevertheless, many of the imported books spread the ideas of the Enlightenment, ideas that challenged authoritarian control and championed individual rights and democratic participation. Newspapers and pamphlets published in the colonial period also conveyed those ideas.

The printing establishment in the colonies represented networks of trained printers, some of whom were connected by family ties, and of business partnerships. Benjamin Franklin, for example, financed the development of newspapers in areas distant from major urban centers; he also published books and helped establish libraries.

seditious libel: Criticism of the government. In colonial times, criticism was considered libelous even if true.

precedent: A legal decision that sets a standard for how subsequent cases are decided.

Mary Katherine Goddard

In colonial times, printing and newspaper publishing were usually family businesses, with everyone sharing in the hard work. About thirty colonial women were known to be publishers, printers, and typesetters. Some women acted as official printers for colonial and city governments; others published newspapers, pamphlets, and tracts. Many took over businesses when their husband died or controlled them until the children were old enough to do so.

One of those women was Mary Katherine Goddard, born in Connecticut on June 16, 1738. After her father died in 1762, Goddard and her brother, William Goddard, continued working with their mother, Sarah Updike Goddard, in the family printing and publishing business in Providence, Rhode Island. In 1765, the family began publishing the *Providence Gazette,* a weekly newspaper. Then from 1768 to 1773, Goddard and her brother ran a printing plant in Philadelphia, Pennsylvania. Three years later, Goddard moved to Baltimore, Maryland, at her brother's request, where she published the *Maryland Journal* while he was away in other colonies, setting up the forerunner of the present postal system.

Goddard turned the *Maryland Journal* into a highly influential voice during the colonial rebellion. In addition, she ran a successful printing, bookbinding, and bookselling business. Furthermore, Goddard was Baltimore's postmistress from 1775 to 1789, the first woman ever appointed to a federal office.

In 1777, when advancing British forces made the Continental Congress move from Philadelphia to Baltimore, the congress commissioned Goddard to print the first Declaration of Independence—with all the signers' names. Throughout the hard times of the American Revolution, she managed not only to keep the *Maryland Journal* afloat but to turn it into one of the colonies' most successful newspapers, publishing extras on the Battle of Bunker Hill and the Continental Congress's call to arms.

After Goddard made the *Maryland Journal* profitable, her brother resumed control—creating an argument that led to a permanent split between them. Although Goddard had been postmistress for fourteen years and had made the postal system profitable, the new postmaster general, Samuel Osgood, decided to remove her in favor of a man. The only reason given was that duties might be harder "than a

woman could undertake." The two hundred signatures by leading citizens on Goddard's petitions and her personal appeals to President George Washington and the U.S. Senate went unheeded.

For the next twenty years, Goddard ran her bookshop and a store. She died at age 78 in Baltimore, on August 12, 1816.

SOURCES: Maurine H. Beasley and Sheila J. Gibbons, "Mary Katherine Goddard," *Taking Their Place: A Documentary History of Women and Journalism* (Washington, D.C.: American University Press, 1993), pp. 51–55; Phyllis J. Read and Bernard L. Witlieb, "Mary Katherine Goddard," *The Book of Women's Firsts* (New York: Random House, 1992), pp. 177–178; Joseph T. Wheeler, *The Maryland Press, 1777–1790* (Baltimore: Maryland Historical Society, 1938), pp. 11, 14; Margie Luckett, ed., *Maryland Women,* vol. 1 (Baltimore, 1931), p. 169.

Although the industry was dominated by men, many women were typesetters in family operations, and sometimes women edited newspapers after their husbands, who had been the previous editors, died. The publishing of books, pamphlets, and newspapers, along with attempts to make printed material more accessible to a general populace, gave impetus to the colonists' move toward independence.

Printers at first were politically cautious, hoping to increase their profits by serving all political constituencies, but as the century moved forward they allied themselves with specific political factions. When the British Parliament passed the Stamp Act, which assessed a tax on paper, newspaper publishers rebelled. The tax was designed to help pay for the French and Indian War, but colonists argued that they had no say in whether or

Keyconcept

The Enlightenment and a Free Democratic Press: The colonial era in America coincided with the rise in Europe of the Enlightenment, a philosophical movement with new ideas about scientific reasoning, democracy, rule by consent of the governed, and free criticism of government. Such ideas, spread by print media, rapidly promoted the concept of a press free of most government controls.

how the war should be fought and should therefore not have to pay the tax. Some printed woodcuts with skull-and-crossbones emblems; other ceased publishing, refusing to pay the tax. By the time of the Revolution, printers were notoriously patriotic. Lack of tolerance for diversity of political opinion characterized most communities, and printers loyal to the British Crown were quickly exiled. Despite protestations against British control of the press, colonists readily exercised the control of public opinion in exiling those who published unpopular opinions. The resistance to free expression during times of stress became a characteristic of American media during the next two centuries, with the media often feeling free to demonize and stereotype America's enemies in times of social strife or war.

Newspaper editors and pamphleteers such as Thomas Paine, who wrote, "These are the times that try men's souls," as Washington's troops were mired in winter snows in Trenton, New Jersey, offered eloquent pleas for steadfastness during the struggle for independence.

Communication and nation building

Once independence was acquired, the nation faced many years of building a political structure and establishing economic stability. During the years of the early republic, editors helped forge political ideologies that became the basis for the Constitution and the political-party structure. As that structure solidified, editors turned toward economies of scale and responded to increased national products and markets with a changed emphasis on buyer-beware advertising, a change that fostered the growth of advertising as an industry. A national market structure produced a commercial emphasis that took little responsibility for the truth of published claims. Through the first half of the nineteenth century, technological changes included the steam press, photography, and lithography. The invention of the telegraph broke the first link between communication and transportation: no longer could information travel only as fast as a horse or a steam engine. News collection could be almost instantaneous. By the end of the nineteenth century, publishing—including books, magazines, and newspapers—was big business. Editors such as New York's Joseph Pulitzer and William Randolph Hearst commanded huge circulations and celebrated all aspects of city life through sensationalized copy that appealed to a broad range of social classes.

The fight for political dominance

Although the states ratified the Constitution with no provision for a free press, within three years—in 1791—a Bill of Rights was added to ensure civil liberties: the right to assemble, to choose a religion, to speak and write freely, and to be tried fairly, among others. Chief among the Bill of Rights was the First Amendment:

Congress shall make no law respecting an establishment of religion, or prohibiting the free exercise thereof; or abridging the freedom of speech, or of the press; or the right of the public peaceably to assemble, and to petition the government for a redress of grievances.

From 1790 to 1830, during the fight for ratification of the Constitution and the establishment of political parties, newspaper editors informed the public about the different positions espoused by the Federalists, who wanted a strong central government, and the Anti-Federalists, who argued vociferously for preserving the powers of the states. The period has been labeled the Dark Ages of American Journalism by many historians because of the rabid political rhetoric that was used. Republican Benjamin Franklin Bache, the grandson of Benjamin Franklin, accused the revered George Washington of having "debauched" the nation and argued that "the masque of patriotism may be worn to conceal the foulest designs against the liberties of a people." Bache was so outrageous that even his friends at times turned against him. But he stuck to his political principles, "in which he said that government officers were fallible, the Constitution good but not obviously 'stampt with the seal of perfection,' and that a free press was 'one of the first safeguards of Liberty.' "[5] A vituperative editor on the Federalist side, William Cobbett, called Bache black-hearted, seditious, sleepy-eyed, vile, and perverted.

The Dark Ages label was attached by modern-day historians who tried to impose current journalistic standards—including the twentieth-century emphasis on objectivity—on newspapers of the early period. However, those political newspapers did not value objectivity as an ideal. Editors, often members of the elite and appointed by a politician, helped establish the function of the press in a newly created democratic society.[6] Editors sometimes overstepped the boundaries of good taste, but they established the right of newspapers to comment on political competition, a right that has fueled the political process ever since.

This 1801 political cartoon attacked the administration of President Thomas Jefferson. These types of cartoons were popular in the wide-open style of political combat common to the period.

Politicians did not always favor outspoken political dissent. And despite the First Amendment, a Federalist Congress in 1798 passed the restrictive Naturalization, Enemy Alien, and Sedition Acts. The Sedition Act made it possible to indict those who "shall write, print, utter, or publish . . . false, scandalous and malicious writing or writings against the Government of the United States, or the President of the United States, or either house of the Congress . . . with intent to defame . . . or to bring them into contempt or disrepute." Those who were convicted could be punished by a fine of not more than $2,000 and could be imprisoned for two years. Republican editors across the land were indicted and jailed, and only when Thomas Jefferson took office as president of the United States were those editors released. The Alien and Sedition Acts indeed marked a low point with their restrictions against the criticism of government in a time of peace. Since those acts were passed, such restrictions generally have been reserved for times of war.[7]

Congress recognized early the importance of the press system in distributing information to the nation, and from the beginning, newspapers secured a favored position in the postal system. Federalists and Anti-Federalists argued over newspaper rates, with Federalists wanting to favor large city newspapers and thereby establish a national in-

53

formation system. Republicans (or Jeffersonians) wanted to maintain local control and to protect local newspapers from dominance by city or national newspapers. Although the argument was repeated during many sessions of Congress, each postal act passed did create favorable rates—far cheaper than letter rates—for newspapers. Magazines did not fare as well, and the lack of postal support hindered their growth until the mid-nineteenth century.

Publishing and a diversified society

The media in the United States have always reflected tension between mainstream culture and competing subcultures. In the colonial period, people such as James Franklin struck out against a colonial elite. Some newspapers focused on political issues while others confronted social and cultural issues that represented the diversity of the new and thriving society. When people moved west and trade routes developed across the Alleghenies, ethnic newspapers developed alongside English-language publications. Immigration patterns produced ethnic enclaves that naturally created concentrated market segments for ethnic media.

Keyconcept

Subcultures in the Media: Regional, ethnic, and social groups that are not part of the dominant culture of a society make up subcultures or minisocieties within larger societies. These groups often use media to gain recognition and self-expression.

From as early as 1739, foreign-language newspapers provided immigrants with news from home. German-language newspapers were among the first to appear. They dominated the ethnic-press field until World War I, but French, Welsh, Italian, Norwegian, Swedish, Spanish, Danish, Dutch, Bohemian, Polish, Portuguese, and Chinese newspapers all appeared during the nineteenth century.

The social and political dilemmas of the society are apparent in early publications by Native Americans and by African Americans. Native Americans, who relied primarily on oral communication, recognized that whites were able to sustain certain advantages because of their written language. Because of that, Native Americans developed written vocabularies. The best known was Sequoyah's syllabary, developed and spread between 1812 and 1828. Printed in English and Cherokee, the *Cherokee Phoenix* during the 1830s and 1840s informed Native Americans of actions by whites as well as about tribal concerns. Samuel Cornish and John Russwurm printed the first known black newspaper, *Freedom's Journal,* in 1827. The newspaper carried poetry and reprinted articles, as well as original articles about slavery in the United States and other countries. Several other black newspapers were developed in the 1830s; in the 1840s, some of the best-known newspapers, such as Frederick Douglass's *Ram's Horn* and the *North Star,* were issued.

Official support through postal rates did not come as easily to magazines and books as it did to newspapers. Although the right of political debate had emerged through the need to guard against arbitrary power, officials were not so ready to support magazines and books that ventured outside the political realm. Books—particularly light fiction—remained a source of concern for keepers of the social order. Ministers worried, for ex-

Samuel E. Cornish was an American clergyman and abolitionist who was co-editor of Freedom's Journal.

John Brown Russwurm edited Freedom's Journal, *an abolitionist newspaper, and became governor of Maryland Colony in Liberia.*

Frederick Douglass, a freed slave, became an eloquent spokesman for the Anti-Slavery Society, traveling in England and the United States. He published a newspaper to argue for the emancipation of slaves.

54 ample, that women might waste their days reading insignificant stories instead of caring for their husbands and children. Nevertheless, magazines and books gained a small market niche. Magazines carried articles about public life, travel, and politics. Books, too expensive to mail, were distributed by book peddlers.

■ Growth and expansion

From the 1830s through the end of the nineteenth century, communication industries expanded not only in terms of the audience they served but also in types of communication products and technology. The expansion reflected spectacular changes in the economic and social fabric of the country. As railway lines spread throughout the massive geographic area that was to define the United States, products were marketed nationally. The new transportation lines provided new circulation routes, and national marketing ensured a wide advertising base for at least the mainstream publications. Circulations expanded, and the distribution of newspapers, magazines, and books spread throughout the country. Urbanization marked the last part of the century, with cultural emphasis on individual accomplishment and the growth of education.

NEWSPAPERS AND URBAN LIFE By the 1830s, the commercial nature of newspapers began to outdistance their political nature—so much so that for years historians described the period as the beginning of the commercial press, the era of the penny press. Publishers such as Benjamin Day, who published the *New York Sun,* saw business opportunities in publishing. They sold their newspapers for a penny and relied more significantly on advertising for revenues as they began to target a wider group of readers. The growing populations of the cities, increased public education, and the development of railroad transportation that resulted in nationally distributed products created new classes of readers and new opportunities for advertising.

Publishers increasingly adopted a let-the-buyer beware approach to advertising and became conveyors rather than endorsers of advertisements and those who manufactured the products advertised. The boom in advertising created the basis for an advertising industry in which buyers bought space at a discount in volume from publishers and then sold it to advertisers, with a heavy markup in price. The practice, often called **brokering,** in many situations today is illegal.

Editors soon realized that their growing audiences looked for information about the cities they occupied. The public's need for information and its desire for entertainment required dynamic content. Courtroom drama and controversy over public services became standard newspaper fare. Publishers hired reporters to seek out information and no longer relied on letters and political documents as their main source of content. Newspapers in the cities were hawked by newsboys on street corners. However, the old model of politically oriented newspaper fare dominated the local market for years, and the penny press of the urban metropolis did not represent a model for the nation as a whole. Well into the twentieth century, newspaper editors were heavily involved in partisan politics, and the cry of independence reflected a financial independence from party support rather than an intellectual independence from party allegiance. The technology of the steam press and other improvements allowed newspaper publishers to target large audiences and to increase the circulations of 2,000 common to newspapers in 1820 to several hundred thousand. By the end of the nineteenth century, the New York papers reached as high as a million in circulation.

Keyconcept

Buyer-Beware Advertising: Early advertising in the media was completely unregulated, with no legal restrictions on what could be advertised or on what advertisers could tell consumers about products. The buyer, who was expected to be on guard against lies or deception, had no protection against false claims.

brokering: The practice of buying space at a discount from publishers and selling it at a higher rate to advertisers.

■ Telegraph breaks transportation link

In 1844, when Samuel Morse opened the nation's first telegraph line with the question "What hath God wrought?" he also broke the link between communication and transportation. No longer could communication travel only as fast as a horse could gallop; it could travel from its point of origin to a publisher's desk via wires, instantaneously. By 1846, newspapers in upstate New York were using the wires to transmit news from the state capital of Albany to western cities. In 1848, a group of New York newspapers, including the *Courier and Enquirer,* the *Sun,* the *Herald,* the *Journal of Commerce,* the *Tribune,* and the *Express,* hired a steamer to retrieve news from the major port of Halifax, Nova Scotia. The papers also negotiated a joint arrangement to use telegraph lines to transmit news from Boston to New York. Those ventures resulted in the establishment of the Associated Press, which, along with other wire services, expanded the flow of news until the Civil War. After an interruption caused by the war, the wire services became important conveyors of information not only nationally but internationally as well. The Associated Press remained the dominant wire service, experiencing little competition until the 1900s.[8]

PUBLICATIONS ADVANCE CAUSES Special-interest publications, primarily newspapers and sometimes magazines, served geographically disparate but ideologically similar audiences. Often those publications fought against the established social order and countered stereotypical depictions in mainstream media. Antislavery societies published pamphlets and newspapers, uniting those who opposed slavery. Those societies used new plate-making devices and printing presses to expand their circulation of materials, and in 1835, the Anti-Slavery Society mailed more than a million pieces of literature. Radicals such as William Lloyd Garrison and Elijah Lovejoy gained national reputations. Garrison in *The Liberator* denounced the U.S. Constitution as a proslavery document, and Lovejoy, a martyr in the anti-slavery cause, was killed in Alton, Illinois. Women, such as Angelina Grimke, who fought for suffrage, broke the societal barrier that forbade women to speak in public forums, and women wrote political pamphlets and reproduced slave emblems, recognizing that pictures had greater impact than words. Slave emblems were illustrations used in books and pamphlets and on objects, such as cameos.

Once again, despite the guarantees of the First Amendment, censorship became a part of public life as postmasters regularly burned antislavery materials and Congress imposed a gag order on the discussion of slavery. At times, just as it had during the Revolution, public opinion remained the strongest form of censorship and those who espoused the antislavery cause were exiled from their homes.

MAGAZINES AND BOOKS THRIVE The mid-1850s also witnessed a magazine revolution. Many of the same factors that promoted the broadened newspaper industry—the development of the penny press, for example—affected the magazine industry as well. Beginning in the mid-1800s, high-quality magazines such as *Scribner's, Harper's,* and the *Atlantic Monthly* catered to upper-middle-class audiences with travelogues, historical articles, biography, and fiction. Nationally marketed products produced advertising for nationally marketed magazines, and in 1879, Congress finally passed postal regulations that made magazine distribution through the mails less expensive. Women's magazines also expanded, forming the core of the magazine industry that continues to the present.

From 1800 to 1850, the number of books available to U.S. readers increased dramatically. Books, like newspapers, served an audience that expanded beyond the cultural elite. Novels, travel accounts, etiquette books, and religious and educational volumes circulated throughout the country. An act by Congress in 1851 that admitted books as mailable objects boosted distribution. Books, such as *McGuffey's Reader,* endorsed cultural norms that advocated public education and modes of conduct such as honesty and

Antislavery Visuals

S lave emblems, or visuals depicting the horrors of slavery, were first used in England. In 1787, the Committee to Abolish the Slave Trade posed a black male slave as a supplicant, with the question, "Am I not a Man and a Brother?" Josiah Wedgewood designed a cameo using the emblem, posing the black slave on a white background. Wedgewood sent some of the images to Benjamin Franklin, who realized that the emblems would be powerful political tools. In 1838, American abolitionists created a similar image, this time posing a woman, half nude, chained and kneeling. The inscription was "Am I not a Woman and a Sister?" Those emblems led to the use of graphics in publications. Angelina Grimke believed that graphics would convey better than words the debilitating conditions of slavery. Grimke wrote, "Until the pictures of the slave's sufferings were drawn and held up to public gaze, no Northerner had any idea of the cruelty of the system . . . and those who had lived at the South . . . wept in secret places over the sins of oppression."

SOURCE: Jean Fagan Yellin, *Women and Sisters: The Antislavery Feminists in American Culture* (New Haven: Yale University Press, 1989), p. 3.

punctuality. The 1851 serialized publication of *Uncle Tom's Cabin* and its subsequent publication in book form advanced the antislavery movement, garnering huge support in the North and the label of a "slanderous work" in the South.[9]

COMMUNICATION AND CAPITALISM The four-year War Between the States—the Civil War (1861–1865)—arrested development of parts of the communications industry, but after the war, the development of traditional communication forms paralleled the growth of industry as a whole. Advertising and public relations, industries that had their roots in the mid-nineteenth century, generated new clients and new products with the growth of capitalism.

During the war, the newly developed Associated Press cut its lines between North and South, censorship emerged once more, and Southern newspapers found it difficult to acquire supplies and paper on which to print. Despite those restrictions, however, the news business flourished. Northern metropolitan newspapers sent reporters into the field and published eyewitness accounts of the conflict. Mathew Brady took his portrait photography business on the road and hired photographers to record camp scenes, famous individuals, and some, although limited, action. Brady's efforts at photography were among the first to document the battlefield through photography, not just through words.

After the war, rapid developments in printing technology paralleled growth in manufacturing as a whole. Paper was now more easily made from wood pulp rather than from rags. **Stereotyping** provided for printing with a papier-mâché mat rather than from type forms, ensuring that type would last longer and enabling editors to experiment with graphics. And most significantly, the **Linotype** machine allowed **compositors** to cast letters in a line of type rather than set each letter by hand.

By the end of the nineteenth century, publishing was a leading industry, part of a corporate capitalism that began to dominate the nation's production of goods and services. Publishers began to conceive of themselves not only as political and cultural voices but as extensions of the nation's marketing system. Advertising became the vehicle for promoting an economy of consumption. Magazines and newspapers editorialized that readers' roles in public affairs was declining. The periodical industry, as well as government, was dominated by business interests. Advertisers promoted brand-name products to make teeth whiter, bodies cleaner, and appearances more acceptable. The emphasis on national brands and the development of department stores created a new industry of advertising agents and agencies, an industry that moved beyond the attempts at basic communication made earlier in the century to a more specialized approach of persuading the consumer. Although editors often supported business, they also saw some of the problems it was creating, and they struggled with how to curtail corruption in city services and government. As the press expanded in numbers and in size, critics questioned the reform positions of editors, asking whether indeed some editors were not captains of industry themselves.[10]

Mathew Brady and his photographers chronicled the Civil War. Magazines such as Frank Leslie's Illustrated Weekly *carried engravings of the photographs to inform the nation of the carnage of the war.*

The rise of the department store provided advertising for newspapers, which remained a mainstay through the 1980s. Much of the copy originally was written in-house by the stores' own staff. With that exception, however, most of the manufacturing community turned toward the advertising agency for help in selling its products. At first ads were informational, but by the 1920s, advertising agencies began to experiment with psychological concepts to help promote products.

stereotype: Process of creating metal plates with raised letters; used for printing before offset printing was developed.

Linotype: Machine that set an entire line of type, eliminating the need to set each letter of each word by hand.

compositor: The person who sets type and composes the plates from which a newspaper is printed.

Key concept

Public Relations and the Media: Nineteenth-century companies used the print media for early forms of public relations—the management of information between an organization and its public.

The growth and expansion fueled the revenues for the massive metropolitan dailies such as Hungarian immigrant Joseph Pulitzer's *New York World* and the affluent William Randolph Hearst's *New York Journal.* Those newspapers reflected the growth of the city and the division of social classes. Competing with their sensationalistic style was the steady *New York Times,* which sought to create a reputation based on the information it presented.

57

Marconi Supplies News to *New York Herald*

Newspaper publishers welcomed the arrival of the telegraph. They saw it as a critical tool that would help them deliver faster, more complete news. James Gordon Bennett, Jr., a controversial character, announced on Sunday, October 1, 1899, that Guglielmo Marconi would use the wireless to cover the America's Cup Yacht Races for the *Herald*. The story that announced this innovation carried the headline "Marconi Will Report the Yacht Races by His Wireless System." The story included illustrations of Marconi's wireless apparatus, the race course, and the inventor.

The *Herald's* article described how the wireless would combine with newspaper technology to tell a story quickly. Two steamships equipped with the wireless would relay the progress of the race to stations at the Navesink Highlands and Thirty-Fourth Street in New York. Waiting reporters would send the news across the United States and the Atlantic by telegraph and cable. Although the last America's Cup race had been reported via a submarine cable, the *Herald* noted that this time the messages would "come rushing through the air with the simplicity of light."

Marconi and Bennett charmed New York's newspaper readers when they kept them informed, within seconds or minutes, of the progress of the race. Articles in the *New York Times* and *Popular Science Monthly* praised technology and commented on its ability to bring people together. "The nerves of the whole world [were] so to speak, being bound together, so that a touch in one country [was] transmitted instantly to a far-distant one," read the account in *Popular Science*.

SOURCE: Susan J. Douglas, *Inventing American Broadcasting, 1899–1922.* (Baltimore: Johns Hopkins University Press, 1987).

In the newly affluent business world, corporate capitalism became a target as well as a sign of progress, and business sought to advance its own interests, borrowing techniques from social-movement leaders to create positive publicity. Although public relations in the modern sense is defined as the management of information between an organization and its public, in the late 1800s, it reflected primarily promotional techniques and press agentry. The railroad industry, concerned about its image, issued free passes to local editors and paid for "puffery pieces" to be inserted in magazines and newspapers.

The modern world of communications

Many forms of media assumed increasing importance in the twentieth century. Newspapers maintained their position as the primary conveyors of news until television newscasts reached maturity in the late 1950s and early 1960s; magazines multiplied in number and through midcentury were significant conveyors and enforcers of social norms; radio, which began as person-to-person communication, discovered that advertising could enable it to "broadcast" its message to a large audience; books remained important vehicles for passing cultural information, as well as knowledge, from one generation to another. Advertising grew as an industry when individuals began to have increased leisure time and disposable income. Public relations also gained a more significant role as business and government sought to inform and persuade the public to adopt technological and political change. During the last half of the twentieth century, electronic media became the dominant conveyors of national and international news, magazines turned toward specialized audiences, and books increased in sales and widespread distribution. Newspapers still dominated in local news delivery, although throughout the 1980s, they began to lose their favored profit position. By the mid-1990s, broadcast technologies were being challenged by cable, computerized databases, and **interactive information sharing.**

■ Magazines as a social force

During the second half of the nineteenth century, three classes of magazines served the populace. The staid, literary magazines of the midcentury, such as the *Atlantic Monthly* and *Harper's,* commented on the leisure activities of the upper class and the polite political dilemmas of diplomacy. These **quality monthlies** were supplemented by women's magazines, such as *Harper's Bazaar,* that grew in popularity.

But the dramatic social force on the magazine front were the inexpensive **muckraking magazines.** Despite massive economic growth and an improved standard of living during the late nineteenth and early twentieth century, a growing recognition of corporate greed and political corruption provided the raw material for a literature of exposure. The magazine industry began to attack corporate giants and their struggle for political power. Theodore Roosevelt, despite his own inclinations toward reform, named these writers "muckrakers." He claimed they lacked the optimism necessary for the development of the country. Roosevelt likened the writers to the man with the muckrake in John Bunyan's seventeenth-century *Pilgrim's Progress:* "A man who could look no way but downward with the muckrake in his hands; who was offered the celestial crown for his muckrake, but would neither look up nor regard the crown he was offered, but continued to rake the filth of the floor." Through the ten-cent magazine, crusading journalists reached almost three million readers. They used the magazines as responsible tools for public education, describing the close relationship of politics and government, and pointing out the advantages of the wealthy and privileged classes. Such magazines—including *McClure's,* the *Munsey,* and the *American Magazine*—thrived until the start of World War I.[11]

■ World War I restrictions and propaganda

With the advent of World War I, reform as a subject lost its high appeal. Although newspapers and magazines vigorously debated whether the United States should enter the war, once the country declared war, most publications offered unqualified support. For those that did not, the consequences were severe. In 1917, Congress enacted restrictive legislation that made it a crime to "write or publish any disloyal, profane, scurrilous or abusive language about the form of government of the United States," the Constitution, the military or naval forces, the flag, or the uniform, or to bring any of them into disrepute or contempt. The German-language press was hard hit, and when editors who had produced newspapers in small communities for years failed to file proper translations with the government, their publications were suspended. One elderly Wisconsin editor died in jail.

interactive information sharing: Use of computers or broadcast technology to transmit information back and forth between individuals or between professional communicators and members of an audience.

quality monthlies: Name given to staid political and literary monthly magazines popular in the mid-nineteenth century that set the tone for prestigious cultural values.

muckraking magazines: Magazines that emerged in the 1890s and exposed corruption while trying to educate the public about reform.

60 Socialist publications also were highly suspect, and the widely popular *Masses* was closed down. In *Schenck v. the United States,* Supreme Court Justice Oliver Wendell Holmes noted that statements made during times of war differed substantially from those made in times of peace; and in articulating the famous **clear and present danger rule,** he wrote that what had to be ascertained was whether words used in particular circumstances would "create a clear and present danger which would have brought about substantive evils which Congress had a right to prevent." Schenck, general secretary of the Socialist party, was convicted for sending out fifteen thousand **propaganda** leaflets to men who had been called to military service, urging them to oppose the draft.

Keyconcept

Wartime Press Controls and the Committee on Public Information: During World War I the U.S. government's efforts to control public communication were centralized in the Committee on Public Information. Many of their information management techniques formed the basis for the development of public relations after the war.

Chief among efforts to control information during the war was former newspaperman George Creel's Committee on Public Information (CPI). Creel earned $8,000 a year for his efforts to intensify national support for the war. In the two years of its existence, the CPI mailed six thousand news releases that generated about twenty thousand columns of newsprint each week. It organized a speaker's bureau to travel to small towns, a war bond campaign, a newsletter for schools, and a foreign-language division. The committee also solicited more than $1.5 million in free advertising in periodicals.

Although public information and public relations techniques had been used before the war by President Theodore Roosevelt as well as by some social-movement groups, Creel's level of organization surpassed all prior efforts. For that reason, his committee is often credited with being the precursor to modern public relations campaigns.[12]

The radio revolution

By the close of World War I, the communications industry was facing a revolution, although few magazine or newspaper publishers realized it. The establishment of the telegraph had broken the first link between communication and transportation. By the early twentieth century, the advent of radio had broken the second link: not only could news travel from its source to an editor's desk as fast as the wires could carry it, news could travel from the editor or commentator to the public as fast as it could travel across the air waves.

Technological developments paving the way for radio had begun as early as 1870, and by the end of World War I, radio technology was well understood. Few had conceived of the radio as a broadcasting—or mass-communication—tool; it had been used primarily in ship-to-shore communications or by amateur operators. Radio had been strictly regulated by the U.S. Navy during the war, and that branch of the military had been increasingly aware and uncomfortable that the British-owned American Marconi Company dominated as a supplier of radio parts. At the end of the war, the U.S. Navy strongly opposed returning the rights to Marconi, and with what historian Christopher Sterling labeled "tacit government approval," Owen D. Young, president of General Electric, organized a new corporation to hold all American patents. General Electric, together with American Telephone and Telegraph, United Fruit, and Westinghouse Electric, formed the Radio Corporation of America (RCA) and created a $2.5 million fund to buy out American Marconi.[13] The companies operated together until 1926. That type of arrangement set the stage for further radio development, organized and controlled by big business and government.

clear and present danger rule: Created by Justice Oliver Wendell Holmes at the close of the Schenck case in World War I. Holmes argued that to suppress material one must be able to argue that such material presented a clear and present danger to the country that the government had a right to prevent.

propaganda: Efforts to influence and persuade the receivers of a mediated message.

Farm families heard news of the world, as well as classical music and comedy shows, over their radios. For the first time, the distribution of information was not tied to the speed of transportation.

As Westinghouse, General Electric, and RCA established stations in the early 1920s, radio became so popular that RCA sold $11 million worth of receivers in 1922 alone. By 1927, 700 stations were operating, and $135 million worth of sets was sold in 1929. In 1923, only 7 percent of U.S. households owned a radio set; by 1930, almost 35 percent owned sets.

Technological interference and arguments over who would control which patents created controversy in the industry, and Secretary of Commerce Herbert Hoover urged Congress to pass new legislation. After several national conferences and years of attempts to pass legislation, in 1927 Congress enacted the **Radio Act** and established the Federal Radio Commission. Congress adopted most of the regulations suggested by the commercial radio industry, including assigning licenses, limiting the number of stations, abolishing low-powered stations (many of which were educational), and supporting trade-name advertising. Congress, believing that radio was too valuable a resource to be held as a monopoly, stated that stations must operate in "the public interest, convenience, or necessity." Thus was established a private, corporate world of broadcasting.

Governmental regulation represented a strict departure from the world of print, which had survived basically without regulation except during times of war. Licensing was justified on the principle of "scarcity of the airwaves," with Congress arguing that there simply were not enough airwaves to go around. Educational channels and nonprofit broadcasters were nearly excluded from the system. Between 1927 and the passage of the **Federal Communications Act of 1934,** which allowed for regulation of developing technologies, nonprofit broadcasters fought for a greater presence in the radio world. They lost the battle when President Franklin Roosevelt signed the act solidifying private and, particularly, network control of broadcasting. The number of nonprofit stations continued to decline and not until the 1960s did Congress establish public radio and television stations.[14]

Radio drama and music were mainstays by the end of the 1930s, and news consisted primarily of short newscasts and reports of elections. The ability of radio stations to gather news was severely hampered by attempts by newspapers to keep wire services from selling news to radio. However, in 1932, despite continued opposition from publishers, the wire services, fearing competition, agreed to provide news to radio. By the end of the 1930s, eight hundred radio correspondents from the United States reported from around the world, and *Fortune* magazine noted that Americans increasingly relied on the radio for news. Radio solidified its news position during World War II when Edward R. Murrow broadcasted commentary from London. But radio remained cautious about expressing controversial opinions during the war years, not wanting to challenge President Roosevelt, who had declared a limited national emergency.[15]

Keyconcept

Radio and the News Wire Services: In the early days of radio, the growth of broadcast news depended on breaking the newspapers' exclusive access to news reports from private telegraph wire services. This breakthrough was finally achieved in the early 1930s.

Radio Act of 1927: Law that governed the regulation of radio by government until the 1934 Communications Act.

Federal Communications Act of 1934: Provided the basis for federal telecommunication and television regulation until the 1996 Telecommunications Act.

■ Film and cultural values

Feature films created extensive public discourse almost from the beginning. They were the most convincing form of media ever produced. In the late 1920s when sound combined with celluloid, middle-class mothers and ministers worried about the social effects of film on adolescents. Sitting in a dark room, confronted with talking images and portrayals of values that did not originate in a local community, what would happen to the nation's daughters? Gender was a strong theme. Could the nation protect women in a society permeated by film images?

Keyconcept

Oligopoly in Media Industries: In the early days of film-making, ownership was concentrated in as few as five dominant companies. As these giant studios came to control the supply of films, they created a system of economic near-monopoly known as an *oligopoly*. This pattern also occurred in other media industries.

During World War I, the film industry, which was established before the war in France, Germany, Great Britain, Denmark, and Italy, flourished in the United States while other countries diverted photographic supplies such as cotton, nitric acid, and sulfuric acid into the manufacture of explosives. The United States, which was involved in the war for a much shorter time, provided a large domestic audience for films. In 1915, David Wark Griffith's three-hour *Birth of a Nation* established the importance of feature films. Film as part of the social fabric of the nation became a reality with *Birth of a Nation,* which created great controversy because of its "outrageously racist" message. Although the early years of the film industry were marked by competition, struggle, and attempts at monopoly, by the end of the 1920s, seven major studios dominated the industry, and an oligopoly was firmly established. By 1929, five companies controlled the industry: Paramount, Warner Brothers, Fox, MGM, and Radio-Keith Orpheum (RKO). **Vertical integration** of the industry allowed for control from the top down, from design and production to the selection of stars, to distribution and showings in theaters.

The movie industry was set apart from publishing, however, when the Supreme Court ruled that movies were not protected by the First Amendment. In 1915, in *Mutual Film Corp. v. Industrial Commission of Ohio,* the court ruled that exhibiting film was a business, not "press." The Supreme Court eventually reversed its position—but not until 1952. Therefore, the movie industry dealt with local and state censorship boards and codes for thirty-seven years. To combat the problem, the industry established self-censorship, hoping to avoid further government regulation or public sanctions. The voluntary code was administered through the Motion Picture Producers and Distributors of America (MPPDA) and forbade sex, excessive violence, and vulgar language. The code remained in effect until 1968, when the industry adopted the present ratings that designate intended audiences.

Movies initially were designed to appeal to working-class audiences, who attended them in local theaters, where the electronic medium was only part of the show. The evening's entertainment was supplemented by stage shows and local talent tryouts. However, as movies were standardized through the Hollywood studio system, the live shows disappeared. Movies moved from local communities to the glitzy urban uptowns during the 1920s, with the creation of palatial movie theaters.

During the 1930s, movie palaces became lavish centers of entertainment.

vertical integration: The control of production from obtaining the raw materials to the distribution of the product.

Keyconcept

Consumer Culture and the Media: Some observers believe that the consumer culture of modern technological society is motivated, perhaps even exaggerated, by the pervasive role of advertising in the media, as well as by entertainment content that reinforces acquiring consumer goods as a cultural value.

During the worldwide depression of the 1930s, film corporations suffered: Warner Brothers lost $14 million in 1932 alone. But the talkies that had been introduced in the late 1920s were exceedingly popular, and people still flocked to the movies when they could spare the bit of cash required. Gangster films, with crime-doesn't-pay morals, musicals, and Shirley Temple comedies attracted audiences. In 1948, the Supreme Court ruled that major film corporations violated antitrust laws. The companies agreed to limit coercive strategies such as **block booking,** which required theaters to accept packages of films rather than contract for individual movies from the film companies.[16]

Communication and consumer culture

At the end of World War I, the United States, weary of foreign wars and sacrifice, plunged itself into a celebration of consumer culture. Media helped promote that culture, with advertising benefiting from the development of full-scale ad agencies. Agencies developed specialized services, no longer selling mere space but designing ads and writing copy that would appeal to the emotional and physical needs of its audience. Stanley Resor, a Yale graduate in economics, pioneered the use of market surveys, and Helen Lansdowne, who went to work for Procter & Collier after graduating from high school, developed new copywriting techniques. During the 1920s, advertising promoted brand names. Striving to police itself and gain public recognition as a profession, as well as to avoid government regulation, advertisers established groups such as the Associated Advertising Clubs of America. Advertising copywriters transformed Fleischmann's yeast into a health product and Listerine into a cure for bad breath (the term *halitosis* was coined by copywriters), convincing women that poor first impressions would doom their husbands' careers.[17]

News in print

The big business environment of the early twentieth century enveloped newspapers, and the number of chain newspapers doubled between 1923 and 1933. In 1933, the six largest chains were Hearst, Patterson-McCormick, Scripps-Howard, Paul Block, Ridder, and Gannett. They controlled almost 70 percent of the nation's daily chain circulation and 26 percent of its total circulation.

Intellectual critics argued that news was becoming a commodity that could be controlled by giant organizations that had business interests outside the news industry. Nevertheless, diversity still characterized the business. Not only did independents control a large portion of circulation, but small newspapers representing specialized interests continued to succeed. The *Chicago Defender,* begun by Robert Abbott in the early 1900s as a small black newspaper, grew to a commercial success that gained circulation throughout the South. Some historians believe that the newspaper encouraged at least a portion of the large southern migration to Chicago in the 1920s. Women in the suffrage movement also created newspapers to bridge the geographical space that separated women who shared a community of ideas.

Newspapers suffered declines after 1910: the number of dailies declined from 2,580 in 1914, to 2,441 in 1919, to 2,080 in 1933. The number of weeklies also declined. Circulations, however, continued to grow until 1929. Dailies were concentrated in the big cities: 41.8 percent of the nation's Sunday papers originated in only six cities.

block booking: An illegal activity by movie studios that required theaters to rent packages of several movies, rather than being able to choose one or two.

64

Media history in our lives

■ **1600s.** African, European folk, and religious music arrive in America.
■ **1690.** *Publick Occurrences* published in Boston.
   ■ **1704.** First newspaper advertisement in America.
   ■ **1741.** First magazine published in America.
     ■ **1826.** First permanent photograph taken by Joseph Niepce in France.
     ■ **1830s.** The penny press becomes first truly mass medium in the United States.
       ■ **1892.** Thomas Edison's lab develops the kinetoscope.
        ■ **Early 1900s.** Mass production records developed.
        ■ **1915.** *The Birth of a Nation* marks start of modern movie industry.
          ■ **1920.** KDKA in Pittsburgh gets first commercial radio license.
          ■ **1923.** Edward Bernays writes *Crystallizing Public Opinion.*

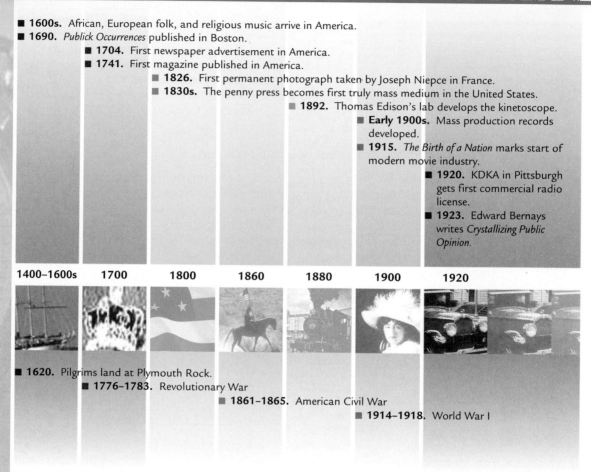

| 1400–1600s | 1700 | 1800 | 1860 | 1880 | 1900 | 1920 |

■ **1620.** Pilgrims land at Plymouth Rock.
   ■ **1776–1783.** Revolutionary War
     ■ **1861–1865.** American Civil War
       ■ **1914–1918.** World War I

During the 1930s, because of their perceived failure to inform people adequately about the onset of the depression, newspapers and magazines turned more toward interpretation. The role of the magazine as social reformer, established early in the century, was reinforced as news magazines that attempted to synthesize each week's events appeared—*Newsweek, Time,* and *U.S. News and World Report.* Henry Luce was not only successful with *Time;* he recognized the potential of the developing photographic industry and its technical advances, and launched *Life* magazine, a showcase for photojournalists. The magazine not only became a photographic treasure; it became known for its significant commentary on social and political issues, particularly the civil rights movement. Newspapers introduced the signed political column, and radio introduced programs such as the pseudodocumentary *March of Time.* The show popularized news events with dramatic—and often controversial—re-creations. Critics rebelled at the mixture of fact and fiction, which predated by many years the infodramas that now are current fare.

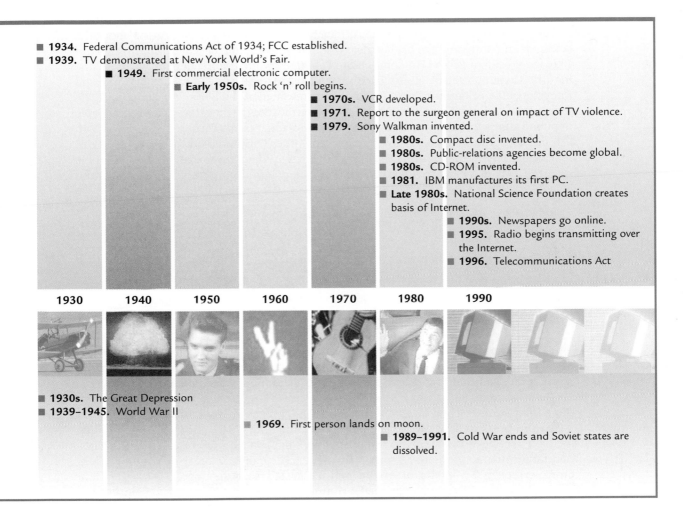

- **1934.** Federal Communications Act of 1934; FCC established.
- **1939.** TV demonstrated at New York World's Fair.
  - **1949.** First commercial electronic computer.
    - **Early 1950s.** Rock 'n' roll begins.
      - **1970s.** VCR developed.
      - **1971.** Report to the surgeon general on impact of TV violence.
      - **1979.** Sony Walkman invented.
        - **1980s.** Compact disc invented.
        - **1980s.** Public-relations agencies become global.
        - **1980s.** CD-ROM invented.
        - **1981.** IBM manufactures its first PC.
        - **Late 1980s.** National Science Foundation creates basis of Internet.
          - **1990s.** Newspapers go online.
          - **1995.** Radio begins transmitting over the Internet.
          - **1996.** Telecommunications Act

1930   1940   1950   1960   1970   1980   1990

- **1930s.** The Great Depression
- **1939–1945.** World War II

- **1969.** First person lands on moon.
  - **1989–1991.** Cold War ends and Soviet states are dissolved.

News media and society

Although small independent outlets still existed, by the early 1940s, many media companies qualified as big business. Newspaper conglomerates, publishing companies, and radio networks operated in an arena often characterized by business principles rather than by journalistic ethics. How well the press served society became a major issue during the postdepression and World War II years, and government was quick to act to suppress what it considered subversive information. In addition, the press often cooperated with government. Critics, however, were concerned not only about the relationship between journalists and politicians but about the economic impact of journalism as business. Critics charged that the press was not self-critical. The media faced criticism and possible efforts to control content from two sides: the government, which sought to advance its own interests, and elements of society that sought to make the media more socially responsible.

The Hutchins Commission

Criticism of the press began during the late nineteenth century, partly as an outgrowth of the reform movement that challenged some of the developments of a capitalist society. With the advent of radio, critics became increasingly concerned about the commercial nature and the big-business orientation of the media. In 1942, University of Chicago President Robert Hutchins chaired an inquiry into the freedom of the press; the inquiry was supported by Henry Luce, chairman of Time, Inc., and funded by Time and Encyclopediae Britannica, Inc. The findings, presented at the close of World War II, addressed the "role of the agencies of mass communication in the education of the people in public affairs." The commission poured over documents and recorded interviews with 225 members of the industry, government, and other entities associated with the press. It also elicited testimony from members of the press. When the commission released the report in 1947, it listed five "ideal demands of society for the communication of news and ideas":

1. A truthful, comprehensive, and intelligent account of the day's events in a context that gives them meaning.
2. A forum for the exchange of comment and criticism.
3. The projection of a representative picture of the constituent groups in the society.
4. The presentation and clarification of the goals and values of the society.
5. Full access to the day's intelligence.

The commission claimed that not only did the nation's news media not fill those "ideal demands" but that the freedom of the nation's press was in jeopardy. The commission charged that few people had access to communication channels because the channels were either owned by or licensed to only a few large corporations. Although the commission warned about the possibility of increased government regulation, it urged the press to adopt the principle of "accountability." To assume accountability, media would need to accept the responsibility of being a "common carrier" of information rather than to promote personal viewpoints. The commission also encouraged vigorous criticism by media of media and suggested that an ongoing, independent commission be created to handle media complaints. It promoted increased communication research and the concept that the public had a responsibility to ensure continued freedom of the press.

The American Society of Newspaper Editors and the industry as a whole rejected all the recommendations. Owners objected to the commission because no reporters or editors had been included in its membership; further, they rebelled at the thought of a permanently established independent commission watching over the press. Despite the negative reaction, the Hutchins Commission's findings have remained a source for discussion of the role of the media in modern society. Some scholars believe that professional journalistic behaviors such as social responsibility and objectivity stem from the Hutchins Commission's report.[18]

Government and press

The Hutchins report was issued at the end of World War II, a period during which the press cooperated extensively with the government, although it sometimes also chafed at the restrictions the government imposed. Print and broadcast media adopted voluntary codes of behavior that supported the war effort and protected military information. The radio industry forbade editorializing and requested the avoidance of "horror, suspense and undue excitement." The federal government organized an Office of War Information that issued propaganda, information designed to promote wartime patriotism, while the Office of Censorship sought adherence to the voluntary censorship code and monitored news entering and leaving the country. The government also put pressure on the motion-picture industry to ameliorate racial tensions, and the Justice Department worked to secure cooperation by the black press. In 1940, Congress passed the Smith Act, designed to prohibit advocacy of the violent overthrow of the government. The act was rarely used before 1949, when public opinion turned violently anticommunist. It still exists, however, as a threat to free speech in times of crisis.

COLD WAR CONTROLS Although government censorship officially ended with the war, government control reared its head repeatedly throughout the postwar Cold War. In the midst of an anticommunist scare and a witch-hunt, headed by Wisconsin Senator Joseph McCarthy, for communists in all organizations, the motion-picture and broadcast industries were under siege. The motion-picture industry caved in quickly to government pressure, meeting in late 1947 to declare that it would clean house, publicize a list of artists to be prohibited from working, or blacklisted, and thereby protect the industry's reputation. The broadcast industry also institutionalized blacklisting: CBS required a loyalty oath, and NBC established security channels in its legal department. A number of newspapers, including the *Christian Science Monitor,* the *Washington Post,* and the *Milwaukee Journal,* and the magazine *Time* challenged McCarthy, but it took four years and a final television challenge by the famous World War II broadcaster Edward R. Murrow to end McCarthy's reign. On March 9, 1954, Murrow devoted his *See It Now* program to a portrait of McCarthy. Murrow's challenge ended with an eloquent statement:

Keyconcept

Cold War Controls and the Media: The Cold War era brought new social and political pressures on the U.S. media to promote democratic values as well as opposition to Communism.

> We will not walk in fear, one of another. We will not be driven by fear into an age of unreason if we dig deep in our history and our doctrine, and remember that we are not descended from fearful men, not from men who feared to write, to speak, to associate, and to defend causes that were for the moment unpopular. This is no time for men who oppose Senator McCarthy's methods to keep silent, or for those who approve. We can deny our heritage and our history, but we cannot escape responsibility for the result. . . .[McCarthy] didn't create this situation of fear, he merely exploited it— and rather successfully. Cassius was right: "The fault, dear Brutus, is not in our stars but in ourselves."[19]

Edward R. Murrow

During the postwar period, the print media also cooperated with the government in an effort to establish worldwide access to information. Frustrated by the difficulty of obtaining information in both friendly and enemy countries during the war, the American Society of Newspaper Editors, the Associated Press, and the United Press strived to establish international accords that would grant correspondents freedom to travel, to gain access to information, and to transmit information freely to their own countries. At a 1948 Geneva Conference on Freedom of Information, representatives from various countries found that they could not agree on issues such as accreditation of correspondents, permissible levels of censorship, and sanctions for violations. Other countries also used the 1947 Hutchins Commission report to charge that the U.S. press was in the hands of a monopoly. By the early 1950s, the State Department and the press organizations abandoned the crusade for worldwide access and reporting standards.[20]

WATCHDOGS EMERGE The heavy-handed governmental presence of the 1950s shifted in the 1960s and 1970s as the Supreme Court responded to a libel challenge to the *New York Times* from an Alabama police commissioner. The *Times* had published an advertisement that contained a number of errors regarding a student demonstration at an Alabama college. Justice William Brennan overturned an Alabama court decision in favor of Police Commissioner L. B. Sullivan. Brennan argued that minor errors should not be used to restrict open discussion of important matters, but that "debate on public issues should be uninhibited, robust, and wide-open." The court ruled that in order for public officials to claim damages for libel they must prove that the statements were made with "actual malice"—that is, with "knowledge that it was false or with reckless disregard of whether it was false or not." This decision reaffirmed the right of the media to criticize the government without fear of reprisal in case of legitimate error.

The Supreme Court recognized that the government needed a watchdog, and President Richard Nixon discovered he had not one, but two, when two young *Washington Post* reporters, Carl Bernstein and Bob Woodward, exposed Nixon's illegal campaign tactics. In 1974, after two years of investigation, Nixon resigned. The government also attempted in the early 1970s to stop the publication of the Pentagon Papers, a history of the Vietnam War fashioned from a forty-seven-volume set of classified historical materials leaked to the press. As you will read in a detailed description of both cases in Chapter 12, "Regulation," both involved an attempt by the government to withhold information because it would be personally—or governmentally—embarrassing.

By the end of the 1970s, however, the public appeared to be tired of war, corruption, and exposure, and sought often to blame the messenger rather than to question the message. Credibility of the press dropped, and by the 1980s, President Reagan had earned the label the Teflon President because criticism by the press did not seem to affect his public image.

The government and the military, believing that an uncontrolled press helped lose the war in Vietnam, controlled reporters to a much greater degree during the invasions of Grenada, Panama, and the Persian Gulf. During the Gulf War, Pentagon personnel, who had been trained to master media appearance techniques, provided pictures of "smart bombs" that were such good television video fare no television director could—or was willing to—resist using them. Reporters in the field were assigned military escorts, their travel was restricted, and some questions they tried to ask of military personnel were deemed inappropriate. Eventually, enterprising television reporters went off on their own and some were captured. Once the war was on the ground rather than in the air, it was harder for the military to control media coverage.

PUBLIC RELATIONS GOES INTERNATIONAL Within the Gulf War framework, corporate public relations earned high dollars and played an important role in creating images of a free Kuwait in the public mind. Public-relations agency Hill & Knowlton helped shape the testimony of the fifteen-year-old Nayirah, who testified that she had seen Iraqis throw babies out of incubators. Later Kuwaiti hospital officials said the incident had not occurred. The public-relations firm received $11.5 million from the Kuwaiti government-financed Citizens for a Free Kuwait in exchange for its efforts to create a positive image of the country in the United States.

Mass media and society

Once television arrived, an expanding consumer society, the prosperity of the post–World War II era, and new technology came together to create an environment for media as creators of consumer culture. The media attracted mass audiences, and the fare they provided helped homogenize that audience, stripping it of regional characteristics, dialects, and mores.

■ Television and its impact

By the early 1940s, television was on the air in Europe, and six experimental stations were broadcasting in the United States. Numbers of stations and sales of sets increased steadily, and in 1948, the FCC froze the processing of new license applications while it resolved a number of engineering and policy questions, including which color system to adopt. The commission then extended the freeze on licenses through the Korean War. However, as you will read in Chapter 9, "Television," when the freeze ended in 1952, television enjoyed substantial growth. By 1958, 42 million homes in the United States had television sets. The three major networks—ABC, CBS, and NBC—controlled between 50 and 60 percent of all local programming and 95 percent of all evening programming. Such control by the networks fed the continuing concern that the nation's media were dominated by a few companies.

Keyconcept

Popular Culture as Media Creation: New media technology, together with an expanding consumer society after the 1950s, have generated an environment in which the media create as well as reflect popular culture.

IMPACT ON RADIO With the advent of television, radio faced severe losses, both of advertisers and listeners. But radio proved to be an adaptable medium. The popularity of the automobile in the 1950s and the portability of radio sets allowed radio to change its tune—to music. Music had always been popular programming for radio, but it had aired between live drama, news, and comedy. As the 1950s witnessed a revolution in music styles with the advent of Elvis Presley and rock 'n' roll, the disc jockey became paramount: teenagers carried their portable radios from bed to bath to school. **Payola** scandals shook the industry in the late 1950s when the government investigated payoffs by record companies and advertisers to disc jockeys who agreed to play certain records in return for liquor, money, and other gifts. Music is still the primary programming for radio, although all-news and talk-show stations exist in most major markets as well.

Charles Van Doren was first a celebrity, then an outcast, on the TV quiz show, Twenty-One. *Quiz shows, many of which were proven to be fraudulent, attracted wide audiences.*

As radio shifted, television adapted many of the old radio dramas. Live drama graced the screen during the 1950s, and quiz shows attracted large audiences. By 1957, quiz shows claimed thirty-seven hours of television's weekly schedule. *Twenty-One, The $64,000 Question,* and imitations of those successful programs aired during the decade, but in 1959, Charles Van Doren, a contestant on *Twenty-One,* admitted that producers had given him the answers to the questions before he appeared on television. Investigations by Congress soon revealed similar scandals involving most of the popular quiz shows.

payola: Paying disc jockeys and radio stations to play certain songs so recording sales will increase.

70

ADVERTISING During the early days of television, advertisers sponsored entire shows, but by the end of the 1950s, with rising costs and concern about advertiser control, the networks began to sell time, rather than shows, to advertisers. Television was an advertiser's dream: gross advertising expenditures during the 1950s grew by 75 percent, a rate higher than the growth of personal income or the gross national product. In 1947, the J. Walter Thompson advertising agency billed its clients more than $100 million. By 1950, at least four agencies were billing more than twice the 1947 figure. Such advertising growth invited criticism, and in 1957, Vance Packard, with a compelling book, *The Hidden Persuaders,* questioned the impact of advertising and its promotion of a consumer culture on individual motivation and group social interaction.

TELEVISION NEWS Television news occupied little airtime during the early days of the new medium. But in 1956, newscasters David Brinkley and Chet Huntley captured the ratings for NBC; and in 1963, CBS introduced a middle-aged wire-service reporter who commanded respect and trust from his television audience. Walter Cronkite anchored the half-hour news show that attracted and held viewers for nearly twenty years. Each evening the show ended with the standard Cronkite ending, "And that's the way it is," a summary statement that strived to make television news look like a true and objective account of the day's news. Cronkite gave substance and credibility to television news. By 1967, all three networks had expanded the evening news from fifteen to thirty minutes.

During the Cronkite years, television gained enormous credence as a news medium. The big stories of the decade were civil rights, the space race, and Vietnam, and all appeared live on the television screen. As the Freedom Fighters marched in the South under the direction of Martin Luther King, Jr., *Life* magazine covered the unfolding story.

Keyconcept

New and Old Media: The advent of television in the 1950s forced print media, radio, and film to rethink their approaches to news and entertainment. As a new medium develops, the definitional lines of all media are altered.

But it took the television cameras in the 1960s to make the story truly public. Journalists Robert Donovan and Ray Scherer observed in the book *Unsilent Revolution: Television News and American Public Life,* that "police dogs looked like police dogs in newspaper and magazine photos, but on television the dogs snarled."

The Vietnam War also became a big television story as the conflict escalated during the 1960s. News reporters enjoyed freedom from censorship in that undeclared war, but they had difficulty knowing where the next story would unfold and how to travel in a country with few passable roads. Government officials provided misleading information; reporters had to find the accurate stories themselves. Although research subsequently showed that negative news coverage of Vietnam paralleled increased public dissent and increased official government dissent, politicians and the general public adopted the idea that the United States lost the Vietnam War because it was fought in the living rooms of America. The documentaries made in Vietnam carried an impact unrivaled by print media.[21]

REGULATION Despite the advances in news credibility, television remained the target of critics. Newton Minow, appointed in 1961 as chairman of the FCC by President John F. Kennedy, attacked the industry at a National Association of Broadcasters meeting, calling it a "vast wasteland." Minow argued for longer newscasts and improved children's programming. The reform years of the 1960s had a major impact on television, leading to increased regulation and the passage of the act that created the Corporation for Public Broadcasting. The accompanying funds supported local education stations that ultimately formed the Public Broadcasting Service and National Public Radio.

During the Reagan years, television experienced deregulation; by 1993, the 1940s Fairness Doctrine that required stations to broadcast various sides of an issue was no longer enforced by the FCC. In 1992, however, Congress overrode President George

Bush's veto of cable regulation and passed a Children's Television Act. Those pieces of legislation indicated lack of satisfaction with some results of the deregulation milieu. Further, the public seemed almost more than willing to tolerate government management of news during the Persian Gulf crisis. The establishment of press pools and severe restrictions against travel by journalists in the Persian Gulf area gave the Pentagon and military commanders a heavy advantage in shaping the news.

71

The 1970s and 1980s were boom years for television networks. NBC, CBS, and ABC continued to dominate the industry, but Ted Turner introduced his Cable News Network and the Australian Rupert Murdock introduced Fox Television. During the 1990s, cable and new networks took viewers from NBC, CBS, and ABC, and people increasingly bought small satellite dishes to receive television programs.

■ The world of print

The postwar world also witnessed a boom in the book-publishing industry. The founding of book clubs such as the Literary Guild and the Book-of-the-Month Club during the mid-1920s had cultivated a middle-class audience for fiction and nonfiction. Publishing houses also forged relationships with film companies to use books as the raw material for film scripts. When soldiers returned to the nation's colleges and universities to take advantage of the GI Bill, which financed their education, the textbook business mushroomed. In fact, the book business has done surprisingly well across the twentieth century, despite critics' claims that nobody reads anymore. The total volume of sales has increased from $435 million in 1947, to more than $25 billion in 1995. With the advent of the large chain bookstores, increased numbers of volumes sell each year. Borders, one of the newest of the large chains, has turned the bookstore into a coffee-shop experience for potential customers to sit and read as they consume cups of premium coffee. The smaller companies common to the industry in 1945 are now typically merged in large conglomerates.

Throughout the 1960s and 1970s, newspapers increasingly became part of chains, and by 1970, one-half the nation's dailies, representing two-thirds of newspaper circulation, were produced through chains. Newspapers experienced a steady growth in advertising revenues and circulation, relying heavily on department-store and other local advertisers, but they also faced increasing costs of paper and ink. A series of extensive strikes caused shutdowns; often those strikes resulted from debates about new technology. Teletype setters ran Linotypes, eliminating the need for many Linotype operators; offset printing, using photographic plates rather than stereotyped plates, required retraining of composing room personnel. Automation also affected mail rooms and accounting systems. During the late 1970s and the 1980s, computers revolutionized newsrooms, changing the relationship of editors and writers, and of editors and composing room personnel. The introduction of computers created another shift in patterns of hiring and in negotiations with trade unions, which were not always willing to adapt to new technology.

Throughout the late 1980s and the early 1990s, newspapers saw their share of advertising decline from the high levels they had enjoyed before television. Department-store failures and an economic recession cut advertising revenues; circulation, while remaining stable, lost in terms of the percentage of households subscribing to newspapers. *USA Today,* Al Newharth's experiment in magazine layout and color for the newspaper, along with bright writing for the "news you can use" department, targeted a national audience. Many newspapers moved quickly to copy the lively graphic techniques. But the industry still faces the need to increase its **household penetration** and assure

household penetration: Term used to describe the percentage of houses in a market that a newspaper, cable channel, or other media form reaches. Newspaper personnel are concerned about declining household penetration.

72

its continuance in a generation of young people who have not developed the newspaper habit.

Television probably affected magazines more than it did newspapers. The large general-circulation magazines could no longer survive after advertisers realized that reaching consumers via television was less expensive than trying to reach them via magazines. But magazines, like radio, proved to be an adaptable medium. They also changed their tune—but not to music. They embraced the concept of specialization. Now *Tennis* magazine garners a smaller but more similar audience of readers than a general-interest travel or sports magazine might and provides an exceptionally well targeted audience for the manufacturers of tennis rackets, tennis shoes, and tennis vacation spots.

The current media picture

The current media picture—and its economic, technological, and cultural development—is the subject of the rest of this book. Probably the most significant developments of the past several decades have been the issuing of public stock by media companies; new developments in distribution, including satellite technology; competition between cable and broadcast television; the advent of the video cassette recorder (VCR); and new computer technologies adapted to the delivery of information. The passage of a new broadcast, cable, and telephone regulatory act in 1996 indicates the importance of converging technologies and the complicated issues such convergence raises.

Begun in the 1960s by the *Wall Street Journal,* the practice of going public has expanded to include companies such as Gannett, Knight-Ridder Corporation, New York Times Corporation, Washington Post Company, and the Tribune Company (Chicago). Critics argue that the trend means that the news business is now more business than news and that owners will worry more about how well their stock is trading on a given exchange than about how the news is covered. Further, trading on the exchange means that newspapers have yet another—and powerful—constituency to please: their stockholders. This phenomenon, coupled with an increasing trend of mergers between formerly separate companies, triggers blasts from critics concerned about monopolistic control of the media.

Cable, initially used to boost reception from broadcast stations, soon mushroomed into a business of its own that challenged the networks and created new dilemmas for the FCC. If one hundred channels became available with cable, was "scarcity" still a justifiable tenet under which to regulate television? According to the National Cable Television Association, 96 percent of homes could access cable, and there are 61 million residential cable subscribers. No longer does cable simply boost reception; it originates material of its own

The "VCR revolution," which altered the home market for movies and television, reflects only the beginning of viewer controlled alternatives for accessing movies and other content on television and computer screens.

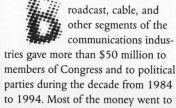

broadcast, cable, and other segments of the communications industries gave more than $50 million to members of Congress and to political parties during the decade from 1984 to 1994. Most of the money went to members of the House and Senate Commerce Committees, which regulate the communications industry.

Those who introduced legislation that made it easier for regional Bell telephone operating systems to enter the long-distance arena and for telephone companies and cable companies to compete were top recipients of the industry's political action committee funds. The largest contributors were AT&T, GTE, BellSouth, the

Lobbying Congress Is Big Business

National Cable Television Association, and the National Association of Broadcasters.

The National Association of Broadcasters has the advantage of other powerful lobby groups, including plenty of money and access to power. But it has an additional advantage—it receives little media coverage when it lobbies in favor of the broadcasting industry. In the 1995–96 election cycle alone, the NAB contributed $861,714 to 177 congressional candidates.

The NAB has effectively slowed the introduction of technologies that are similar to or compete with broadcasting, such as cable television, by arguing that broadcast stations are the only universally available medium required by the federal government to serve the public interest.

SOURCE: *Broadcasting & Cable*, May 2, 1994; Paul Farhi, "Their Reception's Great," *Washington Post*, H1, 5, February 16, 1997.

and establishes a base for movie channels, the ever-popular MTV, and all-news stations such as Cable News Network. In August 1996, the combined ratings for cable channels exceeded the ratings of the most watched commercial network.

The advent of satellites accelerated the flow of international news and created a technological environment in which companies such as Ted Turner's Cable News Network could successfully challenge the dominance of the major networks. CNN, begun in 1980, by 1990 reached 60 percent of all homes. The news station gained significant credibility during the Persian Gulf War, with its instant accounts of the war in progress. Such news coverage again raised questions for critics. What is the role of the journalist in high-speed delivery of news, especially when the news is enhanced by smart-bomb pictures provided by the Pentagon brass? The development of the VCR gave audiences even greater control over television watching. Now viewers could speed through commercials, tape shows broadcast during the day for viewing at night, or shun television programming altogether by renting or buying tapes at a video store. That development worried advertisers and movie theater owners, but was gratifying for the young parent for whom movie going was an expensive proposition.

At issue in the late 1990s is how much consumers will adopt computer technologies for delivery of information. Will they prefer the newspapers delivered to their front door, or will newspapers have to provide menus so that individuals can order selected information to be delivered via their computer printers each morning? Will television succeed with new interactive formats, or will it become an old mass-entertainment medium?

As we near the end of the twentieth century, the U.S. media system is an enormous business enterprise, with stock traded on the exchanges, media companies held in large conglomerates, and sophisticated technology used for delivery of messages. No longer is the newspaper a fledgling enterprise representing the efforts of one man, as John Campbell's Boston *News-Letter* indeed did. No longer does the industry represent a single entity, the press. Rather, the forms are multiple, including books, magazines, newspapers, pamphlets, political tracts, television, radio, motion pictures, and computer-delivered information. But even those forms of media do not comprise the whole of the industry. The related advertising agencies, graphics-design firms, recording companies, public-relations agencies, and political consultants all own a piece of the media industry. Even more significant is that the media are less distinguishable from one another than they used to be. Newspapers use telephone lines to distribute information; television is rapidly becoming intertwined with computer technology. What remains constant, however, is a commitment to the First Amendment as a goal, if not a reality, that grants to all the right of free expression. Few might argue that the framers of the Constitution intended the First Amendment to provide a broad umbrella of protection to such new developments as satellite transmissions. However, many would contend that the intent to create a society that governs itself includes a permanent guarantee of the right to criticize the government. In a modern society, creating a delicate balance between individual rights and societal rights is often a dilemma. Making the hard decisions about news and entertainment content and the role of media continues to be a challenging and significant task. Editors and station managers of today—like John Campbell of yesterday—must make the difficult decisions each day.

Summary

- The John Peter Zenger case represented a powerful call for freedom of expression in the United States.

- An important theme underlying the justification for freedom of expression was the colonists' belief that they should be able to oppose arbitrary government power.

- The invention of movable type and the printing press turned the marketplace of ideas into a commodity market.

- Newspapers and pamphlets played an important role in the colonists' struggle for independence from Britain and in establishing a political party system in the new nation.

- In the nineteenth century, commercial development and product manufacturing fostered the growth of the daily newspaper.

- New technology and graphics were used by the American Bible Society and by the antislavery societies in their efforts to free American slaves.

- As a consumer culture developed during the second half of the nineteenth century and the early twentieth century, national magazines thrived because of national advertising.

- Public relations became an increasingly important aspect of business during the second half of the nineteenth century as businesspeople became aware of the need to inform the public about business practices.

- Radio became a mass medium after World War I. Radio regulation introduced the concepts of "scarcity of the airwaves" and operating in the "public interest."

- Radio regulation resulted from agreements among the major components of the industry, not from arbitrary government controls on business.

- In 1947, the Hutchins Commission issued a report that challenged the press to become "socially responsible" and to present news in the context of each day's events.

- Film was not protected under the First Amendment until 1952.

- *New York Times v. Sullivan* made it easier for reporters to comment on the activities of public officials without worrying that a slight error would position them for a libel suit.

- During the Vietnam War, the press published news without official military censorship. Despite evidence to the contrary, many military and government officials believe the media lost the war.

- During the Persian Gulf crisis, the military used positive media coverage of its activities and strategic media plans to gain public confidence.

- The 1980s was a time of consolidation and mergers. Newspaper circulation stabilized, the networks competed with cable, and magazines became even more specialized than in the past.

- Issues for the future include the issuing of public stock by media companies; new developments in distribution, including satellite technology; competition between cable and broadcast television; and adaptation of new computer technologies to information delivery.

Navigating the Web

Media history on the web

Historians can browse the World Wide Web for archival material or for historical documents, as well as for media historians and new media developments. The following sites will help you understand the field:

| Media History Project | http://www.mediahistory.com |

This is a great site for finding reviews of recent books about media history, links to archival sites, syllabi for media history courses, and articles like "1928: What's on TV?"

| U.S. Historical Documents | http://www.canet/~brad/doc/index.htm/ |

At this site you can read historical government documents, such as the Constitution, the Declaration of Independence, or government edicts about the French and Indian War.

Here you can see reproductions of some issues of the *Lady's Book* and read articles such as "19th Century History and Fashions" or "The Manufacturing of Gun Powder," from the June 1861 issue.

▧ Questions for review

1. Where did movable type originate?

2. What was the relationship of transportation to communication?

3. How did the political party press influence the writing of the Constitution and the development of political parties?

4. How did the introduction of television affect magazines?

5. Why were films treated differently by the Supreme Court than were other media? What happened in 1952 to change the situation?

6. What questions have converging technologies posed for the future of media?

▧ Issues to think about

1. What were the societal ramifications of the introduction of movable type and the printing press to western Europe and later to the British colonies in North America?

2. Describe the different types of print media in the United States.

3. What is the relationship between the development of capitalism and a consumer culture and the growth of print and electronic media? What is the role of advertising?

4. If publishers and broadcasters followed the suggestions of the Hutchins Commission, what changes would you see in today's media?

5. Are journalists adequately prepared to be good "watchdogs" for society?

6. Does the development of the Internet create new opportunities for existing media? New challenges? New competition?

▧ Suggested readings

Baldasty, Gerald. *The Commercialization of News in the Nineteenth Century* (Madison: University of Wisconsin Press, 1992).

Barnouw, Erik. *A Tower in Babel: A History of Broadcasting in the United States to 1933* (New York: Oxford University Press, 1966); *The Golden Web: A History of Broadcasting in the United States, 1933–1953* (New York: Oxford University Press, 1968); *The Image Empire: A History of Broadcasting in the United States since 1953* (New York: Oxford University Press, 1970).

Ewen, Stuart. *Captains of Consciousness: Advertising and the Roots of Consumer Culture* (New York: McGraw-Hill, 1976).

Schudson, Michael. *Discovering the News: A Social History of American Newspapers* (New York: Basic Books, 1978).

Tedlow, Richard. *Keeping the Corporate Image: Public Relations and Business, 1900–1950* (Greenwich, Ct.: JAI Press, 1979).

Vincent, Theodore G., ed. *Voices of a Black Nation: Political Journalism in the Harlem Renaissance* (San Francisco: Ramparts Press, 1973).

Books

Maxwell Perkins,

in 1919, put his

career on the line

to persuade his

superiors to sign

F. Scott Fitzgerald

to a contract for

his first novel, *This*

Side of Paradise.

Classic novels, such as Little Women, often provide the context for movies.

In 1926, Perkins had to do a repeat performance to get Hemingway published. Charles Scribner, head of the publishing house, was afraid that *The Sun Also Rises* was just another dirty book and that publishing it would destroy the reputation of his quite respectable publishing house.[1] Both Fitzgerald and Hemingway, of course, became classic writers of the 1920s generation and are still read by high school and college students as a part of their literary education.

Since merchants first began to sell books to the general public, critics have wondered whether the desire for profit would overcome good judgment. But definitions of quality and a publisher's ability to discern quality have always been elusive. Publishing *The Sun Also Rises* may have seemed like pandering to the popular taste at the time, but it resulted in the preservation of an enduring classic. It was an economic success for the publisher, and despite its enduring quality, some may still argue that it's nothing but a dirty book. On those grounds, people have even urged that the book be banned, that political control be exerted.

Charles Scribner's concern reflected more than the caution of a respectable man. It reflected a continuing publishing dilemma. That dilemma includes the following issues:

- In a market system driven by popular acclaim, is there a relationship between quality and profit?

- Who defines quality? Are literary elites in a better position than the general public to define quality? Is there a relationship between quality and popular acclaim?

- What are the social and economic impacts of publishing decisions?

- What is the role of books in creating stories? How do books function as the basis for electronic media content?

Growth of literary culture

In nearly all cultures, books have been viewed both as the transmitters of knowledge and as tools of radicals. During medieval times, the reproduction of books was restricted by the Church, for the most part, to monasteries, where scribes hand-copied treasured manuscript books that then made up the important libraries of Europe. In that closed culture, copying books was an art, which we can appreciate when we look at rare books on exhibit in museums. Scholars often had to travel across Europe to the famous libraries to have access to knowledge. Such scarce books rarely, if ever, were owned by individuals, and students relied on teachers to read books to them, producing the "lecture" system of education that is still prevalent in American and European colleges and universities. When your professor lectures to the class, he or she is reenacting an ancient tradition born of necessity.

With the advent of the printing revolution in the mid-1400s as a result of Gutenberg's cast-metal moveable type, books became objects to be printed and sold. They moved out of libraries and into the domain of public culture. Soon books, printed in lots of 200 to 1,000 copies, circulated among the wealthy classes. The production of books opened the way for printer-merchants, who published books and searched for new markets for their products.

Key concept

Scribal Culture: In the Middle Ages, before the invention of the printing press, written material was reproduced almost exclusively by monks who served as scribes, or copyists. As the sole repository of books, the medieval church was able to control what information reached the population.

The Bible, soon printed in English as well as in Latin, circulated freely. No longer did the educated classes depend on the authorities to interpret the word of God; they thought themselves capable of their own interpretations. The circulation of books threatened the power of church and state because knowledge, a powerful tool and weapon, was accessible to anyone who could read. In European towns, the printer's shop became a meeting place and educational center. As the British settled the North American colonies, bookshops there also became important cultural centers.

Books in your life

Judging Their Quality

You be the judge. If you're familiar with any of these books, give them a couple of letter grades: A, B, C, D, F. Judge their quality and their popularity according to how you think most of your friends would rate them. Think about whether quality and popularity can be combined in the same package. Do you think your parents and your professors would give these books the same ratings you do?

BOOK TITLE	QUALITY RATING	POPULARITY RATING
The Bridges of Madison County (Robert Waller)		
A Clear and Present Danger (Tom Clancy)		
Little Women (Louisa May Alcott)		
Peachtree Road (Anne Rivers Siddons)		
Beloved (Toni Morrison)		
For Whom the Bell Tolls (Ernest Hemingway)		
Waiting to Exhale (Terry McMillan)		

As you read this chapter, you will find these books mentioned in connection with important issues for the book industry, including the apparent dilemma of quality versus popularity. Do you think quality and popularity are mutually exclusive?

Because of the perceived power of books, nearly all governments and societies at one time or another have sought to restrict the printing or distribution of books. From the early 1500s until the end of the 1600s, printing in England was strictly controlled by the monarch. In 1529, Henry VIII issued a list of prohibited books and imposed a system of **prior restraint** that required printers to have a license before printing. However, in spite of the severe punishments that were handed down to those who printed outside the system, by the mid-sixteenth century in England, nearly one-third of all books were printed outside the official channels. In 1695, the British Parliament allowed the licensing system to expire, and newspapers and books flourished throughout London and the provincial towns.[2]

Books in American life

As the printing business expanded into the provinces in Britain, it also expanded in the British colonies in America. Information was a highly prized commodity in British America, and colonists bought books to read for pleasure as well as to maintain their connections to the British homeland. Because books were expensive, the industry at first ap-

prior restraint: Restricting publication before the fact rather than banning material or punishing an individual after the material is already printed.

pealed to elite sensibilities and to those who had extra money and leisure time. However, throughout the nineteenth and twentieth centuries, the book industry was democratized. Today, books are produced cheaply and quickly and appeal to all classes of people.

Throughout the seventeenth century, almost all books in the colonies were imported from Europe, although a few religious books and histories were published in Cambridge, Massachusetts. Later, as colonists sought more books, printers such as Benjamin Franklin helped to establish public libraries. Franklin and a group of his Philadelphia friends contributed forty pounds in British sterling to start the Library Company in Philadelphia in 1731 to import books for reading and discussion. The colonists imported mostly religious books, but they also asked for professional books to expand their knowledge of law, medicine, and navigation. Fiction and poetry also were popular. All of those books provided a link between the colonists and their English past. Popular literature also was imported and then published in the colonies. Chief among the popular books were cheap forerunners to paperbacks, known as **chapbooks,** and almanacs and **broadside ballads.** The chapbooks included tales of pirates and highwaymen, cookbooks, household manuals, fortune-telling attempts, and even primitive weather forecasts. By the late 1700s, bookshops such as Franklin's in Philadelphia sold imported and locally produced books, catering to an ever-wider audience.

> **Key**concept
>
> *The Quality versus Quantity Question:* Book publishers traditionally have faced an apparent dilemma: Must they choose between publishing high-quality material or publishing to maximize their profitability? Different publishers have responded to this dilemma in different ways. Some have found that they can make a profit by producing work of high literary quality; others choose to produce work that appeals to more stereotyped and fleeting tastes.

Books posed a problem when it came to circulation. They were bulky and expensive to distribute, and postage rates did not favor distribution through the mails. Before the Civil War, many books were circulated by book peddlers, who traveled from town to town with a horse and cart, selling books or exchanging stock with other dealers. Romantic novels, as well as the traditional religious, professional, and historical books, were sold throughout the rapidly expanding United States. The industry was well enough developed by the mid-1850s to play an important role in social movements and in creating a popular culture.

■ Books and social change

Harriet Beecher Stowe propelled the issue of slavery into the popular culture of the 1850s and in the process created the first mass-market best-seller in the American book business. She published *Uncle Tom's Cabin* in book form about two weeks before the last installment appeared in **serialized** form in the magazine *National Era.* Within three weeks, twenty thousand copies of the book had been sold, and by January 1853, that number had grown to two hundred thousand. Stowe received more than $10,000 in royalties on three months' worth of sales of *Uncle Tom's Cabin.* No American or European author had made so much money from a single book. Although Stowe was criticized by some authors as being too sentimental in depicting the life of slaves and their mistreatment, James Russell Lowell and Ralph Waldo Emerson, both noted New England authors and antislavery writers, wrote her congratulatory notes. Students at the University of Virginia publicly burned the book, and peddlers were sometimes driven from southern towns as they attempted to distribute it.[3]

The expansion of the book-publishing industry provided outlets for other antislavery voices as well. Frederick Douglass, a slave born of a white father and a black mother, escaped from slavery and became one of the principal lecturers for the Massachusetts Antislavery

chapbooks: Cheaply printed paperback books produced during the 1700s.

broadside ballads: Songs and poems printed on single sheets of newsprint.

serialized: A book printed in parts in a magazine or newspaper over a certain period of time.

The first national best-seller, Uncle Tom's Cabin, *was a sentimental depiction of the evils of slavery and intensified the national discussion over slavery.*

Society. He first wrote for newspapers, but in 1845, when he was only twenty-seven years old, he wrote an autobiography, *Narrative of the Life of Frederick Douglass.* Between stints as a newspaper editor, he wrote *My Bondage and My Freedom* (1855) and then took his message abroad. Douglass's voice was one of only a few black voices that found its way to the pages of the published book; his work represented a nineteenth-century practice of authors writing and updating their life stories while they were still alive. After the Civil War, Douglass continued to fight for black voting rights, urban development, social justice, and women's rights.[4]

PAPERBACKS REFLECTING SOCIAL AND ECONOMIC CHANGE The development of the paperback book industry crystallized the social concerns surrounding book publishing. Books had belonged to the elites, and access to "refined" and "socially respectable" forms of reading had reinforced elite values. The development of inexpensive paperbacks created the perception of pandering to popular taste and appealing to those who could be entertained by formulaic fiction. Accessibility to reading material helped to expand the middle class, but it also challenged elite social control.

Keyconcept

Elite Dominance of Cultural Norms. The book-publishing industry initially sold its products to the wealthy social elites of developed countries. These upper classes used books to dominate the norms of culture and social behavior, thus controlling the distribution of information that reached the marketplace of ideas.

Economic and political conditions fueled the development of paperbacks. First distributed before the Civil War, paperbacks benefited from the less expensive printing technology associated with newspapers and from lack of government regulation. Because the U.S. government refused to recognize foreign **copyrights,** books from other countries could be cheaply reproduced as paperbacks.

Further, newspapers printed cheap editions of French and English novels that masqueraded as newspapers so they could be distributed by newsboys and sold through the mail under inexpensive newspaper rates. Competition from paperbacks threatened the young hardback book industry because of the low prices and wide distribution systems.

THE DIME NOVEL After 1845, the federal government refused to allow paperback books to be mailed under inexpensive newspaper rates, but the demand for paperbacks continued to grow. Soon publishers encouraged an inexpensive, relatively short kind of fiction that became known as the **dime novel,** a form well suited to popular taste. During the Civil War, soldiers in the field wanted to fill their time, and reading provided portable entertainment. The Beadle Brothers sold four million copies of dime novels between 1860 and 1861. These pocket-

copyright: A law that protects authors, playwrights, composers, and others who construct original works and keeps others from reproducing work without permission.

dime novel: Cheap, paperback fiction produced in the mid-nineteenth century.

The availability of dime novels expanded reading for the middle- and working-class. Heroic tales appealed to men and women.

size novels were written with specific plots to specific lengths and concentrated on romance and violence, similar to the plots of television entertainment or the romance novel of today.

During the last half of the nineteenth century, new printing and paper technology fueled the distribution of cheap literature in the form of **pamphlet books.** This time, publishers tried to qualify for low mailing rates by claiming that the paperbacks were magazines. The practice ended in 1901 when the Postmaster General declared that book publishers could not use second-class mailing rates under any conditions. Publishers took their case to court but ultimately lost. Already, the issues of quality and quantity were hotly debated, and in 1884, *Publishers Weekly* reported, "In the rage for cheapness, we have sacrificed everything for slop, and a dainty bit of bookmaking is like a jewel in the swine's snout."[5]

Paperback stories reflected the entry of men and women into factories and fictionalized the situations they might encounter in that new world of work. The stories were produced through what writers often called the **fiction factory,** in which publishers dictated the story lines, characters, plots, and sometimes specific scenes. The stories were aimed at the working class: mechanics, farmers, traveling salesmen, boys in shops and factories, secretaries, and domestic servants. The story lines included traditional heroic stories of war and the frontier, as well as tales of outlaws, detectives, male factory operatives, and young women who worked in the mills. Religious themes declined, but the virtue of women remained a hot topic. "Fiction that heroized women outside the domestic sphere," wrote Christine Bold, "offered working-class women some kind of accommodation and justification, some means of negotiating the transition from private to public."[6]

New York publishing houses also promoted the popular **Horatio Alger** rags-to-riches novels of individual achievement, which soon gave way to adventures of athletes and western heroes. Science fiction also gained readership, attesting to the development of technology, although the **genre** often endorsed traditional value systems. Heroes were those who resisted: the detective who resisted the temptation of sex and crime to solve the murder, the cowboy who left the adoring virgin to pursue the bandit, the loner who solved the ills of the community and then fled.

Keyconcept

Democratization of Knowledge: As books became more accessible in the 1800s, knowledge spread widely among the middle and lower classes, creating an increasingly democratic reading public. Wide distribution of books depended on cheap postal rates, inexpensive book production, and portrayal of varied classes of people in fictional works.

pamphlet books: Books without hard covers printed to look like magazines in the 1800s. Publishers wanted to get cheaper mail rates given magazines.

fiction factory: Late nineteenth-century publishing of formulaic books, in which publishers dictated story lines.

Horatio Alger story: Began as a real story of how Horatio Alger worked his way up the social and economic ladder, but soon developed into a term to represent the glorification of individualism in American life.

genre: A category of fiction distinguished by a definite form or style. The term is also used to categorize other forms of artistic endeavor.

Global *Impact*

Book Piracy

No cannons fired and no blood flowed, but in May 1995, American publishers won an important victory in the worldwide battle against book piracy. Prentice-Hall and Harcourt Brace settled a lawsuit against Anhui Science and Technology, a Chinese publishing company, and six Beijing bookstores over the violation of copyrights for English-language texts.

In the growing global economy, that seemingly dull event generated shock waves. Although companies in China (along with many other countries in Asia) continue to violate copyrights, the victory was the first official step toward controlling those abuses.

The copyright debate centers on the conflict between the need to reward creators for their work and the need for accessible information. On the one hand, most people and companies will not create information without making a profit. Copyright laws protect the author's and publisher's commercial interest. On the other hand, overly strict control can limit the flow of information and ideas in the marketplace of ideas.

An early hint of change in the Pacific Rim area came in 1992 when publishers from China, Taiwan, and Korea bought large numbers of copyrights for translated versions of books from other countries. Then the United States informed China that trade expansion would not be allowed unless China agreed to recognize intellectual property rights, which include copyrights, patents, and trademarks. In March 1995, the United States and China signed an agreement for tougher enforcement of intellectual-property violations.

Battles to protect the creators of books and other material are being won, but the war, which dates to the 1500s in England, continues. The digital transmission of text and visuals with computers makes piracy even easier. Information will play a key role in the global economy, both as a product and as a way to correlate economic activities. Developing countries that want to participate in that global economy will be required to respect information ownership.

By 1914, books finally gained a favored mailing status that promoted distribution. In 1913, Congress had established a separate parcel-post mailing rate for packages but had failed to include books. Nevertheless, the following year, the Postmaster General simply moved books to the fourth-class parcel-post rate, which allowed books to be delivered through rural free delivery, established in 1896. The move laid the groundwork for the development of book clubs in the 1920s, a creation that promoted popular consumption of best-sellers, as well as of histories and biographies. During World War II, President Roosevelt administratively lowered the book rate, and Congress officially passed the lower rate in 1942. Cheaper postal rates for books ensured that they would be available to a wide audience, not merely to an elite.

Book publishing enters the modern era

The founding of book clubs—the Book-of-the-Month Club in 1926 and the Literary Guild in 1927—allowed publishers to reach a national but targeted group of readers through direct-mail promotion techniques. Such distribution opened the markets for an astounding array of new titles. Publishing figures rose steadily through the 1920s and then declined between 1931 and 1933, the years of the Great Depression. During the late

86

Books in our lives

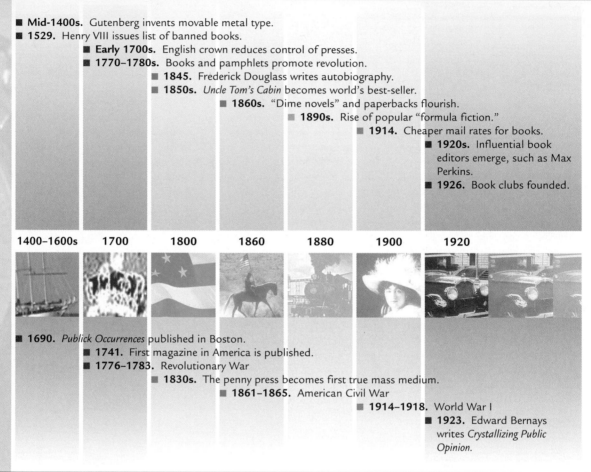

- **Mid-1400s.** Gutenberg invents movable metal type.
- **1529.** Henry VIII issues list of banned books.
  - **Early 1700s.** English crown reduces control of presses.
  - **1770–1780s.** Books and pamphlets promote revolution.
    - **1845.** Frederick Douglass writes autobiography.
    - **1850s.** *Uncle Tom's Cabin* becomes world's best-seller.
      - **1860s.** "Dime novels" and paperbacks flourish.
        - **1890s.** Rise of popular "formula fiction."
          - **1914.** Cheaper mail rates for books.
            - **1920s.** Influential book editors emerge, such as Max Perkins.
            - **1926.** Book clubs founded.

| 1400–1600s | 1700 | 1800 | 1860 | 1880 | 1900 | 1920 |

- **1690.** *Publick Occurrences* published in Boston.
  - **1741.** First magazine in America is published.
  - **1776–1783.** Revolutionary War
    - **1830s.** The penny press becomes first true mass medium.
      - **1861–1865.** American Civil War
        - **1914–1918.** World War I
          - **1923.** Edward Bernays writes *Crystallizing Public Opinion.*

1930s, figures again rose as prosperity returned, but the number of new titles declined during World War II. Immediately after the war, however, came a new publishing boom.

The postwar publishing years were characterized by specialization. Publishers significantly increased the number of scientific and technical books, with a shift of emphasis to subjects that emerged from war-time trends. Themes reflected the struggle of individuals to maintain their individualistic, small-town American values while taking advantage of new technology. Americans were ready to move forward technologically. Popular subjects included science fiction, aeronautics and aircraft manufacture, automotive construction and maintenance, radio, television, navigation, and radar. Books that probed the human personality, including those in the areas of psychology, psychiatry, and psychoanalysis, flourished. "How-to-do-it" books in home construction, furniture design,

Keyconcept

Book Distribution: The ability to produce and distribute more books to more people depended on book distribution—the process of making books known and physically available to potential readers. Wealthy social elites tended to favor limiting wide distribution and opposed low postal rates for books. However, cheap postage and improved marketing techniques eventually made books accessible to large numbers of readers.

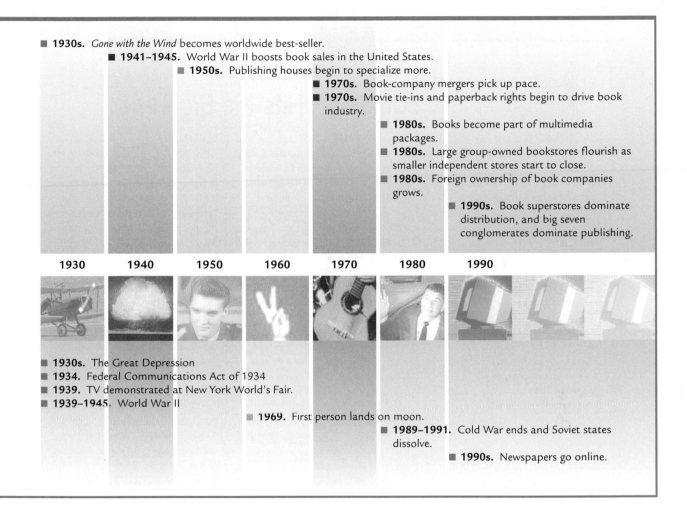

■ **1930s.** *Gone with the Wind* becomes worldwide best-seller.
  ■ **1941–1945.** World War II boosts book sales in the United States.
    ■ **1950s.** Publishing houses begin to specialize more.
      ■ **1970s.** Book-company mergers pick up pace.
      ■ **1970s.** Movie tie-ins and paperback rights begin to drive book industry.
        ■ **1980s.** Books become part of multimedia packages.
        ■ **1980s.** Large group-owned bookstores flourish as smaller independent stores start to close.
        ■ **1980s.** Foreign ownership of book companies grows.
          ■ **1990s.** Book superstores dominate distribution, and big seven conglomerates dominate publishing.

| 1930 | 1940 | 1950 | 1960 | 1970 | 1980 | 1990 |

■ **1930s.** The Great Depression
■ **1934.** Federal Communications Act of 1934
■ **1939.** TV demonstrated at New York World's Fair.
■ **1939–1945.** World War II
    ■ **1969.** First person lands on moon.
      ■ **1989–1991.** Cold War ends and Soviet states dissolve.
        ■ **1990s.** Newspapers go online.

and interior decoration catered to those faced with housing shortages or lack of skilled labor, as well as to people interested in manual craftsmanship. Expansion of secondary schools and the creation of the GI Bill, which financed higher-education programs for returning GIs, created a demand for educational texts. College enrollment, which was one million students before the war, mushroomed to 12 million during the 1960s and 1970s. A variety of federal legislation packages created programs that expanded libraries, both in and out of schools, thereby creating an even larger demand for more books. Most of the major book publishers developed extensive education divisions.

Today's market structure

The major issues in book publishing—quantity, profits, and quality—are debated today, even as the market structure changes. Although critics lament that nobody in the United States reads anymore, the book-publishing industry thrives, publishing more books in

Best-selling author Tom Clancy struck it rich on publication of his first novel, *The Hunt for Red October.* Clancy's book was first published by the obscure Naval Institute Press, but Clancy soon moved to Putnam-Berkley Group, Inc. and increased sales with each successive book. Altogether, Putnam-Berkley has shipped more than 31 million copies of his books.

The success of Clancy's book indicated a demand structure that supported the successful development of not only one novel, but of a series of "technological thrillers" in the context of real-life political events. Clancy's work was in demand by larger publishers because they recognized the work would support a more mainstream "product line" than Clancy had originally imagined.

Clancy wrote *The Hunt for Red October* on an IBM Selectric typewriter in his office during the afternoons and at home on the weekends. When it was finished, he told his wife, Wanda, to lock herself in the bedroom and read the book while he watched the kids. She read it reluctantly, fearing it would be terrible and she'd have to tell him so. "I thought he was crazy when he started writing the book," Wanda told a reporter for the *Saturday*

Unknown Hits the Big Time

Evening Post. But once Wanda had read the book, she changed her mind, predicting that it would sell far more than the 5,000 copies Clancy hoped for. She anticipated the demand. In 1984, when Clancy was earning $100,000 from his insurance business, *The Hunt for Red October* hit the bookstores, and Clancy's income jumped to a reported $15 million, representing an economic boon to the author and to his publisher.

He received an eight-figure advance for his 1992 thriller, *The Sum of All Fears.* By 1994, the 47-year-old writer was living with his wife and four children in a 16,000 square foot mansion on an estate that used to be a boys' camp. Clancy keeps hitting the big time. After *The Hunt for Red October* came other technological thrillers: *Patriot Games, Red Storm Rising, The Cardinal of the Kremlin, Clear and Present Danger, The Sum of All Fears,* and *Without Remorse.*

The Clancys' lives changed quickly. Invitations arrived daily, including one to dinner at the White House with President Reagan. Clancy's daughter Michele says that some people expect her to be a snob just because her parents have money. Clancy says it was easier to keep his new-found wealth and popularity in perspective, however, because he was in his thirties before it arrived. But fame did have an impact, and in April 1995, Clancy and his wife separated. By the end of the year, however, they had reunited. Despite some of the complications of a wealthy and more leisurely life, however, nobody in Clancy's family wishes he were still selling insurance.

Clancy continues to turn out novels, CD-ROMs, and recently did a stint as a space reporter. His versatility earns him about $16 million a year.

SOURCES: Dick Victory, "Clancy's Game: How Tom Clancy has Turned the Novel of Revenge Into Earnings of $16 million a Year," January 1997, *Washingtonian,* p. 49; Tom Reeves, "Corporate America's Most Powerful People," *Forbes,* May 25, 1992, p. 160; and November 9, 1992; *Publishers Weekly,* August 10, 1992, p. 9; and Christopher Phillips, "Red October's Tom Clancy: After the Hunt," *Saturday Evening Post,* September 1991, p. 16.

every passing year. In fact, the total volume of sales increased from $435 million in 1947 to more than $25 billion in 1995. Although only about 10,000 titles were sold annually in the mid-1950s, by the early 1990s, about 50,000 titles were sold each year. Table 4.1 shows the increase in number of titles from 1993 to 1994, broken down by field.

Paperbacks are a significant staple in the book business. In 1995, in an average 24-hour period, 27 percent of Americans aged 30 to 59 reported having read a paperback book, up from 17 percent in 1987. The numbers in younger and older age groups

TABLE 4.1 Books Published in the United States, 1993–1994, by Subject Field

SUBJECT FIELD	1993	1994	SUBJECT FIELD	1993	1994
Agriculture	558	532	Literature	2,169	2,356
Art	1,540	1,621	Medicine	3,094	3,147
Biography	2,071	2,197	Music	377	364
Business	1,442	1,616	Philosophy, Psychology	1,764	1,741
Education	1,247	1,310	Poetry, Drama	1,004	1,065
Fiction	5,419	5,415	Religion	2,633	2,730
General Works	1,870	2,208	Science	2,678	3,021
History	2,317	2,507	Sociology, Economics	7,502	8,038
Home Economics	881	1,004	Sports, Recreation	1,146	1,161
Juvenile	5,469	5,321	Technology	2,247	2,085
Language	669	700	Travel	487	556
Law	1,143	1,168	**Total**	**49,727**	**51,863**

Source: Gary Ink, "Output Bounced Back in '94," *Publishers Weekly,* April 29, 1996, pp. 32–34.

Reprinted from the April 29, 1996 issue of *Publishers Weekly,* published by Cahners Publishing Company, a division of Reed Elsevier, Inc. Copyright © 1996 by Reed Elsevier, Inc.

remained about the same, as did the number reading hardback books. Consumers cite books as one of the best values for their money, far ahead of cable television, live entertainment, restaurant meals, VCR movies, and magazines.[7] Individuals buy books in a variety of stores, not just in bookstores. Table 4.2 indicates the type of stores and numbers of books bought there.

Although the number of fiction titles has stabilized, sales of individual volumes have increased substantially. From 1990 to 1995, each year broke the sales records of the previous year. The top ten best-sellers of 1983 sold fewer copies than did the 1993 top seller, *The Bridges of Madison County,* which sold more than 4.3 million copies in 1993 alone. *Bridges* remained on the *Publishers Weekly* best-seller list until October 1995, for a total of 161 weeks. In 1993, nine books sold more than a million copies each. The number of fiction and nonfiction books with sales of more than 100,000 copies also set a record: 157 titles, excluding religious books. Most of the growth was in fiction.[8]

Nevertheless, book publishers are fully aware that their market is narrow. The biggest buyers of literature are people under twenty-five, probably spurred by requirements leveled

TABLE 4.2 Kinds of Stores Where Books Are Sold in the United States

TYPE OF STORE	NUMBER OF STORES
Antiquarian	2,328
College	3,523
Comics	340
Computer software	363
Department stores	2,372
General book stores	7,223
Gift shops	388
Juvenile book stores	467
Mail order	1,348
Museum, nature, and educational	990
Other	3,746
Religious	4,026
Paperback	465
Used	931
Totals:	**28,510**

Source: Adapted from "Retailer Categories in the United States and Canada," *American Book Trade Directory,* 41st ed., 1995–96 (New Providence, NJ: R. R. Bowker, 1995–96).

African American Best-Sellers

When literary agents refused to handle a book that Faye Childs had written, telling her there was no market for it because African Americans don't read, she didn't just go home angry, she went home determined. In August 1991, she syndicated a newspaper column, "Blackboard: African American Bestsellers." Her column is endorsed by the 9,000-member American Booksellers Association, the nation's largest book-publishing organization.

Childs's book, *Across the Creek,* is still unpublished. She says that her column absorbs the time she needs to complete the revisions. But the initial rejection is what spurred Childs to action. She found that few African American authors, with the exceptions of stars Toni Morrison, Alice Walker, and Alex Haley, have appeared on best-seller lists. Morrison's books, such as *Beloved* and *Song of Solomon,* and Terry McMillan's *Waiting to Exhale,* appeal to white as well as black audiences.

Childs and Debbie Wade, a friend and partner, contacted twenty-two bookstore owners in thirty cities and asked them to report their best-selling books by or about African Americans in a monthly survey. Today, fifty-five bookstores (60 percent of which are African American–owned) participate in her continued surveying. Childs's goal is to get the word out about African American authors who are not superstars, to boost sales of African American books, and to raise cultural awareness about the content of those books.

Her complaint may not be specific to African American authors. Authors routinely complain that best-seller lists are limited to sales in the mega-bookstores. Stores that handle books outside the popular mainstream fare rarely get to report their sales to the best-seller lists. One exception to this was *The Bridges of Madison County,* which gained its initial sales momentum in independent stores. Mainstream marketing techniques sometimes obscure audience demand and slow the pace of distribution.

Childs would like to see "Blackboard" expand into a television show that would feature book reviews, interviews with authors, and industry gossip. She believes that books by African American authors would provide rich material for much-needed African American films.

SOURCE: Joy Duckett Cain, "Faye Childs: Charting Our Books," *Essence,* May 1994, p. 64.

by college professors, and the biggest buyers of popular fiction are over sixty-five. Moreover, a vast majority of book buyers are white. In a nation in which the minority population is growing faster than the majority, subsequent generations of booksellers will need to target new audiences if they are to continue to experience market growth.

Media conglomerates in the book business

Book publishing has undergone radical economic and structural changes since World War II. During the 1940s and 1950s, publishing was almost a cottage industry, with, as John Baker writes, "a comparatively small business producing a comparatively limited number of books for a cozily elite readership whose access to bookstores was limited by geography."[9] Like many other companies, small, independent book publishers were swallowed up by conglomerates, although a variety of small, new firms still are

TABLE 4.3 Ranking the Big Publishing Houses, 1996

PUBLISHER	NUMBER OF HARDCOVER BOOKS	WEEKS ON BEST-SELLER LIST IN 1995
Random House	44	319
Bantam Double Day Dell	28	251
Simon & Schuster	24	176
Putnam Berkley	20	136
HarperCollins	16	225
Time Warner	14	200
Penguin USA	5	65

Source: Reprinted from the January 6, 1997 issue of *Publishers Weekly,* published by Cahners Publishing Company, a division of Reed Elsevier, Inc. Copyright © 1997 by Reed Elsevier, Inc.

being created today. The large inventories needed after World War II to supply increasing demand required larger capital investments. Capital came from a variety of sources, including **public investment**; books, like newspapers, went public. Magazine publishers and motion-picture magnates plowed some of their profits into the book industry; electronic companies, in anticipation of the computer revolution, also invested. Ownership went international. By 1992, five of America's largest book publishers were foreign owned.[10] Even more significantly, a few publishing houses dominated the industry. In 1996, seven conglomerates—Random, Inc., Bantam Doubleday Dell, Simon & Schuster, HarperCollins, Time Warner, Putnam Berkley, and Penguin USA—accounted for about 88 percent of the hardcover slots and about 80 percent of the paperback slots on the best-seller lists. Table 4.3 indicates the power of the big houses.

The Simon & Schuster story indicates what consolidation has meant to the industry. Begun in the 1920s, Simon & Schuster developed a solid reputation as a publisher of scholarly, scientific, and artistic books that appealed to popular taste. In 1944, the Chicago department-store magnate Marshall Field bought a substantial interest in the company and simultaneously invested in Pocket Books, a paperback publisher. In 1966, Simon & Schuster acquired Pocket Books, and in 1976, both companies were brought under the Gulf + Western umbrella, which later became Paramount Communications. In 1983, Simon & Schuster acquired Allyn and Bacon; in 1984, it acquired the venerable publishing firm of Prentice-Hall; and in 1991, it acquired Macmillan Computer Publishing. Then in 1993, Simon & Schuster, under the umbrella of Paramount, acquired Macmillan, a publishing firm with English origins dating to 1843.

Books, records, toys, and games are only a few of the spin offs created when a book or movie is successful. Media are large businesses, often with many subsidiaries, all of which may play some part in promotional efforts.

public investment: The buying of stock in a company by the general public.

But the story doesn't end here. In February and March of 1994, Viacom, Inc., and QVC Network, Inc., battled for control of Paramount. Viacom won by bidding more than $10 billion. The purchase affected all media industries, not just publishing, because in addition to its vast publishing holdings, Paramount also owned Paramount Pictures and an 890-title movie library (*Wayne's World, The Firm,* and *Sunset Boulevard*), television studios, a theme park division, the New York Knicks National Basketball Association team, and the New York Rangers of the National Hockey League. Viacom also has many other holdings, including MTV, VH-1, and the Nickelodeon networks. In 1994, as a unit, Viacom and Paramount owned twelve television stations, fourteen radio stations, Showtime, the Movie Channel, syndicated reruns such as *Cheers,* and 3,790 films. They controlled 1,927 movie screens, 3,500 home video stores, and 507 music stores.[11]

■ Conglomeration and media convergence

The building of conglomerates has resulted in the production of packages in which books, movies, television programs, and other products are viewed as parts of the same media package. In some cases, however, conglomerates are loose coalitions in which one arm—say, the broadcast arm—might not know what the other arm—say, the book-publishing division—is doing. Dan Lacy, former president of McGraw-Hill, notes, for example, that Little, Brown, a book publisher owned by the same conglomerate as Book-of-the-Month Club, will market a book to Literary Guild if the Guild offers a better deal.[12] Moreover, authors often work through agents who demand the "best deal" rather than an in-house arrangement. However, the trend is definitely toward generating packages, in particular, those that showcase "star" writers, leaving less money for the nonstars. In addition, power has moved from editors toward those who deal with subsidiary rights. Despite the looseness of the coalition, the position of the conglomerate is significant. Corporations often exercise a fair amount of allocative control—allocating funds to various divisions or sections of divisions. Division heads often have a great deal of autonomy when it comes to operations, but they are heavily controlled by the budgets given to them by corporate business managers.

Concentration has advantages and disadvantages. Book publishing is a risky business; only 20 to 40 percent of books published make a profit. Therefore, concentration allows for greater profit by producing fewer books in large quantities. However, it also tends to contribute toward homogenization. If one type of book is successful, publishers will look for a similar book that will appeal to the same broad audience. This, in turn, can negatively affect the marketplace of ideas; fewer ideas are out there for discussion.

Keyconcept

Media Consolidation: From the 1960s onward, books, movies, and other media products have increasingly become linked as part of the process of consolidation—the merging and combining of diverse companies under the same ownership. A few large corporations now control many publishers, film studios, and other media outlets. Although the consolidated companies may produce more books and movies, limited ownership of media may restrict the types of information transmitted to the public.

Audience demand in book publishing markets

The market can be divided by types of publishing houses, as well as by types of books. Publishing houses can be further divided by size. Large publishers often have several divisions and publish different types of books within each division. A large house such as Simon & Schuster, for example, may have a **trade book** division as well as a **textbook** division. Trade publications, or books published for general distribution, include (1) hardcover books, (2) quality paperbacks, and (3) mass-

trade book: Most mass marketed books sold at bookstores or through book clubs. Excludes textbooks.

textbooks: Books used for elementary school, high school, and college classroom work.

specialized publishers: Publishing houses that produce a particular type of book, such as religious and children's books.

[profile]

Stephen King

More movies have been made from Stephen King's novels than from any other writer's. So far, twenty of his thirty best-sellers have hit the screen. His editor says that King's success is partially because he can see the relationship between books and screen.

King grew up a poor child of a single mother. His father left the family when King was two, and his mother took whatever jobs she could find. She brought home secondhand paperbacks, which she called "cheap, sweet vacations." Mother and son read murder mysteries. When he was seven, King sneaked into drive-ins to watch horror films. When he was eleven, he and his brother started a local newspaper, which included film reviews and science-fiction stories.

By age fourteen, King had submitted several stories to professional publications. After a number of rejection letters, King published a story in *Startling Mystery Stories*. He was twenty years old and a student at the University of Maine, majoring in literature and taking courses in creative writing and rural sociology.

King married his college sweetheart, Tabitha, and had two small children. By the time he was twenty-five, he had typed out five novels and received as many rejections. His few published short stories couldn't pay even the telephone bill.

However, in 1973, while King was working at a laundry, his wife fished one of his novels out of the trash. Her intuition was good. *Carrie* brought a near-record sum of $400,000 in paperback sales. Three years later, the novel was made into a movie. King followed *Carrie* with *Salem's Lot* and *The Shining*, both of which also made it to the big screen.

King says that the difference between a talented writer and a successful one is a lot of hard work. He should know. By 1990, he had written twenty-five books; by 1996, he had published forty.

King's success is based on talent but also on sheer output: He churns out 2,000 words a day, often before lunch. He writes enough to produce seven novels a year. He composes novellas, comic books, short stories, novels, and literary dissertations. Not all of them are tales of hor-

ror. Some of them are published under the pseudonym of Richard Bachman, which he uses to prove that he can produce good literary work without the Stephen King label.

SOURCES: Nancy Pate, "It's Double Trouble by Stephen King," *Sun-Sentinel* (Fort Lauderdale), September 4, 1996, Section Lifestyle, p. 3E; Andy Beckett, "A Career Written in Blood," *The Independent,* March 10, 1996, Section Comment, p. 19; John Millar, "Kingdom of Horror," *Scottish Daily Record & Sunday Mail Ltd.*, March 7, 1996, p. 22; Nick Hasted, "Old King, New King," *The Irish Times,* February 18, 1995, Weekend Supplement, p. 12.

market paperbacks. Textbook divisions include (1) college textbooks, (2) high school textbooks, and (3) elementary school textbooks. In addition, some houses, such as Macmillan (now under the ownership of Paramount), traditionally included a division (in Macmillan's case, the Free Press) for publishing scholarly books. Other scholarly books, particularly those that sell only in limited numbers to professors and libraries, are published by university presses. In addition to scholarly books, **specialized publishers** also produce children's books, religious books, and professional books. "**Niche publishers**" target tiny

niche publishers: These are smaller publishing houses that serve very narrowly defined markets.

specialized audiences, such as antique collectors. Publishers strive to supply the demand within a well-defined market.

Financing and convergence

Books traditionally have relied little on advertising for financial support but rather have been financed by individuals, by those of us who buy books. Increasingly, the book industry is supplying the content for packages that include several media. Movie rights, television specials, and other related products often boost the proceeds for a publisher and an author. When Winona Ryder was nominated for best actress in the film *Little Women,* book sales of the nineteenth-century children's story got a new boost. Such packaging represents one type of media convergence, a blurring of definitions between media—here, between books and films.

During 1996, Oprah Winfrey became a new force in the book industry. Oprah began a reading club for her television program, and the selection of a book for Oprah's show pushed it to the top of the best-seller's lists. The first book selected for the reading club was *The Deep End of the Ocean* by Jacquelyn Mitchard. It went from 100,000 copies in print to 640,000 within weeks. This example shows the power of celebrity, but it also illustrates a potential new source of demand for books.[13]

Since Oprah Winfrey created her book club, books succeed often on the basis of whether she chooses them. Here Oprah and Maya Angelou gather with friends to discuss The Heart of a Woman.

Market dimensions of a best-seller

Published in April 1992, Robert James Waller's *The Bridges of Madison County* is a success not only as a book but as a package. The novel was short and the author was unknown, but the romantic tale of a *National Geographic* photographer and a farm wife caught the eye of booksellers, as well as the novel-reading public. By August 10, it had made the *Publishers Weekly* best-seller list, and a week later it was on the *New York Times* list. Less than a year after its publication date, it had been reprinted nineteen times, for a total of 274,500 copies. In early 1993, Warner Hardcover Books, the publisher, promoted it with Valentine's Day bookstore displays, National Public Radio interviewed the author, and *Cosmopolitan* published an excerpt. Those promotional efforts, its place on the best-seller lists gained by sales at independent book stores, and the NPR interview garnered big orders at the chain bookstores. (See Figure 4.1 for a summary of the promotional efforts and spin-offs from the book.) By May 29, 1993, *The Bridges of Madison County* was the top seller at two of the national chains, and Warner had gone back for a thirty-fifth printing. Television helped. That May, author Waller appeared on an Oprah Winfrey show filmed in Madison County, Iowa; on CNN's *Sonya Live;* and on the *Today* show. During May and June of 1993, sales of the book at Barnes & Noble and Waldenbooks were close to 250,000 copies, a figure that most publishers would be happy to achieve during a twelve-month—let alone an eight-week—period.

Aaron Priest, Waller's agent, who handled the book and got Waller a $35,000 advance for a first major-market work, also hammered out a deal with Atlantic to record *The Ballads of Madison County,* an eleven-song album that included four original songs by Waller plus some old favorites such as "Autumn Leaves." Warner and Atlantic cooperated on the deal so that the album was available in bookstores as well as through music retailers. The book spawned travel articles on Madison County and Winterset, Iowa, where the book is set. *Travel-Holiday* published a 1,300-word piece, "Bridges to the Heart," touting the small farming community as reminiscent of a 19th-century painting and the town of Winterset as a product of the 1950s. By late 1993, the book had sold 4.7 million copies, and by January 1996, sales had passed 6 million copies. The book sold more copies than any novel since *Gone with the Wind,* published in 1936. Kathleen Kennedy bought the movie rights, MPI Home Video produced a video travelogue about the Iowa bridges, and A-Vision marketed a video to promote the ballads on its sister label, Atlantic Records. In 1995, Clint Eastwood and Meryl Streep appeared on screen as the central characters in the movie version of the novel. Waller's second book, *Slow Waltz at Cedar Bend,* was published in November 1993 and also hit the top of the charts. Twentieth-Century Fox bought the film

FIGURE 4.1 Example of Book Promotion and Spin-Offs

By January 1996, 6 million copies of *The Bridges of Madison County* were sold in the United States. It has been translated into five languages. More books by Waller include: *Slow Waltz in Cedar Bend, Border Music,* and *Puerto Vallarta Squeeze.*

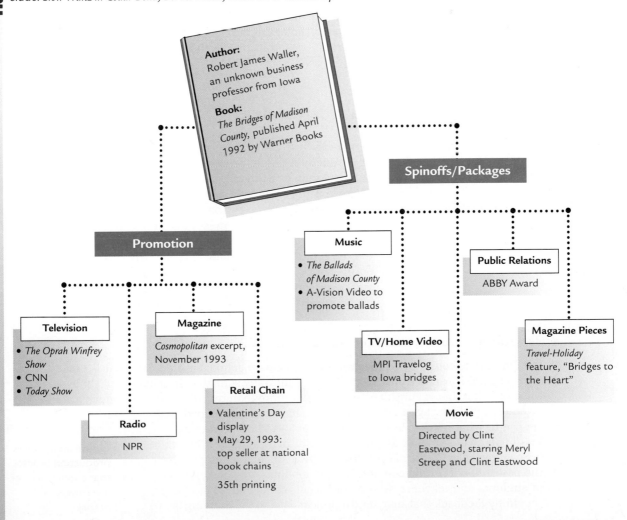

rights. In addition, Waller received the 1993 ABBY Award for the book that booksellers of the American Booksellers Association most enjoyed selling during the year. When the book hit the big time through promotion by independent bookstores, it became a multi-media production, with film, video, recording, and publishing all seeking to profit from Waller's popular romantic tale. In 1995, it remained on the best-seller lists. In this case, the book was the bedrock for spin-offs by many media, an example of the convergence of technologies to spread ideas rather than the combination of technologies for distribution.

■ Enduring themes in audience demand

Religious and inspirational books are enduring categories in the book business. In 1994, books heading the fiction list were James Finn Garner's *Politically Correct Bedtime Stories: Modern Tales for Our Life & Times* and James Redfield's *Celestine Prophecy,* a psychological New Age quest story. The *Catechism of the Catholic Church* sold about two million copies during the last half of 1994, and William Bennett's *Book of Virtues: A Treasury of Great Moral Stories* made *Publishers Weekly*'s charts forty-nine out of fifty-one weeks. *Publishers Weekly* speculates that the current popularity of spiritual and moral themes may be due to the aging baby boomers, the excesses of the '80s, or a reaction to corruption in politics.[14] Those enduring themes account for the success of Anne Rivers Siddons's books, such as *Peachtree Road.* Siddons taps the romantic nature of her readers and ties her themes to current social and psychological themes. Other popular titles that sell well over time include romantic novels, how-to books, home-improvement books, and cookbooks.

Supplying the audience's demand

Books are produced for different markets by different types of publishers; trade books and textbooks are published through distinctly different processes. Trade books gain greater publicity than do textbooks, but textbooks and professional books comprise the bulk of the book-publishing market. When Harcourt Brace cut back its trade division, few noticed that trade books represented only 3 percent of its sales; in the book industry as a whole, trade books constitute no more than 25 percent. The rest are textbooks, scientific books, reference and scholarly publications, Bibles, and other specialized books.[15] Figure 4.2 shows consumer expenditures for books by type of publication.

> **Key**concept
>
> *Markets and Processes in the Book Industry:* The book industry is set up in different ways to serve the distinct market needs of general consumers, educators, and professionals. The processes of book production and distribution can be varied to fit these distinct markets.

■ Textbooks

Producing books for elementary and secondary schools is a process that is exceedingly **capital intensive** and politically and culturally sensitive. In school publishing, authors play the role of consultant–contributor more than that of writer, to produce a book or educational package that is constantly shaped and reshaped in response to what market leaders want, as analyzed by marketing professionals. The process is predominantly driven by the big state bureaucracies in California and Texas, which are large enough to have the power to determine content. Sample modules are tried on groups of students and teachers, who record what works and what doesn't, providing feedback that may send a project back to the drawing board

> **capital intensive:** A production process that requires a large investment of money.

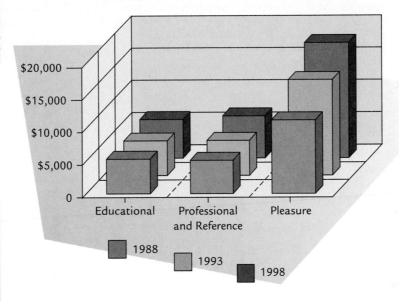

FIGURE 4.2 Consumer Expenditures for Books (in millions of dollars)

Source: Book Industry Trends, 1994. Book Industry Study Group, Inc., 1994.

Note: 1998 figures are estimated. Educational includes elementary, high school, and college textbooks. Professional and reference include professional, university press, and subscription reference. Pleasure includes trade, mass-market paperback, book clubs, and religious books.

before a final huge investment is made. Sometimes special editions are printed to cater to local demands if the scale justifies the printing cost. Often, videotapes or CD-ROMs are given away or sold at cost to encourage schools to adopt specific books. Because at the public elementary and secondary level, taxpayers usually pay for the books, culturally sensitive issues often hit the media and become political footballs for citizens' pressure groups of all kinds. The danger, of course, is that catering to the educational demands of large states such as California and Texas also requires catering to the cultural needs and demands of powerful groups in those states. How accurate is a history textbook? How much room is there for diversity? How much room for interpretation?

Although the college book industry also is market driven, there are significant differences between it and the public school market. In the college market, authors are writers; students, rather than taxpayers, usually pay for the books; the economic stakes are much lower; and books that grate on culturally sensitive nerves sometimes are used for a purpose. Although professors often generate ideas for college textbooks, sales representatives and editors evaluate whether those ideas will produce books that are competitive with other books in the field. The author's primary responsibility in the college textbook field is producing the manuscript. The contract between the publisher and the author determines who will locate photographs, provide rough sketches for charts and graphs, write photograph captions, and provide an index.

Once the book is finished, it is marketed through the publisher's marketing teams. For public school adoptions, the marketing professionals contact curriculum committees in states and municipalities; for college adoptions, they contact professors in various colleges and universities who might choose to adopt the book for their classrooms or departments.

98

Thus the publisher assumes almost all the financial responsibility for the book, as well as for production and promotion. The publisher selects what will be published, produces the book, advances the financing for production, promotes and distributes the book, and, if the book is successful, makes a profit. The authors risk time. They produce the copy, examine the changes made by copyeditors, sometimes locate photographs, read page proofs, and sometimes provide an index.

The trade market: Fiction and nonfiction

Trade books can be broadly classified as fiction and nonfiction. Nonfiction books usually start with a proposal. For both fiction and nonfiction, an author usually hires an agent to market a proposal. However, in an exceedingly small number of cases, authors send completed manuscripts to a publisher. A manuscript is read by a reader hired specifically to scan incoming manuscripts. The manuscript is then forwarded to an editor and accepted for publication (or rejected). Sometimes an author is successful first with a small publisher, and then a larger publishing house will entice the author away, as happened to Tom Clancy.

In the case of *The Bridges of Madison County,* author Robert James Waller took a leave of absence from his position as a university professor to write his first novel. When he finished the manuscript, he sent it to some friends to read, and one of them got him in touch with an agent, Aaron Priest. After several publishers rejected the book, Warner Books offered Waller a $32,000 advance.[16] Well-known authors, such as Stephen King, receive much larger advances, sometimes as high as $1 million.

Once a book is accepted, an editor is assigned to work with an author. In trade divisions, the editor has a great deal of power and often helps the author to shape the book. Through the 1960s, editors helped to develop great writers. Probably the best-known editor was Maxwell Perkins, who in the 1920s and 1930s worked with F. Scott Fitzgerald, Marjorie Kinnan Rawlings, Ernest Hemingway, and Thomas Wolfe. Editors such as Perkins regarded themselves as part of the literary class and were aware of their roles as developers of culture and literature and as contributors to the marketplace of ideas. During the past twenty years, power has shifted to some degree from those editors to people in subsidiary rights and marketing. Although editors are still influential in shaping a work, they tend to have less power in the organization and often remain anonymous to the general public. Nevertheless, many editors helped shape the best-sellers listed in Table 4.4.

PRODUCTION Book publishing has long made use of the process of contracting out work. Before the Paramount merger, Macmillan's staid office building on Third Avenue in New York City housed very few of the company's actual operations. It was primarily an office building, with some design studios. The typical pattern is for a book to be formatted into one of several standard designs produced by in-house artists and designers or to be designed by an independent firm under contract to the publisher. If a design contract is commissioned especially for a project, the author may work with the designers in all phases of the production process. Freelancers usually copyedit, typeset, and print a book. Those freelancers may be individuals, or they may be production or printing firms outside the geographical confines of publishing centers. With the evolution of word-processing programs that allow documents to be converted into type fonts and page designs directly on the computer, this "outsourcing" trend will probably continue. The publisher therefore has access to specialized skills without having to hire full-time employees for what may be seasonal work, does not have to pay the benefits associated with full-time employees, and does not have to provide office space or other amenities such as child-

TABLE 4.4 Publishers Weekly 1996 Hardcover Best-Sellers

TABLE 4.4

Best-sellers tend to fall into categories. Popular fiction includes thrillers, romances, horror tales, and inspirational books. Nonfiction often includes cookbooks, self-help, popular psychology, inspirational, and celebrity stories. Best-selling authors tend to appear on the list more than once. These lists show the hardcover best-sellers for 1996 and the number of weeks they appeared on the *Publishers Weekly* lists.

FICTION	NONFICTION
1. *The Celestine Prophecy* by James Redfield (Warner), 48 weeks.	1. *Men Are from Mars, Women Are from Venus* by John Gray (HarperCollins), 52.
2. *Primary Colors,* by Anonymous (Random House), 31.	2. *The Zone,* by Barry Sears with Bill Lawren (Regan Books), 41.
3. *The Horse Whisperer,* by Nicholas Evans (Delacorte), 25.	3. *The Seven Spiritual Laws of Success* by Deepak Chopra (New World Library), 39.
4. *The Tenth Insight,* by James Redfield (Warner), 25.	4. *Simple Abundance,* by Sarah Ban Breathnach (Warner), 39.
5. *The Runaway Jury,* by John Grisham (Doubleday), 23.	5. *Emotional Intelligence,* by Daniel Goleman (Bantam), 38.
6. *How Stella Got Her Groove Back,* Terry McMillan (Viking), 21.	6. *Midnight in the Garden of Good and Evil,* by John Berendt (Random House), 37.
7. *Executive Orders,* by Tom Clancy (Putnam), 18.	7. *Undaunted Courage,* by Stephen E. Ambrose (Simon & Schuster), 36.
8. *Absolute Power,* by David Balducci (Warner), 17.	8. *The Dilbert Principle,* by Scott Adams (HarperBusiness), 35.
9. *Moonlight Becomes You,* by Mary Higgins Clark (Simon & Schuster), 16.	9. *Rush Limbaugh Is a Big Fat Idiot,* by Al Franken (Delacorte), 24.
10. *Gods and Generals,* by Jeff Shaara (Ballantine), 15.	
11. *The Deep End of the Ocean,* by Jacquelyn Michard (Viking), 15	

Note: Rankings are determined by sales figures provided by publishers; the numbers generally reflect reports of copies "shipped and billed" in calendar year 1996.

Source: Reprinted from the January 6, 1997 issue of *Publishers Weekly,* published by Cahners Publishing Company, a division of Reed Elsevier, Inc. Copyright © 1996 by Reed Elsevier, Inc.

care facilities. Specialized employees are able to work from their homes, which can be advantageous for parents and other groups but which often means lack of benefits such as health insurance.

DISTRIBUTION Distribution has undergone major changes since World War II, with chain bookstores accounting for almost half of bookstore sales. Today, the top six chains in sales are Waldenbooks, Barnes & Noble, Crown Books, Borders Books, Books-A-Million, and Encore Books. The marketing of books through suburban bookstores affiliated with these chains actually has historical roots: Nineteenth-century novels were published in greater numbers as the middle class, especially women, began to read for leisure. Waldenbooks specifically targets suburban, middle-class readers, many of them women. Furthermore, the chain stores provide statistics on sales that often are used by

Magazines and books can survive only if they are properly distributed, a process which is highly controlled by a few distribution companies.

publishers to determine in advance the number of books to be printed. Surveys show that the average per-book press run is 10,000. To appear on a best-seller list, a book must sell about 70,000 copies. Unless the suburban book chains carry the book, it is unlikely to appear on such a list.[17] *The Bridges of Madison County* defied this trend by selling well at small, independent bookstores. Nevertheless, the book's amazing success (sales of more than six million copies) occurred only after the chains picked it up.

Trends and innovations

Book industry analysts suggest the industry will see (1) increasing involvement with electronic and computer technologies, (2) increasing use of multimedia packages and multimedia promotion, (3) increasing growth of the superstore, and (4) a continuing realization that content still is a basic determinant of success. Those trends will continue to pose questions about quality versus popularity. As books increasingly become the content base for other media, potential profits in the movie or television sector may directly influence book content.

Electronic publishing

Although electronics industries invested heavily in the book industry in the 1970s, the computer revolution has only recently begun to affect book publishing as much as some anticipated. Computerized typesetting and production, comparable to but more sophisticated than word-processing technology, has worked its way more slowly into the publishing of complex books than it did into the periodical business. Because the book industry deals with nonstandard formats and sometimes small printing runs, it was difficult for publishers to justify early investments in page-making software. One result of the new technology, however, has been more streamlined and sometimes "instant book" production, such as those following the conclusion of the O. J. Simpson trial. By now the use of computerized artwork, cover designs, and promotion pieces is standard. Skill, or at least familiarity, with computerized technology is rapidly becoming a requirement for entry-level professionals, who must use technology-related tools such as specialized graphics and database software.

CD-ROM brings books to the computer screen. This technology allows readers to search reference works for specific words and phrases.

BOOKS ON DISK The book-on-disk concept has remained somewhat elusive. In 1992, transportation alone accounted for 40 percent of the cost of books, starting with the transportation of lumber to the mill and ending with the transportation of books between warehouse and bookstore. Such costs indicate that computerized books are just around the corner; indeed, the CD-

Sumeria Reborn

book publishers are experimenting with CD-ROM and other new technology. Some are attempting to use new technologies merely to expand the marketplace for content already present in more traditional forms of media; others are trying to establish new technologies as new forums for creativity.

In 1992, after fifteen years of working in magazines, Jerry Borrell left the world of print publishing to found a company that would publish in new, digital media formats. He named his company Sumeria because, he wrote, it seemed appropriate "homage to a culture of 4,000 years ago that shaped the written communication of Western Civilization."

During the first year and a half of Sumeria's existence, the company published fourteen books and magazines as CD-ROM titles. The company developed CD-ROMs for other publishers, reor-

ganized itself three times, laid off staff three times, and finally had its products accepted by a national distributor. By late 1993 Sumeria had begun to make "a respectable amount of money," but Borrell said it still didn't find bankers or venture capitalists willing to jump to its aid.

Borrell designed Sumeria to be driven by the aesthetic values of print design, rather than by multimedia or electronic-game design:

"We struggle to incorporate video, sound, and interactivity into a digital media framework, trying to bring a complex texture to the publications that we create at the same time that we disguise that complexity in simple and elegant products.

Our CD-ROMs are used in three ways: to be viewed as we publish them much like a book or a magazine to be read; as a source of materials by our readers, who can extract and reuse the text, pic-

tures, and video for their own purpose; or to be played like a videotape, to be viewed in a passive, TV-fashion.

In my nightmares, I see used-up stars promoting self-help videos or cosmetics on CD-ROM, or large media conglomerates, evolved into science fiction mega-corporations, sucking the world's visual assets into anonymous databases to be replayed at their will and for their profit.

In my good dreams, I see the CD-ROM products with the quality of the PBS series "Nature" transformed into something that the reader can reshape and explore in ways never imagined by their creators, allowing readers to travel the real information highway, the pathways of the mind."

SOURCE: Jerry Borrell, "Digital Media Boom in the City," *San Francisco Examiner,* May 6, 1994, p. D-5.

ROM is rapidly inhabiting libraries that are increasingly short of funds and storage space. The goal is to increase available data for customers. Writes Joseph L. Dionne, president of Nova Systems,

> There's a myth that customized printing is somehow optional for our profession. This reminds me of how the once-mighty railroads considered the DC-3 and two-axle trucks as mere irritants, failing to recognize these upstarts would eventually drain the lifeblood from the business. As publishers, we must recognize that advances in technology can liberate us from the comparative inflexibility of expense of producing the traditional textbook—the 'tyranny of the printing press.' We can't mistake the book we want to publish for the market we want to serve. We can't fall in love with our own products and give short shrift to the actual needs of our customers.[18]

However, marketers are not convinced that very many people want to read by sitting at a computer screen. Print remains a relatively cheap, popular, portable, and accessible medium. It is hard to envision leisurely reading a popular novel on a computer screen while sitting in a lounge chair at the beach.

Audiobooks

At the less sophisticated end of electronic technology, however, is the audiobook. Audiobooks have expanded enormously since their introduction about fifteen years ago. Video stores and supermarkets, together with truck stops, offer audiobooks for sale and rent. Three audiobook clubs, formed by companies such as Columbia House and Doubleday, are enjoying some success. But in 1995, standard growth rates varying between 25 and 40 percent declined to 1.4 percent. Some publishers, however, reported substantial sales and growth, and argued that the industry has matured, resulting in consolidation and stability that account for the overall flat growth rate. The audio industry recognizes its need to grow, however, and is using new technology to generate sales. Many companies have World Wide Web sites designed specifically to promote the sales of audiobooks.[19]

Multimedia products

The second trend, that of multimedia packaging and promotion, is increasingly successful in boosting a book to the best-seller charts, especially when the book is promoted by someone of celebrity status. When Oprah Winfrey's cook produced *In the Kitchen with Rosie: Oprah's Favorite Recipes,* the book set a record for the fastest-selling book of all time. It was published in April 1994, with a 400,000-copy first printing. Ten months later, after thirty trips back to the press, copies in print totaled 5.6 million. The book was largely successful because of Oprah Winfrey's television presence, a strong marketing plus for those promoting the book.[20]

A strong movie tie-in is one of the best predictors for best-seller success. Winston Groom's book *Forrest Gump* sold widely in the paperback version after the popular Tom Hanks movie opened. Simon & Schuster then published *The Wisdom of Forrest Gump,* and Oxmoor House packaged *The Bubba Gump Shrimp Co. Cookbook. Schindler's List* is another example of a book with sales that were boosted by a popular movie.

Furthermore, books are reaching the consumer as multimedia packages. The Freedom Forum, a nonprofit foundation that supports journalistic research and conferences, produced its annual report in 1995 both in book form and on disk. Cookbooks sometimes come with CD-ROMs. Reference books, such as the *American Heritage Dictionary* and *Roget's Thesaurus,* are sold with other reference works as a CD-ROM package.

Superstores

A significant trend during the past few years has been the book superstore: Borders, Crown Books, Books-A-Million, Barnes & Noble. The superstores feature a wide selection of books, comfortable browsing surroundings, and coffee shops. Their sales increase daily. In 1995, superstores increased their share of the bookstore retail market to 23 percent and increased sales nearly 45 percent. Table 4.5 shows sales in millions of dollars and numbers of superstores.

The superstores have made an enormous impact in medium-size cities with good economies and appealing demographics. Austin, Texas, is one example. In 1993, no big bookstores existed in the city, but by October 1996, Borders Books and Music, Barnes & Noble, and Book People (a local company) had planned or opened four stores. Those

TABLE 4.5 Superstore Sales and Outlets
(sales in millions of dollars)

COMPANY	1994		1995	
	SALES	STORES	SALES	STORES
Barnes & Noble	$952.7	268	$1,350.0	358
Borders	$412.5	75	$683.5	116
Crown Books	$167.2	70	$190.0	84
Books-A-Million	$110.0	46	$180.0	66

Source: "Superstore Sales Up 45% to $2.4 Billion in '95," *Publishers Weekly,* May 6, 1996, p. 10.

thirty-thousand- and forty-thousand-square-foot stores are designed for browsing. Many offer coffee and pastries in addition to books, magazines, newspapers, and audio products.[21] Opening a superstore is an expensive venture, requiring about $1.1 million in capital expenditure and another $140,000 in pre-opening expenses. Costs to the store for initial inventory are about $800,000.[22]

By the beginning of 1997, some book industry analysts showed concern that the superstore chains were overbuilding. During 1996, these companies closed 180 mall stores, which about equaled the number of superstores they opened. But the mall stores are much smaller. The net gain was a 20 percent increase in floor space devoted to books in the United States. Increasingly, the superstores were being built in smaller cities, such as Fargo, North Dakota, Santa Rosa, California, Boise, Idaho, and High Point, North Carolina. Doubters don't question that people in these cities want books, but rather whether superstores, and how many superstores, are needed to serve these and similar cities.[23]

Content is key

Despite the focus on technology and distribution, companies recognize that books are an important source of information and inspiration. "Content is king" is a concept that book publishers have not abandoned. Heads of publishing companies anxious to do multimedia deals and produce electronic products repeatedly say that "the book is the beginning in the content chain that leads to other products," "books are the seeds in the soil from which other projects spring," and "the core assets for many of these new delivery systems come from print." Time Warner's trade group chairman Larry Kirshbaum notes that "everything starts with a story and our role is to be the originator of those stories."[24]

Summary

- Books are the oldest commercial form of mass media. They have evolved from serving a highly elite audience to serving a form of popular culture that has spread throughout most literate societies.

- Publishing as an economic enterprise moved from the control of the church to small printers in European cities and then to the provinces, including the American colonies.

104

- Throughout history, publishers have been confronted with a quality-versus-quantity dilemma. However, publishers have been willing to risk profits to publish controversial or idea-provoking works, both in the history of ideas and in popular fiction.

- The advent of the paperback in the nineteenth century, the development of book clubs in the 1920s, and the current widespread publication of all types of books in paperback form have all helped to democratize the book industry.

- Book publishing has moved from business conducted in the atmosphere of a "gentlemen's club" to conglomerate ownership.

- The high costs of books are still borne primarily by individuals. Therefore, books continue to appeal to a predominantly middle-class audience.

- With the development of conglomerates, the book industry has become more multimedia oriented. Book success is often related to technological convergence. Successful films and audio or video products can hike book sales.

- Books often provide the stories, or content, for other media.

Navigating the Web

Books on the web

Book-oriented World Wide Web sites take two forms: some promote books and bookstores; others provide information about books and the industry. You can find information about the art and commerce of publishing on the following sites.

Bookwire	http://www.bookwire.com

Bookwire deals with a wide range of book issues and also has links to several good sites about books and the industry. It is a server for reviews, and it has a database of books, best-sellers, and publishing companies.

Book Industry Study Groups, Inc.	http://www.bookwire.com/bisg/

This industry association is concerned with a variety of publishing issues. The site carries news releases about the industry, including yearly data.

Publishers Weekly Interactive	http://www.bookwire.com/pw/

This is the online version of the leading trade publication for the industry. The site gives access to a wide range of articles about authors, publishing companies, and the industry itself.

The following sites carry extensive reviews of books.

Hungry Mind Review	http://www.bookwire.com/hmr/
The Quarterly Black Review of Books	http://www.bookwire.com/gbr/

Questions for review

1. What developments signified the emergence of mass-market best-sellers in the United States?

2. What trends in book production were represented in the fiction factory?

3. What were the first two book clubs, and when were they founded? Why were book clubs a significant development?

4. What is a media conglomerate?

5. What is the difference between a trade book and a textbook?

Issues to think about

1. During the American colonial period, information was a highly prized commodity. Do you think it is still so highly valued? How do converging technologies affect this concept?

2. Discuss the evolution of postal policy that affected the distribution of books in the United States. Why is postal policy an important factor in the development of print media?

3. Discuss the importance of the paperback industry to widening access to fiction and other printed works.

4. What does the trend toward multimedia packaging mean for the book industry?

5. What are the implications of producing school books for children and young adults that are targeted to the most populous states of the nation? Who makes the decisions about those books? Why are the decisions sometimes political?

6. How does consolidation of the book industry affect the circulation of ideas in an intellectual marketplace?

Suggested readings

Coser, Lewis A., Kadushin, Charles, and Powell, Walter W. *Books: The Culture and Commerce of Publishing.* (New York: Basic Books, 1982).

Davis, Kenneth. *Two-Bit Culture: The Paperbacking of America* (Boston: Houghton Mifflin, 1984).

Dessauer, John. *Book Publishing: What It Is, What It Does* (New York: R. R. Bowker, 1981).

Stern, Madeleine B. *Publishing for Mass Entertainment in Nineteenth-Century America* (Boston: G. K. Hall, 1980).

Newspapers

When Helen Moody
retired in 1990,
the 102-year-old
Almena Plaindealer
retired with her.
It was the last
newspaper in
Kansas that was
still being set
with a Linotype—

Reading newspapers is a shared cultural activity. From small towns in Kansas to the Ukraine, people read newspapers for information and entertainment.

a typesetting machine introduced in the late nineteenth century—
and printed on a hand-cranked, sheet fed press, also a nineteenth-
century relic.

But Almena's citizens missed their newspaper. So in 1994, with the
help of a group of Kansas State University students and the Huck Boyd
National Center for Community Media, Becky Madden and some
other Almena volunteers started to put out a newspaper, the *Prairie Dog Press.* In March
1995 they were still going strong, and twenty-six volunteers in the community were helping
to produce the newspaper.[1] The *Prairie Dog Press* reports on local 4-H activities, baseball,
and the city council; describes school board meetings; and records deaths, accomplish-
ments, and reunions. It provides a vehicle of communication for a small community.

Newspapers traditionally have been local vehicles of mass communication. There have been
some exceptions, such as *USA Today,* but for the most part, newspapers are local commodities. And
although much media criticism focuses on highly visible daily newspapers, weeklies remain a substantial segment of the industry. Of the 9,435 newspapers in existence in 1996, about 7,915 were weeklies.

newspapers

Although many newspapers are highly profitable, they confront an uncertain future. Today's newspapers must respond to several changing conditions:

- Newspapers must deal with changing reading patterns. Readers increasingly say they don't have time every day to read a newspaper. The percentage of households subscribing to a daily newspaper has fallen since the 1950s; the percentage receiving weekly and Sunday newspapers has grown.

- Newspapers must redirect their content to new audiences because demographics in the United States have changed. The percentage of the white, middle-class population that represents the traditional newspaper reader is declining. The minority population is growing; women who used to have the leisure time needed to read a newspaper are in the workforce in increasing numbers.

- Newspapers must reach younger people, who do not read newspapers as often as their parents do. Less than 30 percent of people between the ages of eighteen and twenty-four read a newspaper daily, while more than 60 percent of adults over age forty-five read a newspaper daily.[2]

- Newspapers must explore new types of content and evaluate what people want and can use. Newspaper readers want different types of content than they used to. Political news isn't enough to satisfy today's readers. Market research indicates that readers want information they "can use" to make better decisions about their lives, such as developing careers, choosing schools, and planning retirement.

- Publishers and editors must entice today's mass-media consumers to read the newspaper. Some argue that newspapers must be more entertaining, though others believe the newspaper must retain its detailed, analytical approach to politics and world affairs. Some newspapers are experimenting with new ways of solidifying their relationship to their communities.

- Publishers must confront new technologies, such as the Internet, and determine whether newspapers should continue in their traditional print formats or shift to electronic editions or supplements.

Increasingly, readers use their limited leisure time to choose from the menu of items that newspapers provide, rather than read the entire newspaper. The feature, "Newspapers in Your Life," invites you to evaluate different ways that you use the newspaper. As you read the rest of the chapter, you will encounter questions about readership that have important implications for the newspaper industry, including issues about how to reach a wider audience.

Newspapers in American life

Local communities have always believed that newspapers belonged to them—that newspapers were products of their towns, their counties, their cities. Since the founders began to shape the laws of this country, Congress and publishers debated whether newspapers should be local entities or whether they should be the fabric that bound the nation together. Should newspapers be the vehicles of communication that would enable communities to identify themselves as part of a nation and a federal government? The establishment of postal rates for newspapers, books, and magazines was pivotal in the debate because out-of-town newspapers were distributed by mail. If mailing a big city news-

Newspapers in your life

What Are Your Newspaper Reading Habits?

Some of the things you look for in a newspaper depend on who you are, how old you are, and what things are important in your life. After you've registered your opinion here, look in the chapter for evidence of what editors think about their readers' interests.

	NATIONAL AFFAIRS	INTERNATIONAL AFFAIRS	TRAVEL	SPORTS	BUSINESS TRENDS	COMICS	LOCAL NEWS
Which sections of the newspaper do you read most?							
What parts of the newspaper do you like best?							
What parts of the newspaper do you like least?							

paper to a rural area was expensive, not many people in smaller communities would subscribe to them. How cheaply a newspaper or magazine could be sent within counties, across states, and even across mountains reflected whether a member of Congress supported local or national control and identity. The different rates charged for magazines and books also reflected attitudes about the content of different media.

During early years of the republic, Congress debated postal rates for newspapers and magazines. Although magazines didn't gain favorable postal rates until the mid-nineteenth century, newspapers were considered, from the beginning, important vehicles of public communication. The fight was not over whether to give newspapers favored status. It was over whether economic favoritism should be used to preserve local voices and traditional values or whether big city newspapers and forces for modernization should be given the advantage. In an effort to give the advantage to urban newspapers, some members of Congress attempted several times during the early 1800s to abolish newspaper postage altogether. If postage did not exist, the urban newspapers could freely distribute their newspapers to wide geographic areas. But the U.S. Post Office Committee argued that such a move would allow city papers to displace local papers. Committee members made dire predictions, arguing that city papers "will depress, and eventually supplant, the smaller establishment." The decline of the rural papers, they said, would mean that "freedom, that manliness of spirit, which has always characterized the great body of the common people of our country, and which constitutes the safeguard of our liberties, will gradually decline."[3]

Congress resolved the postal rate issue with a compromise that ensured the survival of the local paper while minimizing the hardship for city newspapers that circulated throughout the countryside. The debate continued until 1852, when a new postal law greatly simplified newspaper rates. In-county newspapers could be distributed free, but any newspaper could cross the continent for a penny.[4]

The early postal battle over newspapers established an important principle: that newspapers were significant factors in the building of a society across wide geographical

110

territory and across the social boundaries of varying value systems. Congress recognized the value newspapers had for the new nation.

Newspapers as local commodities

In the early 1700s, John Campbell began the first continuous newspaper in the English colonies, the *Boston News-Letter.* Campbell's newspaper served first the town of Boston and later the towns along the trade routes that developed outside Boston. Campbell, who was Boston's postmaster, published his *News-Letter* "by authority," which meant

Key concept

Prior Restraint: Authorities sometimes try to prohibit or restrict publication of a story before a newspaper can get it into print. Because prior restraint keeps information from the marketplace of ideas, it is considered one of the most insidious forms of publication control.

that he allowed the government to censor his newspaper in return for free postage. His newspaper followed Benjamin Harris's *Publick Occurrences, Both Foreign and Domestick,* which survived only one issue before being closed down by a displeased government. So Campbell operated under prior restraint, summarizing news that he received from dispatches from abroad, from the government, and from private businesses. His goal was not to present timely accounts but to present complete historical summaries of news from abroad. Being postmaster gave a publisher a number of advantages, including free distribution and government allotments. Despite these monetary contributions, Campbell never made a profit on his newspaper. In 1719 he lost his postmastership and his government assistance to William Brooker.

Brooker started the *Boston Gazette,* and two years later, James Franklin introduced the *New England Courant* to the Boston newspaper mix. Brooker's paper contained slightly more local news than did Campbell's, but it was really James Franklin who instituted the first local newspaper. Franklin is often credited with starting the first newspaper crusade because he took on the local Puritan establishment and introduced items of wit and humor. Thomas Leonard writes, "Defiance was the soul of the *Courant,* the spirited cry of newcomers bumping against an old elite, of artisans mocking the more

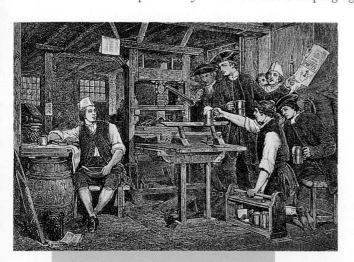

Benjamin Franklin—colonial printer, inventor, and diplomat—financed the beginning of several early American newspapers, extending his printing dynasty from Pennsylvania to South Carolina along the major trade routes of the colonies.

respectable classes, of provincials picking up the language of London coffee houses, and of eighteenth-century men recovering the nerve to mock and amuse in the face of the grave."[5] When Franklin turned his satirical pen toward the government, however, he landed in jail. While there, he continued to run the newspaper through his brother Benjamin. James Franklin was released, but only on the condition that he not publish his newspaper. In 1726, he moved to Rhode Island and became a government printer.

Benjamin Franklin, who introduced satirical essays to the *Courant* under the pen name of Silence Dogood, went to Philadelphia, where he established a prominent newspaper to compete with the established printing dynasty of the Bradford family. Franklin ran a bookshop, printed a newspaper and various pamphlets, attempted publication of a magazine, and helped to found a public library system. He extended his printing network to the southern colonies by financing printers so that they could start bookshops and printing establishments in growing cities.

He gained fame both for the lightning rod experiments that later earned him a place in elementary school science books and for his "Join or Die" snake, a graphic representation of the need for the colonies to stick together in their fight against England or undergo separate deaths. Franklin's role in the colonies and the early republic as an editor, political spokesman, and businessman was unsurpassed. He was a significant figure not only because of his own newspapers, but also because he helped to extend the newspaper network to southern colonies that lacked them.

Newspapers as political entities

From the 1730s until 1776, when the Declaration of Independence was signed, newspapers flourished in the colonies. Besides dispensing news from abroad and reporting local concerns, they became significant voices in revolutionary rhetoric. As you read in Chapter 3, John Peter Zenger was jailed because he printed James Alexander's criticism of the royal governor. Combined with political pamphlets, which were often printed by the same editors who drafted the newspaper columns, newspapers intensified political argument. However, though patriot publishers railed against unfair control by the British, tolerance did not characterize their own behavior during the Revolutionary period. Publishers who dared to publish views that were unpopular in patriot eyes were often tarred and feathered or driven from town. Meanwhile, the Continental Congress met in secret, and only selected printers received early news of their decisions.

Once the war was over, newspapers became vitriolic and highly political, supporting either the Federalist or the Anti-Federalist party. The Federalist party's political spokesman was Alexander Hamilton, who believed in a strong central government. Thomas Jefferson, an ardent Anti-Federalist, argued eloquently that such a government would be despotic and that the Constitution should contain a bill of rights to preserve civil liberties. The dispute was one primarily of national versus local control, and newspaper publishers often were strong party loyalists who argued their party's point of view vociferously. This period, often labeled "the Dark Ages," was, as you read in Chapter 3, a period of newspaper involvement in nation building. "News" during this period was not limited to "true" facts; it included partisan pleading. Such political argument still appears in many newspapers today outside the United States; it is a particularly strong element of newspapers in developing countries that have recently experienced revolution or that are working to change their governments. The nation-building years of the United States were characterized by a lack of tolerance; and the Federalists used the **Alien and Sedition Acts** to try to silence the voice of the Anti-Federalists.

Competition in a new century

During the nineteenth century, many towns supported newspapers that competed on the basis of political orientation, business orientation, and sometimes even language. In Philadelphia, for example, German-language newspapers were available from the earliest days of the republic. Newspapers viewed local communities in different ways. During the 1840s, Washington, D.C., supported a variety of competing newspapers. The *National Intelligencer* focused on politics, and one hardly knew that the city itself existed from reading the *Intelligencer.* Washington was—by the *Intelligencer*'s definition—Capitol Hill. However, the *Georgetown Advocate,* though it followed politics, was more interested in city development and constantly covered the expanding city services and street pavings that were of major concern in the business community. Because the harbors at Georgetown and nearby Alexandria, Virginia, were busy trading ports in the 1840s, the *Alexandria Packet* and the *Advocate* also covered shipping news. In ad-

Alien and Sedition Acts: Federalist laws passed in 1798 to restrict freedom of information.

Newspapers in our lives

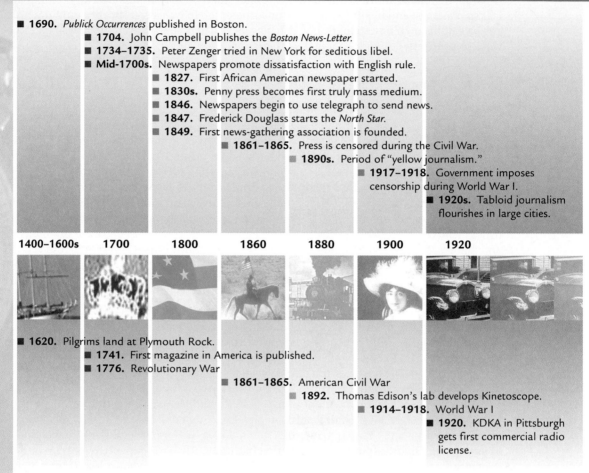

- **1690.** *Publick Occurrences* published in Boston.
  - **1704.** John Campbell publishes the *Boston News-Letter*.
  - **1734–1735.** Peter Zenger tried in New York for seditious libel.
  - **Mid-1700s.** Newspapers promote dissatisfaction with English rule.
    - **1827.** First African American newspaper started.
    - **1830s.** Penny press becomes first truly mass medium.
    - **1846.** Newspapers begin to use telegraph to send news.
    - **1847.** Frederick Douglass starts the *North Star*.
    - **1849.** First news-gathering association is founded.
      - **1861–1865.** Press is censored during the Civil War.
        - **1890s.** Period of "yellow journalism."
          - **1917–1918.** Government imposes censorship during World War I.
            - **1920s.** Tabloid journalism flourishes in large cities.

| 1400–1600s | 1700 | 1800 | 1860 | 1880 | 1900 | 1920 |

- **1620.** Pilgrims land at Plymouth Rock.
  - **1741.** First magazine in America is published.
  - **1776.** Revolutionary War
    - **1861–1865.** American Civil War
      - **1892.** Thomas Edison's lab develops Kinetoscope.
        - **1914–1918.** World War I
          - **1920.** KDKA in Pittsburgh gets first commercial radio license.

---

dition, Washington, D.C., supported a temperance newspaper, which viewed all action in light of the evils of alcohol and gambling, and a penny newspaper, the *Saturday Evening News and General Advertiser*. This penny paper printed business cards on at least one full page of the four-page newspaper and published comment about prison reform, public education, and almshouses for the poor, as well as city improvements and debates over where to locate public buildings. The *Saturday Evening News* described the social city of Washington beyond the boundaries of politics and business. Each newspaper had a distinct role as a local arbiter of cultural values. The *Intelligencer* catered to the political elite; the Georgetown and Alexandria newspapers promoted local business; and the *Saturday Evening News* recognized a society in the city that was not necessarily intellectual, business-oriented, or wealthy.

Keyconcept

Penny Press: In the early 1830s a new class of newspapers earned the name "penny press" because they were sold for a penny a copy to lower- and middle-class audiences. In addition to traditional news about commerce and politics, they included lively stories about social life in the city.

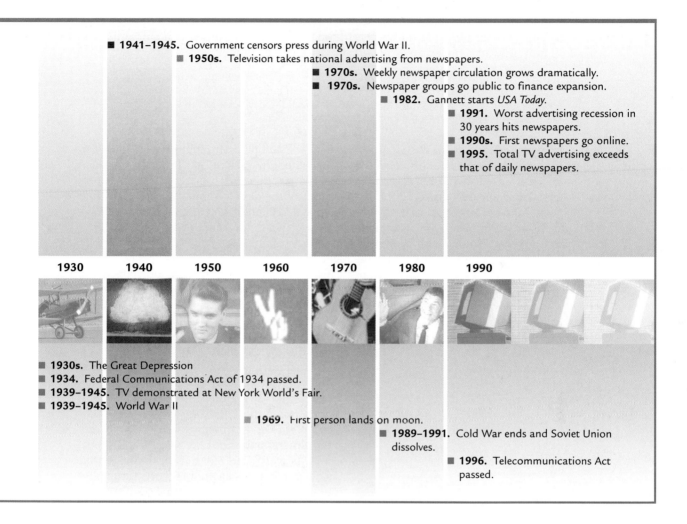

■ **1941–1945.** Government censors press during World War II.
  ■ **1950s.** Television takes national advertising from newspapers.
    ■ **1970s.** Weekly newspaper circulation grows dramatically.
    ■ **1970s.** Newspaper groups go public to finance expansion.
      ■ **1982.** Gannett starts *USA Today*.
        ■ **1991.** Worst advertising recession in 30 years hits newspapers.
        ■ **1990s.** First newspapers go online.
        ■ **1995.** Total TV advertising exceeds that of daily newspapers.

1930   **1940**   **1950**   **1960**   **1970**   **1980**   **1990**

■ **1930s.** The Great Depression
■ **1934.** Federal Communications Act of 1934 passed.
■ **1939–1945.** TV demonstrated at New York World's Fair.
■ **1939–1945.** World War II
  ■ **1969.** First person lands on moon.
    ■ **1989–1991.** Cold War ends and Soviet Union dissolves.
    ■ **1996.** Telecommunications Act passed.

■ Rise of the penny press

By the 1830s, New York City was the undisputed center of newspaper activity. It had replaced the important colonial city of Boston in economic and political importance, becoming the nation's largest commercial city. New York City spawned a variety of competing newspapers, edited by men who championed different social classes in the city and by men who intended to make a profit. Before 1830, most newspapers had **circulations** between two thousand and three thousand and appealed to the commercial interests of the city. But Benjamin Day, who started the *New York Sun* in 1833, and James Gordon Bennett, who established the *New York Herald* in 1835, increased their circulations by selling their newspapers cheaply—for one cent a copy. Publishers no longer relied on letters from abroad, political documents, or letters written by members of the elite for news. They hired reporters and managing editors and began to seek news. They recognized the power of timely news

circulation: The number of copies sold by a newspaper during its production cycle (week or day).

114

and cultivated reporters to get the **scoop,** or to beat the competing newspaper to a good story. The era of the penny press intensified the focus on local communities.

The penny press newspapers targeted middle-class audiences involved in trade, transportation, and manufacturing. However, they were no longer bound to commerce and politics; they reflected the increasing social activity in their urban surroundings. Benjamin Day announced his *New York Sun* with this comment:

> The object of this paper is to lay before the public, at a price within the means of every one, ALL THE NEWS OF THE DAY, and at the same time afford an advantageous medium for advertising. The sheet will be enlarged as soon as the increase of advertisements requires it—the price remaining the same.[6]

Day hired George W. Wisner, a young reporter, and paid him four dollars a week to rise at 4:00 in the morning to cover daily police court sessions. Wisner turned police court charges of spousal assault and petty debt into action and drama for the *Sun*'s news pages. Crime stories reinforced the social values of the day by showing what happened to those who broke the rules, but they also appealed to an interest in "bad people." Wisner was an ardent abolitionist, so he used his position to try to sneak antislavery editorials into the *Sun* along with his police reports.

When Wisner left New York for Michigan, Day hired Richard Adams Locke, an educated man who was interested in scientific discovery. Locke is famous in journalism history for his 1835 series exploiting the discoveries of Sir John Frederick William Herschel, the greatest astronomer of his time, who had established an observatory near Cape Town, South Africa. Locke reported that Herschel, through the use of a new telescope, had discovered planets in other solar systems and had seen the surface of the moon, with vegetation, animals, and winged creatures that resembled men and women. Locke cited the *Edinburgh Journal of Science* as his source and managed to fool not only the general public but the scientific community as well. The *Sun* defended the **hoax,** saying that it was useful in diverting the public mind from such worrisome issues as the abolition of slavery. The Moon Hoax as it came to be called, is often used to illustrate the claim that penny editors were less concerned with fact and objectivity than with entertaining their public. Sometimes a little fiction was useful in building an audience.

The New York Sun *fascinated its readers in the 1830s with stories of observations of winged creatures on the moon. The stories, and the illustrations, turned out to be fakes.*

Some critics speculate that Locke was trying to upstage the staid, political papers of New York City, which had rejected the penny press as sensationalistic. These papers couldn't ignore Locke's story, and most of them printed it. When the hoax was revealed, the papers had little argument with which to defend themselves against the penny press upstarts.[7]

The penny press newspapers sold for a penny a copy, were financed primarily by advertising rather than by subscription, and were sold by boys on street corners. The newsy and entertaining little sheets were the fruit of expanding literacy, improved technology, and

scoop: Publishing the story of a news event before another news organization does.

hoax: An act or story intended to deceive; a tall tale; a practical joke or serious fraud.

the belief in egalitarianism that permeated the 1830s in rhetoric, if not in fact. The notion that individuals should have an equal opportunity to make their way in the world created a new realm of content for New York editors, who appealed to the lower and middle classes making their way through the social labyrinth of New York City.[8]

The national stage

By the 1890s, newspapers in towns as small as Emporia, Kansas, where William Allen White edited the *Gazette,* accepted national advertising and carried national and international news provided by the Associated Press or other wire services, thus becoming more national in scope. Nevertheless, White and like-minded editors still regarded the local community as the audience for their newspapers. In larger cities such as New York, Boston, Philadelphia, and Chicago, newspapers played on a larger stage, but their audience remained primarily local. During the 1850s, Horace Greeley marketed his *New York Tribune* to westerners as well as New Yorkers, and later in the century, William Randolph Hearst with the *New York Journal* and Joseph Pulitzer with his *New York World* played to the nation by commanding large circulations and claiming influence with major political figures. Nevertheless, New Yorkers were their main subscribers, and New York advertisers paid most of their bills.

Advertising took on a national scope during the mid-1800s. Editors carried advertisements for nationally distributed brands as well as local products. For editors such as William Allen White, this posed a dilemma. To accept national advertising was to encourage readers to buy from larger surrounding cities and from mail-order houses rather than from merchants in their hometowns. White carried national advertising but constantly exhorted his readers to "buy at home."

Key concept

Yellow Journalism: In the late 1890s, in a battle for readership, William Randolph Hearst's *New York Journal* hired the artist who drew the popular cartoon "The Yellow Kid" away from Joseph Pulitzer's *New York World.* The *World* retaliated by hiring a new artist to draw the cartoon. Thus began the "Yellow War," in which the two papers published increasingly lurid stories with bold headlines and lots of graphics. The term "yellow journalism" is still used to denote content that is considered irresponsible, unethical, or lacking in professional standards of news judgment.

Meanwhile, technology was changing, allowing large printings—and large circulations. The rotary press, which printed from rolls of paper rather than from sheets, new folding machines, and new techniques for making plates into paper mats that could be bent around a cylinder to accommodate rolls of paper all contributed to newspaper expansion.

In the expanding market, newspaper editors competed for circulation, using information, entertainment, and sensationalism as their tools. Henry Raymond, who had started the *New York Times* before the Civil War, appealed to the business classes of New York and Washington and established a reputation for solid information without entertainment. Charles Dana, who bought the *New York Sun* in 1868, advocated artisan republicanism, a philosophy maintaining that all people, including the working class, should have equal rights and full participation in the political system. Ultimately, however, Dana could not compete with Joseph Pulitzer's *New York World.* Pulitzer and William Randolph Hearst, with his *New York Journal,* played to the crowds. Catering to the working and middle classes, their newspapers hummed with the vitality of New York City life. They covered stories that had not been covered before, reporting New York gossip among the social set as well as political debates over the organization of labor and the rights of property owners. These newspapers were highly sensationalistic, although Pulitzer, except during the most highly competitive years, operated from a sense of journalistic integrity. Pulitzer introduced an editorial platform that called for taxing luxuries, inheritances, large incomes, monopolies, and privileged corporations, which he viewed as tools of the rich. He also called for reforming the civil service and

Newsrooms have always been semipublic places where reporters worked under noisy conditions to produce stories on deadline.

punishing corruption in office. The *New York Times* countered the sensationalists with a sober writing style and point of view.

The New York City papers were not the only ones to capitalize on new developments. E. W. Scripps offered a different kind of competition. Avoiding the urban cities of the Northeast, he established dailies in medium-size cities in the Midwest, supporting organized labor and advocating independence from powerful advertisers. After acquiring a number of newspapers in Ohio, Scripps expanded to the West Coast. With his midwest papers and significant holdings in Oregon, Washington, and California, he shaped one of the first effective newspaper chains. Scripps required his editors to operate on a very small budget. His formula included heavy reliance on subscriptions and on revenues from multiple advertisers because he feared the power large advertisers might gain if a newspaper relied too heavily on them. Scripps, who disliked the sensationalism of Hearst and Pulitzer, sought to provide local information as the mainstay of his smaller newspapers.[9]

■ Growth and maturation

Shortly after the turn of the century, the number of daily newspapers began to decline. Advertisers were looking for efficient advertising, and they sought placement for their ads in the largest newspapers. Those newspapers that were not as successful experienced a decline in advertising and thus in profit. Shortly after this decline began, newspapers confronted a new form of competition in radio. With the stock market crash of 1929 and the Great Depression of the 1930s, critics charged that newspapers had not adequately warned the public about the economic crisis that enveloped not only this country, but many countries in Europe as well. Newspapers introduced interpretation in response to their critics. Through the 1950s, newspapers continued to be major conveyors of information, focusing as always on local communities and supported primarily by local advertising.

Competition from radio increased during World War II. Both newspapers and radio faced some government censorship, but on the whole they cooperated with the government in reporting the war effort. Radio's role in news became increasingly important, particularly in reporting international events. President Franklin Delano Roosevelt's "fireside chats" and reports from London by Edward R. Murrow challenged newspaper superiority in reporting on the war. Nevertheless, it was not until the 1960s, when news of civil rights and subsequently of the Vietnam War exploded on the television screens of American homes that newspapers faced the ultimate challenge from television news.

With some exceptions, the strength of newspapers is still the local audience. National newspapers have difficulty achieving financial stability, let alone high profit margins. During the 1960s, the *National Observer* acquired a national, politically sophisticated audience with its well-written interpretive pieces, but it never obtained the advertising that would have enabled it to succeed in its appeal to a relatively elite national readership. The *Wall Street Journal* succeeds as a specialized national newspaper, appealing to the business community across geographical boundaries. *USA Today* targets a middle-class national audience, but despite attractive graphics and readable stories, it struggles to maintain its advertising base. The *New York Times,* while definitely targeted toward New Yorkers, also maintains a loyal audience among intellectuals across the nation and at times has exerted major influence nationwide. For example, *New York Times* v. *Sullivan,* a landmark libel case, resulted when an Alabama police commissioner sued the newspaper because he resented the influence the *New York Times* had in the civil rights movement.

Today's market structure

Newspaper **markets** have been defined in a variety of ways. Newspapers have been considered vehicles of mass communication that target generalized audiences within a local geographic area. However, exceptions are common. The *Wall Street Journal,* for example, targets a national market when defined by geography, but a specialized market when defined by editorial or advertising content. Furthermore, communities are being identified differently from the way they were in the past; suburban dailies not only compete with metropolitan newspapers but also supplement them with even more local news and information. In the Washington, D.C., metropolitan area, residents of the Northern Virginia suburbs often subscribe not only to the nationally renowned *Washington Post* but also to one of the suburban *Journal* newspapers. For example, the *Fairfax Journal* prints swim team scores, stories on the actions of the Fairfax County board of supervisors, and notices of road repairs and construction. The *Post,* despite its weekly sections for Northern Virginia and nearby Montgomery County, Maryland, cannot compete with the level of detail that the *Journal* newspapers provide.

Keyconcept

Market Structure for News: The market relationship between newspapers and their buyers is based on costs, competition, and availability of substitute products, such as other newspapers or television news programs.

Market structure determines the degree of competition in a market and therefore how responsive newspapers must be to readers. The market structure for newspapers has three components.

The first component is how many choices are available within the market. Residents of Lawrence, Kansas, a town centered between Kansas City, thirty miles to the east, and Topeka, thirty miles to the west, have several choices. They can buy the *Kansas City Star,* the *Lawrence Journal-World,* or the *Topeka Capital-Journal.* Because Kansas City straddles the Missouri-Kansas state line and is a large city, the *Star* offers more cultural news for the area, Missouri state government news, national and international news, and advertisements for shopping in a larger city. The Topeka newspaper offers a larger amount of Kansas state news. The Lawrence newspaper will offer the best local news. Now the question becomes, "How will residents deal with this choice?" Will they buy one newspaper? Several newspapers?

The second component is the probability that buyers will substitute products. For example, what is the probability that a person living in Lawrence will buy the *Kansas City Star* instead of the *Lawrence Journal-World?* The component of substitution becomes increasingly important when different types of media are available. Then people have the ability to substitute television, for example, for newspapers.

markets: Major markets are markets defined by a metropolitan area and many media choices; outstate markets are those with some diversity that are removed from metropolitan areas, but are not rural; isolated markets include rural areas in which traditional media choices are exceedingly limited.

118

The third component is the number of barriers new firms face when trying to enter the market. In any major market area, new publishers find it exceedingly difficult to crack an already established newspaper market with a newspaper that competes for the same audience and the same advertisers as an existing newspaper. To challenge the *Washington Post,* for example, requires enormous resources. Although the *Washington Times* has spent huge sums of money, it has been unable to successfully compete with the *Post*'s broad advertising and subscription base.[10] The *Post* serves its advertisers better than the *Times* does, because the *Post* can reach more potential buyers at less cost. The overwhelming advantage held by most established newspapers in major markets remains the most important barrier to new competition.

Audience demand in newspaper markets

Editors and owners are having increasing difficulty determining what content readers want, in part, because they do not understand the components of market structures that were discussed in the previous paragraphs. In the 1950s, white male editors of the mainstream newspapers concentrated on the city beat and basic suburban themes such as road development, schools, and protection from crime and focused on a middle-class white audience. The newspaper included a women's section that focused on fashion, food, and children. Ethnic and minority newspapers targeted specific audiences. However, the composition of the United States has changed dramatically in ethnic diversity, the distribution of power, the number of women working, and the makeup of the typical family. Editors have to address a wider audience, and they are having greater difficulty determining what specific segments of their market want to read. For example, professional women may want newspaper content that is more similar to what professional men read than to what women who work at home read. Although market research is increasingly used to explore readers' needs and preferences, this "fuzziness," or blurring of the boundaries of desired content, increases the difficulty of identifying the factors that would make an individual or family buy a particular newspaper rather than turn to another source of news.

In the 1990s, the newspaper editor is no longer guaranteed that most middle-class households will subscribe to a newspaper. Indeed, **household penetration**—the number of households subscribing to a newspaper compared to the number of potential households—has steadily declined, though circulation figures have remained relatively stable. Between 1975 and 1996, the percentage of the adult population reading a newspaper daily fell from 71 percent to 59 percent. During

household penetration: Percentage of households in a market subscribing to a newspaper.

Financial indicators for newspapers are difficult to interpret. In 1994, expenditures for advertising in newspapers hit a record high, showing the largest percentage gain in eight years. But newspapers' share of all advertising dollars continued to decline. Household penetration also continued to slide, and during the first quarter of 1995, weekday circulation for nine of the ten biggest metropolitan dailies lost ground. In 1995, 64 percent of all adults read a newspaper every day, compared with 77.6 percent in 1970.

Profits are still healthy at most newspaper companies, although a nearly 50 percent increase in the cost of paper in 1994 and 1995 sent shock waves through the industry. However, paper prices leveled off in 1996. Publishers also said that the baseball and hockey strikes of 1994 and early 1995 deprived them of important sports coverage.

Indicators Are Mixed

Between 1995 and 1996, of the ten largest metropolitan newspapers, only the *Boston Globe* showed a small increase in weekly readership. *USA Today,* a national newspaper, also showed a small increase but no overall profit. (*USA Today* occasionally shows a quarterly profit.) However, *USA Today* is an unusual case because of its reliance on national, rather than local, advertising.

Some publishers said that the circulation declines also represented an effort by newspapers to maintain the type of subscription base that advertisers want; publishers were cutting "fringe" circulation that, because of geographical distance from the newspaper's home base or because of demographics, were less attractive to advertisers. Because fewer copies were being printed, the eco-

nomics of supply and demand meant higher subscription and single-copy prices.

Cathleen Black, former president of the Newspaper Association of America, said that newspapers must build their publications' brand identities with the public to compete in the new media marketplace. We must see ourselves, she said, "as a brand or as a channel of communications" and reposition ourselves "into a force that can break through the barriers to the new era of communications."

SOURCES: William Glaberson, "Newspapers Are Advised to Build Their Brand Identities," *New York Times,* April 25, 1995, p. D4; William Glaberson, "Circulation Drop Continues at Most Large Newspapers," *New York Times,* May 2, 1995, p. D8.

the same period, the number of daily newspapers declined by two hundred. As you can see in Table 5.1 on page 120, this decline continues. Nevertheless, newspapers still reach nearly 60 percent of all American households.[11]

This loss of a guaranteed audience results from a new diversity in the potential market and from changes in the nature of competition. The advent of radio and television, with their ability to inform and entertain even while the consumer is eating, working, or performing some other task, has presented new choices for newspaper readers. Television and radio have the advantage of providing dramatic visual or auditory images. They are also instantaneous; world events are presented to viewers and listeners in real time. Furthermore, people may choose not only from the traditional media of magazines, books, newspapers, network television, and radio, but also from specialized information sources, including online services. Added to this mix are cable television, public radio and television programming, trade magazines and newsletters, and local and regional publications.

TABLE 5.1 Declining Circulation: Weekday Circulation Declines at Large Metropolitan Newspapers

NEWSPAPER	SIX-MONTH CIRCULATION ENDED MARCH 31, 1995	PERCENT CHANGE BETWEEN MARCH 31, 1994, AND MARCH 31, 1995
Newsday	669,739	-7.03%
San Francisco Chronicle	499,526	-5.18
New York Daily News	725,599	-5.00
Chicago Sun-Times	500,969	-4.34
Los Angeles Times	1,058,498	-4.18
Detroit Free Press	531,825	-3.39
Philadelphia Inquirer	470,693	-3.15
Miami Herald	397,943	-2.29
Minneapolis Star Tribune	404,757	-1.86
Washington Post	840,232	-1.41
New York Times	1,170,869	-1.38
Houston Chronicle	413,717	-0.55

Some industry officials argue that circulation losses represent better audience targeting, but other factors included the baseball strike of 1995 and higher newsprint costs.

Source: "Circulation Drop Continues at Most Large Newspapers," New York Times, Tuesday, 2 May 1995, p. D8.

The result of increasingly diverse market structures is that newspapers can no longer count on the generalized mass markets that supported their development throughout the nineteenth and early twentieth centuries. The diversity of audience and choice is greatest in "major market" metropolitan areas. It is in these areas that editors have the most difficulty determining what the audience demands in terms of content. Newspapers such as the *Philadelphia Inquirer* are increasingly aimed at a metropolitan elite, rather than at the entire population of Philadelphia.[12] Following this trend, some reporters for the *New York Times* say that they write not for the general public, but for the political and intellectual elite—as well as for other newspaper reporters and editors.[13] By the year 2000, newspaper publishers will have to decide whether to continue as mass media or to turn increasingly toward segmented audiences. If newspaper managers adhere to the basic concept of a newspaper as news for everyone, they will need to identify themselves as suppliers of information, not just of news, because the demand for content will be wide-ranging. If they turn instead to specialized audiences, their markets may be easier to define. They can choose, for example, to aim at the political elite; at business entrepreneurs; or at the under-thirty, entertainment-oriented upper middle class.

Newspapers have some advantages over other media. Their role in the community has a historical tradition as well as solid First Amendment protection. To maintain that traditional role, however, newspapers will need to be seen by community members as essential reading. Newspapers may have to modernize their forms of delivery, using fiber optics, telephones, satellite transmission, and computers. Diversifying newsrooms in terms of the lifestyles, economic backgrounds, gender, education, and ethnic origins of reporters and editors can help newspapers respond to audience demand.

Supplying the audience's demand

After more than two centuries of steady circulation growth, the newspaper industry entered a period of decline in the late 1940s, resulting in major restructuring of the industry after 1980. During this forty-year period, newspapers came increasingly under group ownership, other forms of media expanded, and competition among newspapers declined. However, after 1980, regional and weekly newspaper competition increased while other forms of mass media—such as network television—became more fragmented.

■ Ownership

Two basic types of ownership exist. Under the first—independent ownership—a person or family owns one newspaper. A second type is group ownership, which may mean that ownership is still private, as in the independently owned single newspaper, or it may mean that stock is available to the public. A group owns two or more newspapers. Ownership groups also vary from those that own just newspapers to media groups that own several types of media, such as Warner or ViaCom, to media conglomerates, in which a corporation owns both media and nonmedia companies. The number of groups and the percentage of newspapers owned by groups have both increased, as Table 5.2 shows.

Newspapers have been desirable commodities for both group and independent owners, and despite recent declining profits, they still generate more than twice the rate of profit of most businesses. However, group ownership of newspapers has increased because of several factors. Business trends toward consolidation favor group ownership. In addition, families who own newspapers sometimes have difficulty resolving tensions among their members about how the business should be run, and the tax structure encourages families to sell inherited property rather than keep it. Further, it is much easier for a group to acquire a newspaper and manage it successfully than to start a new one. *Newsday* is the most recent successful metropolitan newspaper started from scratch, and that was in the early 1940s. In Washington, D.C., the *Washington Times* was started to compete with the *Post*, but the *Times* has yet to earn a profit. (It continues to exist because it is subsidized by the Unification Church.)

TABLE 5.2 The Growth of Groups

YEAR	NUMBER OF GROUPS	NUMBER OF PAPERS OWNED BY GROUPS	PERCENTAGE OF NEWSPAPERS OWNED BY GROUPS
1920	31	153	8
1940	60	319	17
1960	109	560	32
1980	158	1002	57
1986	127	1158	70
1994	115	1215	75
1996	126	1124	74

Source: John C. Busterna, "Trends in Daily Newspaper Ownership," *Journalism Quarterly, 65,* 833; Raymond B. Nixon and Jean Ward, "Trends in Newspaper Ownership and Inter-Media Competition," *Journalism Quarterly, 38,* 5; and *Editor & Publisher International Yearbook, 1997* (New York: Editor & Publisher, 1997), pp. 1-457–1-458.

[profile]

Robert Maxwell

Robert Maxwell was an international legend who became one of Great Britain's most powerful millionaires, building a media empire almost single-handedly. Although Maxwell had little formal education, his energy and leadership abilities helped him to create an empire with two major public companies (Mirror Group Newspapers and Maxwell Communication Corporation) and 400 private firms.

Maxwell was born Jan Ludwik Hoch on June 10, 1923, the seventh child of poor Jewish agricultural workers in a Czech village. When Germany invaded Czechoslovakia in 1938, Hoch joined the Czech resistance. He was captured, but he escaped and fled the country. His father was shot by Germans, and his mother died at Auschwitz. He joined the British Army and emerged from the war with a commission (captain) and a British medal for gallantry.

During the war he changed his name to Ivan du Maurier (after a favorite brand of cigarettes), to Leslie Jones, and then to Robert Maxwell. He married Elizabeth Meynard, a French interpreter, and learned to speak nine languages fluently.

From 1964 to 1970, Maxwell represented the Labour Party in Parliament. When he was found guilty of exaggerating the profits of his company, Pergamon Press, he was cited by the Board of Trade as unfit to run a public company. Undaunted, Maxwell persevered. In the 1970s, he turned the fledging British Printing Corporation into his profitable British Printing and Communication Corporation. In the early 1980s, he bought and strengthened the influential Mirror Group Newspapers.

Firmly established as a British media millionaire, the power-hungry Maxwell went global in 1988. He bought the *Official Airline Guides* from Dun & Bradstreet and engineered the takeover of Macmillan Publishing Company. In 1990, he started a European newspaper, hoping to take advantage of merging European interests and identities.

Many of Maxwell's ventures were not successful. His moves into satellite and cable came to dead-ends, his stock in Central Independent Television had to be sold, and his attempt at a twenty-four-hour-a-day London newspaper failed.

In November 1991, Maxwell's house of cards tumbled. He died on November 5 in a mysterious fall from his yacht. His companies were found to be bankrupt, and he had misused their pension funds. He had committed fraud against scores of banks and had established a record of borrowing, lending, transferring, converting, and tax evading.

SOURCES: Steve Briggs, "Mad World and Its Master: Maxwell," *Scotland on Sunday,* February 11, 1996, Sec. Spectrum, p. 12; "Ghost of Robert Maxwell Lives on after Acquittal," Reuters World Service, January 19, 1996; Maurice Weaver, "Robert Maxwell: An Attractive Monster with a Touch of Genius," *The Daily Telegraph,* November 6, 1991, p. 3; Raymond Snoddy, "Robert Maxwell," *Financial Times,* November 6, 1991, Sec. I, p. 28.

Group ownership has been criticized since the first chains were formed. Community leaders and journalists tend to fear that group ownership will standardize products so that they will lose their local distinctiveness, that absentee owners are less likely to invest in the newsroom, and that ownership groups will impose their editorial will on a local newspaper. Supporters of group ownership argue that financial strength makes groups less vulnerable to manipulation by advertisers or political groups, that groups have more money to invest in staff and equipment, and that when managers are moved from one location to another, they are less likely to become part of the local power establishment with policies and interests to protect. Researchers have found that much of the criticism has little to do with whether a newspaper is owned by a group or by an individual or family. The difference is in ownership commitment and style—two elements that vary among newspapers, whether owners are groups or individuals. However, recent research indicates that publicly held ownership can negatively affect local newspapers. The more stock is owned by the public, the higher profit rate a newspaper company will pursue.[14] The high profit keeps stock prices up, but the result is reduced newsroom budgets that can lower the quality of the local coverage.

123

The ownership issue has a political as well as an economic dimension. People who support local control of government entities tend also to support local control of newspapers and see group ownership of newspapers as another loss to a national, rather than a local, focus.

Competition

Direct competition among daily newspapers has all but disappeared. In 1920, 42.6 percent of 1,295 cities had two or more dailies owned by different people. By 1960, only 4.2 percent of 1,461 cities had separately owned and operated dailies. Currently, about a dozen cities out of 1,500 have daily newspapers that are separately owned and operated. Why this downward trend?

Newspapers have more than one audience. The reading audience is diverse and chooses from a variety of media sources. Another audience, as shown in Chapter 2, is composed of advertisers. These advertisers want to reach the most people possible for the least amount of money per individual. That means that advertisers buy newspaper space according to the number of readers. This factor is referred to as cost-per-thousand, or the amount it costs to reach 1,000 subscribers. In a two-newspaper town the newspaper with fewer readers has a higher cost-per-thousand, so advertisers leave for the better buy at the other paper. Because readers buy newspapers for ads as well as for news, readers of the trailing newspaper end up buying the competing one. Once a newspaper begins to lose readers, it also loses advertisers, and as it loses advertisements, it also loses readers. A downward spiral begins. One newspaper gains a disproportionate amount of advertising, and before long, a two-newspaper town becomes a one-newspaper town.

Competition is an important factor in newsroom quality. Research shows that competition gives the reader choice and therefore power. Usually, then, as the intensity of competition increases, publishers spend more money on the newsroom, resulting in better-quality reporting. With more news and advertising space available in each market, advertisers get lower advertising rates, and reporters and editorial writers strive for new ideas for stories. The existence of two editorial sections also increases the possibility that the marketplace of ideas will become more lively and that readers will have access to varied points of view.

With these competition factors in mind, Congress in 1970 created the Newspaper Preservation Act, which allows two newspapers in the same town to combine all of their operations, such as business and circulation, with one exception: the newsroom. Originally, nineteen newspapers set up Joint Operating Agreements (JOA). In 1996, only seventeen existed; Of those, fifteen were from the original JOAs.

Research indicates that the quality of JOA newspapers is not as good as that in competitive markets but that it is much better than the quality in cities with one daily newspaper. Within the JOA framework the financial commitment continues as in competitive markets, but it shows some decline. Two editorial voices remain, as does the healthy

124

competition among reporters. However, JOAs do not end the downward circulation spiral, they tend to increase ad rates, and they don't stop newspapers from going out of business.

Newspaper competition also was affected by the development of television. TV's cost-per-thousand for common items, such as household soaps and soft drinks, was much lower than that of newspapers. Newspapers lost much of their national advertising while retaining local advertising. However, as the big mass market newspapers declined, other portions of the industry began restructuring. The number of weeklies has grown dramatically, and regional competition has become a factor. Many suburban dailies are becoming twice-weekly or weekly newspapers. Metro dailies have responded to competition from suburban dailies by **zoning** their coverage. For example, the *Washington Post* includes a Fairfax County and a Montgomery County section once each week to compete with the *Journal* papers. Such sections also allow local advertisers to circulate to smaller, geographically zoned areas for lower prices. Zoning has earned profits for newspapers only when the zones are designed narrowly and the sections carry information that readers want and believe they can use.

Minority and ethnic press

Social groups often have information needs that are not met by large commercial newspapers. Historically, immigrants and other minority groups used their newspapers to protest treatment by the mainstream society or to fight for changes in laws. These newspapers not only serve as political tools, but they also reaffirm membership in communities and reinforce ties to native cultures. For example, African American newspapers that developed after the Civil War challenged segregation laws put into place in the 1870s, and they printed news of social events, engagements to be married, and weddings. During the 1960s **Chicano** movement, Spanish language newspapers fought discrimination against Hispanics. The ethnic and minority press is an important part of society today as well as historically, and immigrants who speak no English start newspapers in their native tongue just as they did 100 years ago.

AFRICAN AMERICAN PRESS The first African American newspaper was *Freedom's Journal.* Started by Samuel Cornish and John Russwurm, in 1827, the paper included articles, poetry, and news about slavery inside and outside the United States. Like most African American newspapers during this period, *Freedom's Journal* lasted only a couple of years. However, it established a precedent. Later, Frederick Douglass used newspapers to battle slavery as he rose to national prominence. In 1847 he started the *North Star,* which became *Frederick Douglass' Paper* in 1851. Throughout his life, Douglass used the press to battle for equal rights for African Americans and women.

The African American press has always struggled for financing. In a system in which advertisers want the largest audiences possible, publications that have small audiences suffer. When this financial prejudice problem is combined with bigotry, the result is that most newspapers last only a few years. Barbara Henritze estimates that the United States has had more than 5,539 African American newspapers since 1827; about 500 African American papers were being published in 1994.[15]

The struggle for adequate financing continues today. African American newspaper publishers in 1989 reported that their papers would continue to exist but that a lack of advertising and a lack of starting capital were serious problems.[16] These papers also face the

zoning: Printing an edition of a newspaper for a specific geographic area (or zone) that has content aimed at that area, usually in a specific section of the paper.

Chicano: A U.S. citizen of Mexican descent.

same problems other newspapers face: increasing newsprint prices and declining circulation. Nevertheless, publishers believe that as long as racism exists, the United States will have an African American press.

125

NATIVE AMERICAN PRESS Like the African American newspapers, many early Native American papers grew from mistreatment by European Americans. The *Cherokee Phoenix* began as a weekly in 1828 and served to communicate the Cherokee nation's cultural heritage.

As with most weeklies during the 1800s, preservation of Native American newspapers was erratic, and an exact count of the number of titles is impossible. One scholar estimated that 250 papers were published in the Indian Territory before 1900.[17] A 1984 bibliography of Native American and native Alaskan periodicals identified 1,164 titles between 1828 and 1982.[18] Most of the publications that continue today take the form of newsletters. This format is more appropriate for the small Native American audience served by these publications. The audience size reflects a historically important difference between African Americans and Native Americans: The African American population grew during the 1800s and 1900s, while the native American population declined.

HISPANIC PRESS Hispanics made up the fastest-growing segment of the U.S. population during the 1990s. However, Hispanics constitute diverse groups, having come from a variety of Spanish-speaking countries at different times in the nation's history. Because the United States seized large amounts of land from Mexico, the largest group of Hispanics are of Mexican descent. Newspapers serving these descendants are called the Chicano press and are printed in Spanish, English, or sometimes both languages.

The Chicano press can trace its roots to the area that is now Texas. Newspapers such as *La Gaceta* and *El Mexicano* were printed in the 1810s as Mexico sought independence from Spain.[19] The number of Chicano papers is difficult to determine, but Herminio Rios and Guadalupe Castillo have estimated that 372 Mexican American newspapers, mostly weeklies, were established before 1940.[20] The 1960s saw growth in the Chicano press as Hispanics battled for political power and civil rights. This growth has continued with the expansion of the Mexican American population.

Latino presses have become tools of political and social activism as well as social control and strive to reflect ethnic culture and values.

Chicano newspapers play a variety of roles in their communities. Felix Gutierrez lists three such roles: as an instrument of social control, as an instrument of social activism, and as a reflection of Chicano life.[21] Besides the same monetary problems that the African American newspapers face, the Chicano press must deal with language barriers. Publishing in just English or Spanish limits readership, but publishing in both languages doubles the cost. Despite problems, the growing population of Mexican Americans seems likely to guarantee the survival of a Chicano press in its diverse forms.

Newspapers as organizations

By the mid-nineteenth century, newspapers had begun to expand their staffs. The small papers of the colonial and early republic years generally were four pages long and were published by a printer-editor or by a printer who compiled writings by anonymous behind-the-scenes editors. As newspapers expanded in size and circulation, editors began to hire reporters. Throughout the nineteenth century the reporter was a hired hand, paid space rates—by the column inch—and given no job security and no benefits. The few women who were hired as reporters had the same lack of security. During the late nineteenth and early twentieth centuries, reporters joined together in press clubs to establish themselves as professionals. Their desire for professional status reflected a growing movement in many of the occupations of the day.

■ Staffing patterns

As the number of reporters increased, newspaper staffs were organized hierarchically, with editors supervising reporters. By the beginning of the twentieth century the positions of **wire editor** and **city editor** were well established. Today, most newsroom organizations follow patterns that were established in those early days. Staffs generally are divided into four areas: advertising, editorial, production, and circulation. Sometimes, production and circulation are combined into a single business department. Advertising staffs on small dailies often consist of an advertising manager, one or two advertising salespeople, and a classified advertising clerk. The advertising manager or one of the salespeople may do the ad layouts. Often, a part-time design person will create the local advertisements. National ads usually arrive as **camera-ready copy.** On weeklies, jobs may be combined across area lines. For example, an advertising manager might also be in charge of circulation. Or a publisher-editor might be in charge of most aspects of the newspaper, with only a few production and editorial assistants.

On the editorial side, a publisher-editor may serve as chief editorial writer, though many publishers do not take an active role in the production of the newspaper. A managing editor may direct the major operations of the small daily, assigning stories to two or three reporters and consulting with a society/lifestyle editor, a sports editor, and perhaps an education editor in allocating space in the paper. The managing editor may double as the page makeup person, who designs the newspaper either on a **dummy sheet** or on a computer screen. The managing editor also may be responsible for photography. On larger staffs a photo editor directs the photography operation. A press foreman directs press and folding operations. A circulation manager handles subscriptions and organizes delivery, usually with the help of part-time clerks.

As the size of the paper increases, so do the level of specialization and the number of positions. For example, the advertising departments of larger newspapers employ several people who specialize in classified advertising, salespeople, and designers, as well as people who specialize in demographics and client relations. On the editorial side, the number of editors expands. Large metropolitan dailies tend to be organized by "desks," or departments, which may be labeled national, business, news, city, education, health and science, and real

wire editor: An editor assigned to edit the material that comes from wire services and news services.

city editor: An editor who manages the "city desk," which is the group of journalists who report and write about the city in which the newspaper is located.

camera-ready copy: Collection of stories (copy), photographs, and headlines that have been edited and placed on a large page. Ready to be photographed and made into a plate for printing.

dummy sheet: A sheet of paper that is used to design a page for the newspaper.

estate. Reporters are assigned to each desk, and the editor in charge of that department ensures that reporters cover regular beats, such as the police department, county courthouse, city hall, or statehouse. General assignment reporters pick up developing stories, **spot news,** and **features.** Circulation departments also become more complicated as circulation increases. A circulation manager is in charge of hiring independent distributors, who deliver the newspapers to various locations where they are picked up for individual distribution.

Entry-level positions are available in all departments: advertising, editorial, production, and circulation. Editors frequently seek students who have business experience or knowledge to enter management-training programs. Copy editors are always in greater demand than are reporters, and students who have computer design skills are highly sought after by editorial and advertising departments.

The bureaucratic structure of newspapers has been highly criticized in recent years; some critics believe that the traditional structure creates barriers to innovative stories and coverage. In their attempt to regain a prominent position, newspapers have been struggling to reorganize so that reporters will better understand their audience's needs, as you will see later in this chapter.

■ Newspaper content

Newspapers contain a variety of information, most of which is not news. This information falls into three broad categories: advertising, opinion material, and news. Each of these three categories has several subcategories.

ADVERTISING Advertising includes classified ads, display ads, and inserts. Classified advertisements are the lists of ads set in small type sizes that advertise jobs, items for sale, and garage sales. Display advertisements, found throughout the paper, incorporate photographs, drawings, and large type. For example, when the movie *Independence Day* arrived in theaters in 1996, many newspapers carried large display ads for the film. Inserts, which are similar to small catalogues, most often advertise merchandise for sale at department stores and supermarkets.

OP-ED A second category of content involves opinion material. This information appears on the editorial and op-ed (short for "opposite the editorial") pages. On these pages, editorial writers, political **pundits,** and local citizens express their opinions about current political and social issues. These pages make up the heart of the marketplace of ideas. For example, the opinion pages of the *Lansing State Journal* carry letters, columns, and editorials about conflicts between Michigan State University students and permanent residents in East Lansing. Permanent residents want limits on late-night parties, while students want lower-priced housing. Ideas exchanged through editorial material allow the community to explore better ways for these two groups to live together.

NEWS The bulk of nonadvertising information is news. News can be soft, hard, or deep. Soft news includes a variety of feature stories, such as the story of the first woman to serve as drum major of a university band or the story of the birth of a Siberian tiger at the local zoo. Soft news also includes advice columns, such as Dear Abby. Hard news focuses on current events that have serious effects on people, such as crime, politics, and disasters. If a child dies in a house fire, the story is hard news. In-depth news requires the story to go beyond breaking events to incorporate background details and trends. Inves-

spot news: News based on one-time events, such as an accident or crime.

features: Stories that emphasize activities of people and do not involve "hard news events," such as crime and disasters.

pundit: An expert about a particular topic, a person consulted because of his or her wisdom.

The unusual is newsworthy, and when members of the Coney Island Polar Bear Club come ashore in midwinter, they make the feature, or soft news, pages.

tigative articles often fall into this category. A series of stories about the impact of changing federal regulations on student loans is an example.

Most news in newspapers comes from three sources: the newspaper staff, wire and news services, and feature **syndicates.** Syndicates emphasize opinion and softer material, such as comic strips and columns. Staff and news service reporters share similar standards for selecting what events and issues become news. These standards are called *news values,* and their application to particular stories is called *news judgment.*

Over time, several news values have evolved. The following values are usually cited as the reasons behind news selection and are even taught in reporting courses in journalism school.

- *Impact* applies when a large number of people are affected by an event or issue or when a small number of individuals are intensely affected. News stories of demonstrations, for example, always include an estimate of the crowd size. These estimates are considered important in evaluating the significance of an event and often are disputed by the participants, who may believe that their numbers—and thus their importance—have been underestimated.

- *Proximity* deals with the geographic location of an event. The more local the event, the more news value it has. A hurricane that affects a large number of people and has enormous impact will be reported across the nation and perhaps internationally. A small storm that destroys valued old trees in a community will be covered locally. The story has importance because of its proximity.

- *Prominence* concerns how notable or famous a person is. Politicians, sports figures, and entertainment stars are prominent figures. The marriage of any movie star is newsworthy; so is the decision of a prominent political figure to run for office, not to seek an office, or to support a particular issue.

- *Novelty* reflects the public's interest in the unusual and bizarre. A story about an alligator that eats several expensive hunting dogs is novel. Unusual Christmas decorations or construction of an oddly shaped house provides material for novelty stories.

- *Timeliness* deals with how recent an event or issue is. Newspapers strive to get the news to people as quickly as possible. Because newspapers tend to focus on **breaking stories,** they are often criticized for missing stories about trends or long-term issues.

- *Conflict* relates to disagreement among people. The conflict can be physical, as in crime and war, but it need not be. Much political news involves conflict in the marketplace of ideas.

- *Disaster* includes both natural calamities such as earthquakes and human-caused catastrophes such as an oil spill in the ocean.

- *Human interest* relates to personal details that intrigue readers. The story of an eighty-year-old woman who drives a school bus and is called "Grandma" by elementary students has human interest.

News values may change as society changes. The penny press, for example, emphasized crime news, which contained conflict and impact. A more recent type of news is called *coping information.* Life in the United States has grown more complicated. More readers want infor-

syndicates: Organizations that sell content, such as stories, cartoons, and photographs to media outlets.

breaking stories: News stories that are continuing to develop as they are covered.

mation that will help them to live more efficiently. Articles about how to stay healthy through better eating and exercise help people to cope with daily stress.

A story can have more than one news value. The more of these values in a story, the more likely it is that people will read it. In addition, some values are more important than others. Because newspapers tend to emphasize local news, proximity is important for most staff-prepared stories.

Journalists don't sit with a checklist of news values when picking events to be covered. Rather, they internalize these values and judge whether stories will be of interest to their readers. As the audience changes, however, the match between journalists' and audience's news values can change. Coping information emerged in newspapers because readers wanted it.

> **Key**concept
>
> *News Values:* Newspaper editors and owners try to develop standards of value for determining what events and issues are newsworthy, that is, deserving of being given space in the paper.

Many readers criticize newspapers for emphasizing too much *bad news,* another term for conflict and disaster. Journalists counter that some bad news is important and must be understood if people are to be effective citizens in a democracy. The Los Angeles riot that stemmed from the Rodney King beating case certainly qualified as bad news, but it had to be covered because it qualified as news by all reasonable definitions.

COMICS AND POLITICAL CARTOONS Although information graphics have proliferated in both print and broadcast media during the past fifteen years, comics and political cartoons are still the mainstay of newspaper graphics. More than 70 million people in the United States read newspaper comics and look at political cartoons every day. *Comics* are drawings that are provided primarily as entertainment for readers. *Political cartoons* are drawings that comment on political, social, and cultural events and the people who influence those events. Comics are aimed at the consumer market; political cartoons contribute to the marketplace of ideas.

Any newspaper editor can explain the importance of comic sections to readers. A 1987 study found that 95 percent of all daily newspapers carried a separate and identifiable comics section on Sunday. Sunday comics were more common than sports sections and editorial pages.[22] Another 1987 study found that 58 percent of newspaper readers read comics regularly. This was greater than the percentage that regularly read sports, editorials, letters to the editor, food pages, and in-depth investigative reports.[23]

The use of graphics boomed in the 1980s primarily because of offset printing and the use of computers. However, three other factors contributed to the spread of graphics at newspapers. First, the development of *USA Today* as a national paper provided a model for other papers. Second, the fact that the Gannett Company, which started *USA Today,* also owned more than eighty other daily newspapers reinforced the use of graphics around the country. Third, competition among dailies in larger markets resulted in more use of color and visuals, such as graphics, to make newspapers more appealing to readers, particularly in competition with television.

The growing use of graphics substantially increased the number of graphic artists in the newsroom and improved their salaries. In 1979 the Society of Newspaper Design started with 22 members; by 1991 it had 2,300 members. The salaries of graphic artists in the early 1990s ran 20 to 25 percent ahead of salaries of reporters and copy editors.

PHOTOJOURNALISM Photojournalism, which integrates words and photographs, attempts to explain people's behavior and the nature of the world. Photojournalism uses this integrated form to communicate photographically and report news to a mass audience. The form involves skilled editing and assumes that informing the public is essential.[24]

Photojournalism is capable of powerfully affecting an audience's interpretation of an event and often defines public memory. Certain photographs of the Kennedy assassinations, police dogs attacking civil rights activists, and the Saigon police chief shooting a

Viet Cong soldier in the head politically defined a decade for the generation that came of age during the 1960s.

Photojournalism may be more critical to society than other forms of photography because its goal is to alter our vision of the world and it is mass distributed. Photojournalism opens up arenas of action and images that people would never see otherwise.

Trends and innovations

During the 1980s, the nation's newspapers changed from drab, gray, and serious layouts with more text than graphics, to livelier news and graphics formats. Accompanying these superficial changes were changes in content. These and other alterations reflect newspaper publishers' attempts to address changes in their audience and their competition.

As newspaper publishers and editors began to recognize that they were losing readers and failing to gain new ones, they enlisted the help of market research firms. These firms conducted surveys and reported that readers wanted news they could use. Newspapers responded by broadening their content.

Newspapers are aggressively experimenting with new technologies. Although electronic delivery systems are showing a profit for newspapers only in rare instances, publishers recognize the importance of being involved at the experimentation stage. The questions of whether to place stories on the Internet, to connect to a commercial online service, or to develop one's own online service are under consideration.

A third trend has to do with organization. Many newspapers are experimenting with *team reporting* approaches that attempt to break down the barriers of the old bureaucratic structures.

A fourth trend is related to some of those already listed because it involves content and how content is determined. It is a trend labeled *public journalism,* and is a distinctive and controversial effort to find ways to reconnect newspapers to their communities.

Content and design

USA TODAY The trend toward more readable news and graphic displays began with the introduction of Gannett's *USA Today* in 1982. The newspaper now claims to have six million readers, but it still has difficulty making a profit, probably because of its orientation to a national market and its reliance on national advertising. However, as one of the nation's largest chains, Gannett is in a unique position to support the financial risk of a marginally profitable but interesting experiment such as *USA Today.* This newspaper was a wake-up call to the nation's newspaper editors, serving notice that readers would respond to "news you can use" and to graphic displays that made information more accessible. *USA Today* also has pioneered technological developments, using new digital photographic techniques and satellite distribution to regional printing plants, as described in Figure 5.1.

CHAINS' ATTEMPTS TO REFASHION CONTENT Beginning in the late 1980s, several newspaper chains made serious attempts to come to a clear understanding of what readers wanted. Market research and **focus groups** were instrumental in the changes.

In 1989, aware of major changes in the South Florida population, Knight-Ridder launched a project labeled 25/43 (because it was an attempt to reach readers in that age group) with the Boca Raton *News* as a pilot. The project illustrated a significant trend in the newspaper business: Publishers wanted to find out, in a scientific fashion, what readers would read. With this in mind, the *News* established several

focus groups:
Groups of individuals representing different interests who are assembled to discuss a topic. A form of research used to get in-depth information, but not information that is representative of an entire audience.

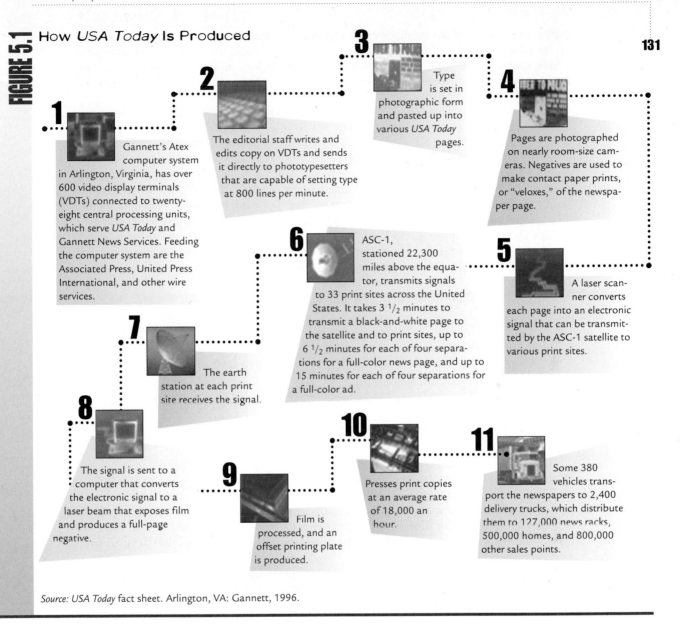

FIGURE 5.1 How *USA Today* Is Produced

1 Gannett's Atex computer system in Arlington, Virginia, has over 600 video display terminals (VDTs) connected to twenty-eight central processing units, which serve *USA Today* and Gannett News Services. Feeding the computer system are the Associated Press, United Press International, and other wire services.

2 The editorial staff writes and edits copy on VDTs and sends it directly to phototypesetters that are capable of setting type at 800 lines per minute.

3 Type is set in photographic form and pasted up into various *USA Today* pages.

4 Pages are photographed on nearly room-size cameras. Negatives are used to make contact paper prints, or "veloxes," of the newspaper page.

5 A laser scanner converts each page into an electronic signal that can be transmitted by the ASC-1 satellite to various print sites.

6 ASC-1, stationed 22,300 miles above the equator, transmits signals to 33 print sites across the United States. It takes $3\frac{1}{2}$ minutes to transmit a black-and-white page to the satellite and to print sites, up to $6\frac{1}{2}$ minutes for each of four separations for a full-color news page, and up to 15 minutes for each of four separations for a full-color ad.

7 The earth station at each print site receives the signal.

8 The signal is sent to a computer that converts the electronic signal to a laser beam that exposes film and produces a full-page negative.

9 Film is processed, and an offset printing plate is produced.

10 Presses print copies at an average rate of 18,000 an hour.

11 Some 380 vehicles transport the newspapers to 2,400 delivery trucks, which distribute them to 127,000 news racks, 500,000 homes, and 800,000 other sales points.

Source: USA Today fact sheet. Arlington, VA: Gannett, 1996.

focus groups to lay the groundwork for a new newspaper. In 1990 the newspaper staff redesigned its product, with stories that were short and did not jump from one page to another, dramatic photographs, grids for classified advertising and movie listings, and national and world maps to indicate where news was happening. The *News* also developed seven daily feature tabloids called "Essentials"—news designed for the baby boomers who populate Boca Raton. The topics range from "Business" to "Parent and Child."

The new design, which was based primarily on market research, particularly the preferences of the focus groups, earned the scorn of media critics and editors, who believed they should decide what readers needed, not cater to what their audiences wanted. *Los Angeles Times* media critic David Shaw told a *Quill* writer that although these changes might attract audiences, they were not the types of changes he believed a newspaper should focus on: "The Boca Raton paper and *USA Today* attempt to emulate tele-

132

vision, rather than make themselves more distinctive from television." What newspapers do best, Shaw said, "are long, thorough, careful, analytical looks at serious problems. That's something television can't do. The more we go for emphasis on color and graphics and short stories, seems to me the more we are going to ultimately render ourselves unnecessary to our readers."[25]

The move away from editor-inspired coverage to reader-inspired or market-research-determined coverage concerned media critics. However, the Boca Raton *News* editor argued, "Newspapers have failed to treat readers as customers and tailor the product to the interests and expectations of those customers. We have to do what Chevrolet and Ivory Soap do when their products no longer appeal." Editor Wayne Ezell noted about the first issue of the redesigned newspaper, "Champagne Prices Soon To Explode—we're the only paper in America to do an eight-inch story on that. For baby bloomers who go to a lot of champagne parties, that's more interesting than whatever Jack Kemp had to say today."[26] Critics were happy to see less than spectacular circulation increases at Boca Raton. Knight-Ridder, however, saw the project as inspiring to its other papers. They encouraged their member papers not to duplicate the Boca Raton *News,* but rather to evaluate their own audiences and tailor their newspapers to particular communities. Knight-Ridder's research showed that the following topics were **hot buttons** for baby boomer readers:

- Substance over style
- The environment
- Issues related to local development
- Competent and affordable child care
- Health/fitness/well-being
- Quality of education
- What's happening in schools

- Delivery of government services
- Ways to save time
- Ways to save money
- Lists of things to do
- Traffic and transportation
- Workplace issues
- Getting ahead[27]

Another major effort by a chain to get its newspapers in touch with their readers was Gannett's News 2000 project. In June 1991, Gannett introduced the program to 230 Gannett executives, instructing each publisher to address the issues that were in the minds of the community. Using surveys, focus groups, and readership studies, Gannett staffs developed comprehensive designs for each paper. Many of the changes involve presentation, with more dramatic designs, **breakout boxes,** and fewer stories that jumped from page to page.

Newspaper publishers are increasingly interested in the needs of young adults, because they will form the readership group for the twenty-first century. A focus group of sixteen-year-olds conducted by the Survey Research Lab at Northwestern University suggested the following topics as ideal newspaper subjects:

- Crime but not a lot of violence
- World events and how they affect me
- Money (how to make it, how to save it, how to spend it)
- Earth issues and the environment
- Social issues and how I can help
- Analysis, perspective, and explanations of events and controversial issues
- New products and technology
- Fashion, with ins and outs
- Sports and in-depth interviews with sports stars
- News of upcoming concerts
- Music reviews by people my age

hot buttons: Timely topics that elicit an emotional reaction from the audience.

breakout boxes: Shorter pieces of information, often direct quotes, that are connected to the larger story being covered. They are used to emphasize specific points and for design relief.

- Lists of things to do
- Getting along with people who are different from me
- Careers and life after high school
- Shopping[28]

Convergence and the newsroom

In early 1995, William Randolph Hearst III, grandson and namesake of the William Randolph Hearst who had broken new ground with the *New York Journal* and *San Francisco Examiner,* left his post as editor and publisher of the *Examiner* to become a partner at Kleiner, Perkins, Caufield & Byers, a twenty-three-year-old venture capital firm in Silicon Valley. Hearst had been introduced as a teenager to the possibilities of computers and, as publisher of the *Examiner,* recognized that newspapers needed to go beyond the traditional print product delivered once a day. He experimented with subscription services such as America Online and Prodigy but later turned to the World Wide Web of the Internet because of the flexibility it offered. In 1994, during the San Francisco newspaper strike, Hearst more fully recognized the possibilities of the Internet when a group of striking *Examiner* and *San Francisco Chronicle* reporters began to post their work on the Web. *Wired* magazine noted, "It's hard to miss the symbolism of Will Hearst's career switch. It marks a vote of confidence in new media from a man whose family heritage is deeply rooted in the old."[29]

Other newspaper companies are experimenting with services that increase access to their information resources. No longer does the consumer have to rely on the editor's judgment about what to include and exclude; each reader can construct her or his own range of information. The Nando Times, presented by the *Raleigh News and Observer,* the respected regional daily in Raleigh, North Carolina, offers continuously updated national, international, sports, business, and technology news, as well as advertising. Nando.net also provides access to the Internet. For a small monthly fee, subscribers can get high-speed Internet connection as well as access to all the information in the *News and Observer* and additional material from the newspaper's staff and wire services.

The *New York Times* may be viewed on the World Wide Web. Also, a daily eight-page summary of the *New York Times* can be downloaded from http://nytimesfax.com/. This electronically delivered version of a *New York Times* digest, called *TimesFax,* is sent daily to 150,000 readers around the world. It can be downloaded in ninety seconds and then printed out on a desktop printer. The *New York Times* also is available through Nexis-Lexis, an information database that is offered for a hefty subscription fee.

Cox Newspapers also have incorporated new technologies in the newspaper framework. Some of the Cox newspapers, including the *Austin American-Statesman* and the *Atlanta Journal and Constitution,* have developed fax services that provide additional detailed information in specialized areas. Readers simply call to request the faxed information. The Atlanta paper, for example, no longer publishes Stock Options and Commodity Futures tables but publishes a number for the free fax service. Nearly all Cox newspapers are offering telephone information services, which allow readers to dial up for additional information, such as sports scores.[30]

By the beginning of 1997, more than 1,630 newspapers worldwide were available online. Of these, 875 originated in the United States. About 95 percent were accessible over the World Wide Web. In the future, the majority of newspapers going online will pick the World Wide Web for distribution.[31]

Newspaper publishers know how to deliver their information through electronic services, but they are still experimenting with how to make money through these services. Charging subscription fees is becoming more common on the Internet, which traditionally has provided information free. However, the graphic nature of the World Wide Web

The *New York Times* and America Online

In February of 1996, America Online and the New York Times Electronic Media Company signed an exclusive agreement that gave America Online subscribers not only access to the *New York Times* daily content and regular updates throughout each day, but to additional programming created specifically for America Online.

New programming will include an expanded version of Science Times, crossword chat rooms, and a monthly "*Times* Looks Back" feature. In addition, AOL subscribers will have access to standard *Times* favorites, such as the *New York Times Magazine.*

New York Times Electronic Media Company President, Martin Nisenholtz, was quoted in *Editor & Publisher Interactive* (*Editor & Publisher's* web site): "As more and more Americans get their news and information online, we anticipate a growing need not only for content customized to specific interests and needs, but also the demand for greater interaction among newsmakers, news gatherers and analysts and news consumers."

The *New York Times* has been a leader in online newspaper experiments, winning two of *Editor & Publisher's* Best Online Newspaper Service awards. In addition to the AOL agreement, New York Times Electronic has launched Times File, a Windows users program that provides for easy retrieval of *New York Times* content with a free download of Times File at http://www.nytimes.com/partners/hotpage.

SOURCE: Walter Brooks, "Best Read News Nuggets," *E&P Interactive,* February 26, 1997.

has expanded advertising possibilities. Progressive publishers know they must adapt; they are simply searching for the right formula.

Reorganizing the newsroom

To reorient their reporters to focus on people's needs rather than traditional reporting beats, some newspapers have reorganized their staffs. Traditionally, a metro editor supervised reporters who covered city hall, county council, police, and courts. This type of coverage focused on institutions rather than on people, and it assumed that most news of importance issued from traditional institutions—usually political ones. Increasingly, newspapers are experimenting with staffing patterns that stress topical, rather than institutional, coverage.

Key concept

Organizing Principles for Reader-Focused Newspapers: Many modern newspapers are reorganizing their newsrooms to address the needs of their communities and their current and potential readers. Newsroom organizations built on traditional hierarchies and territorial/geographic boundaries are giving way to structures that address topics rather than institutions.

In Columbia, South Carolina, *The State* reorganized its newsroom into coverage "circles" to encourage reporters to broaden their definitions of news, to knock down the traditional barriers between news desks, and to become more flexible and responsive. *The State's* coverage circles include "Passages," "Quality of Life," "Transactions," "Leisure," "Governance," "City Life," "Sports," and "Community Roots." A copy desk, a graphics desk, a library, a design desk, and a photography desk complete the news staff.[32] The paper's managers also increased emphasis on six key issues: education, race relations, environment, poverty, effective governance, and economic development. They vowed not to raise territorial walls, but to use an interdisciplinary—or interdesk—approach to developing ideas and collecting information for stories. Furthermore, reporters are supposed to explore the culture of Columbia, South Carolina, as an anthropologist would—always beginning with people rather than with institutions.[33]

The public journalism controversy

Newspapers have always gathered their strength from local readers and local advertisers. But during the mid-twentieth century, community journalism lost respect. Reporters viewed working for big papers such as the *New York Times, Chicago Tribune,* and *Washington Post,* as the road to professional advancement and career success. On a smaller scale, journalists left the small towns for papers in the state capitals. Urban journalists could adopt the professional values of being detached, objective, tough, critical. They stood apart from the community they served.

As their audience and their competition changed, newspapers found themselves with diminishing circulations and a lack of connection to their communities. Seeking to reestablish their identities, some newspaper editors, as well as academicians, began to explore a philosophy of public journalism. The *American Journalism Review* lists as the components of public journalism

Keyconcept

Public Journalism: By creating a public conversation through journalism, modern news media hope to inspire consumers of news to become more involved in their own communities. The media encourage citizens, officials, reporters, and editors to identify and respond to the issues that confront their neighborhoods and their cities.

asking readers to help decide what the paper covers and how it covers it; becoming a more active player and less an observer; lobbying for change on the news pages; finding sources whose voices are often unheard; and, above all, dramatically strengthening the bonds between newspaper and community. At its heart is the assumption that a newspaper should act as a catalyst for change.[34]

Davis "Buzz" Merritt, Jr., was one of the first editors to embrace the concept in modern times. Dismayed with the low voter turnout in the 1988 election, Merritt established a Voter Project for the *Wichita* [Kansas] *Eagle* during the 1990 election campaigns. The paper conducted surveys and focus groups to determine what readers thought the crucial issues were. The newspaper tried to keep candidates focused on those issues and downplayed campaign rhetoric. Reader satisfaction with the *Eagle* jumped more than 12 percent.

One key goal of public journalism is to involve readers—as news sources, in focus groups, as critics of the newspaper. The idea is that journalism cannot be measured by professionals alone but must involve the people who buy and use the product.

But words such as "involvement" invoke specters of political corruption from the past, and editors fear that trying to influence the outcome of public action will affect the newspaper's credibility. In addition, some editors see the new approach as a loss of control over one's own product. One outspoken opponent has been Leonard Downie, Jr., executive editor of the *Washington Post,* who advocates a strict policy of not being involved. Downie has said that he doesn't vote, rarely reads editorial pages, and tries not to form opinions on matters covered by the *Post.* Marvin Kalb, director of the Joan Shorenstein Center on the Press, Politics and Public Policy at Harvard University, while acknowledging that the public journalism movement "is not a flash in the pan phenomenon," urges caution: "A journalist who becomes an actor, in my view, is overstepping the bounds of his traditional responsibility."[35]

The public journalism movement is one response to reader alienation. Many newspaper editors view the struggle to get the community involved as a lifesaving measure in a time when newspapers have been gaining few, if any, new readers.

The Charlotte Project has been an innovative experiment in public journalism by the Poynter Institute for Media Studies, a journalism think tank, and the *Charlotte Observer* in cooperation with WSOC-TV, the ABC affiliate in Charlotte, North Carolina. Discouraged with the style and content of the coverage of the 1988 presidential election, the Poynter Institute decided to work with a newspaper to "take campaigns out of the hands of spin doctors and give them back to the voters." The Institute staff believed that focusing on Willie Horton, a flag factory, Boston Harbor, and the Pledge of Allegiance during the Bush-Dukakis campaign had not served the voters well. The Institute decided to establish new types of coverage in connection with a television station and newspaper that were respected in their own communities and in the national journalistic community. In this way, the Institute believed, they could get citizens more involved in elections and thus reinvigorate American politics.

The *Observer* and WSOC-TV conducted a comprehensive opinion survey. The *Observer* then ran a front-page story on six major issues identified by citizens, a column of local voter opinion, and a column and two full inside pages analyzing the various issues. For the next six weeks the *Observer* analyzed the issues, telling the stories through the eyes of the readers, posing possible solutions, portraying candidates in relation to the issues, expanding coverage beyond politics, and presenting the material in a readable, organized fashion. Throughout the election coverage the *Observer* involved readers in shaping the news, explained to its readership what it was doing, reminded readers that they had helped to decide which issues to focus on, and framed stories in terms of citizens rather than in terms of candidates. The newspaper made a deliberate attempt to cover issues, not a horse race. For the 1992 election, voter turnout in Mecklenburg County (metro Charlotte) was up 32 percent over the previous record. County Elections supervisor William Culp, Jr., credited the *Observer's* coverage for the increase.

Five hundred people were active on the *Observer's* Citizen Panel, and more than 2,500 people interacted with the newspaper during the campaign through letters, phone calls, or interviews. Editor Rich Oppel, who is now Washington Bureau Chief for Knight-Ridder, said after the election, "For us, it meant a reinvigoration of the creativity of the paper. We do things now in an atmosphere of enterprise and innovation that probably wasn't there before."

The Poynter Institute concluded that although the project had mixed results, journalism's allegiance to objectivity does not need to come at the expense of community understanding and engagement. In the name of objectivity, journalists have often excused themselves from participating in the activities of their own communities. The Institute argues, "Communities need journalism's insights, skills, experience, disciplines, ethics, perceptions, hard work, and, above all, passion to be involved. All can be compatible with the traditional values of journalism."[36]

The Charlotte newspaper has continued its involvement in public journalism. In 1996 a major project focused on crime-plagued neighborhoods. Reporters asked people living in the communities what they thought they needed to improve their living conditions. Reporters became immersed in the communities, trying to understand life through the eyes of the residents. The *Observer* published recommendations by the citizens rather than exclusively by social planners. In early 1996 the Pew Memorial Trust, which funds a variety of public journalism projects, recognized the *Observer's* unique experiments by giving the paper a James K. Batten Award.

Who are America's journalists?

In striving to become more responsive to their readers, newspaper executives have become more aware of who is writing America's news. The predominantly white and male newsroom staff is being joined by increasing numbers of minority members and women.

TABLE 5.3 Statistical Profile of the "Typical" U.S. Journalist

Daily newspaper journalist (55%)	Attended public college (57%)
Male (66%)	Did not major in journalism (61%)
Married (60%)	Works at group- or chain-owned organization (65%)
White (92%)	
36 years old (median)	Works with news staff of 42 (median)
Protestant (54%)	Has worked in journalism 12 years (median)
Democrat (44%)	Does not belong to a journalism organization (64%)
Has bachelor's degree (82%)	

Includes all types of journalists, including broadcast, magazine, etc. Of the 1,156 journalists included in the sample, 798 were newspaper journalists.

Source: David Weaver and Cleveland Wilhoit, *The American Journalist in the 1990s,* funded by the Freedom Forum. Undated handout.

However, the changes have been slow, and newsroom managers and minorities often have different perceptions of newsroom reality. A survey conducted by the National Association of Black Journalists (NAJB) indicates that African American journalists feel that they work in an unfriendly, unsupportive environment. Although 94 percent of newsroom managers said that their organization showed a serious commitment to retaining and promoting black journalists, 67 percent of the black journalists disagreed. NABJ's investigation of the coverage of the 1992 Los Angeles riots found that the lack of black decision makers in determining story coverage was a critical problem, according to black reporters who were assigned to cover the riots. Many black reporters indicate that they are afraid to bring up race issues because they believe it will hurt their careers. Although many newsroom executives seemed surprised at this claim, Geneva Overholser, former editor of the *Des Moines Register,* said that it is not just blacks who are afraid to speak up in newsrooms: "Women are afraid to speak out, young people are afraid to speak out. I certainly know that people of color are afraid to speak out."[37] Table 5.3 shows the characteristics of the typical journalist.

Summary

- Newspapers historically focused on their local communities and provided information about local events. Nevertheless, they also carried national and international news, and Congress early debated the relative merits of local versus national circulation of newspapers.

- During the revolutionary period, newspapers helped to develop political rhetoric that supported independence. In doing so, they were seldom tolerant of competing voices.

- With developments in manufacturing during the nineteenth century, newspapers began to carry national advertising and expanded their markets.

- Newspapers competed with each other through formulas that capitalized on information and sensation.

- Newspaper markets today are determined by several components, including the number of choices within a geographic area, the probability of product substitution, and barriers to entering the market.

- Changing demographics make it difficult for newspaper editors to understand the components of the market. Publishers can no longer assume that middle-class readers will subscribe to the newspaper.

- Newspaper readers now have many choices. They can choose to read a newspaper, subscribe to cable television, listen to the radio, watch network television, or subscribe to a computer online database service.

- Newspaper content includes advertising, opinion material, and news.

- Newspaper content comes from newspaper staff reports, wire and news services, and feature syndicates.

- Journalists apply news values in determining what stories to assign and write. Many of their judgments are made almost unconsciously but tend to follow a predictable pattern.

- To combat changes in the markets, newspaper executives are trying new approaches. Some newspapers use survey research and focus groups to determine the needs of their particular communities and then target their reporting and writing to those needs. Other organizations have revamped their news-gathering operations, relying less on institutional news and more on topically defined news.

- Newspapers will remain an important component of the media mix, as long as they take advantage of new technologies and revamp their content to serve their audiences.

- Newspaper publishers recognize the opportunities of online delivery of information, but they have not yet determined how to make a profit using this new technology.

- Some newspapers are engaging in public journalism in an attempt to involve their readers and to make themselves essential to their communities.

Navigating the Web

Newspapers on the web

Web sites about newspapers contain information about the industry and online versions of newspapers. With the Internet, a person can access newspapers from all over the world and find articles and data about the industry.

Newspaper Association of America	http://www.naa.org

The NAA represents more than 1,500 newspapers in the United States and Canada. Its site provides a variety of information about marketing, public policy, diversity, and operations in the newspaper industry. The NAA "Facts About Newspapers" page carries detailed data about the industry in the United States and Canada.

E & P Interactive	http://www.mediainfo.com

The leading newspaper trade publication, *Editor & Publisher,* runs this site about electronic newspapers. The site contains regular columns and articles about newspapers on the Web as well as links to an extensive list of online newspapers around the world.

| Express Newspapers | |
| Research Department | http://www.research.expressnewspaper.co.uk/intronn.html |

This site contains a research article about the national newspaper industry in Great Britain. It contains a description and details about types of newspaper in England. The Express Newspapers are part of a larger corporation, United News and Media.

The following are sites for online newspapers.

The *Washington Post*	http://www.washingtonpost.com
The *New York Times*	http://www.nytimes.com
The *Times of London*	http://www.the-times.co.uk
Clarin Digital, Buenos Aires, Argentina	http://www.clarin.com.ar

■ Questions for Review

1. Discuss the levels of tolerance that colonial newspaper editors practiced. Discuss the significance of their participation in revolutionary rhetoric.

2. List the characteristics of the penny press.

3. What is a newspaper market?

4. If most newspapers are making a substantial profit, why are publishers worried?

5. List the most common news values that journalists include in their reporting.

■ Issues to think about

1. If newspapers have traditionally appealed to local audiences, what should they do to attract younger audiences that will make up the buying public during the next ten to twenty years?

2. Why is it difficult for newspapers to target audiences?

3. What kinds of news are less likely to be covered because they do not fall under the traditional news value umbrella?

4. How does a newspaper engage in public journalism and maintain a level of objectivity at the same time?

5. In what ways can newspapers respond to and use new technologies to enhance the quality of news reporting, editing, and production?

■ Suggested Readings

Bagdikian, Ben. *The Media Monopoly,* 3rd ed. (Boston: Beacon Press, 1990).

Bogart, Leo. *The Press and the Public: Who Reads What, When, Where and Why in American Newspapers,* 2nd ed. (Hillsdale, NJ: Erlbaum Associates, 1989).

Gruley, Brian. *Paper Losses* (New York: Grove Press, 1993).

Halberstam, David. *The Powers That Be* (New York: Alfred Knopf, 1979).

Underwood, Doug. *When MBAs Rule the Newsroom: How Marketers and Managers Are Reshaping Today's Media* (New York: Columbia University Press, 1993).

Magazines

When Jennifer stopped to buy some food at a convenience store near her campus, she noticed the most recent issue of *Tennis* and wondered if it could give her some tips on her game.

Then she spotted the new issue of *U.S. News & World Report,* which featured a story about international politics and the balance of trade. She remembered a discussion in her political science class and decided to buy the magazine to update the material in her textbook. That afternoon at the student health clinic, Jennifer found magazines scattered about the waiting room, and although the issue was dated, she began to browse through a Florida travel magazine, thinking of the spring trip she was planning. After receiving her flu shot, Jennifer went to see her adviser to discuss her interest in journalism. She left with an issue of *Quill*—the magazine published by the Society of Professional Journalists—to help her decide how interested she actually was in journalistic issues and in becoming a journalism major. When she arrived home, Jennifer found that her new issue of *Wired,* a magazine about the online world of information and games, had arrived.

Magazines traditionally coordinated the various activities of society by commenting in words and pictures on politics, social issues, and events of the day. In the 1990s, they more often appeal to special interests.

The kinds of magazines Jennifer encountered highlight some of the trends in the industry today. Women's magazines, such as *Harper's Bazaar,* and general-interest magazines like *Reader's Digest* have been popular for decades. Today, however, the industry is depending more and more on specialized magazines—those devoted to particular interests, like sports or travel or specific professions or computers. Specialized magazines are also being aimed at different age groups. Publications like *Word,* which bills itself as the authority on "issues, culture, and spandex," appeal to the twenty-something generation. At the same time, *Modern Maturity* thrives because it targets baby boomers turning fifty. *Modern Maturity* was redesigned in late 1995 "to reflect what the magazine is about, and the magazine is about change." Its editor says, "Readers' lives are fraught with change. They're getting married, remarried, divorced. Some are starting new careers, some are going from empty nesting to renesting."[1] So we see that even traditional magazines are adapting to new demographics, the characteristics (like age and income) of the population. Furthermore, magazine content is increasingly appearing on the Internet and on online services. And small magazines, called zines, are appearing online, bypassing paper publication altogether.

Throughout our nation's history, magazines have been the collectors, producers, and distributors of contemporary social knowledge. Magazines have helped connect different aspects of society, explaining to millions of readers how small bits of information fit into a larger context. With today's trend toward specialized magazines, however, that traditional function may be in jeopardy.

Magazine publishing is a risky industry that generates billions of dollars. Consider these findings by Mediamark Research Inc. About 88 percent of adults read one or more magazines each month. Each person passes an issue to about five other people. The average reader is thirty-nine years old; 60 percent of readers are married, and 40 percent have at least a high school diploma.

Many magazine start-ups occur each year, and many magazines fail. In a world in which individuals have increasing choice about which media to buy and use, magazine-industry personnel have to find answers to these issues:

- How will converging technologies affect magazine content, audience, and distribution?

- As the U.S. population ages, how will magazines adapt to changing demographics?

- As business goes through a cycle of downsizing, will downsizing by magazine publishers enhance the growth of magazines or shrink it?

- Will specialized magazines—which are so successful today—be able to function as conveyors of social knowledge? Will they continue to connect people?

Magazines in American life

The magazine business, like all business ventures, has been dependent on supply and demand. Once magazines became established in the British colonies in America, they successfully occupied a niche within the world of print and publishing as the nation's conscience, the conveyors of social knowledge. While newspapers supplied quick information and books offered professional materials and fiction, magazines provided the long, thoughtful essays that encouraged people to think about politics, to plan their travels, and to engage in debates about social policies. At first, magazines catered to the elite, but they soon began to reach a broader class.

Magazines in your life

Do Magazines Bring People Together?

As you read this chapter, consider whether magazines connect people. Think about the types of magazines you, your friends, and your family read. Are your family's magazines so specialized that you don't enjoy them? What about your magazines? Would your parents or your children read them? Or do you think that magazines are so specifically targeted to special interests and to age groups that they've lost their ability to bring people together? What kinds of magazines bring people together?

TYPES OF MAGAZINES	TITLES YOU READ	TITLES YOUR FAMILY READS	OTHER PEOPLE WHO READ YOUR MAGAZINES
News			
General Interest			
Specialized			
Men's			
Women's			

■ Magazines experience slow growth

The colonists were eager for information from their home countries and from adjacent colonies, where they had family and friends. They imported books from England and read the fledgling newspapers in the colonies. Magazines developed more slowly because they were expensive, postal regulations did not favor their distribution, and a professional class of writers was required to supply articles.

Key concept

Magazines and Correlating the Parts of Society: People from various social groups have used magazines to discover and make sense of the behavior of other groups. Information about others in magazines may help a group to bring into perspective, or correlate, the actions of one part of the society with the actions of another.

In fact, it was a full fifty years after the first newspaper was published in the colonies that Andrew Bradford sold the first magazine. Titled *American Magazine, or A Monthly View of the Political State of the British Colonies,* it appeared on February 13, 1741. Although Benjamin Franklin had intended for his *General Magazine, and Historical Chronicle, for All the British Plantations in America* to be the first magazine in the colonies, Bradford's was published three days earlier. Bradford's magazine lasted three issues; Franklin's survived six.

The first American magazines boldly published articles that appeared in British magazines. Local content was the exception rather than the rule. Magazine covers, when used, were made of light-colored **stock** that displayed an elaborate illustration or the table of contents.

Reading magazines was a pastime of the colonial elite, who not only had the education to read but also the time. Most colonists were engaged either in subsistence agriculture or the trades, and they worked from dawn to dusk. Thus, few people had time to read magazines. Inadequate distribution and printing methods contributed to

stock: A term used to refer to types of paper.

144

the slow growth of magazines. Magazines never enjoyed the favored postal rates that newspapers quickly grew accustomed to. To reach audiences outside the growing towns of Boston, Philadelphia, and New York, magazines traveled by stagecoaches, which had to contend with rough and sometimes washed-out roads. Most publishing operations were family owned, sometimes with husband and wife sharing equal responsibilities, and profits could be earned more easily by printing, stationery sales, or newspaper publishing, than by publishing magazines.

Magazines in the nineteenth century

Although only twelve magazines existed at the beginning of the nineteenth century, nearly 100 were in existence by 1825; by 1850, the numbers had grown to about 685. This growth was fostered by changes in technology and manufacturing that followed the **Industrial Revolution** that began in England in the eighteenth century. Expanded literacy and public education also produced a larger middle-class audience.

The change from an agricultural- to industrial-based society affected the United States in the years following the Civil War. The development of machine technology that spawned the Industrial Revolution made magazines cheaper, more attractive, and more efficient to produce. New technologies, including the steam press, **stereotyping,** and **electrotyping,** speeded production. These innovations also reduced the amount of heavy labor needed and often allowed young women, who could be paid less, to handle many aspects of publishing, thus reducing labor costs. Papermaking machines allowed paper to be produced in continuous rolls. Photographic and engraving developments also were important to magazines because they allowed publishers to use engravings and drawings more frequently at less cost.

Keyconcept

The Industrial Revolution in Magazine Technology: In the mid- to late nineteenth century, developed societies were completing a transition from an economy based on handwork and agriculture to one based on mechanized industry. The shift from handwork to machinery and mechanized production increased efficiency and radically lowered the costs of printing, making magazines and newspapers affordable for a large population.

Technology also improved transportation and contributed to a more advanced postal system that enabled faster and less expensive distribution of magazines across wider geographical spans. Newspapers could rely on local forms of distribution, but magazines were expensive and needed a wider geographical base from which to attract readers.

Changing postal regulations improved magazine distribution during the nineteenth century. In 1845, a five-ounce magazine cost six and one-half cents to mail; by 1852, the same magazine could be mailed for five cents. If postage was paid in advance, charges were reduced by half. By 1863 postal laws were even more favorable, setting the rate at one cent for four-ounce magazines published less than weekly, with rates rising proportionally for each additional four ounces.[2]

A rapidly growing population and a steady move toward cities helped consolidate the audience for magazines. As manufacturing made the transition from locally produced products to nationally distributed brand names, magazines became the perfect national advertising vehicle. They circulated to all regions, thus appealing to national businesses.

Magazine audiences were not merely groups of consumers; they were avid and active readers who also shaped the culture of the society. Magazines gave meaning to situations and helped readers under-

Industrial Revolution: The period during the late 1700s and 1800s when America and Europe moved from an agriculture-based economy to a manufacturing based economy.

stereotyping: The use of a paper mat to make cylindrical molds for printing.

electrotyping: A metal plate used in letterpress printing, made by electroplating a lead or plastic mold of the page to be printed.

Advanced printing technology and an upwardly mobile population with discretionary income encouraged the development of magazines. Readers sought information in magazines that would help them interpret a rapidly changing society.

stand significant social, economic, geographic, industrial, and educational events. The search for social knowledge was important to those who wanted to be upwardly mobile. With this historical context in mind, think about the magazines you listed in Magazines in Your Life on page 143. Can you think of magazines you read today that help you understand significant social and political events?

Social knowledge was considered critical in a democratic nation. By 1830, many of the northeastern states provided cheap or free public education for the middle class as well as for the elite. Children were expected to read in order to become good citizens, and young adults strived to expand their knowledge in order to gain promotions in the ranks of salespeople and clerks.

Expanded literacy and the growing middle class fueled the magazine business. The audience for magazines often overlapped with the audience for books, but magazines sought a particular niche. Their widespread distribution through the mails and their less expensive format fostered a wider audience, connected different groups of people, and helped transmit social heritage.

Thus emerged a budding industry that influenced the economics of literature and art. Many of the early magazines were begun in conjunction with book companies. *Harper's Monthly Magazine* was an excellent advertising vehicle for the new books published by Harper Brothers. Magazines promoted books in other ways as well. Many books were first printed as serials, or installments, in magazines; thus, books and authors obtained recognition and publicity. Magazines also influenced reading habits by summarizing or reviewing books and other published works.

Keyconcept

An Era of Democratic Reading: By the mid-nineteenth century, thanks to the availability of cheap publications, all classes of society felt encouraged to become readers. The new democracy of readers eagerly devoured newly created magazines and newspapers.

The showcase magazines of the mid-nineteenth century were the quality monthlies, known for their travelogues, light fiction, and political material, as well as for their elegant covers and finely drawn illustrations. Among these were *Century, Scribner's, Atlantic Monthly,* and *Harper's.* Those magazines helped to develop a class of American writers and created a forum for criticism of American art and literature. By 1870 *Harper's,* which relied heavily on British authors, had a circulation of 150,000. The *Atlantic Monthly* was one of its chief competitors, building its reputation on American authors, especially those of New England.

ECONOMIC DECLINE Economic hard times during the late 1850s and the Civil War era stifled the magazine business. An audience hungry for news was not always able to afford it, and demand declined. Soaring paper prices closed down many magazines, especially those in the South. A few magazines, such as *Harper's Weekly,* thrived on the war, providing news and illustrations for the news-hungry population. Nevertheless, newspapers benefited from the war more than magazines did because newspapers were cheaper to produce and were more timely.

ECONOMIC RESURGENCE AND CULTURAL CONTROVERSY Mass industrialization and economic growth after the Civil War spurred the development of magazines as a business. The

146

period saw overall business expansion, with an increased emphasis on national production and the distribution of named products. Printing technology and mass-distribution methods also fostered the growth of magazines. By 1885 the industry had experienced a sharp turnaround, and 3,300 magazines were in circulation.

Advertising provided the funds for growth but also provoked social and cultural controversy. Some magazine publishers shunned advertising, believing that ads for such items as **patent medicines** cheapened their product. "Lower-class" publications sold space publicizing contraceptives and abortion-producing drugs. Middle-class women consumed patent medicines loaded with alcohol, and ads for abortion-inducing medicines forced readers to face the facts of unwanted pregnancies.

The economic growth of the magazine industry provided an outlet for the work of American short-story writers and novelists. But magazine writing did not provide a substantial income. Publishers comprised an elite class who believed that writing was an avocation, not a trade. They were reluctant to pay the young, middle-class writers who wanted and needed money for their work. Eventually, the situation improved. *Atlantic Monthly* paid the average rate, which was $5 a page, to new writers, $6 a page to published writers and $50 for a poem. Louisa May Alcott was paid $50 for her first story; Ralph Waldo Emerson, $50 per essay; and Harriett Beecher Stowe, $400 for her "Uncle Tom's Cabin" series. During the nine months that Stowe's "Uncle Tom's Cabin" ran in the *National Era,* the antislavery journal sold a magazine record of one million copies. As the number of professional writers or "magazinists" grew, so did the practice of paying writers.

Although general-interest and women's magazines were the most popular magazines of the nineteenth century, publishers began to recognize the value of **market segments,** or specific categories of readers, and toward the middle of the century they developed specialized magazines, targeting particular social and economic interests. Even before the Civil War, periodicals focused on subjects such as Southern living, public affairs, agriculture, antislavery, medicine, law, education, banking, and the insurance industry. By the end of the century, specialized audiences included druggists, hardware dealers, railroad enthusiasts, telegraphers, coach makers, children, and literary types. In the twentieth century, targeting specific market segments enabled magazines to survive economic hard times and competition with new media such as radio and television.

Keyconcept

Specialization in Publishing: As early as the mid-nineteenth century, magazines adopted the practice of targeting specific segments of an audience rather than appealing to the general public. Magazines are continuing this trend as the twenty-first century approaches.

Probably the best example of large-scale specialization and technological innovation appeared in an unlikely place—in philosophy and religion. As a result of a widespread religious revival, by 1860 the leading religious organizations had twenty or more periodicals. Groups that published religious magazines, such as the American Bible Society and antislavery societies, often were the first to use technological innovations. They used newly developed, cheap methods of printing to expand the distribution of their messages and to create the illusion that their movements were larger than they really were.

■ Mass production and assembly-line magazines

By 1890, 4,400 magazines were being published and circulated to 18 million readers. Fifteen years later circulation reached 64 million. In 1915, advertising revenues for general-interest and farm publi-

patent medicines:
Packaged drugs that can be obtained without a prescription. Before the Food and Drug Administration was created, these drugs often contained large amounts of alcohol and sometimes opium.

market segments:
The target audience. The group of individuals a magazine selects to target as a readership group.

cations combined topped $28 million. The **gentlemen's club** magazines of the nineteenth century, such as *Harper's,* and the refined ladies' magazines, such as *Godey's Lady's Book,* gave way to mass-produced, assembly-line products.

The revolution in magazines was symptomatic of a revolution in society, and magazines grew by exploiting the social trends and changing values that emerged with a rising middle class. Public education, opportunities for college education, and business had expanded. More significantly, business had gone national. The number of trademarks registered with the U.S. Patent Office, for example, jumped from 1,721 in 1910 to 10,282 in 1920. In this new world of rapidly developing products and new technology, national advertisers bought magazine space to appeal to the middle-class potential consumers of new products.

Big-circulation magazines profited because publishers began to realize that as magazine circulation increased, they could charge higher rates for advertising because they gave advertisers wide exposure. Advertising could provide an increasing percentage of magazine revenues, and subscribers

Before television became a nationwide visual medium for mass audiences, general interest family magazines, such as the Saturday Evening Post *or* Collier's, *were dominant and accessible forms of visual information.*

could pay a lower percentage of the costs, thus widening the circle of likely readers. Magazines such as *Youth's Companion* and *Harper's* began to use rotary presses, printing many copies at lower costs. Economic and technological change once again combined to produce cultural change.

Magazines began to define their audiences more broadly, although magazines remained an expensive medium in comparison to newspapers. Circulation boomed, although only one magazine, *Comfort,* had a circulation of one million at the turn of the century. The *Ladies' Home Journal* passed the million mark in 1904, but until World War I few magazines fared as well.[3] Among those that did were *Collier's, Cosmopolitan, McCall's* and the *Saturday Evening Post.* Most of the top fifty magazines during that decade and the following ones were general-interest magazines such as *Collier's Weekly, McClure's Magazine, American Magazine, Independent, Literary Digest, Leslie's Weekly, Scribner's Magazine, Century Magazine,* and the *Saturday Evening Post.*

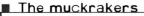

The muckrakers

Among the general-interest magazines was a new class of **dime magazines** marketed to a middle-class audience and highly critical of what they perceived to be an "unholy" alliance between government and business. These magazines, labeled muckrakers by President Theodore Roosevelt, reflected a societal concern about corrupt business practices and exploitation of the masses for the good of business and government. Roosevelt chastised magazines such as *McClure's, Munsey's,* and the *American Magazine* for a position he considered to be too critical of American society.

Although exceedingly popular, the muckrakers were relatively short-lived. Getting their start during the depression of the 1890s, they peaked at the turn of the century, and then fell from favor by 1915.

gentlemen's club:
Magazines produced in offices occupied by middle-aged white males. The atmosphere was similar to that of a gentlemen's club.

dime magazines:
Magazines that cost 10 cents and appealed to a broad class of readers. These magazines were less expensive than the quality monthlies that preceded them.

148

Muckraking as a social phenomenon has been the focus of critical dispute about the role of magazines and how they reflect, respond to, or influence social and economic forces. Muckraking magazines came of age during a period of general dismay over business practices. During the early 1900s, Congress passed the Pure Food and Drug Act, the Clayton Antitrust Act, the Federal Trade Commission Act, and other pieces of legislation to curb business excess—or at least to create the appearance of doing so. That period saw social-reform issues arise in all media, from the reform press to the photography of social reformers such as Lewis Hines. It is possible that by 1915—when the magazines slipped in popularity—the public was tired of reform or believed that corruption had subsided. Perhaps the public had shifted its attention to the looming war in Europe. Some critics speculate that business deliberately killed off the magazines, starving them for advertising and, in some cases, buying them and changing their editorial policies. Nevertheless, the muckraking magazines were a social force that informed readers about corporate and political behavior inappropriate for a democratic society.

Keyconcept

Muckraking: The label "muckrakers" has long been applied to investigative reporters who dig into backgrounds of people and organizations, often exposing corrupt political or business practices. The label sometimes connotes sensationalized or even irresponsible and unethical reporting.

Photojournalism: Small camera technology and social insights

As the Kodak box camera began to revolutionize public photography after 1900, the development of the 35-millimeter camera and fast film created new opportunities for photojournalism, an extension of the type of photography social reformers had used between 1880 and 1915 to document and fight the negative social effects of the industrial revolution.

Some journalists tried to expose these problems through articles and illustrations. Muckrakers, who often were magazine journalists, and their newspaper counterparts attacked corporations and fought for changes in labor, agricultural, and business laws. Jacob A. Riis and Lewis W. Hine photographed the plight of the poor and homeless to show what can happen to unskilled workers in an unregulated capitalist economic system.

In the 1920s, social documentary photography was greatly enhanced with the introduction of the small Leica camera, made by E. Leitz of Germany. With the Leica, a photographer could work unnoticed while recording a scene. In addition, film became "faster," needing less light—and less time—to record an image. These technological changes led to flourishing picture magazines, first in Germany, then England, and then the United States. Henry Luce's *Life* and Gardner Cowles' *Look* became showcases for photojournalists. Magazines that used high quality paper and printing processes benefited more than newspapers from the new technology. Until the development of **fast film** in the 1960s, **35 millimeter** film was too slow for newspapers and produced pictures that had a grainy look. So newspapers stuck with flashbulbs and large-format Speed Graphics, while general-interest magazines chronicled the Depression of the 1930s, World War II, the prosperous 1950s, and the early moments of the Civil Rights Movement.

Perhaps the most notable group of photographers during this time worked for Roy Stryker and the Farm Security Administration (FSA). Photographers such as Arthur Rothstein, Walker Evans, Dorothea Lange, and Gordon Parks photographed migrant farmers in California, African American sharecroppers in the South, drought-stricken farm-

fast film: Generic term for film photographers use to stop "fast" action. Does not need long exposure to light to capture the photographic image.

35 millimeter: Photographic film that has a frame for exposure 35 millimeters in length. It is used for both still and moving pictures.

The photojournalism magazines captured emotion as no medium had before. Here on the pages of Life, *C. P. O. Graham Jackson plays "Goin' Home", expressing his own and the nation's sorrow at the death in 1945 of Franklin Delano Roosevelt.*

ers in Oklahoma and Texas, and federal work projects throughout the country. The FSA photographers' records of that period demonstrate how effectively a camera can function as a sociological commentator and historical recorder.

Beginning in 1936 and continuing into the 1960s, *Life* magazine showcased the work of the country's premier photojournalists. The magazine, begun by Henry Luce, chronicled the latter years of the Depression and set the standard for war photography during World War II. Unlike photographers in previous wars, *Life* photographers, with their small cameras and fast film, could photograph moving bodies. They conveyed action, blood, effort, and grief, transporting readers to the battlefields of war.

■ Maturation and competition

The boom years of the early twentieth century quickly faded when the United States, in 1930, confronted a massive economic depression. About one-third of U.S. workers were unemployed, the stock market tumbled, and the gross national product (GNP), or value of services and goods, was at an all-time low. Magazines suffered from reduced advertising and intense competition from radio and movies. Within a few years, television introduced additional fierce competition. However, once again magazine publishers responded to hard times by bringing social needs into focus and capitalizing on new technology. News and photo magazines gave subscribers a new look at the news in synthesized and pictorial form. Henry Luce, who later developed the Time, Inc., publishing empire, capitalized on the need for news, the development of the 35-millimeter camera, and the public's desire for interpretation of social and political events. He and Britton Hadden started *Time* magazine in 1922, at first clipping and rewriting items from daily newspapers and later adding their own staff and building the weekly into one of the most renowned news vehicles in the nation. In 1930, when the Great Depression was already underway, Luce successfully founded the business magazine *Fortune.* Although some thought he was foolhardy to initiate such a venture at that time, he recognized that businesspeople and the public needed to understand the consequences of business decisions. Then, in 1936, he created *Life,* based on the model of German picture magazines. The stunning photographs that appeared each week in *Life* captivated an audience that was bewildered by the Depression and concerned about an oncoming war. DeWitt Wallace's *Reader's Digest* (1922) and Gardner Cowles's *Look* (1937) capitalized on some of the same trends.

Magazines in our lives

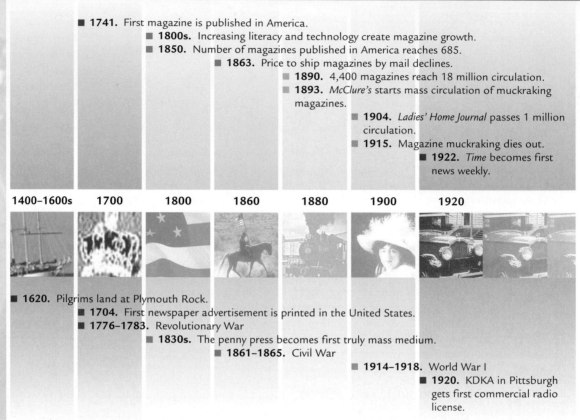

- **1741.** First magazine is published in America.
- **1800s.** Increasing literacy and technology create magazine growth.
- **1850.** Number of magazines published in America reaches 685.
- **1863.** Price to ship magazines by mail declines.
- **1890.** 4,400 magazines reach 18 million circulation.
- **1893.** *McClure's* starts mass circulation of muckraking magazines.
- **1904.** *Ladies' Home Journal* passes 1 million circulation.
- **1915.** Magazine muckraking dies out.
- **1922.** *Time* becomes first news weekly.

| 1400–1600s | 1700 | 1800 | 1860 | 1880 | 1900 | 1920 |

- **1620.** Pilgrims land at Plymouth Rock.
- **1704.** First newspaper advertisement is printed in the United States.
- **1776–1783.** Revolutionary War
- **1830s.** The penny press becomes first truly mass medium.
- **1861–1865.** Civil War
- **1914–1918.** World War I
- **1920.** KDKA in Pittsburgh gets first commercial radio license.

As World War II raged through Europe during the early 1940s, Americans turned to magazines for information about world events. However, diminishing supplies and rationing hindered the growth of magazines—except for those adventure and detective magazines that were sent to military personnel. Responding to financial hardship, publishers conducted market research in an attempt to convince advertisers of the effectiveness of their medium. The end of the war in 1945 generated prosperity, record amounts of buying, and also rising costs, including an 89 percent increase in postal rates. *Life* and *Look* magazines—in addition to movie newsreels—had brought the war home in pictures, making Europe and Asia seem closer. Those vibrant magazines helped people stay informed and understand world and national events.

Media compete for advertising

Advertising—the golden financier of magazines—became a commodity to be fought for. It had fueled the magazine industry, but as radio and television entered the media picture during the mid-twentieth century, magazines began to lose their competitive edge. Now they had to share advertising resources not only with newspapers but also with new and dynamic media that captured people's ears as well as eyes. Between 1950 and 1955, television's share of advertising increased from 3 percent to 11.2 percent. Ads

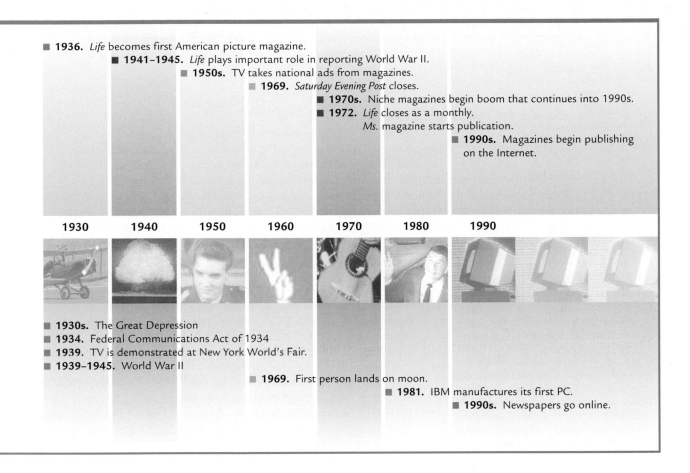

■ **1936.** *Life* becomes first American picture magazine.
■ **1941–1945.** *Life* plays important role in reporting World War II.
■ **1950s.** TV takes national ads from magazines.
■ **1969.** *Saturday Evening Post* closes.
■ **1970s.** Niche magazines begin boom that continues into 1990s.
■ **1972.** *Life* closes as a monthly.
Ms. magazine starts publication.
■ **1990s.** Magazines begin publishing on the Internet.

| 1930 | 1940 | 1950 | 1960 | 1970 | 1980 | 1990 |

■ **1930s.** The Great Depression
■ **1934.** Federal Communications Act of 1934
■ **1939.** TV is demonstrated at New York World's Fair.
■ **1939–1945.** World War II
■ **1969.** First person lands on moon.
■ **1981.** IBM manufactures its first PC.
■ **1990s.** Newspapers go online.

with sound and motion made stronger impressions on consumers than print ads. And the cost for television ads was cheaper: In 1971, the expense per thousand persons reached via *Life* was $7.71; via television, it was about $3.60.

Three historic general-interest magazines died with the growing popularity of television. The magazines failed not because of loss of circulation but because of loss of advertising. Although the *Saturday Evening Post* had a paid circulation of 6 million and a **pass-along rate** of 14 million readers, it ceased publication in 1969. *Look*'s paid circulation was 8 million with an estimated 18 million readers when it folded in 1971. Even *Life,* which boasted a circulation of 7 million and was read by 21 million people, folded in 1972. (*Life* was later revived as a feature magazine published monthly.) These giants had retained huge circulation lists, but they lacked the advertising money needed to keep them afloat financially. Whereas television's share of national advertising more than doubled in the 1960s, from $1.5 billion to $3.5 billion, magazines' share went from less than $1.0 billion to only $1.2 billion.

Specialization, however, kept the magazine industry alive by targeting specific audiences and addressing changing **demographics.**

pass-along rate: The total number of readers who read a magazine regularly, including those who read copies that were given, or passed along, to them.

demographics: Characteristics of an audience for mass media based on age, gender, ethnic background, education, and income.

152

Specialized magazines thrived because, rather than competing for the same audiences as broadcast television, they delivered to advertisers audiences with particular interests and consumer habits. Advertisers can count on subscribers to *Skiing* to buy advertised skiing products. Particularly successful niche magazines have addressed changing demographics, trends, and technologies: They have targeted increasing numbers of working and single women, emphasized fitness and health, and exploited the popularity of computers.

Today's market structure

The magazine industry, like other media industries, is big business. A few conglomerates dominate, especially in the field of large-circulation consumer magazines. Yet the magazine industry is very risky. Most magazines are relatively new: In 1950, there were only 6,960 periodicals in the United States. In 1994 alone 832 consumer magazines were introduced. In 1996, there were 10,466.[4] The volatility is due, in part, to new printing technologies. Computer-driven publishing is easy and inexpensive, allowing companies or individuals to start up magazines without a major capital outlay. However, without adequate market testing and financial planning, publishers are hard put to keep new magazines going. Further, magazine content must keep pace with changes in society—technological, economic, and cultural. Despite the risk inherent in the industry, the total number of magazines has remained relatively stable, and total circulation has increased steadily in recent years.

Specialists categorize magazines in various ways. One common method is to divide them into the categories of consumer magazines, business magazines, and literary journals. Consumer and business magazines dominate the field. In today's magazine industry, small-circulation magazines are growing faster than large-circulation publications. For instance, more than 65 percent of the country's magazines have a circulation of 50,000 or less.

Despite the heavy concentration of magazine ownership, the industry continues to make room for **entrepreneurs.** One innovation is the production of **zines,** low-cost magazines, often with erratic publication cycles, that are created and duplicated using computers, computer printers, and photocopy machines. The content of zines reflects the idiosyncrasies of the publishers. For example, Jeff Potter of Williamston, Michigan, produces *Out Your Backdoor* from his home. In 1995, Potter's zine had forty-eight pages, a circulation of 5,000, and a price of $3. Hundreds of electronic equivalents of zines can be found on the Internet, where production costs are even cheaper. As in the past, evolving technology continues to create opportunities for new magazine publishers.

Changes in the magazine industry are related to the nation's broad economic trends as well as to the publishing industry's specific environment.[5] For instance, magazine publishing has followed the national corporate trends of decentralizing and downsizing. Cost-saving measures have included cuts in full-time staff and and an increased use of freelancers. In 1991, *Time* magazine laid off forty staffers. Four years later, Times Mirror Magazines laid off 125 people, or 20 percent of its workforce. Decentralizing is implied with the geographic changes in publishing, which are shown in Figure 6.1 on page 154.

Keyconcept

Consumer Magazines versus Business Magazines: The two main types of magazine are magazines for general audiences of consumers and magazines for specialized audiences of professionals and business people. Consumer magazines are distributed to the public, through either subscriptions or retail sales, carry advertisements for consumer products, and may cover any general or specialized topic. Business magazines, sometimes called trade journals, are distributed through controlled free subscriptions or paid subscriptions and contain articles and advertisements that are of interest to small target audiences.

entrepreneur: A person who assumes the risk of starting a business.

zines: Inexpensive magazines produced with desktop publishing and usually distributed over the Internet.

Computer magazines exemplify the impact of specialization on the magazine market. In 1988, a computer magazine of any kind would have been considered a specialized magazine. Now, the computer market is divided into its own specialized categories. Computer magazines target the laptop industry, advanced users, novices, people with home offices, users of Windows, and other segments of the computer market. Ownership of computers in American households leaped from 17.7 percent in 1988 to 38 percent in 1996. Analysts predict that by 2000, nearly half of all American households will have computers, and increasingly those computers will be connected to on-line services. While only 8.6 percent

Ziff-Davis and Computer Mags

of computer households owned modems in 1988, by 1994, 30.2 percent owned modems.

The company that has cashed in most successfully on this market is Ziff-Davis, an American company bought by the Softbank Corporation of Japan in 1996. Ziff-Davis markets computer magazines to the world.

In 1995, Ziff-Davis increased its revenues by 11 percent over 1994, sold more than 50,000 advertising pages worldwide, and pioneered with demographic and regional editions. Its most successful magazines in garnering advertising were *Computer Shopper, PC Magazine, FamilyPC,* and *Computer*

Life. Ziff-Davis is having similar success in Germany, France, and the United Kingdom.

Ziff-Davis also has made money from its World Wide Web site, ZD Net, which had gross sales totalling $1.2 million in the second half of 1995.

SOURCES: Veronis, Suhler & Associates, Communications Industry Forecast, p. 313; "Ziff-Davis Magazines Tops in Ad Pages, Ad Revenues, and Ad Page Growth," *IAC (SM) Newsletter Database (TM), M2 Communications, M2 Presswire,* from Lexis-Nexis, January 31, 1996.

Consumer magazines

Consumer-magazine numbers have not varied significantly in recent years, but some changes reflect demographic and lifestyle aspects of today's society. Specialization is still the key to success. Magazines covering computers, health and fitness, pets, and teens are growing steadily; magazines covering entertainment, spectator sports, and general editorial topics have declined slightly in circulation.[6]

Business magazines

The top ten business-magazine categories are computers, health care, engineering and construction, media, automotive, banking and finance, business, building, advertising and marketing, and industrial/manufacturing.[7]

Controlled circulation—sending magazines free to individuals within industry and advertising—was developed as a distribution technique in the specialized business-press arena. Unlike consumer magazines, more than half of the specialized business publications still use

> **controlled circulation:** Technique of sending magazines free to individuals within an industry to increase identification with an organization.

154

FIGURE 6.1 Where Magazines Are Published

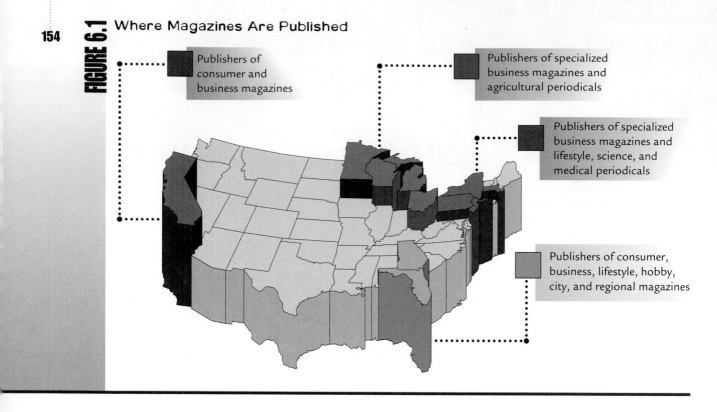

Publishers of consumer and business magazines

Publishers of specialized business magazines and agricultural periodicals

Publishers of specialized business magazines and lifestyle, science, and medical periodicals

Publishers of consumer, business, lifestyle, hobby, city, and regional magazines

controlled circulation. However, controlled-circulation magazines are recognizing that they need to try different approaches to support growth.

Association magazines, in particular, can no longer afford to exist on dues alone. "They have to generate revenues from selling ads and doing all the things that consumer publications do," says Elissa Myers, vice president and publisher of *Association Management,* the 21,400-circulation magazine published by the American Society of Association Executives, based in Washington, D.C. Myers points out that the average association now draws only 40 percent of its revenues from dues, compared with the 95 percent drawn in the 1960s. As a result, more and more association magazines are beginning to tap non-members as subscribers.[8]

Who owns magazines?

Despite the growth in small-circulation magazines, magazine publishing is big business, and a handful of **conglomerates** dominate as they do in other industries. Some owners publish in a variety of subject categories while others specialize. Market analysts predict that the pace of consolidation will slow, but magazine publishers will continue to realize benefits by being big. Size brings decided advantages in marketing and distribution. However, companies are more concerned about whether a particular magazine fits the company's business profile. Those that don't fit into an apparent long-term strategy may be sold off.

Conglomerates also have the advantage of staff pools. When one of the conglomerate's magazines is successful, its editor may be moved to

association magazines: Magazines published by various associations to publicize their activities and communicate with their members.

conglomerate: A corporation formed by merging separate and diverse businesses.

TABLE 6.1 Top Four Magazine Publishers, Based on Annual Advertising Revenues

Time Warner: *People, Time, Fortune, Sports Illustrated*	$1.6 billion
Hearst Magazines: *Good Housekeeping, Cosmopolitan, Redbook, Esquire*	$737 million
Conde Nast Magazines: *Parade, Vogue, Glamour, Vanity Fair, Traveler*	$661 million
New York Times Co.	$569 million

Source: Adapted from "Vital Signs" *Folio,* July 1, 1994, p. 51.

another of the conglomerate's magazines. Nevertheless, critics continue to worry about the standardization that comes with conglomerate ownership. If conglomerates prevail, how will the independent magazines—the *Rolling Stones*—of this decade survive? Industry analysts—and some critics—answer that there will always be room for a good editorial product.

The industry's top fifteen publishing organizations have annual revenues of several million to several billion dollars, mostly from advertising and circulation. Listed in Table 6.1 are magazines with the top advertising revenues.

Audience demand in magazine markets

A magazine has to be in demand to succeed. People can be looking for news on a general topic, advertising about companies or products, or information about new ideas. In response to demand, magazine publishers produce certain kinds of content. The two major markets are consumer, with magazines selling editorial content to readers, and advertising, with magazines selling readers to advertisers. Listed in Table 6.2 are the top paid-circulation consumer magazines.

TABLE 6.2 Top Paid-Circulation U.S. Consumer Magazines

TITLE	CIRCULATION 1996	CIRCULATION 1995
Modern Maturity	20,528,786	21,042,005
Reader's Digest	15,027,260	15,103,830
TV Guide*	13,013,938	13,175,549
National Geographic	9,025,003	7,768,071
Better Homes and Gardens	7,605,325	7,603,207
The Cable Guide	5,260,421	4,737,851
Family Circle	5,239,974	5,007,542
Good Housekeeping	4,951,240	5,372,786
Ladies' Home Journal	4,951,240	5,045,644
Woman's Day	4,508,333	4,707,330

Source: Advertising Age, February 24, 1997

*Weekly publication; other publications are monthly.

Consumer market

All publications need to find a **market niche.** Books contain more in-depth information than magazines. Magazines contain more in-depth information than newspapers. And magazines differ from one another in the audiences they attract. Audiences usually fall into one or more of the following segments:

- Geography—worldwide (*National Geographic*); regional (*Southern Living*); state (*Texas Monthly*); city (*Detroit Monthly*)
- Gender—female (*Victoria, Sassy*); male (*Esquire, Men's Fitness*)
- Ethnic background—African American (*Ebony*); Hispanic (*Hispanic Times*)
- Age—children (*Sesame Street Magazine*); teenagers (*Savvy, YM*); seniors (*Modern Maturity*)
- Lifestyle—raising children (*Parents Magazine*); owning a home (*Practical Homeowner*)
- Occupation—*Farm Journal, Nursing, Chemical Engineering News, Editor & Publisher*
- Hobby or sport—*Art & Antiques, Game & Fish Magazine*
- Socioeconomic background—wealth (*Fortune*); education (*Harpers*)
- Application—entertainment (*TV Guide*); surveillance (*Newsweek*); decision making (*Consumer Reports*)
- Ideology—liberal (*Mother Jones*); conservative (*National Review*)
- Topic areas—*Dog World, Astronomy, Guns & Ammo*

Almost every literate person in the country is a potential magazine consumer. Many market segments overlap, but rarely do two magazines target the identical audience. For example, audiences for *Working Women* and *Working Mothers* overlap, but some readers of *Working Women* are not interested in motherhood. Similarly, some readers of *Redbook,* a magazine targeted at young mothers, also read *Working Mothers.* Furthermore, *Modern Health Care* might also compete for the audience of any of the three women's magazines mentioned.

Keyconcept

Market Segments for Magazine Advertisers: Each magazine strives to sell content and advertising to a specific segment of the total population that the publisher has selected as the target readership. The tastes of the target audience determine the nature of the magazine's offerings.

Changes in audience demand force magazines to respond with changes in content. Therefore, as social change enabled more African Americans to earn higher incomes, advertisers began to recognize that African Americans had increased purchasing power. Publishers then began to target magazine content to specific African American interests, convinced that they could attract advertisers for the new market. Thus economic and cultural forces intertwine—as do consumer and advertising markets.

Advertising market

Initially, magazine publishers relied primarily on subscriptions for revenues. However, they soon recognized that they could broaden their audience by allowing advertisers to pay part of the costs. Today, advertisers search for media that are most appropriate for their product and message. Magazines compete with all media for consumers and for advertising. However, a few magazines, such as *Ms.* and *Consumer Reports,* publish without advertising because their publishers wish to avoid advertiser control and also have found that some subscribers support content that does not appeal to advertisers.

market niche: Portion of the audience a particular magazine gains as subscribers or buyers.

Advertisers target specific audiences through magazines. The teen magazine, for example, is a prime advertising medium for products aimed at fashion-conscious teenagers. Specialized sports magazines, such as Tennis, *market products aimed at specific interest groups.*

Magazines allow companies to match their messages to specific audiences. For example, suppose that a national software company that publishes an interactive database for evaluating entry-level jobs wants to reach people in their late teens and early twenties. Radio and newspapers tend to be too local, and national television advertising costs too much. That leaves national magazines that appeal to young people. *Working Women* would allow the software company to reach young women, and *Details* would allow it to reach young men.

Cultural Impact

Teen Magazines

Probably more than any other type of magazine, the teen magazines reflect and shape changes in society. *Seventeen,* which was fifty years old in 1994, in 1996 had a circulation of 2.3 million. Gruner & Jahr's *YM* in 1996 was closing in on *Seventeen,* with a circulation of 1.9 million. Those two magazines dominate the market, but *Teen* and *Sassy,* both owned by Petersen Publishing Company, until September, 1996 had a combined audience of over 2 million. *Sassy* recently was folded into *Teen. YM* claims to be a fashion and beauty magazine, but *Seventeen*'s editor says that *YM* has a sensationalist approach, with cover lines like "I Slept with My Best Friend's Boyfriend," that *Seventeen* avoids.

The teen market is growing. Two other teen magazines—targeting both young men and women—entered the market in 1994: *Tell,* a joint Hachette-NBC product, and *Mouth 2 Mouth,* financed by Time, Inc. According to the U.S. Census Bureau, the teen population, now estimated at 25 million, will grow at nearly twice the rate of the rest of the population. *Dallas Morning News* writer Tom Maurstad notes, "These teens are coming of age in

the Age of AIDS, the Age of Media, the Age of Marketing, the Age of Multiculturalism and Political Correctness." Teen magazines have articles on body piercing and tattoos, on sex— including AIDS and sexual abuse—and on the fame, power, and money of celebrities.

Seventeen, which began publication in 1944, brought a new self-awareness to girls. "I read it in the mid-'50s and it was like the Bible. If you were wondering what was going on in the teenage world, that was it," says Margaret Boone, 52, a Cobb County, Ga., interior designer. Despite new publications that push the boundaries, eleventh-grader Jenny Towns says she prefers *Seventeen*. "It's not so trashy as *Sassy* or *Teen,* and it addresses more elegant topics."

SOURCES: Deirdre Carmody, "Petersen Will Restart *Sassy* with Push for Older Readers," *New York Times,* December 8, 1994, p. D19; Janet Ozzard, "Teens: Survival of the Fittest: These Days, Everyone's Making a Run at *Seventeen,*" *Women's Wear Daily,* October 28, 1994; Tom Maurstad, "Fashion! Dallas: Something Different," *The Dallas Morning News,* August 24, 1994, p. 3E; Jean Marbella, "Attacking the Teen Market–By Design," *Baltimore Sun,* March 26, 1994, p. 1D; Valerie Seckler, "Who's Making Money?" *Women's Wear Daily,* October 28, 1994, p. S18; Angela D. King, "*Seventeen* Editor Gets Top Spot at New York," *New York Daily News,* October 10, 1996, p. 73.

158

Supplying the audience's demand

To continue making money and survive as a business, magazine organizations have to keep in touch with their readers. As society changes, so do readers' wants. For example, *Seventeen* magazine caters to teenaged females. Every few years, the magazine's audience "ages out," and *Seventeen* has to recruit new readers. The magazine targets not a set of particular women, but a particular age group whose demographics, backgrounds, wants, and needs are always changing.

The readers change, and so do the topics that interest them. Today's *Seventeen* includes stories and information that were not considered necessary or even proper ten or twenty years ago. While *Seventeen*'s August 1994 story "She's Your Sister" ("You love her, you hate her, and you're stuck with her for life") might have appeared ten years ago, chances are that gun violence in the schools and beepers for staying in touch wouldn't have occurred to an editor as possible topics. Even if your older sister or aunt read *Seventeen* when she was a high school student, she probably read a far different magazine from the one teenagers read today.

A magazine's operations, organizational structure, content, advertising, design, production, circulation, and delivery all depend on the characteristics of its current audience.

■ Creating a new magazine

Ideas for new magazines start with a concept that gets refined through reactions and suggestions of others.[9] Only one in every ten ideas presented to publishers makes it to the start-up stage, and even then, market success is not guaranteed. An idea must be original, but not so far outside the mainstream that it won't attract an audience. Further, a magazine must have staying power: If it addresses a trend, the trend must be here to stay. For example, computer magazines have proliferated, addressing a permanent, new development in our society. In 1988, as the computer trend gained strength, about 180 ideas for computer magazines were presented to major magazine publishers. Eighteen were seriously pursued, but only three were still in existence three years later. Of course, many specialized computer magazines now are available on newsstands.

More important than a great idea is its execution; an idea must be packaged as a marketable product. An entrepreneur must be both an editor and a marketer.[10] As marketer, the entrepreneur must secure financial backing. Figure 6.2 indicates the number of magazines started since 1988.

Financial support for starting magazines comes from three sources. Entrepreneurs can seek support from companies already established in the industry—for example, major publishers—to launch a new idea. Second, they can look for **venture funding** from small investors seeking higher risk and bigger payoffs than traditional capital investors. For that, a strong business plan is crucial. Third, start-ups can be funded by private investors who know the publisher and believe in that person's ability to make the magazine work.

> **venture funding:**
> Funding of an enterprise with cash from several investors who are interested in innovative enterprises that carry both risk and the potential for large profits.

■ Financing a magazine

Magazines usually are financed by governments, special interest groups, and commercial companies. The launches shown in Figure 6.2 were supported by a variety of financing sources.

FIGURE 6.2 Magazine Launches, 1988–1994

The number of magazines started each year has increased since 1985, when 231 magazines were started.

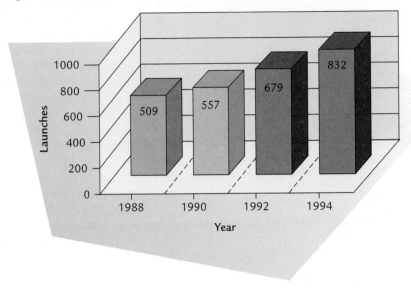

Source: Samir A. Husni, "Folio Ovation Awards," *Folio,* January 15, 1994, p. 64; and Barbara Nachman, "Mags and mags and mags," *Lansing State Journal,* October 9, 1995, p. D1.

GOVERNMENT Although some government agencies publish magazines, these tend to be geared to government employees. Usually government publications are newsletters or pamphlets.

SPECIAL INTEREST GROUPS Some organizations, such as a city Chamber of Commerce or a nonprofit organization, publish magazines. Some associations, such as the National Association of Home Builders, publish magazines that rival commercial publications in quality and cost. Others publish much smaller, less professional magazines.

COMMERCIAL COMPANIES The vast majority of magazines are commercial, with financial support coming from readers, advertisers, or a combination of the two.

■ Advertising

ADVERTISING-FREE MAGAZINES Some magazines survive without advertising; they are supported solely by readers who pay for subscriptions or for issues off the newsstand. These magazines are published by individuals who believe that advertising would compromise the integrity and principles of the magazine. For instance, *Ms.* magazine, after initial disputes with advertisers, reinvented itself as a nonadvertising publication. Because the magazine's editorial stance is that a woman looks and feels best without excessive use of cosmetic products, *Ms.* wanted to avoid the hypocrisy of printing advertising that contradicted the editorial position. The editors also wanted to avoid advertising cigarettes and alcohol, products that the editors had denounced as dangerous.

160

Magazines are financed in a variety of ways. Magazines such as Life *rely on advertising and subscriptions, but other magazines rely solely on advertising. If a single advertiser or group of advertisers control the content of the publication, it loses credibility. Sometimes, however, the editorial content is masked so that it is difficult for the reader to determine the source of the material.*

FREE MAGAZINES WITH ADVERTISING-ONLY FINANCING Although some magazines are supported by readers only, others are financed by advertising only. Consumers read or receive the magazines at no charge. For example, during the 1980s, Whittle Communications took advantage of captive audiences in places such as physicians' waiting rooms. Whittle developed a magazine for a specific health-care company and placed it free in doctors' offices. Although these types of publications continue, Whittle, who was experiencing financial difficulty in his own business, stopped publication of the magazine in 1994.

COMBINATION FINANCING A third type of financing is a combination of advertising and circulation. Magazines that rely on a combination of advertising and reader support traditionally competed for readers, but now they more often compete for advertising dollars. Advertising rates are closely tied to circulation figures, so publishers must be careful not to price their magazines out of the market. If they do, the decrease in circulation will result in a subsequent decrease in advertising revenues. Therefore increased costs often must be absorbed by increased advertising revenue.[11]

ADVERTISING TIE-INS Although prestigious newspapers have established their independence from advertising pressures, magazines have allowed, and sometimes even courted, editorial/advertising **tie-ins. Package deals** are commonplace for many magazine editors who guarantee preferential editorial treatment to advertisers.

Take, for example, one issue of the now-defunct *Lear's,* a magazine for professional, middle-aged women. The front cover featured the close-up face of a woman with blue-gray eyes. Turning the cover, a reader saw a **premium two-page spread** advertising Guerlain's Samsara perfume. Four pages later, on the table of contents, the reader was told that the woman on the cover was wearing Guerlain make-up and Samsara perfume.

Elsewhere on the same page, the reader learned that the cover model was none other than the director of public relations for Guerlain and that her latest promotional project was Samsara. Further into the magazine were two and two-third pages of more Guerlain advertising (for antiwrinkle products).

ADVERTISERS AND EDITORIAL CONTENT Advertisers also specify placement of some ads and react negatively when editorial content doesn't support their products. Many advertisers even hire resident censors who sit in the ad departments of major magazines. Dow specified that ads for its its Spray 'n Wash products had to be ad-

Keyconcept

Magazine Startup and Financing: New magazines may get financial support from government or special interests, but most often the support comes from business financiers who have experience in the industry or are willing to take risks in hope of high returns. Some magazines seek funds from subscribers and patrons only (avoiding ads) or from advertisers only (offering the magazine free to readers), but most magazines get support from a combination of advertising and subscriptions.

tie-ins: The connection made when a magazine runs a story about a product advertised in the magazine.

package deals: A series of media tie-ins.

premium two-page spread: An advertisement that spreads across two pages in the center of the issue.

jacent to pictures of children or editorials about fashion, and ads for its bathroom cleaner next to home-furnishing and family features. Clairol suspended placement of its ads for six months in one women's magazine after the publisher ran an article on the acceptability of gray hair. Revlon refused to advertise in a magazine because the Soviet women on the cover were not wearing makeup. (The story later won a prestigious Front Page Award.) And during the Gulf War, Procter & Gamble successfully stopped *Sassy* from running a page covered with the word *peace.*

However, if a magazine too often crosses the fine line that separates credibility and promotion, the industry and the magazine's readers may lose faith in it. If circulation drops as a result, advertisers lose interest as well, and the magazine is left to wither from lack of reader or advertiser support.

■ Publishing a successful magazine

The masthead, or list of owner, publisher, and staff of a magazine, usually appears near the table of contents in the first few pages of a magazine. The number and size of departments and types of positions vary with each publication; large consumer-magazine staffs may employ several hundred people, while small specialized business publications might have fewer than ten people. The positions and departments listed below are common for all sizes of magazine staffs.

Keyconcept

Magazine Publishing Process: To publish, magazines need the combined efforts of publishers, editors, writers, graphic artists, production staff, printers, ad managers, subscription managers, and distributors. These staff members provide content, physical print production, ad or subscription support, and distribution to the magazine's reading public.

PUBLISHER The publisher, to whom all staff members are ultimately responsible, may also be the magazine owner or editor. The publisher defines the personality of the publication and works to ensure its financial success. Some publishers with particularly forceful personalities and deep pocketbooks can breathe life into a publication or kill it with an easy blow. When *Lear's* ceased publication in March 1994, the *New York Times* reported that the magazine had died as it had lived. "It was created by Frances Lear, who, after a bitter divorce from television producer Norman Lear, was at a crossroads. She invented the magazine for a particular reader: herself. She gave the magazine her vision, her energy, her money and her name. She sustained it with her enthusiasm, and when she lost interest, she pulled the plug."[12]

EDITORIAL Once the publisher has defined the magazine's personality, the editor develops and shapes its identity. To successfully complete an editor's mission, the managing editor, the articles editor, and department editors work together to give readers the information they want. Editors edit and proofread stories, approve design and graphics, accept freelance submissions, and contract with designers.

Most magazines rely solely or partially on freelance work for their articles. Freelancers or their agents (who take 15 percent of the writer's fee in return for time spent selling the idea and the freelancer) send a query letter outlining and justifying a story idea and giving the writer's background and qualifications for doing the story. If the editors like the idea, they commission the freelancer to write the story. Although it is hard initially to get an idea accepted, once a writer does acceptable work for an editorial staff, it is likely to accept the writer's work a second time or even to commission stories. Nevertheless, even for regular writers, freelancing is rarely a road to financial success. For example, *Running Times* pays $25 to $400 for nonfiction, *TV Guide* pays $500 to $1,000 for nonfiction, and *Ladies' Home Journal* pays a minimum of $500 for fiction. Only a few magazine writers, such as Gail Sheehy, hit the big time in terms of money and prestige.

[profile]

Gloria Steinem

Since the founding of *Ms.* magazine in 1971, Gloria Steinem has been a feminist ideal for young women and men. She has devoted her life to persuading all kinds of women to believe in themselves, has lent an influential voice to the cause of immigrant farmworkers in California, and has helped to persuade Democratic political leaders to include women's issues in their platforms.

As a feminist, Steinem has had a major impact on the magazine industry. She developed a solid reputation as a reporter and magazine writer, founded *Ms.* in 1971, and later helped convert it to a no-advertising publication to avoid the impact of sexist advertising on its content.

Steinem grew up in a tenement in Toledo, Ohio. Her emotionally ill mother, Ruth, had once been a newspaper journalist who wrote under a male pseudonym. Steinem's parents were divorced when she was ten.

When Steinem was old enough, she worked evenings and weekends as a waitress and shop assistant. She also tap-danced in chorus lines. While she told the world that everything was all right, she and her mother lived in a rat-infested basement. However, she graduated from Smith College and then spent a year in India with the followers of the spiritual leader Mahatma Ghandi before starting her professional career. She advises women to use their backgrounds to learn and to grow.

When she returned to the United States from India, she wrote for *New York Magazine* and *Esquire,* building a reputation as a reporter and establishing a network. Her political involvement in women's causes began in 1969 at an abortion–law reform rally, where she listened to other women talk about being offended by sexist jokes and about having abortions and other experiences, some of them similar to hers. Inspired, Steinem cofounded the national feminist publication *Ms.*

Today, Steinem continues to be active in women's issues as president of the Voters for Choice Education Fund and through other volunteer work.

SOURCES: Sarah Lyons, "Daughter of the Revolution," *South China Morning Post,* July 6, 1996, Sect. Books, p. 8; Joan Smith, "The Unexplained Feminist," *Financial Times,* May 4, 1996, Sect. Books, p. 11; Rosie Boycott, "Sex and Feminism," *Daily Mail,* April 20, 1996, p. 36; Maureen Freely, "Gloria and Me," *The Guardian,* April 18, 1996, Sect. Features, p. 6; Katie Donovan, "Feminist Enigma," *The Irish Times,* April 9, 1996, Sect. News Features, p. 9.

Sheehy now is the recognized author of several books, including *Passages,* and is the premier writer for *Vanity Fair.*

ADVERTISING Advertising is often a magazine's lifeblood. Because an average magazine loses about 20 percent of its regular advertisers from one year to the next, magazine advertising departments are always seeking new advertisers. Ad revenues are notoriously unstable. Between January and October 1994, for example, *Elle* increased its ad pages by 12.3 percent; *Vogue* lost 103 ad pages during the same period, and *Glamour*'s ad pages were down 6.3 percent. Nevertheless, *Vogue* and *Glamour* sold the most advertising pages among women's magazines.[13] After a consistent decline in advertising revenues during the first half of the 1990s, magazine advertising seemed to be on the rise in 1996. Experts predict that it will level off and fluctuate according to the economy.

Advertising staffs may include only an advertising director and several salespeople. At larger magazines, divisional managers contribute specialized knowledge about readers and advertisers in specific geographic areas or about specific types of products.

DESIGN AND PRODUCTION The design department designs the actual paper product that readers hold. The production staff includes artistic experts, technological wizards, and people who buy supplies for production, such as ink and paper. Magazine production used to be tedious, complicated, long, and expensive, but computers have revolutionized the process. **Desktop publishing** has saved magazines millions of dollars and cut production time. For example, when the National Geographic Society converted from an **Atex system** to Macintosh-based desktop publishing for *National Geographic Traveler and World,* it saved $200,000 annually.[14] With desktop publishing, *TV Guide* cut its production time in half. What used to take seven to ten days now takes three to four days. *TV Guide* prints 20,000 pages in 113 regional editions. Technology also has allowed publishers to print split runs—and use selective binding, in which pages are changed according to geographic locale and advertising copy is based on Zip Code. Geographically divided runs allow publishers to better target their markets.

Computerized page design allows an editor to manipulate text and graphics on the magazine page to create attractive layouts.

CIRCULATION The circulation staff gets the magazine to the reader, through either subscriptions or newsstand sales. Each method has different costs. A new subscription costs publishers about $15 in promotion expenses; each renewal costs about $3. For single-copy sales, every stage of transport between publisher and newsstand takes a percentage of the copy price.

Soliciting subscriptions is one facet of circulation, and experts have become adept at using direct mail to solicit them. Circulation departments buy lists of people's names from various organizations and other publications, and send subscription offers directly to homes. The direct mail novelty of the 1960s was the computerized missive that integrated the recipient's name into the letter. Today computers combine different pieces of demographic background information about an individual in long solicitation letters. The aim is personalized target-market selling.

Magazines continue to seek innovative ways to sell subscriptions.The *New Republic* has chosen to use the Internet. The *New Republic*'s Electronic Newsstand can be seen by a potential audience twenty-four hours a day, seven days a week. On the Internet, readers can find magazines' tables of contents and excerpts of articles. Consumers can send an electronic message requesting a subscription, or they can call a posted 800 number to receive a single-copy example at one dollar over the newsstand price to be paid with a credit card. So far, 3,000 people a day "stop by" the Electronic Newsstand.

desktop publishing: Writing, illustrating, and designing publications with a personal computer.

Atex system: A centralized computer system used for word processing.

164

Magazines sold on newsstands must compete for news-rack space. Some publishers are finding that single-copy sales are leveling or dipping because of limited newsstand space, too many titles on similar subjects, and the high cost of single copies (which has doubled since 1978).[15]

Newsstand, or single-copy, sales go through a variety of stages before hitting the display racks. Each publisher works with one of about ten national **distributors.** The distributor supplies the printer with the mailing labels of some of the four hundred regional **wholesalers.** The printer mails bundles of issues to the wholesalers, which deliver the copies to dealers. Popular newsstand dealers are grocery stores, convenience stores, pharmacies, and bookstores. At the same time that magazines are delivered, the wholesaler picks up and discards the previous week's or month's unsold ones.

MAGAZINE EMPLOYEES In 1996, *Folio* magazine reported that entry-level workers were about 26 years old, earned salaries of about $25,000, and expected a 7.8 percent pay increase that year. They were overwhelmingly white and female, despite the fact that women earn significantly less in the industry. Most had a bachelors' degree, and 36 percent of them got their jobs through a connection with someone in the industry. Magazine employees in the New York City area earned the highest salaries but expected low raises and tended to be less satisfied with their jobs than did workers in other parts of the country.[16]

Trends and innovations

Today's magazines are operating in a climate of massive change. The business climate and technological development indicate that magazines will continue to be geographically decentralized and to operate with smaller staffs and increasing contractual arrangements. Technological change is affecting how magazines address demographic change, as well as increasing the choices for distribution. Social change, intertwined with the growth of the aging population challenges magazine editors to provide new types of content. Increasingly, you, your friends, and your families may not read the same magazines.

In the midst of these changing times, Bruce Sheiman, managing director of the Jordan, Edmiston Group, Inc., in New York City, exhorts editors to remember that magazines provide subtle benefits. He argues that magazines continue to hold a unique place in American society because they "crystallize, articulate and reinforce a person's identity."[17] They offer intimacy and depth not offered by electronic media. Sheiman argues that people relate to magazines as friends, experts, and role models.

Keyconcept

The Future of Magazines in Fragmenting Markets: As rapidly shifting audiences and electronic technology push publications into geographically wider but more specialized segments, questions arise as to how magazines may continue to help to correlate the parts of our society.

Demographics

Magazine publishers are getting ready for the year 2000. Slower population growth, an aging society, changing lifestyles, and an increasingly diversified population will make new demands on magazines. If magazines are to survive, magazine publishers must learn how to satisfy the new demands.

distributors: Companies that help get magazines from the printer to the wholesalers.

wholesalers: Companies that deliver magazines from a warehouse to dealers, such as book stores.

Population growth during the 1990s has been slower than ever before in the United States. Meanwhile, the society is getting older. Despite the teen boom that magazines have addressed, the two fastest growing age groups today are people aged 45 to 54 and 85 or older. Publishers targeting today's baby boomers (ages 37 to 52) with active lifestyles will have to redirect their titles to attract tomorrow's aging baby boomers. Furthermore, the number of people living alone is increasing faster than the number of those married with children, and numbers of minorities are becoming greater.[18] Recent publications targeted to a niche market include *Emerge,* a news weekly for African Americans; the *Senior Golfer,* targeted at aging baby boomers; and *Skiing for Women.*

Publishers will concentrate on improving editorial content by offering selective sections geared to the specific needs and interests of readers. These sections add editorial and advertising value to a magazine. Selective binding techniques permit publishers to create customized editions of a single issue of a magazine. *Prevention* now has two editions, one for readers over 55 and one for those under 55.

Advertising and information markets may further blend as more publishers join with companies to produce magazines for consumers of particular products. IBM's *Profit* and *Beyond Computing* are being published in a partnership arrangement with the New York Times Company; Gruner + Jahr USA is producing *Target the Family,* for Target stores.

Customizing is increasingly tied to new technologies. *TV Guide,* using sophisticated database technology, began in July 1995 to bring the production of its 113 weekly versions of the magazine in-house. By December, it was producing final, digitally imposed pages ready for output for 82 editions. The cost of this technology? More than $7 million for development alone. Nevertheless, the new technological approach allows *TV Guide* to create 22,000 to 25,000 new pages each week, with a closing time of just two days.[19]

■ Economic and social change

The adaptation of magazines to social and economic change has enabled them to continue to connect people and events. In 1969, *Life* magazine published pictures, letters, and interviews with friends of 220 of the 245 men killed in Vietnam during the week of May 28 to June 3, 1969. The magazine received 1,300 letters from readers praising and criticizing it for this personal look into the reality of war. The massive pictorial essay represented a distinct change in attitude toward the war by Time, Inc., and generated a national conversation about the gains and losses of the war in Vietnam.[20]

In the 1990s, magazines are increasingly addressing the needs of an aging population. As people live to be older, they look for different content in their magazines. For example, seniors and those caring for them need to know more about health care and financial planning.

Take the case of 85-year-old Sarah K. Goldstein who threw her back out while shoveling snow. Her daughter, Carol Abaya, who ran an advertising and public relations business, found it almost impossible to get information about health-care systems and to cope with the needs of her mother as well as those of her own demanding life. In 1992, she started a magazine, the *Sandwich Generation,* designed to provide information to the nation's 76 million baby boomers who were caring for more than 32 million people aged 65 or older. The magazine originally circulated only in Monmouth and Ocean counties of central New Jersey, but it now circulates in forty-two states. Abaya claims that her circulation has increased 500 percent since the first year, and her distributor says that her growth is 15 percent ahead of the national average for newsstand magazines. Abaya was invited to testify before the U.S. House Ways and Means Committee in January 1995 to discuss the relationship among elder care, tax credits, and the Republican Contract with America.

166

Social issues affect not only the content of magazines but their production as well. Recycling, for example, has become an important issue. Many publishers are aware that the magazine industry must initiate a voluntary recycling program to keep Congress from enacting mandatory recycling requirements for the industry. Some major publishers are still reluctant to use recycled paper because of its higher cost, lower quality, and limited availability. However, as publishers demand higher-quality recycled stocks, paper producers will attempt to push the technology to produce what is in demand.

Magazine development is tied to economic change. The mid-1990s witnessed a significant increase in paper costs, leading to price increases and a potential decline in circulation. Coupled with slower growth or a leveling off of advertising revenues, increased costs indicate a difficult time ahead for magazines. Nevertheless, old media, even in the face of new technologies, remain strong.

Combined technology offers more choice

Technology is driven, at least in part, by economic need. As publishers see the need for innovation in order to maintain profits, they finance the development of technology. At other times technological developments in fields other than publishing are tools to be adapted for innovation.

Computer publishing has greatly decreased the cost of producing magazines. But an even more costly area has been distribution. The news weeklies pioneered satellite transmission of electronic pages to tighten editorial deadlines but still meet distribution schedules. Now *Vanity Fair* can close some pages just hours before press time because it uses totally electronic page composition and transmission to its printer. Publishers also take advantage of the Internet and online systems.

ONLINE SERVICES Magazines benefit from taking advantage of online services. Consumers have accessed magazines and newspapers on commercial online services, such as CompuServe Information Services Inc., since the mid-1980s. The number of magazines appearing on online services increases daily. In some cases online distribution has enabled magazines to survive. When Sheryl Huggins could no longer sustain her New York City–based *Shade,* a magazine for twenty-something African Americans, she turned to New York Online because publishing online was less expensive than publishing on paper.[21]

CD-ROMS Magazines often find an advantage over newspapers through multimedia products, often stored as CD-ROMs. These compact discs have color, graphics, text, animation, and sound. *Newsweek* magazine, owned by the Washington Post Company, began producing quarterly CD-ROMs in mid-1993. The first *Newsweek* CD-ROM centered on the environment, included a full-length story, seven sidebars, 189 photographs, twelve charts, ten minutes of video, a thirteen-minute narrated documentary, five hours of radio interviews from the weekly program *Newsweek on Air,* 20 columns from the *Washington Post* newspaper, and three recent months of *Newsweek* magazine searchable by keywords.

CD-ROM companies also license material from magazines, produce CDs, and then pay royalties to magazine companies. Such is the case for Creative Multimedia, which licenses material from *U.S. News & World Report, Sports Illustrated for Kids, Consumer Reports, Travel & Leisure, Life, Smithsonian,* and *Golf Digest.* Len Jordan, Creative Multimedia president, says that the company pays royalties in the range of 8 percent to 12 percent. Most titles sell between 20,000 and 30,000 copies, with a typical retail value of $30. This arrangement allows magazines to take advantage of a new technology without risking large amounts of capital.[22]

Magazines and Consumer Choice

During the 1850s, Harper Brothers recognized that new technologies and mass marketing could fuel the magazine industry. Magazines were cheaper to produce than they had been before, and mass marketing provided an advertising base that would promote national circulation. Harper Brothers used its new magazines, *Harper's* and *Harper's Weekly,* not only to take advantage of a growing medium but also to promote the books that had been the mainstay of the company.

During the 1990s, many magazine publishers are exploring new technologies to determine how they might best sustain the magazine industry that was hit hard by the recession of the late 1980s and early 1990s. Although by 1993 revenues had begun to

increase once more, magazine publishers recognized that changes in technology would provide new competition and new opportunities for the nearly 200-year-old industry. Magazines had survived economic competition from television and radio by becoming specialized. Now publishers have to discover how best to use CD-ROM, computer online services, and other forms of electronic delivery.

Usually, the solution is to embrace the new technology rather than to avoid it. Time Warner, the giant cable, entertainment, and publishing company, now offers versions of *Time* online. During the past five years, it has experimented with other projects as well, testing a fully interactive full-service network in Orlando, Florida. The system provides

movies; news-on-demand with information from Time, Inc., magazines; home shopping; and electronic classified ads.

Playboy offers *Personalities and Profiles: The Playboy Interview Collection,* as well as a personal planner, on CD-ROM.

U.S. News & World Report offers an extension of the magazine's annual college issue and the popular *Best Colleges* guidebook on CD-ROM.

Converging technologies mean increased choice for the consumer. Rather than spelling the death of magazines, technology provides new delivery systems that recruit additional readers.

SOURCES: *Advertising Age,* March 7, 1994; *Folio,* January 1, 1996, p. 38.

FAX Using the telephone dial as a keypad and the fax machine as a printer, consumers can request and receive information from magazines around the clock. For example, *Car and Driver* magazine has a road test request service that lists telephone numbers, car, and year codes so that readers can dial up and request, for a fee, reprints of more than 300 road tests that have appeared in the magazine for the past several years.

International markets

Mailing costs and lack of access to lists of potential foreign consumers have slowed the growth of international circulations, but those difficulties may be overcome as international readers begin to show more of an interest in U.S. consumer magazines. Some publications already have successful foreign markets. *Reader's Digest* is read in about 163 countries; *Time* produces about 34 foreign editions; and in April 1994, *Cosmopolitan,* on

168

sale in about 84 countries, became the first major women's magazine published in the former Soviet Union. Recently, Rodale Press, publisher of *Runner's World,* and General Media International, publisher of *Longevity,* launched South African editions of their publications through joint ventures. *Ms.* magazine began distributing in the United Kingdom, Australia, and New Zealand. *National Geographic* and *Time* are exploring the feasibility of launching Japanese-language editions of their magazines. Hearst Corporation has joined with Televisa S.A. of Mexico to have more of its titles translated into Spanish-language editions for the Latin American market. Currently, Spanish-language editions of Hearst's *Cosmopolitan, Harper's Bazaar, Popular Mechanics,* and *Good Housekeeping* are distributed in Latin America. A Canadian edition of *Sports Illustrated,* launched in 1993, encountered protests from Canadian magazine publishers. Under new Canadian government regulations, U.S. companies will have to obtain government approval for future Canadian editions of their magazines. The Canadian government restricts Canadian editions because of its fears about the impact of those magazines on Canada's economy and on Canadian culture.

Media markets are global. This 1997 Time *magazine cover reports the story of global trade; at the same time it represents a commodity traded on the open market.*

Even the very American launching of *George* magazine in September 1995 represents internationalism in the magazine industry. Hachette Filipacci Magazines invested $20 million in *George,* the magazine that combines politics, entertainment, and celebrity worship under the guidance of John F. Kennedy, Jr. The cover of the first issue showed model Cindy Crawford dressed as George Washington. What could be more American than a magazine named after the first U.S. President being run by a former President's son? Not much, except perhaps an American owner of the magazine.

Hachette Filipacci, which publishes twenty-two magazine titles and ranks fourth among U.S. magazine companies, is a subsidiary of Hachette Filipacci USA, Inc. HF USA is associated with Marta-Hachette, a French publishing conglomerate that has become one of the most active media companies in Europe. Marta-Hachette has several subsidiaries involved in selling mobile telephones and satellite services around the world, distributing magazines and books in Canada, developing Europe Online, producing French films, and even producing CD-ROM reference works, such as encyclopedias.

Marta-Hachette, in turn, is controlled by the Lagardere Group, which also owns Marta Defense. This company produces Exocet missiles, which were used by Iraq in 1987 to kill thirty-seven sailors on the USS *Stark.*

Connecting John F. Kennedy, Jr., to Exocet missiles defies logic, but the elaborate web of corporate connections found in the Lagardere companies illustrates the growing complexity of global media conglomerates and their associated businesses. Which company owns which media in which countries with what effect has become an important issue.

Summary

- Magazines developed in colonial America as a forum for the essay. Magazines helped to develop the nation's social conscience.

- Limited technology and lack of an economic base, together with a primitive postal system, hampered the development of the American magazine industry.

- Rapidly advancing technology and mass marketing of goods reduced production costs and created an advertising base that fostered magazine development.

- A rising middle class, increased public education, and the opportunity for social advancement encouraged a reading audience. By 1900 that educated middle class used magazines as the medium for social protest.

- Magazines survived competition from radio and television by targeting groups of readers. This specialization was attractive to both the audience and the advertiser.

- In today's market, specialization is key. Consumer magazines and literary journals make up the bulk of magazine publishing.

- Huge business conglomerates are the primary owners of magazines. However, in response to the recession of the early 1990s, magazine publishers are downsizing and decentralizing.

- Many new magazines do not survive. Those that do have solid financial backing, a specific advertiser base, and a staff of highly trained professionals.

- Demographic changes force magazines to attract new audiences. Magazines must meet the needs of changing audiences and of advertisers.

- Combined—or converging—technologies foster new methods of production and distribution. Magazine publishers increasingly are enhancing their products with CD-ROM delivery or add-ons, online magazines, and fax sections.

- Despite the impact of new technologies, magazines will continue to function as important generators of a national conversation about political and social issues.

Navigating the Web

Magazines on the web

Magazine Web sites include sites for the magazines, sites for companies that publish magazines, and sites for information about the industry. Although industry information and company sites are usually free, some magazine sites require users to purchase a subscription.

The following sites provide information about the industry and companies:

| Veronis, Suhler & Associates Magazine Industry Data | http://www.vsacom.com/pr/prmagcif96.htm |

This site carries summary data about the magazine industry, including income figures and predictions about the industry.

| Miller Freeman, Inc. | www.mfi.com |

This is the home page for the Miller Freeman Corporation, which publishes seventy business and trade publications. It contains information about the magazines and the company.

| Ziff-Davis Magazines | www.zdnet.com/home/filter/mags.html |

Ziff-Davis is one of the largest publishers of computer and electronic media magazines. This site connects to the texts of magazines published by Ziff-Davis, including *PC Magazine* and *Family PC.*

Some magazines online:

People	http://pathfinder.com/@@tz8pjwQAvidU1ffg/people/
Business Week	http://www.businesweek.com
PC Magazine	http://www.pcmag.com

Questions for review

1. Why were magazines slow to develop in early America?
2. How did mass production affect magazines?
3. How are magazines financed?
4. How is technology used for distribution?

Issues to think about

1. What social roles have magazines occupied?
2. How are economics and cultural issues intertwined in magazine development?
3. Should magazine editors and consumers be concerned about influence on content by advertisers? If so, why?
4. What are the advantages and disadvantages of conglomerate ownership?

■ Suggested readings

Fredette, Jean M. *Handbook for Magazine Article Writing* (Cincinnati: Writer's Digest, 1988).

John, Arthur. *The Best Years of the Century* (Urbana: University of Illinois Press, 1981).

Rivers, William L. *Free-Lancer and Staff Writer* (Belmont, CA: Wadsworth Publishing Co., 1992).

Vincent, Theodore G., ed. *Voices of a Black Nation: Political Journalism in the Harlem Renaissance* (San Francisco: Ramparts Press, 1973).

Wilson, Christopher. "The Rhetoric of Consumption: Mass-Market Magazines and the Demise of the Gentle Reader, 1880–1920," in *The Culture of Consumption,* Richard Wightman Fox and T. J. Jackson Lears, eds. (New York: Pantheon, 1983), pp. 39–64.

Wilson, Harold S. *McClure's Magazine and the Muckrakers* (Princeton, NJ: Princeton University Press, 1970).

7 The Movies

When I was a child, my grandmother often entertained us children by telling stories about going to the movies. She vividly recalled standing in front of the box office, holding her brother's hand, waiting to pay the dime it took to get into a movie. Movie houses in the cities were elaborately decorated with gold paint and velvet curtains, yet the weekend matinees catered to children. In summertime, the movie house offered a cool respite from the beating sun. Once she was in the movie house, my grandmother said, she could believe she was Greta Garbo or Lauren Bacall, elegant and beautiful, full of courage and fancy-free. My grandmother's fantasies, cultivated assiduously during adolescence, were played out in the plots and characters of the dramatic films she so loved.

The suspense of movies such as Twister *transports the audience to another place. Movies have served as dream factories and flights of fancy for generations of Americans.*

The popular movie epitomized the American hope for success. "Above all, Hollywood captures the popular imagination," wrote Douglas Gomery, "because it is still the nation's (and the world's) 'dream machine,' projecting private hopes and fantasies and fears onto a big screen for all to see and share."[1]

Child psychologist Dr. Bruno Bettelheim wrote that as an adolescent he went to the movies as often as he could and that they "provided unique opportunities for letting down one's defenses and experimenting with being in love. . . . I do not recall having ever laughed as heartily and unrestrainedly as I did when watching funny scenes in these pleasure palaces. In fact, watching the movies thus carried me away so that I was no longer quite myself. Instead, we were part of the world of the moving picture."[2]

Fascination with the moving picture has focused on the way in which entertainment appeals to certain psychological needs: to have a fantasy life, to be loved, to be beautiful, to take one's place in the world. Films have helped to create culture as well as perceptions of society and culture. However, because films have been financed by commercial, often large corporate interests, the cultural perspectives are related to the industry's desire for profit. From the beginning, critics were interested in the impact of film, although they usually worried more about declining standards of morality than about commercialization. Parents, community censorship boards, voluntary associations, and religious interests all believed that film would have a major impact on the nation's youth. Today, critics are still concerned about the cultural influence of film.

As you read this chapter, consider the following issues facing film makers and those who are interested in the impact of movie making and moviegoing:

■ Does film viewing have economic and cultural impacts on American life? If so, how would you describe these impacts? Are films significant in shaping the culture of our future?

■ Economic interests are an important component of film making. How do you think corporate interests and the studio system have contributed to (or limited) the subject matter and impact of film?

■ Increasingly, film production houses are internationally owned. How will this increased international economic concentration affect film as a "culture machine"?

■ How do you think new technologies will affect the production and delivery of film and its convergence with other media?

Film viewers can choose different settings in which to see films in a variety of technological formats. "Movies in Your Life" outlines some of the choices available and points out that different types of viewing may serve different functions.

Film in American life

Louis Giannetti and Scott Eyman wrote that moving pictures were, for some, "art, science and schooling all in one."[3] They also are—and have been since 1920—big business. The emergence of moving pictures was part of American experimentation with entertainment during the 1880s and 1890s that included concert saloons, peep shows, and vaudeville variety acts.

Technological and economic development

The fascination with pictures in motion goes back to ancient Greek and Arab civilizations, but not until the mid-1800s did technology make such pictures available to broad audiences. Motion pictures evolved from two sets of developing technologies: experimentation with photographic processes and development of moving picture devices.

Movies in your life

How Do You Watch Movies?

College students are major consumers of movies. How important are they to your life? As you read this chapter, think about the different ways in which you view movies. Do you think these habits of you and your friends influence the movie industry? What do your friends think?

FORM OF VIEWING	TYPE OF FILM	TIME/DAY	PURPOSE OF VIEWING
Movie Theater			
Broadcast TV			
Cable TV			
VCR/Rental			
VCR/Own Film			
VCR/Library			
Computer			
Other (please specify)			

Take a moment to think about how the form, type, and function of movies you view are intertwined. Do you view movies on videocassette for relaxation and in a theater for social reasons? Do your goals differ when you view movies in different places? Are the results different? For example, do large-screen films viewed in a theater have a greater impact on you than does a film viewed on a VCR? Is form—or the convergence of technology—affecting the impact, the content, or the use of film? As you read this chapter, you will see that the movie industry is concerned about some of the very same considerations that influenced you in responding to these issues.

Photographic processes that evolved in the mid-nineteenth century paved the way for moving pictures. By the late nineteenth century, a French scientist had developed a camera that produced twelve pictures on a single plate. The development of gelatin emulsions and the production of celluloid during the 1880s furthered photographic technology. In 1878, Eadweard Muybridge achieved a sense of motion by positioning cameras at different intervals along a race track and arranging for the shutters to click in sequence. In 1892, Thomas Edison's labs produced the **Kinetoscope,** a device that moved loops of film over a series of spools.

A contemporary observer wrote,

The ends of the film are joined, forming an endless band passing over two guide drums near the top of the case. One of these drums is driven by motor and feeds the film along by means of sprocket teeth which engage with perforations along the edges of the film. Just above the film is a shutter wheel having five spokes and a very small rectangular

Kinetoscope: A box-like mechanism used to view short films during the late 1800s. The viewer looked into an opening and watched film move past a light bulb.

opening in the rim directly over the film. An incandescent lamp . . . is placed below the film between the two guide drums, and the light passes up through the film, shutter opening, and magnifying lens . . . to the eye of the observer placed at the opening in the top of the case.[4]

This new technology set the stage for the peep show, which featured short films that could be viewed by looking through a viewfinder on a machine about the size of an upright piano. Kinetoscopes became popular in hotel lobbies and other public places, but they never produced the great profits Edison had anticipated.

Keyconcept

The Vaudeville Show as Early Movie Theater: In the early 1900s, popular comedy, dramatic skits, or song-and-dance entertainment was presented in local vaudeville theaters. Early silent films, usually with piano accompaniment, were also shown in these theaters.

Vaudeville provided the entertainment milieu in which technical projection developed as a form of theater. Vaudeville acts were popular from the beginning of the nineteenth century, though their form and acceptance varied with specific historical periods. Until the 1880s, vaudeville was considered legitimate theater and appealed to all classes. During industrialization in the late 1800s, audiences developed a greater sense of class consciousness, and upper-class theatergoers began to object to the "lower class" that cheered and booed from the galleries. The upper class then excluded the working class from theater, and variety acts became more important as entertainment in working-class neighborhoods, often in saloons. However, entertainment entrepreneurs, not content to appeal only to a drinking crowd, sought to establish vaudeville in its own theater environment that would attract working-class and middle-class audiences. Once variety moved back to the stage—this time as its own genre rather than as an extension of theater—it was established as vaudeville with high appeal to the middle class. In this environment, entrepreneurs marketing new technologies made inroads.

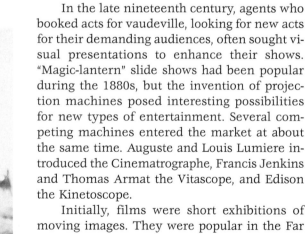

Short action films were among the first popular films to appear in theaters of the early 1900s. One of these, Edwin Porter's The Great Train Robbery, *helped to launch the popularity of the cowboy movie.*

In the late nineteenth century, agents who booked acts for vaudeville, looking for new acts for their demanding audiences, often sought visual presentations to enhance their shows. "Magic-lantern" slide shows had been popular during the 1880s, but the invention of projection machines posed interesting possibilities for new types of entertainment. Several competing machines entered the market at about the same time. Auguste and Louis Lumiere introduced the Cinematrographe, Francis Jenkins and Thomas Armat the Vitascope, and Edison the Kinetoscope.

Initially, films were short exhibitions of moving images. They were popular in the Far East, Europe, and the United States. Between 1896 and 1903, travelogues, local features, comedy, and news often were the subjects of short films. Depictions of movement also were used to create a physiological thrill. In 1903, Edwin Porter produced two American films, *Life of an American Fireman* and *The Great Train Robbery.* These twelve-minute productions pioneered storytelling techniques in film and led the way to the development of feature films.

The Lion King and New Technology

Just as the Kinetoscope was an important technological development for showing films, so is computer technology—this time in the form of the CD-ROM. But for thousands of children who opened their Christmas packages in 1994 to discover *The Lion King* on CD-ROM, disappointment reigned supreme. Many of the CD-ROMs didn't work.

Disney, the trusted producer of media for kids, had been struggling hard to match the advances of companies such as Broderbund and Electronic Arts in children's software. So for Christmas of 1994, Disney spent $3 million in advertising to promote the 300,000 CD-ROMs stocked in the Kmarts and Wal-Marts of America. The campaign was timed to coincide with the rerelease of the hit film *The Lion King.*

Disney ran into trouble because it released the CD-ROM with known glitches, falsely assuming that the glitches would affect only a few out-of-date computers. Disney was wrong. From December 26 onward, angry messages flooded Disney by mail and telephone, as well as through the new technology of the computer.

Nevertheless, kids who got CD-ROMs that were compatible with their home computers loved the program. Preliminary testers at *Home PC* magazine loved the eighteen screens of narrative and three interactive games.

SOURCE: Frederick Rose and Richard Turner, " 'Lion King' CD-ROM Takes a Bite out of Disney," *The Orlando Sentinel,* January 29, 1995, p. H-1.

Films were shown in the vaudeville theaters and by traveling showmen, who projected them at tent shows or fairs. By 1906, storefronts known as **nickelodeons** exhibited films that attracted working-class audiences. To broaden their audience, nickelodeon operators began moving their operations into theaters and adding one or two vaudeville acts to broaden the attraction. This small-time vaudeville relied more heavily on motion picture entertainment and less on live acts than did the traditional variety show. By 1910, nickelodeons attracted 26 million Americans each week, a little less than 20 percent of the national population. By 1914, the weekly audience had increased to 49 million.[5] The moving picture was now considered respectable middle-class entertainment, and theaters expanded in middle-class neighborhoods and small towns.

In 1908, a variety of companies were competing in the movie industry. Industry leaders were spending so much energy defending their patents and jockeying for position that, in an effort to increase profit and to standardize the industry, they decided to form a monopoly. Led by the Edison Manufacturing Company and the American Mutoscope and Biograph Company, they formed a trust called the Motion Picture Patents Company (MPPC). Creating trusts was a common business strategy in the late nineteenth century to acquire and pool patents. For a short time, the MPPC controlled production of raw film, manufacture of motion picture and projection equipment, distribution, and exhibition. All members were required to purchase film from the Eastman Kodak Company, and the company refused to sell to outsiders.

nickelodeon: Small storefront functioning as a theater; popular about 1910. These preceded the grand movie palaces.

178

The trust was dissolved in 1915 because of the government's success in *United States v. Motion Picture Patents Co.,* an antitrust case against the MPPC. The MPPC certainly had increased its own profits and was known for its strong-arm tactics, which included raiding independent studios and smashing equipment. However, it had also ended squabbles among different segments of the American film industry and had improved film quality. Through competition and standardized distribution and exhibition practices, the MPPC helped to create an internationally competitive motion picture industry.[6]

Although members of the MPPC had tried to eliminate independent movie production, its standardization of production and distribution became too rigid. The MPPC clung to the concept of short films and at first rejected the multiple-reel feature films that became successful during the teens. Independents saw big feature films as a way to gain a market niche and sought financing on Wall Street. By 1915, the MPPC was gone and independents were producing feature films. Film exhibition moved from the storefront nickelodeon and the small vaudeville houses to theaters that were designed exclusively for the showing of movies. The movies had become big business.

Movie palaces like this one in New York attracted upper class audiences.

The audience and new expectations

When D.W. Griffith's long, controversial and popular feature film *Birth of a Nation* opened in New York's Liberty Theater on March 3, 1915, it established the importance of feature films. The three-hour film was based on a popular novel published in 1905 that had become a successful play. This story of the aftermath of the Civil War roused enormous controversy because of its underlying racist message. The film depicted a Northern family and a Southern family adapting to the post-war period, but the point of view was decidedly Southern. African Americans who were not loyal to their Southern masters were depicted as subhuman. The last half of the film was dominated by Ku Klux Klan activity that would never

Pioneer film maker D.W. Griffith perfected the art of cinematic continuity and storytelling necessary for the modern feature film. His film Birth of a Nation, *a controversial story dependent on racial stereotypes, was a box-office hit, but his subsequent film* Intolerance, *loaded with pacifist scenes, failed to gain an audience on the eve of World War I.*

be condoned today. Nevertheless, the film opened to a packed audience. Each audience member paid two dollars for a reserved seat, an orchestra accompanied the performance, and costumed ushers handed out souvenir programs. The exhibition format resembled that of an upper-class theater. The film played for forty-four consecutive weeks at the Liberty and showed in leading theaters across the United States, breaking records and generating controversy because of its racist tones. The three-hour production yielded $5 million on an investment of less than $100,000.

Griffith's follow-up picture, *Intolerance,* ran three and one-half hours, and although the film is regarded as an artistic classic, it failed miserably to reward its financial backers. Griffith, who personally stood behind the losses, never recovered financially.

Why did *Intolerance* fail? Critics debate the issue. Griffith's message of love, tolerance, and the uselessness of war might have been popular before 1916, when Americans were resisting involvement in what many considered a European war. However, by 1916, when the film was released, the message alienated many viewers as the United States prepared to go to war.

Griffith made other successful films, but he was a poor businessman and always struggled with finances. By 1920, he was one of the few filmmakers left on the East Coast, and his films were no longer regarded as ground-breaking. Nevertheless, Griffith's innovative film techniques redefined the expectations of film audiences. He created grand epics with spectacular scenery and introduced lighting and **editing** techniques that established film as a medium for exploring social and cultural themes.

Sound and money

Companies that experimented early with adding sound to motion pictures were the first to realize vast profits from introducing the technology, but this introduction also changed the industry economically. Once big money was needed for big technology, few companies could make the switch without help from the bankers. The adoption of sound also signaled a solidifying of big business interests.

As audience reaction to feature films and the appearance of stars ensured that movies would indeed continue to be an important entertainment medium, companies such as Western Electric, Warner Bros., and Fox experimented to develop technology for sound, hoping that it would accelerate profits. Although some critics thought such investments were a waste of money, sound soon became accepted through an economic process of invention, innovation, and diffusion.[7] In 1926, Warner formed the Vitaphone Corporation in association with Western Electric, a subsidiary of American Telephone & Telegraph Co., to make sound pictures and to market sound production equipment. Although Warner lost $1 million in 1926, the loss was anticipated and was necessary to finance the expansion. Vitaphone initiated a sales campaign to encourage exhibitors to introduce sound equipment. Such planning paved the way for the success of *The Jazz Singer,* which premiered in October 1926. Because Warner was first to market sound, it earned extraordinary profits. During the last half of the 1920s, Warner was able to solidify its position by acquiring other companies with production and exhibition facilities.

After the success of *The Jazz Singer,* most of the major companies rushed to switch to sound. RCA, which had developed a competing sound system called Photophone, merged the new sound company with a motion picture giant, the Radio-Keith-Orpheum Corporation, and the Keith-Albee-Orpheum circuit of vaudeville houses into a massive firm. Major companies had signed long-term, exclusive contracts with AT&T, but RCA challenged the giant with unlawful restraint of trade and reached an out-of-court settlement in 1935. By 1943, RCA supplied about 60 percent of all sound equipment. Production costs rose as a result of the

editing: The joining of two pieces of film; this technique allows for moving images into different time sequences.

180

new technology. The major companies and studios were able to make the capital investment needed to switch to sound, but smaller independent companies did not have enough financial backing or capital to make the transition. Many of the independents simply closed their doors or sold out to the bigger companies. By 1930, the industry was an **oligopoly.**

The studio system

By the 1920s, the movie industry had moved to California, where the studios could use nearby locations to depict desert, mountain, or ocean scenes and the weather permitted year-round filming. However, many decisions affecting the industry were made in New York offices by film company executives. The corporate CEOs (such as Harry Warner, Nicholas Schenck of Loew's/MGM, and Joseph M. Schenck of Fox) made the most important decisions, such as the number of films to be produced in any given season, total production budgets, the number of **A and B pictures,** and, finally the pictures themselves. Once the president had prepared a release schedule, the head of the studio took over. But those who controlled the business aspects of the industry made the most important creative and business decisions. Because they valued stability, they stuck with popular stars in familiar roles. In this way, economic structures affected film style and content.

Unlike the CEOs, the heads of the studios were familiar to the public: Louis B. Mayer at MGM, Darryl Zanuck at Twentieth-Century Fox, and Jack Warner at Warner. The heads promoted and negotiated contracts with the stars, ensured that production schedules were met, and assigned material to producers.

Stars, despite their glamour, had little control over their own lives; the studios controlled many of their personal and private actions. Their contracts usually ran for seven years, the studio being able to drop or renew the contract yearly. A star who rebelled could be loaned out to work for other studios on pictures that had little chance of succeeding. Further, stars were cast repetitively in similar roles. Once the studio discovered someone with star potential and groomed the actor, it tried to stay with the winning formula. Such formulaic casting made it difficult for stars to get more demanding roles. Publicity departments at the big studios promoted the stars and worked to make sure the public would view each star in a particular wholesome but glamorous light.

Domination by the big five

By 1930, five companies dominated United States movie screens: Warner Bros.; Loew's, Inc., the theater chain that owned Metro-Goldwyn-Mayer; Paramount; RKO; and Twentieth-Century Fox. Each company was vertically integrated, producing motion pictures and operating worldwide distribution outlets and a theater chain. Three other companies—Universal, Columbia, and United Artists—had significant holdings but no chain of theaters. Universal and Columbia supplied pictures to the majors, and United Artists was a distribution company for a small group of independents. Theaters owned by the

Keyconcept

The Star System: By the 1930s and 1940s the New York–financed Hollywood studios had developed a system for ensuring financial stability based on movies featuring popular stars in familiar roles. Iron-clad contracts forced actors and actresses to accept scripts that enhanced the particular image the studio wanted the star to project. Stars were also required to behave as their fans expected them to, both inside and outside the studio.

oligopoly: A business situation in which a few dominant companies control enough of the business that each one's actions will have a significant impact on actions of the others.

A & B pictures: Studios commission or produce two types of films. A films are usually high budget films that studios expect to be box office hits. B films are low budget films that are basic money-makers. Studios invest little money in their production and marketing.

big five companies took in more than 75 percent of the nation's box-office receipts. Through the 1930s and 1940s, these eight companies defined Hollywood.

The Depression of the 1930s caused movie revenues to plummet. The major studio companies had difficulty meeting their financial obligations. They had overextended themselves in a market that was declining rather than expanding.

When President Franklin D. Roosevelt introduced the National Recovery Act, with provisions for cutting competition among industries, the federal government allowed the big five to continue practices that they had already established to limit competition. These included **block booking** (requiring all theaters to buy a season's package of films rather than individual productions) and **blind booking** (forcing a theater owner to rent a season's package of films sight unseen). The NRA also allowed the companies to continue the **vertical integration** they had established, which brought them great profits. In return, the studios were supposed to make certain concessions. Although the studios had vociferously opposed unionization, now they readily recognized trade unions of production personnel, which formed some of the least expensive parts of the business, as a way of complying with the act. However, they continued to fight to keep creative personnel outside the collective bargaining system.

Growth in the domestic market

When World War II began, the film industry lost most of its worldwide business that had been established during the late 1930s, despite an attempt to appeal to Latin American audiences. But the domestic market improved dramatically, since Americans were earning relatively high wages and had few commodities on which to spend them. Movies were affordable and available. Domestic **studio film rentals** for the eight major studios increased from $193 million in 1939 to $332 million in 1946. In this peak year, an average of 90 million Americans, or 75 percent of the population, went to the movies each week.

Key concept

The Domestic Film Market and the Big Five: By 1930 five giant Hollywood studios dominated world filmmaking: Metro-Goldwyn-Mayer (MGM), Paramount, RKO, Twentieth-Century Fox, and Warner Bros. World War II cut Hollywood off from film markets abroad, but demand for movies intensified in the domestic market, that is, the market within the United States.

Post–World War II decline

The movie business declined at the end of the war—even before the rise of television. Returning soldiers bought houses in the suburbs, went back to college on the GI bill, and started families. The decline in movie attendance paralleled a restructuring of the industry after the Supreme Court in 1948, in *United States* v. *Paramount Pictures, Inc., et al.,* forced the companies to divest themselves of their theater chains and thus limited the vertical integration that had been the norm for thirty years. The Supreme Court's *Paramount* decision ended block booking, fixing of admission prices, and other discriminatory practices, which were declared to be in restraint of trade.

With the *Paramount* decision came increased freedom for producers and stars. Although the major companies continued to dominate the industry, the number of independent producers more than doubled from 1946 to 1956. In response, the major studios competed to provide space and facilities for such producers. Foreign films had

block booking: The practice of forcing a theater to book movies as a package, rather than individually. Declared illegal in the 1940s.

blind booking: Marketing strategy common in the 1930s and 1940s that required theaters to book movies before they were produced.

vertical integration: A system in which a single corporation controls production, distribution, and exhibition of movies. Declared illegal in the 1940s.

studio film rentals: Studios rent films they produce to distributors and/or theaters.

182

more access to the U.S. market, and small **art theaters** sprang up, particularly in university towns and large urban areas. Stars were more reluctant to sign long-term, exclusive contracts, so their talent became more widely available.

Nevertheless, the big companies continued to dominate the production business, both at home and abroad. Because access to American movies had been limited during the war and many European production facilities were shut down, studios made huge profits from European rentals. Foreign operations, both rentals and production, continued to gain importance; by the 1960s, more than half the revenue of the major studios came from operations overseas.

■ Response to television

By the early 1950s, the movies had a major contender for audiences' time: television. For young families with children, television was simpler and less expensive than going to the movies. For older people, television did not require as much effort. The motion picture industry was forced to respond, using its natural advantages. Studios produced more films in color, experimented with screen size and introduced **Cinerama** and **3-D.** The most lasting innovation was **Panavision,** introduced by Fox in 1962, which gave the illusion of depth without seeming contrived.

More significantly, the industry began to collaborate with television. In 1949, Columbia converted a subsidiary into a television department that produced programs for *Ford Theater* and the comedy series *Father Knows Best.* In 1953, when television made the transition from live to filmed production, Hollywood became the center for television production.

By 1955, Hollywood was also releasing many of its older pictures for television broadcasting. For example, RKO sold its film library to a television programming syndicate for $15 million. During the 1960s, however, the studios realized that they had undervalued their old films. ABC paid Columbia $2 million for the 1957 film *The Bridge on the River Kwai,* and when the film was shown on television on September 12, 1966, sixty million people watched. Television became a regular market for films, and competitive bidding continued to rise.

In the late 1960s, studios began producing made-for-television movies. In television movies, production costs were kept low, and these movies soon glutted the market and diminished the demand for older movies. Between television movies and acquired film libraries, the networks discovered that they had enough films stocked for several years and stopped bidding for studio productions. The studios retrenched, but by 1972 they were again selling to the networks. ABC, the youngest network, increased its ratings and forced CBS and NBC to be more competitive. The three networks bid the prices of movies such as *Alien* as high as $15 million. When cable became widespread in the 1980s, movies became an even hotter commodity. Film ultimately benefited from converging technologies. The coming of television and cable increased film viewing.

Keyconcept

Film Competition and Collaboration with Television: In the 1950s the movie industry, desperate to recapture audiences lost to television, competed by offering technical novelties, including 3-D, which remained a novelty, and wide-screen Panavision, which was a success. Soon Hollywood also collaborated with television, providing studio facilities for making innovative TV series.

art theater: Theater that shows films designed for their artistic quality rather than for their blockbuster audience appeal. These films usually are produced by independent companies rather than by the big studios.

Cinerama: Trade name for process that produces wide-screen images.

3-D: Film technique that produces 3-D images; required viewers to wear special glasses.

Panavision: System of lenses used in filming. It enables a film shot in one wide screen version (Cinemascope, for example) to be shown in a theater without the lenses for that type of projection.

183

The movie industry responded to television first with denial, then with cooperation. An early Hollywood made-for-television mini series was crafted from The Thornbirds, *a popular romantic novel by Colleen McCullogh. The four-episode broadcast starred Rachel Ward and Richard Chamberlin.*

The development of cable television and direct satellite broadcasting has altered the use of movies on television. Home Box Office (HBO), a cable television channel that began operation in 1972, allowed its subscribers to see movies after their theatrical release but before the major broadcast networks could acquire them. HBO's success led to the establishment of other premium channels, such as Showtime and Cinemax.

In the 1990s, the expansion of channels made possible by fiber-optic cable allowed cable companies to offer pay-per-view movies. These differ from premium channels in that the viewer pays for each viewing. Pay-per-view makes films available to the cable subscriber at the same time as the movie appears in video stores, before it appears on a channel such as HBO. Some hotels even offer pay-per-view showings of movies that are currently in first-run movie theaters.

Increasingly, movies, whether made for theaters or directly for television, have become a basic building block of television content. The strong film libraries held by Disney, TBS, and Time Warner were important factors in the mergers between Disney and Capitol Cities/ABC and between Turner Broadcasting System and Time Warner. Television and theaters are no longer competitors. Instead, they are different distribution systems for reaching viewers.

Cultural and political development

Until 1952, movies did not receive First Amendment protection; the rationale was that they were not a "significant medium for the communication of ideas," but a simple amusement, like a circus. At the same time, civic and religious groups fought against movies and tried to institute censorship because they feared the power of the movies. Early research labeled movies as emotionally powerful. These contradictory views persist. But through the generations, the movies—America's dream factories—have given generations of children, adolescents, and adults the opportunity to escape from routinized work, from inhibition, and from the doldrums of everyday life.

Movies as art and social commentary

The studio, the star system, and a system of genres enabled the Hollywood studios to maximize profits. They also guaranteed that a certain type of movie would emanate from Hollywood. Americans left intellectual movies to foreign producers. During the silent era, slapstick comedies, westerns, and melodramas were the most popular **genres.** However, D. W. Griffith and his contemporaries in the teens and early twenties introduced more sophisticated narratives dominated by characters who were not only goal-oriented, but also in a hurry to succeed. These narrative structures were linear and came almost directly from the stage. Griffith's *The Birth of a Nation,* for example, was a stage play before he adapted it to film.

genre: A kind or style of movie.

184 (M)ovies in our lives

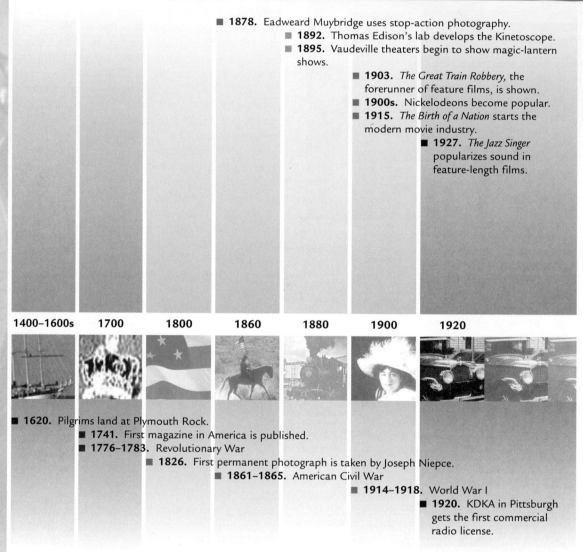

■ **1878.** Eadweard Muybridge uses stop-action photography.
■ **1892.** Thomas Edison's lab develops the Kinetoscope.
■ **1895.** Vaudeville theaters begin to show magic-lantern shows.
■ **1903.** *The Great Train Robbery*, the forerunner of feature films, is shown.
■ **1900s.** Nickelodeons become popular.
■ **1915.** *The Birth of a Nation* starts the modern movie industry.
■ **1927.** *The Jazz Singer* popularizes sound in feature-length films.

| 1400–1600s | 1700 | 1800 | 1860 | 1880 | 1900 | 1920 |

■ **1620.** Pilgrims land at Plymouth Rock.
■ **1741.** First magazine in America is published.
■ **1776–1783.** Revolutionary War
■ **1826.** First permanent photograph is taken by Joseph Niepce.
■ **1861–1865.** American Civil War
■ **1914–1918.** World War I
■ **1920.** KDKA in Pittsburgh gets the first commercial radio license.

Gangster pictures, musicals, and screwball comedies became popular during the talkie era, and the studio and star systems propelled Hollywood to produce big-budget spectaculars. Yet despite the emphasis on popular culture films and the box office, Hollywood managed to produce, sometimes by accident, lasting classics such as *Mr. Roberts* and *The Maltese Falcon.* Certain artistic directors earned international recognition. For example, Orson Welles wrote, directed, and starred in *Citizen Kane* in 1941, when he was twenty-six years old, and became known throughout the world for his contribution to cinematic technique. *Citizen Kane* was based loosely on the life of newspaper tycoon William Randolph Hearst. Welles included unusual camera angles, backlighting, and condensed time sequences and introduced other film techniques that continue to influence movie

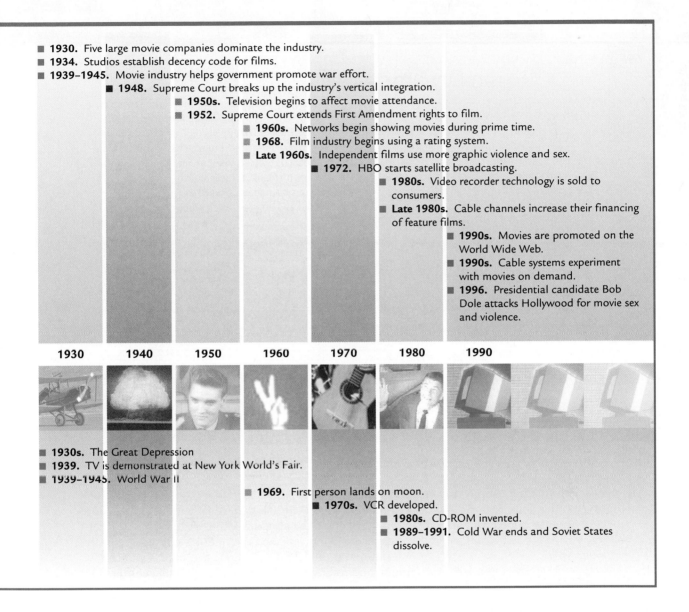

■ **1930.** Five large movie companies dominate the industry.
■ **1934.** Studios establish decency code for films.
■ **1939–1945.** Movie industry helps government promote war effort.
　　■ **1948.** Supreme Court breaks up the industry's vertical integration.
　　　　■ **1950s.** Television begins to affect movie attendance.
　　　　■ **1952.** Supreme Court extends First Amendment rights to film.
　　　　　■ **1960s.** Networks begin showing movies during prime time.
　　　　　■ **1968.** Film industry begins using a rating system.
　　　　　■ **Late 1960s.** Independent films use more graphic violence and sex.
　　　　　　■ **1972.** HBO starts satellite broadcasting.
　　　　　　　■ **1980s.** Video recorder technology is sold to consumers.
　　　　　　　■ **Late 1980s.** Cable channels increase their financing of feature films.
　　　　　　　　■ **1990s.** Movies are promoted on the World Wide Web.
　　　　　　　　■ **1990s.** Cable systems experiment with movies on demand.
　　　　　　　　■ **1996.** Presidential candidate Bob Dole attacks Hollywood for movie sex and violence.

| 1930 | 1940 | 1950 | 1960 | 1970 | 1980 | 1990 |

■ **1930s.** The Great Depression
■ **1939.** TV is demonstrated at New York World's Fair.
■ **1939–1945.** World War II
　　■ **1969.** First person lands on moon.
　　　■ **1970s.** VCR developed.
　　　　■ **1980s.** CD-ROM invented.
　　　　■ **1989–1991.** Cold War ends and Soviet States dissolve.

makers today. Many film critics consider *Citizen Kane* to be the greatest American film ever made. However, it was a box-office failure when it was released because Hearst used his immense power in the newspaper and entertainment industries to encourage negative reviews and to force theater owners to boycott the film.

From the 1940s to the early 1960s, films used a narrative structure that featured wholesome heroes and heroines. Although there were attempts at **social realism,** such as Tennessee Williams's *A Streetcar Named Desire,* positive tones and outcomes dominated the big screens. In *Streetcar,* Marlon Brando played Stanley Kowalski, a brooding, unkempt anti-hero who brutalizes both his wife and her sister. With the 1960s, film

social realism: Films that are critical of the social structure.

Hoop Dreams

*T*he film production process, an unstable merger of commerce and art, dependent on collective initiative and collective response, is intimately interwoven with the mentalité of society. What succeeds at a given time in the movies and what is remembered later (often two separate things) obviously offer historians significant clues to the tastes, hopes, fears, myths, interior vibrations of the age.

—ARTHUR SCHLESINGER, JR.

Hoop Dreams, a hit documentary in 1994, "intimately interwoven with the mentalité of society," was a comment on the ghetto society and commercial exploitation that drive young black men to see playing professional basketball as the only possible way to succeed. The documentary is based on the legendary inner city basketball courts where young black men perfect techniques to attract mostly white coaches, agents, and corporate executives. Watching

Hoop Dreams, no viewer can "quite emancipate himself from his age and country."

Hoop Dreams is the story of two young black men, Arthur Agee and William Gates, who are recruited from different parts of Chicago by a suburban private high school to play basketball. Because of financial problems, Arthur must drop out of the suburban school. At his inner city public schools, he neglects his studies. He endures family upheavals caused by his father's drug problem, fathers two children, and ends up at a junior college because he cannot pass his SAT tests with the minimum score required by the NCAA. William remains at the suburban school and becomes a basketball star until his knee is injured. He also fathers a child, but he is determined that life will be different for his daughter. Recruited by many colleges, he chooses Marquette University.

Reviews of *Hoop Dreams,* a comment on the classic struggles of people in search of a dream, revealed the "mentalité of society" as much as did the film itself. The right-of-center *American Spectator* called the film sentimental: "It is sentimentality that has taught them that they are entitled to the most wildly fanci-

---

content and character changed in dramatic ways. Some critics date the shift to the 1967 production of *Bonnie and Clyde,* a movie about two 1930s gangsters, which critic Pauline Kael described as a film of violence that "puts the sting back into death."[8] The strident films of the 1960s reflected the nation's conflicts over the Vietnam War, youthful rebellion, the civil rights movement, and militant black power efforts. Social conflict and social statement films dominated the decade and the early 1970s. After 1977 and the production of *Star Wars,* a science fiction epic, many films turned to escapism. Film makers also moved away from the structured narrative that had dominated through the 1960s to more episodic narratives with less foreshadowed endings. Heroes were sometimes amoral, and sex, often fused with violence rather than with romance, moved onto the screen in unprecedented fashion. *M*A*S*H* (1970) depicted interrelationships between characters thrown together in a medical unit during the Korean War. The exploits of the medical team were told in episodic fashion.

Many traditional film themes are repeatedly played out in film making today. The classic western with loner good-guy cowboy repeats itself in films about loner heroes in

Key concept

Movie Genres and the A and B Picture: By the 1930s and 1940s the most profitable American film genres included such types as cowboy and gangster movies, featuring strong narratives dominated by characters who were in a hurry to succeed. The studio star system fueled big-budget, *A pictures,* which were of high quality and had well-known stars, while *B pictures* with smaller budgets often appeared as the second movie of a *double feature*—two movies for one price.

ful of ambitions, which then become the excuse for a lifetime of failure and self-deceit."

But *Commentary* also noted, "Aside from the church, there are no 'mediating institutions' to serve the social needs of the population, no organizations to soften the blows of poverty while also ensuring that the poor are equipped to become functioning members of society. It seems, indeed, that the only connections between the Chicago of Arthur Agee and William Gates and the outside world are basketball scouts and welfare checks."

This documentary, widely acclaimed as a modern social statement, failed to be nominated for best documentary by the Motion Picture Academy, the group that awards the Oscars. During the first four months of its release, *Hoop Dreams* earned almost $4 million at the box office, less than most feature films but more than most documentaries. Some critics argued that the Academy spurned it because of its financial success. "It's a crime," fumed Wendy Finerman, a producer of *Forrest Gump*, which received thirteen nominations. "This was one of the best documentaries of all time. The film makers were robbed."

What happened to Arthur and William in real life? In late 1994, both were still in college and playing ball. Arthur Agee's brother was killed in a drug-related shooting. William Gates earned a 3.0 average at Marquette during the spring semester of 1994. He married the mother of his daughter and dropped out of basketball for a while, only to come off the bench at Marquette during his senior year.

SOURCES: Arthur Schlesinger, Jr., "Film and History: An Equivocal Relationship," Patricia Wise Lecture at The American Film Institute, Washington, DC, February 8, 1984, cited in *Hollywood: Legend and Reality,* Michael Webb, ed. (Boston: Little, Brown and Company, 1986), p. 33; James Bowman, "Sweet Dreams," *American Spectator* (December 1994); "Hoop Realities," *Sports Illustrated,* December 12, 1994, p. 18; Richard Corliss, "How The Winner Lost," *Time,* February 27, 1995, p. 66; Mark Gerson, "Hoop Dreams," *Commentary* 99:3 (March 1995), p. 56+.

a postnuclear anarchical society. An Australian film, *The Road Warrior,* exemplifies this category. But characterization varies over time, and moviegoers today see much more complex characters than appeared in the films of the past. During the 1940s "Golden Age of Hollywood," Jimmy Stewart took on corrupt Washington in Frank Capra's *Mr. Smith Goes to Washington,* and Henry Fonda cleaned up Tombstone as Wyatt Earp in John Ford's *My Darling Clementine.* Stephen Amidon in the *Sunday Times* wrote that the regular-guy hero—the competent family man who maintains good humor under stress, whose values are reinforced, and who triumphs over adversity—is no longer the leading Hollywood hero. Rather, the hero who is "a tangle of neurosis and buried trauma" has taken over. "Think," writes Amidon, "of Michael Douglas's sweaty, brutal, unpredictable wanderer in *Falling Down,* or his horny, unprincipled cop in *Basic Instinct.* Think of Mel Gibson's self-mutilating Vietnam vet in *Lethal Weapon.*"[9] Of the highest-grossing films, only a few come from decades before the 1990s. Table 7.1 details these successful films.

Hollywood movies during the 1990s offered a wide variety of choices for viewers. Families helped to push Disney's profits higher and higher with a succession of successful films including *Beauty and the Beast, Aladdin, The Lion King,* and *Pocahontas. Forrest Gump,* a bittersweet look at the 1960s, not only made hundreds of millions of dollars, but also won the Academy Award for best picture of 1994 and gained Tom Hanks a second straight Oscar for best actor.

188

Despite the variety of films being made, **action films** continue to dominate the movie industry. *Independence Day* topped the box office in 1996 with $306.1 million from U.S. theaters. This placed it sixth on the all-time box office films. Close behind in 1996 was *Twister* with $241.7 million in U.S. sales. This trend continued into 1997 with the return of the Star Wars Trilogy. The first of the three, *Star Wars,* grossed $98 million in the first three weeks and became the top grossing domestic film of all time, passing *ET.* This top position seemed short-lived as movie audiences waited for the summer 1997 release of the sequel to *Jurassic Park.* The mid-1990s saw an increase in the use of graphic violence in serious films. Just as *Bonnie and Clyde* earlier shocked viewers with its violence, *Pulp Fiction* and *Natural Born Killers* sparked a discussion about the role of violence in film. Directed by respected film makers Quentin Tarantino and Oliver Stone, respectively, these movies resurrected the question of whether movies reflect reality or create it. Does movie violence simply reveal what happens in some areas of society, or does it shape the cultural world? Whatever the reaction to movie violence, the critical and financial success of these movies will most likely influence other serious directors during the remainder of the decade.

TABLE 7.1 Top Grossing Films in Domestic Market, February 1997

TITLES	IN MILLIONS
Star Wars (1977)	$447.8
ET (1982)	$399.8
Jurassic Park (1993)	$357.1
Forrest Gump (1994)	$329.1
The Lion King (1994)	$312.8
Independence Day (1996)	$306.2
Home Alone (1990)	$285.8
Return of the Jedi (1983)	$263.7
The Empire Strikes Back (1980)	$262.9
Jaws (1975)	$260.0

*Figures not adjusted for inflation.

Sources: Mark Tran, "Force of *Star Wars* Relaunch Dislodges *ET* as Top U.S. Grossing Film," *The Guardian,* February 15, 1997, p. 24; "The Box Office Force Was With Us," *Orange County Register,* January 31, 1997, p. F7.

Movies and the marketplace of ideas

Hollywood has rarely produced explicitly political films. Despite the cultural and social impact of movies, the motion picture was not considered "speech" until 1952 and therefore was not protected by the First Amendment to the U.S. Constitution. In 1915, in *Mutual Film Corp.* v. *Industrial Commission of Ohio,* the U.S. Supreme Court declared that exhibiting films was a business pure and simple. To avoid including film under the protection of the First Amendment, courts for nearly forty years adhered to the "simple business" standard and did not recognize movies as "a significant medium for the communication of ideas." However, in 1952, *Burstyn* v. *Wilson,* the Supreme Court declared that film content entertained and informed and therefore was subject to First Amendment protection.

In 1922, the motion picture industry organized the Motion Picture Producers and Distributors of America (MPPDA) and named Will H. Hays as its president. The move was designed to avoid government regulation and to combat negative publicity about stars, divorce, and the prevalence of drugs in the industry. Twelve years later, a group of American Catholic bishops organized the National Legion of Decency to develop lists of films that were acceptable and not acceptable for

action film: A type of movie that emphasizes physical activities, such as car chases, fighting, and explosions. Such films usually have simple plots and only limited development of the characters. These films often succeed internationally because their simple plots transfer across cultural boundaries.

Catholic viewers. Hollywood responded by establishing a production code that forbade sex, excessive violence, and vulgar language. Violators of the code were to pay a $25,000 fine to the MPPDA, although the fine has never been publicly invoked. The code, although often skirted or challenged, remained on the books until 1968, when the industry adopted a ratings system. The ratings system shifted responsibility to the movie viewer by specifying the type of audience the movie had been designed to attract. In 1984 and again in 1992, the industry revised specific ratings, but the principle of alerting the audience rather than controlling admission remained as the guide.

Key concept

Production Codes and Rating Systems: The film industry, constantly facing pressure to produce exciting films yet avoid moral injury to young audiences, developed a production code, or set of rules, for producing movies to comply with various local government restrictions on immoral entertainment. In 1968 the industry switched from controlling content to informing audiences about the content. The production code was replaced by a system of ratings to identify levels of sexual and violent content and adult language.

Government opinions of the motion picture industry's activity during the war were mixed. Major producers cooperated to produce war films on what they termed a nonprofit basis. Nevertheless, during 1941 and 1942, the Army Pictorial Division alone spent more than $1 million in Hollywood. Critics claimed the producers filmed for the government during slack times, or when the studios otherwise would have stood idle, and that by cooperating, the industry managed to remain relatively untouched by the war. Therefore, despite Walt Disney's portrayal of Donald Duck as a duck willing to pay taxes with patriotic enthusiasm and Frank Capra's direction of the "Why We Fight" series designed to train new soldiers, the motion picture industry still had a variety of enemies in Congress.

The Motion Picture Bureau, a division of Office of War Information (OWI), attempted to influence Hollywood producers to support the war effort. Among its tasks was to try to motivate producers to incorporate more realistic pictures of black life into films. A 1942 survey conducted by the Office of Facts and Figures indicated that 49 percent of Harlem blacks thought they would be no worse off if Japan won the war. In response to this evidence OWI wanted Hollywood to tone down its racist images of blacks to foster a sense of unity in the country.[10]

Although the industry had catered to the Legion of Decency and various economic groups, when OWI attempted to promote more positive images of blacks, the industry cried censorship. For example, MGM in 1938 had hand carried its script of Robert Sherwood's antifascist play, *Idiot's Delight,* to Italy for approval after drastically altering it to avoid offending Benito Mussolini. Warner Bros.' coal mining saga, *Black Fury,* was altered to blame labor unrest on union radicals rather than on mine operators after the National Coal Association protested.

OWI efforts to promote positive African American images had little effect. A 1945 Columbia University study found that of 100 black appearances in wartime films, 75 percent perpetuated stereotypes, 13 were neutral and only 12 were positive. OWI hesitated to push very far, claiming the war came first.[11]

Congressional frustration with the film industry was not limited to its concern about treatment of minorities in wartime. In the late 1940s and 1950s, conservative members of Congress attacked the industry in hearings before the House Committee on Un-American Activities. This committee and Senator Joseph McCarthy's parallel committee in the Senate pummeled the media industries, taking special delight in attacking the motion picture and broadcast industries. Congressman and committee chairman Thomas Parnell intended to prove that the film industry had been infiltrated by Communists who introduced subversive propaganda into the movies.

At the 1947 hearings, ten screenwriters, later dubbed the Hollywood Ten, refused to say whether they had been members of the Communist Party, invoking the First Amendment guarantee of freedom of the press and freedom of association. The Hollywood Ten all went to jail for contempt of Congress. Although recent research shows that these writers had in no way tried to formally propagandize or commit any type of subversion, Hollywood did not stand behind them. Rather, it panicked. Many Hollywood liberals, such as Humphrey Bogart and John Huston, supported the writers initially, but most support disappeared when the heads of the large studios threatened the supporters' careers. The Hollywood Ten were suspended from work, and executives invited Hollywood's talent guilds to help them eliminate any subversives from their ranks.

An anti-Communist witch-hunt fueled attacks on Hollywood stars during the late 1940s and early 1950s. Ten film writers were jailed for refusal to answer trumped-up charges of communist affiliation. A chill-effect followed, with panicky Hollywood executives refusing work to many actors and producers.

From 1951 to 1954, a second round of hearings investigated Hollywood further. Director Elia Kazan, who would later win an Academy Award for *On the Waterfront,* eagerly testified and lost many friends. The result of the hearings was an informal blacklist of actors, directors, writers, and producers whom the major studios would not hire. A few found work with independent production companies, often using false names. The actor Kirk Douglas hired Dalton Trumbo, who had been one of the Hollywood Ten, to write the script for his 1960 blockbuster *Spartacus,* but more than 320 people were blacklisted by the studios.

Once the national scare ended and Senator McCarthy was exposed as an irrational manipulator of fear, the film industry enjoyed relative freedom from government interference and regulation. Even during the 1990s, with renewed emphasis by some special interest groups on family values, Congressional rhetoric and action focused more intensely on the television industry than on film. While campaigning for the Republican presidential nomination in 1995, Senator Bob Dole attacked Time Warner for its production of violent films, but within the context of the entertainment industry as a whole.

Keyconcept

Politics and the Movies: Even before McCarthyism and the Red Scare of the 1950s, some politicians saw films and television as sources of corruption of Americans' political or moral values. The U.S. film industry, seeking to avoid such criticism, has typically discouraged controversial political content in movies.

Despite varying degrees of freedom, the American movie industry usually avoids explicitly politically oriented movies. Exceptions, such as Frank Capra's 1941 *Meet John Doe* and Tim Robbins's 1992 *Bob Roberts,* can be found, but movies' main contribution to the marketplace of ideas has been in the area of social and cultural issues.

■ The role of women in movie history

For years, most women in the movie business played second billing to men. A female actor could not open a movie, which means "attract a large audience," by herself. Even acclaimed actresses such as Katherine Hepburn and Bette Davis were defined in most films as much by their leading men as by their own star power. Few women were executives, and even fewer directed films.

Today, opportunities are better for women, if not great. Actresses such as Whoopi Goldberg, Meryl Streep, and Sandra Bullock open films, attracting large audiences. Women sit on the executive boards of major studios, and female directors produce excellent, money-making movies. Penny Marshall, who starred in the TV series *Laverne and Shirley,* directed *Jumpin' Jack Flash* and *Big,* and was executive producer for *A League of Their Own.* Her films have won critical praise and large profits.

[profile]

Jodie Foster

Jodie Foster has been called the most powerful woman in Hollywood. She is one of the few actors who can virtually ensure worldwide box-office attention.

Foster began working at the age of three to help support her mother and three siblings. Many people fondly remember Foster's first job as the little Coppertone girl in pigtails whose swimming suit bottom was being pulled down by a mischievous dog. Others may remember her in television shows such as *The Courtship of Eddie's Father*. After that came Disney movies, including *Freaky Friday* and *Candleshoe*.

While other children were watching her in Disney movies, Foster and her siblings were watching French and Italian movies. Her mother chose similarly offbeat movies for Foster to act in. The most memorable, garnering Foster an Oscar nomination when she was only fourteen, was *Taxi Driver* (1976). It also made her the obsession of John W. Hinckley, Jr., who attempted to assassinate then President Reagan in 1981. *Taxi Driver*, rereleased

in 1996, starred Robert De Niro as a Vietnam veteran turned late night taxi driver in New York City. He becomes obsessed with rescuing a twelve-year-old prostitute played by Foster and goes on a bloody killing spree in an attempt to cleanse the city of moral degeneracy.

After Foster graduated from the Lycee Francais in Los Angeles, she became an honors student in comparative literature at Yale. On her return to Hollywood, she had to stand in line to try out for movie parts. She had been away from the industry too long for her name to be an automatic box-office draw.

Foster's star power was still there, however. In 1988, she won an Oscar for best actress for her role as a rape victim in *The Accused*. Her second Oscar came three years later in *Silence of the Lambs* for her portrayal of an FBI agent trying to get information from one vicious killer in order to find another. In addition to acting, Foster has focused her talents on directing. In her first feature film as director, *Little Man Tate* (1991), the story of a bril-

liant child, she also acted. The movie is more about character than plot. Her second directing success was *Home for the Holidays* (1995), a story about a young woman who goes home to have Thanksgiving with her dysfunctional family.

Foster has been pragmatic in managing her career and is known for her sense of perspective about life. Reviewers repeatedly comment that success does not corrupt her. CEO of her own production company, she is an accomplished producer, director, and actor.

SOURCES: Stephen Rebello, "Jodie Foster: Nice Girls Do Finish First," *Cosmopolitan* 220:4 (April 1996), p. 176.

Despite advances, women still face problems in Hollywood. Young actresses often feel typecast in roles that depend more on looks than on talent. Such typecasting reflects assumptions that men's viewing habits determine a film's monetary success and that men are not interested in films about independent women. The 1991 movie *Thelma and Louise* was labeled male bashing, mostly by male columnists, because it showed two strong women refusing to be intimidated by men.

The conditions that women face in Hollywood are exemplified by writer Sheila Benson's opening to a story that appeared in *Variety:*

> The UN's decade of the woman was 1975–1985. The International Year of the Woman was 1991. The Academy Awards officially saluted women in 1993.
>
> Old-line Hollywood's response to such fanfare can be summed up in this true story: When a female executive presented a woman-oriented project at her studio, the studio male CEO said, "When is this f—————Year of the Woman going to be over?[12]

192

Discussions of movies and race often dwell on the treatment of African Americans in movies made by white film makers. These discussions inevitably conclude that, with a few exceptions, African Americans have not been accurately portrayed in films made by whites. During the 1930s and 1940s, the movie image of blacks was one of lazy and slow-thinking people. This stereotype has been called the "Step'n Fetchit" role. The name comes from the stage name of Lincoln Perry, who made a career out of playing this type of character.

Often ignored in history are the films made by African American film makers. The first black film company was the Lincoln Motion Picture Company, formed in 1915 in Los Angeles to showcase black talent. In 1916, the Frederick Douglass Film Company formed on the East Coast to counteract the anti-black images in the movie *The Birth of a Nation*.[13]

Hampered by financing and distribution problems, both companies closed during the early 1920s. They were replaced by other African American film companies. Oscar Micheaux became the best-known black film maker of this period, producing dozens of silent and talking films. Many of these films dealt with racial issues and presented African American life in greater variety than was found in major studio films.

Key concept

Stereotyped Film Roles for Women and Minorities: Despite a steady evolution toward more positive roles and the elimination of the most insulting stereotypes of gender or ethnic behavior on screen, most movies continue to show only relatively narrow ranges of behavior and few substantial roles for minority and female actors. Rarely are African Americans, Hispanic Americans, Asian Americans, or Native Americans portrayed in films outside a small set of social settings, and seldom are women shown in strong or dominant roles.

From the late 1930s to the 1950s, a variety of companies produced movies with all–African American casts for the segregated theaters of the black community. These films tended to imitate white-produced films and were made cheaply. As film historian Daniel J. Leab said, "The leads remained very Caucasian-looking and spoke good English; the villains and comic figures, who were more Negroid in features and darker skinned, tended to speak in dialect."[14] The failure to present African Americans in a more realistic fashion in these films can be largely attributed to the financial and distribution control that whites continued to hold over the black film industry. Films about African Americans had to fit white stereotypes to be seen.

In the 1960s, major studios discovered that African American actors could make money at the box office. Sidney Poitier became an acclaimed actor and bankable star. The change in Hollywood reflected the changing mood of a nation whose consciousness was being raised by the civil rights movement. The late 1960s and early 1970s saw the arrival of the black action film. *Shaft,* directed by famous black photographer Gordon Parks, came out in 1971. It was a violent film, not unlike similar white-oriented detective movies. It cost $1.1 million to make and made $6.1 million.[15] Hollywood understood these figures, and similar films followed, including two *Shaft* sequels. Although these films starred African Americans, they were produced by major film studios, and some critics said they exploited the anger black audiences felt about the lack of changes in society. In fact, they are now referred to as "blaxploitation movies." These films were no closer to the average African American's life than the James Bond films were to the average white person's life. But white people saw a larger variety of self-images in film than did people of color.

In the 1980s and 1990s, young African American filmmakers such as Spike Lee and John Singleton gained financial support from major studios. Lee's *She's Gotta Have It,* an independent production, attracted the interest of Columbia Pictures, who financed half his second film, *School Daze* (1988). However, black filmmakers' projects typically receive less financial support than do projects by white directors. Lee's later films, such as *Do the Right Thing* (1989) and John Singleton's *Boyz N the Hood* (1991) received critical acclaim and made a profit. Despite the high quality of acting, writing, and produc-

Acclaimed African American director Spike Lee's early work explored some of the dynamics of white-black interaction in such movies as She's Gotta Have It. *Some critics fear that if Lee and others concentrate too much on exploring violent roles for African American males or on ghetto settings, they may promote still another Hollywood stereotype for African Americans in film.*

tion, some critics see in many of these films new stereotypes that continue to reflect the financial control of white-run studios. Film scholar Jacquie Jones concluded:

> Unfortunately, even a cursory examination of the recent wave of black films financed with studio capital reveals that age-old ghettoization of black products remains unchanged. The industry's wholesale investment in films that explore only ghettoes and male youth ignores the existence of a black community beyond these narrow confines—inclusive of women as valuable participants—as well as films that refuse to cater to these prescriptions."[16]

The 1996 release of *Ghosts of Mississippi* and *A Time to Kill* created controversy about the way the 1960s civil rights movement is being portrayed in films. *Ghosts of Mississippi* concerns the conviction of the man who killed Medgar Evers in 1963. The film spends little time on Evers, who was an activist in the civil rights movement. The star is Alec Baldwin, who plays the white prosecutor who convicted the killer. Other films such as *A Time to Kill* and *Mississippi Burning* have de-emphasized the roles of African Americans in the civil rights movement, concentrating instead on heroic white men. Director Spike Lee claims that such films are about the moral dilemmas of white liberals, not about the lives of black people. Lee says that because Hollywood executives believe they need a white lead to bring the audience in, the true story lines are corrupted.

Today's market structure

The film industry is still dominated by a group of major studios. It has survived repeated challenges, including the breakup of theater networks; the rise of television, cable, and pay-per-view; and the popularity of the videocassette recorder (VCR). The studios haven't just survived; they have adapted, prospered, and grown. For example, Rupert Murdoch, the Australian press lord, merged Twentieth-Century Fox and combined it with his chain of metropolitan television stations acquired from Metromedia Television. The Fox television stations give the corporate family instant access to wider distribution of a film after it appears in the nation's theaters.[17] In 1985, Ted Turner bought MGM and acquired its film library for his superstation before reselling the movie company. The major studios still control about 80 percent of the business in the United States and about half the market in Sweden, West Germany, several other Western European nations, and Asia. Although the number of independent producers has increased during the last twenty years, all of them contract with the studios to distribute their films.

The key to the studios' success continues to be their domination of distribution. The growth of new theater chains paralleled the advent of drive-ins during the 1950s, which were attended not only by adolescents fascinated with the freedom and privacy of the automobile, but also by young parents who could keep an eye on their children in the

194

backseat while watching a new release. The number of drive-ins peaked in 1958 at about 4,000 nationwide. Today only about 870 continue, with most of these in warmer climates. The biggest culprit in the decline has been the value of real estate. Land that once housed drive-ins makes more money when it is used for malls and apartment buildings. With the growth of the shopping center during the 1970s came the cineplex, a movie theater with three to twelve screens in one location. During the deregulatory years of the Reagan administration, studios once again invested in theaters, this time with the quiet acquiescence of the Justice Department. Movie theater admissions reached their peak of 4.5 billion in the golden years of the 1940s, then dropped to about one billion during the 1960s. They have remained relatively stable since that time, despite the advent of VCRs and cable television.

Audience demand in movie markets

In the early days movies catered to the family audience. From the era of the nickelodeon to the age of Panavision, mothers, fathers, and kids flocked to neighborhood movie houses and to the theater palaces in the cities. After the advent of television, as couples settled down to raise kids in the suburbs, the movies were not so attractive. For parents, going to a movie meant paying for a babysitter, tickets, and transportation; many chose to stay home and watch television. Slowly, the audience changed, and from the late 1960s until the late 1980s, the seventeen-year-old was the most reliable moviegoer. Demographics have changed, however, and in the late 1990s, aging baby boomers far outnumber teenagers in the United States and present a viable group for studios to target.

In 1981, 24 percent of moviegoers were between the ages of sixteen and twenty, according to the Motion Picture Association of America. By 1992, only 15 percent of admissions were in that age group, and admissions of viewers between the ages of forty and forty-nine had risen from 6 percent to 16 percent. Since 1991, middle-aged adults have gone to the movies in increasing numbers.[18]

Nearly half of teenagers go to the movies at least once a month, compared with just one in four adults. Young people rarely wait for recommendations and reviews but go to movies as soon as they open. They attend movies as part of their social activity with friends, choose a movie on impulse, and are heavily influenced by television advertising. By contrast, older adults attend movies selectively, preferring films that represent more sophisticated fare than they can find on television. They choose movies after reading reviews and listening to their friends' recommendations.

Adults also accompany young children to family movies and appreciate the music, acting, story lines, and animation. Adults, as well as the children they accompany, are partly responsible for the success of movies such as *Beauty and the Beast, Aladdin,* and *Home Alone.* In general, films rated G and PG earn more money than do films rated R or NC-17. According to *Variety* magazine, from 1972 to 1991, movies with G or PG ratings earned the most at the box office. Nevertheless, R movies increased from 39 percent to 61 percent of all movies. R movies appeal to youth, particularly urban youth, who report in focus groups that they want movies dealing with the reality of their lives, which often are violent and surrounded by drug use.[19] Despite this growth, the financial success of non-R-rated films has promoted a recent trend toward more PG and PG-13 movies.

Keyconcept

Audience Demographics and Current Rating Formats: The moviegoing public, which originally consisted largely of family audiences, had an average age of seventeen during the 1970s but slowly shifted to an older, more diverse age demographic in the 1980s and 1990s. The current rating system incorporates labeling for this varied audience: G: general audiences; PG: parental guidance suggested; PG-13: special guidance for children under thirteen; R: people under seventeen must be accompanied by an adult; NC-17: no one under seventeen admitted.

The Business of Profit

Aspiring script writers can learn an important lesson from *Forrest Gump:* Do what Winston Groom and Eric Roth, creators of Gump and the screenplay failed to do—get a percentage of gross profits. Forget about the net.

Believe it or not, one of the most popular movies of all time has lost money—according to Hollywood accounting standards, at least. Paramount Pictures' *Forrest Gump* has grossed more than $657 million at box offices around the world. Add to that figure the videocassette and soundtrack revenues, licensing fees on products—Forrest Gump wristwatches, Ping-Pong paddles, and cookbooks—and the film could generate up to $350 million more for Paramount's parent company, Viacom, Inc.

Nevertheless, on Paramount's books, *Forrest Gump* lost money—$62 million through December 31, 1994. When Paramount had finished splitting the box-office take with theater owners, subtracting 32 percent of gross profits for a distribution fee, counting off $67 million for additional distribution expenses (throwing parties, advertising, storing film reels), the studio recorded no profit.

What is a distribution fee? Pure profit for Paramount, couched in the language of losing money. According to Paramount, the combined types of distribution fees were higher than the $112 million cost of producing the movie.

Actor Tom Hanks and director Robert Zemeckis knew well enough to negotiate a percentage of gross receipts. Forget about profit; their 8 percent gained them each $20 million within a year after the film was released.

Paramount has already been to court once over a dispute over what constitutes profit and loss. Art Buchwald sued the company for his 19 percent of the profits on *Coming to America,* which another court had ruled was based on Buchwald's work. Paramount claimed that it had made no money on the film. Buchwald appealed to the Los Angeles Superior Court, where Judge Harvey Schneider ruled that Paramount's standard net profit participation contract was "unconscionable" and awarded Buchwald and his producer, Alain Bernheim, $900,000 plus $150,000 to cover court costs.

After this, Paramount decided to pay Winston Groom, creator of *Forrest Gump,* $250,000 as an advance against royalties and bought the rights to his sequel for a seven-figure sum.

SOURCE: Nina Munk, "Now You See It, Now You Don't," *Forbes,* June 5, 1995, p. 42; and Marla Matzer, "Hollywood's Starving Artists," *Forbes,* July 17, 1995, p. 16.

Increasingly, the American audience—in all its various segments—is only a portion of the audience to which American movies are directed. Profits can be doubled by showings in the international market. Furthermore, studios are measuring popularity of particular stars and genres in the international markets before film scripts are even developed.

Supplying the audience's demand

Movies meet the demands of the audience and make profits not only through traditional showings at theaters, but also through release to the international market, pay-per-view television channels, home videos, premium channels, and television networks. Movie theaters usually split box-office receipts with **distributors,** which also charge booking fees to movie makers. Exhibitors make a good deal of their

distributors: The people of the movie industry who arrange to book movies in theaters, then on television.

money, however, on food and drink, which often are marked up by 60 percent over their wholesale cost.

The movie industry had its best year in 1996, selling more than $5.8 billion in tickets. In the previous best year, 1995, $5.5 billion in tickets were sold. Industry observers credited the growth to increased numbers of screens in the multiplex theaters and to the action films, such as *Independence Day, Twister,* and *Mission Impossible,* that look much better on big screens.

Since the advent of sound in the 1920s, financial investors have become increasingly important in movie making. Profits from prior movies, investor groups, and banks finance film making. Creating the dream machine—and keeping it alive—is big business.

■ Product placement: Supplying the advertising market

Advertising has never played a large part in the financing of movies. However, concerned about young people's increasingly cynical response to television commercials, companies constantly search for ways to sell their products more effectively. One strategy is to use product placement, that is, depicting a popular star in a film drinking not just a soft drink, for example, but a clearly identifiable can of Pepsi. Critics argue that product placement is deceptive because the viewer doesn't recognize the ad for what it is. Industry spokespeople have another point of view: Director John Badham notes that film budgets have become so large that producers need to look for new types of revenue. "From a producer's or a director's view, product placement is a great way to reduce the budget and keep the studio quiet."[20]

Keyconcept

Movie Production and Product Placement Advertising: Movie production has been financed primarily by admission revenues rather than sponsored ads. However, since the 1980s, significant indirect advertising income has come from the product placement system, whereby a product such as a Coca-Cola can is clearly discernible in the movie.

The technique is not new. In 1945, film star Joan Crawford downed Jack Daniels bourbon whiskey in the Warner Bros. production *Mildred Pierce.* However, in 1982, product placement hit the big time when sales of Reese's Pieces soared 66 percent in three months after the candy was showcased in Steven Spielberg's *E.T. the Extraterrestrial.* Hollywood-featured releases became an important element of every consumer marketing program. [21] Now more than a dozen companies have been organized to expedite the placement of products in Hollywood films.[22] And studios, like Disney's Buena Vista Pictures, are aggressively seeking product placements for forthcoming pictures.[23]

Subtle advertising in feature films is known as "product placement" and is created by using well-known brands. Casual use of such products, for example, Ray Ban glasses worn by Will Smith, is intended to inspire those who admire the characters to use the same brands.

■ The videocassette revolution

When Sony introduced the Betamax home videocassette recorder in 1976, few people anticipated the impact that the VCR would have on the film and television industries. This piece of technology would allow viewers to control *when* they watched *what* programs on television and, with the advent of video rental stores, would keep even more viewers home from the movies. However, the high cost kept many people from purchasing the VCRs. JVC introduced VHS technology a few months later and provided the competition that drove the cost down and led to the eventual demise of the Beta format. Today, VCRs can be purchased for less than $200.

The VCR was not a popular piece of equipment among movie moguls. Jack Valenti, president of the Motion Picture Association of America, called the VCR a "*parasitical* instrument."[24] However, the studios quickly adapted. At first, they attempted to sell movies on videocassettes to the public, but high costs made that impractical. Sensing a business opportunity, some entrepreneurs bought the expensive videocassettes and rented them out at affordable rates. As rental stores began to spring up in neighborhood locations, film studios capitalized on the new market by releasing more and more films on video. As more videos became available, more people bought VCRs. Today, popular family movies such as *Home Alone* first make money at the box office; theater popularity prompts buyers to pay $15 to $25 for a movie their children will watch over and over again. Less popular films do better as rentals. Top video sales include children's and family movies. Table 7.2 shows the videos with the highest sales in 1995.

Keyconcept

The VCR Market: Since its appearance in the mid-1970s, the videocassette recorder-player (VCR) has become a common piece of home entertainment equipment. Because it enables people to watch movies at home at a time of their choice and to record from television, the VCR was originally perceived as a threat to the traditional film industry. As with television, however, the industry quickly learned to join the revolution, profit by spinoff sales of tapes of popular films, and eventually discover ways to create products directly for the videocassette market.

The Walt Disney Company has been one of the true entrepreneurs in the videocassette business. The company has excelled both at marketing popular theater movies and at using those movies to sell less-expensive videos directed at the home market. For example, after amazing success with the film and video versions of *Aladdin,* Disney began selling *The Return of Jafar,* a home video sequel, in May 1994 and moved 1.5 million cassettes in the first two days. Although *Jafar* never showed in movie theaters and was panned by critics, industry experts predicted that it would sell more than 10 million copies, thus ranking among the ten top-selling videos of all time.

Jafar was successful because of *Aladdin*'s popularity. By late 1994, *Aladdin* had grossed $486 million worldwide in theaters. Disney's merchandising for *Aladdin* was greater than any previous Disney film, with a record 24 million videocassettes sold, a triple-platinum soundtrack album, 20 million story and activity books in print and a Sega Genesis video game with sales pushing 1 million copies. *Aladdin* reportedly garnered $1 billion in revenue for Disney during its first year after release.

Disney's success in the home video market may signal a change in the types of movies released for the home market. Previously, exercise tapes, stories for preschoolers, and B-grade movies have been the primary fare aimed directly at the home market, or "sold through" to consumers.

TABLE 7.2 Top 10 Video Sales of 1996

1. *Babe* (Uni Dist. Corp)
2. *Apollo 13* (Uni Dist. Corp)
3. *Pulp Fiction* (Buena Vista Home Video)
4. *Playboy: The Best of Jenny McCarthy* (Uni Dist. Corp)
5. *The Aristocrats* (Buena Vista Home Video)
6. *Batman Forever* (Warner Home Video)
7. *Jumanji* (Columbia TriStar Home Video)
8. *Pocahontas* (Buena Vista Home Video)
9. *Cinderella* (Buena Vista Home Video)
10. *Heavy Metal* (Columbia TriStar Home Video)

Source: Billboard, January 11, 1997, p. 39.

198

The production of direct home video has obvious advantages. The budget for *Jafar* was about $5 million, considerably more than the $500,000 Disney spends on a half-hour of animated television programming but considerably less than the estimated $30 million spent on *Aladdin.* Although critics argue that there is a creative loss, producers claim that the product can get to the market quickly and inexpensively without the cumbersome creative and financial restrictions of film making.[25]

Supplying the international market

International revenues increasingly are considered as studios decide which films to fund and which stars to hire. Genre and star identity often determine a film's success overseas. For example, Bruce Willis's *Die Hard with a Vengeance* earned $100 million in U.S. revenues and cost $90 million to produce. Willis's salary was $15 million. Did the studios take a loss? Definitely not. Overseas grosses were expected to be between $225 and $275 million.[26] Action is the most foolproof genre for overseas sales, and films like *Die Hard* will gross almost as much in Japan as in the United States, which has twice Japan's population.

Some films encounter international political barriers, however. *Schindler's List,* which grossed $100 million in Europe, Asia, and Latin America, was barred from many Arab and Islamic nations. Director Steven Spielberg told the *New York Times* that the banning was disgraceful. "It shocks me because I thought the Islamic countries would feel this film could be an instrument of their own issues in what was happening in Bosnia."[27]

International film

Film has always been an international medium. In 1895, the first public screening of short films occurred in France, the United States, Germany, and Belgium.[28] Today, despite the dominance of American-made films in most markets, movies remain essentially international. Three trends demonstrate the global nature of films: strong domestic film industries in many countries, growing exportation of films from many countries, and increasing coproduction of films across national boundaries.

Strong domestic film industries

Many countries with growing populations have developed their own film industries to meet the increased demand for entertainment. The Indian film industry outproduces all other countries with 800 or more films a year, about twice the number produced by Hollywood. The Indian industry peaked in 1990 with 945 films in twenty-one native languages. As you can see in Table 7.3 on page 200, the United States ranks second in film production and has not been the leading producer since the 1950s.

The **three Chinas** experienced similar growth in films during the 1980s and 1990s. China reopened the Beijing Film Academy in 1978, with a resulting growth in the film industry. In the 1990s, about 120 domestic films a year have been produced in China. In 1990, *Ju Dou,* a film directed by Zhang Yimou, was nominated for an Academy Award

Keyconcept

U.S. Films Abroad versus Indigenous Industries: The international sale of films has been an important source of profit for the U.S. movie industry, which sometimes earns more on violent or sensational U.S. movies abroad than at home. Some countries see American movies as a threat to their domestic film industries. However, several nations have vigorous movie traditions of their own, and British, French, and Chinese film styles have influenced American film making.

three Chinas: The term refers to China, Taiwan, and Hong Kong. Before the twentieth century, all three were classified by Europeans as China.

Global *Impact*

Icon with an Attitude

e's big and he's ugly. On a bad day, he might destroy New York or Tokyo, but he remains one of the most beloved movie stars of all time.

Long before America gave the world the dinosaurs of *Jurassic Park,* the Japanese film industry created Godzilla. Today, more than forty years after his first film in 1954, he has starred in twenty-two movies, has his own fan magazine, and can be accessed through the Internet. During 1995, Americans bought more than three million Godzilla toys.

Despite his international acclaim, many people think of Godzilla as a man in a rubber monster suit crushing miniature tanks. This reflects a problem that many movie stars endure: a concentration on their lesser efforts. The original Godzilla film, entitled *Godzilla,* included some of Japan's top actors and made a serious statement about the hazards of nuclear weapons (Godzilla, a dinosaurlike creature, was created by American hydrogen bomb tests). Two years later, the film was recut; scenes of Raymond Burr playing an American journalist in Japan were added. The American version, *Godzilla, King of the Monsters,* played down the nuclear weapons element.

As Godzilla's career evolved, the films became more campy, especially the American versions. But American and Japanese audiences remained attracted to the monster that had changed from a bad guy into a creature who defended Japan from a variety of alien and monster threats. In 1993, *Godzilla vs. Mothra* was the highest-grossing domestic film in Japan. TriStar Pictures owns the rights to make an American version of Godzilla and was pursuing that goal in the mid-1990s, but with computer imaging.

The old Godzilla may not have the computer sophistication of a *Jurassic Park* raptor, but his staying power makes him the king of prehistoric movie creatures and a true international movie icon with an attitude.

SOURCE: Steve Ryfle, "Godzilla Lives," *Chicago Tribune,* August 17, 1995, Sec. 2, pp. 1,2.

---

for the best foreign-language film released in the United States. This film, a story about a peasant woman who is forced to marry an old factory owner, was banned in China because of its focus on individualism. Throughout the 1960s and 1970s, Hong Kong produced more than 120 films annually, mostly martial arts movies, for domestic and international markets. During the 1980s, some film makers moved toward more complex plots. Taiwanese films, which were similar to those released from Hong Kong, also moved toward more socially meaningful themes during the 1980s and 1990s.[29]

Growing exportation of films

In addition to growing domestic markets, several countries have seen growth in the exportation of their films. Australian and New Zealand movie companies have found both financial success and critical acclaim in the United States. The string of successes included Australia's *My Brilliant Career* (1981), the "Mad Max" movies, and *Crocodile Dundee* (1986). Following the success of these films, several members of the Australian movie industry, including actor Mel Gibson and director Peter Weir, moved to Hollywood. In 1993, *The Piano,* a New Zealand film starring a New Zealander and two Americans, was nominated for an Academy Award for best picture.

TABLE 7.3 Leading Country in Production of Feature Films

TABLE 7.3

YEAR	TOP COUNTRY	NO. FILMS PRODUCED	SECOND COUNTRY	NO. FILMS PRODUCED
1922	United States	748	Germany	474
1932	Japan	498	United States	489
1942	United States	488	India	173
1952	United States	391	Hong Kong	259
1962	Japan	537	India	315
1972	Japan	421	India	411
1982	India	763	Japan	322
1991	India	910	United States	279

A feature film is at least one hour in length. These rankings do not include made-for-TV movies. During the last few decades, India and Japan have consistently produced the most films. However, the United States continues to be the leading exporter of films.

Source: Patrick Robertson, *The Guinness Book of Movie Facts & Feats* (New York: Abbeville Press, 1993).

An important element of the growing exportation of films from a variety of countries is the number of serious film makers practicing throughout the world. Beginning in the 1980s, Satyajit Ray of India, Aki Kaurismaki of Finland, Luis Puenzo of Argentina, and Pedro Almodovar of Spain have represented a new wave of serious directors. These film makers and others use film to explore personal problems and social relations in a way that transcends geographic boundaries.[30]

International coproduction

Increasingly, movie companies from different countries are combining to make truly international films. French financiers, for example, funded *The Oak,* a 1992 Romanian film written and directed by Lucian Pintilie. During the 1980s and 1990s, Akira Kurosawa, one of Japan's greatest film makers, directed films that were financed by companies in the Soviet Union, United States, and France.

Today, it is common for a film crew from a variety of countries to work on a movie that is financed by multinational companies. A film's financial and artistic prospects are more relevant issues in the quest for financing than are the countries in which the director, producer, and actors live.

Trends and innovations

As it has in the past, the movie industry will surely continue to take advantage of new technologies and respond not only to changes in demographics of the U.S. population, but also to the demands of the international markets.

The conglomerates that own numerous media companies are experimenting with the concept of movies on demand. Such services include not only pay-per-view movies on a particular cable channel, but also the selection of films from a library of movies to be ordered and watched at the viewer's preferred time.

The availability of movies on demand is being affected by two factors: the integration of computer and television technology and the deregulation of telephone companies. Deregulation enables telephone companies not only to provide technology for transmitting messages, but also to design and provide entertainment and information services. Bell Atlantic has already begun testing **information services** in large urban areas. If regional telephone companies begin to provide such services, cable companies will face a huge challenge.

Demographics

Demographics have always been an integral part of the movie business. Film producers and distributors aimed first at the family audience, then at teenagers. Recently changing demographics favor older groups of moviegoers. Merchant-Ivory Productions, for example, produces movies that appeal to the older American audience. Films such as *Howard's End* (1992) feature the typical qualities of Merchant-Ivory production: "good taste, a strong narrative line, impeccable period detail, and superb performances."[31] Martin Scorsese, who in 1976 targeted 25-year-olds with the culturally critical *Taxi Driver,* in 1993 gave American middle-aged baby boomers an adaptation of Edith Wharton's novel, *The Age of Innocence.*

Women emerged in the mid-1990s as an important demographic group. In 1996, for example, *The First Wives Club* earned $105 million because its tale of three women gaining revenge on their former husbands appealed to women. Conversely, the critically acclaimed *The People vs. Larry Flynt* failed at the box office after criticism from feminists that it degraded women. Industry sources explain that teenage males tend to pick the movies for dates, but women play the dominant role in selecting movies for people in the 30 to 50 age range.[32] The growing strength of women as movie consumers may pressure Hollywood to offer more managerial opportunities for women in the movie industry.

Influences of international market

Because the market is lucrative, international audience demand will continue to affect the types of films that are produced in the United States. Currently, it seems that this will sustain an increase in action films such as *Independence Day.* Comedies rarely sell well internationally because humor is often culturally bound, but a recent film, *While You Were Sleeping,* appears to be an exception. The key factors in its success seem to be the actress Sandra Bullock and the popular theme of romance.

Bullock's success indicates another influence of the international market: enhancement of the traditional American star system. Stars are known quantities and are easier to sell than concepts. The international market is more willing to take a risk on a film if it features a star.

The success of the American film industry through world wars, regulation, public opinion, and changing economic and social conditions reflects its ability to adapt. How it responds to new markets and new technologies will lay the groundwork for the film industry of the twenty-first century.

Summary

- American film making has been dominated by large studios since the early years of the industry.
- Films first targeted family audiences, then, with the advent of television, switched to the teenaged audiences that spent their money indiscriminately on movies.

information services: Services that provide entertainment and information via telephone lines or through other technologies. Before 1996, telephone companies were prohibited from entering the information business. They now compete with cable companies and other service providers.

- Film represented two lines of technological development: the perfection of the photographic process and the fascination with moving pictures.
- Vaudeville influenced the content and style for the first projected shorts.
- Edwin Porter's 1903 short films *Life of an American Fireman* and *The Great Train Robbery* pioneered storytelling techniques that led toward feature-length films.
- The Motion Picture Patents Company controlled early film production. Although it edged out independents, it also stabilized a fledgling industry.
- During the teens and early twenties, film became middle-class entertainment, and studios introduced the star system to attract large audiences.
- By 1930, five movie companies dominated the U.S. film industry.
- The peak year of movie attendance in the United States was 1946.
- After World War II, the domestic audience dwindled, with a population shift to the suburbs, a baby boom, and ultimately more attention to television. However, the foreign audience increased and by 1960 provided nearly half the American film industry's revenues.
- Movies constitute art, social commentary, and entertainment.
- Movies were not given free speech protection until 1952.
- Movies usually target a young audience, although aging baby boomers constitute a dynamic secondary market.
- Product placement is a form of advertising in which identifiable brand-name products are consumed or used by characters in movies.
- The advent of the VCR created a new challenge for the film industry, but the industry responded by supplying videos through rental stores and directly to the consumer, increasing revenues by $15 billion.
- Merchandising products is a successful profit-making venture of movie studios.

Navigating the Web

Movies on the web

Movies and film are at the top of the popular culture list of Web sites, and the collection addressing these topics is one of the largest. Sites cover the *history, business,* and *criticism* of *film.* Many are created by interested individuals; others are produced by the large movie corporations. Some experimentation will be done with *movies on site,* but as yet they are still more suited to the television set or the big screen for general viewing.

The following sites contain research material about movies and their history.

Movietone	http://www.iguide.com/movies/movitone

This site contains photographs and short film clips from the archives of the Movietone newsreels. Before television news appeared, these newsreels were the main form of electronic news and were shown in theaters between movies.

Film 100	http://www.film100.com

The 100 most influential people in film history are listed here, along with material about them and their contribution to the film industry.

Women in Cinema: A Reference Guide	http://poe.acc.virginia.edu/~pm9k/libsci/womfilm.html

This site contains bibliographies, reviews, and comments about the role of women in movies. It also contains links to other pages addressing the subject.

The following sites are examples of locations where information about studios and the current state of the movie industry can be found:

Disney Studios	http://www.disney.com
The Hollywood Reporter	http://www.hollywood.reporter.com
Premiere	http://www.premieremag.com

▨ Questions for review

1. What type of technology did magic-lantern shows use?

2. Which studios have retained dominance over time?

3. Why was the First Amendment not applied to film until 1952?

4. Why is *Bonnie and Clyde* sometimes considered a turning point in the development of modern film?

5. What types of movies are most popular today?

▨ Issues to think about

1. Some people argue that movies have been the American dream machine. As more films are made with an international audience in mind and more international films are imported into the United States, how will the dream machine transmit social and cultural heritage?

2. How does the technological form of film watching affect the content and reaction? Do you react differently if you watch a film on a VCR at home or in a dark theater? With friends or parents?

3. How has the Hollywood system affected the development of American film?

4. What do you think the technology of the future will be? How will it affect the production, distribution, and marketing of movies?

5. What are the implications of product placement?

▨ Suggested readings

Adair, Gilbert. *Flickers: An Illustrated Celebration of 100 Years of Cinema* (Boston: Faber & Faber, 1995).

Corrigan, Timothy. *A Cinema without Walls: Movies and Culture after Vietnam* (New Brunswick, NJ: Rutgers University Press, 1991).

Ellis, Jack C. *A History of Film,* 2nd ed. (Englewood Cliffs, NJ: Prentice Hall, 1985).

Giannetti, Louis D. *Flashback: A Brief History of Film,* 3rd ed. (Englewood Cliffs, NJ: Prentice Hall, 1996).

Gomery, Douglas. *Movie History: A Survey* (Belmont, CA: Wadsworth, 1991).

Radio

Key concepts

- Broadcasting
- Network Broadcasting
- Commercial and Noncommercial Stations
- Airwave Scarcity
- Radio-Newspaper War
- Drive-Time Broadcast Markets
- Radio Markets for Information and Advertising
- Radio Station Types
- Former Colonial Radio Systems

Late at night in the middle of the Cultural Revolution, Lumen Huang climbed to a lonely spot in the mountains in southern China, carrying a shortwave radio set, on which he listened to Voice of America (VOA) broadcasts.

Radio is still the medium of choice in many countries. It's inexpensive, it's portable, it plays music, and it brings information to young and old.

From those broadcasts he perfected the limited English he had acquired. Learning English in the early 1970s in China was dangerous, and listening to the VOA was punishable by years of hard labor. Nevertheless, listening to VOA broadcasts was an extremely popular clandestine activity. Today, students in China can listen to the radio without fear. For example, every evening at 10:00 P.M., students of English at Yunnan University tune in to a two-hour VOA program. The students have little money and live in Spartan conditions in university dormitories, but nearly all of them have radios, which cost about $60. It's a rare luxury.[1] China has changed its position on learning English, and the students have responded with great fervor.

Meanwhile, in East Lansing, Michigan, bookstore owner Davis Matson switches on the radio in his small office. His college bookstore just opened, and he wants to hear the store's first radio ad. The introductory jingle is followed by a promise to beat any textbook price offered by competitors. The same promise appeared in the local daily and student newspapers, but Davis knows that buying advertisements on pop, alternative rock, and classic rock stations will get the word to more students about his new store.

These examples illustrate two of radio's many faces. Radio can be a powerful political tool that transcends borders and creates new avenues of information for people living under coercive governments. Radio can also be an inexpensive advertising medium that can reach specialized audiences, particularly those composed of people under the age of thirty. Radio has had other faces as well. This powerful medium once was an innovative journalistic tool that brought a war home to listeners around the world. In countries where television is not widely available, radio is still a primary source of news and entertainment. It remains one of the most portable mediums available, as well as one of the most influential information and propaganda tools. Perhaps the most notable characteristic of radio is its availability. According to UNESCO, in 1993 the least developed countries had one radio receiver for every ten people, compared to one TV set for every 100 people. The most developed countries had 968 radio receivers and 494 TV sets for every 1,000 people. Radio is everywhere.

The most consistent characteristic of radio has been the ability to survive in emerging competitive markets. Radio began as a medium for live entertainment and short news broadcasts. It developed situation comedy programs and dramatic fare that eventually transferred to television. After television sapped the best performers and programs from radio, radio altered its format, turning primarily to music, news, and talk. In the 1990s, especially in developed countries, radio faces increased competition from computer-based interactive technologies. Listeners can play music on CD-ROMs that are integrated into computer video. Progressive Networks' RealAudio software allows online listeners to hear live and recorded music broadcasts from rock and blues clubs. Users of the Internet and online services can access the latest news on demand. Even radio's grip on talk could be loosened as individuals communicate with each other over the Internet. As radio continues to compete with other media and enters the world of converging technologies, the major issues will be the following:

▓ Will computer-based, interactive programming force domestic radio to shift its content, or will radio's music, talk, and news format still appeal to tomorrow's population?

▓ How will radio reflect or contribute to cultural life?

▓ What role will radio have in political campaigns and decision making in the United States? Will the growth of "talk radio" have an effect on political debate?

▓ Will radio continue to be significant as a carrier of international news and information, crossing boundaries of countries that try to block external influence?

radio

Radio in your life

How Many Roles Does Radio Play?

Think about your own use of radio: What purposes does it serve for you, your family, and your friends? Do you use it for news? For entertainment? For background study music? Do you listen to the talk shows? Do you find yourself using the computer for some of the same purposes you use the radio for?

TYPE OF STATION	USE	HOURS PER DAY	OTHER MEDIA USED FOR SAME PURPOSE
Rock			
Alternative rock			
Country			
Rap			
Classical			
Jazz			
Talk			
News			
Public radio			
Other			

Radio in American life

Radio was the first national electronic mass medium, and politicians, corporate managers, and advertisers were quick to recognize its potential power. Radio allowed millions of people throughout the country to listen simultaneously to the same carefully tailored message. Despite the introduction of newer technologies, people throughout the world still use radio more than any other mass medium for information and entertainment. Even in the United States, where television seems to dominate the mass media, radio retains a significant audience—and significant political and social influence. In 1997, the United States had more than 12,000 licensed radio stations, compared to about 1,500 licensed television stations. Delivery of news is a critical radio function; the number of U.S. radio journalists about equals that of television journalists.[2] Among the top five radio stations in almost any large media market is at least one news and talk station. Radio's ability to deliver music is also important; in fact, music, especially music heard on the radio, has defined several generations of youth.

The magic starting point

As with most technology, finding an exact starting point in radio history is not easy. Radio was not invented by one person. Rather, a variety of inventors contributed to spe-

208

cific aspects of radio development. The scientific understanding gained by James Clerk Maxwell and Heinrich Hertz during the 1870s and 1880s furthered radio's development. Nathan Stubblefield experimented with transmitting voice and foresaw radio not merely as a point-to-point communication form, but as a method of transmitting news.[3] In 1895 Italian inventor Guglielmo Marconi produced a device that sent a message without wires. The message, however, was in code, like that of the telegraph. For radio to be a significant force, voice and wireless transmission had to merge.

Others contributed as well. John Ambrose Fleming developed a type of vacuum tube, Lee de Forest made amplification possible, and Reginald A. Fessenden experimented with the technology and began broadcasting. Edwin Howard Armstrong and de Forest fought bitterly in court over the patents to the regenerative circuit—a circuit that used the **Audion** as a transmitter, amplifier, and detector in a radio receiver. Although engineers familiar with the technology believed that Armstrong understood the process far better than de Forest did, the court awarded de Forest the patent. Armstrong later invented **FM,** but its development was halted by Radio Corporation of America (RCA). Armstrong committed suicide after losing his legal battles and watching FM languish in the shadow of television development.

By 1915 the technology to send and receive music and voice was well established. On September 30, 1915, David Sarnoff, then a lowly employee of American Marconi

Company but later president of RCA, wrote a memo to his boss. He predicted that the "Radio Music Box" would become as common in households as the piano or phonograph. But it took more than five years for radio to become a commercial enterprise because the demand had not yet developed and because of patent infringement disputes.[4]

The development of the radio station ensured that radio would be a mass medium, sending content to a large number of radio receivers, rather than remaining a wireless telephone. Several stations claimed to be "first." The first experimental license after the Radio Act of 1912 was given to St. Joseph's College in Pennsylvania. The University of Wisconsin was granted an experimental license in 1919, two years after it first broadcast music; this license became a regular license in 1922.[5] KDKA in

David Sarnoff—airwave pioneer and radio czar—began his career in radio's infancy. His role in forming Radio Corporation of America (RCA) and the NBC network dramatically shaped the broadcast industry as a commercial medium.

Pittsburgh was the first radio station to schedule programming and to offer continuous voice service. It received a commercial license on October 27, 1920, to experiment with voice transmission for a year. KDKA's first broadcast was election returns from the Harding-Cox presidential race. The station also broadcast church services, sports, and market reports. Less than a year after KDKA started broadcasting regularly, and shortly before its experimental license was converted to regular status, WBZ in Springfield, Massachusetts, received the first regular broadcasting license.

Audion: A three-electrode vacuum tube amplifier that was the basis of the electronic revolution that permitted the development of radio.

FM: Stands for frequency modulation.

■ Radio as a mass medium

Radio became a mass medium during the 1920s. This decade saw rapid growth and change in the number of stations, the percentage of U.S. households with radio receivers, the forms of financing radio, and the nature of programming.

The United States went from thirty licensed commercial AM stations in 1922 to 618 by 1930. Despite radio's development as a broadcast medium, the influence of the telephone company persisted. American Telephone and Telegraph (AT&T) invented the broadcast network, simultaneously broadcasting on January 4, 1923, over its stations in New York and Boston. Two years later, AT&T had a regular network of twenty-six stations from New York to Kansas City.[6]

In 1926, AT&T withdrew from the radio industry and sold its radio subsidiary to RCA. RCA soon acquired all stock in the National Broadcasting Corporation (NBC) and began to build a dominant network. Starting with nineteen stations in 1926, NBC had fifty-six stations two years later. The network grew to 154 stations in 1938 and 214 by 1940. NBC's network was actually two: the Red and Blue networks. The Blue network's flagship station was WJZ, NBC's first station in New York. The Red flagship station was WEAF in New York, which NBC acquired from AT&T. Each network offered its own programming.

Keyconcept

Network Broadcasting: Broadcasting stations are usually linked in a cooperative system involving a formal business relationship, shared program content, and sometimes common ownership. These commercial networks shaped and dominated the U.S. radio industry from its infancy.

NBC soon had competition, as the Columbia Broadcasting System (CBS) became the second network. CBS had sixteen stations in 1929 and expanded to 113 by 1938. In 1934, Mutual Broadcasting Network entered the field with four stations; by 1940 it had 160 outlets. Mutual differed from other networks in that it did not own any stations but shared programs among independent member stations. In 1943, when the FCC, in an effort to reduce the power of the networks, forced NBC to sell one of its networks, the American Broadcasting Corporation joined the competitive field. Table 8.1 shows that the number of AM stations grew steadily through 1993 and then declined slightly. FM stations continue to proliferate, although growth has slowed.

Networks provided programs for less money than it would have cost individual stations to produce equivalent programs; this meant higher profits. From an advertiser's perspective, networks simultaneously connected homes throughout the United States. A company could reach millions of people with the same message at the same time. A modern mass medium had arrived.

TABLE 8.1 Growth in the Number of Radio Stations

YEAR	NUMBER OF AM STATIONS	NUMBER OF FM STATIONS	TOTAL NUMBER OF STATIONS
1922	30		30
1930	618		618
1940	765		814
1950	2,144	691	2,835
1960	3,483	741	4,224
1970	4,228	2,126	6,354
1980	4,559	4,193	8,752
1993	4,954	6,466	11,420
1997	4,906	7,095	12,001

Sources: The FCC as reported in Lawrence W. Lichty and Malachi C. Topping, eds. *American Broadcasting: A Source Book in the History of Radio and Television* (New York: Hastings House, 1975), p. 148; and "By The Numbers," *Broadcasting and Cable,* January 27, 1997, p. 86.

210

Although networks could connect the people in the United States, people had to want to be connected—and they did. Demand for radio receivers expanded as fast as radio stations did in the 1920s. With radios selling for as low as $9, the percentage of households with radios rose from about 7 percent in 1923 to 20 percent in 1926 and 35 percent in 1930.[7]

Advertising arrives

As late as 1922 the primary purpose of radio programming was to sell radio sets. Without programs, no one would buy radio receivers. That year, AT&T started *toll broadcasting,* or the selling of time, at WEAF in New York. Secretary of Commerce Herbert Hoover feared that a speech by the President would "be used as the meat in a sandwich of two patent medicine advertisements." Nevertheless, station owners quickly envisioned a future of broadcasting financed by advertising. By 1929, advertising had been included in the first National Association of Broadcasters code of standards. NBC made more than $15 million in advertising that year.[8]

Because radio was new, the audience responded even to relatively simple and inexpensive programs. On 1920s radio, dance music reigned supreme. Many stations broadcast bands and orchestras live. Religious programming was also popular. University stations and, to some degree, networks broadcast educational material. Educational programming declined during the 1920s as university stations closed from lack of funding and commercial stations, whose owners actively opposed educational licenses, got control of more **radio frequencies.**

Order Now! for delivery Christmas Morning
Let Majestic's
COLORFUL TONE
flood your home with
year 'round enjoyment

Majestic
R A D I O

Radio was initially conceived as a technological device to be experimented with in garages and workshops, but as programming developed, the device was encased and moved into the living room as a piece of furniture. Radio was advertised as a cultural device that could bring the best symphonies into every middle-class home.

Early regulation

Technological chaos ruled in the early days of radio. Stations attempted to broadcast over the same frequencies, resulting in noise rather than useful programming. The problem of allocating stations to the limited number of airwaves led to several regulation efforts. The Radio Act of 1912 gave the Secretary of Commerce and Labor the right to license radio stations and assign frequencies. However, failing to anticipate that demand would far exceed availability, the act created no criteria for licensing.

Keyconcept

Commercial and Noncommercial Stations: The goal of commercial stations is to make a profit, usually by selling advertising. Noncommercial stations do not try to make a profit but have other goals, such as education. These two types of stations make up the radio industry.

Finally, Congress passed the Radio Act of 1927 and established the Federal Radio Commission (FRC) to regulate broadcasting. Such legislation represented a major departure from the government's stance toward the press. Regulation of radio was justi-

radio frequency: An electromagnetic wave frequency used in radio transmission.

fied on the basis of **scarcity of the airwaves,** and the commission was instructed to act in the "public interest, convenience and necessity." However, this departure was acceptable to industry representatives. The Radio Act represented the culmination of many discussions between the industry and government and ensured that commercial interests would dominate the medium, networks would retain power, and government would not interfere too directly. The number of educational licenses fell from 129 in 1925 to 52 in 1931.[9]

Even though the FRC reduced the chaos in the radio industry, several agencies still shared regulation of radio, telephone, telegraph, and cable; this overlap created confusion as to which regulations applied. Congress passed the Federal Communications Act of 1934, establishing the Federal Communication Commission (FCC) as the regulator of wire and wireless communication. Congress also charged the FCC with recommending action on the longstanding debate between educational and commercial broadcasting, but the pattern set by the 1927 act persisted. The commercial forces, well financed and well organized, dominated the debate. Noncommercial interests were unable to create a unified front that would present a cohesive message to Congress. It would be decades before frequencies would be set aside specifically for educational purposes.

Keyconcept

Airwave Scarcity: Radio signals can be carried only on certain frequencies of the electromagnetic spectrum. Because the *airwaves,* as these frequencies are informally called, are considered public space, the government has regulated their use. Recent technological developments have enabled more signals to be broadcast on the airwaves, but government still has a role in helping to determine how the expanded capacity can best be used.

Radio's golden age

During the 1930s, radio matured as a mass medium. Through the 1940s, radio was the electronic bridge to world affairs, quality entertainment, national sports events, and urban progress. It was a Golden Age for radio. The number of homes with receivers, the interest of advertisers, and the types of programming expanded rapidly. News, comedy, drama, mysteries, and "entertainment news" emerged in radio programming. As the medium matured, audiences began to regard radio as a reliable source of news and information. The World Series was carried by some stations as early as 1922.

Drama was a favorite, and in 1934 the *Lux Radio Theater* began presenting radio adaptations of films, using movie stars to provide the voices. Soon, more than 30 million people listened weekly. Because of radio's credibility, influence, and popularity, when Orson Welles and his *Mercury Theater* players broadcast an updated version of H. G. Wells's *War of the Worlds* on Halloween night in 1938, some listeners did not realize that it was meant to be entertainment. The program started with dance music, which was interrupted by a realistic-sounding news flash announcing that Martians had landed in New Jersey. Although the program contained periodic statements identifying it as a dramatization, tens of thousands of listeners reacted as if it were real.

In the early days of radio, sponsors supported an entire program, such as Truth or Consequences. *The system gave way to spot advertising in an effort to keep content under the control of the producers rather than the advertisers.*

The mix of drama and news entertained and informed, and some early radio programming foreshadowed the television docudrama. *The March of Time,* which began in 1931, dramatized news, using actors to recreate—sometimes in altered form—actual

scarcity of the airwaves: Concept that because there are only limited airwaves, they must belong to the people and therefore be regulated by government, not owned by broadcasters.

212 **R**adio in our lives

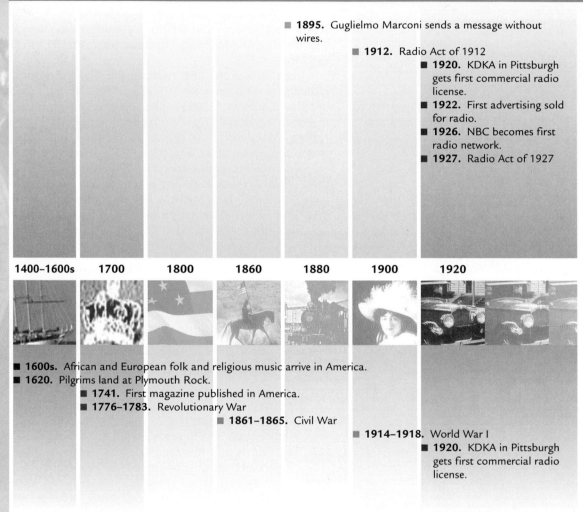

- **1895.** Guglielmo Marconi sends a message without wires.
  - **1912.** Radio Act of 1912
    - **1920.** KDKA in Pittsburgh gets first commercial radio license.
    - **1922.** First advertising sold for radio.
    - **1926.** NBC becomes first radio network.
    - **1927.** Radio Act of 1927

1400–1600s	1700	1800	1860	1880	1900	1920

- **1600s.** African and European folk and religious music arrive in America.
- **1620.** Pilgrims land at Plymouth Rock.
  - **1741.** First magazine published in America.
  - **1776–1783.** Revolutionary War
    - **1861–1865.** Civil War
      - **1914–1918.** World War I
        - **1920.** KDKA in Pittsburgh gets first commercial radio license.

news events. *The March of Time* was broadcast on and off for the next fourteen years, reaching as many as 9 million homes at one point, and spawned several imitators.

During the day, soap operas such as *Guiding Light* and *Backstage Wife* attracted a primarily female audience. At night, game shows such as *Twenty Questions* and *Truth or Consequences* were family listening fare. Mysteries, crime shows, westerns, and comedy series added diversity. Comedy shows ranged from *Amos 'n' Andy,* which used racist stereotypes of African Americans, to *Blondie,* which featured a bumbling, unlucky husband named Dagwood Bumstead. The king of the radio comedians was Jack Benny. By 1938, Benny had an audience of 7 million families and was making $25,000 a week.

The growth of radio listening during the 1930s reflected an increase in radio ownership and a hunger for news and entertainment spawned by the Great Depression. Be-

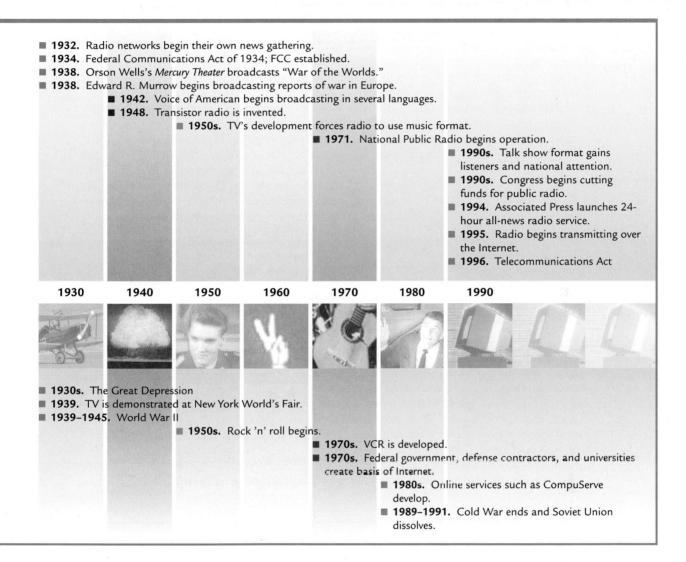

■ **1932.** Radio networks begin their own news gathering.
■ **1934.** Federal Communications Act of 1934; FCC established.
■ **1938.** Orson Wells's *Mercury Theater* broadcasts "War of the Worlds."
■ **1938.** Edward R. Murrow begins broadcasting reports of war in Europe.
　　■ **1942.** Voice of American begins broadcasting in several languages.
　　■ **1948.** Transistor radio is invented.
　　　　■ **1950s.** TV's development forces radio to use music format.
　　　　　　■ **1971.** National Public Radio begins operation.
　　　　　　　　■ **1990s.** Talk show format gains listeners and national attention.
　　　　　　　　■ **1990s.** Congress begins cutting funds for public radio.
　　　　　　　　■ **1994.** Associated Press launches 24-hour all-news radio service.
　　　　　　　　■ **1995.** Radio begins transmitting over the Internet.
　　　　　　　　■ **1996.** Telecommunications Act

1930　　**1940**　　**1950**　　**1960**　　**1970**　　**1980**　　**1990**

■ **1930s.** The Great Depression
■ **1939.** TV is demonstrated at New York World's Fair.
■ **1939–1945.** World War II
　　■ **1950s.** Rock 'n' roll begins.
　　　　■ **1970s.** VCR is developed.
　　　　■ **1970s.** Federal government, defense contractors, and universities create basis of Internet.
　　　　　　■ **1980s.** Online services such as CompuServe develop.
　　　　　　■ **1989–1991.** Cold War ends and Soviet Union dissolves.

tween 1930 and 1940 the number of radio sets in the United States increased from 13 million to 51 million.[10] During the Depression, people bought the relatively cheap radio receivers and sought escape from their everyday difficulties.

As radio matured as an advertising medium, companies bought time to sponsor particular shows rather than simply airing commercials. For example, General Foods' Jell-O sponsored Jack Benny. Networks rented time to companies, which were responsible for the content of the entire program. This enabled advertisers to dictate the type of programming that aired. A similar pattern dominated the early years of television. However, after a series of television scandals in the 1950s (see Chapter 9), advertisers were no longer allowed to control entire programs. Television and radio developed their own programming and simply sold *spots* of time to advertisers.

■ **Beginnings of radio journalism**

Early radio news programs were tied to newspapers. In July 1922 the *Norfolk* [Nebraska] *Daily News* started the first regularly broadcast noon news program. These broadcasts often used wire service material that was available from newspaper sources. During the 1920s the news services—the Associated Press (AP), United Press (UP), and the International News Service (INS)—waffled in their stance toward this potential competitor. They were unsure whether supplying news to radio should be part of their newspaper service or whether radio was a threat.

However, when radio networks used wire service material to beat newspapers in delivering election results of the 1932 Roosevelt–Hoover presidential race, the war between radio and newspaper was officially declared. In that election, broadcast replaced newspapers forever as the primary source of election night coverage. After the election, the AP, a newspaper-based and -funded service, refused to sell news to radio networks, ordered newspapers with radio stations to limit broadcasting of AP news to brief bulletins of thirty words, and charged additional fees for the use of its material on radio. UP and INS created similar constraints on radio.

Keyconcept

Radio-Newspaper War: During the late 1920s, as radio became more established, it challenged newspapers for the role of delivering news. Newspapers, fearing radio's ability to reach the public quickly, tried to control access to news reports from private telegraph wire services. In the mid-1930s, radio stations succeeded in breaking the newspapers' hold on the wire services and increased their own news-gathering operations.

The news service actions led to the growth of separate radio news-gathering organizations. CBS started the fledgling Columbia News Service soon after the AP decision, though it was discontinued when NBC and CBS signed an agreement to end the radio-newswire war. This agreement, which limited the networks' ability to gather their own news, lasted less than a year. The wire services provided only limited copy to the networks and maintained a structure that favored newspapers. The radio industry was not strong enough to consider staffing its own worldwide bureaus.

Competition emerged from a new service that was not tied to the newspaper industry. Transradio Press Service, begun in 1934, acquired 150 clients during its first year and provided news from other wire services such as Havas in France and England's Reuters as well as domestic news. The service sent an average of 10,000 words a day.[11] Fearful of the competition, the wire services declared independence from newspaper dominance and sold news to radio stations. The networks also returned to gathering their own news.

■ **Radio and World War II**

Radio made its journalistic mark with its dramatic and complete coverage of World War II. Before radio, war news took hours, days, or even weeks to reach the general public. Radio was instantaneous. Furthermore, print could never match the immediacy of Edward R. Murrow broadcasting from London as German bombs ripped through the city.

The first taste of radio war coverage came in 1938 when Germany invaded Austria. Murrow set up the first simultaneous broadcast with reporters in Vienna, London, Paris, Berlin, and Rome. By the time Hitler invaded Poland in 1939, CBS and NBC had placed experienced reporters throughout Europe. By 1943 the amount of radio news in the networks' evening programming had tripled, and a majority of people in the United States rated radio as more accurate than newspapers in war coverage.

Radio coverage of World War II trained an entire generation of broadcast journalists, many of whom helped to found television news. Hans Von Kaltenborn, Mary Marvin Breckinridge, and Eric Sevareid all covered the war. Murrow, who set up the network of CBS war correspondents, later set up the CBS television news department. He set a standard of broadcast journalism to which many journalists still aspire.

Although news was the cornerstone of radio war coverage, entertainment programs also contributed to the war effort. Celebrities sold war bonds over the radio to help finance the war. Soap operas got into the act by including special appeals for blood donations and by incorporating the war into existing series. Despite such contributions to the war effort, critics have argued that the commercial nature of radio kept entertainment programs from contributing as much as they might have.[12]

Radio competes with TV

At the end of World War II, radio was at the height of its dominance as a mass medium. By this time, 14.6 percent of advertising expenditures went to radio, up from 6.5 percent only ten years before. Ten years later, the percentage had dropped to 6.1 as television moved into households across the nation.[13]

The advent of television caused a rapid decline of comedy and drama shows on radio. As radio stars such as Jack Benny and George Burns and Gracie Allen moved to television, many critics predicted an end to radio as a mass medium. But radio reshaped itself and survived, becoming the music box of a new generation. Radio created a forum for ethnic music. And further, millions of young baby boomers found rock 'n' roll, which distinguished them from their parents' generation.

New technology recreates the "music box"

The development of FM radio and the creation of the transistor, which made portability possible, combined to recast radio as the music box it had once been. FM had three major advantages: (1) it had better sound quality than AM; (2) smaller communities would have access to frequencies; and (3) with its wider **wave band,** FM could carry the new **high fidelity** and stereo recordings that were enhancing the quality of recorded music. The **transistor,** invented in 1948, made possible portability and better car radios. By the late 1950s, teenagers could listen to rock 'n' roll anywhere and just about any time they wanted.

AM radio stations send long wave length, low frequency radio signals, and FM stations send short wave length, high frequency signals. The longer the wave length, the greater the distance the signal will travel because it is not easily absorbed by the ground and other solid objects. This explains why a person in Montana can pick up an AM station in Forth Worth, Texas, late at night when atmospheric interference is low. High frequency signals, on the other hand, produce higher quality sound.

FM stations dominate radio ratings today because of the higher sound quality. Music is the primary format on radio, and FM provides higher fidelity for stereo radio. Nevertheless, AM radio staged a comeback in the 1990s, as talk radio boomed. Talk and information do not require high quality transmission and the longer reach of AM opens up a bigger market for the talk shows.

Today's market structure

By the end of the 1960s, as television became the favorite mass medium for national advertising, radio lost its mass appeal. Local stations began to tailor their formats to attract specialized audiences. The shift has been a lucrative one. In 1995, radio received $11.3 billion in advertising revenues, compared to $1.2 billion for cable television.[14] In the early 1990s, about 77 percent of the average station's revenue came from local advertising, 22 percent from national and regional advertising, and 1 percent from **network compensation.** Most com-

wave band: An electromagnetic wave within the range of radio frequencies.

high fidelity: Reproduction of sound with minimal distortion.

transistor: A small electronic device containing a semiconductor. A key component of an integrated circuit. Paved the way for portability.

network compensation: Money paid by the networks to the local stations for running network programming.

Country: Country music in a variety of forms: traditional, contemporary, and country-rock. Appeals to ages 25 to 64 with a variety of socioeconomic backgrounds.

News/Talk: Twenty- to thirty-minute cycles of local, state, national, and international news and a variety of talk and call-in shows. Targets listeners between 25 and 65 and can narrow the group according to content.

Religion: Music, information, and talk designed to appeal to people who support the religious beliefs of the organization that runs the station. Aimed mostly at adults.

Adult Contemporary: Current and former popular music. Attracts wide range of adults between 18 and 35.

Oldies: Mostly rock and roll hits from the 1950s and 1960s. Targets people over 35.

Top 40: Current top-40 selling rock and pop songs. Targets ages 18 to 24 but has many younger listeners.

Middle of the Road: Variety of music and information. Music list includes contemporary popular music. News, sports, weather, traffic, and talk are included in the mix. Attracts 25- to 45-year-olds.

Album-Oriented Rock: Emphasizes current and old hits of particular artists. Album cuts and entire sides are played. Particularly attractive to people 18 to 35, especially men.

Alternative Rock: Plays rock music from lesser known groups and singers who would not appeal to Top 40 listeners. Aimed at people in the 18 to 30 age group.

Spanish: Variety of music, news, and talk in Spanish. Aimed at Spanish-speaking people in a particular market.

Urban/Black: Black-oriented music, ranging from soul, gospel, and rhythm and blues to jazz and rap. Aimed at African Americans between 18 and 49. Also attracts many white listeners.

Classic Rock: Music mostly from the 1960s, 1970s, and 1980s, with an emphasis on particular artists. Aimed at those older than 35, especially men.

Easy Listening: Slow, instrumental versions of current and older hits. Aimed at older listeners.

Jazz: Jazz music, from big band to fusion. Appeals to a limited number of upper-income listeners.

Classical: Recorded and live opera, symphony, and chamber music. Aimed at educated groups.

munities have the choice of a number of stations in several formats. Rural areas, of course, have access to fewer stations and formats.

Keyconcept

Drive-Time Broadcast Markets: Significant audiences are available to broadcasters during the morning and afternoon periods when people are driving children to and from school and are going to work. These *drive times* represent prime markets for radio—and for radio advertisers.

These formats, which are described in Table 8.2, deliver a particular type of audience to advertisers, who buy time to present their goods and services. The audience for each format is carefully defined by music or content taste, age, lifestyle, and buying habits. Stations use a variety of strategies to build a loyal audience, often creating programming around distinctive **on-air personalities.** Stations with similar formats compete for advertisers, particularly during the highly lucrative drive times—6:00 to 10:00 A.M. and 3:00 to 7:00 P.M.

Syndicated programming increasingly dominates radio, especially in non-drive-time periods. A disc jockey at a central location plays songs and provides chatter that is supplied to stations around the country through telephone lines and by satellites. Standardized programming, which sometimes eliminates the DJ, is often less expensive and of higher quality than local programming. However, this type of programming lacks local flavor and reduces diversity.

on-air personalities: One of the attractions of radio has been the ability of listeners to identify with a personality who comes to them regularly from radio. Whether a person who reads the news or announces music, the on-air personality gives a station a singular identity.

syndicated programming: Nationally produced programming that is supplied to stations through telephone lines and by satellite.

Radio stations often promote local products and services, with announcers becoming local celebrities. Radio now mixes nationally syndicated material with local programming and advertising targeted at specific age groups.

Radio station organization

Organizational patterns are similar for AM and FM stations. A general manager supervises the entire operation, makes business decisions with the assistance of other department heads, and runs the business department, which handles payroll, hiring, billing of advertisers, and buying of supplies.

At least three departments—programming, sales, and engineering—report to the general manager. The programming department and its manager select and produce all of the station's programming. If a station has a news format or substantial news programming, it may have a separate news department and news director.

The sales department sells radio time—and, implicitly, the attention of its listeners—to advertisers. A sales manager runs the department, and account executives sell time and serve the advertisers. This service includes helping advertisers to pick the best time for their ads to air and helping them to develop the advertisements.

The engineering department, headed by the chief engineer, is responsible for the technology at the station. This includes a variety of equipment, from CD players to **modulators** and antennas. Members of this department make sure the station's broadcasting meets the requirements of the FCC.

The **traffic** manager works with the sales and programming department. She or he prepares a log of what is supposed to play every day and keeps a record of what actually goes on the air. The traffic manager supplies the information that is used to bill advertisers for time on the radio.

Larger stations may have additional departments, such as a promotions department that is in charge of advertising and public relations for the station. At smaller stations the general manager usually handles these responsibilities.

Who owns radio?

Even though large media corporations own many radio stations, independently owned stations are still common. The radio industry has traditionally been less concentrated than many other media. However, deregulation by the 1996 Telecommunications Act brought a boom in mergers and station acquisitions.

modulator: Device that modulates, or processes the carrier wave so that its amplitude or frequency varies. Amplitude modulation (AM), is constant in frequency and varies the intensity, or amplitude, of the carrier wave. Frequency modulation (FM) is constant in amplitude and varies the frequency of the carrier wave.

traffic: Department that controls movement of programming through the day, logs what goes on the air, and supplies information for billing advertisers.

E ver since television grabbed the national audience, people have predicted the death of radio. However, radio survives because it has adapted to changes in its environment. Begun first as a local entity, radio responded to the demands of advertisers and listeners and became the first national mass medium. When television became the national advertising medium of choice, radio returned to its local origins, and each station in a market developed a niche. Today, technology and economics are pushing radio back to the future by increasing the national reach of the medium through syndication and satellite delivery.

National networks originally developed because stations could afford higher-quality programming by pooling resources. If each radio station had produced all of its own programming during the 1930s, the Golden Age of Radio would never have existed. No

Return of National Radio

one station could have afforded the salaries paid to performers such as Jack Benny and Bing Crosby.

The strong networks of the 1930s and 1940s will not return, but the same underlying concept is at the heart of a growing radio syndication business. Syndicates deliver the same program by satellite to several stations around the country. The program may be a talk show, such as Larry King's or Howard Stern's, or it may be music, such as "Z-Rock." These shows cost stations less than producing their own programs.

The trend toward more syndication started because lower programming costs equal higher station profits. However, critics argue that syndicated radio, which has no local flavor, fails to serve the communities

where stations are located. The critics warn that radio stations will no longer be responsive to their communities' needs, nor will they employ as many local people. Broadcasters reply that radio stations must decrease costs because of increasing competition.

Proponents of local radio programming faced another problem in 1997, when the FCC approved rules governing satellite digital radio. Digital satellite radio service (DARS) allows the same station to reach the entire country by using satellites to distribute it. People with DARS systems will pay to get up to twenty channels anywhere in the country. Critics say the system will not function well in urban areas because of interference from buildings and other objects.

Radio stations are generally owned by four types of companies:

1. Independent companies that own one station or perhaps an AM-FM combination.

2. Groups or companies that own more than two radio stations but no TV stations. In 1994, 446 out of 522 radio companies fit this category. An example is American Radio Systems, which owned ten AM and fifteen FM stations.

3. Broadcast groups that own radio and TV stations. Seventy-six companies fit this category in 1994. For example, CBS Broadcasting Group owned eight AM stations, thirteen FM stations, and seven TV stations in 1994.

4. Multimedia groups. Multimedia groups owned at least two radio stations and some form of print media, such as newspapers or magazines. In 1994, Capital Cities/ABC Broadcast Group owned nine AM stations, ten FM stations, eight TV stations, eleven daily newspapers, sixty-nine weeklies, twenty-six shopper guides, and dozens of magazines. Sixty-eight companies owned both radio and print outlets that same year.[15]

The low operating costs and low **profit margin** of radio stations make them relatively cheap buys for someone wanting to own a media firm. Between 1990 and 1993, 2,763 radio stations sold for an average price of $965,000. During the same time, 314 TV stations sold for an average price of $15.3 million. AM stations typically sell for about half the price of FM stations. Congress drastically changed ownership rules for radio stations with the 1996 Telecommunications Act. Before the act, companies could own no more than thirty stations, and those stations could not have more than 25 percent of the national audience. The new law removed all national limits on audience and stations. The law also expanded the number of stations a company could own within a particular market. The number varies with market size, as shown in Table 8.3.

TABLE 8.3 Ownership Rules Under the 1996 Telecommunications Act

NUMBER OF STATIONS PER MARKET	NUMBER OF STATIONS ONE COMPANY MAY OWN	NUMBER OF SINGLE TYPE (AM OR FM)
1–15	5	3
16–29	6	4
30–44	7	4
44+	8	5

The changes represented efforts to increase radio companies' profits, but not everyone was pleased. Smaller markets could now be dominated by two or three companies. This placed power in the hands of companies to increase advertising prices, to reduce jobs by combining operations, and to limit access to the airwaves. Some critics have argued that profitability could have been enhanced and accessibility maintained with lower ownership limits.

Audience demand in radio markets

Radio does not aim for the mass. It aims for targeted audiences. Station managers strive to identify content that will appeal to dedicated listeners with particular demographic characteristics. Gaining a loyal and identifiable segment of the audience, rather than trying to attract a large percentage of the total available audience within a given geographic area has enabled radio to survive in a competitive media environment.

Consumer market

Radio listeners in the 1990s express a demand primarily for music, news, and talk. A few nostalgia stations continue to carry radio drama and comedy, and college stations may broadcast sports, but music makes up the bulk of programming.

DEMAND FOR MUSIC Music programming provides background for people's daily lives. Students study, mechanics repair cars, and commuters drive—all to the sound of radio music. Music helps us to endure exercise and to transcend boring tasks, and it bonds us with people who share common interests. It is the shared interest that makes the format approach work. In general, people who want to listen to country music tend to have some common characteristics—characteristics that can be associated with certain buying habits that attract advertisers. Without correlations between demographics and music and demographics and buying habits, radio advertising would lose its effectiveness.

profit margin: The cost of goods sold, minus that of goods that are returned, yield net sales. The net sales, minus the cost of the goods sold, is the gross profit. Gross profit is divided by net sales to get the profit margin, expressed as a ratio or percentage.

Radio stations often sponsor concert series that appeal to specific age groups.

Demographics that lead to demand for a particular type of music might involve education level, race, or gender, but they most often reflect age. Music has been the language of adolescence, and the various demographic groups have been given names that reflect their music tastes in adolescence. The members of the so-called "Generation X" tend to share musical tastes, as did the "Bobbysoxers" and "Baby Boomers" before them. The "Xers" have rap and grunge, the "Boomers" had folk-rock and acid-rock, and the "Soxers" had Frank Sinatra and swing. The radio and recording industries have addressed the music of each generation, capitalizing on the ability of radio to create and spread popular music to those who want to listen. As a result, the radio and recording industries share a symbiotic relationship that makes both prosper financially. The recording industry provides the content to meet musical demand.

DEMAND FOR NEWS AND TALK Radio news ranges from the in-depth reporting of national and international news found on National Public Radio to a quick survey of the city's most important stories. In between falls extensive coverage of local news. Large markets have enough demand for these types of news to support either an all-news or a news-talk station. Smaller markets must often rely on public radio stations to meet the demand for news.

■ Advertising market

Advertising demand is expressed by the potential advertiser, not by the audience. Demand for radio advertising can be local or national. A family-owned pizza parlor could buy a fifteen-second commercial that would be aired with a thirty-second spot for Chevrolet. Because each radio station targets a demographically defined group of people who listen to a specific format, no station can deliver an audience that would include all the people a business might want to reach. Therefore, businesses often buy radio advertisements as a part of a total media package. A pizza parlor might run a coupon in the local newspaper and buy radio ads on one, two, or several stations to tell people about the special price. One study of two medium-sized cities found that the average company bought ads from about five different media.[16]

Advertising rates reflect an independent assessment of audience size. Advertisers learned early not to rely on media companies to estimate audience size and supported the rise of ratings companies, whose sole job is to measure audiences. Arbitron, the primary radio ratings service, assigns counties to 250 geographic regions, labeled **areas of dominant influence (ADI),** and reports listener data for these areas and smaller geographic components on either an annual or a quarterly basis.

The numbers of listeners are reported in two forms: rating and share. A *rating* is the percentage of *all people in a market* who are listening to a particu-lar station during a 15-minute segment. A *share* is the percentage of *people with their radios on* who are listening to a particular station during a 15-minute segment. The data came from surveys in which randomly selected listeners are asked to fill out a week's worth of daily logs detailing their radio listening.

To understand ratings and shares, look at The Pit Viper's hard rock drive-time program on station JIMI. The rating service estimated that 10,000 people listened to the Viper's show from 8:15 to 8:30 A.M. on

areas of dominant influence (ADI): Areas defined by the ratings company Arbitron for purposes of reporting listener data.

TABLE 8.4 Ratings and Shares

This chart shows how the rating and share is computed for the Pit Viper's hard rock listeners.

	TOTAL MARKET (BASIS FOR RATING)	TOTAL LISTENERS WITH RADIO ON DURING SEGMENT
May 15 Segment: 8:15 A.M. to 8:30 P.M.	1,000,000	100,000
Pit Viper's hard rock listeners	10,000	10,000
	Rating: $\frac{10,000}{1,000,000} = 0.01\ (1\%)$	Share: $\frac{10,000}{100,000} = 0.10\ (10\%)$

May 15. Of the 1 million listeners in the ADI, 100,000 were listening to radio at that time. Table 8.4 shows how the rating and share for the show is computed.

Supplying the audience's demand

The job of supplying the demand of the radio audience falls mostly on local radio stations. The powerful national networks of the 1930s and 1940s faded during the 1960s, and even though syndicated content grew during the 1990s, radio remains primarily a local medium.

Radio stations can be classified into eight types as shown in Table 8.5, on the basis of ownership and type of financing: commercial, state-run, public, shortwave, educational institution, community, special-interest, and pirate stations. The types of stations available vary by country, depending on the nature of government and regulation. In the United States, about 85 percent of all stations are commercial, though all eight types can be found. In Asia and Africa, state-run and commercial stations are the most common.[17] U.S. commercial stations program primarily music, and public radio remains the prime source of news and information. Talk radio is emerging as a cultural force, and it is emerging on commercial and public radio, special-interest stations, and shortwave.

Keyconcept

Radio Station Types: The demand for information from various audiences is met by eight types of radio stations in the United States. In addition to the dominant commercially financed stations, there are stations run by governments, public consortiums, community groups, special interests, and educational institutions as well as shortwave operators and unregulated pirate broadcasters.

The public radio system

In 1967, after a period of concern that television was becoming a "vast wasteland," Congress responded to the recommendations of a prestigious study group, the Carnegie Commission, and created the Corporation for Public Broadcasting (CPB). In 1969–1970, CPB joined with public television and radio stations to form the Public Broadcasting Service (PBS) and National Public Radio (NPR). These organizations provide programming for noncommercial stations.

TABLE 8.5 Types of Radio Stations

Commercial: These stations seek to make a profit. Programming is mostly music, interview and call-in shows, and news.

State-run: Owned and operated by governments with direct control of content on a day-to-day basis.

Public: Noncommercial stations that receive money from the general public, private foundations, and governments. Receive government grants but are shielded from day-to-day government intervention.

Shortwave: Shortwave radio is used to beam international programming. During 1995 it gained new attention in the United States because of its use by the militia movement.

Educational: Educational radio stations are owned and operated by universities, colleges, and even high schools. More than 800 U.S. educational institutions have broadcast licenses.

Community: Low-power stations that promote community participation in solving local problems. In the United States, many serve ethnic communities.

Special-Interest: Financed by noncommercial groups that advocate particular political or religious beliefs.

Pirate: Unlicensed stations. For example, WTRA/Zoom Black Magic Liberation Radio in Springfield, Illinois, battled the Federal Communication Commission (FCC) over the right to broadcast without FCC approval. The low-power station promoted communication among people who lived in a low-income housing project.

Sources: Carolyn Weaver, "When the Voice of America Ignores Its Charter," *Columbia Journalism Review,* November–December 1988, pp. 36–43; Michael C. Keith, *Radio Production: Art and Sciences* (Boston: Focal Press, 1990), p. 228; Robert Chapman, *Selling the Sixties: The Pirates and Pop Music Radio* (London: Routledge, 1992); and Ron Sakolsky, "Zoom Black Magic Liberation Radio: The Birth of the Micro-Radio Movement in the U.S.," in *A Passion for Radio,* Bruce Girard, ed. (Montreal: Black Rose Books, 1992), pp. 106–113.

NPR started in 1971 in one room with part-time journalists. Early programming was offbeat, and the small budget encouraged an emphasis on feature stories. One reporter—writing in a closet—commented on whether Wint-o-Green Life Savers spark in the dark when someone bites them.[18] By the early 1990s, NPR had a news budget of more than $15 million and was carried by more than 350 stations. Its combination of features and in-depth news programming such as *All Things Considered* and *Morning Edition* has brought it millions of regular listeners. As NPR has become successful, its product has been criticized for becoming too much like commercial radio news. However, NPR programs are often the only radio news available in smaller towns and cities. As such, they are serving the purpose envisioned by noncommercial radio proponents as early as 1920.

Most of NPR's financing comes from listeners' contributions and payment from member public radio stations. In 1993, about 35 percent of a public radio station's funding came from the public, 16 percent from the CPB, and the remaining 49 percent from universities, private businesses, and foundations.

NPR makes up an important part of public radio, but the 622 local member stations produce the bulk of programming. Public radio stations produce local news, and most have talk shows on a variety of topics, from sports to building a house to current events. Classical music and jazz also make up a significant proportion of program time on many stations. Public radio stations tend to reflect the needs and wants of those in the community who supply the money that allows the station to operate, a practice that has opened the system to charges of elitism.

Each public station operates independently as a public corporation. Each station originates its own programming but also carries NPR programs about national and interna-

The Car Talk guys represent only one aspect of talk radio and one aspect of public radio, which has provided an alternative to commercial formats.

tional issues. Stations may choose which NPR programs to carry, depending on available funding and local needs.

The public broadcasting system appeared to be in jeopardy in mid-1995 after Republicans devoted to cutting the national deficit took over Congress for the first time in forty years. Congress decreased CPB funding by 12 percent in 1996, from $312 million to $275 million. Funding for 1997 dropped by 17 percent, from $315 million to $260 million.

Producers of entertainment for public radio fear that the cuts will hurt the independent artists and experimental music that commercial stations shy away from. One person who is already speaking out is folksinger Iris DeMent, who is defending what she believes is public radio's true service: providing an oasis from the barrage of commercial messages and commercially motivated programming that create a false impression of Americans. "That's not an accurate picture of who we are as a people," says DeMent. "Public radio maintains that balance."[19]

The Republican Congress, headed by Speaker Newt Gingrich, argued that funding public broadcasting is not an appropriate use of taxpayers' money. Lawrence Jarvik of the Centre for the Study of Popular Culture says that it is unfair to use tax money to support television and radio, especially in times of fiscal stringency. "I don't think we need a domestic Voice of America," he says.[20]

Content is also an issue. Conservative critics complain that NPR programs have a liberal bias and that their social content is too controversial. Ironically, when CPB first was funded, the primary concern was whether public funding would mean government control. Public stations now carry more material that is critical of government than do commercial stations, and the primary criticism of the public broadcasting system is that it is too liberal.

Commercial radio news

The growth and development of NPR coincided with a decline in the amount of commercial radio news, especially in smaller markets. The growth of television, the development of FM radio, and deregulation all combined to restructure radio news after 1960. However, commercial radio news continues to survive and even shows signs of resurgence.

Commercial radio stations provide two forms of news. First, about two dozen all-news stations, located in major markets, and about 200 commercial stations that mix news and talk provide news throughout the day. Typically, these stations have ongoing news packages that summarize important happenings around the world, nation, state, and local areas. The motto is "give us 22 minutes and we'll give you the world." The second form of commercial radio news is a short news summary.

Deregulation and increasing competition for radio advertising have hurt smaller news operations. Before the deregulation of the 1980s, most radio stations provided news every thirty minutes as part of their public service requirement for a license. When the public service requirement was dropped, about 8 percent of the stations dropped news.

224

The increasing number of stations chasing after dwindling advertising funds in the early 1990s contributed as well. Many stations simply could not afford news.[21]

Despite predictions of doom, surveys by the Radio-Television News Directors Association and Associated Press show that about 80 percent of radio stations have a news operation of some sort.[22] Research also shows that listeners turn to their radios for news about major crises. The Gulf War illustrated this point as ratings increased by 50 percent or more for most major market news stations during the 1991 war.[23]

The Associated Press launched a twenty-four-hour all-news radio service in 1994. Other networks and news providers also expanded their offerings, focusing on providing FM stations with more news, while using satellite distribution and digital automation to reduce costs.[24]

Talk radio

Between 1990 and 1995 the number of stations that devote the bulk of their programming to talk almost tripled, from 405 to 1,130. With talk, radio stations have discovered a new way to boost their ratings and bring in advertisers.

Talk radio provides new profits, but only a few stars, such as conservative political talk show host Rush Limbaugh and the outrageous Howard Stern, generate huge sums. Limbaugh alone produces $30 million in revenue for his syndicator, EFM Media Inc.[25] Rush Limbaugh attracts 20 million listeners each week on 660 stations. Talk radio trails only country music as the nation's most pervasive format; it attracts more than 15 percent of radio's fragmented audience.[26]

Talk radio as a format was developed in the 1960s by conservatives Joe Pyne and William Buckley. Murray Levin, a Harvard professor who wrote *Talk Radio and the American Dream* in 1980, told a *Los Angeles Times* reporter in 1995 that talk shows today capitalize on emotional subjects in much the same way they did in the 1960s. "When I studied talk radio," Levin said, "there was no issue that aroused as much anger and emotion as homosexuality. The talk-show hosts, they knew this. They would talk more about it than the subject warranted. They'd get heated debates and would push people to further extremes. That boosted ratings."[27]

Because talk is so popular, the collection of hosts has expanded to include former political figures, celebrities, and infamous characters. Former governors, such as Douglas Wilder of Virginia, Lowell Weicker of Connecticut, and Mario Cuomo of New York, and presidential candidates such as Ross Perot and Pat Buchanan test the popular sentiment via the airwaves, trying to connect with "the people," checking the election landscape, and earning—on occasion—big dollar rewards.

In the mid-1990s, talk shows came under new scrutiny as public figures accused talk show hosts of exploiting social issues such as race and militancy. In 1995, President Clinton denounced the shows as "purveyors of hatred" after the bombing of the Alfred P. Murrah Federal Building in Oklahoma City. Clinton and other critics have argued that talk show hosts contribute to a climate of violence and polarization, rather than to rational debate and resolution of issues.

In 1993, political scientist Richard Hofstetter surveyed San Diego County and found that about one-third of adults had listened to political talk shows at one time or another. Those who were more interested in political issues and well informed about candidates were more likely to listen. Most were mainstream in their views, Hofstetter said. Eighty percent said that they disagreed with the talk show host at least occasionally, but 30 to 40 percent said that they disagreed often. "That was surprising," Hofstetter told the *Los Angeles Times*. "That suggests this is a sort of titillating, cheap thrill for these listeners. I think what's happened is people stuck in automobiles want to listen to something besides music."[28]

Shortwave Radio

Shortwave radio is a technological and cultural phenomenon. Shortwave radio is access to the world. It's also a handy tool with which to reach the world. Shortwave, or "ham," operators receive a license from the FCC, which is granted on the basis of technical competence and intended primarily for broadcast to an international audience. Shortwave traditionally was conceived of as radio for person-to-person communication, or *narrowcasting,* but it has also been used by the VOA and other news and cultural services to broadcast across national boundaries. It's often valuable in times of disaster, when telephone lines are destroyed by high wind or other acts of God. Shortwave radio operates on frequencies that standard AM and FM receivers can't access.

However, shortwave has recently become identified in the United States with the militia movement and with the Christian Right. Powerful 100,000-watt shortwave stations such as WWCR (World Wide Christian Radio) out of Nashville and less powerful stations such as WRNO in New Orleans and WINB in Red Lion, Pennsylvania make it possible for someone to buy half an hour of air time for as little as $150. This person can then broadcast programs from his or her living room via cassette, a satellite patch, or even a direct telephone link.

Linda Thompson of Indianapolis used this method to promote her video *Waco: The Big Lie,* which attempted to show a government tank shooting flames into the Koresh compound. Although the video's claims later were widely discredited, many people in the patriot-militia movement accepted it as fact. Another popular shortwave broadcaster, "Mark from Michigan," was pulled from the airwaves in the spring of 1995 after the bombing of the Alfred T. Murrah Federal Building in Oklahoma City. WWCR station manager George McClintock said he pulled the program temporarily because it was in the best interests of the country. Mark Koernke, a thirty-seven-year-old maintenance man at a University of Michigan dormitory, had been broadcasting his "intelligence" report via a telephone satellite link on weeknights for two years.

Shortwave radio has not been the only communications tool used by the radical right—or left. The Internet and cable access TV stations also provide outlets for the expression of their beliefs. Nevertheless, shortwave radio remains one of the cheapest ways to get specialized information. A $200 digital receiver is easy to tune and gives access not only to extremist thought, but also to the BBC, Radio Havana, Radio Australia, Radio Japan, The Voice of the Andes, and many others. Cultural programming from the world—as well as political diatribes—is readily available.

SOURCES: Rogers Worthington, "Terror in the Heartland," *Chicago Tribune Online,* April 26, 1995 and April 29, 1995; Jill Smolowe, "Radio Business Report," Time, Inc., America Online, May 2, 1995; Robert A. Masullo, "Shortwave Radio Still Best Link to Far-Reaching Places, People," *Sacramento Bee,* April 2, 1995, p. EN2.

Talk shows are not all conservative, although those at the top of the ratings are. Mike Malloy hosts a liberal talk show on Atlanta's WSB, several black nationalists talk on New York's WLIB, and Tammy Bruce, a lesbian feminist and head of the Los Angeles chapter of the National Organization for Women (NOW), runs a weekend show on Los Angeles's KFI.

The popularity of talk radio has caused critics and scholars to speculate about why it has been so successful. Critics differ on how influential the shows are. Some gave talk show hosts credit for the Republican landslide of 1994. A more interesting argument is cultural, rather than political, and embodies the idea that talk radio is the new town

[profile]

Howard Stern

Broadcast talk shows have sprung up like mushrooms. In 1954, Steve Allen developed the first TV talk show. Today, television has more than twenty-five daytime talk shows and numerous late-night ones. Allen's original *Tonight Show,* which was filled with wit and intellect, is a far cry from talk programs such as Ricki Lake's noisy in-your-face format. However, a talk show is perhaps the cheapest way to draw an audience and the easiest way to fill a time slot.

Radio's call-in format was developed in the 1940s, when hosts had to paraphrase callers' comments and questions. In 1960, KABC in Los Angeles, the first all-talk radio station, began airing callers' comments directly. Today, there are about 850 AM and FM radio talk shows. Rush Limbaugh's and Howard Stern's shows lead the pack.

Howard Stern grew up in Long Island. His father Ben, a radio engineer, took Stern to task for being a "moron." Stern says his father was not mean-spirited, but genuinely concerned. However, Stern says he sometimes feels he is still seeking his father's approval.

Stern's style is angry, bombastic, and assaultive. When the popular Tejana singer Selena was murdered, Stern talked in detail about having sex with her in her coffin and the taste of her corpse. After he claimed that Mexicans liked having sex with animals, several stations dropped his show. When a Chicago station dropped him for his crude comments and declining listenership, Stern retaliated by announcing on the air that he hoped Larry Wert, the station manager, would be raped by two gay bikers in a gas station bathroom, contract AIDS, cut himself shaving, and bleed in his children's food, and that once the family died, the dog would eat the corpses.

Stern's syndicated program, carried on about twenty stations, reaches about 13 million listeners across the country. Many social groups have filed complaints against Stern's programs. In September 1995, Stern and his company paid the federal government $1.7 million—the largest amount a broadcaster has paid the federal government—to settle several indecency complaints sparked by Stern's comments about minorities, women, and homosexuals.

Stern moved into the realm of Hollywood in 1997 with a semi-autobiographical movie called "Private Parts." The film was the top grossing film during its first week of release, bringing in $14.6 million. However, some industry analysts said the movie, with its $26 million price tag, would not be the blockbuster the studios had hoped for.

SOURCES: Jenny Hontz, "Howard Stern Gets Dumped from Chicago's WCKG-FM," *Electronic Media,* October 9, 1995, Section News, Page 3; Arlene Rodda, "Talk Radio: The Phenomenon and Some of Its Leading Personalities," *RQ,* 35:1 (September 22, 1995), p. 19; Patrick McCormick, "Is America Running Off at the Mouth?" *U.S. Catholic,* 60:5 (May 1995), p. 46; Jerry Crowe, "Latinos to Stern," *Los Angeles Times,* April 11, 1995, Section Calendar, p. F2; and Ed Masley, "Mr. Nice Guy: Is He the Antichrist or Is Bad Boy Howard Stern Just A Big Pussycat?" *Pittsburgh Post Gazette,* Arts and Entertainment Section, p. 4.

meeting of a fragmented society whose members never meet in person but use electronic media such as radio and the Internet to connect. In this town meeting, the populace speaks rather than relying on official voices. In fact, in *Talk Radio,* Levin attributes the public fascination with talk radio to an increasing distrust of official institutions.

Critics often attack talk radio as a negative force. Peter Laufer, in *Inside Talk Radio,* concludes that many hosts put forth "fallacy" as "fact," "uninformed opinion" as "thoughtful commentary," and "groundless innuendo" as "investigative journalism."[29] Critics suggest that talk radio exploits and fans groundless fears and feeds paranoia.

TABLE 8.6 Radio Sets per 1,000 Inhabitants for Regions of the World

REGION	1970	1980	1993
Africa	51	103	173
Asia	37	98	179
Europe	476	595	628
Latin America	160	260	358 (1991)
North America	1,347	1,875	2,009 (1991)
Oceania	526	865	987

Source: UNESCO Statistical Yearbooks, 1993 and 1995.

International radio

Radio is a powerful medium in many countries. Even with new technologies, radio continues to be significant because programming is inexpensive to produce, can be transmitted across borders, and does not rely on expensive receiving equipment. These features, combined with portability, make radio a tool both for governments and for those who seek to challenge governments. In countries where print media are not widely distributed or where governments deny access to news, portable radios often form the only connection to factual information. Table 8.6 shows the availability of radio sets in different parts of the world.

Broadcasting across borders

Broadcasting across borders dates to 1926, when the Soviet Union ran a brief radio propaganda effort against the government of Romania. The first ongoing broadcast for people outside a country occurred in 1927, when Holland directed domestic programming to Dutch citizens living abroad. During the next seven years, Germany, France, Great Britain, the Soviet Union, and Japan created their own "colonial" broadcasts.[30]

During World War II, several combatant countries broadcast programs aimed at the enemy's population, trying to undermine opposition, lower morale, and create confusion. Germany, for example, broadcast anti-British messages into India in eight Indian languages.

Known personalities tended to attract listening audiences. One of the most famous of the radio personalities, "Tokyo Rose," broadcast to the allied troops in the Pacific in an effort to lower their morale. After the war, an American typist, Iva Togura, was convicted of treason and spent ten years in prison for being the infamous Tokyo Rose. Togura, who was trapped in Japan during the war, admitted to working for Japanese radio. In reality, Tokyo Rose did not exist. The name had been applied to every woman announcer on Japanese radio.

From the end of World War II until the late 1980s, the Cold War, a war of ideology, relied heavily on the dissemination of information and propaganda. The western and eastern bloc countries fought for domination through propaganda extolling the virtues of one political system over the other.

The two dominant broadcast units for the West were the BBC and the Voice of America (VOA). The BBC began broadcasting to the Soviet Union in 1946, and the VOA followed a year later. The VOA reached its zenith under President John Kennedy in the early 1960s, when it also received its greatest support from Congress.

Voice of America and the Internet

During the 1990s the ability to deliver radio messages through the World Wide Web made the government's Voice of America broadcast operation available to a domestic audience, as well as to its traditional international audience, and created a new legal dilemma for the agency.

In 1942, the Voice of America (VOA) began broadcasting radio programs in several languages; these were carried on privately owned shortwave stations, which the U.S. government took over for its own use during World War II. A few government-owned transmitters aided the broadcast effort. By the end of the war, VOA was a massive production and broadcast operation under the umbrella of the Office of War Information. More than 1,000 programs were issued from New York alone. After the war the operation moved to the State Department, then to the U.S. Information Agency, which was created in 1953 to promote the U.S. government.

The VOA traditionally provided news through shortwave radio broadcasts to populations whose governments control and withhold information. In the late 1990s, VOA reached an audience of 100 million people, broadcasting in forty-six languages from studios in Washington, D.C., and had twenty-five correspondents stationed around the world. Although ten countries had once interfered with VOA broadcasts, only Cuba—and sometimes China—were still jamming them.

Now Internet users can access digitized VOA newscasts in fifteen languages. By early 1994, VOA was uploading text from many of its broadcasts to the Internet; in September 1994 the agency began supplying audio files as well.

Converging technologies have created a new legal dilemma. The 1948 Smith-Mundt Act specifically prohibited the VOA from disseminating information domestically. However, for years, anyone with a shortwave radio could pick up VOA broadcasts, and those with satellite dishes could receive VOA's WorldNet Television. Now the VOA can be accessed domestically by Internet users. Not only can individuals read the transcripts of news stories, but with the proper equipment they can download actual broadcasts and play them.

Some critics believe that the prohibition of domestic access should be ended—that the 1940s fear of brainwashing the public is out of date. They argue that Americans are capable of reaching their own conclusions about government broadcasts.

On average, 9,000 users log onto VOA's server every day through the Internet to access program schedules, frequency information, and satellite downlink instructions for the VOA and the U.S. Information Agency's World-Net Television.

The VOA's gopher address is gopher gopher.voa.gov. The World Wide Web address is *gopher://gopher.voa.gov.* If you send electronic mail to *info@voa.gov* with the message "send help," the computer will automatically respond with instructions on how to receive lists of broadcasts and other information.

SOURCES: John Schwartz, "Over the Net and Around the Law? U.S. Computer Users Gain Access To Voice of America Broadcasts," *Washington Post,* January 14, 1995, p. C1; David Lamb, "VOA Vies for Ears of World, Tests Water in New Markets," *Los Angeles Times,* September 6, 1994, p. A5; James M. Smith, "More Users Log onto Multilingual Digital VOA Newscasts," *Government Computer News* 13(20), September 5, 1994, p. 18.

It is difficult to say how much international broadcasting contributed to the changes that swept the world during the past decade. However, western radio broadcasts to other countries claimed audiences in the tens of millions through- out the Cold War period. Chinese immigrants talk about listenting to the broadcasts while they were banished to the villages during the Cultural Revolution, and others profess to have learned English by listening to the broadcasts.

Europe

Most European countries have mixed systems with both public and commercial stations. Public stations are financed by license fees, which theoretically represent licenses to obtain radio content but in practice are fees for using a radio receiver. Commercial stations raise revenue from advertisers, and during the 1980s they increasingly took advertising revenues from other media. In Austria, Ireland, Portugal, France, and Greece a higher percentage of advertising dollars is spent on commercial radio than in the United States.[31]

Programming on European public networks includes classical to popular music, sports, news and current affairs, and educational material. As in the United States, commercial stations in Europe target segmented audiences, and during the 1980s, European radio became less national and more local.

Africa

African radio systems continue to mimic the BBC and French radio systems that were common when the African countries were European colonies. The BBC-derived systems are run as public operations with boards of governors appointed by the national government, and they operate nationally and regionally. Typically, 70 to 80 percent of revenue in these systems comes from advertising, the rest coming from government through the boards.

Keyconcept

Former Colonial Radio Systems: In many undeveloped countries, radio systems were built from communication networks originally set up by European governments and businesses that colonized and exploited Africa, Asia, and Latin America.

The French-derived systems have less autonomy than the British-derived systems, carry less advertising, and receive more direct government subsidies. They are usually run by the country's Ministry of Culture or Ministry of Information. The number of stations has remained relatively small in most African nations because it is in the interest of the elite class to limit the number of stations and, therefore, access to information and power. A few African nations, such as Nigeria and Madagascar, experimented with privately owned radio stations during the mid-1990s. The effort, however, has remained limited in scope.

Latin America

Despite Latin America's colonial background, its radio system differs greatly from Africa's and Asia's. Most Latin American countries have diverse systems, with state-owned, special-interest, educational institution, community, and commercial stations. The difference between radio in Africa and radio in Latin America probably reflects the dominance of the BBC in Africa and the generally stronger economies of Latin America. Latin America had 358 radio receivers per 1,000 inhabitants in 1991, compared to 170 per 1,000 inhabitants in Africa and 182 per 1,000 inhabitants in Asia. Commercial stations are strong in Latin America because the greater number of receivers and higher standard of living, compared to Africa, help to sustain a system funded by advertising revenue.

Commercial programming in Latin America is similar to that found in North America, with an emphasis on music and entertainment. Some countries saw a growth in community and pirate radio stations during the 1980s. During this period, hundreds of illegal FM stations sprang up in Argentina. They served people in smaller communities by running local information and education programs and by offering advertising to smaller businesses. Until 1991, when politicians discovered that these stations provided an effective way to reach voters, the central government tried to close them down.

Asia

Radio in Asia has similarities with radio in both Latin America and Africa. Because of European colonial influence, countries such as India have adopted systems modeled after the BBC. However, Asian radio systems, like those in Latin America, provide more diverse programming than do African stations. Some Asian nations, such as Singapore, have highly developed commercial systems. Some, such as South Korea, have radio systems with extensive religious programming. In China the government maintains tight control of radio at both national and local levels.

The variety of systems reflects variations in economic and political development. In 1989, the number of radio receivers per 1,000 inhabitants ranged from a low of 15 in Bhutan and 41 in Bangladesh to a high of 1,003 in South Korea and 895 in Japan. The importance of radio as a mass medium varies as well. In some isolated parts of China, radio is the primary source of national news. In Japan a highly developed television system has replaced radio as a primary source of information.

Radio is still the most accessible medium, with radio sets and broadcast networks available in remote parts of the world. In China, in 1997, those who could not get inside the Tiananmen Square gates for a memorial service listened instead to a radio broadcast.

Australia

Australia, with its vast geography and scattered population, has a natural demand for radio. The distances between population centers far exceed the broadcast capabilities of nonsatellite television. In 1989, Australia had 1,262 radio sets per 1,000 inhabitants, second in the world behind the United States.

The Australian radio system is overseen by the Australian Broadcasting Commission (ABC), which also provides programming through a network of stations. The programming is similar to that of public stations in the United States, with music and news making up most of the content. During the 1980s, ownership rules were changed to allow more stations per company, and commercial radio grew in popularity.[32]

Although music and listener attitudes resemble those in the United States, the government's ability to produce content remains closely tied to the British BBC system.

Trends and innovations

Radio remains financially healthy heading into the twenty-first century. Total revenue for the U.S. radio industry broke $10 billion in 1994, increasing by 11 percent over 1993. The strong showing corresponded to growing numbers of radio listeners in a media environment that was becoming more and more fragmented.

A strong financial position usually means that content will not change drastically. People don't fix things they don't think are broken. Talk radio will probably continue to attract high ratings, but music will still dominate radio formats in the near future. Content does change slightly, however, with new types of music formats. The fastest growing rock music format is alternative music. Part of this growth represents a change in the nature of the music, as well as an increase in the number of stations playing traditionally defined alternative music. Groups and performers, such as Stone Temple Pilots and Soundgarden, who were once labeled alternative, are now being played on mainstream rock format.

Some observers say the "alternative" label doesn't really fit anymore because of the mainstreaming of the once fringe groups. Others argue that the music is maturing and as it does, it will splinter into a variety of alternative rock formats, just as rock 'n' roll splintered in the late 1960s.[33]

Whatever the name, the movement to adopt emerging talent represents an effort by radio stations to attract the younger music listeners. The effect is to make radio more open to new groups and performers who previously had difficulty getting play time on radio.

The most important trends will concern the way in which radio reaches its audience. In this electronic age, the pressing questions involve radio's role on the information highway. Will the medium that entertains people on regular highways light up fiber-optic roads as well?

On January 17, 1995, Radio 927 GNR in Perth, Australia first broadcast online through the Internet. During the broadcast, the station received e-mail from Finland, Germany, and other countries around the world. The broadcast included the station's regular Tuesday night program about computers.

Broadcasting on the Internet or any online service opens radio to international interaction. No longer must the audience be limited to the reach of airwaves. A person anywhere in the world with a computer can listen. Online audio also allows interaction through text and voice. A voice can provide the sense of intimacy that many people find lacking on computer bulletin boards.

Online radio will grow with the technical improvements of computer audio. As more computers incorporate stereo sound systems and better software is developed, satisfaction with online radio will improve.

Although online radio strives to create larger communities, music available through cable systems may work in the opposite direction. Many cable systems already provide music channels. In the future they could provide music on demand. If a person wanted to hear an hour of country recording artist Vince Gill, she or he would simply place an order by telephone. The listener could pick the time to receive the music on a designated cable channel.

The technical possibilities of online and cable music on demand could drastically change radio. Personalized cable music probably would be paid for by the listener and would contain no advertising. Cable and online music certainly would compete with traditional radio as background music. Of course, the impact on traditional radio would depend on how radio reacts to such competition. Radio stations, with their recording libraries, could even become the providers of personalized music programs.

Summary

- Radio began as a point-to-point communication form before becoming a mass medium during the 1920s.
- Radio became the center of home entertainment during the 1930s, much as television is today.
- During World War II, radio news provided speed and intimacy to war coverage that had never existed before.
- A central debate throughout the history of radio is whether it should be a commercial medium serving owners or a public medium serving society.
- In the United States, radio has become a medium that attracts demographically defined audiences and sells the attention of those audiences to advertisers.

232

- Music makes up most of radio's programming, but news and talk radio remain important, especially in large markets.
- Almost two dozen music formats are available to radio stations.
- There are eight types of radio stations: commercial, state-run, public, educational institution, community, special interest, shortwave, and pirate.
- Radio remains the most used medium throughout the world.
- International broadcasts grew during the 1980s, as more countries used improving technology to communicate their ideologies.
- Radio will expand its distribution system in the future as it moves into digital delivery systems such as online services.

Navigating the Web

Radio on the web

Radio on the Web is growing more and more as stations set up Web sites. The availability of RealAudio software will increase the broadcasting of radio on the Web in the near future. RealAudio can be downloaded at

    http://www.realaudio.com

Sites also include information about the history and current state of the radio business.

The following sites contain historical and industry information.

| Old-Time Radio | http://www.old-time.com |

Programming logs, pictures, and catalogues of tapes from the Golden Age of Radio are available at this site. It contains historical material about the 1930s and 1940s.

| The Museum of Television and Radio | http://www.mtr.org |

This page is an introduction to the two museums about radio and television. One is located in New York and the other in Southern California. The site contains information about the museums and what is inside them. The museums have scholarly material about the history of radio and TV.

| Television and Radio News Research | http://www.Missouri.edu/~jourvs/index.html |

Professor Emeritus Vernon Stone of the University of Missouri maintains this page. It contains a large amount of research conducted by Professor Stone for various electronic news organizations. It has information about radio and TV salaries, internships, and pros and cons of broadcast journalism careers.

The following sites have radio news, music, or information about radio companies.

| Westwood One Radio Networks | http://www.westwoodone.com |

This site is maintained by the Westwood Radio Networks. It contains information about the company, its programming, and its affiliate stations.

This is the home site for the National Public Radio. It contains audio and text versions of news events and information about NPR, its programs, and its affiliates.

This site provides rock music online, information about musicians and record labels, and chat rooms for discussing music and politics.

Questions for review

1. Was radio first conceived of as a broadcasting system?

2. What is a network?

3. When did radio journalism become significant?

4. What is significant about radio formats?

5. List four types of radio ownership.

6. What are the major types of audience demand?

Issues to think about

1. Describe radio's flexibility across the years. How has this contributed to its staying power as a mass medium?

2. Does specialization strengthen or trivialize radio as a news and information medium?

3. What is the significance of the growing interest in talk radio?

4. Does public radio make a unique contribution to the society? How important are Congress's efforts to decrease funding for public radio?

5. Why is radio a significant international medium? How does it differ from other media in this respect?

Suggested readings

Adams, Noah. *Noah Adams on "All Things Considered:" A Radio Journal* (New York: W. W. Norton, 1992).

Chantler, Paul. *Local Radio Journalism* (Oxford, Focal Press, 1992).

Murray, Michael D. *The Political Performers: CBS Broadcasts in the Public Interest* (Westport, CT: Praeger, 1994).

"Radio, the Forgotten Medium," *Media Studies Journal,* Summer 1993 (New York: The Freedom Forum Media Studies Center).

Sklar, Rick. *Rocking America: An Insider's Story: How the All-Hit Radio Station Took Over* (New York: St. Martin's Press, 1984).

Television

"**W**hen I was a child," the student said, "my mother only let me watch *Sesame Street.* She thought I'd grow up smarter."

Americans sat glued to their TV sets as O. J. Simpson's Bronco was pursued by police along a California freeway. Live televisioin provides information simultaneously to an audience that is geographically and ideologically diverse.

"When I was a child," the middle-aged teacher said, "watching television was a social activity. People in the neighborhood used to go to each other's houses to watch TV."

"Aha," said the learned and aged professor. "When I was a child, we created our own pictures in our own heads."[1]

Added an all-too-clever student, "And was television as great a wasteland then as it is today?"

Television has always been a controversial factor in American life. Newton Minow, chairman of the Federal Communications Commission in the early 1960s, called television "a vast wasteland."[2] Critics have argued that television provides not only sound, but also pictures in our heads and that those images destroy the ability to use our imaginations, which is the essence of creativity. Others have long worried that television presents violent behavior as acceptable—or at least normal within society. Some believe that television advertising creates a desire for products and services that people may not need and not everyone can afford. Some believe that television is replacing the vitality and diversity of folk and ethnic cultures with a bland, homogeneous consumer culture.

Television has a positive side as well. It expands the world of people who have limited opportunities to experience faraway places and events. For many, television is the great entertainer and informer. Television also brings the world to our homes and can create common experiences among Americans. These range from entertaining spectacles such as the Super Bowl to tragedies such as the assassination of President John F. Kennedy and the bombing of the Alfred P. Murrah Federal Building in Oklahoma City. Television continued to give us the Oklahoma City story as it followed the legal proceedings surrounding the trials of Timothy McVeigh and Terry Nichols.

As you read through this chapter, you'll see that changing technologies affect how people watch television as well as affecting what they watch. At times, programming pushes cultural boundaries; at other times, it reinforces the status quo. But television content and the amount of television being watched remain concerns for people who are interested in individual development, social change, political life, and the evolution of a democratic society. Consider the following issues:

■ Television in the United States has been, for the most part, a commercial venture. As you read this chapter, ask yourself, just as critics are asking, how the commercial nature of television has shaped its content. Is content shaped by advertisers? By public need and desire? By the overwhelmingly commercial structure of the medium?

■ Until recently, the broadcast television industry was dominated by three networks. Has this oligopoly responded to public need across the years? Has the structure of the industry limited or fostered the development of television?

■ Television is a force for political and social change. How do you think content of television has shaped or changed U.S. culture and society? Has television fostered democracy? Has it turned politics into entertainment? Has it made people more accepting of violence? Has it encouraged tolerance of diversity?

Television in American life

The history of television is a history of technology and policy, economics and sociology, and entertainment and news. Television has never been a static medium. Rather, it has been altered constantly by changing technologies, including changes in presentation (such as programming in color) and distribution (by cable, satellite, and fiber optics), all of which have been affected by government regulation. But television was not merely a technical invention—it changed people's lives, even down to the arrangement of their homes. As Lynn Spigel has demonstrated, for example, American women's magazines of the 1950s discussed how to rearrange household furniture to accommodate the television as a replacement for the fireplace and the once traditional piano. The magazines also noted that television could provide a unifying influence in family life.[3] In later decades, televisions were often placed where they could be watched during meals. Today, many households have more than one television, and family members may watch individually, rather than together.

Television revolutionized not only the home, but also news, politics, and information. Some say that it revolutionized an entire society.

TV
in your life

How Do You Watch Television?

Watching television can be a solitary activity or a group activity. Check here the situations that apply to you. What are your motivations for watching? What are the motivations of your friends and family?

MOTIVATIONS	WATCHING ALONE	WITH FAMILY	WITH FRIENDS	AS A DATE
To see people I can identify with and enjoy				
To see people who are different from me				
To escape and relax				
To watch action, adventure				
To find good role models				
To learn ways to solve daily problems				
To learn about different cultures and lifestyles				

■ Development of television

No one person invented television. What we enjoy today is the result of a long line of early experiments by many inventors, including Vladymir Zworkin, Philo T. Farnsworth, Edwin Armstrong, and Lee de Forest. The finished product represents the efforts of combined technologies and vicious patent disputes. Although experimentation began a century ago, the first test broadcasts did not begin until the mid-1920s. Development of television was not an exclusive American phenomenon; television was on the air in England in the mid-1930s.

Battles between the network and electrical giants determined the course of television in the United States. David Sarnoff of Radio Corporation of America (RCA) became the dominating force in both radio and television network development. In 1933, Sarnoff opened the RCA Building in midtown Manhattan, which included a studio designed to provide live TV programs. RCA first demonstrated its all-electronic television system to the **trade press** in 1935, and television sets went on sale in a Bronx furniture store in 1938. In 1939 many Americans saw their first television on five- and seven-inch screens at the New York World's Fair.

Television arrived in the home and changed not only people's vision of the world, but the spatial arrangements of their homes. Household furniture was shifted to accommodate the television as a replacement for the fireplace and the once traditional piano.

trade press: Periodicals that target a specific industry. *Broadcasting & Cable* magazine, for example, targets the broadcast and cable industry and is an example of a trade magazine.

238

During 1939, several radio companies, including General Electric, RCA, CBS, and Du-Mont, began transmitting from experimental television stations in New York. RCA and DuMont, which manufactured early receivers, slowly increased the size of the viewing screen to twelve inches. After several years of debating technical standards, the FCC authorized a standardized system for resolution quality and transmission.[4] By the end of 1941, television's initial year of commercial operation in the United States, CBS and NBC had converted their New York stations from experimental to commercial status, and about 10,000 sets were sold.

Early regulation

Industry players cooperated with the government to ensure a profitable, commercial broadcast system. By 1934, regulation of broadcasting had been assigned to the Federal Communications Commission, created by the Communications Act. Broadcast regulation is treated thoroughly in Chapter 12, but it is important to note here that the basic outlines of radio regulation were applied to television, guaranteeing that it, too, would be primarily a commercial medium. The act extended principles of the 1927 Radio Act that assigned licenses to "trustees" of the airwaves and charged broadcasters with operating in the public interest.

Keyconcept

Broadcasters as Trustees of the Airwaves: Basing its regulations on the concept that airwave scarcity produces a common space that is subject to public laws, the U.S. government has long required that broadcasters function as trustees of the airwaves, operating by license in the public interest.

World War II and postwar challenges

Television's progress came to a halt in 1942 as manufacturers devoted themselves to war production. New television sets could not be made, and old ones could not be repaired. Only six experimental stations stayed on the air, and these for only an hour or so a week.

Although the technology was in place and regulation allowed for expansion, commercial television faced major challenges at the end of the war. First, TV station startups were expensive, requiring $1.5 million (about $7 million in today's dollars) or more. Second, the nation still suffered a shortage of critical materials. Third, advertisers were wary of television's high costs. Owners correctly expected their stations to operate at a loss for several years before a large enough viewing audience began to attract advertisers.

Each segment of the industry was reluctant to commit resources because of uncertainty in other segments. Station owners were concerned about whether consumers could afford sets to receive their broadcasts; set manufacturers needed on-air programming to entice set buyers; programmers needed advertisers' financial support; and advertisers needed viewers. One entity had to create the impetus for the other players to take the plunge, so development was slow. Nevertheless, the potential market encouraged risk-taking, and each segment stumbled its way to success.

Postwar boom

After World War II, television began to emerge as a mass medium, with networks rapidly becoming the dominant force in shaping station ownership and programming. In 1948, wanting to avoid the signal interference that had characterized early AM radio, the FCC froze the granting of television station licenses while it deliberated where and how sufficient frequencies could be allocated. Until it ended in 1952, the freeze limited stations to the 108 that were already in operation. During the freeze, a few big cities had several stations, and many had none. In areas that had no television, people used ingenious methods to get signals. In some communities, companies built tall antennas on hilltops to receive station signals and then transmitted those signals through **coaxial cable** to subscribing homes, thus initiating cable television. By 1952, about 15 million homes (10 percent of the U.S. population) had TV sets, and advertising revenues were about $324 million. Total advertising revenues for radio in the same year were about $445 million.

By late 1948, four television networks were in operation, broadcasting from New York with limited links west to Chicago. Three of the networks—ABC, CBS, and NBC—were based on radio networks; the fourth, which was television only, was run by DuMont with help from its partner, United Paramount Theaters of Hollywood.

Good programming and solid local affiliate stations were the main ingredients for a prosperous network. CBS and NBC offered the strongest programming and so gained the most affiliates. ABC and DuMont competed for the rest. DuMont was the only network that had no radio connections; its financial support came from a successful television-manufacturing business. DuMont hoped to pick up stations along the Atlantic seaboard and then move inland as the number of receivers increased and as the AT&T coaxial cables necessary for carrying television signals moved west. But the new stations tended to affiliate with one of the major networks. Unable to compete financially, DuMont closed its doors in 1955.[5] ABC, CBS, and NBC continued to dominate television until the coming of the Fox network in the late 1980s.

During the 1950s CBS and NBC competed for top spot. One of their early battles was played out through color. CBS and RCA, among others, had experimented with color systems from 1940 on. As often happens with innovative technologies, technical standards clashed. In 1948, CBS claimed that its system was ready for implementation, but RCA argued that further experimentation was necessary before standards could be set. In 1950, after considerable political pressure from Congress and from CBS, the FCC first chose CBS's partly mechanical color system. However, in 1953 the FCC reversed its earlier decision and authorized the all-electronic RCA system, which was compatible with black-and-white sets. David Sarnoff, chairman of the board of RCA, announced on television that color had arrived. "This day will be remembered in the annals of communications," he said, "along with the historic date of April 30, 1939 when RCA–NBC introduced all-electronic black-and-white television as a new broadcast service to the public at the opening of the World's Fair in New York. At that time we added sight to sound. Today, we add color to sight."[6] However, Sarnoff's claim was mostly public relations hype, and it was not until the mid-1960s that color receivers became widely available as all three networks began to offer more and more color programming.

Keyconcept

Community Antenna Television (CATV) as a Cable System: The first form of cable system, CATV was created in 1948. It used signals that were beamed to widespread communities via hilltop antennas; coaxial cable then carried the signals to households. The CATV system brought television signals to many rural areas that previously were unable to get them or received only poor-quality signals.

Keyconcept

Network Affiliate: A television station typically contracts to carry one network's programming and commercials; the station thus becomes an affiliate of that network. In return, the network pays the station for use of its time. The big three networks—CBS, ABC, and NBC—historically gained much of their strength through powerful affiliation agreements.

coaxial cable: Cable that contains two conductors: a solid central core surrounded by a tube-like hollow one. Air or solid insulation separates the two. Electromagnetic energy, such as television transmission signals, travels between the two conductors.

Policy and politics

As technical standards were developed, challenged, and established, the infant television industry also confronted policy decisions and faced challenges from people who sought to control television's social and political impact.

240

POINTS OF VIEW The FCC argued that editorializing might not serve the public interest because broadcasters might propagate their own opinions without providing air time for opposing points of view. Therefore, in a 1941 broadcast licensing hearing, the FCC ruled in the *Mayflower Decision* that a broadcaster could not advocate a specific point of view. In 1946 the FCC codified much of its previous thinking into a document titled "Public Service Responsibility of Broadcast Licensees," generally referred to as the "Blue Book." This document outlined the rationale for FCC programming regulation and set standards for public service. It also argued that some profits should be reserved for public service programming. The TV industry attacked the Blue Book, arguing that the FCC was moving too close to censorship, which is prohibited by the U.S. Constitution. In 1948–1949 the FCC reconsidered its position on editorializing and encouraged reasonably balanced presentation of responsible viewpoints.[7]

THE COMMUNIST SCARE In the aftermath of World War II, fear of Communism infected American society. Legislators, business groups, and others attacked the film and television industries, labeling performers, producers, actors, and writers "fellow travelers," or sympathizers with those who advocated bringing Communism to the United States. In the atmosphere of anti-Communist hysteria fostered by Wisconsin Senator Joseph McCarthy, the entertainment industry faced sharp challenges from the House Un-American Activities Committee.

In 1950, Counterattack, a right-wing political group, published *Red Channels: The Report of Communist Infiltration in Radio and Television,* naming many writers, performers, and other broadcast employees as Communist Party members or sympathizers. This and other **blacklists,** many of which went unpublished, destroyed the careers of many aspiring broadcasters because those named on the blacklist were denied employment in the industry.

Keyconcept

"Fellow Travelers" in Broadcasting: During the period of intense fear of Communism in the 1950s, many people in the broadcast and entertainment industry were unfairly accused of being *fellow travelers,* that is, of sympathizing with the beliefs of the Communist Party.

Entertainment programming

During the late 1940s, television programming was successfully adapting radio's best offerings. **Anthologies** quickly became standard fare. *Kraft Television Theater, Studio One,* and *Fireside Arena Theatre,* produced live from New York, mimicked live stage performances. With live television, "every night was opening night," recalled costume designer Bill Jobe, "with fluffed lines, ties askew, flies open, and overstuffed merry widows."[8] Critics acclaimed the tasteful performances, and sponsors seeking sophisticated audiences raced to finance independently produced high-quality programming.

Comedy-variety shows hosted by successful radio comedians, quiz shows, dramas, and westerns were standard prime-time television fare. Local programming also increased as stations began to broadcast during the daytime hours. "Every station had its cooking expert; a late afternoon children's program host, usually a cowboy or a clown; a general interview host for daytime shows; and a small local news staff."[9]

By the late 1940s, the networks had added situation comedies ("sit-coms"), again mostly borrowed from radio. One of radio's most popular comedies was *Amos 'n Andy,* which debuted under the name of *Sam 'n Henry* in 1926. In 1931, the two white radio actors who spoke as *Amos 'n Andy* on radio starred at the *Chicago Defender*'s second an-

blacklist: A list of individuals compiled with the express purpose of forcing them out of their jobs. Used during the 1950s to label certain individuals as Communists and to force them out of the information and entertainment industries.

anthology: A favorite television format of the 1950s was the anthology series, which consisted of stage plays that were remade for TV.

Television comedy borrowed from its predecessor, radio. The Red Skelton Show specialized in slapstick that contained vestiges of vaudeville.

nual picnic. The *Defender* was Chicago's nationally known black weekly newspaper. But even as actors Charles Correll and Freeman Gosden appeared at the *Defender*'s picnic, another prominent black newspaper, the *Pittsburgh Courier,* attacked *Amos 'n Andy* for being demeaning to African Americans.

Amos 'n Andy became a television hit in 1951, with black actors replacing the white radio voices. It was the first television show to have an all-black cast. The black community was split in its response. The NAACP denounced *Amos 'n Andy* for depicting "the Negro and other minority groups in a stereotyped and derogatory manner" that strengthened "the conclusion among uninformed or prejudiced people that Negroes and other minorities are inferior, lazy, dumb, and dishonest." But the *Pittsburgh Courier,* which had panned the radio show, found the television version to be "well-paced, funny more often than not, directed and produced with taste." *Amos 'n Andy,* the television show, won an Emmy nomination in 1952, but CBS did not renew the program for a third season. CBS syndicated the show, however, selling it to local stations and foreign countries until 1966. Correll and Gosden continued to act a radio version of the program until 1960.[10]

Other popular sit-coms soon became part of television fare. *I Love Lucy, Father Knows Best, Our Miss Brooks,* and *Burns and Allen* enjoyed long runs. However, many programs lasted only a few months.

Live performances continued to dominate television programming through the mid-1950s, but broadcasters soon realized that the medium of television lent itself to the use of recorded programs. Filming programs for later broadcast was efficient and economical. By the late 1950s, the national programming from New York and much of the creative local programming that had originated in Chicago had moved to Hollywood. There, television producers had access to the technology and talents of the film studios, and the climate allowed outdoor filming all year. Film was the primary recording method; videotape did not have widespread use until the early 1960s.

The influence of advertising on programming

From the beginning of television, advertising and programming were intertwined—through network personnel and through sponsorship. For example, Harry Ackerman, appointed vice president to head network programs for CBS in Hollywood in 1951, had worked at CBS radio and then for the prestigious Young & Rubicam Advertising Agency. At first, television programs were owned by advertisers, which based the content of the shows on the interests of the audiences they wished to reach. The names of the anthology dramas reflected their sponsors: *Kraft Television Theater* and *Goodyear TV Playhouse,* for example. The sponsor's advertising agency bought time from a network, and the agency produced and controlled the program and supporting ads. Sometimes the line between advertising and entertainment blurred. "A girl breaks into song," the *New Yorker* reported, "and for a moment you can't quite pin down the source of her lyrical passion. It could be love, it could be something that comes in a jar."[11]

242

Through the 1950s, networks and advertisers struggled over who would control content. NBC introduced the concept of *magazine programming,* which meant selling time to several advertisers to share the support of a single show. The networks improved their production facilities and brought more production in house. As the expense of programming and advertising rates increased, TV networks and stations increasingly sold time, not shows. At first only one product or service appeared in each commercial break, but later each break contained multiple ads.

The downfall of the single-sponsor system came with the 1950s **quiz show** scandals. These popular shows were cheap to produce because they required little in the way of sets or staging. Individuals appeared on stage and answered questions, much like *Jeopardy* contestants do today. The shows appealed to large audiences. The famous *$64,000 Question,* developed by an advertising agency and sold to Revlon, achieved one of the highest ratings of the decade. But the *$64,000 Question* and other highly rated quiz shows, including *Twenty-One,* were rigged to make them more exciting. The scandal broke during the summer of 1957. In the fall of 1958, Charles Van Doren, star contestant on *Twenty-One,* confessed that the producers (and by implication the sponsors) had given him advance answers to the questions he would be asked.[12] (Van Doren's story was the basis for the 1994 film *Quiz Show.*) Although the networks were in some cases reluctant to take over the management of advertising and programming, they used the scandal to claim that because sponsors were too greedy for high ratings, the networks themselves should control programming.[13]

Keyconcept

Sponsor System: In the early days of television, a single advertiser often sponsored an entire show. This system declined as television time became more expensive and the reputation of sponsors suffered from the quiz show scandals of the late 1950s.

■ Television Journalism

By the mid-1950s, television was firmly entrenched in the world of news and information, as well as election coverage. By the 1980s, it had combined with political change to reshape the nature of political news.

Television news, as first developed by NBC, combined the dramatic visual images of **newsreels** and announcer/interview techniques of radio news. Even in its earliest days, television news sought ways to become more visual, to show more than mere **talking heads.** NBC presented the experimental *Esso Television Reporter* in 1940. This program, sponsored by Standard Oil, offered printed titles between news items, still pictures to illustrate the announcer's words, and decorous organ music in the background. During World War II, the FCC halted network news experimentation, but in 1945, NBC set up an organization for production of news film.[14] The *NBC Tele-Newsreel* relied on newsreel film from companies serving movie theaters, but in 1948 the network presented *NBC Newsroom,* a program produced by radio journalists and broadcast from the NBC radio newsroom. Critics argued that pictures of a man reading the news didn't add much to understanding world affairs, but ratings were sufficient to keep the program on the air and attract competitors. The networks also attracted audiences with their coverage of presidential conventions in 1948 and later and with Senate hearings on organized crime in 1951.

Newsreel companies competed with the networks to produce news film for television. In 1947 the R.J. Reynolds Tobacco Company signed a contract with 20th-Century Fox to produce an NBC news program, *Camel Newsreel Theater.* Two years later, NBC persuaded Rey-

quiz show: Show on which contestants answer questions that show their knowledge of selected material.

newsreel: Film depiction of news events. Some were composed of real footage, others of dramatized events.

talking head: Use of a person on television, usually as an expert. The visual consists of a shot of the individual's head and shoulders as he or she talks.

nolds to cancel its contract and replace the program with the network-produced *Camel News Caravan,* a fifteen-minute nightly program starring John Cameron Swayze. CBS inaugurated a similar program, *Douglas Edwards with the News.*

Camel News Caravan solidified NBC's news operation for the short term. By May 1951, forty stations carried the program, which mixed newsreel footage with visual reading of the news. NBC Television News established bureaus in New York, Chicago, Washington, Cleveland, Los Angeles, Dallas, and San Francisco. It recruited **stringers** from abroad, hired camera crews and photographers, and signed exchange agreements with affiliate stations for news film. However, in 1952–1953, as production costs increased and NBC's news programs encountered financial difficulty, the network dramatically reduced its news division

Meanwhile, CBS expanded its news operations. William Paley, along with his second-in-command, Frank Stanton, shaped CBS into a leader in entertainment and news programming. Paley solidified CBS's financing, then demonstrated an uncanny skill for negotiating with affiliates and with stars. He was willing to allocate resources to programming, and it didn't take Paley long to ensure that CBS would surpass NBC as a leader in news and information programming.[15]

Veteran newsmen remember the Edward R. Murrow days as the Golden Age of Television News, when money flowed through CBS newsrooms and news shaped the reputation of the individual network. Murrow, famous for his radio news broadcasts during World War II, debuted in television in 1951 with the first network public affairs series, *See It Now.* In later years, Murrow made CBS famous for its documentaries, such as "Harvest of Shame," which depicted the plight of migrant farm workers. Bill Leonard, the former president of CBS news programming who initiated *60 Minutes,* remembered Murrow as a "remarkable force." Leonard told an interviewer,

> Superficially, the most remarkable thing about Ed Murrow was his voice, which was unique. It had a resonance, but that was really, of course, minor. His absolutely pure-blue-flame integrity was important, and his courage—his absolute standards. He was a fine broadcaster; a good writer; not the greatest writer, just a very, very good one. But he had an absolute standard of integrity that shone through and he had all of the courage that a man can have.[16]

In 1963, only a few weeks before the assassination of President John F. Kennedy, whose funeral made television history, NBC expanded its evening news coverage from a mere fifteen minutes to a thirty-minute newscast featuring the anchor team of Chet Huntley and David Brinkley. CBS followed suit with a news program anchored by Walter Cronkite. ABC, whose newscasts were at best a fledgling operation, didn't expand to a half hour until 1967. Since the 1960s the networks have often explored expanding their evening newscasts to an hour. However, the affiliated stations continue to run their own profitable local newscasts in the lead-in time slot (usually 5:00 to 6:30 or 7:00 P.M. EST) while retaining the time slot following the network news for profit-making syndicated shows such as *Wheel of Fortune* and *Jeopardy.*[17]

Despite the limited time devoted to national news and occasional documentaries, by

Television networks sought news anchors with star quality that would attract loyal viewers. Walter Cronkite was once voted the most popular man in America and was the mainstay of the CBS Evening News.

stringer: A part-time or contract employee who works as a reporter on a story-by-story basis or on the basis of column inches.

244 Television in our lives

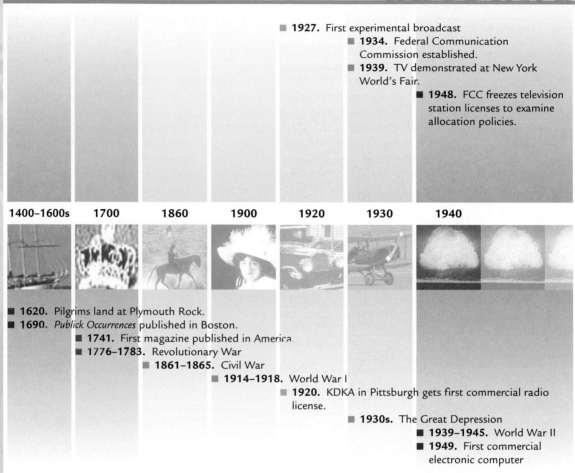

- **1927.** First experimental broadcast
- **1934.** Federal Communication Commission established.
- **1939.** TV demonstrated at New York World's Fair.
- **1948.** FCC freezes television station licenses to examine allocation policies.

| 1400–1600s | 1700 | 1860 | 1900 | 1920 | 1930 | 1940 |

- **1620.** Pilgrims land at Plymouth Rock.
- **1690.** *Publick Occurrences* published in Boston.
- **1741.** First magazine published in America.
- **1776–1783.** Revolutionary War
- **1861–1865.** Civil War
- **1914–1918.** World War I
- **1920.** KDKA in Pittsburgh gets first commercial radio license.
- **1930s.** The Great Depression
- **1939–1945.** World War II
- **1949.** First commercial electronic computer

the end of the 1960s, television had become the country's dominant medium for the visual display of social controversy. Television broadcast Kennedy's funeral, with no advertising.[18] The civil rights movement, the war in Vietnam, environmental damage, and women's demands for equality were big stories of the decade. Television covered them all. In 1969, even Vice-President Spiro Agnew, who despised and feared the power of television, admitted that

> [t]he networks have made "hunger" and "black lung disease" national issues overnight. The TV networks have done what no other medium could have done in terms of dramatizing the horrors of war. The networks have tackled our most difficult social problems with a directness and immediacy that is the gift of their medium. They have focused the nation's attention on its environmental abuses . . . on pollution in the Great Lakes and the threatened ecology of the Everglades.[19]

Key concept

Syndication: Local television stations can control content by contracting for programs that are syndicated, or made available for sale directly to stations rather than being distributed by networks to affiliates. For example, before it started the UPN network, Paramount syndicated its popular series *Star Trek: The Next Generation* to independent stations. Discontinued network shows that have had long successful runs are also candidates for syndication, as are earlier seasons of current network hit shows.

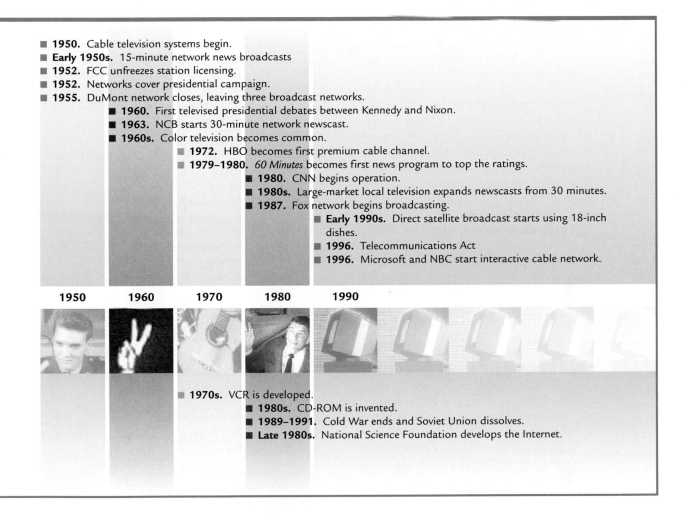

- **1950.** Cable television systems begin.
- **Early 1950s.** 15-minute network news broadcasts
- **1952.** FCC unfreezes station licensing.
- **1952.** Networks cover presidential campaign.
- **1955.** DuMont network closes, leaving three broadcast networks.
  - **1960.** First televised presidential debates between Kennedy and Nixon.
  - **1963.** NCB starts 30-minute network newscast.
  - **1960s.** Color television becomes common.
    - **1972.** HBO becomes first premium cable channel.
    - **1979–1980.** *60 Minutes* becomes first news program to top the ratings.
      - **1980.** CNN begins operation.
      - **1980s.** Large-market local television expands newscasts from 30 minutes.
      - **1987.** Fox network begins broadcasting.
        - **Early 1990s.** Direct satellite broadcast starts using 18-inch dishes.
        - **1996.** Telecommunications Act
        - **1996.** Microsoft and NBC start interactive cable network.

1950   **1960**   **1970**   **1980**   **1990**

- **1970s.** VCR is developed.
  - **1980s.** CD-ROM is invented.
  - **1989–1991.** Cold War ends and Soviet Union dissolves.
  - **Late 1980s.** National Science Foundation develops the Internet.

Expansion of network news came not in the prestigious and expensive evening hours, but in morning news, in which a softer format appealed to audiences. The definition of news also expanded to include **news magazines** such as *60 Minutes,* begun in 1968 but not achieving a permanent slot on the weekly schedule until the late 1970s, and late-night news programs such as Ted Koppel's *Nightline,* which ABC introduced in 1979 during the height of the crisis arising from Iranian militants' seizure of hostages in the U.S. embassy in Teheran. In the late 1980s, the number of news magazines in prime time grew. By 1997, ABC, NBC, and CBS were producing seven or more news magazines a week. This trend reflected the long-term success of CBS's *60 Minutes,* which in 1979 was the first news show to reach the top of the ratings, and ABC's *20/20.* The news magazines also represented the changing economics of television; these programs cost less to produce than did an hour of dramatic television.

news magazines: Fifteen- to twenty-minute news segments put together to form hour-long electronic magazines such as *60 Minutes* or *Dateline.* These programs combine soft features with hard-hitting investigative reporting.

■ TV and American politics

Just as television restructured American entertainment patterns and the process through which Americans got their news, so it also reshaped the process of electing government officials. Television combined with expanding education, increasing mobility, participatory democratic legislation, and sophisticated research methods during the 1950s and 1960s to weaken America's political parties and increase the role of the media in selecting leaders.

In 1952 the networks covered the presidential campaign, a race between the popular General Dwight D. Eisenhower, a hero of World War II, and Illinois Governor Adlai Stevenson, one of the nation's foremost intellectuals. During this race, politics began to conform to the requirements of television. Stevenson's long commentaries bored too many of his listeners; Eisenhower, although anything but a polished television star, at least learned the value of short spots.

Soon after being named Eisenhower's running mate, Richard Nixon was accused of being the beneficiary of a secret trust fund set up by wealthy businessmen. The public was scandalized. Fearing that Eisenhower would drop him from the Republican ticket, Nixon chose television as the medium for his defense. In what became known as "the Checkers speech," Nixon detailed his financial condition and vowed that, though his children's dog Checkers had been donated by an admirer, the family loved the dog and "regardless of what they say, we're going to keep it." This personalized use of television built on what Franklin Delano Roosevelt had accomplished with his "Fireside Chats" over radio before and during World War II. Politicians began to go directly to the public, rather than having information first sifted through reporters and editors for newspapers and magazines.

THE IMAGE Image has always played a role in American politics. Image helps to define candidates for voters. Television, with its strong visual impact, enhanced the ability of media and politicians to manipulate political images.

John Kennedy used presidential debates and press conferences to shape his image. His ready wit and handsome smile made him a natural for the cameras. In the first televised presidential debate between Kennedy and Richard Nixon in 1960, Kennedy established himself as a man with a vision for leadership and placed Nixon in the position of defending the status quo. In his opening statement, Kennedy recalled images of Abraham Lincoln:

> In the election of 1860, Abraham Lincoln said the question was whether this nation could exist half-slave and half-free. In the election of 1960, and with the world around us, the question is whether the world will exist half slave and half free, whether it will move in the direction of freedom, in the direction of the road that we are taking or whether it will move in the direction of slavery. . . . I think it will depend in great measure upon what we do here in the United States, on the kind of society that we build, on the kind of strength that we maintain.[20]

President Richard Nixon struggled with his media image throughout his campaigns and his Presidency. After alienating the press in earlier years, in 1968 Nixon hired people who had mastered the art of television advertising and whose job was to improve the Nixon image.

The Kennedy-Nixon debates set a precedent for future presidential campaigns. Debates are now an expected part of the campaign process, and their effectiveness or lack of it is widely debated. In the 1992 elections, the questioning of candidates in a town hall format, with citizens rather than journalists asking questions, gained more attention than did formal debates, but as the 1996 election debates showed, formal encounters will continue to be a significant part of presidential campaigning.

Key concept

Televised Presidential Debates: Debates between candidates in front of television cameras or audiences have become significant factors in presidential elections. Televised debates for primary candidates in key states, as well as in national elections, can earn respectable ratings and appear to be an important way for the public to see candidates interact and talk about issues.

In his 1964 campaign against Barry Goldwater, Lyndon Johnson used television advertisements that presented powerful, emotionally charged images. One of Johnson's ads showed a small girl in a field of flowers; the following image was the mushroom cloud of a hydrogen bomb. The ad ran only once, but it implied that Goldwater might push the United States closer to a war with the Soviet Union. Another ad depicted a red phone, presumably the "hot line" to the leader of the Soviet Union, ringing on a desk, with the message that the phone rings only "in a serious crisis." The ad didn't mention Goldwater, but the implication was that the Republican candidate might be trigger-happy and force the United States into a world crisis.

In 1968, Richard Nixon hired people who understood the art of television advertising, and paid media became a significant force in political campaigning. Nixon's people knew how to research public taste and to create advertising. Although disarray in the Democratic Party in 1968 aided Nixon's victory, some critics charge that without the mastery of the television image devised by his advisors, Nixon might never have become president.[21]

Today, political candidates work hard to control their images through advertising and arranged appearances. Many candidates limit their exposure to journalists, preferring to display a crafted image rather than having to respond to impromptu questions. Whenever candidates do respond to the press, their **spin doctors** work to get the candidate's interpretation of an event or issue into journalists' stories.

President Ronald Reagan became famous for the *photo opportunity,* a controlled appearance that was designed to present him in his best light. Journalists were allowed to take pictures but not to ask questions. When journalists screamed questions at Reagan as he walked toward the noisy presidential helicopter, audiences viewed the journalists as badgering the president. Thus the image of the journalist declined as that of the president rose.

The promotion of image rather than issues and substance is also fostered by some of the current production values of television. News values that promote higher ratings through ever shorter **sound bites** allow candidates to shape a planned, desirable television image, no matter what their actual political history is.

spin doctor: A public relations specialist employed to put the most favorable interpretation on a politician's comments or activities or to minimize damage caused by charges against the politician.

sound bite: A short quotation used on radio or television to express an idea.

POLITICAL PARTIES AND TELEVISION During the early 1900s, political parties controlled politics by controlling much of the vote. In return for being voted into power, a party helped people to find jobs and offered police protection and clean streets. Even when the power of this kind of "machine politics" declined, party organizations controlled the way candidates were nominated, and so candidates had to toe the "party line." As Americans became more educated and more mobile, they were less influenced by party dictates. In addition, democratic reforms such as the ballot initiative, the referendum, and the direct primary weakened party power even as television increasingly allowed candidates to reach a mass audience without party backing. Although parties still play an important role in raising money for candidates and in turning out the vote, television has significantly decreased the parties' power, increased the power of paid and free media, and increased the ability of a candidate to emphasize image over his or her political record on the issues.

Ross Perot, in his attempts to become president in the 1990s, exemplifies the use of media power rather than political party power. Perot used money and his reputation as a successful businessman to gain media exposure. In 1992, he bought expensive thirty-minute prime time television slots to explain his views, using simple visual tools such as charts and graphs. Though he gained only a small percentage of the popular vote and did not carry a single state, Perot forced mainstream politicians to take him and his ideas seriously.

Today's market structure

Until the mid-1980s, television was dominated by three major networks. CBS, NBC, and ABC regularly attracted 90 percent of the viewers in prime time. Cable was targeted at a small, largely rural audience. However, in the 1980s, cable companies took advantage of satellite technology to expand their distribution. They found that even urban viewers, with a range of network affiliates and small local stations to choose from, would pay to receive noncommercial channels, **superstations,** and premium channels offering special sports, music, or movie programming. Besides the growth of cable, CBS, NBC, and ABC faced new competition from a fourth network, Fox, which successfully challenged their dominance and paved the way for other new networks.

Keyconcept

Superstation: Some large TV stations have the capacity to reach hundreds of markets throughout the country through satellite distribution of their signals to cable systems. Such "superstations" have been significant in supplying cable systems with nonnetwork content, thereby reducing the power of the historically dominant networks.

Shifting status of the networks

Although networks had long dominated television, by the early 1990s, forecasters were predicting their death. The share of the prime-time viewing audience held by ABC, CBS, and NBC eroded from a high of 91 percent in the 1978–1979 season to less than 50 percent in fall 1996. The lost audience moved to the three new networks—Fox, UPN, and WB—and to cable. However, predictions of the networks' deaths were premature. Networks remain strong as a result of deregulation in the 1990s. They continue to attract the largest audiences of any medium.

Murdoch's new network

Rupert Murdoch, who started his career managing a family-owned newspaper in Adelaide, Australia, managed to do in ten years what no American had been able to do in the past—pose a serious competitive challenge to CBS, NBC, and ABC. Targeting a young audience, Murdoch took advantage of the FCC's desire to foster competition against the networks and used his own resources and nerve to battle the dominant business structure of U.S. television.

Murdoch built his single paper into a chain of tabloid newspapers, then moved to London in 1969 to buy a tabloid weekly, *News of the World.* By 1985, Murdoch and his News Corporation had collected a group of powerful media companies in Britain, including *The Sun,* the

superstation: A station that reaches hundreds of markets throughout the country by means of satellite distribution of a signal to cable systems.

From the mid-1980s to the mid-1990s, media critics announced the pending death of the networks. But the networks—although no longer the only players in the television industry—are far from dead. CBS is a good example. Throughout its history, CBS set records. Renowned for its news division in the 1950s, 1960s, and 1970s and for its popular prime time programming, CBS was the preeminent network for decades. In the 1990s, however, CBS lost its luster; it fell from being the marginal winner of the prime time ratings game in 1992–1993 to third place two seasons later, barely beating Fox in average weekly share of viewers.

Despite declines in ratings and increasing competition, the networks remain strong financially because they

Networks and Profits

are not just networks. The big four (ABC, CBS, Fox, and NBC) own radio networks, radio stations, television stations, and cable systems in addition to the network programming system. As a result, they remain very profitable. In 1996, the top four networks had $3.36 billion in profits, which was up 24 percent from 1995. About half of the total profit comes from owned and operated stations, most of which are located in the large markets.

On the surface, it appears that the dominance of television stations as the profit centers for networks might reduce the importance of the network programming, but this is not the case. The success of the network owned and operated stations is based on the

continuing appeal of their network programs. If these stations did not have the benefit of original network programs such as *ER, Home Improvement,* and *60 Minutes,* they would not generate such large profits. The strength of network programming is why media writer and journalism professor Douglas Gomery says the "real economic action still centers" on the networks.

SOURCE: Douglas Gomery, "Dinosaurs Who Refuse to Die," *American Journalism Review,* March 1995, p. 48; Steve McClellan, "Big Year for Big Four (or Was It?)," *Broadcasting & Cable* (March 3, 1997): p. 4.

nation's largest-circulation daily, and the prestigious *Times,* and had begun laying the groundwork for a satellite television service called Sky Channel, which beams programs to cable systems throughout Europe.

In the United States, Murdoch bought the *New York Post,* the *Boston Herald,* the *Chicago Sun-Times,* the *Village Voice,* and *New York* magazine. He eventually sold all these publications, but in 1993 he bought back the *Post.* He also acquired *TV Guide,* one of the nation's largest-circulation magazines, for $3 billion. In 1985, Murdoch's News Corporation moved into electronic media with purchase of Twentieth-Century Fox Film Corp., with its rich film library. In the same year, Murdoch bought six big-city television stations from Metromedia in New York, Los Angeles, Chicago, Dallas, Houston, and Washington, D.C.[22]

Murdoch's deal needed approval by the FCC, but he was not a U.S. citizen, and the Communications Act restricts ownership of American broadcast stations by foreigners. Murdoch changed his citizenship as soon as legally possible, and the FCC seemed to ignore the fact that his News Corporation was made up primarily of foreign investors. In addition, Murdoch needed a waiver from the FCC to own a newspaper and television station in the same city. The FCC, which had long cultivated opposition to the three networks, readily granted the waiver.

Ten years after Murdoch started the network, which he named the Fox Network, the foreign ownership issue resurfaced. After an eighteen-month investigation, the FCC reversed its 1985 decision, declaring that Murdoch's company, despite his citizenship switch, was indeed a foreign company. However, the FCC simultaneously granted Murdoch a waiver from the foreign ownership rule, allowing him to continue business.[23]

Fox has become a highly profitable enterprise with total profits of $570 million in 1996. Of this, $410 billion came from the owned and operated television stations. The network earned $90 million in profits. Overall profits increased by 25 percent from 1995 to 1996.

The network built its financial success by appealing to eighteen- to thirty-four-year-olds with *Beverly Hills 90210* and its spin-off, *Melrose Place,* but in 1995 it announced that it was broadening the basic audience to include eighteen- to forty-five-year-olds. Although inclusion of programs aimed at older audiences at first seemed successful, some critics worry that Fox will lose the focus that has distinguished it from the other networks. Younger viewers draw massive advertising, but top prime time advertisers tend to target the thirty-four- to forty-five-year-old group.

Fox's success created more competition. Two new networks joined the field during 1994–1995. United Paramount Network (UPN) scheduled five programs on Monday and Tuesday nights, including *Star Trek: Voyager* and *Platypus Man.* Warner Bros. Network (WB) offered four programs on Wednesdays and Saturday morning programming for kids, including *Batman,* with *Superman* being added the next season. During their first season, UPN, with *Star Trek: Voyager,* reached an average of about 4 percent of the households, and WB reached about 2 percent.

The Fox network captured the young adult market with shows like Melrose Place, *to boost its standing among the more traditional networks.*

The future of these two new networks is uncertain. Each lost millions of dollars in its first year, and financial analysts predict that one or both will fail because both networks aim at younger audiences and there is a limited amount of advertising money available to support all television programming.

■ Television operations

In 1997, about 93 million households in the United States had one or more television sets. About 62 million households subscribed to cable. However, after the introduction of eighteen-inch satellite dishes in the spring of 1995, a growing number of households began to subscribe to a direct broadcast satellite (DBS) system. But as of 1997, DBS subscribers remained only a small percentage of total viewership.

BROADCAST STATIONS The United States has about 1,550 **full-power** television stations. Some 1,150 are *commercial,* in business primarily to make a profit. They are licensed by the FCC, transmit programs over the air, and carry commercial messages to pay costs and make a profit. *Noncommercial* stations, often referred to as educational or public television, are not operated for profit. These 365 stations are financed primarily by grants from foundations, viewers' donations, and

full-power: A station that reaches a large percentage of houses in its market and that must broadcast a schedule of programs.

New Television Behaviors

The widespread adoption of VCRs and remote controls has changed the way people watch television. New behaviors allow viewers more control over time and the television content they watch. They also have given new meanings to some old words:

Zapping involves using a VCR to remove advertisements while recording. By turning the VCR off during commercials, the viewer zaps the ads from the videotape.

Time shifting lets a person record a program to watch at a different time.

Channel surfing or *grazing* occurs when a viewer uses a remote control to go from one channel to another. A channel surfer pauses at each station only briefly before going on to look for something new and different.

Cannibalizing is characterized by *zapping* commercials from a program and saving the program for future viewing.

---

government funds and carry no traditional advertising. *Low-power broadcast* stations serve limited areas because the station's signal cannot reach long distances. There are about 1,600 low-power broadcast stations. Broadcast operations can be further classified according to their spectrum location in the very high frequency (VHF) or ultra high frequency (UHF) band.

CABLE INDUSTRY The $21.5 billion cable industry includes cable distribution systems, superstations, cable networks, and the programming they carry. The cable industry profits mostly by selling cable service to subscribers, although many systems and networks also sell advertising. Cable systems originally functioned as boosters for broadcast signals, but in the 1950s they began to augment programming, producing limited local programming and importing television signals from distant cities with the use of microwave transmission. Later, cable companies offered additional features, such as movies without ads, for an extra charge to their subscribers.

By the mid-1960s, broadcasters began to fear the power of cable competition and asked the FCC to design protective regulation that would keep cable operators from competing with traditional broadcast stations. From 1966 until the late 1970s the FCC imposed heavy restrictions on cable development. However, such regulations did not hold up under Supreme Court scrutiny, and during the late 1970s the FCC reversed its position on cable regulation. In 1984, Congress passed a strongly deregulatory Cable Communications Policy Act, which limited interference in cable operations by local communities, state governments, and the FCC. The longest-running battle probably was over the "must-carry" rule, which required cable channels to carry local broadcast signals without charge. In March, 1977, the Supreme Court upheld the "must carry" rule. Recent disputes over cable have centered primarily on subscriber rates, with a fair amount of government and private concern directed toward the rapidly increasing costs of cable television to the consumer.

Cable television has expanded possibilities for programming and usually targets specific audiences. Planet Groove *is Black Entertainment Television's prime time music video show.*

Deregulation paved the way for cable superstations. In 1976, Ted Turner turned the lowest-rated Atlanta TV station, UHF Channel 17, into superstation WTBS. He contracted with a satellite company to **uplink** his signal to RCA's SATCOM I for distribution to cable systems. At first, only twenty systems **downlinked** WTBS; but within two years more than 200 systems downlinked programs from the station, and by 1979 more than 2,000 systems were participating.[24] Using WTBS, Turner made the Atlanta Braves, which he also owns, one of the most popular baseball teams in the United States.

Today, cable is a mass medium, with more than 11,000 systems and 62 million subscribers. Cable advertising revenues are the fastest-growing segment in the communications industry. In 1981, cable television had less than 1 percent of the total television advertising pie. By 1994, its share had risen to nearly 9 percent while the broadcast networks' share fell by the same amount.[25] Table 9.1 illustrates how broadcast stations and cables get their revenues.

Cable offers advertisers an edge that the networks don't provide: a narrowly segmented audience. However, with more than forty-five established cable networks, each promising to deliver a specific demographic market, the sell is getting more difficult. Furthermore, the cable market seems to have reached its peak; the number of new cable subscribers now decreases each year.

In 1997, the average cable system offered fifty-four channels, but this average includes systems that have 100 channels and systems that have thirty. Efforts to increase channels with fiber optics continue, but new services seem to pop up to fill these openings. Also, the contracts of most cable systems include a commitment to local programming, so the systems devote some of their channels to government, schools, and other local organizations. Pay-per-view often takes up a half dozen to a dozen channels.

Cable networks are reacting in a variety of ways to the limited channel capacity. Increasingly, new networks pay to get access on a cable system. Fox News Channel, Home & Garden Network, the Cartoon Network, and others paid Tele-Communications Inc. (TCI) millions of dollars for channel space in 1996 and 1997. Some networks are using times, such as after midnight, when other networks do not program, and others are trying to take over public access channels.[26]

Decisions about which networks to run and which to leave off have created controversy. A national letter-writing campaign began in 1996 when a Texas cable system dropped Lifetime, the only cable network specially devoted to women, to make room for another news network. The efforts of Fox News to get on the Time Warner cable system in New York City were unsuccessful at the beginning of 1997. Time Warner owns Cable News Network, a competitor of Fox News. New York City officials implied that Time Warner might have trouble renewing its cable franchise in 1998 because of the dispute.[27]

There is no indication that the channel squeeze will end anytime soon. People's interest in specialized information and entertainment seems almost limitless, and companies are always eager to supply such demand if it can be done for an adequate profit.

uplink: Transmitting an electronic signal to a satellite for storage or further distribution.

downlink: Transmitting an electronic signal from a satellite to a ground facility.

TABLE 9.1   Revenue Sources for Television (in millions)

Because the Communications Act of 1934 guaranteed a commercial environment for television, broadcast TV has earned almost all of its revenues from advertising. Cable receives revenues from consumers (subscribers) as well as from advertisers.

YEAR	CONSUMER REVENUES FOR CABLE TV	AD REVENUES FOR CABLE TV	AD REVENUES FOR BROADCAST TV	TOTAL REVENUES
1984	6,955	538	19,310	26,803
1986	8,786	855	22,026	31,667
1988	11,834	1,196	24,487	37,517
1990	15,274	1,789	26,619	43,682
1992	17,520	2,155	27,220	46,895
1994	20,823	2,930	30,780	54,533
1996*	19,100	3,415	34,890	57,405

*Projection.

Source: Veronis, Suhler & Associates, *Communication Industry Forecast,* 1995.

■ Television ownership patterns

When buyers consider purchasing a television station, they must first look at the other media they own within that market. FCC regulations limit multiple ownership of the same medium and cross-ownership of other media (radio and newspaper) within the same market. The intent is to prevent a controlling media monopoly and to encourage a variety of voices within the marketplace.

GROUP OWNERSHIP Of all ownership types, network-owned and -operated ("O and O") groups receive the most attention. The O and O stations tend to be in larger markets, such as Chicago, New York, and Los Angeles, because they will attract larger audiences and profits than they would in smaller markets. The four major networks (ABC, CBS, NBC, and Fox) generate or acquire programming that runs on their own stations and on affiliated stations. The networks make money by selling advertising time at their stations. The profit margins generated by the network owned-and-operated stations by selling advertising for local and other nonnetwork programming is higher than the margins networks make selling advertising during network programming. Thus, networks are dependent on their owned-and-operated stations for a good deal of revenue.

Other groups besides the networks own stations. Some of these companies are major players in the industry. For example, Gannett Company's acquisition of Multimedia, Inc. in 1995 added Multimedia's five network-affiliate TV stations to the ten stations Gannett already owned, expanding coverage to 14 percent of the country. The merger placed Gannett among the ten largest broadcast group owners.

Stations that are owned by groups can be affiliated with networks. Affiliates make money from networks, which pay them to run programming, and by selling advertising at their stations. Affiliated stations also buy syndicated programs to run as well as using network shows.

The relationship between affiliates and networks has changed during the history of television. When only three networks were available, the networks had the upper hand in the relationship. However, stations now are powerful enough that they can negotiate for the best network deal. Some cities have experienced the complete reshuffling of networks among their local stations. In Baltimore, for example, the station that had been an ABC affiliate for many years became a CBS affiliate, the former CBS affiliate became an NBC affiliate, and the former NBC affiliate contracted with ABC.

News-gathering technology also has played a role in network-affiliate relations. Before the development of satellite news-gathering equipment, local stations depended on the network news departments for video from other parts of the nation and world. Often the networks would save the best video for their network newscasts and provide lesser-quality video feeds to local stations. With satellite technology, a local station can send its own reporter or contract with a service to cover an event anywhere in the world. Networks have responded by offering better video feeds from the network news departments.

INDEPENDENTLY OWNED STATIONS Independently owned stations are not affiliated with a network but can be associated with other ownership groups. Independently owned stations must rely on their own programming, syndicated fare, and other sources. Programming can be expensive for stations that do not have a network to rely on. However, independent stations have total freedom in deciding content, and much creative programming has originated at these stations.

MULTIPLE SYSTEM OPERATORS Even though the United States has more than 11,000 cable systems, most of them are owned by a few companies. These multiple system operators (MSOs) control cable systems located throughout the country. The two largest MSOs are Time Warner and Tele-Communications Inc. (TCI). In 1996, each served more than 11 million subscribers with their cable systems. Both also own a variety of other media. Time Warner owns HBO and Cinemax. TCI owns shares of Court TV, E!, the Family Channel, Discovery, Black Entertainment Television, the Learning Channel, and a variety of other cable networks. The ownership of cable networks by MSOs explains why some cable systems carry certain networks and not others. An MSO cable system is likely to carry networks that the MSO owns.

PUBLIC TV STATIONS Public broadcast stations do not carry direct advertising; they are supported mostly by tax revenues, grants and private donations, and corporate underwriting. Corporate underwriting, in which a large company or corporation provides funding for a series, a program, or a particular time slot, is reflected in statements such as "This program is sponsored in part by. . . ." Public television is known for its long-running popular educational programs, such as *Sesame Street, This Old House, The Frugal Gourmet,* and explorations of nature and science. In addition, its multipart social and cultural programs, such as Ken Burns's *The Civil War,* often attract large audiences of people who do not regularly watch public television. Public television is also known for carrying important Congressional proceedings such as the debate about whether to support the Bush administration in the Gulf War and the Senate Judiciary Committee's confirmation hearings when Clarence Thomas was nominated to the Supreme Court. However, C-SPAN and CNN now generally provide more thorough coverage in this area.[28]

When the federal government looks at cutting its budget, public television is always a political target. In 1996 the federal government allocated $275 million to the Corporation for Public Broadcasting, which, in turn, partially funds 1,000 public radio and television stations. In addition, local and state tax money is used to support stations. With some of this money, public stations produce or buy programming. Television stations buy

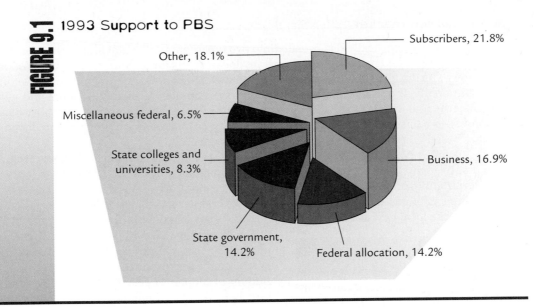

FIGURE 9.1 1993 Support to PBS

- Subscribers, 21.8%
- Other, 18.1%
- Miscellaneous federal, 6.5%
- State colleges and universities, 8.3%
- Business, 16.9%
- State government, 14.2%
- Federal allocation, 14.2%

shows such as *Wild America* and *The News Hour with Jim Lehrer* from Public Broadcasting Service (PBS), a network created by the Corporation for Public Broadcasting (CPB). Theoretically, public stations are free from advertisers and can present all points of views. However, because about 43 percent of the total public television budget comes from one form of tax money or another, it remains a target for those who see television as an entity that should be privately funded. However, critics argue that if federal funding were cut or eliminated, many smaller stations might die. Figure 9.1 shows where public television gets its money.

A 1995 poll by the Opinion Research Corporation showed that people support public television: 84 percent wanted to increase or maintain the current level of federal funding; 82 percent thought that public television was of higher quality than commercial television; 86 percent said that public television was an important resource to the nation; 90 percent thought that PBS was more educational and informative than most television; 92 percent believed that PBS was more suitable for the whole family; and 90 percent said that PBS offered something for everyone, regardless of education or income.[29] However, ratings indicate that more people say they support PBS than actually watch it.

The strong public support for public television prevented Congress from eliminating funding, but the amount being set aside has been declining. In 1996, Congress decreased CPB funding by 12 percent and mandated further decreases.

Audience demand in television markets

Television caters to the advertising market and the consumer market with news and entertainment. Networks, cable systems, direct broadcasters, and syndicates provide programming that supplies the demand. The chief goal, except in public television, is to make profits, which is usually done by achieving high ratings. However, high profits are increasingly associated with targeted audiences rather than mass audiences. In such cases, lower ratings can still attract advertisers. For example, golf events on television earn low ratings but are still attractive to advertisers because people who watch golf on television are high earners with disposable income to spend.

TV shows can be divided broadly into two types: entertainment and news. Most television stations and networks have separate departments for providing these types of programs. The distinction does not mean that news cannot and should not be entertaining. Traditionally, the distinction has been that entertainment is mostly fictional and news concerns real events. This difference seems less identifiable, however, as reality-based programs such as *Cops,* magazine programs such as *Entertainment Tonight,* and docudramas based on recent news events have proliferated.

People's demand for news reflects an interest in international, national, and local affairs. In nightly newscasts, networks provide national and international news, but stations traditionally broadcast local news as well. In the early days of TV news, the lack of portable cameras and the use of ordinary, fixed news sets led to low production quality. Often, the local newscast represented no more than a station's effort to satisfy the FCC's policy of serving the public interest. However, in the 1980s, the realization that local news programs could make enormous profits prompted stations to adopt new portable technologies and to hire consultants to redesign and expand their news formats. Now local news ratings of stations in big markets rival those of network news. Large-market stations regularly include national and international news, using satellite technology.

Demand for entertainment is as diverse as the population. Most entertainment programming falls into standard categories such as comedy, drama, sports, talk, game shows, children's programs, documentaries, and reality-based shows. Within these categories there can be great variety. Drama includes weekly series, such as *Melrose Place, NYPD Blue, ER,* and *X-Files,* and miniseries such as *Lonesome Dove.* Comedy programs can be equally disparate, ranging from *Murphy Brown* to *Beavis and Butthead.*

America's Most Wanted involves viewers in the content by asking for their participation and help. Fugitive Jeffrey Sibley, who was arrested after being featured on the show, is escorted off an airplane by law enforcement officials.

In addition to prime time programming, most of the networks or their stations provide morning shows, such as *Today* and *Good Morning America,* daytime soap operas, and late-night shows such as *Nightline* and *Late Show with David Letterman.* Local stations usually fill the remaining time with syndicated material, such as *Oprah Winfrey* and *Ricki Lake,* movies, cartoon shows, and reruns of old prime time programs.

Cable stations run prime time reruns, movies, sports, music videos, and syndicated programming, but they may also produce original material. In 1993, HBO was praised for producing a movie called *And the Band Played On,* which was based on journalist Randy Shilts's book about early AIDS research. The broadcast networks had turned down the idea because they thought it would be too controversial. As the number of cable channels proliferates, cable networks will generate greater amounts of original programming to draw viewers from broadcast networks.

There is no adequate theory of audience demand for news and entertainment programming. Although ratings reflect how audiences choose between available programs that are *already* on television, they do not reflect what *could be* on television. Audience research has been designed primarily to find out how viewers react to what is available, not to find out what viewers might like to watch if they had the chance.

Advertisers use media to persuade possible buyers. Television advertisers have traditionally addressed a mass market, and products that are advertised on television reflect such an audience. A popular actress, Betty Furness, opened refrigerator doors on television repeatedly during the 1950s to advertise Westinghouse refrigerators to housewives; Procter & Gamble advertised its various cleaning products on Ed Sullivan's Sunday night variety program in the 1950s and 1960s; and a new line of automobiles rolled across the screen each year on Dinah Shore's variety show sponsored by Chevrolet.

With the development of multiple cable channels, advertisers increasingly use television to target audiences through use of **demographics** and **psychographics.** Although traditional demographics give advertisers some guidance in targeting audiences, some larger audiences are bound together more by attitude than by demographics. The Discovery Channel, for example, has "different demographic groups but they share a psychographic tie that binds them together," says Chris Moseley, senior vice president of marketing and communications for Discovery. "They want information and they want to be entertained." Through research, Discovery divided its audience not merely into people over and under fifty years of age, but into categories that included "scholars," "practicals," and "boy's-toys."[30]

> **Key**concept
>
> *Demographic and Psychographic Approaches to Broadcast Marketing:* Research analysts looking for TV advertising markets identify program preferences by using two common approaches: Demographic approaches stress statistical links between program features and such factors as age, education, income, and gender. Psychographic approaches stress links between programs and potentially measurable factors in audience lifestyles or in categories of personal likes and dislikes.

ADVERTISING AND TELEVISION CONTENT Company sponsorship of individual television shows, a practice that began in radio programming, declined in the 1960s after the quiz show scandals. Today, it is rare for an entire program to be sponsored by one advertiser. Rather, networks or stations sell time for ads—*spots*—during a show. Does this mean that advertising has little impact on programming? No, the influence remains, but it is more subtle. Individual advertisers occasionally affect content, but advertising as a form of financing has a more pervasive impact.

Because cable television fragmented audiences during the 1980s, advertisers increasingly aim at precise demographic groups. To provide efficient advertising within these groups, programs need to attract as large a proportion of the targeted group as they can. A company selling jeans to eighteen- to twenty-four-year-olds wants to reach as much of that audience as it can with one program, since having to buy ads on several programs cuts into the company's profit margin. Therefore the company may prefer a program that concentrates on sex, action, and violence, which have a visceral impact that attracts many viewers in the target age group.

Such programming sometimes targets the lowest common denominator, but some programs, such as the hospital drama *ER,* are high-quality shows that may include sex and violence but don't rely heavily on them. The muscular chests and jiggling breasts of the lifeguards in *Baywatch,* for example, attract viewers, while the occasional shot of Detective Sipowicz's buttocks probably does not significantly increase the audience of *NYPD Blue.* High-quality dramatic shows attract viewers with more complicated plots, greater character development, and more sophisticated writing.

NYPD Blue provides an example of the declining influence of advertisers on adult programming. The program first aired in the fall of 1993 amidst controversy over its language, violence, and occasional nudity. During its premiere season, automotive, food, and beer advertisers stayed away, frightened by protests from some organizations. As it turned out, the violence did not exceed that found in the

demographics: The study of the characteristics of human populations and population segments.

psychographics: The study of lifestyles, attitudes, and values.

[profile]

Bill Cosby

Bill Cosby has achieved a lot in a relatively short time: In his thirty years as an entertainer, he has been a stand-up comedian; broken racial barriers as costar of the 1960s television series *I Spy;* changed the face of television situation comedies with *The Cosby Show;* sold four million copies of his first book, *Fatherhood,* and two million of his second book, *Time Flies;* had two comedy albums in *Billboard*'s Top 10; and been awarded eight gold records and five Grammy awards as well as Emmy awards for *I Spy* and *Cosby.*

Much of Cosby's work is based on his family life and his experience as a father—areas he says he knows best. Cosby believes in keeping comedy and situation comedies clean, and he has been successful doing so.

Cosby was born in Philadelphia on July 11, 1937, and was the first of three boys. The family lived in a housing project, where, he says, their needs were met and there was no place for prejudice. His mother Anna Pearl Cosby, his proclaimed role model, raised the boys while working sixteen hours a day as a domestic. His father served in the Navy.

Cosby was the captain of his high school track and football teams, but he dropped out of school in his sophomore year. He joined the Navy, finished high school through a correspondence course, and received his GED. He went to Temple University on a track scholarship but quit three years later to concentrate on his comedy career. He later obtained his degree from Temple and went on to obtain master's and doctorate degrees in education from the University of Massachusetts. His wife, the former Camille Hanks, also has a doctorate in education. The Cosbys have four daughters; their son Ennis was murdered in 1997.

Cosby played the first minority lead role in television when he starred with Robert Culp in *I Spy* from 1965 to 1968. Before the series was over, he had won three Emmy Awards. Cosby went on to perform in other TV shows, several specials, and many successful concert performances. He also recorded more than twenty comedy albums and wrote four books.

Then came *The Cosby Show,* a family show in which the parents were strict but loving and children and parents learned from each other. Cosby took his idea to all three networks, but only NBC accepted it. By its second season, *The Cosby Show* was the highest-rated weekly television series, attracting 60 million viewers. The show ran for eight years, from 1984 to 1992.

Today, Cosby is one of the richest people in the entertainment business. He has been Number 1 on *Forbes*'s list of top-earning entertainers several times, with a recent estimated worth of $325 million. In the 1996–1997 season, NBC introduced *Cosby,* a new situation-comedy series.

However, Cosby's success as a creative entertainment and his financial wealth have not protected him from tragedy. On January 16, 1997, his son Ennis William Cosby, a doctoral student at Columbia University, was found shot to death near his car on the side of a road in California.

SOURCES: Don Heckman, "Common Cos," *Los Angeles Times,* June 11, 1995, Section Calendar, p. 8; Bob Thomas, "Cosby Talks," *Good Housekeeping* 212:2 (February 1991): p. 167; Todd Klein, "Bill Cosby," *Saturday Evening Post* 258 (April 1986): p. 42.

earlier *Hill Street Blues,* and the language could be heard daily on talk shows. The sex, while racy by traditional network standards, proved to be mild by cable standards. Two years after its inception, *NYPD Blue* was awarded an Emmy for best drama of 1994–1995 and consistently ranked in the top ten programs on television. Advertisers flocked to reach its audience.

AUDIENCE MEASUREMENT AND STATION SURVIVAL: THE RATINGS GAME Measuring audience demand for particular programs is important because prices charged for advertising are based on the number of households and people watching. The measurement also helps programmers to evaluate the demand for various types of shows. If dramas about police departments get high ratings one season, more such programs will surely appear the next season.

A.C. Nielsen Media Research dominates the audience measurement business; the American Research Bureau (Arbitron) withdrew from measuring television audiences in the mid-1990s. Nielsen measures viewing of programs and breaks down the number of viewers into a variety of demographic and psychographic categories. Using statistical techniques, the Nielsen reports can tell an advertiser how many people between the ages of eighteen and thirty-four who make more than $40,000 a year watched *Seinfeld* on Channel 10 in Lansing, Michigan, on September 12, 1996.

Nielsen uses a variety of techniques to measure audiences. These include diaries, personal and telephone interviews, audimeters, and people meters.

Ratings determine whether shows continue or die. This event, where supporters of the television show Ellen *view her coming out, was sponsored by the Gay and Lesbian Alliance Against Defamation.*

- *Diaries.* This method requires viewers to keep journals detailing what they are watching. Although the results might seem quite precise, a diary measures only what a viewer is willing to write. It reflects the viewer's perceptions, not an actual response.

- *Interviews.* Personal or telephone interviews are designed to inquire about watching habits. Interviews rely on individual recall, which is sometimes faulty, and, like diaries, are reports of perceptions rather than measurements of actual behavior.

- *Audimeters.* A sample of homes within large television markets are connected to audimeters. These indicate when a set is turned on, which channels it is tuned to, and for how long. The audimeters provide quick responses—ratings are obtainable overnight. However, they do not provide information about the person watching the show. Advertisers don't know whether their product ad is reaching a mother, a child, or an empty room.

- *People Meter.* People meters can distinguish who in a household is watching a program. Each member of the household is assigned a different number to press on a control when watching or changing shows. Again, a drawback is that some people, especially children, might not push the button every time they change shows.

The proliferation of cable channels and videocassette recorders (VCRs) has complicated the ratings process. Many people don't watch programs at scheduled times but record them for viewing later. People also watch one program while recording another. A company cannot say that audiences rated one program over another if viewers plan to watch both, but at different times.

Nielsen Media Research measures audiences and reports findings in the form of ratings (percentage of TV households in a market watching a program). Nielsen found out, for example, that during the week of June 24 to 30, 1996, *Seinfeld* was watched by more people than any other program, with a rating of 14.4. Because one rating point equals 970,000 television households, 14 million households had *Seinfeld* turned on.

Nielsen also reports its findings in the form of shares (percentage of households watching TV that are tuned to a particular channel). Shares are significant figures because they show how watching is distributed among channels, and they can be compared across markets. The *Seinfeld* program, with its 14.4 rating, had a share of 27. The next closest program during the same time period was *Rescue 911,* with a share of 11.[31]

The accuracy of audience measurements continues to be a controversial issue. Different methods can produce different ratings and shares. This is particularly important to local stations because their advertising rates are connected to Nielsen audience measures. Advertisers require that the ratings be measured by an independent company because stations might inflate their own audience measures to increase ad rates.[32]

During the 1990s, network executives began criticizing Nielsen Media Research for inaccurate ratings. These executives believed that some of the decline in network ratings reflected problems in collecting data about viewing habits. The participation rate among households contacted by Nielsen had dropped below 50 percent. The level of response rate affects how well the households used for determining ratings represent all households.

As a result of the dissatisfaction, Statistical Research Inc. (SRI) of New Jersey developed a system of rating programs that is less intrusive than the older Nielsen system. In 1995 tests, the SRI system got a response rate above 50 percent. Nielsen did not take the experiment by a competitor lightly. It increased the number of households in its sample, increased its participation rate, and worked to make its data collection system less obtrusive. The impact of these changes remained unclear as executives continued to express concerns about Nielsen during late 1996.[33]

Supplying the audience's demand

Supplying the demands of the information market and supplying the demands of the advertising market are intertwined. Sometimes, while trying to target (attract) a certain segment of the audience, television executives manage to deter other segments, causing lower ratings and decreased advertising support, as in the following example.

In 1992–1993, the networks experienced the largest growth in advertising since 1988. The Olympics and political advertising contributed to the increase, but so did steady viewership. The combined network advertising growth would have been higher if ratings for NBC hadn't fallen in the last quarter.[34] What happened was this: Combined network ratings and audience shares for the 1991–1992 prime time season (September through April) were the highest since 1985–1986. The Winter Olympics and the end of the Gulf War may have helped the increase, but so did overall good programming. Then, in the 1992–1993 season, NBC experienced a decline in ratings, which accounted for most of the rating decline for all networks. In fall 1992, NBC decided to change its programming to target eighteen- to thirty-four-year-old viewers. When it replaced *Golden Girls, Matlock,* and *In the Heat of the Night,* older viewers changed channels, turning their attention to Discovery, A&E, and CNN. After reviewing ratings and shares, NBC returned to its previous "a program for everyone" mode in fall 1993. Fox also announced that it would move from a young target audience to a more general one.

Station organization

Most television stations comprise six core departments. How extensive each department is depends on how big the station is. The engineering department manages the technical equipment used by all departments, especially the news and programming ones; the news department produces newscasts and public affairs reporting; the programming department buys and produces content to attract viewers for advertisers; the advertising or sales department solicits advertisers; the business office maintains financial records; and the promotions department uses advertising, special events, and public service to attract viewers and develop a positive image of the station.[35]

■ Television technologies

Television, just like newspapers and magazines, has to be distributed to the audience. Television transmission technologies can be either wireless, such as broadcast, microwave, and satellite, or wire-based, such as coaxial or fiber-optic cable. Many of these technologies are used in combination with each other.

■ Broadcast Transmission

Broadcast television is similar to broadcast radio in that the information is transmitted from a station antenna on a specific spectrum frequency or channel to a receiver, usually a TV set's antenna. Each TV station has a designated channel on which it transmits. The spectrum space needed for television is 6 MHz, larger than radio, because more information is transmitted.

MICROWAVE Microwave is a focused line-of-sight transmission mode that uses much higher frequencies than does broadcast transmission. Tall microwave towers are needed about every thirty miles to efficiently receive, amplify, and relay its point-to-point signals.

In recent years, on-the-scene TV reporters have used microwave transmitters attached to the tops of their vans to immediately relay reports to their stations for taping or broadcast.

SATELLITES Satellites provide a relatively inexpensive way of transmitting information nationally or globally and have made instantaneous global communication possible. Most communications satellites are launched into space to orbit 22,300 miles above the equator. At this distance they appear to remain stationary over one point on earth. This enables them to continuously receive signals from and send signals to ground stations. Large ground dishes uplink signals to satellites on frequencies that are much higher than regular broadcast signals. The satellite transponder then downlinks the signal to stations on the earth.

A satellite usually has twenty-four transponders, with which it can receive and transmit twenty-four different TV channels simultaneously. Digital video compression increases the channel capacity by at least threefold.

Keyconcept

Satellite Transmission via Uplinks and Downlinks: Communication satellites have the capability to receive electronic signals by an *uplink* process for storage or further distribution. Signals can then be distributed by a *downlink* process from a satellite to a ground facility.

WIRE TRANSMISSION Cable television transmits its programming through coaxial or fiber-optic cables instead of broadcasting it over the air.

Cable transmission has several advantages: Cables, strung on telephone poles or laid underground, are not subject to line-of-sight obstruction or most other electronic interference; two-way interaction back and forth along the same cable is possible; and a subscriber can receive many channels, typically 35 but sometimes as many as 200, from one cable system instead of one channel from one broadcast station.

Disadvantages for cable operators are often financial. Because the initial cost is so high, a number of households must subscribe for it to be financially viable to bring cable into a neighborhood. In rural areas, the distances between houses greatly increase the

262 cost of laying cable, so many rural areas do not have access to cable. Furthermore, cable operators must employ salespeople and pay for promotions to encourage people to buy the service. Broadcast operators, by contrast, worry only about transmission costs because households buy their own antennas to catch signals and broadcast television is directly supported by advertisers, not consumers.

FIBER OPTICS The hair-thin strands of glass known as fiber-optic cable carry audio, visual, and digital information on lights produced by laser. More information is carried more quickly and in a narrower space by fiber optics than by coaxial wires. For example, one inch of coaxial cable can carry more than 400,000 telephone calls simultaneously, but one pound of fiber-optic cable can carry eighty times more information than one pound of coaxial cable can.[36]

Television signals and digital computer signals must be transmitted either by airwave or wire. Fiberoptic cable is more expensive to install than the traditional coaxial cable, but allows for a high volume of signal traffic.

Although fiber-optic technology has been available for some time, its installation has been slow. First, suitable attachments are needed to connectors, which amplify and relay signals. Some strands are miles long, and the signals need to be strengthened at connector points along the way, or else all the information dissipates. Whereas copper wire can be welded to connectors, glass cannot. Second, technology standardization is needed. Information often passes through the optic strand in analogue form, the same form in which information goes through a telephone wire. Audio, video, and digital information must be encoded into analogue at the origination point and then decoded back into digital form at the end point. Unfortunately, the encoding and decoding technologies, developed by different companies, are not always uniform devices that understand each other's signals.

DIRECT BROADCAST SATELLITE Direct broadcast satellite (DBS) takes TV signals from earth stations and downlinks them to houses that have receiver dishes. For almost two decades, travelers have noticed the eight-foot satellite receiving dishes in rural areas that cable and broadcast stations could not reach. However, since spring 1995, eighteen-inch receiver dishes, about the size of a large pizza, can receive more than 150 channels with high-quality digital reproduction. As a result, cable television now has competition in urban areas.

Keyconcept

Analogue TV Transmission versus Digital Technology: Traditional TV transmission uses a continuously varying, wavelike signal system, known as analogue, corresponding to the light or sound waves originated by the source. Newer digital technology changes visual and audio content into a series of zeroes and ones that are computer readable. These digital signals are transmitted and then decoded into visual and audio content at a reception point.

The new DBS systems offer a variety of viewing packages at prices comparable to those of expanded cable packages. However, DBS has two disadvantages when compared to cable. First, the DBS subscriber must buy or rent the dish. The cost of buying a dish dropped to under $200 by 1996, with company rebates. Second, the DBS systems do not include local TV stations. To receive local news, viewers must use either cable systems or a broadcast antenna. Despite these two problems, early sales of small satellite dishes exceeded expectations, and the number of households with DBS increased by one-third during the first ten months of 1996. Cable systems reacted to the competition by offering lower prices for some packages, providing better service to customers, and broadcasting ads that emphasized the limitations of DBS.

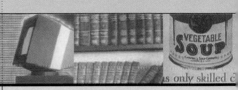
The Brave Continuing World of Interactive TV

nteractive television is not new. In the early 1950s, children urged their parents to buy a special plastic screen for the television set so that they could draw on the screen and interact with a clever children's cartoon program, *Winky Dink and You*. Winky Dink, chased by a tiger to the edge of the cliff, could be saved only if the child drew a bridge to the next mountain to help Winky Dink escape.

Interactive technology has been experimented with intensively since 1964, when AT&T demonstrated a picture telephone at the New York World's Fair. But thirty years later, the picture phone has not become a household item. The quality of the image was poor; cost of the service was high; and owners could communicate only with people who also owned picture phones. Perhaps most important, individuals didn't always *want*—and almost never *needed*—to see each other on the telephone. Using the

telephone for business, however, does create demand for teleconferencing via video phone, and varied combinations of video and telephone are still being experimented with.

Today, interactive technology is becoming commonplace. Personal computers, automated teller machines, VCR remote-control keypads, and information kiosks at airports, hotels, and tourist attractions rely on interactive technology. For interactive video technology to be successful, however, the quality of the image must attract viewers, the content must entice them to participate, and the cost must not exceed that of similar devices. Also, technology experts and programmers must distinguish between computer-style and television-style uses. For tasks that require the user to lean forward and work, select items, and respond, the computer remains the instrument of choice. For activities that can be accomplished while relaxing in an enter-

tainment mode, television outranks the computer.

Various corporations have experimented with interactive television for almost twenty years, but experts have yet to find the right combination of programming, technology, and cost to drive people to adopt the innovation. When the FCC opened the programming doors to telephone companies, a new wave of interactive experiments began. By early 1997 it was possible to purchase a device such as the Philips-Magnavox WebTV that allowed the user to browse the web on a television set. TV set manufacturers are predicting the availability of digital sets by 1998, which makes the converging of the World Wide Web and television not far off.

SOURCE: John Carey, "The Interactive Television Puzzle." Technology Paper, The Freedom Forum Media Studies Center, New York (undated).

MULTICHANNEL DISTRIBUTION SERVICE Multichannel distribution service (MDS), also called wireless cable, uses higher broadcast frequencies than traditional broadcast television frequencies and a converter box to send multiple channels of cablelike programming. Initially designed for cities that did not receive cable because initial installation and start-up costs were less expensive, MDS faces an uncertain future because most cities now are wired for cable and DBS also provides competition.

LOW-POWER TELEVISION Low-power television (LPTV) is comparatively inexpensive to both producer and viewer because it operates on conventional television broadcast frequencies at very low power, covering distances less than fifteen miles. LPTV's local nature,

264

more defined target audience, and cost are advantageous; however, competition makes financial stability difficult. Since large numbers of consumers watch network broadcast and cable television, advertisers are less inclined to spend money reaching the small audiences of the low-power stations. To overcome the competition obstacle, groups of LPTV stations are forming to offer larger audiences that will attract advertisers.

Supplying news: The world in our living rooms

Local stations, national networks, CNN, and news syndicates generate news programming. Local stations usually produce their own community news; if they are network owned or affiliated, they also carry national network news. CNN, through cable and satellite technology, provides twenty-four-hour access to news. TV news syndicates take the form of either a video exchange by local stations joined in a cooperative or a pay service. CONUS, a cooperative formed in 1984, has more than 100 member stations. Reuters and Associated Press, which provide video services for subscribers, are pay services.

Technology has greatly influenced how stations supply news. In the 1970s, news gathering became portable as small videocameras and microwave equipment enabled reporters to broadcast live. A limiting factor was the nature of microwaves, which went in straight lines and could be blocked by the earth and other objects. Satellite development in the 1980s led to portable equipment called satellite news gathering (SNG) equipment, allowing reporters to bounce their signals off satellites. Now stations can send reporters all over the globe and no longer have to depend on networks for nonlocal news. However, SNG equipment is too expensive for most stations outside the large metro areas to buy. By the beginning of the 1990s, however, stations could rent SNG equipment on an as-needed basis. Medium- and small-market stations can cover news that affects their viewers regardless of where the news happens.

Television continues to be regarded as the most credible news medium. Figure 9.2 shows the results of a survey in which people were asked who they would be "most inclined" to believe when offered different or conflicting reports of the same news story.

EVENING NEWSCAST The evening news format, as exemplified by the network shows featuring Peter Jennings, Dan Rather, and Tom Brokaw, is the most basic news presentation model. Chet Huntley and David Brinkley popularized the anchor format, in which one or two anchors read the news, usually with video or other visual accompaniment. This format later became identified primarily with former UPI reporter Walter Cronkite. Cronkite became the evening CBS anchor in 1963 and soon ranked in public opinion polls as the most trusted person in the United States. Since Cronkite's retirement in 1981, no newscaster has enjoyed such a high level of credibility.

Keyconcept

TV Newscast Formats: Television newscasts have evolved a variety of formats ranging from the traditional evening and morning news shows to variations to documentaries, interviews, and weekly news magazines.

Local stations have their own news teams. These are usually headed by a pair of anchors, with supporting team members who report on local weather, sports, and other topics of interest, such as health and consumer information. Station reporters are shown on location at sites of stories of local interest, such as a controversial legal trial or a crime scene. There may also be remote feeds, usually from stations affiliated with the same network, for stories of special interest. For example, during the criminal and civil trials of O.J. Simpson, many local news broadcasts around the country featured live reports from California.

DOCUMENTARY Documentaries evolved from a tradition of news and exposure that was prominent in film during the 1930s. They moved to television in the 1950s as thirty-

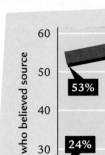

TV News Leads in Credibility

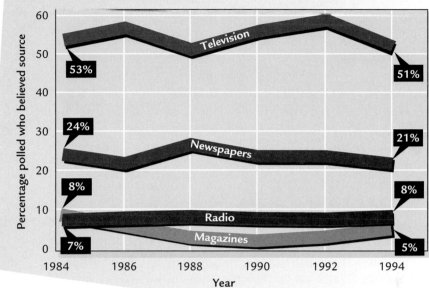

Source: Roper Starch Worldwide for the Network Television Association and the National Association of Broadcasters, 1995; published in The Freedom Forum *Media Studies Journal,* "Media Critics," Spring 1995.

minute or one-hour programs concentrating on a single issue. The purpose of a documentary is to provide depth and context for important public issues. Some memorable documentaries are *Harvest of Shame* (1960), which exposed mistreatment of migrant workers; *The Selling of the Pentagon* (1971), which centered on the use of federal money to promote the military; and *The Guns of Autumn* (1975), which documented abuses in gun ownership and hunting. The number of network documentaries has declined because controversial issues are rarely attractive to advertisers. Today, documentaries are most often associated with independent production companies, cable channels such as Discovery, and public television, which does not depend on advertisers for financial support.

WEEKLY NEWS MAGAZINES Magazine programs contain several stories in each weekly segment. The longest-running and most popular magazine show, *60 Minutes,* first appeared in 1968. Although *20/20* also gained a strong following, it wasn't until the 1990s that news magazines reached the level of prominence they enjoy today. Magazine programs such as *Dateline NBC* air more than once a week, and it is common to find seven or more prime time magazines per week.

The shows vary in the degree of hard and soft news they carry and in the degree of sensational treatment. However, they are profitable because they cost less money to produce than a prime time drama and they allow the networks to share the high salaries of news personalities among several programs.

The intense competition among these programs can lead to some embarrassing problems as each program tries to outdo the other. For example, *Dateline NBC* admitted to staging the explosion of a pickup truck in one segment, and ABC lost the initial round of a $5.5 million law suit to Food Lion, a supermarket chain. The ABC *Primetime* reporters had done a story about unsanitary conditions with hidden cameras. The network lost the case because of its reporting practices, such as using faked resumes to get jobs in Food Lion stores.

INTERVIEW SHOWS *Meet the Press* and *Face the Nation,* in which journalists interview one or more prominent people in the news, are some of the longest-running programs. They provide the public with the opinions of prominent politicians, military leaders, and other important public figures. In doing so, these programs serve the marketplace of ideas.

MORNING NEWS SHOWS Morning news shows have completed a circle, arriving where they were when the *Today Show* started on NBC in 1952. The early *Today Show,* hosted by Dave Garroway, provided news, but in a very broad sense of the term. Celebrity interviews, a large picture window where people on the street could hold up signs of greetings, and even chimpanzees named Mr. Kokomo and J. Fred Muggs greeted viewers in the morning. Eventually, the *Today Show* spawned a variety of imitations. The morning shows took on a harder edge during the late 1960s and early 1970s. But *Good Morning America* started a return toward softer news in the mid-1970s. This sometimes sensational news approach became the norm for morning shows after 1979, when *Good Morning America* replaced the *Today Show* as the ratings leader for morning news shows. CBS has struggled in the morning news market, featuring *CBS This Morning* but never gaining a solid audience for the show.

TABLOID TELEVISION Tabloid television includes confessional talk shows such as *Oprah Winfrey,* gossip shorts such as *A Current Affair,* and so-called reality based shows such as *Night Beat, Cops, Top Cops, American Detective,* and *America's Most Wanted.* These are cheap to make, easy to syndicate, and wildly profitable. Tabloid shows, such as *Hard Copy,* came under fire from numerous critics during the 1990s because of their emphasis on sex, reenactments, and the practice of paying sources. As a result, *Current Affair* producers announced in June 1995 that they would stop reenactments and paying sources as a common practice. If sources were paid, this would be stated on air.[37]

Supplying entertainment

Because it is difficult for programming directors to predict the success of shows, they rely on what seems to have worked in the past. Costs are high, and risks are great. When a network's new show pulls good ratings, other networks will quickly produce shows with similar plots or casts of characters. This *copy-cat programming* increases the chance of success. Thus programming often goes through three stages: *invention,* in which new genres or types of shows are developed; *imitation,* or copy-cat programming; and ultimately *decline.* Prime time television has been through Old West periods, war periods, doctor periods, and police periods. In the 1994–1995 television season, for instance, ABC added its hospital show *Medicine Ball* to the existing line-up of CBS's *Chicago Hope* and NBC's *ER,* but *Medicine Ball* failed. Other recent fads include single-parent households headed either by a dad or a mom and groups of urban singles such as *Friends* and *The Drew Carey Show.*

Low-budget programs are a mainstay, especially during daytime programming. Low-budget programs include soap operas, game shows, and interview shows. Soap operas hire actors who often begin (and end) their careers in

Keyconcept

Entertainment Formulas: Because of financial risks, producers of broadcast entertainment tend to rely on standard entertainment patterns or formulas that have been successful in the past. They often extend adult formulas into entertainment for children; if violent programs attract young adult audiences, a similar violent format may be used in children's programs.

TV Land Versus Real Life

n a research project called "Distorted Viewing: TV's Reflection of Life," *USA Today* staffers found that "any similarity between life as depicted on television and as lived in the United States appears to be coincidental." Some of their observations include the following:

- *Gender is misrepresented.* Women are shown as only 37 percent of television characters, yet women make up more than half of the population (51 percent). Male characters dominate television shows (63 percent) while being less than half the population (49 percent).

- *Employment is misrepresented.* Professionals/executives and law enforcement characters are overrepresented on television (60 percent and 10 percent); in reality they comprise 26 percent and 2 percent of the workforce, respectively. Labor/service/clerical workers are underrepresented on television (21 percent), whereas they are 72 percent of the workforce in real life.

- *Age is misrepresented.* Children, teens, and older people make up only 18 percent of television characters but represent 43 percent of U.S. society. Young adults and middle-aged adults are vastly overrepresented, making up 82 percent of TV-land population, whereas they make up 57 percent in U.S. population.

- *Race/ethnicity is misrepresented.* Native Americans, Asians, and Hispanics are shown as only 3.4 percent of TV characters, but they make up 13 percent of U.S. society. Blacks represent 13 percent of TV characters, just 1 percent more than reality. Whites comprise 84 percent of TV characters while making up 76 percent of the real-life population.

- *Physical differences are misrepresented.* Characters are rarely handicapped (1 percent compared to 17 percent in society), overweight (10 percent compared to 68 percent in society), or wear glasses (14 percent compared to 38 percent in society).

- *Violence is misrepresented.* TV violence—the number of assaults and killings—appear much more often in "TV Time" than they do in society in "real time." Of the 94 nonnews programs watched, 48 showed 276 acts of violence.

SOURCE: "Distorted Viewing: TV's Reflection of Life," *The Detroit News,* Thursday, July 22, 1993, p. 3E.

soap operas, with a salary that reflects their starting position. Game shows and interview shows need only one set and use amateurs, who are less expensive than professional actors.

Entertainment programming includes prime time network shows, which run between 8:00 and 11:00 P.M. Eastern time. Syndicates' prime time shows are first-run shows that are sold through syndicates and not by networks. Other programming is composed of syndicated reruns, which are former or current successful prime time shows that produced enough episodes to run five days a week. Still other programming includes movies, sports programming, and public broadcasting.

Who produces entertainment programming? Overwhelmingly, television shows have been produced by Hollywood studios. However, freed from regulation during the early 1990s, networks began producing more of their own television programs. This allowed them greater control of the program content, but it also raised concerns among independent producers. With network-produced shows taking up more time slots, networks will buy fewer independent programs.

268

Although First Amendment considerations prevent government action in most content areas, Congress and public interest critics have repeatedly raised concerns about the impact of sexual and violent content on television, particularly on children.

Programs aimed at teenagers typically emphasize relationships between boys and girls, which translates on television into sex. Fox has been successful with programs such as *Melrose Place* and *Beverly Hills 90210* in attracting highly sought-after young viewers, who spend much of their money on consumer goods and services. These programs target teenagers who conceive of themselves as young adults. Proponents argue that these programs introduce social issues and teach teenagers how to deal with them. Critics are quick to point out that dilemmas are usually solved within the hour and that choices made by the characters seldom have lasting consequences.

The public and Congress express even greater concern about the impact of programming on young children, particularly in regard to violence. Some people argue that parents should monitor what their children watch, others support installing electronic chips that can block specified programming, and still others advocate outright control of content production. During the early 1990s, the FCC outlawed advertisements that were extensions of programs, arguing that young children could not distinguish between a G.I. Joe cartoon and an advertisement for a G.I. Joe product. As you will read in Chapter 12, which discusses regulation in all media, in the early 1990s, Congress passed legislation that regulates some of children's television content.

Increased concern about the influence of television content on children and the impact of violent programming on society led to a television program rating system in 1996. The television industry developed the system not out of altruism but because the 1996 Telecommunications Act mandates a system that can be used with a computer chip. The industry hopes the rating system will help to blunt any further efforts to control content.

The Motion Picture Academy of America helped to develop the ratings system, which is similar to the one used for movies. The system has been adopted by the networks and most basic cable channels. The system has six levels that appear as icons in the upper left corner of the TV set during the first fifteen seconds of the program. The levels are based on age and run from TV-Y, which means that the program is suitable for all children, to TV-M, which means that it is not suitable for children under 17. Table 9.2 lists all of the new ratings.

The television industry in 1997 developed a series of ratings similar to those for movies in an effort to sidestep political demand for intervention in broadcasting. However, the rating system proved controversial as some broadcasters viewed it as a restriction of free expression.

The ratings system has not received unanimous support. Critics argue that the ratings should address content more specifically and that separate ratings should be available for sex and violence. Others argue that determining the suitability of TV content should be left to parents, not a ratings system.

Surveys conducted in the six weeks following the introduction found that many parents were not using the system. In one poll, 86 percent said that they supported having a ratings system, and 73 percent said that they were aware of the new system. However, only 37 percent said that they had used it to help select programs.[38] As the V-chip portion of the Telecommunication Act moves through the courts, the use of ratings and the particular system being used will continue to be debated.

TABLE 9.2 Television Ratings

TV-Y—All Children: The program is suitable for all children. It should not frighten younger children.

TV-Y7—Older Children: Designed for children age 7 and older, may contain mild physical or comedic violence that may frighten children under 7.

TV-G—General Audiences: Program is appropriate for all ages. It contains little or no violence, no strong language and little or no sexual dialogue or situations.

TV-PG—Parental Guidance Suggested: Program may contain limited sexual or violent material that may be unsuitable for younger children.

TV-14—Parents Strongly Cautioned: Program may contain some material that many parents would find unsuitable for children under 14 years old.

TV-M—Mature Audiences Only: Program is specifically designed to be viewed by adults, and therefore may be unsuitable for children under 17.

■ Supplying the advertising market

Several different entities—networks, groups, individual stations, and cable systems—sell advertising time. The price of the time varies with the geographic location and type of audience, which varies in kind and number with the time of day. For example, advertising time within a network show is much more expensive than time within a local show because of the larger, national audience that the network can reach. The price for an ad within a Chicago local program would depend on the size and demographics of the audience. Advertisers may pay more to reach people with higher incomes because these people have more money to spend.

Advertisers are always interested in knowing how much it costs to reach a single consumer. The number of viewers a particular program attracts determines the fee that the network or station charges advertisers. The formula for determining such costs is called the *cost per thousand (CPM),* which is the dollar amount it costs to reach a thousand viewers with an ad. Take, for example, a thirty-second advertisement on *Seinfeld.* The charge for such a spot was about $400,000 in 1995. On a good night, the program might have 40 million viewers. The cost per thousand viewers would be $10. Here is the formula broken into two parts:

$$\frac{\text{Total number of viewers}}{1,000} \qquad \text{Example: } \frac{40,000,000}{1,000} = 40,000$$

$$\frac{\text{Cost of ad}}{\text{Result of first equation}} \qquad \text{Example: } \frac{400,000}{40,000} = \$10 \text{ per thousand}$$

The same formula can be used for radio, magazines, and newspapers. Thus the cost of reaching a thousand people with a TV program can be compared to the cost of reaching the same number of people in other media. The higher a show's rating, the more a station can charge for a minute of advertising, as long as the CPM does not become too much higher than that of other media.

Television regulation also affects how stations and networks supply the advertising market. For example, cigarette advertising is prohibited. Cigarette manufacturers got around the ban on TV advertising by putting cigarette ads in football stadiums, baseball parks, and basketball arenas, which appeared on TV. The Justice Department said that Philip Morris had ads placed near the field or scoreboards in fourteen football stadiums, fourteen baseball parks, and five basketball arenas. In 1995, Philip Morris agreed to remove such advertisements.[39]

However, in other instances, deregulation has favored advertisers. Since the early 1990s, advertisers have been permitted to develop program-length commercials. Advertisers can purchase a period of time equal to that of a regular program and broadcast advertising videos, many of which look like news shows. Critics are concerned about whether consumers will differentiate between paid time and news time.

Keyconcept

Cost per Consumer in the TV Advertising Market: The key factor in selling TV advertising is how much it costs to reach a single consumer. Therefore the number of viewers a particular program attracts determines the fee charged to advertisers. Some of the most expensive ad spots are in Super Bowl broadcasts, which attract enormous audiences.

The latest move toward regulating advertising concerns liquor advertisements. From 1948 until 1996, the companies that produce distilled spirits voluntarily refrained from advertising on television. But in fall 1996, Seagrams ran advertisements for Chivas Regal Scotch in Texas and Massachusetts, sparking discussion among FCC commissioners and members of Congress about regulating liquor advertising. Beer and wine producers, which spent $391 million on TV advertising during the first seven months of 1996, were concerned that such regulation might include them.

Television and the international market

Technology and corporate activities continue to make television an international medium. During the 1990s, satellite transmissions of video material and changing government systems opened up areas of the globe that once had limited access to television. Soon, Tim "The Tool Man" Allen may be recognized on the streets of Buenos Aires as well as on the streets of Detroit.

Keyconcept

Market Factors in International TV: Satellite transmission technology and international corporate mergers have made TV a worldwide force. Key factors are ownership and availability of satellite services, broad access to content through mergers of production companies, and development of international television content through cooperative global conglomerates.

The growing globalization of television involves four issues that will determine the nature and extent of this trend: the availability of distribution systems, the availability of programming, cultural resistance, and international corporate cooperation.

Availability of distribution systems

At the center of global television are companies such as Hughes Communications, which owns DirectTV and is developing satellite services for Japan and Latin America, and News Corp., Rupert Murdoch's company that controls Sky TV in Great Britain and Star Television, which serves Asia from Hong Kong. These and other satellite companies use eighteen-inch satellite dishes to provide packages of channels to viewers in a variety of countries and are able to reach audiences without the expensive task of laying cable. Such corporations wield enormous power. Although NBC challenged Murdoch's News Corp., arguing that it violated FCC regulations because it was foreign owned, NBC dropped its complaint after Murdoch agreed that NBC could use Star Television's satellite to reach Asian markets.

Availability of programming

Offering 150 channels won't attract viewers unless the programs have appeal. With the proliferation of channels, content becomes an increasingly important issue, and some of the communications mergers of the 1990s sought to broaden access to content. For example, the merger of Time Warner and Turner Broadcasting Systems combined the MGM and Warner Bros. film libraries to create the biggest collection of films and videos in the world. In 1995, News Corp., with its satellite system and NFL football games, joined Tele-Communication Inc., which has several regional sports cable companies, to create a worldwide sports network. The new network competes with Disney's ESPN.

Many countries' governments help to supply the demand for content. The European Union spends about $60 million a year to develop television programming. Canada invests in film and video and has emerged as the biggest foreign supplier of television programming in the United States.

Cultural resistance

Not all countries embrace expanding access to television. Many countries in developing areas fear that Western programming will corrupt the morals of their people and forever alter indigenous cultures. They see the expansion of television as a form of cultural imperialism, the forcing of Western culture onto non-Western countries. In 1995, Iran banned satellite dishes because of concerns about the clash of American programs such as *Baywatch* with Muslim beliefs.

Several Asian countries limit the use of programs that are produced outside the country. For example, Taiwan requires that 70 percent of its programming be domestically produced; South Korea limits imported television programming to 20 percent of available time.

Fears about cultural imperialism are economic and cultural. Both stem from the popularity of American programming. With their high production values, focus on action, emphasis on sex, and simple plots, many American television shows and movies attract audiences across cultures. Economically, imported programs undermine indigenous television production. Such programming often contradicts cultural values. For example, in a country where older individuals are held in high esteem, an American program that caters to a young audience by portraying older people as inconsequential could be offensive.

International cooperation

Because resistance to external video programming is widespread and shows no sign of subsiding, global conglomerates have turned to pursuing cooperative ventures for developing international television content. Time Warner and France Television have agreed to develop programs for French TV. BMG Entertainment, Warner Music, and HBO Ole combined in 1995 to develop a twenty-four-hour Spanish-language music channel, YA TV, to compete in Latin America with MTV Latino. In Japan, several companies have joined forces to offer a fifty-channel direct satellite broadcast system.

As the world moves toward 200-channel satellite and cable systems, programming demand increases. If 200 channels averaged eighteen hours of programming apiece each day, the system would require more than 10,000 hours of programs per month. In an entire season the four major American television networks provide only about 500 hours of new programs.

Trends and innovations

Trends and innovations in television can be categorized according to technology, ownership, and content. Just as they have been in the past, the three elements are, and will continue to be, interdependent. Economically, the survival of television is assured. Researchers concluded that each person in the Unites States spent $40.36 on all television in 1984 and about $82.58 in 1990; in 1994, researchers estimated people would spend $102.09 in 1997. The rest of the billion-dollar television industry is financed principally by advertisers. Total broadcast advertising was expected to increase from $25.8 billion in 1992 to $34.0 billion in 1997; cable advertising and subscriptions were expected to increase from $19.7 billion in 1992 to $24 billion in 1997.[40]

Technology

Technology and economics will drive many of the changes that are expected. Interactive television is on the horizon, but marketers have not yet determined exactly how much interactivity audiences want, what types of interactive programs they will watch, how willing they are to use complex technologies, and how much they will pay for it. Interactive trial runs have been inconsistent. Although some experiments have been welcomed in households, few consumers seem willing to pay for the service once the free trial is over. The most popular services seem to be movies-on-demand, games, children's services, and content created specifically for interactive television.

Thanks to an FCC decision in April 1997, the next generation of television sets likely will have a higher-quality picture and will connect more easily to the Internet. After years of debate and experimentation, the FCC began allocating additional spectrum space for high-definition television (HDTV). HDTV uses digital technology to improve the quality of the TV picture by increasing the number of lines on the screen. Eventually, each television station will send two signals for about nine years. One signal will be the current analogue signal, and the other will be the same programs in digital form. After nine years, the only signal will be digital. Anyone who has not replaced his or her old set with a digital one will have to buy a converter.

Initially, HDTV was developed just to improve picture quality, but the growth of the Internet pushed the new system toward digital transmission. The move to digital may be the most important element in the adoption of HDTV because it will lead to PCTVs, combinations of personal computers and television sets. These PCTVs will connect homes to electronic distribution systems, such as the Internet, without having to have both a television and a personal computer. The development of HDTV as a way just to improve picture quality would have faced much greater opposition than developing HDTV as a way to connect households to growing electronic distribution systems.

Television set manufacturers have indicated that HDTV sets will be available in 1998, but it is unclear how interactive these sets will be. Even if sets are available by 1998, HDTV will not be in every household overnight. Initially, the prices of such sets will probably run $1,000 to $1,500 more than traditional sets. The prices will decrease with time as more people buy HDTV sets.

The future of interactive television is connected to two developments: HDTV and the creation of digital video disk (DVD). At some point during the next decade, households will be buying PCTVs. The movement toward these converged technologies will probably be made more quickly with the introduction of DVD in 1997. The DVDs look exactly like the audio disks that replaced records except that they hold seven times more data than the audio disk. DVDs most likely will become the standard way of watching movies at home because they have much higher reproduction quality than videocassettes and are cheaper than laser disks. In addition, DVD allows for interactivity with films. Viewers can select different languages and even the format in which a film will be viewed. Initially, DVD players were selling for $500 to $1,000, and DVDs were selling for about $20 to $25, which is competitive with videocassettes. One drawback of the

DVD is that it cannot be used for recording from television. However, this is expected to change by 1999.[41]

The movement toward PCTVs will be helped by DVDs once they can record. The current VCRs are analogue based, while the DVDs are digital, perfect for the new digital television technology. Just how quickly the transition to digital PCTVs will occur depends on how quickly the prices for these televisions and the digital disk decline. However, it is safe to predict that within the next decade the television systems we currently use will disappear and be replaced by higher quality and more interactive television.

■ Ownership and delivery of services

The development of technology is never separate from the issue of ownership. Just as David Sarnoff at RCA had an enormous impact on development of radio and broadcast television, so will companies that currently hold licenses or deliver services to television. After the telephone companies were given greater access to delivering services in 1995, they experimented in test markets with information and entertainment services to be delivered to households. Although many of the companies halted the experiments in late 1995, such services will likely challenge the dominance of the networks and cable companies in the future. The mix of service providers in interactive television is particularly broad, including cable operators, telephone and computer companies, movie studios, and traditional broadcast networks.

With the passage of the Telecommunications Act of 1996, ownership and the mix of delivery services are almost guaranteed to undergo massive change. The act changed regulations governing television ownership, programming, and cable rates. The far-reaching law affects all areas of the television industry and will alter the nature of the industry well into the twenty-first century.

Old rules limited companies to ownership of twelve television stations reaching up to 25 percent of the national audience. The 1996 Act eliminated the limit on the number of stations one entity could own and increased to 35 percent the national audience a company's stations could reach. Companies began immediately to take advantage of the change. Benedek Broadcasting, based in Illinois, owned twenty-two stations in small and medium markets less than a month after the law passed.

As a result of the act, networks and TV stations can now own cable systems, and cable systems may own TV stations. A network can own a second network, provided that it starts the second one rather than buying an existing network. The new law also requires the FCC to consider whether it should relax the rule against a broadcaster only owning one TV station in a market. The FCC has taken a liberal stance toward ownership of a TV and radio station in the same market.

These changes are certain to increase the concentration of ownership within the broadcast industry, with fewer companies owning more stations and cable systems. Supporters of the Telecommunications Act believe that because of cable, the markets will remain competitive despite increased concentration among broadcast stations. Critics expressed skepticism about this point because cable is not available to everyone.

Perhaps the most drastic changes are in the cable industry. Rate regulations established in the early 1990s ended immediately in 1996 for cable systems that had fewer than 50,000 subscribers and were not affiliated with a large cable systems operator such as TCI. Larger markets are to be deregulated within three years or when a telephone company begins competition in any way other than direct broadcast satellite.

The success of cable rate deregulation hinges on telephone companies providing programming. These regional operating companies can deliver programs as a cable system, which will require a franchise agreement from local government, or as an

open video system. Open video systems do not have to get local franchise agreements and are subject to limited federal cable regulations. In return for more freedom, these open systems will make cable channels available to unaffiliated programmers without discrimination in either of two ways: The system operators will rent entire channels to programmers and have no control over the content; or the systems can make a channel available that will vary in its content. A person or group could buy an hour of time on a given day to broadcast any message that falls within the limits of the law.

Open video systems allow greater access to people and organizations that are not affiliated with an existing network or television station. Economists would say that this lowers barriers to entry for nonestablished businesses and will make content more diversified.

Just as telephone companies can enter the cable business, cable companies can begin to provide telephone service. Existing telephone companies must negotiate with new service providers about interconnections and a variety of other issues required to keep telephone use simple.

■ Content

The next issue is whether these changes will affect content. What will these multiple technologies deliver to individuals? Will the content differ from that currently available? Or will consumers simply have more control over what they can receive at a given time? If a telephone service gives the consumer the ability to order a specific movie to be shown at the consumer's convenience, the viewer may switch from her or his standard cable service to a new delivery technology. Viewers may receive the same or similar programming as before, but they may be able to make better choices within their viewing time frames.

Keyconcept

The Future of Television: The development of new TV technologies, closely linked to mergers and other changes in ownership, is especially evident in rapid developments in the cable industry. The next few years are likely to bring important changes in the services and formats from which viewers can choose.

The most controversial parts of the 1996 Telecommunications Act involved content regulation. Under the law, cable systems must scramble programs that a subscriber deems unsuitable for children. In addition, cable operators can reject programs that they deem indecent or obscene. This is important because the fine for sending out obscene material either over cable or by broadcasting was increased from $10,000 to $100,000. Supporters of the bill argued that this gives people more control over programming that comes into their home; opponents say that it provided the FCC with the ability to affect content by threatening fines.

An even more controversial part of the Telecommunications Act is the V-chip. The law requires every new TV set to have an electronic chip that can screen programs for sex and violence on the basis of a ratings system embedded in the programs. Supporters of the V-chip argue that it will reduce exposure of children to sex and violence. Opponents say that this provision is censorship and violates the First Amendment, and some have challenged the section of the law in court.

On a practical level, TV set manufacturers are waiting to see what happens before they start building sets with V-chips. By March 1997, the FCC had not set technical specifications, and the public was not supporting the ratings system developed in late 1996. Estimates were that the V-chip would increase the cost of a set by about 15% and an adapter for existing sets would sell for about $40.

open video system: A system that rents entire channels or time on channels to unaffiliated programmers without discrimination. Designed to provide access for those who don't own their own channels.

Summary

- Television, as a medium and as content, has always been controversial in American life.

- Television technology has been the result of many concerted scientific efforts, not the effort of a single inventor.

- Television station licensees are charged with operating in the public interest.

- Getting the television industry on its feet after World War II was difficult because each important element—station owners, set manufacturers, programmers, consumers, and advertisers—was waiting for someone else to begin the process.

- Although blacklisting did not alter the structure of the television industry, it did remind television executives of their vulnerability and underscored the necessity for free expression.

- Three large networks, CBS, NBC, and ABC, dominated television for its first forty years. This dominance declined during the late 1980s and early 1990s because of cable television and the advent of Fox and other new networks.

- Early television programming borrowed from radio and was broadcast live.

- Early advertising took the form of sponsorship, with advertisers controlling the content of specific programs.

- Network television journalism began as fifteen-minute evening newscasts but has expanded to include a variety of news formats.

- Television has combined with changes in the political landscape to shift power from political parties to television. The emphasis is on the candidates' images rather than on substantive discussion of the issues or investigation of the candidate's past positions.

- Broadcast stations profit by selling an audience to advertisers, whereas cable stations profit mostly by selling programming to subscribers.

- Television involves a variety of distribution technologies such as broadcast, cable, satellite, microwave, fiber optics, and combinations of these and other transmission processes.

- Ownership categories include group ownership, independents, public stations, and multiple-system cable operators. Some stations are owned and operated by networks; others are affiliated with networks; and some are independent, broadcasting local and syndicated programming.

- Some people in the United States cannot receive cable because the nearest cable company has decided that laying cable to these potential subscribers is not profitable. Often the decision not to lay cable affects the poorest individuals in urban areas.

- Although a program may have many viewers, the broadcast station might choose not to broadcast it the next season because it doesn't attract the consumers that certain advertisers wish to reach.

- Audience measurement, such as ratings and shares, affect programming because they affect an advertiser's willingness to buy time in connection with specific programs.

- Technology, economics, competition, and regulation are interdependent in the television industry.

- Innovations will occur as the result of changes in technology, ownership and service patterns, and content. These elements are interdependent.

Navigating the Web

Television on the web

You can find sites related to your favorite television programs, or you can use television Web sites to find information about the industry. There also are sites that lead you to current news and information and station promotion.

Ultimate TV	www.ultimatetv.com

Ultimate TV provides information about a variety of programs, including network prime time, sports, syndication, and cable, as well as some specialized material.

Broadcasting & Cable	http://www.broadcastingcable.com

Broadcasting & Cable is the television trade magazine. This online version contains information about the print version as well as some content from the current print edition.

Television News Archive, Vanderbilt University	http://tvnews.vanderbilt.edu/

Since 1968, Vanderbilt University has collected evening newscasts by ABC, CBS, and NBC as well as other special news events broadcasts. This page contains information about the archive of tapes and transcripts that are available.

In 1996, Microsoft and NBC went on the air and online with a news program that was aimed to compete with CNN but be interactive. CNN already had a Web site. Here are the addresses for both.

CNN Interactive	http://www.cnn.com
MSNBC	http://www.msnbc.com

▉ Questions for review

1. Who were David Sarnoff and William S. Paley?
2. Distinguish between cable systems and broadcast stations.
3. What was the *Mayflower* decision?
4. Why were the quiz shows of the 1950s significant?
5. Why was Edward R. Murrow a significant figure in broadcasting?
6. What is the significance of the Fox network?

▉ Issues to think about

1. How has the primarily commercial ownership of television in the United States affected its development?
2. What changes do you see in politics since the advent of television? Do these changes foster democracy?
3. Has television content deteriorated, or is it merely the reflection of a new age?
4. How do varying distribution technologies affect the development of television content?
5. As cable and new networks compete with ABC, CBS, and NBC, what changes do you foresee?
6. What will be the impact of interactive television?
7. What will be the impact of the Telecommunications Act of 1996?

▉ Suggested readings

Barnouw, Erik. *The Golden Web: A History of Broadcasting in the United States, 1933–1953* (New York: Oxford University Press, 1968).

_____. *The Image Empire: A History of Broadcasting in the United States since 1953* (New York: Oxford University Press, 1970).

_____. *Tube of Plenty: The Development of American Television* (New York: Oxford University Press, 1975).

_____. *The Sponsor: Notes on a Modern Potentate* (New York: Oxford University Press, 1978).

Benjamin, Burton. *Fair Play: CBS, General Westmoreland, and How A Television Documentary Went Wrong* (New York: Harper & Row, 1988).

Cantor, Muriel, and Pingree, Suzanne. *The Soap Opera* (Beverly Hills, Sage, 1983).

Douglas, Susan. *Inventing American Broadcasting, 1899–1922* (Baltimore: Johns Hopkins University Press, 1987).

Gitlin, Todd. *Inside Prime Time* (New York: Pantheon, 1985).

Kisseloff, Jeff. *The Box: An Oral History of Television, 1920–1961* (New York: Viking, 1995).

Music and the Recording Industry

Key concepts

- The Minstrel Show Tradition
- The Folk Ballad Tradition
- The Tin Pan Alley Tradition
- Rock 'n' Roll
- The Popularization and Commercialization Process
- Colliding Technologies and Audio Recording Disks
- Recording Giants versus Independents
- Integrated Markets for Music in Media
- The Recording Process
- Revenue from Licensing
- Record Promotion and Distribution
- The Payola Factor in Music Promotion
- Multimedia Packages and New Media Channels for Music

In the faint urban light, a half-dozen street kids sleep under a bridge in Seattle. Over their heads, on the concrete wall, is a message in three-foot spray painted letters: "Cobain lives in us."

Two thousand miles away, amid souvenir shops and traffic, the thousands of tourists who visit Graceland see fans' feelings scrawled in marker, ink, and paint on the stone wall that runs along the street: "I love you Elvis. Please come back." "Elvis, we miss you."

Music creates idols who achieve mythical status after death; music also sells hamburgers. It calls on deeply embedded emotions and delivers mind-numbing background noise. Music gives life rhythm. It has the power to create shared experiences by serving as part of cultural rituals and ceremonies. Although concerts enable people to experience music as a live performance, most music reaches its audiences in mediated forms. The average person listens to three hours of music a day through radio, tapes, or compact disk. Many fans of Elvis Presley and Kurt Cobain never attended a live performance.

Music has been an important cultural force in all countries. In the United States, some forms of music have been categorized as "elite" and others as "popular." Further, as diverse groups entered the society, different forms of music came with them. Because the lyrics and rhythms of songs that are popular among the young tend to push the boundaries of contemporary culture, they often are controversial. In the 1960s, "Beatlemania" offended at least some of the older generation; now music videos on MTV draw the wrath of critics.

Controversy over music increased once music could easily be disseminated through mass media. Recording technology took music out of the carefully controlled parlor with its piano or phonograph into the automobile with its portable radio. Adolescents were able to listen to music far from the ears of their parents. Today, parents often don't know what their children are listening to. Unwilling to listen to the "noise," they leave it to their children to choose their own artists, songs, and lyrics. The ability to listen outside parental influence and issues of taste have caused dilemmas for the recording industry; for radio broadcasters, who balance specific audience needs and tastes with broader cultural boundaries; and for advertisers, who seek to attract adolescents who have money to spend on recorded products.

The economics of the music industry have also changed. In recent years the recording industry has become more concentrated. Music promoters and broadcasters, seeking to please audiences and advertisers, tend to favor established artists. Concentration of the industry means fewer independent recording companies and may signal a more difficult time for entrepreneurs and new artists to break into the business.

Besides economics, changing technologies affect the distribution of recorded music and people's relationship to music. In addition to broadcasting concerts over the Internet, artists can carry on correspondence with fans, send messages to each other, and use World Wide Web sites to promote their own identities. The emergence of music videos, especially with the development of MTV, combines visual imagination with rhythm and lyrics.

In this world of mediated music, economics and technology pose significant issues, such as the following:

■ Music is a cultural force. Critics wonder whether music can continue to push the cultural boundaries of society without encountering crippling political and social resistance. Are the bounds of good taste and artistic innovation at odds? Do cultural clashes represent the differences between generations and social classes?

■ The recording industry is, for the most part, a corporate world. Will the industry's focus on profits mean more promotion of mainstream music and the exclusion of aspiring artists who experiment with varied musical forms and lyrics? Will independent musicians and small companies be strong enough to continue innovation?

■ Will converging technologies alter the form of music itself? Will video images and self-promotion made possible by technology destroy music in its purest forms? Or will it make a wider variety of musical forms accessible?

recording

industry

Printed and recorded music in American life

Europeans brought their own music with them to America. Clinging to familiar traditional forms, they disregarded the music that existed on this continent long before the Europeans first arrived. Native American music, like that of Europeans, was central to religion, but it also served as oral history. Most tribes had no written language, so music helped them to remember and teach the stories that make up their histories.

Music in your life

Music as Rhythms and Ideas

Music can be listened to merely for entertainment, but it may also educate. Think about how music has affected your life. Why do you listen to it? What does it do for you?

As you read this chapter, think about the many ways in which music pervades American life. Think about how you use music—to tell stories, to relax; to worship. Also try to relate some issues to the commercialization of music and the impact of corporate music makers on popular content.

WHAT YOU LEARN	TECHNOLOGIES YOU USE	PEOPLE YOU LISTEN WITH	PURPOSES OF MUSIC
New ideas	Radio	Friends	Religion
About people who are different from you	Television	Date	Excitement
About people who are like you	Compact disks	Family	Making friends
About the world around you	Tape/records	People in restaurants/ bars/store	Relaxing
About emotions	Internet/computer	Colleagues at work	Other

Native American music is still not a key ingredient of American popular music.[1] Most of the music that has become popular through piano sheet music, phonograph, radio, television, and compact disks has two major cultural strains: African American music forms, which evolved into blues and jazz, and European religious and popular music, which evolved into bluegrass and country music. Ultimately, strains of all the popular forms made their way into a blend called rock 'n' roll.

■ African American music

African music arrived in Virginia aboard slave ships even before the *Mayflower* landed in New England, and it appeared in printed form during the Civil War. It evolved into black spirituals, work songs, blues, and jazz. Although the slaves sang tribal songs with a **syncopated beat** that was foreign to most European songs, during the 1700s and 1800s the slaves blended these songs with European religious music to create spirituals. The first black spiritual appeared in printed form in 1862, and the first collection of black spiritual sheet music was published five years later.[2] African Americans sang work songs on the docks and in the cotton fields of the South. These songs had no instrumental accompaniment, and workers used them both to help them bear harsh working conditions and as clandestine protest songs, creating the base of the blues tradition.

Blues songs were personal—simple music about an individual's troubles. After the Civil War, wandering musicians helped to spread

syncopated beat: In syncopated rhythm, the regular metrical accent shifts temporarily to stress a beat that is normally weak. Syncopation is important in African and African American musical traditions and is considered the root of most modern popular music.

Early jazz music developed from the ragtime and blues played in New Orleans and was spread northward by musicians such as Louis Armstrong, whose career paralleled the growing popularity of jazz. Elements of jazz ultimately became a critical element in rock 'n' roll.

the spontaneous music with impromptu lyrics, and at the turn of the century, W.C. Handy immortalized the genre with his song "The St. Louis Blues." The song was so popular that it earned Handy $25,000 a year in royalties forty years after it was written.[3]

African Americans also composed music for entertainment and dancing. These fast-paced banjo songs were adopted by white performers in the traveling **minstrel** shows that were popular among white audiences from the 1840s to the early twentieth century. In these shows, white men blackened their faces with burnt cork and sang black songs. Successful songwriters such as Stephen Foster gained fame by imitating the songs of black Americans, who were not allowed to perform their own music. Such music eventually made a successful transition from performance to motion picture. Al Jolson, famous for his blackface movie roles, carried the minstrel tradition into the twentieth century.

In the late 1800s, the minstrel shows also gave rise to ragtime, which originated in the African American dance music called the cakewalk. Ragtime emphasized intricate syncopated rhythms in march tempos. Ragtime composer Scott Joplin, who first studied classical European music, stunned his audiences with songs such as the *Maple Leaf Rag.* Ragtime developed as commercial music, particularly in urban areas with large concentrations of African Americans.

At the turn of the twentieth century, African American musicians performed in the bars and brothels of the Storyville section of New Orleans. They combined ragtime and blues forms, creating jazz in the relatively tolerant environment of the southern port city.[4] City authorities closed down Storyville in 1917 under pressure from the U.S. Navy, which had a large military base in New Orleans. New Orleans' loss was the country's gain as jazz spread through the nightclubs of Chicago, St. Louis, New York, Kansas City, Memphis, and San Francisco. As the country entered the 1920s, the economy boomed, young people looked for excitement, and jazz thrived.

A decade later, jazz became the basis for the Big Band—or swing—sounds of the 1930s and 1940s, played by black, white, and mixed bands. Many jazz musicians criticized swing because it sanitized jazz to make it more commercial. Nevertheless, jazz flourished and grew in complexity. It underwent a revitalization in the 1950s and is found in a variety of forms today.

Key concept

The Minstrel Show Tradition: Minstrels were traveling musicians in Europe during the Middle Ages. In the United States in the 1800s, the term "minstrel shows" was applied to traveling stage shows that featured music, entertainment, and comedy, often with real or imitation African American performers and dancers. Some of these entertainers also performed in later vaudeville shows.

European American music

Europeans brought both religious and folk music with them to America. The religious songs came with the settlers, many of whom were escaping religious persecution in Europe. The folk songs came with the sailors and adventurers who saw the New World as a way to make money and with the peasants and farmers who settled on the expanding frontiers. Serious music did not gain a foothold until

minstrel: An entertainer, with blackened face, performing songs and music of African American origin.

Keyconcept

The Folk Ballad Tradition: In colonial times, American popular music was strongly grounded in lyrical or narrative ballad songs, usually with a verse and chorus format, the tunes often originating in England, Scotland, or Ireland. These story songs gradually merged with other traditions to form distinctive American musical forms such as bluegrass, country, and western music.

the first half of the nineteenth century, when an elite class began to look toward European forms of entertainment.

Because of the efforts to break away from Europe, patriotic songs were popular in early America. British soldiers used "Yankee Doodle" to taunt colonists, but during the Revolutionary War it became a standard sung by Americans on the battlefield. Patriotic songs remained popular throughout the 1800s, reaching their peak with the marches of John Philip Sousa in the latter part of the century.

ORIGINS OF WESTERN, BLUEGRASS, AND COUNTRY MUSIC European folk music blended with other traditions. In some urban areas, folk ballads were integrated into African American minstrel music, and in the West they formed the basis of western songs, expressing the tales of the lonesome cowboy. Hill music—bluegrass, hillbilly, and country—had its roots in European folk music. In the mountains of Tennessee, Kentucky, Virginia, and North Carolina, people used folk tunes and religious songs, played on traditional instruments such as the fiddle and banjo, to ease the burdens of life.

URBAN POPULAR AND TIN PAN ALLEY The popularity of music culminated in the late 1800s in Tin Pan Alley, which was both a place and an approach to commercial music. The popular music industry was centered in New York City, around Union Square. Here, the music houses employed people to write songs for sheet music, vaudeville, and theater.

Keyconcept

The Tin Pan Alley Tradition: The sound of pianos in the commercial music district of New York gave the name "Tin Pan Alley" to the industry that produced popular songs for sheet music, vaudeville and minstrel performance, and early recording in the United States.

Writers incorporated classical and folk melodies and wrote their own tunes to please the taste of the average person. In 1893, the music producers moved to West 28th Street. Monroe H. Rosenfeld, a press agent and journalist, named the street Tin Pan Alley after the sound made by a piano that had been modified with newspaper strips woven through its strings to muffle the noise.

Tin Pan Alley dominated popular music for almost twenty-five years, producing thousands of mostly forgettable songs for sheet music sales. It died in the 1920s as radio, phonographs, and movies began to distribute not only notes and lyrics, but sounds as well. Today the term describes formula commercial music aimed at pleasing large numbers of people.

ELITE MUSIC Although serious music did not develop as quickly as popular and religious music in the United States, it made giant strides from 1865 to 1920 and even today is significant as a form of music available through radio, tape, compact disk, and even television.[5] The increased availability of higher education, the expansion of the middle class during the Industrial Revolution, and the invention of the phonograph created larger audiences for serious music. Private citizens funded conservatories and concert halls, and by 1920, symphony orchestras had been established in New York, Philadelphia, Chicago, Cincinnati, Minneapolis, Pittsburgh, San Francisco, Cleveland, Detroit, and Los Angeles. Opera did not fare as well, with only two permanent opera companies performing in 1920.[6]

From the 1930s to rock 'n' roll

By the middle of the 1920s, African and European music had become interwoven, forming specific strains of popular music. Radio had entered American life and allowed the wide distribution of popular forms of music. America had jazz, blues, country,

284 **M**usic **in our lives**

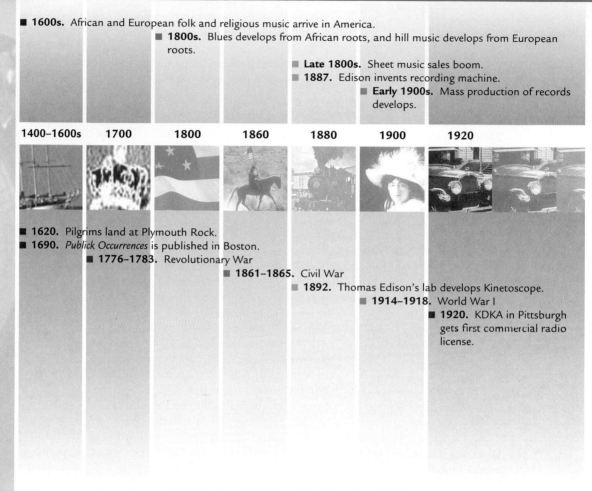

- **1600s.** African and European folk and religious music arrive in America.
  - **1800s.** Blues develops from African roots, and hill music develops from European roots.
    - **Late 1800s.** Sheet music sales boom.
    - **1887.** Edison invents recording machine.
      - **Early 1900s.** Mass production of records develops.

| 1400–1600s | 1700 | 1800 | 1860 | 1880 | 1900 | 1920 |

- **1620.** Pilgrims land at Plymouth Rock.
- **1690.** *Publick Occurrences* is published in Boston.
  - **1776–1783.** Revolutionary War
    - **1861–1865.** Civil War
      - **1892.** Thomas Edison's lab develops Kinetoscope.
        - **1914–1918.** World War I
          - **1920.** KDKA in Pittsburgh gets first commercial radio license.

western, theatrical and movie songs, Tin Pan Alley tunes, and dance music. Jazz entered the mainstream musical arena and paved the way for rock 'n' roll.

The hot jazz of the 1920s, born in the brothels of New Orleans, gave way to **swing** during the late 1920s. Gone were the small improvisational groups, replaced by bands of more than a dozen musicians. Some African American swing musicians, such as Duke Ellington, garnered an audience and a reputation during this period, but swing was dominated by predominantly white bands headed by Benny Goodman, Glenn Miller, and Artie Shaw.

Even as mainstream singers such as Frank Sinatra, Bing Crosby, and the Lennon Sisters sold millions of records during and after

Keyconcept

Rock 'n' Roll: The increased demand for varied radio and recorded music in the post–World War II era encouraged a blend of styles that eventually merged the African American, urban popular, and country traditions to form rock 'n' roll in the 1950s.

swing: Big band music played with a jazz rhythm that was popular during the 1930s and early 1940s.

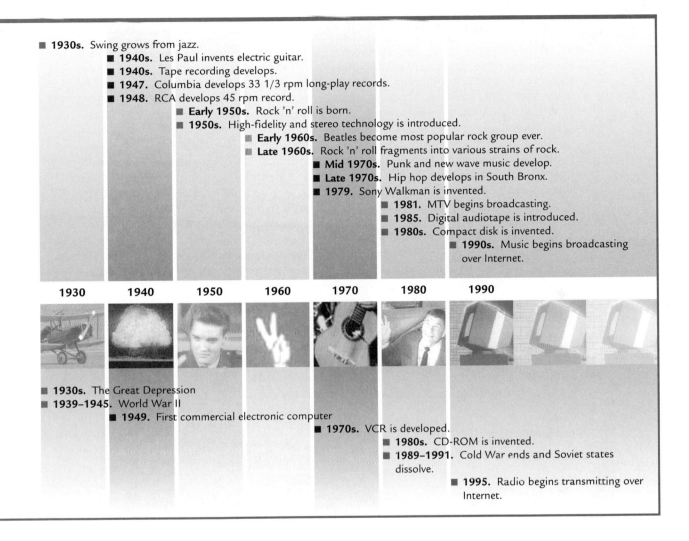

■ **1930s.** Swing grows from jazz.
■ **1940s.** Les Paul invents electric guitar.
■ **1940s.** Tape recording develops.
■ **1947.** Columbia develops 33 1/3 rpm long-play records.
■ **1948.** RCA develops 45 rpm record.
■ **Early 1950s.** Rock 'n' roll is born.
■ **1950s.** High-fidelity and stereo technology is introduced.
■ **Early 1960s.** Beatles become most popular rock group ever.
■ **Late 1960s.** Rock 'n' roll fragments into various strains of rock.
■ **Mid 1970s.** Punk and new wave music develop.
■ **Late 1970s.** Hip hop develops in South Bronx.
■ **1979.** Sony Walkman is invented.
■ **1981.** MTV begins broadcasting.
■ **1985.** Digital audiotape is introduced.
■ **1980s.** Compact disk is invented.
■ **1990s.** Music begins broadcasting over Internet.

1930 **1940** **1950** **1960** **1970** **1980** **1990**

■ **1930s.** The Great Depression
■ **1939–1945.** World War II
■ **1949.** First commercial electronic computer
■ **1970s.** VCR is developed.
■ **1980s.** CD-ROM is invented.
■ **1989–1991.** Cold War ends and Soviet states dissolve.
■ **1995.** Radio begins transmitting over Internet.

World War II, some areas of music were changing. In jazz, African American artists such as Charlie Parker and Dizzy Gillespie reacted against swing and the white commercial exploitation it represented. They developed **bop,** which returned jazz to its improvisation roots and boosted its ability to compete in the recording industry.

The bop movement represented only one genre of African American music that flourished. Count Basie gained white fans with his **jump music,** and blues singers such as Blind Lemon Jefferson and Big Mama Thornton recorded hits. The term "rhythm and blues" (R&B) was applied to all kinds of black music, replacing the term "race music."[7]

Country music flourished along with rhythm and blues. The lonesome songs of Hank Williams, the western songs of Gene

bop: Jazz that developed during the 1940s as a reaction to big band swing music. Usually performed by small groups with fast tempos and conflicting rhythms. Also called bebop.

jump music: Small band music that merged swing and electric blues during the late 1940s. Jump developed into rhythm and blues music.

Autry, and the foot-tapping bluegrass of Bill Monroe made country music commercially attractive for the recording industry.

■ Blending music to make rock 'n' roll

People disagree about who invented rock 'n' roll, but everyone agrees that it vitalized the recording industry. Many say that Louis Jordan's rhythm and blues music of the 1940s was rock 'n' roll. Others argue that Bob Wills and his Texas Playboys' western swing of the 1930s was the root of rock 'n' roll. Other influences include urban blues singers such as T-Bone Walker, who adopted Les Paul's solid-body electric guitar during the late 1940s.[8] Elements of gospel music can also be heard in early rock 'n' roll.

Without question, however, rock 'n' roll was born in the deep South. It was here that young musicians heard the black R&B and white hillbilly music that formed the core of rock 'n' roll. Two streams emerged. One involved identifiable rock 'n' roll music from rhythm and blues, by musicians such as Little Richard, Bo Diddley, and Chuck Berry. The other stream was the rockabilly music, which dated to Bob Wills but incorporated more rhythm and blues. Early rockabilly musicians included Johnny Cash, Carl Perkins, Buddy Holly, and Elvis Presley.

Alan Freed, a Cleveland disk jockey, helped to popularize the music in the North. His show boomed in popularity after June 1951, when he began playing the R&B records he had heard on black radio stations. Freed called the music "rock 'n' roll."

Though early rock 'n' roll made African American rhythms more acceptable to white audiences, the major recording companies resisted. Company executives saw no future in music that adults considered too loud, and the sexual energy demonstrated in rock 'n' roll dancing alarmed adults. This was "trash" music to most white people older than age eighteen. Production and distribution of rock 'n' roll were left to smaller record companies such as Sun Records of Memphis and Chess Records of Chicago. Figure 10.1 illustrates the evolution of rock 'n' roll and other strains of music in the United States.

FIGURE 10.1 The Evolution of Rock 'n' Roll

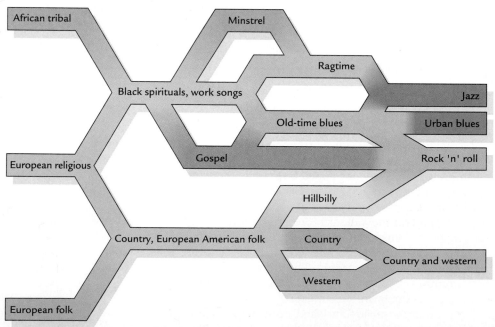

Social and cultural impact

Three elements have guided the evolution of twentieth century popular music in the United States: rebellion, the blending of different types of music, and commercialization. These elements signify the controversial nature of music distributed by mass media and its impact on social change. Rarely was a musical form adopted by the mass media without enormous controversy. Even elites who wanted classical music to dominate argued that trying to broadcast classical music would diminish its quality; they believed that only in a concert hall or parlor could an audience truly appreciate the nuances of classical music. Political figures and social reformers balked at putting jazz on the radio. They were afraid that such forms of music would corrupt society's youth, encouraging them to dance cheek-to-cheek—and more. The same arguments were made when rock 'n' roll began to climb the charts. Most recently, gangsta' rap has come under attack by parents, Congress, and public figures.

■ Music and rebellion

Music—particularly music as a form for mass media—has served for each generation as a forum for rebellion against the status quo. As rock spread into a variety of subgroups defined by varying ethnic backgrounds, cultures, and class, its successes and barriers in the recording industry represented cultural tension, not merely a change in musical form.

As each generation matures, its members see the world with a new perspective and with new values. The lyrics and music written by artists who are members of this new generation often express these values, which inevitably conflict with values held by their parents. When Bob Dylan wrote "The Times They Are A-Changin'" in 1963, he told parents "your sons and your daughters are beyond your command," and asked the parents to "please get out of the new one (road) if you can't lend your hand."[9] Dylan's words were adopted by many baby boomers as an expression of their discontent with what they saw as an unjust and valueless society. Three decades later feelings of alienation among the children of baby boomers found expression in the rebellious lyrics of grunge and rap.

The Supremes attracted black and white audiences who rebelled against the previous generation by listening to "crossover" Motown soul music.

Sometimes the rebellion in music expresses itself through lyrics; in other times the music itself is rebellious, as was the syncopated beat that made early rock 'n' roll different. Often the music represents the results of social change. The same generation that embraced the rebellion in folk music associated with Dylan accepted the blues of Ray Charles, which led to soul music and to the Motown sound from Detroit. The Supremes, Aretha Franklin, Four Tops, Temptations, Stevie Wonder, and Smokey Robinson and The Miracles sold millions of records to young white people whose parents would have condemned the music as "race music" just a generation before. The times did change.

The rock 'n' roll musical rebellion of the 1950s affected Europe as well as the United States. Young British rock 'n' rollers listened to American music on Radio Luxembourg and cheered when

Buddy Holly and the Everly Brothers toured Britain during the late 1950s. The Beatles brought British rock to America and became the best-selling musical group in history. Hard rock, pop, and psychedelic rock boomed during the 1960s. Bands like the Grateful Dead and Jefferson Airplane carried the rebellious hippie culture of the San Francisco Bay area to mainstream America.

Convergingtechnologies

The Beatles Return

More than twenty-five years after the group disbanded and fifteen years after one member died, the Beatles reunited in 1995. Adapting to the latest in media packaging and using new technologies to enhance music recorded long ago, the Beatles proved that they could still top the charts and create controversy.

The three surviving Beatles—Paul McCartney, George Harrison, and Ringo Starr—created a package of media products that extended into 1996 and beyond. First came a three-part television documentary in November 1995. Two days later, the Beatles released a double album, *The Beatles Anthology Vol. 1*. Two new songs in the TV show were based on a 1977 demo tape of an unreleased song by the late John Lennon. Paul, George, and Ringo added vocal and instrumental tracks, giving the impression that they were singing with Lennon. In addition to the television documentary and double album, the Beatles' return

included plans for future volumes of songs, a book, and a home video.

The Beatles' golden touch remains. *Anthology Vol. 1* sold more than a million copies during the first week. More than 200,000 copies were sold at stores that normally do not carry recordings. The first installment of the documentary, watched by an estimated 47 million Americans and 25 million British viewers, whetted appetites and spurred sales. The Beatles could gross more than $100 million from the entire package.

The staggering amount of money that they stood to earn led to controversy. Some music critics said the entire project was designed merely to pull nostalgic heartstrings to make a profit. Others argued that the songs based on Lennon's never-released demos were mediocre and should have remained unreleased. But others claimed that even mediocre Beatles music was better than most rock music and that their return would introduce a new generation

to the most significant mainstream band in rock history.

Music listeners voted with their money. The *Anthology Vol. 1* album sold more copies in a week than any other album, eclipsing Pearl Jam's *Us* album, which had sold 950,000 copies in a week in 1993. By early 1997, Vol. 1 had sold 8 million copies. Vols. 2 and 3 also sold more than 3 million units.

SOURCES: Adam Sandler, "Morisette, Braxton, Prince Hit Milestones," *Daily Variety* (March 4, 1997): 16. Clinton Manning, "The Big Pound 240M Apple: How Ex-Beatles Are Making a Fortune from a New Wave of Beatlemania," *Daily Mirror* (December 8, 1995) Features 3, 31; Mark Tran, "Beatlemania Back in the US Even Bigger than Before," *The Guardian (December 1, 1995) The Guardian City*, p. 23; and Greg Kot, "The Beatles . . . not again!" *Chicago Tribune* (November 19, 1995) Section 7, pp. 1, 18, 19.

Live Fast, Die Young

In the Who's song "My Generation," Roger Daltrey sang, "I hope I die before I get old." Unfortunately, this wish has come true for a number of rock stars. As the following list shows, many died from unnatural causes, such as drug overdoses, suicide, murder, and accidents. The uncommon amount of travel and the problems of coping with the impact of fame contributed to many of these deaths. Nevertheless, the early deaths of many stars leaves them etched permanently in the world's memory as eternally young.

2/3/59—Buddy Holly, Ritchie Valens, and the Big Bopper, early rock and roll stars, died in a plane crash.

12/10/67—Otis Redding, singer and songwriter, was killed in a plane crash.

7/3/69—Brian Jones, guitarist in the Rolling Stones, drowned in his swimming pool after taking drugs.

9/18/70—Jimi Hendrix, guitarist and songwriter, died of suffocation from his own vomit after taking barbiturates.

10/4/70—Janis Joplin, singer, died of a heroin overdose.

7/3/71—Jim Morrison, singer for the Doors, died of heart failure after years of drug and alcohol abuse.

10/29/71—Duane Allman, leader of the Allman Brothers Band, was killed in a motorcycle accident.

9/20/73—Jim Croce, singer and songwriter, died in a plane wreck.

7/29/74—Mama Cass Elliot, of the Mamas and the Papas, died of heart failure.

8/16/77—Elvis Presley, singer, died of a drug overdose.

9/7/78—Keith Moon, Who drummer, died of a drug overdose.

2/2/79—Sid Vicious, bass player for the Sex Pistols, died of a heroin overdose.

9/25/80—John Bonham, Led Zeppelin drummer, died of alcohol poisoning.

12/8/80—Beatle John Lennon was shot and killed.

7/16/81—Harry Chapin, singer and songwriter, was killed in a car accident.

12/28/83—Dennis Wilson, member of the Beach Boys, died in a swimming accident.

4/1/84—Marvin Gaye, singer, was shot to death by his father.

3/4/86—Richard Manuel, member of the Band, committed suicide.

5/5/87—Paul Butterfield, leader of the Paul Butterfield Blues Band, died of a drug overdose.

8/27/90—Stevie Ray Vaughn, guitarist, was killed in a helicopter crash.

4/8/94—Kurt Cobain, lead singer of Nirvana, committed suicide.

8/9/95—Jerry Garcia, singer and guitarist in the Grateful Dead, died of heart failure.

Three rock forms stood out during the 1970s and 1980s. Taking its name from the discotheque (dance club), disco music had a relatively short life but made a big splash on television and in the movies. Disco, sung by groups such as the Bee Gees, was based on a heavy beat that was easy to dance to. It lacked the soul of other types of rock and, like Tin Pan Alley music, became crassly commercial.

A second form, heavy metal, evolved from the acid and hard rock of the late 1960s. Led Zeppelin and Queen led the movement, and other groups, such as Van Halen, Judas Priest, and Def Leppard, carried it through the 1980s. Heavy metal underwent a resurgence in 1994, with Megadeth, Pantera, and several other groups.

290

During the late 1970s, punk rock emerged as a reaction to the commercial success of rock. Groups such as the Sex Pistols and the Ramones played angry, nihilistic music that projected little hope for the future. A somewhat milder form of rebellion against traditional rock came in the form of new wave groups, such as the Talking Heads.

Grunge and hip hop carried the punk tradition into the 1990s. Grunge rock, led by groups such as Nirvana, originated in the Northwest United States and projects images of a painful, materialistic, and uncaring world created by the earlier rock generations. The success of grunge is a contradiction because of grunge musicians' disdain for materialism. One of grunge rock's leaders, Kurt Cobain of Nirvana, killed himself in April 1994, becoming, at least for some, a cult figure and martyr.

Although grunge rock appealed primarily to white young people, hip hop music emerged from the African American tradition. Hip hop developed in the South Bronx during the late 1970s and formed the backdrop for 1980s **rap music.** DJs such as South Bronx's Lovebug Starski and Grandmaster Flash experimented with turntables as musical instruments, deftly stitching together pieces of different songs, which tended to have a heavy beat. Some DJs would rap while the music played. The first rap single, "Rapper's Delight," was released in 1979 by Sugarhill Gang. Rap and hip hop have their roots in African call-and-response music and, more recently, the Watts poets in 1960s Los Angeles, Bo Diddley and Cab Calloway.[10]

As rap moved into the 1990s, it diversified and attracted political attention. Some rappers, such as M.C. Hammer, had a softer sound, while gangsta rap, with its emphasis on harsh ghetto conditions, has a violent edge. Gangsta rap came under fire from Congress because of its emphasis on violence and its demeaning attitude toward women.

■ Blending musical forms

A second defining feature of American music is the blending of forms. Often, this has happened casually, as musicians adopted features of music that they had heard. Sometimes, however, musicians have searched deliberately for exotic styles of music. Singer and songwriter Paul Simon has stayed in style according to *Newsmakers 1992*, "precisely because he is continually 'rediscovering' musical styles—from folk-influenced rock ballads to rollicking gospel, blues, jazz, and reggae-fueled tunes to an eclectic brand of 'world music.'" However, Simon's blending of styles became controversial when he chose to cross cultural lines.

Introduced by a friend to the *township jive* songs of black South African musicians, Simon was so impressed that he traveled to Johannesburg and recorded several partial tracks with prominent South African musicians. These tracks became the basis for a highly acclaimed album, *Graceland.* Winner of the 1987 Grammy Award for best album, *Graceland* experimentally mixed the distinctive mbaquanga beat of the South African musicians with Simon's lyrics. It received little airtime but was a commercial and critical success. *Graceland* and its accompanying tour exposed enormous audiences to South African variations of **world music.** The album gave Western audiences the opportunity to hear such musicians as Ladysmith Black Mambazo, Hugh Masekela, Youssou N'Dour, and Miriam Makeba. Robert Browning, director of the World Music Institute, called *Graceland* a "milestone."

However, Simon's tour created intense political controversy, showing once again that music is not just music, but a form of communication and often a political statement. A number of groups attacked Simon for traveling to South Africa and recording there;

rap music: African American music with a rhythmic, repetitive beat and spoken lyrics. Gangsta rap reflects urban conditions and incorporates references to drugs, violence, and sex.

world music: Generally used to refer to non-English-speaking musicians singing in their native language. Usually applied to music originating in developing countries. Often songs of protest.

Members of the South African singing group, Ladysmith Black Mambazo, dance with their founder, Joseph Shabalala in Chicago. This group typifies "world music," the ultimate blending of continental African music with rock 'n' roll sounds.

these groups considered those activities a refutation of the cultural sanctions that the United Nations had in place against South Africa before **apartheid** was overthrown. In addition, when Simon performed in 1987 in Zimbabwe, two exiled South African musicians, Hugh Masekela and Miriam Makeba, joined Simon before a racially mixed crowd. Simon wrote a letter to the U.N. Special Committee Against Apartheid explaining that he had refused to perform in South Africa and that he unequivocally supported the boycott.

By the time Simon performed in Johannesburg in 1992, the U.N. General Assembly had lifted the cultural boycott against South Africa. However, a radical black consciousness group, feeling that genuine political reform had not yet occurred in South Africa, joined with the Pan Africanist Congress and threatened violence, if needed, to stop Simon from performing. Nelson Mandela's African National Congress (ANC) and the predominantly black South African Musician's Alliance supported Simon's efforts to perform, which he did, despite a grenade attack on the office of the concert's promoters. In spite of the controversies caused by this tour, Simon refused to back down under outside pressures, even violent ones. As he once explained to *Esquire,* "By nature I'm a tenacious person."[11]

Another prominent musician who has successfully blended styles and changed through years of performing is rock musician Van Morrison, an Irish son of a jazz singer, who has blended Celtic music, blues, jazz, gospel, and folk rock into music that is singularly his. The ability to blend styles allows an artist to speak to succeeding generations rather than staying within the confines of his own age cohort. Van Morrison began playing as a teenager. By the time he was twenty-three he had recorded *Astral Weeks,* an album that Greil Marcus, in the *Rolling Stone Illustrated History of Rock and Roll,* described as "a strange, disturbing, exalting album" for which there was little precedent in rock 'n' roll history when it was released. Marcus wrote,

> Tempered by jazz restraint . . . and three levels of string arrangements, the disc moved with a rock beat and a rock feel. It was as serious an album as could be imagined, but it soared like an old Drifters 45. With *Astral Weeks,* Morrison opened the way to a new career, and established himself as a performer who deserved to be ranked with the creators of the very best rock and roll music.[12]

Jimi Hendrix, Simon's and Morrison's contemporary, created his own blend of music. Starting from his rhythm and blues roots, he combined a unique style of playing electric guitar and a lyric sense like Bob Dylan's to create the Jimi Hendrix Experience. He blasted onto the rock music scene at the 1967 Monterey Pop Festival, playing guitar by a new set of rules and then setting his guitar on fire with

apartheid: Strict racial segregation. Usually associated with South Africa's political system that was overthrown in the early 1990s.

[profile]

Janis Joplin

To many rock-and-rollers, Janis Joplin was the most exciting performer of her generation and the greatest female rock singer of her era. "She was not just a singer, but a symbol of the liberation and excess of hippy San Francisco in the late '60s," reminisced Harper Barnes, who had reviewed Joplin's performance in front of 11,000 fans at the outdoor Mississippi River Festival in Edwardsville in the summer of 1969. "Joplin simply tore the place up. . . . She flings herself into every song, her voice scooping up notes and slamming them down, her body moving like a bawdy majorette. At one point, she looked out at the audience with the grin of a naughty child and said, 'Now do you know what rock 'n' roll is all about?' "

Janis Joplin was born into a middle-class family on January 19, 1943, in Port Arthur, Texas, an oil town on the Gulf of Mexico. It seemed that the plain, chubby girl and then teenager was often unhappy and had trouble fitting in with others her age. After graduating from high school, she attended the local college briefly, then set out to San Francisco. In North Beach,

where the beat writers such as Jack Kerouac had gathered, Joplin sang in bars and coffeehouses, experimenting with folk and blues songs before settling into rock 'n' roll.

For a while, Joplin gave up music. She returned home and started school again—this time in Austin, Texas—but left after a short stay. Friends in the fading band Big Brother and the Holding Company convinced her to join them in San Francisco in 1966. The band's new sound combined an energetic beat with Joplin's powerful blues- and gospel-influenced voice.

Joplin pursued pleasure with the same energy, and life became an incessant whirl of sex, alcohol, and drugs. When she was not too strung out to sing, she "drove audiences into a frenzy with her harsh yet soaring voice and the highly charged, openly sexual energy of her performances," wrote Barnes.

By 1967, Janis Joplin was a star. She, Jimi Hendrix, and Otis Redding were the hottest American performers in rock 'n' roll. When the album *Cheap Thrills* came out in 1968, she became world famous. Over time, however, the alcohol and $200-a-day

drug habit took their toll. In 1970, at the age of twenty-seven, Joplin died of an accidental overdose of heroin. Jimi Hendrix had died from suffocation related to drug use a month earlier.

Some of Janis Joplin's most famous songs included "Summertime," "Ball and Chain," "Piece of My Heart," and "Turtle Blues." Three months after her death, "Me and Bobby McGee" was released and became Janis Joplin's first song to be Number 1 in the pop charts.

SOURCES: Harper Barnes, "Full-Tilt Boogie Janis Joplin Came and Went Like a Texas Tornado," *St. Louis Post Dispatch,* October 14, 1992, Section Everyday Magazine, p. 1F; Susan Whitall, "Polishing the Tarnished Janis Joplin," Gannett News Service, October 14, 1992.

lighter fluid. Twenty-five years after his death, his unique mix of music and words continues to sell a quarter-million CDs and cassettes per year.

■ Commercialization

The third trend in popular music is commercialization, a process that tends to move power from the artists to the recording executives and audiences. Popular music has two purposes. It can be an expression of an individual's vision and emotions, like Bruce Springsteen's songs, or it can be a processed product aimed at a specific demographic

Keyconcept

The Popularization and Commercialization Process: Music that has the potential to attract a wide audience traditionally undergoes a process in which individual expression is converted into a form that is designed to appeal to a specific demographic group. The commercialization process tends to move power from the artists to the recording executives and audiences.

group, like the disco music of the BeeGees. Although many people regard music that incorporates an individual's vision as more sincere than processed music, for recording companies, the music of individuals is risky. It is difficult to predict just whose music will have immediate popularity and whose will gain stature over the long course. To reduce risk and retain power, recording companies often look for the short-term profits of processed music. This was the approach of Tin Pan Alley, and it has been the approach of many recording companies since.

Other forms of popular music

Rock has come to dominate the popular music scene in the United States, but that domination is far from complete. Country—in its many forms—is next in popularity to rock. Traditional country music, such as that played at the Grand Ole Opry during the 1940s and 1950s, flourished until the mid-1970s, when Willie Nelson, a songwriter who had enjoyed limited success as a singer in Nashville, led a revisionist movement. His simple-sounding lyrics in songs such as "Crazy" evoked powerful emotions and memories of Hank Williams's songs of the 1940s and 1950s. Nelson, Waylon Jennings, Jerry Jeff Walker, and Kris Kristofferson incorporated rock, western swing, and blues in their songs and helped to reshape country music.

Country music today has a new set of stars, including Garth Brooks, Reba McEntire, Mary Chapin Carpenter, Vince Gill, and LeAnn Rimes. They represent a revival of traditional country that started with Randy Travis in the mid-1980s.

Jazz, too, continues to change. The bop of the 1940s and 1950s gave way to three types of jazz in the 1950s and 1960s: cool, hard bop, and free jazz. Cool jazz had an intellectual quality, with sophisticated arrangements. Hard bop combined bop jazz with old jazz forms from New Orleans. Free jazz dropped the rhythm and tune of jazz and explored personal, impromptu music.[13] Since the 1960s, jazz also has incorporated rock elements. This fusion music continues today, as jazz begins to merge with hip hop and rap music.

Serious music

Music for elite audiences has always had difficulty acquiring popular support and financing in America. This holds true in the 1990s, but serious music still survives as a segment of the music and recording industry. In the 1990s, the sales of classical music recordings and the number of classical music radio stations declined. Declining support from the National Endowment for the Arts, labor disputes among orchestras, an aging of the audiences, and the closing of some prominent civic orchestras in cities such as Sacramento and San Diego indicate difficult times ahead for serious music.[14]

However, attendance at recitals by well-known artists increased and opera attendance grew. *Chicago Tribune* music critic John von Rhein offered a prescription for the serious music artists and business people in 1997:

We must accept the fact that serious music is in a state of change, and change can be unpleasant, even downright brutal, sometimes. The days of classical music preaching to the already-converted elite, and doing so in the same old manner, are fast disappearing. All aspects of the music business will need to reinvent themselves, to a degree, if they want to be useful and enriching to more than a privileged elite of the most educated citizens.

In short, classical musicians and presenters must get out of their ivory towers and learn to adapt better to the social, economic and cultural shifts of the world in

294

which it exists. Their challenge will be to devise ever more creative tactics to attract new consumers while keeping the integrity of the music foremost.[15]

The recording industry

The technological and economic processes for creating and delivering music come together in the recording industry. A small portion of the industry involves producing non-music recordings, such as books on tape and motivational recordings. However, for the most part, the recording industry and music continue the symbiotic relationship that has existed since the first records were pressed.

The precursor to recording technology was the printing press. During the 1880s, entrepreneurs cranked out sheet music to sell to budding pianists and singers. Some songs sold more than a million copies, and in 1910, two billion copies of sheet music were sold.

The phonograph hit the sheet music industry hard. By 1877, Edison had developed a machine that could record on a tinfoil cylinder, but it was not until the 1890s that Emile Berliner developed a way to engrave a zinc disk and mass produce copies of records. He joined forces with Columbia Phonograph, a company that developed a method of creating disks with wax in the early 1900s. The modern recording industry was born.

The famous opera singer Enrico Caruso became the first recording star to earn big royalties in the industry. He began recording records in 1901 and accumulated more than $2 million in royalties between 1904 and his death in 1921.

The recording industry boomed between 1910 and 1920. Industry sales reached $158 million in 1919, but the banking depression killed the boom. After World War I, radio promised to revive the industry, but the worldwide depression of the 1930s stunted its growth. In 1927, 104 million records were sold; in 1932 the figure dropped to 6 million. The economic recovery and improving technology during the 1930s and 1940s brought the recording industry back to prosperity.

Keyconcept

Colliding Technologies and Audio Recording Disks: The 1950s saw an interruption in the steady advance that major recording companies had developed in marketable audio technology—from zinc to wax to shellac to plastic disks. When an explosion of new technology confused buyers with three competing turntable speeds and two record disk sizes, the major recording companies decided on a standard (33 r.p.m.) disk to regain the market. The smaller (45 r.p.m.) record remained as a secondary format until the 1970s.

Phonographs and records

After World War II the recording industry experienced a period of rapidly improving technology. Within a thirty-year period, companies moved from the 78 rpm record to 33 1/3 rpm LPs (long-playing records) and 45s—the inexpensive "singles" that music-loving young people collected. Eventually, magnetic tape recordings were perfected, and even amateurs could copy records for their own listening pleasure—or to trade or sell illegally.

Like many industries, the recording industry encountered competing technologies. The first records played at 78 revolutions per minute (rpm), and we get the term "album" from those days, when a long work or collection of songs consisted of several 78 rpm records packaged in a cardboard case that resembled a photo album. In 1947, Columbia developed the long-playing record that, at 33 1/3 revolutions per minute, could play for an hour or more. The next year, RCA introduced the 45 rpm record, which played for only a few minutes, about as long as the old 78 rpm records. The 45 had one song per side and required an adapter to play on most record players, but RCA wanted to recoup its investment. The company pushed ahead in the battle of the speeds.

With so many types of records, the public was confused, and sales dropped dramatically until 1950. Columbia and RCA called a truce, and machines were manufactured to play both 45s and LPs. The 78s disappeared almost immediately, and the 45s slowly gave way to the LPs, which could hold many more songs, as the most popular record speed.

Audio tape and digital technology

With radio available to broadcast music, inventors searched for new ways to preserve live performances. Early efforts to record on wire were scratchy and unreliable. During World War II the Germans developed magnetic tape recording technology. Americans smuggled those machines to the United States, and U.S. engineers improved on them. In 1946, Bing Crosby—who wanted to have more time for his golf game—tape recorded his radio show, proving that a star could be successful without performing live.

Competing record formats during the late 1940s and early 1950s confused the public, but once the 45 rpm small-diameter record went on sale, it became the favorite of teenagers and soared to popularity.

During the late 1940s the Minnesota Mining & Manufacturing Company (3M) perfected plastic recording tape, and Ampex developed better tape recorders. However, the recorders and tape players remained expensive and cumbersome to use. In the 1970s, reel-to-reel recorders gave way to portable cassette players for personal use, and their popularity skyrocketed after Sony introduced the Walkman in 1979. Portability, as well as quality, was now a characteristic of recording machines.

Despite the increased use of magnetic tape, entrepreneurs aimed to improve record quality as well. High fidelity, a side benefit of wartime English sonar technology, could pick up a wider range of tones; it was followed by stereo records, which were introduced in 1958.

Records, cassette tapes, and **eight-track tapes** dominated the market during the 1970s, but in the mid-1980s they lost ground quickly to the compact disk, with its almost flawless reproduction. Sales of CDs soared from $17.2 million in 1983 to $930 million in 1986. As a result, the major companies closed their record plants; most new vinyl records now being produced are novelties. CDs are also swallowing the market for prerecorded cassettes, which are found in shrinking numbers in most record stores.

The recording industry viewed the development of magnetic tape in cassettes during the 1970s skeptically. The industry feared that the simplicity and portability of tape dubbing would increase album pirating—and they did. Estimates of losses from pirating run from $350 million to $1.5 billion. The industry's concern led to several hearings before Congress. The Sound Recording Act of 1971 made copying for one's own use legal, and in 1984 the Supreme Court ruled in favor of home recording in the Betamax case. It seemed that the fears had died down until 1985, when the Japanese introduced digital audio tape (DAT). The fear reemerged because DAT can make perfect copies from CDs and would become a better way of pirating.

Congress resolved the DAT controversy with the Audio Home Recording Act of 1992. DAT recorders sold to consumers now have a microchip that allows the owner to make one digital recording of a

eight-track tape: A plastic cartridge that holds a continuous recording tape. Invented primarily for automobile play during the 1960s, its eight tracks allowed high-quality stereo reproduction in an easy-to-handle cartridge.

prerecorded tape. It also prevents further copies from being made from the copied tape. In addition, the law allows a tax on DAT recorders and blank cassettes, which is paid to recording artists for lost royalties.

This solution seems like overkill; DAT never took off as a consumer recording technology, and other digital recording technologies have developed. Sony developed the MiniDisc (MD) as an alternative to CDs. The MD is only 3 1/2 inches in diameter, compared to the 5-inch CD. It is durable and easy to carry, but MD players will not play larger CDs. However, many radio stations are converting to the MD. About the same time, digital compact cassettes (DCC) were introduced as an alternative to current analogue cassettes. The DCC recorder will play analogue cassettes and is related to DAT technology.

The exact form that digital technology will take in the future remains unclear. However, CDs should remain popular, at least partly because an agreement among electronics firms in 1995 created the enhanced CD, which is a standardized compact disk that works in audio players and in computer CD-ROM drives. Enhanced CDs can contain video and other multimedia content, allowing CD-ROM users to do more than just listen to the music. There is still no standard digital cassette technology.

The future of standardized digital recordings might lie in DCC or in some form of recordable minidisk, or standard-sized enhanced CDs may become the standard for the recording industry. The buying habits of music listeners will be the determining factor.

The history of technology adoption has been one of creating technology that serves the listener. The adoption of new technology speeds up as more people buy, demand spurs manufacturing, and the price decreases from mass production. Because consumers have not rushed to buy the newer digital equipment, it seems that they are waiting to see just which new technology might replace CDs and analogue tape.

Today's market structure

By media industry standards the recording industry is small but growing steadily. Between 1984 and 1995 its revenues almost tripled, from $4.4 billion to almost $12 billion, and its percentage of all media increased from 3.7 to 4.8.[16] But it is an important industry, and the figures are misleading because they ignore the need for music and its impact in other media industries, such as radio, television, and movies.

The industry is dominated by six major recording companies, though independent companies fill an important niche that often is more innovative than the territory dominated by the majors. The six major U.S. recording companies—Sony, Warner, Polygram, Capitol/EMI, RCA, and MCA—produce and manufacture about 75 to 80 percent of the best-selling cassettes and CDs in the United States. The concentration of the recording industry has increased since the early 1960s, when four companies produced about 50 percent of the albums; it has declined slightly since 1982.[17]

Independents, often termed "indies," have taken risks when the majors were reluctant. Rock 'n' roll finally hit the charts because indies produced records when the majors thought rock 'n' roll was a dangerous fad. Even today, independents often can offer exposure to regional groups that otherwise would be ignored. For example, grunge might well have remained a local fad if Subpop Records had not offered recording contracts to Soundgarden, Nirvana, and other Seattle bands.

The recording industry is global, and although worldwide data are elusive, estimates suggest that five recording companies, owned by American, British, and Japanese corporations, controlled about 70 percent of recorded popular music worldwide in 1990.[18] The industry's concentration in these countries reflects the concentration of buyers. The United States, Japan, Britain, Germany, and France accounted for 68 percent of all records and tapes sold during the early 1990s.

Who Gets the Money?

Among the talk about budget deficits and contracts with America, the U.S. Congress took time during 1994 to talk with members of the rock group Pearl Jam. The issue had nothing to do with the 2.7 million copies of *Vitalogy* the band sold that year. It concerned how much people pay to see a band in concert and who gets the money.

The U.S. Justice Department began to investigate the $1.4 billion ticket distribution business in 1994 after Pearl Jam filed an antitrust complaint against Ticketmaster. Pearl Jam accused Ticketmaster of overcharging for concert tickets because the giant ticket distributor adds a $5 to $8 service fee to each ticket it sells. The Justice Department wanted to determine whether this service fee allowed Ticketmaster to pay the large concert locations and promotion companies for exclusive rights.

If this is the case, rock and country music acts must work with Ticketmaster if they want to perform in the best stadiums and concert halls. Pearl Jam filed the complaint because they said the Ticketmaster service fee meant the band would have to charge higher ticket prices than they felt their fans should pay for their 1994 summer tour.

A congressional subcommittee held hearings on the ticket distribution system in June 1994, following the Justice Department's announced investigation. Besides Pearl Jam members, many of the business people who run the music industry testified.

The Justice Department dropped the investigation in summer 1995, saying that new companies were entering the ticketing business and alternative tour sites could be booked. Some critics of Ticketmaster noted that the alternative sites were often small and located in out-of-the-way places. Although it dropped the investigation, the Justice Department said that it would continue to "monitor competitive developments in the ticketing industry."

SOURCES: Michael J. Sniffen, "Reno defends Ticketmaster ruling," *Lansing State Journal* (July 7, 1995) p. 5A; Reuters, "Pearl Jam ends boycott of Ticketmaster services," *The Orlando Sentinel* (July 6, 1995) p. 2A; and Gary Graff, "Ticketmaster has a big jump on other methods," *Detroit Free Press* (March 5, 1995) p. 4G.

Market concentration shows no sign of abatement. Media corporation mergers have flourished since the early 1980s, as large companies have acquired other large corporations. Sizable companies have favorable production and distribution economies that allow them to offer lower prices per unit than independents. This ability, along with solid financial backing that allows large companies to open new markets and finance new ventures, gives them a strong edge in the market. Currently, the majors are actively using their financial resources to invest in formerly Communist-dominated countries that promise new, and potentially lucrative markets.

The market edge held by the majors makes it more difficult for independents to operate. Nevertheless, lower production costs from less expensive technology resulted in a slight increase in independent shares of the recording market during the mid-1990s. In 1997 in Chicago, for instance, more than 30 independent labels recorded music

Key concept

Recording Giants versus Independents: With their deep pockets and their ability to mass-produce copies of recordings at low average costs, the six largest recording companies have the economic advantage over independent companies. The independents try to counter this by promoting relatively unknown musicians who are creating new and exciting kinds of music.

298

ranging from jazz and blues to punk rock and country. The long-term success of indies depends on their ability to find creative new musicians and to push the acceptable boundaries for musical innovation.

Audience demand in recording markets

People demand music for entertainment and for affirmation of cultural values. Music can distract people from boring or difficult tasks; listening to a song while mowing grass or cleaning a room can make those jobs easier to finish. Music also plays important social roles, fostering rebellion, blending forms to make new cultural statements, and promoting certain cultural norms through commercialization. It contributes to ceremonies and rituals that define social groups. National anthems praise and affirm the glory of a country. Weddings, funerals, graduations, and other life passages incorporate music as a basic element. Music gives generations of people an identity because the shared values expressed in music create feelings of commitment and membership and help to pass on the social heritage. Music from distant lands can bring foreign cultures to people who have never left their own country.

Music conveys information while it entertains. During the 1960s the simple melody and lyrics of Bob Dylan's "Blowin' in the Wind" captured the feelings of many of the people who were working in the Civil Rights movement. In 1993, Bruce Springsteen's theme to the movie *Philadelphia* expressed the isolation from society that people with AIDS often feel. As information, music's strength is its ability to combine the rational and the emotional through lyrics, melody, and beat.

The demand for music encompasses formal music, such as classical, and the many styles of popular and religious music. A current form of demand that we might label *integrated* involves combinations of media. Such integration can be seen in the incorporation of music into movies, television programming, and advertisements.

Changes in musical taste can be sudden and dramatic. The rapid growth in the demand for rock 'n' roll during the 1950s caught many music companies off guard. But a decade later, the music system had adjusted. Table 10.1 shows how demand for music can change in just four years. Between 1988 and 1992 the percentage of money spent on rock music dropped from 47.5 percent to 33.2 percent. The growth in country music offset this decline, as the percentage spent on country grew from 6.8 percent to 16.5 percent. During the same period, urban contemporary saw a 5 percentage point increase in sales as rap music moved toward the mainstream and rhythm and blues sales grew. Pop music experienced a slight decline in sales during this period.

Keyconcept

Integrated Markets for Music in Media: As one way to deal with unpredictable changes in popular taste, recording companies seek ways to integrate their music into other media—movies, videos, advertising, games, and recently the Internet—to exploit fads, extend the life of the companies' products, and diversify audiences and markets for music.

TABLE 10.1 Percentage of Expenditures on Music by Type

TYPE OF MUSIC	1988	1990	1992
Rock	47.5	37.4	33.2
Urban Contemporary	11.7	18.3	16.7
Country	6.8	8.8	16.5
Pop	14.7	13.6	11.4
Classical	4.8	4.1	4.4
Jazz	4.9	5.2	4.0
Gospel	2.4	2.4	2.7
Soundtracks	0.7	1.0	0.9
Children's	0.4	0.4	0.5
Other	6.1	8.8	9.7

Source: Veronis, Suhler & Associates, *Communications Industry Forecast,* 1993.

Changes in demand for music often reflect changes in the music itself. The demand for country music changed as country adopted a rock beat and new superstars emerged. Change also occurs with societal change and with pop trends.

Supplying the audience's demand

The recording industry supplies demand for music in a number of ways. Recordings can be supplied on a variety of disk, tape, and vinyl forms. However, all recording forms start with the recording process, and all forms require financing, distribution, and promotion. Some companies handle all of these processes; other companies may be involved in only one or two. Regardless of ownership structure, the recording process remains the same.

The recording process

Musicians create music, but creating music does not guarantee that it will be heard. It must be recorded. Recording as a technical process can be divided into two types: multitrack and direct recordings. *Multitrack recording* involves recording the various elements of the music—singer, rhythm, and lead instruments—at different times and combining them through an electronic mixing process. Natalie Cole's CD *Unforgettable* is an example of multitrack recording. This popular CD blends the voices of Natalie and her father singing "Mona Lisa" and other songs made famous by Nat King Cole. Her recent recordings have been blended with the older songs recorded by her deceased father. In 1995 the three surviving members of the Beatles used multitrack recording to record two songs that included John Lennon, the fourth Beatle, who had died in 1980. Multitrack recording also is routinely used to record several layers of instrumental and vocal tracks. In fact, multitrack recording is more common than single-track recording.

The demand for music often results in a blending of styles to make new cultural statements. Zydeco music from Louisiana originated as a symbol of cultural survival for the Acadian French but now has a far wider appeal.

In *direct recording,* all the parts are recorded together at the same time. The direct process involves six steps:[19]

1. *Session preplanning:* This includes getting the studio technology ready, preparing music for musicians, and discussing how the session will be run with the musicians in charge.

2. *Creating the sound quality of the recording:* A dress rehearsal is conducted, and factors affecting sound quality are adjusted. A tape of the rehearsal is made.

3. *Consultation with musicians:* The person in charge of recording meets with the musicians, and they go over the rehearsal tape to determine whether any changes in sound quality are needed.

300

4. *Recording session:* The music is recorded in sections. Each section will have more than one **take.** These takes continue until at least two usable takes are recorded. Technicians work on the quality elements of the recording during this process.

5. *Selection of takes:* The person in charge of recording and the musicians listen to the takes to select the best one for a master recording.

6. *Editing to compile master tape:* Any changes that were decided upon during the take selection are made at this time, and a final master tape of the recording is made for reproduction.

Multitrack recording is similar, except that the various tracks are recorded at different times and must be mixed. This mixing can be complicated and involves the input of the person in charge of recording and the creative artist.

The amount of time involved in the recording process varies greatly with the type of recording and the artist involved. The Beatles' *Sgt. Pepper's Lonely Hearts Club Band* album required more than 700 hours in the recording studio because of the amount of overdubbing and multitrack recording used.[20] The result was an album that changed rock 'n' roll.

A new era in the recording process was signalled when the popular Beatles group produced the breakthrough album, Sergeant Pepper's Lonely Hearts Club Band. *It featured layered sounds using high-tech blending techniques.*

■ **Financing**

Financing the recording industry takes many forms. People buy CDs and tapes, which is a direct source of income. Because recording production, distribution, and promotion are expensive, most recording titles that are released do not make a profit. This is why the profit potential of blockbuster recordings is so important.

A secondary source of revenue comes from licensing existing music. Someone who uses a copyrighted piece of music must pay the copyright holder. Copyright owners receive revenue, known as royalties, under three conditions. Under *performing rights* the copyright holder is paid every time a song is performed. *Mechanical rights* ensure that the copyright holder is paid when the song is recorded. *Public performance rights* require that the copyright holder be paid when an actual recording is played commercially.[21]

These rights are overseen by music licensing organizations such as the American Society of Composers, Authors, and Publishers (ASCAP) and Broadcast Music Incorporated (BMI) in the United States, the Performing Rights Society (PRS) in England, Gesellschaft für Musikalische Aufführungs (GEMA) in Germany, and the Société des Auteurs, Compositeurs et Éditeurs de Musique (SACEM) in France. The organizations act as agents for the publishers and composers of music who join them. The organizations collect fees and distribute money on the basis of formulas that incorporate

take: One effort to record a piece of music.

several factors, such as the number of performances of a particular song and the writer's prestige and seniority.

Licensing rights can be important revenue sources, especially in the case of rock 'n' roll artists who died prematurely and are later "discovered" by new fans. For example, during the first six months of 1993, recording companies sold 750,000 copies of recordings by Elvis Presley, 500,000 copies by the Doors, and 450,000 copies by Jimi Hendrix.[22]

■ Distribution

The two keys to a hit recording are play time on radio and television and getting adequate distribution of copies. Play time involves promotion, which is the attention-grabbing side of the industry. Distribution tends to be rather mundane in comparison, but it is no less important.

Distribution can take several forms. Recordings are sold in record stores, such as Where House Records; in department and discount stores, such as Kmart; by mail clubs, such as Columbia House; and over television, as in the ads for a singer's greatest hits or songs of a certain era. The latter two forms often involve direct selling, which means that the production company handles the distribution without another company between it and the buyers. The other two forms involve at least one intermediate company.

Since the early 1970s, the six major recording companies have expanded their distribution branches. These branches sell directly to record stores and to rack jobbers. *Rack jobbers* handle sales of recordings in department and discount stores. They stock the CD and tape racks and split the sales money with the store. Other independent distributors also serve the industry by distributing independently produced recordings and even some recordings from major companies.

Keyconcept

Record Promotion and Distribution: Companies traditionally promote a record by making people aware of it through performance on radio and television. They distribute a record by selling it directly to record stores or indirectly to discount and department stores. The latest electronic technology offers new opportunities for promotion and distribution. Many record stores provide listening stations that allow customers to sample records before buying them. The Internet offers sampling and downloading of music, online music stores that carry a variety of music and real-time radio broadcasts.

In the competition for distribution the majors have an advantage. They can provide large numbers of copies of hit recordings; they can afford expensive national promotions; and they have strong financial backing.

Throughout the twentieth century, music has been delivered to people either by radio or through some recording technology. The 1990s introduced a new distribution form: the computer. Initially, the use of music on computers was limited by the poor quality of the audio, but today computers provide digital-quality stereo sound. CDs, online audio, and broadcast radio have converged at the computer.

CDs provide music through CD-ROM technology. The computer's CD-ROM drive plays music as well as providing text and graphics. Enhanced CD-ROM technology allows people to listen to a Beethoven symphony while viewing the sheet music on the screen and learning more about the composer. Computers can also receive audio through online services and the Internet. Increasingly, radio stations are broadcasting through the World Wide Web. For listeners, Progressive Networks provided its Real Audio Player free, though it now charges for an enhanced version.

Computers can also function as radio receivers. Phillips Smart Radio software places a radio receiver card in computers that can pick up text, data, and audio broadcast from specially equipped radio stations. In 1995 the Electronic Industries Association started a $1 million campaign to get stations in the top twenty-five markets to install hardware encoders. Computer software will allow a person to select stations on the basis of artists, call letters, and even song titles, using a screen that resembles the front of a radio/stereo CD player.[23]

Sales of records or sheet music have always depended on making the largest number of people aware of the music's existence. When sheet music dominated the industry, vaudeville performers increased sales of a particular song by performing it. As radio attracted more listeners, radio play time became essential to a record's reaching the charts. Today, exposure on television, as on a music video channel, is also useful in promoting recordings.

Because of the limited number of television music channels, radio remains the best promotion tool. If a recording can get extensive play time on radio stations across the country, it has a chance of making the top-selling recordings list. The station format and the location are crucial considerations in promoting recordings on radio. Contemporary hit radio formats that run recordings from the Top 40 chart provide the best exposure. However, recording companies sometimes select stations with other formats for promotions because those stations fit the recording better. Stations in markets with a **cumulative weekly audience** of more than 1 million are vital for promotion. These markets, such as New York, Los Angeles, and Chicago, generate a high percentage of recording sales. Exposure in these markets can make or break a recording.

Promotion involves traditional **press releases** and **media kits** like those used in any public relations campaign. However, the key link in recording promotions is the independent promoter, sometimes called a "plugger." Independent promoters are hired by recording companies to help increase record sales. They use a variety of techniques to promote recordings, including providing information to media about the artists and the recording, arranging personal appearances by artists, and helping with tours that promote new recordings. The crucial role of the independent promoter is getting a recording played on the radio. During the late 1980s these promoters became very powerful in either getting or stopping play time. Without independent promoters, records face a tough time becoming a hit.

PROMOTION'S INFLUENCE ON MUSIC Because promotion significantly affects the sales of music, it also is a prime source of corruption. A recurring problem in the record industry has been the phenomenon of *payola,* or paying a programmer or disk jockey to play a specific song. In the 1950s the situation became so critical that Congress held hearings that revealed an industry in which payola ruled. For example, 335 disk jockeys reportedly received $263,245 in "consultant" fees.[24] Stations offered deals that were thinly disguised payola plans. One station in Los Angeles offered a "test record plan," which cost $225 a week for eight plays a day, and a New York station had a deal of six plays per day for six weeks for $600.[25] As a result of the congressional hearings, the Federal Communications Act of 1934 was amended in 1960 to outlaw payola. Punishment is one year in jail with a maximum $10,000 fine. However, these hearings concentrated only on rock 'n' roll music—a controversial genre in the 1950s—and ignored payola in other areas of popular music. Furthermore, payola is difficult to monitor. Although it has been outlawed, independent

Keyconcept

The Payola Factor in Music Promotion: A recurring issue in the record industry has been the factor of payola: paying DJs or program producers to run a specific song on a radio station or video channel to enhance the song's popularity. Investigated by Congress since the 1950s, this invisible thread of influence between the recording and broadcast industries is probably impossible to uproot, especially as combined ownership affects more sectors of the media and recording industries.

cumulative weekly audience: The total number of people who listen to radio during a given week in a given market.

press release: An announcement of some event, such as a recording release, sent to various news media outlets.

media kit: A collection of information about a particular event or person, such as a recording release. The kit can include text, photographs, audiotapes, and even computer diskettes and CD-ROMs.

promoters are still known to deliver money, gifts, or more tangible services to those in a position to get music on the radio.[26]

PROMOTION AND CONTROVERSY Controversy over rock music is as old as the music itself. Instead of promoting African American artists, the recording industry used white performers, such as Elvis Presley, who either recorded R&B songs or adapted African American sounds to country and western music. Presley was controversial to many white parents because he had an African American sound and because he wiggled his hips as he sang. The controversy seemed only to sell more records, as young people delighted in the disapproval of their parents.

Although the numerous controversies that have arisen during the years have rarely resulted in successful legal attempts to censor music, society controls its music in the commercial marketplace. Promoters and record companies are reluctant to promote music that offends people and raises the specter of government intervention into radio content. Some rap music continues to face promotion problems because of the emphasis of gansta rap lyrics on violence and misogyny. Concerns over such lyrics led to congressional hearings in 1994 about the recording industry and graphic lyrics. Controversial music can gain some attention through independent companies, which foster cutting-edge music. Nevertheless, success usually requires the involvement of the majors, which often means that a group will have to alter its message and its tune.

Almost every controversial trend in music provokes a countering move or trend in reaction to the original movement. For example, rap lyrics by male-dominated urban groups produced violent images that appeared insulting to women, provoking objections from mainstream authorities, but also producing rap groups such as the Fugees, who countered the original rap style.

Influence of promotion was demonstrated in the early 1960s, when an appearance on the Ed Sullivan Show could enhance a singer's success. Elvis Presley and the Beatles made their first U.S. television appearances here. However, Bob Dylan refused to appear when CBS wanted to censor his politically oriented songs. The Rolling Stones wanted the exposure and saw no problem in altering lyrics. They changed their lyrics from "let's spend the night together" to "let's spend some time together." Both Dylan and the Rolling Stones had long and prosperous music careers.

Fortunately, the power of promotion has a limit. Artists who demonstrate star power early in their careers will have more musical freedom. The Beatles, Bob Dylan, and Bruce Springsteen are examples. If recording companies can profit from controversy, they will support it. Although during the last half of the twentieth century, some musical groups have achieved a measure of independence, no artist ever escaped all influences of the promotion machine.

VIDEO: A NEW PROMOTIONAL TOOL On August 1, 1981, Music Television (MTV), a cable TV channel, began broadcasting. Within ten years, MTV reached more than 204 million homes in forty-one countries around the world. MTV and other music channels provided a new source of income for musicians and recording companies: selling music videos.

304

However, videos have been far more important as a promotion tool than as a revenue source. A well-conceived and well-executed video can boost recording sales considerably.

Video promotion is a creative art. Some videos are constructed with story lines that enhance the music; others merely contain appealing abstract images that may be unrelated to the specific lyrics. In the early 1990s the average cost of producing a music video was about $70,000, although today popular stars often spend more.

However, the nature of MTV and other music networks began to change during the 1990s. Because of declining ratings, video television networks turned to programming other than music videos. MTV's *Beavis and Butthead* developed an almost instant cult following. The two imaginary teens made the cover of *Newsweek* in 1993. Acoustic ("unplugged") instrument concerts filmed for MTV revived the careers of rockers such as Rod Stewart. VH-1 began running more standup comedy shows to attract viewers.

The future of music videos as entertainment remains unclear, but they will continue to have promotional value. However, as available TV time decreases on existing music channels, the nature of videos may change. Pay-per-view for music videos could make music videos bigger revenue producers. Their use as a promotional tool would decline because the audience, rather than the programmer, would control exposure.

Global Impact

MTV: Music Television for the World

Music Television (MTV) changed the face of television in 1981 when it initiated the first twenty-four-hour music channel. The mission was simple: to capture cable viewers between the ages of twelve and thirty-five by adding video to music. The result was a form of television that spread throughout the world.

The idea of combining video and music existed long before MTV. Rock 'n' roll joined television early with dance programs such as *Dick Clark's American Bandstand*. Later, documentaries about musicians combined video and music. Frank Zappa's 1971 movie *200 Motels* visually represented his surreal music. Movies such as *Woodstock* and George Harrison's *Concert for Bangladesh* brought viewers a sense of the live concert experience. Short videos were used to promote music. However, MTV changed the music industry by widely distributing promotional videos through satellite and cable transmission.

Within six years, MTV began creating channels to provide music to the world outside the United States. MTV, now owned by Viacom, provides music television to Australia, Europe, Asia, and Latin America. Dozens of competing music satellite networks are available around the world.

Initially, MTV's ratings rose quickly. In 1986, however, they started to fall, and the network added nonmusic programming. In 1995, MTV's ratings remained lower than those of several other cable channels, such as the Nashville Network, ESPN, and USA. However, MTV remains a cable power because it can deliver the twelve- to thirty-five-year-old audience to advertisers and because it promotes sales of CDs and tapes. MTV play time is crucial for making a song a hit.

SOURCE: Robert M. Ogles, "Music Television (MTV)," in *The Cable Networks Handbook,* Robert Picard, ed. (Riverside, CA: Carpelan Publishing, 1993) pp. 137–142.

Trends and innovations

Trends and innovations in the music and recording industry appear in musical, technological, and economic forms.

Although musical innovations, or changes in the music itself, can easily be labeled once they are developed, predicting them remains almost impossible because they arise from individual creativity. Musicians continually experiment with new styles, though most such experiments never reach the public. When they do, they may achieve short-term, popular success with extensive promotion and radio play time. The record morgues contain recordings by hundreds of such groups, from the Archies in the 1960s to the Bay City Rollers in the 1980s. However, long-term critical and financial success is hard to predict. Few would have guessed in 1963 that four English working-class lads called the Beatles would reshape rock music or in 1980 that South Bronx rap music would capture so large a segment of the African American music business.

Technological innovation in the music and recording industry seems somewhat easier to anticipate. The information superhighway awaits music's contribution. In late 1994 the Rolling Stones broadcast a concert live over the Internet. Though the music and video quality was primitive, the concert suggested the potential in this new form of music delivery. Eventually, listeners will be able to get music on demand, delivered by cable and telephone companies through fiber-optic cable to be downloaded onto digital tape or CDs.

Music today is technological, relying on equipment that records separate tracks, synthesizes, and generates a final product. Artists are showcased and enhanced by technology.

As computer sound and video technology improves, people will continue to use digital forms to listen to music. Questions remain as to whether those forms will be disk or tape, but it seems likely that both will be available for some time to come. Owning recordings continues to have an advantage over having music delivered digitally because the owner of a CD or cassette can listen to that music whenever and as often as she or he wants to at a reasonable cost.

Economic trends also shape the industry. As with all information products, financing determines how and in what form consumers can buy music. Two trends—multimedia packaging and the commercialization of alternative music—will be big factors in the next decade.

Multimedia packaging

Multimedia packaging involves the production and release of recordings with other media products. In the world of commercial music the recording is often just part of the package, which may also include a video, movie, and concert tour. For example, Michael Jackson recorded a song called "Will You Be There" in 1993 in connection with the small-budget film *Free Willy.* The video of Jackson singing the song played at the beginning of the film and on music television. The video, the soundtrack tape and CD, and the movie all promoted each other. The result was success for both the movie and the recording.

Multimedia packaging is not new. Vaudeville acts and sheet music were tied together at the beginning of the twentieth century. Movies and music have a longstanding connection, and movie sound track albums reached prominence in the 1940s and 1950s. Movies have even served to revitalize older music. The soundtracks from *The Big Chill* in 1983 and *Forrest Gump* in 1994 used popular songs from the 1960s and 1970s. Both soundtracks sold hundreds of thousands of recordings.

306

Keyconcept

Multimedia Packages and New Media Channels for Music: Trends in the music industry seem likely to be shaped by heavy investment in two areas: sophisticated packaging of music with other media products, including videos, movies, game CDs, and concert tours, and new uses of the World Wide Web to reach diverse audience markets with specialized alternative music and music on demand.

■ Mainstreaming alternative music

The music industry traditionally has lived with two conflicting needs: to create new products and to maintain and increase profits. Because new musical styles might not catch on, and therefore might decrease profits, the major recording companies like to promote established performers. The independents carve out market niches by developing new artists. The majors then recruit the alternative artists who earn successful profit margins.

However, because the music audience often rebels at established practice, generations of listeners have demanded alternative music forms. This accounts for the success of rock and roll in the 1950s, hard rock and folk rock in the 1960s, punk rock in the 1970s, and rap and grunge in the 1980s. Increasingly, the pace of transition from alternative to mainstream has increased. It took a few years for R.E.M. to move from alternative to mainstream radio. Bands of the 1990s, such as Pearl Jam, Counting Crows, and Veruca Salt, made the transition in months.

The reason is simple. Listeners in the eighteen to thirty age group want distinct music. They want music that makes them feel separate from the Baby Boomers. This younger audience started moving to alternative stations, and the mainstream stations wanted them back because advertisers want them. Radio station's music playlists reflect audience demand. Some observers have even suggested that the mainstream rock station is dying. In its place, stations will have even smaller, more fragmented audiences listening to narrow types of music. The combination of commercialization, demand for alternative forms, and the role of promotion, however, poses a dilemma for artists who want to succeed but maintain their creative edge at the same time. Musicians and audiences alike have asked whether commercially successful artists can retain the creative drive that made them become musicians.

Summary

- Music's primary purpose is to entertain people, but it also serves important social and personal functions.
- Music binds social groups together by creating shared experiences and by serving as part of ceremonies and rituals.
- American popular music evolved by blending music from African and European cultures.

- Popular music depends heavily on the connection between music and young people's rebellion against existing social norms.
- As music has become commercialized, control of the music has moved from the artists to the recording companies.
- The first technology used by the music industry was the printing press to print sheet music during the 1800s.
- During the 1950s, two record formats battled for supremacy. The 33 1/3 r.p.m. long-playing format won over the smaller 45 r.p.m. format, only to lose out to tape and compact disk during the 1970s and 1980s.
- Today's recording industry remains highly concentrated in both the United States and the world, with a few companies producing 70 to 80 percent of all recordings.
- The recording process can be direct, which means recording all parts at the same time, or multitrack, which means recording different parts at different times.
- Copyrights allow the holder of the copyright to be paid for reproduction and performances of music.
- Distribution of recordings occurs through record stores, discount and department stores, television, and mail-order clubs.
- Because of their size, the major recording companies have economic advantages in distributing and promoting recordings.
- Promotion plays a key role in selling recordings, making people aware of the music and encouraging demand. It also creates conditions for corruption.
- Music video emerged during the 1980s as an important promotion tool. As a result, TV music channels now influence record sales.
- The recording industry is global in reach, but most of the recording production and sales organizations are located in Britain, France, Germany, Japan, and the United States.
- Musical innovation is difficult to predict because it depends on the creativity of individual artists.
- Technological trends involve improving existing disk and tape processes and increasing delivery of music through fiber-optic cable.
- Economic trends in the music business include multimedia packaging of music and the transition of music from alternative to mainstream status.

Navigating the Web

Music on the web

Music is a growing presence on the World Wide Web because of improved sound quality. Sites take a variety of forms, from those owned by recording companies to sites where the music of independent artists can be sampled and their recordings bought. The following sites are information sites for the music and recording industries.

Internet Underground Music Archive	http://www.iuma.com

A variety of material and links can be found here, mostly for popular music. Information about music books and links to recording labels and music magazines abound.

University of California San Diego Music Library	http://132.239.120.17/music

This site contains links and material about a wide range of music, including opera and classical.

Rock World	http://www.slip.net/~scmetro/rock.htm

Extensive material about the history of rock 'n' roll and links to other sites related to artists, bands, record companies, and radio stations, among others.

The following sites contain photographs, text, and music of independent artists.

Virtual Radio	http://www.vradio.com

Mammoth Artists	http://www.mammothartists.com

■ Questions for review

1. How did African American music first appear in American life?

2. Why was Tin Pan Alley a significant force in mass mediated music?

3. What cultural strains in American life did rock 'n' roll depict?

4. What three elements have guided the development of American popular music?

5. List several ways in which the recording industry is financed.

6. How do converging technologies affect the distribution of mediated music?

■ Issues to think about

1. If rap, grunge, and alternative rock indicate cultural change, what do you foresee as a natural outgrowth?

2. How does concentration within the recording industry affect musical content?

3. How do promotional needs and efforts shape the music industry?

4. How would you describe MTV as a cultural force?

5. In what ways do you foresee the Internet and other online services affecting the delivery of music?

■ Suggested readings

Campbell, Michael. *And the Beat Goes On: An Introduction to Popular Music in America, 1840 to Today* (New York: Schirmer Books, 1996).

Chanan, Michael. *Repeated Takes: A Short History of Recording and Its Effects on Music* (New York: Verso, 1995).

Dannen, Fredric. *Power Brokers and Fast Money Inside the Music Business* (New York: Times Books, 1990).

Farr, Jory. *Moguls and Madmen: The Pursuit of Power in Popular Music* (New York: Simon and Schuster, 1994).

Hamm, Charles. *Putting Popular Music in Its Place* (Cambridge: Cambridge University Press, 1995).

Santoro, Gene. *Dancing in Your Head: Jazz, Blues, Rock, and Beyond* (New York: Oxford University Press, 1994).

Computers and the Information Highway

Keyconcepts

- Memex and Memory
- WYSIWYG and Computer Access
- The World Wide Web and the Growth of the Internet
- Knowledge Gap
- Implications of Hardware and Software
- Information Society
- Virtual Reality Technology
- Information Highway
- Regulations in the Information Age
- Convergence of Electronic Technology

Jane needed to write a two-page paper for her contemporary life class. It was late Sunday night, and the paper was due at 10:00 Monday morning. Oops! The library was closed.

Jane closed her computer solitaire game, quickly checked her e-mail, then dialed America Online. How could she be so lucky? The dominant feature of the *Atlantic Monthly*'s cover was a headline on Bosnia. Wait—that wasn't all. Here was a comparison of the disturbance in Bosnia today and a crisis there in 1913:

> CRISIS IN BOSNIA. Can the Balkan conflict be understood? See "The Crisis in the Balkans" and compare the *Atlantic*'s articles from 1989 and 1913, in *Flashbacks and Followups*.

With a mouse click, Jane could compare the *Atlantic's* explanation of the Bosnia situation at two time points, seventy-six years apart. She found other articles as well, one in an online encyclopedia and another in the *Nando Times,* the *Raleigh News and Observer*'s World Wide Web site. She downloaded the files, switched to her word processing program, and soon had the paper written.

Now for some real fun. She went back to America Online to play interactive games with several friends around the world.

Jane's computer represents the integration of many media. It stands alone as a medium and as a technology, but it also embodies the convergence of electronic and print media. The merging of graphics, text, and electronic delivery appears most vividly on the computer screen through the many services that connect individuals through electronic mail and provide

311

information and forums. As material is increasingly created specifically for the Internet and online services, computer-delivered information has become part of mass communication. By providing a unique format for conveying information, computer technology becomes a medium rather than a mere form of distribution. It is through this new technology and the services provided that we come to understand cyberspace.

In 1795, information in the form of books and newspapers was a scarce commodity. Creating and distributing these products were slow and laborious processes. Two hundred years later, people get their information from books, newspapers, magazines, letters, movies, radio, television, telephones, VCRs, audiotapes, electronic mail, interactive CDs, and computer online services.

This information revolution has affected almost every process of *communication*—gathering, organizing, presenting, and disseminating information. Some theorists predict that someday we will have a paperless society in which radio and television combine with a computer for a home information system. However, media industry analysts suggest that this process will take considerably longer than some futurists contend.[1] What remains certain is that text, visuals, and sound are converging as the best elements of television and recording industry technology combine with computers.

The term "media convergence" is generally defined as the combination of two or more traditional media into one process. For some industry watchers, media convergence also means the merging of mass media organizations. Traditionally, each medium had one objective. For example, the U.S. Postal Service transported handwritten or typed correspondence from one destination to another. Newspaper organizations presented news and information on newsprint to a reader. Telephone companies made it possible for people in different locations to talk to each other. And television stations provided vivid, moving pictures to viewers. Today, innovative companies combine these functions into one process, using a computer and telephone lines or a combination of television sets and telephone lines. When users turn on their computers and go online, they can send and receive e-mail, read information about a bill that was passed recently in Congress, or watch basketball game videos—all from the same source. With the right technology, they can even talk to each other via the Internet. Some news organizations are combining these technologies on their own; others are merging with a variety of companies representing different media.

The computer has had a major impact on other media and on consumers. For example, newspapers and broadcast news programs can receive their syndicated programs more quickly and easily; public relations practitioners can get information from a database in another country instantly; advertisers can approve faxed designs in minutes; broadcasters can receive newsfeeds via satellite simultaneously; and freelancer writers can interview sources electronically.

The computer also presents the possibility of a society interactively linked by a network. In a networked society, people will be able to access mass media services and communicate individually through the computer. If the connections are vast enough and access is great enough, the world may become an information society—connected by an information highway.

New technology offers not only possibility, but problems as well. The issues here include the following:

- If an information highway does exist, who will have access to it? Will electronic information aid democratic participation or retard it? Will we be an information-rich society, or will some people benefit more than others?

- How is this new technology related to content? Does the new technology simply provide an extended delivery service for old content? Or will it be integrated to create new forms of mass media? To make the old obsolete? To change the old?

- As we travel online, will we be able to preserve the tenets of free speech? How will we make sure that everyone will have access? How will we protect creators of information and individuals from violations of copyright and invasions of privacy? What legal issues will become significant?

Computers in your life

Tools And Toys

Computers are becoming increasingly indispensable for students. Do you use computers? Do you use them for work? For play? As you read through this chapter, think of uses of the computer that we've not yet even dreamed of—or at least have not per-fected the technology for. Computers and the online world have great potential, but most analysts don't yet know how the technology will be used in the mass media mix.

HOW DO YOU USE COMPUTERS?	YES/NO	HOURS/ WEEK
Research for School Assignments		
Word Processing		
Software Games		
Games on a Network via the Internet, World Wide Web, or Commercial Service		
Banking Service		
At Work		
Electronic Mail to Family and Friends		
Electronic Mail to Teachers		

Computers in American life

Computers have profoundly influenced our society by simplifying complex tasks and by informing and entertaining us in new ways. Every day we encounter computing technology, just as we encounter mass media. A computer assists us each time we make a phone call, watch television, listen to the radio, program our VCRs, time our microwaves, drive a car, get cash from a bank's automated teller, have our purchases scanned at the checkout counter, reserve an airplane seat, or pay with a credit card. In the coming decades, we will use computers even more for information and entertainment. The computer is the heart of interactive television, virtual reality, movies on demand, and individualized news delivery. An information or media center in a custom-built home in 2000 may well control not only temperature, lights, and appliances, but also the information that household receives and sends.

Some historians date the computer to the ancient abacus, a hand-held counting device, and mechanical devices were in use by 1900 for tabulating large amounts of data. However, the military demands of World War II produced the first electronic computers. A huge computer, the Colossus, helped the British to break German military codes, and Harvard mathematician Howard Aiken developed a computer to calculate artillery ballistics. When U.S. leaders saw the possibilities for defense

Key concept

Memex and Memory: The memex, an early idea for a mechanical device for storing information to be consulted with speed and flexibility, soon became a conceptual prototype for the computer. The people who developed this first version of a computer envisioned a machine that could extend the power of human memory.

Personal Computer as Hobby

When Micro Instrumentation Telemetry Systems (MITS) produced the Altair computer in 1975 and sold it for $397, Steve Dompier was living in Berkeley, California. When he read the *Popular Electronics* article, he became a man obsessed. This was access. Individuals simply hadn't been able to buy computers before.

Dompier mailed a check for $397 to MITS, but when his Altair didn't arrive soon enough to suit him, he bought an airline ticket and flew to Albuquerque to pick it up. Although he didn't get his computer on that visit, it arrived soon afterward in the mail. However, the Altair had to be assembled. "I received my Altair 8800 in the mall at 10 A.M.," Dompier said, "and 30 hours later it was up and running with only one bug in the memory!"

In April, Dompier showed up at the Peninsula School in Menlo Park, where the Homebrew Computer Club held its meetings. Dompier attracted a crowd. He was going to demonstrate his Altair. After Dompier set up the machine and started programming it, someone tripped on the extension cord and the Altair went dead.

Finally, Dompier finished reloading the computer and ran the code. A radio sitting next to the Altair began to buzz with static. It buzzed the Beatles' "Fool on the Hill." According to legend, when it finished, that it buzzed "Daisy," also known as "Bicycle Built for Two," as an encore. ("Daisy" was sung by HAL, the computer in the 1969 film *2001: A Space Odyssey*.) Dompier had written a set of empty loops whose only purpose was to play music in the static the Altair generated on a portable radio. The crowd went wild.

SOURCE: Swaine, Michael, "The Programmer Paradigm," *Dr. Dobb's Journal of Software Tools*, (January 1995):109+, via Lexis-Nexis.

and space applications of computer technology, they channeled government money to finance computer research and development.

In a landmark 1945 article in the *Atlantic Monthly*, MIT researcher Vannevar Bush suggested that a machine, a "memex," could extend the powers of human memory and association and solve the problem of organizing and accessing information. "A memex," Bush wrote, "is a device in which an individual stores all his books, records, and communications, and which is mechanized so that it may be consulted with exceeding speed and flexibility. It is an enlarged intimate supplement to his memory."[2] Bush envisioned the machine as a desktop device with a keyboard; storage would be on microfilm, and dry photography would be used for input.

Doug Engelbart, a young sailor still on duty in 1945, read Bush's article and recognized the problem he described but realized that the computer, not a microfilm machine, was the answer. The computer could manipulate symbols and allow individuals to compare data.[3] Engelbart went on to direct laboratory research at the Stanford Research Institute and was active through the 1970s in developing computer applications. Engelbart's group at Stanford initiated the field of computer-supported cooperative work and invented **WYSIWYG** word processing, the mouse, multiwindow displays, and electronic meeting rooms.[4]

Although Bush envisioned a mechanical device to sort information, electronic computers were the key to Engelbart's concept of being able to manipulate information. In 1946 the first electronic general-

314

WYSIWYG: Text on a computer screen that corresponds exactly to the printout.

Keyconcept

WYSIWYG and Computer Access: The phrase "What You See Is What You Get" (WYSIWYG) began as a marketing slogan to promote a software feature that soon became standard: screen displays that exactly duplicated what would appear in a printed document. The rise of WYSIWYG programs transformed the workplace computer into an accessible, user-friendly, home-based tool.

purpose computer, Electronic Numerical Integrator and Computer (ENIAC), was developed at the University of Pennsylvania.[5] ENIAC was eighteen feet high and eighty feet long and weighed thirty tons. It used 17,468 vacuum tubes connected by 500 miles of wire to perform 10,000 operations a second. To change its instructions, engineers had to rewire it. The research effort that produced it had been financed by the U.S. government in hopes that a computer would contribute to the war effort, and ENIAC was used to make some of the calculations in the building of the hydrogen bomb in the 1950s.

International Business Machines (IBM) became a leader in the computer industry when its president, Thomas Watson, Jr., realized that IBM's mechanical business machines were on the verge of becoming obsolete. Watson had seen the ENIAC, and he envisioned the future. ENIAC evolved into the Univac computers that today are products of Unisys Corp. In 1954, just as IBM was about to bring out a new computer, it learned that Univac's new machine would surpass it, so Watson rushed development of memory technology that had been planned for later production and had it running in IBM machines within six months. By the 1960s, Watson's efforts had made IBM the leader in computer production.[6] By then the vacuum tubes had been replaced by small silicon chips.

Engineers recognized at the beginning that computers had many possible applications. Not only could they manipulate numbers and sort information by topic, they offered a platform for developing graphics programs that could serve as architectural and design tools. Already in the early 1950s, MIT laboratories were experimenting with **interactive** computing and computer graphics. Ivan Sutherland created "Sketchpad," a graphics program in which the user drew directly on the screen using a light pen. "Sketchpad" introduced software inventions such as the cursor, the window, and clipping. In 1955, IBM released the **computer language** FORTRAN, which was designed to aid scientists in solving engineering problems.

Man won over the computer when Garry Kasparov challenged IBM supercomputer Deep Blue. Computers were first envisioned merely as storage and sorting machines, but their capabilities surpass simple tasks. Later, the computer defeated Kasparov.

Mildred Koss, one of UNIVAC I's initial programmers, commented, "There were no limitations to what you could accomplish. There was lots of vision and new ideas as to where the computer might be used. We looked at the computer as a universal problem-solving machine. It had some rules and an operating system, but it was up to you to program it to do whatever you wanted it to do."[7]

But computers could be problematic as well. Grace Hopper, a mathematician who worked in computer research at Harvard and developed the first commercial high-level computer language, gave a name to those problems. While trying to determine what had caused a computer malfunction, Hopper found the culprit—a dead moth on a vacuum tube. From then on, "bug" became a common computer term.[8]

interactive: Interactive systems involve two-way communication. The information receivers act as senders and vice versa.

computer language: An intermediate programming language designed for programmers' convenience that is converted into machine language.

The move to micro

With the development of the silicon chip in 1959, the computer industry expanded to become a microelectronics industry. The silicon

316

chip and programming languages enabled the electronics industry to develop **micro-computers** for general use. Software, rather than hardware, determined the application. By the early 1960s, this infant industry was garnering annual revenues of more than $1 billion. As computers were used for processing different applications, hardware and software manufacturers began to rapidly develop new products.

In 1974, Intel marketed its first computer chip, the Intel 4004. This chip, which combined memory and logic functions to the microchip to produce a microprocessor, launched the individual computer market. First, workstation terminals that were attached to a large mainframe began to proliferate in the workplace, and then stand-alone desktop computers appeared. However, the personal computer (PC) was designed primarily for ham radio operators and other electronics hobbyists.

In 1975, Paul Allen, a friend of a Harvard student named Bill Gates, was attracted to a newsstand cover of the January 1975 issue of *Popular Electronics.* The cover featured a photo of the very first personal computer, the MITS Altair 8800. After reading that article, Gates left Harvard, and he and Allen started Microsoft Corporation.

The Altair 8800 was the first practical mass market machine, produced by a hobby company called Micro Instrumentation Telemetry Systems (MITS), and sold for $397, about the price of the Intel chip that made its production possible. But there was a catch. To be useful, an Altair required a videodisplay terminal, floppy disks, and a printer, which brought the price into the $5,000 range, but for that price the buyer had a computer that did real work, such as word processing, file management, and running BASIC, FORTRAN, COBOL, and PL/I programs. Programmers entered data with switches instead of a keyboard. Hobbyists and entrepreneurs loved the Altair. Personal computing had arrived.[9]

In 1977, Steve Wozniak and Steve Jobs, two college dropouts, perfected the Apple II, which sold for about $1,300, contained 4 **kilobytes** of memory and came with a jack that converted a television set into a monitor. About the same time, the Tandy/Radio Shack TRS-80s became available; Tandy sported the first truly portable model. In 1981, Osborne introduced a machine with a built-in 24-line monitor, and in 1981, IBM entered the market with the first IBM PC. "Totables" or "luggables" included the Kaypro, which sold for about $1,800, and Compaq's suitcase-style machine, which was about the size and weight of a portable sewing machine.

By the mid-1980s, DOS-based personal computers and the Apple Macintosh had become affordable, revolutionizing not only the workplace, but the home as well. These machines enabled people to use a desktop computer for sophisticated engineering problems and at the same time for other applications such as word processing, graphics, design, **spreadsheets,** and **database** management.

Software revolution

"Software" is a term that covers all the programs that affect how people use computers. Software includes **computer operating systems,** communications software, task-oriented software such as word-processing programs, and entertainment software.

In 1980, **user-friendly** software did not exist. Early versions of word processing programs, for example, required either addressing text

microcomputer: A small computer using a microprocessor as its central processor.

kilobyte: A measure of memory size equal to 1024 bytes.

spreadsheets: Software that allows for organization and tabulation of financial data. Commonly used in planning budgets.

databases: Software for recording statistics. Data can be sorted in categories and reports printed in various forms. Used by businesses who need to sort customers by zip code, for example.

computer operating systems: These are the programs that tell the computer how to behave. DOS and Windows, produced by Microsoft, dominate the world market for operating systems. The Macintosh operating system is second; it is used by about one-tenth as many machines as the Microsoft systems.

user-friendly: Software that is designed for use by individuals who are not familiar with complex computer languages.

[profile]

Bill Gates

Until the mid-1970s, computers took up entire rooms. But in 1975 the first microcomputer kit—the Altair 8800—was developed, making computers more affordable and usable in the home. Unfortunately, the operating system language for the microcomputer was the same as that for large mainframe computers, filling up most of the Altair's small memory capacity and leaving little room for data.

When Paul Allen read about the Altair 8800, he convinced his friend Bill Gates to work with him on developing a condensed operating system language, which the teenaged math geniuses licensed to the makers of the Altair 8800.

One year later, Allen and Gates established Microsoft Corporation. The young founders were convinced that they were in the forefront of a computer revolution. Software, said Gates, was where the money would be.

Microsoft's big break came in 1980 when the industry's leader,

IBM, asked Gates to develop an operating system for its new personal computer. Gates declined at first, then bought a system from another small company for $50,000, reworked it, and licensed it to IBM for $125,000. He named the operating system MS-DOS, for "Microsoft disk operating system." Gates retained ownership and thus was ready to confront the microcomputer revolution. IBM introduced its PC in 1981, and clones (practically identical machines) using MS-DOS soon followed.

Today, Microsoft's operating systems—MS-DOS and Windows—run more than 90 percent of the world's personal computers.

On July 15, 1996, Microsoft and NBC each invested $220 million to launch MSNBC, the Microsoft-NBC news service that is available on cable and online. The companies claim they are preparing for the time when computers and television merge. Gates is now a billionaire, one

of the richest people in the United States.

Sources: Peter H. Lewis, "A Glimpse into the Future as Seen by Chairman Gates," *The New York Times,* December 12, 1993, Sect. 3, p. 7; "Bill Gates," *Newsmakers,* Gale Research Inc., August 1993; Joel Achenbach, "The Computer King's Hard Drive; Billionaire Bill Gates, Cult Hero, Cracks Open a Window on the Secret of His Success," *The Washington Post,* April 14, 1993, p. B1; Cynthia Flash, "Microsoft, NBC Launch News Venture," *News Tribune,* July 14, 1996, p 1.

by numbered lines or learning various combinations of function, control, and letter keys to execute commands. However, everything changed when, in 1980, Bill Gates provided DOS for IBM's landmark PC—and cut a deal. The deal was that Microsoft reserved the right to sell DOS to interested third parties. This deal allowed Microsoft to license the system to other PC manufacturers, which developed the IBM clones that dominate the market today. Microsoft also allowed software developers to base their products on MS-DOS. Once Intel began to provide the **microprocessors** that are the **powertrains** of most PCs and Gates made MS-DOS generally available, DOS-based PC software proliferated.[10]

Personal computers became more user-friendly in 1984 with the introduction of the Macintosh by Apple. The Macintosh provided an easy-to-use format with a mouse and layers of work files (called the desktop) in a small, light computer. However, Apple refused to license

microprocessor: The chip that contains all the components in a CPU. The best known chip in the 1990s was the Intel.

powertrains: Microprocessors—the power behind computers.

the Mac operating system to other computer companies. This kept other manufacturers from cloning the Apple, but it also meant that a limited number of Apples were available to consumers. Furthermore, fewer programs were being written for Apples than for DOS-based PCs. As a result, IBM clone computers that used DOS as an operating system took larger shares of the PC market. By 1995, Apple had only 8 percent of world PC sales; in March, 1997, Apple announced it would be laying off 4,100 employees, a third of its work force.

In 1990, Gates introduced Microsoft's Windows 3.0 (and a 3.1 upgrade), which allowed DOS computers to be as user-friendly as the Macintosh while retaining the power and speed of the DOS microcomputer. Windows had sold 60 million copies by 1995, and Microsoft was supplying 80 percent of the operating systems worldwide. The introduction of Windows permanently stunted IBM's infant OS/2 system and relegated Macintosh to the fringe of the market. Microsoft, with access to Windows developments, leapt into the software market and now provides most of the word processing and spreadsheet programs for Windows PCs and Macs. Today, nearly two-thirds of Microsoft's revenue comes from applications, and the company is by far the biggest, most profitable vendor in the industry. Since the introduction of Windows in 1990, Microsoft's annual profits, revenues, and stock price have soared.[11] The company's most recent coup was Windows 95, launched in August 1995, an operating system that better integrates hardware and software and manages complex directories and files. Windows 95 sold 40 million copies in the first year. Microsoft is now working on yet another operating system that will integrate desktop and Internet functions.

The software revolution, along with the trend toward microcomputers, has made computers a more common household item. A 1995 study by the Times Mirror Center for The People & The Press found that nearly 36 percent of American homes had a personal computer. If 1980 is used as a starting point for when portable computers were available, in sixteen years, computers had experienced 36 percent penetration. For comparison, Table 11.1 shows the number of years it took for some popular technologies to reach 50 percent penetration. The sales of personal computers in the United States are expected to remain fairly stable between 1996 and 1999 at about 8 million units a year. The international sales of PCs will boom, however, as the number of units sold increases from about 72 million in 1996 to about 114 million in 1999.[12]

TABLE 11.1 Number of Years to Reach 50 Percent Penetration of U.S. Households for Selected Technologies

TECHNOLOGY/MEDIUM	NUMBER OF YEARS TO REACH 50% PENETRATION
Newspapers	100+
Telephone	70
Phonograph	55
Cable TV	39
Color TV	15
VCR	10
Radio	9
Black and White TV	8

Sources: EIA, U.S. Department of Commerce, 1996; courtesy of John Carey.

■ Networking

The next major advance will be to **network** all of these different computers at work and home—workstations, personal computers, **laptops,** and mainframes—together to form what Vice President Albert Gore has often referred to as "the information highway." People in different parts of the world will then be able to regularly videoconference, send electronic messages, and share working documents. Already, friends write electronic letters, children download encyclopedia entries, and teenagers play online computer games. Many people, businesses, and their computers are already linked through the Internet and commercial on-line services. Some of these services are professionally oriented. Others are consumer mass products.

THE INTERNET The Internet is a network of computer networks. These networks include computers found in businesses, universities, libraries, government, media companies, and homes.

Radio first made possible rudimentary long-distance education, but new media and satellites make it possible for students to participate interactively with instructors and discussion groups.

The Internet is available today because the federal government wanted to link computers in such a way that in times of disaster—whether created by humans or nature—defense and communications systems could still operate. So a little more than twenty years ago the U.S. Defense Department designed an experimental network called ARPAnet. As the type and number of network systems increased, it became apparent that using some common system that would allow computers to talk to each other would be beneficial to all. In the late 1980s, the National Science Foundation (NSF) created five supercomputer centers. At first, NSF tried to use ARPAnet to connect them, but bureaucracy and staffing problems got in the way. NSF therefore created its own network, connecting the centers with telephone lines. Then, through a chain system, the network linked universities and other commercial and noncommercial computer groups. In each area of the country a group is linked to its neighbor group or institution, rather than every one being fed to a central location. This saves primarily in the cost of telephone lines.

The success of the system came close to being its downfall, as users multiplied rapidly and the telephone lines couldn't sustain the use. In 1987 the old network was replaced with higher-capacity telephone lines.

The most important feature of the NSF network has been its commitment to letting everyone use it, thereby opening up enormous sources of data and conversations for people using computers.[13] What is amazing is that connections occur within seconds, despite being linked from one institution to another across hundreds of miles or around the world.

Keyconcept

The World Wide Web and the Growth of the Internet:
The World Wide Web, a graphic-rich segment of the Internet that is accessed by using Web browsers such as Netscape Navigator, has led to an astronomical growth in the availability of information in graphic, audio, and text forms. The Web's user-friendly graphical format and easy navigation by site-to-site links encouraged not only scholarly research, but also exploration by children, teenagers, educators, business people, and other users in many walks of life.

network: Computers that are connected by communications lines. The computers may be connected within a restricted geographic area, such as a laboratory in a mass communication program. This network is a local area network (LAN). The Internet networks millions of computers worldwide through telephone and fiber-optic lines.

laptop computer: A portable computer about the size of a thick notebook and weighing from five to seven pounds.

ONLINE SERVICES An early experiment in business and consumer applications was a service called "viewdata," developed by Sam Fedida, an engineer of the British Post Office. During the 1960s, Fedida developed a computerized hotel reservation system. He was attempting to facilitate hotel registration procedures and eliminate intermediary hotel clerks, which would save hotels money and personnel time and save the customer time.

Almost simultaneously, James Redmond and Peter Rainer of the BBC were working on a way to display information on television screens, such as captions for hearing-impaired people. Thus computerized information transmitted by telephone lines for display on a remote terminal—originally the television—was born. Early **videotex** experiments in the United States did not succeed. The services required expensive and awkward **dedicated technology,** and consumers could not perceive enough advantage from the system to be willing to spend the money required.

However, with improved technology and a variety of business, professional, and consumer products to offer, online services now are widely available. Users can sometimes subscribe directly to a database or, more commonly, to a vendor of databases. Vendors provide one or more databases that offer up-to-the-minute research information; some provide interactive capability. For example, a user can order airline tickets through one of Prodigy's databases or have flowers shipped for Mother's Day through America Online. The business-oriented vendor Lexis-Nexis provides information access, retrieval, and printing capabilities for business and legal use.

Online services are valuable because of the vast amounts of information they provide access to and because the databases can be updated continuously. In fact, occasionally, if you return to a Lexis-Nexis search a half hour after starting the search, the database will leave you a message indicating that new information has been added since you started the search. In addition, online services can be accessed from any location.

Online services vary greatly. Some, like America Online, combine entertainment and information. An America Online subscriber can talk to other users via a chat room, search an encyclopedia on the web, play computer games, and send electronic mail. Users of Lexis-Nexis have access only to business and information through an extensive database.

The number of online databases has grown phenomenally. About 300 databases existed in 1979. That number zoomed to more than 5,307 in July 1994. In the early days, the number of databases grew by only 100 a year, but from 1992 to 1993 the number increased by 736.[14]

Social and cultural effects

Economists and social theorists claim that the United States and other developed countries have moved from industrial-based economies to information-based economies. Creating and distributing information for entertainment, investing, and economic decision-making account for a large portion of America's national product. In addition, information is a commodity that represents knowledge and the ability to transcend socioeconomic class. As information becomes more specialized, more technology-based, and more expensive, sociologists and political critics worry that the participation of an informed public, necessary to support the foundations of a democracy, may erode even further than it already has. Sociologists are concerned we will become a fragmented society in which there is no longer such a thing as "common knowledge." We might have nothing to say to our neighbors any more because we choose the content and the information sources we want, which might be different from what our neighbors want.

videotex: Online services that provide words and graphics and sometimes allow for interactive capability.

dedicated technology: Piece of equipment dedicated to one purpose; early videotex equipment could be used only for receiving the videotex service, not to retrieve other information or for entertainment. Requirements for dedicated technology hamper development of services.

Research tells us that individuals with higher levels of education generally have more exposure to various channels of mass communication from which they gain ideas and information. People with lower levels of education usually are not exposed to as many kinds of mass communication systems. As mass media technology becomes more sophisticated, individuals with the access and understanding to use it gain information even more quickly, thus widening what is termed "the knowledge gap."[15]

Key concept

Knowledge Gap: Because a democratic society is based on the existence of an informed populace, access to information is a political as well as a social issue. A greater gap or disparity between highly educated people, who typically make use of many types of information, and those with less education and less access to sources of information can make a society more elitist and less democratic.

Such a knowledge gap, exacerbated by an increasing volume of highly specialized, technical knowledge, could lead to an "information-rich, information-poor" society. In such a society, individuals would be categorized in socioeconomic classes according to their access to information.

People who already use computers and online databases at work or who tinker with new entertainment technologies at home are the first to use advanced software and networks. These people are the ones who already understand the logic of using communication tools. They easily adopt sophisticated information technologies because they build on their present knowledge. These are the "information-rich," that is, people who have access to the information.

A second group of people who have an interest in new communication technologies but who have not worked with the hardware and software will take longer to adapt to the technology. They read about technology but do not have the institutional affiliation or finances that enable them to use it. These people might be at a disadvantage unless they gain access to information through new communication technologies.

A third group consists of people who have little knowledge about new communication technologies for a variety of reasons and might never access the information provided. They may not know how to read or might not have access to traditional media from which to obtain information. Many people are not worried about stocks, annual reports, and airplane crashes in another country but are struggling to survive day to day. Even if technology is available, such as computers in public libraries, people in this group may be the "information-poor" because they do not have the knowledge or motivation to access new technology.[16]

Research indicates that the knowledge gap about a particular subject narrows as the topic becomes important to the information-poor.[17] If someone with little education really wants to know about the toxic waste dump a mile away, she or he will seek out that information. The impact of new communication technology on such knowledge gaps will depend on how available the technology is in public libraries and the degree to which electronic media replace print media. If information remains available through print or television, computer technology will not create gaps in areas that remain important to the information-poor.

A democratic society requires an informed public. As information becomes increasingly available through computer services, poor media consumers could quickly lose ground in the struggle for information. Public access to computers—often through libraries—helps to keep the marketplace of ideas open to all.

One way of bringing down the cost of access is using networked computers rather than stand-alone PCs. These computers would have little storage capacity and would temporarily download necessary software from the network as needed. In 1997, Microsoft and Intel introduced the Net PC to compete with the network computer already manufactured by Sun Microsystems. Neither computer uses diskettes, but the

322

FIGURE 11.1

Penetration of Media: 1996

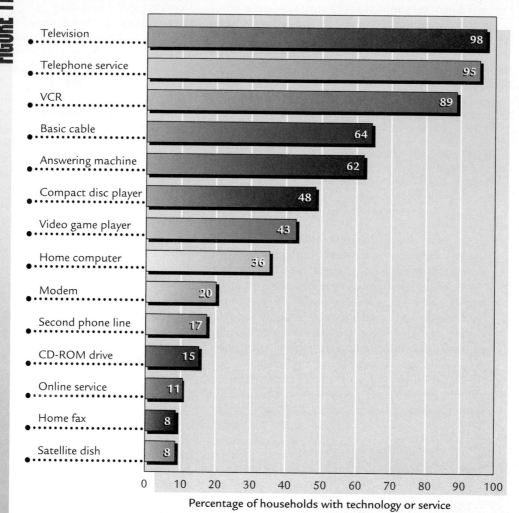

Source: EIA; NY Times; Video Business. Reprinted with permission of John Carey, Greystone Communications.

Net PC has more storage capacity. To start, these "dumb" machines will be used mostly by businesses. Their current prices run about a third to a half of the cost of a stand-alone PC. The impact of these cheaper computers on the general public remains less clear, but some argue lower-cost network computers could provide inexpensive access to the Internet. Figure 11.1 shows what percentage of households at mid-decade had adapted forms of new technology and how these compare to household ownership of television and telephone.

Today's market structure

The computer industry—coupled with information services that make the personal computer valuable—is highly diversified and competitive. The market consists of hardware

TABLE 11.2 Projected Expenditures for Interactive Electronic Communication (in the United States in Billions of Dollars)

TYPE OF INTERACTIVITY	1996	1997	1998
Internet	$1.5	$2.4	$3.7
CD-ROMs	$3.1	$3.3	$3.5
Interactive TV	$0.8	$2.0	$4.2
Kiosks	$0.8	$1.4	$2.2
Video games	$4.0	$4.2	$4.3
Infomercials and home shopping	$3.9	$4.6	$5.4
Total	$14.1	$17.9	$23.3

Sources: Goldman, Sachs & Co., New York; Dataquest, San Jose, CA; Jupiter Communications Co., New York; Inteco Corp., Norwalk, CT; BT Securities, New York; and Paul Kagan & Associates, Carmel, CA, as reported in Debra Aho Williamson, "Building A New Industry," *Advertising Age,* (March 13, 1995) pp. 5–3.

manufacturers, software manufacturers, and providers of online products. Now included in the industry mix is the emergence of telephone companies. Part of the diversification is due to the fact that "the industry" is really many "industries." Table 11.2 shows the dollars spent on some commercial products related to computer use.

Part of the reason that the computer industry has stayed dynamic and has continued to grow so rapidly is that constant change fuels the growth. Computers get smaller and more versatile, software becomes more flexible and accomplishes more complex tasks, and online services provide new types of information in more convenient ways.

Hardware

The boom in personal computers during the 1990s increased growth and profit among computer manufacturers. In 1996, Compaq sold 7.1 million PCs, which was an 18.5 percent increase from 1995. IBM sold 6.1 million, a 27.9 percent increase from 1995, and Hewlett-Packard sold 2.9 million. Dell saw sales increase by 80 percent as its output went from 1 million PCs in 1995 to 1.8 in 1996. The range of revenues in this group is large. IBM's 1996 revenues equaled $75.9 billion, which was more than all other computer hardware companies combined. Contributing to the hardware competition are companies that provide specific parts or peripherals, such as Hewlett-Packard, printers; Intel, computer chips; and Western-Digital, **hard disks.**[18]

Despite advances in hardware, computers remain difficult to use for reading print media such as newspapers, books, and magazines. Many people enjoy reading these at the breakfast table or while riding a subway or bus. Even laptop computers remain too bulky and expensive for this type of use, and many people find print on computer screens hard to read for long. In an effort to make electronic text more available, Knight-Ridder began researching an electronic tablet during the 1990s that would put text and graphics on a portable screen about the size of a notebook. Roger Fidler, who was director of Knight-Ridder Information Labs, predicted that the tablets would be available by the year 2000 at a cost of less

hard disk: Storage capacity built into a personal computer, in contrast to external drives for "soft" storage disks.

Computers in our lives

dateline

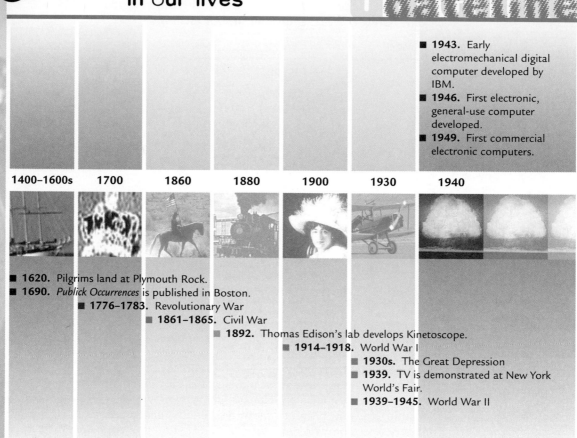

| 1400–1600s | 1700 | 1860 | 1880 | 1900 | 1930 | 1940 |

- **1943.** Early electromechanical digital computer developed by IBM.
- **1946.** First electronic, general-use computer developed.
- **1949.** First commercial electronic computers.

- **1620.** Pilgrims land at Plymouth Rock.
- **1690.** *Publick Occurrences* is published in Boston.
  - **1776–1783.** Revolutionary War
    - **1861–1865.** Civil War
      - **1892.** Thomas Edison's lab develops Kinetoscope.
        - **1914–1918.** World War I
          - **1930s.** The Great Depression
          - **1939.** TV is demonstrated at New York World's Fair.
          - **1939–1945.** World War II

than $400. However, in late 1995, Knight-Ridder closed the lab to cut costs. The future of electronic tablets remains uncertain.

Software

"Software" is a term for programs, or the instructions that tell the computer's processor what to do. Besides operating systems, software includes communications software, task-oriented software, and entertainment software. A PC can use more than one type of software at any one time.

Communication software provides connections from one computer to another. Some programs configure a modem so that a user can fax material, send an electronic message to another person, or access an online service. Other programs, such as Netscape Navigator or Internet Explorer, enable users to browse the World Wide Web, a dimension of the Internet that relies heavily on graphics.

This type of software became hot financially as interest in the Internet grew in the 1990s. Jim Clark, who cofounded Netscape Communication Corporation, became a billionaire in 1995. Netscape started selling shares to the public on August 5, 1995, at $28 each. Within two months, the stock rose above $110. This success attracted several

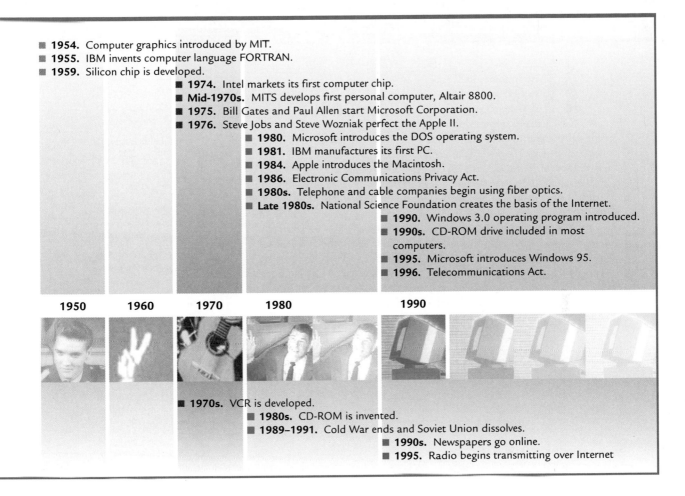

- **1954.** Computer graphics introduced by MIT.
- **1955.** IBM invents computer language FORTRAN.
- **1959.** Silicon chip is developed.
  - **1974.** Intel markets its first computer chip.
  - **Mid-1970s.** MITS develops first personal computer, Altair 8800.
  - **1975.** Bill Gates and Paul Allen start Microsoft Corporation.
  - **1976.** Steve Jobs and Steve Wozniak perfect the Apple II.
    - **1980.** Microsoft introduces the DOS operating system.
    - **1981.** IBM manufactures its first PC.
    - **1984.** Apple introduces the Macintosh.
    - **1986.** Electronic Communications Privacy Act.
    - **1980s.** Telephone and cable companies begin using fiber optics.
    - **Late 1980s.** National Science Foundation creates the basis of the Internet.
      - **1990.** Windows 3.0 operating program introduced.
      - **1990s.** CD-ROM drive included in most computers.
      - **1995.** Microsoft introduces Windows 95.
      - **1996.** Telecommunications Act.

1950   **1960**   **1970**   **1980**   **1990**

- **1970s.** VCR is developed.
  - **1980s.** CD-ROM is invented.
  - **1989–1991.** Cold War ends and Soviet Union dissolves.
    - **1990s.** Newspapers go online.
    - **1995.** Radio begins transmitting over Internet

competitors in the browser business, though only Microsoft is currently threatening Netscape's market position.

Online software also became a battleground in 1995 as Microsoft entered the field. CompuServe, America Online, and Prodigy expressed concern about Microsoft's entry because the Microsoft Network is integrated into Windows 95. The companies feared that Microsoft would use its advantage in marketing Windows to dominate the communication software business as well. However, online services did not experience the expected growth as independent Internet service providers began to offer lower prices and the Web became easier for new users to navigate.

Task-oriented software incorporates all the programs that allow people to create text and images and to organize data. Included are word processing programs, such as WordPerfect; page design programs, such as Quark; database organizers, such as Filemaker Pro; and spreadsheets, such as Lotus 1,2,3. This software allows individuals to create the content that appears on the Internet and online services.

Keyconcept

Implications of Hardware and Software: Computer development involves both changes in hardware, such as the silicon chip, and the evolution of software, such as sophisticated desktop publishing and financial programs. Hardware developments, such as the modem and the CD-ROM, make possible the widespread transfer of information, while software allows even computer novices to manipulate and send information electronically.

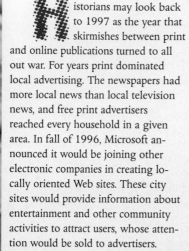

Historians may look back to 1997 as the year that skirmishes between print and online publications turned to all out war. For years print dominated local advertising. The newspapers had more local news than local television news, and free print advertisers reached every household in a given area. In fall of 1996, Microsoft announced it would be joining other electronic companies in creating locally oriented Web sites. These city sites would provide information about entertainment and other community activities to attract users, whose attention would be sold to advertisers.

Microsoft is not the first to set up such city sites. America Online and even daily and weekly newspapers have Web sites that do the same thing. The difference is that Microsoft has a very big bank account that can help them hire good journalists and develop new services. These services could include monitoring areas of special interest to a person and keeping them up to date. For example, if a person likes REM, the city site will select and send information about this group, such as dates of the closest concert and reviews of new CDs, to a person's computer. The computer could even automatically buy and ship a new CD. This technology, which goes out and seeks information for a person, is called "push" technology, because a user doesn't have to seek

Advertising Cyberwars

the information; it will be pushed to the user by a computer.

Newspaper executives are concerned that such sites might take away classified advertising. Currently, about 37 percent of newspaper's advertising income comes from classified ads. These small ads seem to work even better in cyberspace than in print. Computers can search ads for specific products and even let a person order immediately. The computer may monitor the classified ads for a person and tell him or her when a particular product or job is available.

Current print publications will not give up without a fight and even have advantages electronic companies do not. Newspapers typically reach 40 to 70 percent of the households in a community, and advertisers—weeklies with just ads—reach every household in a geographic market. Cyber sites require a computer and a hook up to the Internet, and only 16 percent of the U.S. households were doing that in 1996. Newspapers also produce news about local government, sports, and school activities—areas of coverage not mentioned in connection with the city cyber sites. Such news is attractive to people whether they access it through computers or print.

It is unlikely that the battle for cyber ads will run local newspapers out of business, any more than radio doomed newspapers or television killed radio. However, the war will affect media companies and consumers. Newspapers will have to provide better and more information on line. The competition will force these companies to spend more money on newsgathering to emphasize their advantages over the city sites. Consumers will have more choices for information, and perhaps, companies such as Microsoft and AOL will invest in local journalism to better compete with the online newspapers. So, from a consumer's perspective, the war in cyberspace will provide more choice and more information.

SOURCES: Hoag Levins, "The Online Classifieds Report: New Cyberspace Advertising Technologies To Impact Newspaper Revenues in Three Years," *Editor & Publisher Interactive,* (November 21, 1996), [www.mediainfo.com]; Steve Outing, "Something To Worry About for Alternative papers: Classifies," *E&P Interactive* (June 3, 1996), [www.mediainfo.com]; and Steven Levy, "Rise of the City Sites," *Newsweek* (September 30, 1996): 86–87, 91.

Entertainment software allows consumers access to a variety of media and activities online and from diskettes and CD-ROMs. Such software delivers thousands of stories, poems, photographs, games, and videos to computer users. Simulation games, such as *Simm City,* provide the baseline for spinoffs. They also integrate analytic skill building with entertainment.

Demand for software has mushroomed since the 1980s. Software is bundled as "free" with new computers, sold at book, office and computer stores, and downloaded from the Internet.

Software can be supplied in packages such as CD-ROM and diskettes through online services, or it can be downloaded into the computer from a Web site or electronic bulletin board. The packages are owned by the consumer, and the online software is accessed by paying a monthly charge and a price for the amount of time spent online. Some downloadable problems are free; others are paid for by mail, over the telephone, or directly through the Internet.

Audience demand in computer markets

The demand for computers in business is enormous. Nearly every professional office—whether it be a law office, a public relations agency, or a government agency—relies on computers. Educational institutions constantly struggle to fund up-to-date computer facilities in a rapidly changing technological environment. Stockbrokers and financial analysts use computers to keep up with constantly changing market conditions. In doctors' offices, appointments and medical and billing records are kept on computers. Reporters, advertising personnel, and public relations professionals seek information via the computer and then use the computer as a tool for the production of ads, news stories, public relations releases, and illustrations. And increasingly, the ads themselves are broadcast electronically, as companies sponsor World Wide Web sites.

Demand for home computers grew during the 1990s as costs dropped. By 1997, a family could buy a computer that was capable of handling online services, including a monitor and a printer, for less than $1,000. Though this remains a steep price for the 50 percent of American families who make less than $35,000 a year, about 36 percent of U.S. households had computers in 1996, an increase from 31 percent in February of 1994. More significantly, more than 60 percent of American adults have access to computers at home or at work.[19]

Demand for software

Demand for operating systems correlates with demand for hardware. Each computer needs an operating system to run. As operating systems have become more flexible and users have come to expect more from their computers, the demand for user-friendly systems with graphical interfaces has heightened. Similarly, demand for communication software is related to online service and modem use. The demand for packaged software is greatest in entertainment and task-oriented applications.

The demand for task-oriented software grew during the 1990s as hardware and operating systems made it easier to process complex graphics. The increase also reflected declining prices and the availability of less expensive color printers and easier programs. The number of computer-designed, color Christmas cards and community newsletters proliferated, and now individuals and families are using task-oriented software to design their own Web pages.

Entertainment demand is shifting away from computer diskettes to CD-ROM, since its huge storage capacity allows more interactivity. For example, an interactive CD-ROM game for *Star Trek: The Next Generation* previewed in 1995 for $70. The player can determine the outcome of the game, which contains more than 15,000 lines of dialogue recorded by five of the TV program's actors.

Demand for CD-ROM will increase as the number of computers equipped with CD drives increases and prices for CDs decrease. More than 10 million computers had CD-ROM drives in 1996, but the number will grow quickly because most computers are now CD-ROM equipped. The price of entertainment software will decline as demand increases. Many CD-ROM games now sell for $30 to $40 dollars.

Demand for networked services

The modem is the connection to the networked world. To access a database, a person generally needs the telephone number or ethernet (cable) address of the mainframe computer holding the database, a telecommunications software program to connect his or her computer to the telephone or cable transmission lines, a modem (to convert computer digital information to audio analogue information if using a telephone transmission line), and a computer terminal with which to receive the information.

Network products, or online services, saw a giant increase from the fourth quarter of 1994 to mid-1995 when the number of Americans subscribing to online services jumped from 5 million to 12 million. But today, the online services face heavy competition from Internet Service Providers (ISPs), who sell direct access to the Internet, usually for a flat price. In early 1996, about 54 percent of the people surfing the Internet at home used an online service to get there. Six months later the figure had dropped to 35 percent.[20] As a result, both Compuserve and America Online offered flat rates to users in 1996. The flood of use at AOL made it impossible for thousands of people to gain access to the service and led to threats of law suits in 1997.

The growth of access to the Internet and online services has changed the demographics and uses of people traveling the information highway. One 1995 study showed that most **cybersurfing** Americans are neither social misfits nor teenagers. Sixty percent of those online are over age thirty-five (only 2 percent are over sixty-five), they visit friends and go to the movies more often than other people, and they are avid users of newspapers and television. Also, education is a better predictor than income for who subscribes to an online service.

Fifty-three percent of subscribers rank e-mail as their most common online activity. Others use it for research or communication with colleagues (41 percent); news gathering (30 percent); participation in chat groups, newsgroups, e-mail lists, and online forums (23 percent); locating entertainment and hobby information (19 percent); finding financial information (14 percent); and playing games (7 percent).[21]

A study released by the IntelliQuest Information Group, Inc., in 1997 showed changing demographics of online users. The original gender gap is closing; women made up 45 percent of people going online. Forty-three percent of subscribers rated their satisfaction as excellent or very good. The survey also found that about 11 to 12 million new users planned to explore the Internet or online services in 1997.[22]

cybersurfing: Browsing through the Internet, the World Wide Web, or any online service.

Global *Impact*

Online Services in Europe

t's called the World Wide Web, but they're still working on the "world" part. Less than 1 percent of the world's population has access to the Internet, though computer companies and online services are expanding in Europe, with its large population and advanced economy. Two services, Europe Online and AOL/Bertelsman Online, began tapping into this potentially large market in 1996. AOL now serves many countries, including Germany, Russia, and Okinawa.

Europe lags behind the United States in online services for a variety of reasons, including higher telecommunication costs, lagging software development, and, ironically, the fact that an interactive service already exists in France.

In 1981, the French created the Minitel system, an interactive system that uses a television screen to network with computers. The company is partially owned by the French government, which subsidizes consumers who buy the TV sets. By 1995, Minitel connections leveled off at 6.5 million homes (about a third of all homes).

The Minitel system is slow and has not been as successful as some analysts predicted. It is used mostly to access electronic directories and for banking. The delay in getting computers with modems is partly because of Minitel's availability as an interactive service and the government's part ownership of Minitel. Governments usually prefer monopolies.

For online services to grow in Europe, governments will have to privatize telecommunication industries and encourage competition to lower prices. U.S. companies are pursuing investment in Europe, but as telecommunication experts point out, the online services must cater to European cultures. Modeling European systems on American cultural values may not be a wise economic investment.

Even though European access to online services and the Internet has been slow compared to the United States, Asia use has started to boom. In 1996, Japan replaced the United States as the country with the highest percentage of households using the Internet. About 18 percent of Japanese households used the Internet in 1996, compared to 16 percent of U.S. households. Germany was third with about 12 percent, followed by Hong Kong at about 11 percent and Taiwan at about 10 percent. Some researchers say Asian use of the Net will triple by the year 2000.

SOURCE: Steve Outing, "The European Interactive Publishing Scene," *Editor & Publisher Interactive: The Media Info Source,* [http://www.mediainfo.com] November 21, 1995; "66.6 Million Households on Net by 2000: New World Study Projects Explosive Growth," *Editor & Publisher Interactive,* November 22, 1996; [http://www.mediainfo.com/] and "PC Growth Slows Worldwide," *Internet Week,* February 3, 1997 [http://www.phillips.com/iw/].

Supplying the audience's demand

Audience demand is supplied through software products, including those on disk and on CD-ROM; network products, including Internet connectors such as Netscape Navigator; and professional and consumer online services.

Traditional news organizations are starting to take notice of the growing number of computer users and their willingness to pay for fast, customized information. News organizations are experimenting with the notion that they are in the "information business," not just the "newspaper" or "broadcast news" business. Many mass media suppliers have created Internet or Web sites or are delivering information through commercial online services. In March, 1997, *Newsweek* and the Associated Press agreed to jointly provide content for Audio Highway (http://www.audiohwy.com) through a weekend radio broadcast titled "Newsweek On Air." Audio Highway's portable device called Listen Up, that sells for about $200, can be used to download audio content from Web sites and play it at remote locations.

Content push technology also brings newspaper content to readers, along with other information. By downloading the PointCast network, for example, a computer user has access to a personalized menu of information. A user can load content from the *Philadelphia Inquirer, Tampa Tribune,* and *New York Times,* along with weather and stock quotes. The material can be manually updated during the day, or continuously updated. In addition, attractive video and content from PointCast acts as a screen saver.

Role of mass communication specialists

Journalists, public relations practitioners, and advertising specialists use many different computerized information sources—online databases, the Internet, and electronic bulletin boards—to gather information. These specialists then organize, present, and disseminate that information in traditional mass media formats, such as newspaper, magazine, radio, and television. In reality, the public can gather the same information from the same computerized sources that professional communicators use.

Although some publishers fear that the role of the journalist might be lessened in this new computer world, the public probably still will rely on specialists to organize the mass of available information. Individuals do not have time to sift information, put it into coherent form, and digest its meaning. Also, some services, such as Lexis-Nexis, are too expensive for most consumers. The role of the specialist, however, will undoubtedly change. Journalists may be relied upon increasingly to interpret stories as the available amount of information increases.

Information can crash as it did in the Atlanta Olympic Games, where IBM had to struggle to get its computer act together to avoid misinformation on the screen. Computerized information—when the computers work—is an excellent source of detailed information in sports competition.

The use of online services and the Web by journalists to gather information is gaining momentum. In 1997, a survey conducted by Columbia University School of Journalism and Middleberg & Associates Public Relations found that about one-third of the 600 newspaper and magazines editors said their reporters go online daily to get information, which was up from the 23 percent reported a year earlier. Only 13 percent of the publications did not have access to the Internet; the figure was 37 percent a year earlier.[23]

Software products

CD-ROMs are particularly useful for storing large volumes of information that do not need constant updating. Indexes such as the *Reader's Guide to Periodical Literature,* encyclopedias, and archives of historical documents adapt well to CD-ROM. Librarians

CD-ROM products are proliferating and are used for education, training, and entertainment. CD ROM technology is especially good for archived information that can be used and reused.

find CD-ROMs particularly valuable because they require less storage space. Researchers appreciate them because they can simply pull a CD-ROM from a case on their desk and search it electronically while working on an article, book, or news story.

These resources serve journalists as well as students and other seekers of information. A magazine writer who is interested in safety standards of a local chemical plant might use the OSHA CD-ROM, which contains the electronic text of all OSHA regulations and procedures, selected documents, and technical information from OSHA's computerized information system. Or perhaps an education writer wants to compare local public high school students' SAT scores with national results. That person might refer to ERIC, which contains nearly 700,000 educational citations and abstracts from 1966 to the present. And a CD-ROM of interest to advertisers targeting minority consumers might be the Ethnic News Watch, which is a full-text coverage of selected major ethnic newspapers published in the United States from 1991 to the present.[24]

Keyconcept

Information Society: The United States, and to some extent the world, is in the midst of an information revolution that parallels the industrial revolution in scope. An information-age society faces the serious question of whether the members who have access to electronic equipment and an understanding of technology will become information-rich while others become information-poor.

Although many CD-ROMs contain only text, others include animation, sound, and high-quality graphics. Cost for information on CD-ROM is sometimes as low as a one-time only payment of $30 to $50, such as for Grolier's Encyclopedia (traditionally twenty-one volumes). Other companies charge a one-year subscription price that can run as high as several thousand dollars. The more expensive services that provide specialized up-to-date information often send new CDs every several months. Specialized information targeted at professionals is more expensive than products targeted at individuals.

CDs have proliferated in the home market as well as the business and professional market. Popular programs include Auto-Map, which is designed to help consumers plan vacations and various cookbooks, home encyclopedias, and games. CDs are also becoming an increasingly popular way of storing software programs and loading them into the computer. A word processing program such as WordPerfect might require a dozen disks, but the entire program will fit on a single CD-ROM.

Keyconcept

Virtual Reality Technology: Virtual reality can be used to simulate reality. Currently, because it is expensive and still in development, it is most used in practical situations, such as training pilots and paratroopers. However, if virtual reality technology becomes used for widespread entertainment, propaganda, or a combination of the two, it will pose serious ethical considerations.

Virtual reality products simulate reality, allowing users to "go" places and "do" things they have never done before. Once considered nearly impossible, the ability to simulate real life has significant applications in health care, education and training, as well as in entertainment. One of the earliest uses of virtual reality was in training pilots. When U.S. pilots moved into Bosnia in December 1995, they trained on virtual reality simulators that

Simulation and virtual reality techniques often are used in training, as well as for entertainment. Information superhighway planners emphasize that equal opportunities for professionals to gain training and upgrade computer skills are essential elements of an information society.

turned satellite data into three-dimensional views of Bosnia-Herze-govina, familiarizing them with the terrain even though they had never seen the Balkans.[25] Bill Gates, in his book *The Road Ahead,* writes about how convincing being in a simulator is: "When I was using the simulator my friends decided to give me a surprise by having a small plane fly by. While I sat in the pilot's seat, the all-too-real-looking image of a Cessna flashed into view. I wasn't prepared for the 'emergency,' and I crashed into it."[26] Significant use of this technique also can be important in the training of medical students for surgery. With goggles and helmets, they will be able to perform simulated surgery on patients who are computer creations rather than living individuals.

Virtual reality products are not yet found in the home market because they require powerful and sophisticated computer equipment combined with intricate software. However, this is likely to change. Simplified approximations of virtual reality have already reached the home market. In December 1995, Intervista Software introduced the WorldView 3D Web browser that would allow users to view certain World Wide Web pages in three dimensions. WorldView was the first stand-alone browser to support real-time three-dimensional (3-D) object viewing and interaction on the Internet and enables users to see and manipulate interactive 3-D "worlds." The latest versions of the most popular Web browsers support 3-D software, and several such programs are available.

Commercial online services

Commercial online services are designed for either professional or consumer use. Professional services are usually more expensive because they provide up-to-date, highly specialized information for use by lawyers, corporate public relations practitioners, reporters, and other technologically sophisticated users. Those aimed at mass media professionals may furnish information for television, newspaper, and magazine reporters, or they may provide material that has been processed for immediate publication or broadcasting.

PROFESSIONAL USES Professionals use databases in a variety of ways. For example, a marketing firm may hire a researcher to investigate different types of packaging. That person might connect to Lexis-Nexis and go into its MARKET, an electronic library grouping of databases on advertising, marketing, market research, public relations, sales and selling, promotions, consumer attitudes and behavior, demographics, product announcements and reviews, and industry overviews. Then the user might narrow the search into PACKNG, a database on packaging from January 1989, for the desired information.

Online services vary in cost. Some, but not all, government databases are free to the public because they are supported by the taxpayers' money. Some professional services are extremely expensive. For example, Dialog, a commercial service that contains more than 400 databases and has the full text of more than 1,100 periodicals, costs $36 to $312 an hour, plus an additional $0.10 to $120 to display a searched record. Some companies, such as Lexis-Nexis, also charge two to three cents a line to print out documents. Because of their high costs, these services are mostly commonly subscribed to by companies, rather than individuals.

NEWS SERVICES The most popular general **news service** is the Associated Press (AP) which has several hundred news bureaus gathering information in more than 100 countries and translating it into six different languages. The AP sells its information to more than 15,000 different types of media organizations around the globe. About 75 percent of the news (international, national, and state) that Americans read and see comes from the AP. On one hand, it is cheaper for media organizations to get information from the AP than to set up bureaus or send their own reporters to all countries where newsworthy events are taking place. On the other hand, it is worrisome to know that most of the information that people receive, whether in print or broadcast, comes from the same source.

Other news services at home and abroad have played important roles throughout the years. United Press International, initially formed from William Randolph Hearst's International News Service and E.W. Scripps's United Press, has fought desperately to stay alive. International services such as Reuters and Agence-France Press have provided information through the lens of a different national perspective. Specialized news services such as Dow Jones and the Washington Post–L.A. Times News Service provide in-depth features and explanations rather than the spot news on which the AP thrives.

Computers have helped news sources to get information to their subscribers quickly. Most news services have reporters who use computers to write their stories and transmit them through portable satellite dishes, all of which can fit into a big suitcase. The reports can be dispatched immediately to the news service's headquarters, edited, and sent to computers at the subscribing media organizations. Although satellite transmission helps journalists to avoid censorship, they still must fear at times for their personal safety. Securing a place from which to bounce a signal off a satellite is not always easy in hostile territory.

Computers have also spurred development of online news services by commercial conglomerates and news chains such as Knight-Ridder. Its news organizations transmit every published story to a central database that is available to all Knight-Ridder news organizations. Other organizations also may subscribe.

SYNDICATES Syndicates provide features, entertainment, opinion columns, and cartoons to media organizations for a fee. Syndicates enable you to keep up with "Dear Abby" or follow the same comic strip in different newspapers in any part of the country. Syndicates also provide news and entertainment video clips for use by broadcast and cable TV stations.

Syndicates contract with writers, illustrators, and video artists to provide work that can be sold through the syndicate. Media organizations can select specific items to purchase, much like choosing dishes in a cafeteria line. Computers are influencing the way news organizations get their syndicated features.[27] For example, even as recently as 1993, when computers abounded in the media workplace, syndicated comics were sent by postal mail, not electronically. Comic strips had to be completed six months before publication.

Syndicates now can deliver comics directly into newsroom computers, and publications now electronically paginate comics pages. Cartoonists thus now have tighter deadlines, which are especially important to political cartoonists, who need to closely follow political "hot topics."

news service: Organizations that collect and distribute news and information to media outlets. Some professionals still use the term "wire services."

334

King Features Syndicate, which handles the largest number of syndicated comic strips, has contracted with the AP to distribute comics electronically using the AP's digital and satellite technology. The AP sends its news photos to subscriber media organizations through a high-speed PhotoStream service. Non-AP material is distributed through PhotoExpress, which uses extra capacity on the PhotoStream service.

CONSUMER SERVICES Other online services provide information to home users at reasonable costs. In 1997, America Online offered several pricing plans to its subscribers: a monthly flat fee of $19.95 for unlimited time online; a limited plan for $9.95 a month for five hours online and $2.95 an hour after that; and a light usage plan of $4.95 a month for three hours online and $2.50 for each additional hour after that. America Online and Internet Service Providers are individual-oriented services used for the following purposes:

- Information retrieval for financial and general information such as that found in traditional newsletters, annual reports, newspapers, magazines, radio, and television.

- Transactions, such as shopping in an electronic mall or participating in a public opinion poll.

- Sending messages to people privately with e-mail or publicly in special interest groups called forums.

- Holding conferences with friends or experts at their computers in different locations.

- Computing accounts and finances.

- Playing games.

MEDIA ORGANIZATIONS AND ONLINE SERVICES To some degree, various online services are delivery systems for print and broadcast media. Lexis-Nexis delivers full text of magazines, newsletters, and newspapers as well as some transcripts from congressional hearings and other proceedings. Increasingly, however, traditional print and broadcast media are exploring the possibilities of reaching audiences through electronic delivery systems. These include fax newspapers and a variety of online services. These delivery systems allow newspapers to deliver to a particular member of an audience material on a specialized subject, background information on a story, or selected stories on a specific topic. Media organizations are struggling to create a profit-making formula for such online delivery systems.

One of the oldest and best established online subscription services is the Lexis-Nexis service that delivers key information to professionals in business, journalism, and the law.

■ *Fax Newspapers.* In the United States, 5 million fax machines transmitted about 20.8 billion pages of information in 1992; the number of faxed pages increased to more than 26 billion in 1993.[28] As more fax machines penetrate the home market, some innovative newspapers are experimenting with faxed information.

Faxed information usually falls into two groups: fax on demand and subscription fax. Fax on demand systems allow customers to call a number listed in the newspaper and order a document or report to be sent to their machine. Sometimes the information is free or advertiser-supported. In most cases the customer pays with a credit card or must dial a pay-per-call number. For example, the *Fresno (Calif.) Bee* offers unlimited sports and business faxes for $10 a month. The newspaper also filled 782 faxed orders of Christmas cookie recipes when an editorial and ads promoted the recipes at Christmas. In 1994, the *New York Times* was faxing customers articles from past issues about computers, desktop publishing, and related subjects for $3.95 each.

Fax subscriptions usually entitle customers to regular reports about specific subjects. For example, the *Austin (Texas) American-Statesman* offers fax publications on university sports and skiing reports. The "Downhill Digest" ski report, sent three times a week, is free to subscribers because it is sponsored by a local ski center. The sports publication covers the Baylor Bears, Texas A&M Aggies, and University of Texas Longhorns and offers recruiting reports and a sports column. Depending on how much information a subscriber requests, the subscription cost ranges from $50 to $130.

▨ *Online Newspapers.* By 1997, more than 1,800 commercial and college newspapers worldwide had electronic news products. These were available through local dial-up BBSs (stand-alone electronic bulletin board services), on the Internet, and through online services. Other newspapers were still in their planning stages and had not yet named an electronic route to their product. The oldest online newspaper still in existence is the *Fort Worth Star-Telegram*'s "StarText," which debuted in 1982 and has more than 4,600 subscribers.

■ Internet

Probably the most important Internet service is electronic mail. Electronic mail sent through the Internet allows scholars, friends, relatives, and others to communicate free if they have a free connection to the Internet through their school or workplace. Other people also gain access through an on-line service, such as America Online, or through an Internet service provider.

The Internet offers free databases. For example, NASA SpaceLink on the Internet (telnet *spacelink.msfc.nusu.gov*) provides the latest NASA news, including shuttle launches and satellite updates. Bulletins are posted every fifteen minutes, allowing journalists and others to track a space shuttle's flight.

In addition, the Internet provides access to electronic bulletin boards and Usenet newsgroups where people discuss everything from television programs to which cars to buy. **File transfer protocol** enables people to transfer electronic files such as texts of congressional bills, White House speeches, and software programs to their home computers. Improved Web browsers allow users to download sound files, pictures, and video clips as well as text files and software.

Although much of what is on the Internet is free, increasingly some magazines or other sites will allow free access for experimentation but will then charge a membership fee to continue to receive information.

One problem with the Internet is that it is huge and confusing and can be difficult to search. For this reason, designers have created a variety of tools for navigating the Internet. **Search engines** such as Excite, Lycos, and Alta Vista help users find information and sites.

Probably the most significant part of the Internet is the World Wide Web, a mushrooming group of Internet sites that present their content in a graphics-based format. Each "home page" on the screen

file transfer protocol (FTP): A system of code procedures that enables transfer of text and other files across the Internet.

search engines: Software designed to search computer networks for specific information.

336

contains links that can be used to jump to another screen. Many Web sites have very sophisticated designs, including frames, which allow several pages to be displayed on the computer screen at one time. Thomas, the Web site for the Library of Congress's legislative information, displays a likeness of Thomas Jefferson and menus for searching the library's archives.[29] The Web can be accessed with the browser, Netscape, sold inexpensively as a software package and available through some services such as America Online. Also, commercial on-line services have developed their own web browsers.

■ Bulletin board systems

On-line bulletin boards (BBSs) are similar to traditional bulletin boards, but messages are delivered through the computer. Postings include an amalgamation of public notices, help-wanted signs, for-sale lists, and personal messages. BBS's offer many of the same features as a commercial online service, such as America Online or CompuServe—electronic mail, chat rooms, public forums, shareware, data libraries, and an Internet connection. Many people enjoy subscribing to BBS's because they are smaller, and subscribers learn to know each other. Some electronic bulletin boards fold after only a few months because they do not attract enough users. People are drawn away from BBS's to explore the vast regions of the Internet.

■ Audiotext

Audiotext information services are prerecorded bits of information available to consumers who call a dedicated telephone number. The content may include book reviews, clips from political debates, or sound bytes from CDs reviewed in the newspaper. These may be provided by media organizations, telephone companies, or other entities. Sometimes the call is paid by a media organization, sometimes by a consumer; the information, itself, however, is almost always sponsored by an advertiser (whose commercial or name is noted at the beginning of the call).

Although media organizations have not determined whether audiotext will develop into a profit-making center, some are making money from various services. The *Evansville (Ind.) Courier* and *Evansville Press* (both of the Evansville Courier Co.) generated about $60,000 in ad revenue for their 1993 Homework Hotline program, which was sponsored by a supermarket chain. The hotline drew about 268,000 free phone calls in the first eleven weeks from students wanting information for school assignments.[30]

Trends and innovations

Computers have been used for communication for about three decades. Almost daily, newspapers and magazines contain articles about changes in the Internet, the World Wide Web, and online services. Three areas of development that will shape the trend of computer communication are the following:

1. Development of a national—perhaps international—information highway. What that highway will look like, who will fund it, and who will travel it remain material for discussion. If electronic media are still to have the goal of providing information that helps individuals to function in a democratic society, the highway will have to accommodate all kinds of travelers.

2. Hardware technology will probably increase in flexibility and become even more portable than it already is. Cellular modems, for example, are available, and their

Cultural Impact

Cultural Impact

In Cyberspace

William Gibson, a young American living in Canada, wandered past some video arcades in Vancouver in the early 1980s. He stopped to watch the young players hunched over their glowing video screens. "I could see in the physical intensity of their postures how rapt the kids were," he says. "It was like a feedback loop, with photons coming off the screens into the kids' eyes, neurons moving through their bodies and electrons moving through the video game. These kids clearly believed in the space the games projected."

Gibson, who wrote the 1984 novel *Neuromancer* on a manual typewriter, said he knew little about the world of computers. But he said that the people he knew who worked with computers ultimately came to accept the reality of "actual space behind the screen." Gibson called that place "cyberspace."

SOURCE: Time, Inc., 1995 delivered via America Online.

---

quality will improve. Software will become increasingly integrated, allowing many applications at a given time and the merging of applications.

3. Regulation will emerge to control the information highway. Many issues of the old media—privacy, copyright, and freedom of expression—will be issues for the new media.

The information highway

The dream of an information superhighway is spawning a modern-day Gold Rush as telephone companies, cable TV operators, publishers, movie studios, computer makers, and cellular phone operators hurry to stake a claim on an enormous consumer market that could reach hundreds of billions of dollars.

In late 1993 the National Telecommunications and Information Administration issued a report concluding that connecting computers in people's homes and places of business and allowing nearly universal access to computer systems would enable U.S. firms to surge ahead in the world economy, generating good jobs for Americans and economic growth for the nation. Further, creation of an information superhighway could transform the lives of the American people—lessening the constraints of geography, disability, and economic status and giving Americans a greater measure of equal opportunity.[31]

Keyconcept

Information Highway: The popular image of information flowing along a "highway" suggests that all people will be able to access and use unlimited amounts of information. The building process that is now underway will be important in determining the reach and accessibility of such a highway system. Important considerations include the role of advertising, the extent of regulation, the types of content, how this highway will be accessed and by whom, and how it will be paid for.

One of the major objectives of the President Bill Clinton's administration, beginning in 1995, was to develop policies that would make the United States a leader in the global information age.[32]

Reflecting on the administration's philosophy, reporter Scott Shepard wrote, "The good news is everyone in Congress supports the information superhighway . . . the bad

337

news is that nobody in Congress understands what the information superhighway is."[33] Shepard argued that when telecommunications officials think of the "information superhighway," they generally mean an electronic delivery system that will carry not only traditional cable TV news, sports, and entertainment channels but also movies on demand, interactive shopping, telephone services, and a host of still-undeveloped information services.

Keyconcept

Regulation in the Information Age: The regulation of Internet material has often been compared to law in the Wild West—almost nonexistent. Legal cases such as the challenge to the Telecommunications Act of 1996 that came before the Supreme Court in 1997 will have major influence on how issues such as privacy and freedom of information are addressed.

But when Vice President Al Gore speaks of an "information highway," he means not commercial services, but rather a coast-to-coast grid of computer-linked fiber-optic "highways" transporting knowledge that will form a new foundation of wealth in the twenty-first century.

In 1994, only about half of all Americans surveyed (51.8 percent) had ever heard of the term "information superhighway," and in 1996, just 14 percent of households were accessing the Internet.[34] This lack of cohesion has worried many groups, including the Computer Professionals for Social Responsibility (CPSR). This group of individuals argues that a national information infrastructure should be designed in the public interest.[35] This means that efforts should be made to prevent commercial interests from controlling a national computer network. As CPSR indicated, it doesn't take much to see a "rapid concentration of power and a potential danger in the merging of major corporations in the computer, cable, television, publishing, radio, consumer electronics, film, and other industries." Concerned that individuals be guaranteed access and that commercial interests not dominate, CPSR recommended the following:

- *Universal access.* Technology and training, and therefore information, should be affordable for all—rich, poor, urban, suburban, rural, disabled, technical and nontechnical.

- *Freedom to communicate.* People must have the right to exchange ideas and contribute to discussion. The Bill of Rights should be extended to the information highway, and people who want to exchange ideas should not have to fear censorship.

- *Vital civic sectors.* All individuals should have the ability to participate (not merely vote) in government by designing legislation and formulating policy. People need timely access to government information to actively take part in governmental decision making at national, state, and local levels.

- *Diverse and competitive marketplace.* An open and competitive marketplace among ideas, products, and information providers should be protected.

- *Equitable workplaces.* Computers change the workplace. For workers who have to upgrade their skills to deal with computers or who must find different work because computers replace some tasks, training and guidance should be available.

- *Privacy.* Individuals' privacy must be protected. This is an ever-increasing problem when vast amounts of personal information are gathered and transferred via computer networks. The government should discourage the collection of personal data and wire surveillance, even under the auspices of law enforcement and national security.

- *Democratic policy making.* Regular users, not just telecommunications experts, should be involved with the design and policies of this new information infrastructure. When people who are expected to use the final product are involved with all developmental stages, an acceptable standard is likely to be found more quickly and adopted sooner than when there is no input from the real users.

339

- *Functional integrity.* The national system must be reliable under all conditions. Some day, perhaps very soon, people and businesses will rely on the information highway as the primary conduit for many aspects of life, such as economic transactions and long-distance medicine. The system cannot become antiquated nor experience national failure because of heavy workloads, natural disasters, or other national economic priorities. Breakdowns must be localized and remedied in minutes or hours. To simply say that "the computer is down" won't be acceptable when a whole nation depends on one conduit. Consumer response to AOL's difficulties in serving clients during the early months of 1997 documented consumers' unwillingness to deal with breakdowns.

Fulfilling the CPSR recommendations depends on the availability of technology to people. The image of the information highway running through a fiber optic cable may have to change to one of an information skyway with information bouncing off satellites. Although the residents of highly developed countries such as the United states, Germany, and Japan have access to the fiber optic information highway, most people in the world are unlikely to have a cable running to their homes. The expense is too high. But a plan to use satellites for Internet distribution might solve the problem. In 1997, Teledesic announced plans to launch 840 satellites about the size of a small car. The project will start in the year 2000 and will take two years and $9 billion to finish. These satellites, located about 435 miles above Earth, would allow access to the Internet and other online services from any spot on Earth.

The plan is being financed by Bill Gates and Craig McCaw, a pioneer in the cellular phone business. Traditional communication

Convergence is the future, but critics are still debating whether the technology for consumers will be computer-based or television-based.

Keyconcept

Convergence of Electronic Technology: Some scholars argue that convergence of technology—the blending of television and computers, for example—only creates a new way of distributing information. Others believe that convergence of technology actually creates new styles and modes of information, which has been transformed based on the way it is delivered.

satellites, which orbit 22,300 miles above Earth, are difficult to use for interactive media. It takes about a half second for an electronic message to go from the Earth to these high orbiting satellites. Although this may seem fast, to a packet of Internet information it is more than a lifetime. Information sent on the Internet must be checked to see if it got where it was going. If this checkback process is delayed for even half a second, the information will not get to its destination. The time it takes for an electronic message to go 430 miles does not create this delay, and these satellites can be used to access the Internet. Locating the satellites at 430 miles means more are needed to connect the globe than are needed when they are 22,300 miles up, but the shorter distance also requires less money to launch the satellites. The work of Teledesic indicates the reality of a worldwide web may have to take place in the sky and not under the ground.[36]

New communication technologies and regulation

In some ways, **cyberspace** resembles the Old West—law and order haven't arrived. Although online services have some standards,

cyberspace: The concept of psychological space behind the computer screen.

the Internet is policed only by the social norms of those who use it. The world of communicating and finding information using a computer is exciting partly because there are no rules and regulations telling one what to do or where to go.

The areas that are proving to be most immediately problematic include privacy, copyright, and access to information. Increasingly, censorship has become an issue. The Telecommunications Act of 1996 outlawed transmission of sexually explicit and other indecent materials to minors under eighteen over computer networks. This provision of the act was challenged immediately in court on the grounds that it violated free expression. In June 1997, the Supreme Court ruled that the Computer Decency Act was unconstitutional.

Computer communication has many international implications. The Internet is international; users can reach across borders that are guarded with barricades and guns. But not all countries are happy with a free flow of information. The government of China, for example—in an attempt to control pornography, political expression, and profits—would like to provide citizens with unlimited access to each other but only to "screened links" with the outside. China has discouraged investment by technology companies from outside the country and hopes to funnel profits through its state-run news agency.[37]

PRIVACY ISSUES Almost every move a person makes can be tracked electronically. Databases record when and where you change addresses, subscribe to magazines, and apply for credit cards. The 1994 movie *The Pelican Brief* was realistic in showing that the FBI and others could identify the exact location of the young lawyer as she used credit cards for shopping, hotel accommodations, and ATM machines. The more recent film *The Net* revealed an even darker side of the computer links to a person's identity. Sandra Bullock was consistently—and intentionally—identified as someone other than herself. Her own identity seemed nearly lost.

Available databases that are used for finding a person's location or biographical information include Post Office Change of Address, People Finder, Address Search, Phonefile, and Credit Abstracts. Information in these databases includes a person's name, age, date of birth, Social Security number, spouse's name, current and previous address, phone number (sometimes even an unlisted one), all residents at that particular address, and neighbors and their phone numbers and addresses.

Some of these databases are put together from information found in standard directories, product response cards, and magazine subscription cards. Herein lies an ethical and perhaps legal issue. Private citizens filling out magazine subscription cards and the like assume that they are providing information to one company for the single purpose of receiving a magazine subscription. However, this information is often sold to other companies that use the information to create databases for anyone to buy. The information is not being used for what the individual originally intended, and at least two companies are making a profit from information that a person has provided freely.

COPYRIGHT Privacy and copyright issues arise in obtaining information from bulletin boards and electronic mail. Many mass media professionals scan electronic networks looking for story ideas, information, and sources to quote. They believe that because these electronic postings are public, they can be repeated and used in printed publications or broadcast (and cable) products. However, they may be sued if the source was not asked permission to be quoted and felt that the published story invaded his or her privacy. Web-based documents are easily downloaded and pasted to other documents. The technological ease of copying material, however, does not ensure that such copying is legal. Furthermore, e-mail messages, like letters, belong to the originator, not to the receiver. They are not considered part of the public domain. Although media organizations may win specific judgments, they often lose in money spent on court costs and in time, often months or years, spent in court.[38]

Summary

- Computers are used in every application by traditional mass media organizations. They are also a medium in their own right and are used directly by consumers.

- Convergence—or the combining of more than one communication form into a single distribution process—is increasing rapidly.

- The computer began as an attempt to create calculating machines, then evolved as scientists sought efficient means to organize, retrieve, and process information.

- Although the computer industry is highly diversified and competitive, giants such as IBM and Microsoft have held leading roles and dominated different portions of the industry at different times.

- Computer research and networking have been heavily funded by the U.S. government because of the implications in defense and strategic applications.

- The development of the silicon chip in 1959 made it possible for the computer to shrink in size.

- The modem is the connection to the computerized world, the device that makes possible the concept of an information highway.

- The Internet is a series of computers, each networked to others, that provide the fundamental basis of an information highway.

- CD-ROM technology allows for massive storage of information on small disks, easy access, and periodic updating.

- Commercial online services provide information, usually at a cost, to high-end business users as well as to consumers.

- Bulletin board systems allow users to talk to each other and access information about specialized interests.

- The Internet can be accessed with a variety of navigational tools, including World Wide Web browsers such as Excite and Alta Vista.

- Computers are increasingly used by newspaper and magazine companies to deliver text.

- Audiotext provides prerecorded information to a user. It can be used for advertising, entertainment, or information.

- Most news services and syndicates are now computer based.

- An information age society poses many issues. One is whether people with access to equipment and an understanding of technology will become information-rich, as others become information-poor.

- The information highway could be a speedy interstate full of advertisements and entertainment, or it could become a useful tool in encouraging participation in a democratic society. Who pays for the highway and who travels it will be critical issues.

- Regulation in a computer-age society is like law in the Wild West—almost nonexistent. Privacy and copyright issues are critical. In addition, citizens must guard the rights to freedom of expression through online conversations.

342

Navigating the Web

Computers and the information highway

Obviously, people who use the Web are interested in computers, technology, and the potential of the information highway. On Web sites you can find information on the history of computers, new technologies, and the business of technology.

| Chronology of Events in the History of Microcomputers | http://www.islandnet.com/~kpolsson/comphist.htm |

This site has a list of important dates in the advancement of microcomputers from 1947 onward. Several of the dates also have links to information about that date or the people associated with it.

| Special Interest Group on CD Application and Technology | http://www.sigcat.org |

This group provides a range of information about CD technology. The site includes a bibliography, an archive of press releases, and publications on the topic.

| Internet World Online | http://www.internetworld.com |

This Webzine covers a variety of Internet topics in columns and articles. *Internet World* is also available in print.

| ZDNet | http://home.zdnet.com/home/filters/main.html |

This Webzine comes from Ziff-Davis, the largest publisher of computer magazines. It covers news from computers and the world of online businesses.

| Media Central Interactive | http://www.mediacentral.com/index/Imonitor |

This site is maintained by Cowles Media. It provides in-depth articles about online media and daily short stories about events in a variety of media.

Questions for review

1. What was IBM's role in the development of computer technology?
2. Why is Microsoft a significant player in computer delivery of mass media?
3. What is an operating system?
4. Describe several online services that target professional users.
5. What are the most common consumer uses of online services?
6. How does the World Wide Web compete with commercial online services?

▧ Issues to think about

1. What are some obstacles that will have to be overcome in building an information highway?

2. Describe ethical issues that emerge from virtual reality technology.

3. How is the concept of a knowledge gap related to media and technology?

4. What is the role of the mass media professional in the development of the World Wide Web?

5. If you were designing a newspaper for the future, how would you incorporate new technology?

▧ Suggested readings

Carey, John, "The Interactive Television Puzzle." Freedom Forum Media Studies Center Paper, 1994.

Diamond, Edwin and Stephen Bates, "The Ancient History of the Internet," *American Heritage* (October 1995):34–46.

Gomery, Douglas, "Centralized or Decentralized—Which World Will the Internet Bring?" *The American Enterprise* (March/April 1996), p. 48–52.

Hernandez, Debra Gersh, "Mayhem Online: Congress considers Hate and Violence in Cyberspace," *Editor & Publisher* (June 24, 1995): pp. 34–36.

"Internet, Free Speech and Industry Self-Regulation." Report by The Information Technology Association of America Task Force on Internet Use, November 1995. This report can be obtained from the association at 1616 North Fort Myer Drive, Suite 1300, Arlington, VA 22209. The association's web site is *http://www.itaa.org.*

Negroponte, Nicholas, *Being Digital* (New York: Alfred A. Knopf, 1995).

Powell, Adam Clayton III, "Maintaining Editorial Control in a Digital Newsroom." Freedom Forum Media Studies Center Paper.

Wulf, William A. "Warning: Information Technology Will Transform the University," *Issues in Science and Technology* (Summer 1995).

Regulation

In 1931 the Supreme Court ruled, in *Near* v. *The State of Minnesota*, that Howard Guilford and J. M. Near could continue to publish the *Saturday Press*, a smear sheet that viciously attacked Jews and Catholics.

The *Press* had also charged that gangsters controlled Minneapolis gambling, bootlegging, and racketeering while law enforcement officials turned the other way. Near and Guilford were charged under a Minnesota statute that prohibited anyone from publishing a "malicious, scandalous and defamatory newspaper, magazine or other periodical." The newspaper's language was so scurrilous that hardly anyone wanted to defend the editors' right to publish. They were told to eliminate some of the content found objectionable under a Minnesota law before continuing to publish.

When Near and Guilford's appeal reached the Supreme Court, Chief Justice Charles Evans Hughes ruled that prior restraint might occur in some instances in which obscenity, secret movement of military troops, or incitements

Media content is regulated throughout the world. In the United States, regulators have a particularly difficult time dealing with pornography. The story of Larry Flynt, publisher of Hustler *magazine, as depicted by movie director De Milos Forman in* The People versus Larry Flynt *raised interesting points about where art, the media, and law converge.*

345

to overthrow the government were at question. However, he balanced the right to restrain against the right to publish. Hughes argued that restraining criticism of government would violate the tenets of the free society the founders of the United States had struggled to create. Even if no one wanted to support Near and Guilford for publishing their scandalous sheet, Hughes declared they had a right to continue.

"Freedom" is perhaps the most abused word in the world. No matter what country you visit, its government claims that the citizens are free. Americans are fond of proclaiming that their country is "the land of the free," but freedom is never absolute in any society. Whenever people interact, conflict arises over who can do what. Ethics and social norms provide standards for behavior, but they have no formal power of enforcement. Some entity must balance the rights of individuals and those of governments and corporations. Ultimately, governments determine what behaviors will be punished as illegal and the form of punishment that will be applied. Therefore regulation—the process of enforcing rules that mediate societal conflicts—occurs in all societies.

Because of the media's potential for changing society, media content and the behavior of people who work in the media are regulated throughout the world. A person in the United States cannot legally start broadcasting without permission from the federal government. A Polish journalist can be sentenced to up to eight years in jail for slandering the government of Poland. The degree of speech and press freedoms varies from country to country, but in no country is it absolute.

The issues surrounding regulation are always complex because they involve the rights of society versus the rights of the individuals and they must cope with changing technologies and changing economic factors. Some of the issues addressed in this chapter include the following:

■ As new technologies enter the media world and channels of information proliferate, what justifications will be used to regulate new technologies? Will these be legitimate bases for regulation, or will they merely serve political or economic purposes?

■ As computer delivery of information increases throughout the world, how will governments regulate this activity, which freely crosses national boundaries?

■ How does regulation achieve a balance between the right of free expression and societal concerns about media depictions of violence and sexual activity?

■ Are journalists' rights to access compatible with individuals' right to privacy and freedom from libel?

Regulation in American life

Although few people dispute a government's right to regulate, nearly everyone disagrees about what the regulation should cover. The founders of the United States, fearing that government officials would exercise arbitrary power, created the Bill of Rights to protect citizens from government encroachment on private affairs and to promote the concept that government is by consent of its citizens.

Free speech and your life

Freedom and Restraint

As you read this chapter, think about how free speech has been restrained at different times in society. Can you think of some of your own examples that might enrich a discussion of how free speech is important to your life as a student? As you think about your own examples of when freedom of speech has been restricted, would you say they fit into the five categories discussed below? Or do they fit other categories?

REASONS GOVERNMENTS GIVE FOR REGULATION	EXAMPLES OF RESTRICTIONS
Economic	
Product or company has negative impact on society as a whole	
Product or company has negative impact on individuals that outweighs benefits to society	
To preserve security during war	
Government regulating to preserve its own power	
Other categories	

Reasons for regulation

In the United States, federal, state, and local governments usually regulate people and organizations for five reasons.

1. *Government regulates when people or organizations interfere with the workings of the economic market system.* The United States has a **market economy** based on two assumptions: that competition works best for society and that unfair business practices must not be allowed to reduce competition. Competition has been favored because it is believed to force companies to respond to the demands of the public and keep prices low. Theoretically, the company that produces the best product at the lowest price will continue in business.

Even though competition does not always provide immediate benefits to media consumers, the federal government assumes that in most situations, competition is better than monopoly. Such was the assumption when the courts broke the AT&T monopoly in 1984. AT&T, a giant telephone monopoly, was stifling competition for long-distance services and making monopoly profits through high prices. The largest company in the world at the time, AT&T was forced to split its local telephone services among seven independent regional operating systems. It continued to provide long-

Keyconcept

The Regulatory Concept: Regulation is designed to maintain a balance between the needs and rights of the society as a whole and the needs and rights of individuals. Therefore government may legitimately regulate mass media to ensure that their behavior does not have an impact on society that outweigh their contributions to society.

market economy: An economy in which the interaction of supply and demand determines the prices of goods and services and the levels of production. In a nonmarket economy, government determines prices and production.

347

> Deregulation has expanded the long-distance telephone service market and opened up the possibility for telephone companies to provide news and entertainment content as well as the technology to carry the message.

distance service, competing against providers such as MCI and Sprint, and could enter into unregulated enterprises.

Now long-distance telephone companies compete to set up worldwide communication systems for a variety of businesses. Several of the regional Bell operating systems are exploring mergers with cable companies and moving into the generation, as well as the distribution, of information. The competition has led to experimentation and development of new technology and services in the **telecommunications industry.** As a result of the 1996 Telecommunications Act, AT&T now competes in a variety of ways with the regional Bell operating systems it once owned.

Key concept

1996 Telecommunications Act: This landmark piece of legislation represented the first major revamping of federal telecommunications legislation since the Federal Communications Act was passed in 1934. It acknowledged the information revolution by allowing telephone companies not only to provide transmission equipment, but to produce content as well.

2. *Government regulates when the use of a product or an industry or company's behavior has a negative impact on society as a whole.* The ongoing struggle between the tobacco industry and the government illustrates this point. By the early 1950s the U.S. medical community was convinced that cigarettes posed serious health hazards for the public. The tobacco industry responded with a public relations and advertising effort that clouded the issue and sought to minimize health problems related to smoking.[1] In 1964 the U.S. Surgeon General pronounced publicly that cigarettes cause cancer. Seven years later, Congress passed legislation prohibiting radio and television from carrying cigarette advertising. The federal and state governments have taken several regulatory steps to control smoking, including banning and controlling smoking in public places.

The ability of tobacco companies to influence policy declined in 1997 when cigarette manufacturer, Liggett Group, released about 175 boxes of internal documents to state prosecutors as part of a law suit settlement. Forty states have sued the tobacco industry to recoup the costs of health care for victims who developed cancer from smoking. Liggett released the documents, which were used in other law suits, and admitted that company executives knew cigarettes were habit forming and caused cancer, something tobacco companies had denied for decades. In return, Liggett will set aside part of its profits to pay claims related to smoking Liggett cigarettes.

Some lawmakers across the United States immediately asked that cigarettes be regulated. This effort will not be easy as law suits against tobacco companies continue in state courts and the highly profitable industry continues its history of political donations. The fact that cigarettes have not been banned entirely illustrates the government's reluctance to enact such a controversial law.

3. *Government regulates when a product or behavior has a negative impact on individuals that outweighs its contribution to society as a whole.*

telecommunications industry: Organizations that are involved in electronic media such as broadcast television, cable, radio, telephone or the transmission of information over wires and the use of satellites.

Laws concerning privacy, libel, and slander are examples of this form of regulation. In 1942, *Time* published a story about Dorothy Barber, a woman who ate constantly but still lost weight, calling her a "starving glutton." She sued, and the courts ruled for Mrs. Barber, arguing that the hospital was one place you should be able to go for privacy. Her disease, rather unusual at the time, is now more widely known as anorexia nervosa.

A journalist cannot enter a person's house carrying secret cameras and microphones. When a *Life* magazine journalist and a photographer did this for an article called "Crackdown in Quackery," *Life* was sued for invasion of privacy and lost. The courts ruled that the journalists' entry into a person's home was an illegal intrusion into A. A. Dietemann's privacy, even though he was practicing a questionable brand of medicine in his home.[2]

4. *Government regulates the flow of information during times of war.* The justification is that unrestricted publication and broadcasting could endanger the lives of the country's troops and could affect the outcome of battles and wars. **Censorship** during war is not mentioned in the Constitution, but courts have supported the government's right to censor ever since the Civil War. During that war the U.S. government passed conspiracy laws giving it the power to suppress news and prosecute journalists. Similar legislation was enacted during World Wars I and II, and a combination of government restriction and journalistic cooperation characterized reporting during those periods.

The exact relationship between the press and government during war remains unsettled. Because the Vietnam conflict was never declared a war, formal censorship was never invoked. Since that time the federal government has tried to regulate the media in war informally through the creation of **press pools** and by limiting access to battle areas.

5. *Government seeks to preserve its own security and power.* Government officials sometimes try to regulate information for illegitimate reasons, to avoid political embarrassment, or to hide illegal activities. From the beginning of the United States, officials have tried to control information and to protect against **sedition** in order to preserve political power. The Alien and Sedition Acts, passed in 1798 by a Federalist-controlled Congress, allowed the government to imprison and fine its critics. Representative Matthew Lyon was imprisoned for four months and fined $1,000 for suggesting that President John Adams's administration had "an unbounded thirst for ridiculous pomp, foolish adulation, and selfish avarice."[3] These acts remained in effect for only two years. During the early 1970s, President Richard Nixon used government secrecy acts to hide information that would have exposed criminal activity in the White House. His effort failed, and in 1974 he became the only U.S. president to resign his office.

Most citizens and journalists would argue that using government laws to avoid embarrassment is an improper use of political power. Two important events, widely separated in time—the overturn of the Alien and Sedition Acts and the resignation of President Nixon—came about primarily because most citizens, journalists, and our nation's courts agreed that government officials' use of laws to avoid embarrassment is a misuse of political power.

Sometimes reporters have to look beneath the official reason to determine whether government is acting in a legitimate way or is just trying to cover up its actions. The Defense Department said that it regulated media access to the Gulf War in 1991 to protect troops and journalists. However, the government seemed just as concerned about criticism from both inside and outside the military as it did about protecting the troops.[4]

censorship: Restricting access to information, deleting information from a story, or refusing to let a correspondent mail, broadcast, or otherwise transmit a story.

press pool: A small group of reporters who are selected to gather information and pass it on to the larger group of press people. Used when the number of reporters gathering in one spot is problematic.

sedition: Inciting people to rebel against their government.

The Pentagon Papers

The so-called Pentagon Papers contained a summary of how the United States got involved in the Vietnam War. The papers were commissioned by Robert McNamara, who served as Secretary of Defense for President Lyndon B. Johnson during the period when the United States became deeply involved in Vietnam. The papers were classified top secret, which indicated that their release would endanger national security.

In the spring of 1971, former Pentagon employee Daniel Ellsberg passed copies of the Pentagon Papers to the *New York Times.* Ellsberg had become convinced that the United States was wrong to be involved in the Vietnam conflict.

Ellsberg took the Pentagon Papers without permission, and the *Times's* decision to publish stolen classified documents was not easy. Business managers at the paper and lawyers argued against publishing. They said that the federal government would take legal action against the *Times.* Journalists argued that publishing would not hurt national interest, and their argument prevailed. The first installment of the papers was published on June 13, 1971. The lawyers were right; the White House immediately got an injunction to stop publication by the *Times.*

In the meantime the *Washington Post* had also obtained a copy of the Pentagon Papers from Ellsberg. The *Post's* managers and lawyers debated whether they should publish once the *Times* had been enjoined. The argument against publishing was that it would be seen as a violation of the injunction. Oth-ers argued that not publishing would be seen as buckling under to the government and would leave the *Times* unsupported.

On June 18, 1971, the *Post* published its first report on the papers. It too was restrained from further publication. By this time, several newspapers had copies of the papers. After the *Post* was enjoined, the *Boston Globe* published the papers and was restrained. Eventually, the *Chicago Sun-Times,* the *Los Angeles Times,* the Knight Newspapers service, the *St. Louis Post-Dispatch,* and the *Christian Science Monitor* all published articles about the Pentagon Papers before the Supreme Court ruled on the case.

Finally, on Saturday, June 26, 1971, the Supreme Court heard arguments in the case. The Court extended its session, which was supposed to end on June 28. Shortly after 2:00 P.M. on June 30, the Supreme Court announced its 6–3 ruling in support of the *Times* and the *Post.* The Court recognized the need for secrecy in government but found that the government had not made a case that publication of the Pentagon Papers was a threat to national security. Justice Potter Stewart summarized the problem created by the top secret classification of the Pentagon Papers when he said, "For when everything is classified, then nothing is classified, and the system becomes one to be disregarded by the cynical and careless and to be manipulated by those intent on self-protection or self-promotion."

SOURCES: David Halberstam, *The Powers That Be* (New York: Alfred A. Knopf, 1975) pp. 565–583; James McCartney, "What Should Be Secret," *Columbia Journalism Review* (September–October 1971): pp. 40–44; Jules Witcover, "Two Weeks That Shook the Press," *Columbia Journalism Review,* (September–October 1971): pp. 7–15.

Two historic clashes between the press and government marked the early 1970s. The first was the battle between the press and the government over the Pentagon Papers, historical documents chronicling the Vietnam conflict. The second was the Watergate affair. Both involved an attempt by government to withhold information because it would be personally—or governmentally—embarrassing. In the case of the Pentagon Papers the government tried to justify the secrecy by citing national security concerns.

In the Pentagon Papers case, major newspapers published government documents that they believed had been misclassified, and they were vindicated by the Supreme Court. The government's ability to hide information legally had not been destroyed, but it had been significantly damaged. At the same time the *Washington Post* became a national newspaper with the willingness to clash with powerful government officials. David Halberstam, in his book *The Powers That Be,* wrote that without the decision to publish the Pentagon Papers, the *Washington Post* would never have published the subsequent Watergate stories. History would not have been the same.

The term "Watergate" applies to a wide range of illegal and unethical behavior undertaken by the Nixon White House during his re-election campaign in 1972. These activities included disruption of Democratic campaign activities, burglary, and taking illegal campaign contributions. Nixon and his advisers got even further into trouble when they tried to cover-up all the activities as the Senate held hearings. Nixon resigned when it became obvious that he would have to endure impeachment proceedings if he remained president.

The initial story of a break-in at Democratic headquarters led to a series of investigations by *Washington Post* reporters Bob Woodward and Carl Bernstein. These reporters won the Pulitzer Prize for their stories that revealed the corruption and illegal activity within the Nixon administration.

■ Regulation of media and the First Amendment

Not all media are equal when it comes to government regulation. Print media initially gained their freedom through the First Amendment to the Constitution because the founders believed that a self-governing populace needed a free flow of information. Because the press—as print media—is specifically mentioned in the Constitution, it enjoys a higher level of protection than broadcast and cable media do. The limited number of channels available to broadcast and cable technology and public fear of their power to influence elections and social values have created an atmosphere in which regulation has been thought necessary and beneficial.

First Amendment press guarantees are not unique. Japan, for example, has a constitution that guarantees freedom of the press and speech. Great Britain also has protection for its press, although the protection is more limited than that found in the United States. One difference in the United States is that the balance of power among the executive, legislative, and judicial branches prohibits one branch of government from creating regulation without review. Each branch of government provides a check on the other that limits—although it doesn't prevent—political abuse.

Keyconcept

Freedom of Expression: Freedom of expression is not granted to the press or to broadcasters alone. Rather, it is a fundamental right based on society's need for basic civil liberties. The authors of the Bill of Rights, believing that governments should be prohibited from exercising arbitrary power, granted to individuals rights such as freedom to speak and write, freedom to bear arms, and freedom from unreasonable police search and seizure.

The almost mythical stature the First Amendment has gained over the years hides the controversy that originally surrounded it and the other nine amendments in the Bill of Rights. During the 1787 Constitutional Convention the Federalists argued against inclusion of a bill of rights. They said that it was unnecessary because any powers not specifically given the central government would be left to the states. The Anti-Federalists, who were suspicious of a strong central government, said that the absence of specific protections for individuals' rights would allow the federal government to supersede such rights granted at the state level.

Some states were reluctant to ratify the Constitution without a bill of rights. To secure ratification, the Federalists agreed that such a bill would be added as amendments. This compromise allowed ratification of the Constitution by the original thirteen states. The Bill of Rights was drafted by the first U.S. Congress and ratified by the states in 1791.

New Technology and Regulation

Technology, in the form of computers and fiber-optic cable, poses new questions about freedom of expression and First Amendment rights. New technology that allows people throughout the world to exchange ideas and opinions seems very much consistent with the concept of an open marketplace of ideas. However, such a system has little built-in accountability for abuse, and because of the worldwide ability to communicate, laws of different countries have to be taken into account.

Companies that use the international information highway face a hodgepodge of regulations around the world. Company managers face problems keeping up with varying regulations and in adjusting to those regulations. For example, regulation specifies that 40 percent of songs broadcast in France must be in French. If a fiber-optic cable system distributes music to England and France, does this constitute a broadcast? If so, must the cable system operate under the laws of all the varying countries?

A second problem will develop from the regulator's perspective. Compared to mass media, the new technology is difficult to physically regulate. Traditional mass media content is created and distributed from a few locations. Newspapers can be confiscated, and broadcasts can be jammed. With computers, satellites, and fiber-optic cable the same content can be created and distributed from hundreds of locations. During the Gulf War, computer users in Turkey got information about the war from across the world. During and after the student uprisings in China in 1989, fax machines and computers were used to get information into and out of China.

The development of computer information technology, which easily crosses borders, brings content regulation into the realm of international negotiation. At the same time governments are finding it more difficult to control content.

SOURCE: Bob Ritter, "New Technology & the First Amendment: An Overview of Legal Issues on the Electronic Frontier." Unpublished paper, Marquette University, April 4, 1994.

For almost 200 years scholars have debated the exact reasoning for writing the First Amendment. However, one component is clear. The founders intended to preserve a marketplace of ideas, particularly in the realm of politics. Many who helped to write the Constitution believed that distasteful and unpopular content must be protected so that democracy did not become mob rule. Today, as then, the press is an essential contributor to public debate. A valid fear is that censorship of very unpopular content can become a precedent for censoring a wide variety of material. The slow erosion of protection could result in a tyranny of majority opinion that would damage the vitality of the entire democratic system.

Types of media regulation

Governments in the United States exercise three types of regulation over mass media:

1. Governments regulate the economic behavior of media companies in the consumer and advertising markets. For example, with a few exceptions it is illegal for a newspaper company to own a television station in the same city.

2. Governments regulate certain internal business activities of media companies. For example, a media company must comply with federal laws that prohibit racial and gender discrimination in hiring.

3. Despite the existence of the First Amendment, governments regulate some content and information. For example, a company cannot broadcast a deceptive advertisement that might harm consumers.

These forms of regulation can take place at several levels of government. Local governments pass ordinances about where newspapers may put newsracks. States pass libel laws. The federal government has created the Federal Communication Commission (FCC), which regulates telecommunications, and the Federal Trade Commission, which regulates advertisements. The higher the level, the more power government has to affect content.

Keyconcept

Balancing Theory: The Supreme Court, as well as the Congress, adheres to a balancing theory, which expresses the need for balance between individual rights and the rights of society as a whole. This balance is essential to a democratic government.

Media regulation evolved through a series of legislative actions and court interpretations that are sometimes inconsistent and confusing. A valid libel defense in one state may not be a valid defense in another. One court decision may set a precedent that conflicts with another. The inconsistencies reflect the nature of a democratic style of government and the difficulties of interpreting laws on the basis of a Constitution written 200 years ago. Table 12.1 outlines the sources of regulatory laws, which range from the Federal Constitution to laws created by judicial interpretation. The ability of media organizations to monopolize a market through more efficient technology did not exist when the Constitution was ratified. Nevertheless, one common thread runs throughout all of the ad hoc public policy: Regulation attempts to balance the information needs of society with the rights of media companies and individual citizens.

TABLE 12.1 Sources of Laws

TABLE 12.1

These are listed in order of power. For example, the U.S. Constitution takes precedence over federal statutory laws. Federal statutory laws can be challenged as being unconstitutional.

- *Federal Constitution:* laws established by articles and amendments to the U.S. Constitution.

- *Federal Statutory:* laws passed by the federal legislative body, the U.S. Senate and House of Representatives.

- *Federal Administrative:* laws established by federal administrative bodies that were set up by statute, such as FCC and FTC.

- *State Constitution:* laws established by the various state constitutions.

- *State Statutory:* laws passed by various state legislatures.

- *State Administrative:* laws established by various state administrative bodies that were set up by statute.

- *State Common Law:* laws created by judicial interpretation; few apply to communication law.

Source: Professor Todd Simon, Kansas State University.

■ Economic regulation

Media economics concerns the way media companies produce and sell products in the information and advertising markets. Two types of regulation affect these markets most often: antitrust laws and direct regulation by government agencies, such as the FCC and FTC.

ANTITRUST LAW Antitrust laws are intended to promote competition in markets and to prevent or break up monopolies. They outlaw several practices aimed at closing a company's competitors, including selling a product for less than it costs to make and joining with another company to drive others out of business.

The Sherman Act, passed in 1890, and the Clayton Act, passed in 1914, are the core of antitrust law. Congress passed them in part as a reaction to the "robber barons" of the late nineteenth century. Industrialists J. P. Morgan, Cornelius Vanderbilt, and John D. Rockefeller, among others, used unfair business practices to monopolize markets. As monopolists, they could increase prices and make considerably more profit than they would have if competition had existed.

The underlying assumption of antitrust laws is that competition is good for consumers. Experience shows that competition can reduce prices and allow consumers to influence products through their purchasing choices. This holds for news media competition at a local level. Competition among newspapers and among television news departments lowers subscription prices (for newspapers), increases news department budgets, increases amounts of information, and causes journalists to work harder to get news quickly and accurately. These advantages have a cost. Competition also can result in an emphasis on sensationalism and in unethical behavior to get stories.[5]

Keyconcept

Competition and Media Consumers: Government regulation of economic affairs of media companies is based on the assumption that competition is good, providing a better product to consumers for less cost. Therefore, government regulates media through antitrust law to ensure competition.

The impact of competition in the advertising market is more straightforward. Theoretically, competition keeps advertising prices low and improves service from the media companies. However, competition can increase advertisers' influence over editorial content. For example, because of the high degree of competition in the field, magazines are far more likely to allow advertisers

A series of government actions have challenged the giant Microsoft Company's dominance of the operating systems and software market. The government's role in ensuring a competitive environment is constantly under review as new court cases require pathbreaking decisions.

to influence content than other media might be. If a company does not like what a magazine has written about its product, the company can ask for a change in that content and threaten to take its advertising elsewhere. Research shows that publications with extensive alcohol advertising also contain favorable editorial content toward drinking.[6] In another study, five large-circulation women's magazines with high amounts of cigarette advertising between 1983 and 1987 carried no feature-length articles about the hazards of smoking.[7]

NEWSPAPERS AND ANTITRUST LAWS Despite the early application of antitrust laws to broadcasting and film, some newspapers have enjoyed exemptions from these laws. Initial application of antitrust law to newspapers did not occur until 1945, when the Supreme Court ruled that the Associated Press could not sell its services exclusively to one newspaper in a city. Two decades later, the Justice Department once more applied antitrust law and dismantled an illegal agreement called a **joint operation agreement (JOA)** between two daily newspapers in Albuquerque, New Mexico. (Seventeen other cities had similar agreements.) The Supreme Court supported the Justice Department, ruling that the agreement that allowed the two newspapers to set prices and sell advertising together violated antitrust law.

As a reaction, Congress passed the Newspaper Preservation Act (NPA) in 1970, which allowed two newspapers in the same city to combine all departments and activities except the newsrooms. Senators and Representatives who voted for the NPA said that it would preserve a second editorial voice in cities where two dailies could not survive independently. Some argued that it was the power of newspapers to influence voters that really got the NPA passed.

No matter what the reasons, the NPA preserved editorial voices in only a handful of cities. The same economic forces that have caused direct daily competition to disappear in all but a dozen cities continued to work in JOA cities. Because the NPA doesn't preserve competition in the long run, the daily that has the circulation lead has little incentive to join a JOA. Only seventeen JOA cities existed in 1997. However, as a rule, the quality of JOA newspapers has been higher than that of the average daily newspaper without direct daily competition. The NPA has helped a handful of cities to have better daily newspapers for a slightly longer time than would have happened otherwise.

DIRECT TELECOMMUNICATIONS REGULATION During the early stages of broadcasting, government gave three justifications for regulation: (1) The airwaves are a limited commodity, (2) the airwaves belong to the public, and (3) broadcasters should be responsive to the community and work in its best interest. The first justification reflected the confusion that arose as the number of radio stations grew during the 1920s. Often, two stations would broadcast on the same radio frequency, which meant that one or both could not be heard clearly. Because the stations would not cooperate, Congress decided to regulate signals. The second justification concerns the physics of broadcasting. Radio and television use electromagnetic waves that move through the air. Because the government controls the air, the signal belongs to the public. The third justification reflects the assumption that giving a broadcasting company a license to use the public airwaves means that the company owes the public various kinds of services in return.

Keyconcept

Direct Telecommunications Regulation: Since the early stages of broadcasting, government regulated broadcast in more direct ways than it did print media. Supporters of government regulation argued that the airwaves, which are limited in quantity, belong to the people, not to the broadcasters and that station owners should be responsive to the community and work in its best interest. This is often referred to as the trusteeship model or the scarcity doctrine.

joint operating agreement (JOA): An agreement that allows two newspapers in the same city to operate the business and production sides of a newspaper together in a fashion that normally would violate antitrust law.

A series of congressional acts in 1912, 1927, and 1934 reflected a compromise between the desire to safeguard the public interest and efforts by broadcasters to preserve a commercially oriented broadcasting system.

The Radio Act of 1912 was the first effort to regulate wireless communication. The Radio Act covered regulations for maritime radio behavior and required that the federal government give radio licenses on request. However, the 1912 act did not provide criteria for rejecting licenses, and as the radio industry developed commercially, stations broadcast over the same frequencies, creating chaos in the air.

In 1927, Congress recognized that radio would be more than wireless communication and passed the second radio act. The Radio Act of 1927 reflected the needs of the industry and followed four radio conferences in 1922, 1923, 1924, and 1925. This act created a five-member Federal Radio Commission and gave it the power to assign radio licenses and require records of programming and technical operations.

Congress created the Federal Communication Commission with the Federal Communications Act of 1934. The FCC was given the power to regulate both wireless and wired communications, which at the time included radio and telephone. Most of the procedures developed under the Radio Act of 1927 continued under the FCC. The 1934 act was amended and extended in a variety of ways as new technology developed, but federal communication regulations did not receive a major overhaul until 1996.

Enforcement of telecommunications regulations is the responsibility of the Federal Communication Commission (FCC), which was established by the Communications Act of 1934. This act provided for FCC control of broadcast licenses and ownership rules, as well as for regulation of some types of content.

During the 1960s, citizens began to take an active interest in television content and in access to these channels of information. In this activist period, regulation increased. For example, in *Office of Communication, United Church of Christ* v. *FCC*, citizens gained *standing,* or the ability to take part in a license hearing. In this case, citizens challenged the renewal of a license to a Jackson, Mississippi, television station because of what they believed to be racist policies. Equal time interpretations also were extended. The equal time rule states that if a broadcast station gives time to a candidate for public office, it must provide equal time for the candidate's opponents. Although this rule was designed to promote political discourse, it often results in less political discussion. Because stations are not required to give access to any candidates, they can avoid controversy by denying time to all candidates. During the 1970s, guarantees of equal time to candidates for federal offices were expanded to include equal access to stations and equality in desirability of air time. For example, a station cannot sell prime time to one candidate and only early Sunday morning time to another. Other regulations required broadcasters to document ascertainment, that is, to verify that they were making an effort to understand the needs of the community and to program in response to those needs. Many women's groups took advantage of the ascertainment requirement to gain access to local programming.

Keyconcept

Ascertainment: In the 1970s the FCC extended the trusteeship concept to require television stations to find out (ascertain) the needs of the community and program to those needs. Broadcasters disliked the additional work and recordkeeping, but the regulatory requirement for ascertainment gave women and minorities a way of demanding that broadcasters recognize that many groups existed in each media market.

In the 1980s, technology allowed fifty or more radio stations and a dozen or more television stations in large markets to broadcast without any signal overlap. This improvement in technology, combined with the rapid rise in cable television, caused critics to question whether scarcity of channels was an issue. The political climate also changed. The Republican administrations of Presidents Ronald Reagan and George Bush had a more conservative approach toward federal government policy than previous administrations had had. The FCC reduced its regulation of broadcasting in ways

Cable companies' ability to provide more than 100 channels to a viewer challenges the old notion of broadcasting as a scarce resource, the very principle upon which broadcast regulation was founded.

that reflected the Reagan and Bush administrations' aim to limit government activities in economic markets.

The broadcast industry changed drastically as a result of deregulation. By 1993, companies no longer had to carry public affairs programs; a station's license did not have to be renewed as often as before; a company could own more radio and television stations; and stations no longer had to observe the *fairness doctrine,* a collection of rules that required stations to air opposing viewpoints concerning controversial issues. However, Congress retained the *equal time rule,* which affects political elections.

Key concept

Fairness Doctrine: The collection of FCC rules that was first passed in the 1940s required broadcast stations to air competing views on controversial issues, though earlier regulations had prohibited such debate. The FCC no longer enforces the rules, and some critics claim that the result has been a watering down of public debate.

The law that governs direct telecommunication underwent its first complete revision in sixty-two years with the 1996 Telecommunications Act. The package of regulations that govern broadcast, cable, and telephone companies ended several years of congressional debate and altered the relationships among the various types of media.

The act removed barriers that prohibited cable and telephone companies from competing against each other. Now telephone and cable companies can provide entertainment, information, and telephone service. In addition, the Telecommunications Act allows local Bell telephone companies to provide long-distance service if the local companies have competition for telephone service and the FCC decides that such entry serves the community's interests.

Price regulation for cable ended immediately for small systems, affecting about 20 percent of cable subscribers. Price regulation for all other systems will end by 1999, or earlier if the cable companies have competition.

Ownership regulation changed as well. The number of radio and television stations a company can own nationally is no longer regulated. However, a single company's television stations cannot reach more than 35 percent of all households in the country. Radio stations have no household limit. At a local level, companies could own only one television station, but in 1997 the FCC was reviewing this rule. In radio a company could own multiple stations in a market, but the number varied with market's size. In markets with forty-five commercial stations a company could own up to eight stations but no more than five of a particular type (AM or FM). In the smallest markets, those with fourteen or fewer stations, a company could own five stations but no more than three of a particular type.

Proponents claim that the act will increase competition and lower prices. Opponents argue that it will increase prices because competition does not yet exist in many markets. The long-term impact will depend on how media companies, courts, and media consumers react to and use the new law.

Business organizations reacted immediately to the 1996 Telecommunications Act. The removal of ownership limits on radio set off a buying spree among big companies. In the weeks following passage of the act, Infinity bought twelve stations for $410 million, increasing its total to forty-six.[8] In 1996, Clear Channel bought eighteen radio sta-

Regulation in our lives

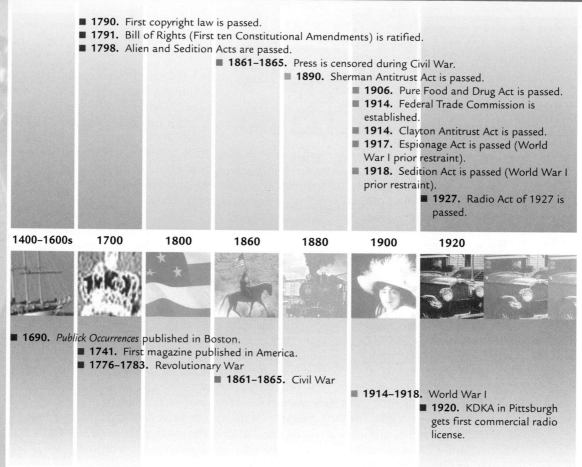

- **1790.** First copyright law is passed.
- **1791.** Bill of Rights (First ten Constitutional Amendments) is ratified.
- **1798.** Alien and Sedition Acts are passed.
- **1861–1865.** Press is censored during Civil War.
- **1890.** Sherman Antitrust Act is passed.
- **1906.** Pure Food and Drug Act is passed.
- **1914.** Federal Trade Commission is established.
- **1914.** Clayton Antitrust Act is passed.
- **1917.** Espionage Act is passed (World War I prior restraint).
- **1918.** Sedition Act is passed (World War I prior restraint).
- **1927.** Radio Act of 1927 is passed.

| 1400–1600s | 1700 | 1800 | 1860 | 1880 | 1900 | 1920 |

- **1690.** *Publick Occurrences* published in Boston.
- **1741.** First magazine published in America.
- **1776–1783.** Revolutionary War
- **1861–1865.** Civil War
- **1914–1918.** World War I
- **1920.** KDKA in Pittsburgh gets first commercial radio license.

tions from Heftel Broadcasting, bringing its total stations to 112, which is almost three times the legal limit before the 1996 Telecommunications Act.[9]

TCI Cable took advantage of rate deregulation almost immediately, increasing its rates in about half its markets; the increases reached 15 to 20 percent in some places. Not only did rates go up, but subscribers now have fewer options for complaining about the acts of cable companies that have yet to face competition. A little-publicized part of the 1996 act stops the FCC from receiving rate complaints from subscribers. The complaints must now go through the franchising authority.[10]

The 1996 Telecommunications Act did not entirely deregulate the cable industry. In 1992, Congress passed the Cable Consumer Protection and Competition Act, which required cable systems to carry the signals of local television stations. Cable operators argued that the law violated their free speech rights because they could not open these channels to other cable networks, such as C-SPAN and Comedy Central. The law helps smaller stations more than larger ones because cable would carry the larger stations anyway. They have large audiences. If the law did not exist, channels used for smaller local stations would likely be used for cable channels and possibly for pay-per-view program-

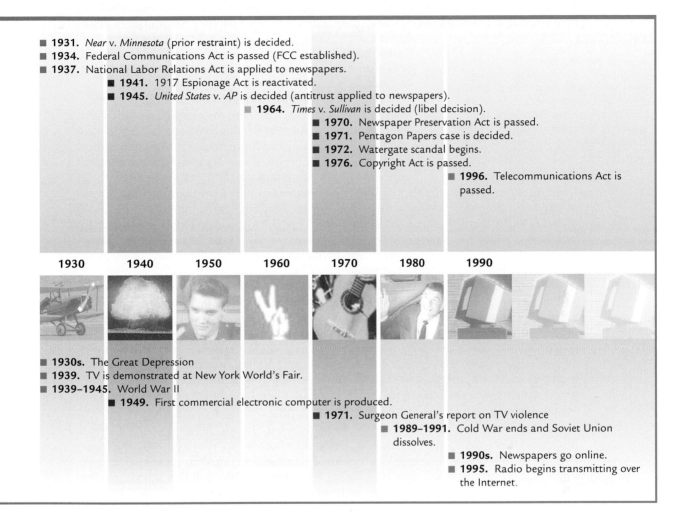

- **1931.** *Near* v. *Minnesota* (prior restraint) is decided.
- **1934.** Federal Communications Act is passed (FCC established).
- **1937.** National Labor Relations Act is applied to newspapers.
    - **1941.** 1917 Espionage Act is reactivated.
    - **1945.** *United States* v. *AP* is decided (antitrust applied to newspapers).
        - **1964.** *Times* v. *Sullivan* is decided (libel decision).
            - **1970.** Newspaper Preservation Act is passed.
            - **1971.** Pentagon Papers case is decided.
            - **1972.** Watergate scandal begins.
            - **1976.** Copyright Act is passed.
                - **1996.** Telecommunications Act is passed.

| 1930 | 1940 | 1950 | 1960 | 1970 | 1980 | 1990 |

- **1930s.** The Great Depression
- **1939.** TV is demonstrated at New York World's Fair.
- **1939–1945.** World War II
    - **1949.** First commercial electronic computer is produced.
            - **1971.** Surgeon General's report on TV violence
                - **1989–1991.** Cold War ends and Soviet Union dissolves.
                    - **1990s.** Newspapers go online.
                    - **1995.** Radio begins transmitting over the Internet.

ming. In 1997, the Supreme Court upheld the law 5 to 4 and required cable systems to continue carrying local station signals. Industry observers had predicted that the Supreme Court would not uphold the act, and further debate on the issue is likely to follow.

Business regulation

While economic regulations govern the interaction among competitors, the concerns of business regulation are less abstract. Business regulations affect the way an organization treats its employees and the impact that it might have on the environment. Business regulations fall into three categories: labor laws, discrimination laws, and other laws that affect media business practices.

LABOR LAWS Treatment of employees makes up a large portion of business regulation. Until the early years of the twentieth century, laborers usually worked six days a week for ten to twelve hours a day. Even children under the age of twelve worked under these

360

conditions. However, in the 1930s the National Labor Relations Act (NLRA) and the Fair Labor Standards Act were passed as part of President Franklin Roosevelt's New Deal package. The NLRA outlawed antilabor activities by employers such as refusing to bargain collectively with employees and firing individuals because they participate in labor unions or publish criticism of an employer. The Fair Labor Standards Act (FLSA) established the minimum wage and set limits on number of hours a person could be required to work.

Keyconcept

Business Regulation: Mass media outlets are usually owned by large corporations. As big businesses, media owners are required to adhere to labor laws, environmental regulations, and such standards as postal law. In many cases, media owners have protested having to abide by these laws, arguing that the laws infringe on their First Amendment rights.

Many media companies fought the application of labor laws to their activities. Although they argued that the First Amendment guarantee of freedom of the press should protect them from having to adhere to laws that affected other businesses, media business owners generally were more concerned with the effect on their profits than on their freedom. The NLRA became applicable to newspapers in 1937 after the Associated Press attempted to fire Morris Watson for trying to form a union. The AP argued, to no avail, that the NLRA abridged freedom of the press. The NLRA was ruled to be applicable to broadcast stations the same year. The Watson case was part of the American Newspaper Guild's efforts to unionize reporters; the Guild, begun in 1933, continues today with contracts at more than 100 newspapers.

The application of labor laws has become intertwined with the question of whether journalists are professionals. Labor laws do not cover "professional" employees, that is, employees who are involved in intellectual pursuits and have a great deal of discretion over their work. Courts have identified some positions in journalism, such as those of columnist and editorial writer, as professional occupations. However, under labor law, general reporters are not considered professionals. Therefore, media organizations are required to pay reporters for overtime; however, many smaller media companies do not keep complete records, and reporters often work long hours without adequate compensation.

DISCRIMINATION LAWS Congress passed a series of laws between 1964 and 1992 that concern discrimination against employees who are members of various groups. The most important law in this area is the Civil Rights Act of 1964. Title VII of this act makes illegal any employment discrimination based on "race, color, religion, sex or national origin." Nevertheless, the percentage of newspaper newsroom employees who are members of racial minorities increased from 4 percent in 1978 to only about 12 percent in 1996. Furthermore, 45 percent of daily newsrooms remained all white.[11] There is also resistance to promoting people of color and women to managerial positions within media organizations.[12]

The American With Disabilities Act (ADA), passed in 1990, prohibits most employers from discriminating against people on the basis of a disability. As the ADA was phased in during the early 1990s, media companies seemed much more prepared to adjust to the law than they did to the Civil Rights Act. A survey of forty-seven media companies in 1991 found that 81 percent would have no compliance problems with the ADA.[13]

OTHER BUSINESS REGULATIONS Two other types of business regulations have important implications for print industries: postal regulations and environmental regulation.

Postal regulations set the cost of mailing items through the U.S. Postal Service. Even in colonial days, Congress argued that newspapers were disseminators of information that was important to building a democracy, so newspapers have long enjoyed low postal rates. Even after the Postal Reorganization Act of 1970, which required that each type of mail be able to pay its cost, newspapers enjoyed a subsidy from the U.S. government.

The government's role in environmental protection has a significant impact on print media, which use vast forest resources and chemical technologies that create disposal and pollution problems. Recycling regulations are a constant concern for these industries.

News media get low second-class rates if they meet certain requirements about content and sorting. Third-class rates, which require senders to do even more detailed sorting, are even lower. Direct mail advertising, which enjoys third-class rates, has taken advertising revenues away from newspapers and magazines. Newspaper owners argue that books of coupons and catalogues get subsidized more than newspapers even though they do not contribute to the marketplace of ideas. The newspaper industry beat back a 1994 effort to increase second-class mailing rates by a higher percentage than other types of mail. Some daily newspapers have started competing with the postal service by using their newspaper carriers to deliver magazines and other material that would usually go through the mail. For example, some advertisers pay to have samples of products such as soap and cereal delivered with the daily paper.

A business regulation that grows in importance every year is *environmental regulation.* During the 1980s, more people became aware of the impact of paper use on the environment. On average in the United States, about 480 million copies of newspapers are printed per week, and about 400 million magazine copies are printed per month. The impact of printed media on forests and landfills is tremendous. Thousands of trees must be cut to provide paper, and all the waste paper must be disposed of. Further problems arise from the chemical nature of ink and paper processing.

As a result of the printing boom of the past thirty years, state governments have passed ordinances requiring newspapers to recycle waste and to use recycled paper. For example, Connecticut passed a law in 1989 that would require newspaper copies to be composed of 90 percent recycled paper by 1998. Whether or not recycling and other environmental laws will stand up to legal challenges remains to be determined. However, many print companies have increased their use of recycled paper and soybean-based ink to reduce the environmental impact and of their products subsequent public displeasure.

■ Content and information regulation

The direct regulation of content emerged from government efforts to balance the free flow of information and ideas against the negative effects of media products. Part of the news media's role, as H. L. Mencken said, is "to comfort the afflicted and afflict the comfortable." Content regulation tries to reduce *unjustified, unnecessary,* and *unreasonable* harm to people from media content. Such regulation can occur before or after distribution. Some types of speech, such as political speech, are more protected than others, such as commercial speech. Figure 12.1 outlines the levels of protected speech.

Keyconcept

Content Regulation: The regulation of subject matter and actual words in a broadcast or print message has been the most controversial area of regulation, because open and robust discussion is considered essential to a democratic society.

REGULATING CONTENT BEFORE DISTRIBUTION Regulation of media content before it is distributed is used to control content in times of war and for economic reasons. Such regula-

FIGURE 12.1 | Levels of Protected Communication

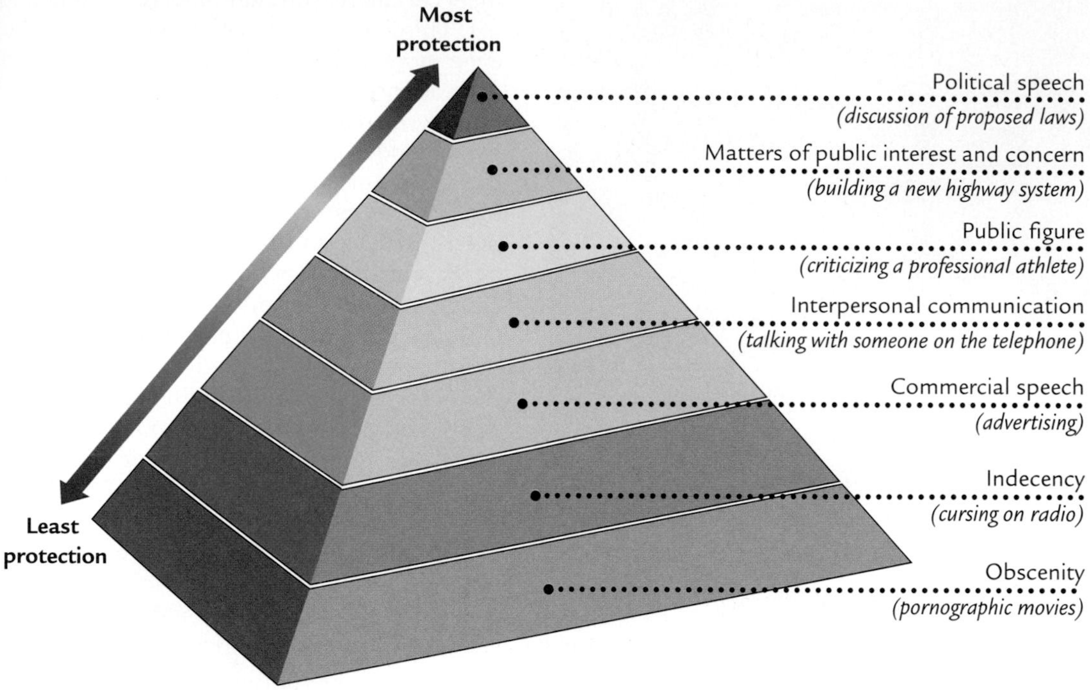

Most protection

Political speech
(discussion of proposed laws)

Matters of public interest and concern
(building a new highway system)

Public figure
(criticizing a professional athlete)

Interpersonal communication
(talking with someone on the telephone)

Commercial speech
(advertising)

Indecency
(cursing on radio)

Obscenity
(pornographic movies)

Least protection

Source: Todd F. Simon, Professor and Director, A. Q. Miller School of Journalism and Mass Communication, Kansas State University.

tion falls into three areas: prior restraint, controlling government documents, and copyright law. The first two concern access to information about governments and their activities, and the third concerns protection of content created by individuals and organizations.

■ *Prior Restraint.* Through prior restraint, a government body prevents the public from getting certain types of information. In some cases the government body reviews content before publication and censors it. In other cases it mandates that some types of content cannot be distributed.

The classic legal case involving prior restraint on newspapers is the case of *Near* vs. *The State of Minnesota,* which was described at the beginning of the chapter.[14] Although the Supreme Court allowed the *Saturday Press* to continue publication and, in effect, struck down the Minnesota "press as public nuisance" law, the court also recognized that these press freedoms are not absolute. It said that prior restraint can be exercised under conditions of national security, situations involving obscenity, and when the public order is threatened through violence. Prior restraint was often exercised during the mid-twentieth century when local and state censorship committees ruled on whether a film could be shown or whether it should be banned because of violence, sexual content, or unacceptable moral prescriptions.

■ *Obscenity.* Prior restraint often has been exercised when obscenity and pornography have been the core issues. Such restraint was employed—sometimes il-

The courts have had a difficult time attempting to define obscenity. Decision making in television content has been most difficult because of the ready access of the medium to children. Mere sexual depiction is not considered obscene, yet many television viewers find it offensive.

legally—by postmasters who took it on themselves to censor the mail they handled. In 1873, Congress adopted the Hicklin Rule, which defined obscenity as anything with a tendency to corrupt people whose minds might be open to immoral influences. Critics later argued that the rule treated all citizens as though they were children. During the 1950s the Supreme Court adopted a new definition, relaxing the standards by which something was deemed obscene. This Roth-Memoirs Rule, named for two Supreme Court cases, declared that material deemed obscene for children was not necessarily obscene for all. This rule also required that the entire work, not just a portion, be considered in judging whether material was obscene. In 1973, with the case of *Miller* v. *California,* the court devised a three-part rule for determining obscenity:

1. An average person, applying contemporary local community standards, finds that the work, taken as a whole, appeals to prurient interest.

2. The work depicts in a patently offensive way sexual conduct specifically defined by applicable state law.

3. The work in question lacks serious literary, artistic, political, or scientific value.

Because the rules are community based, what is deemed obscene in Shreveport, Louisiana, may be determined by community standards in New York City to be purely artistic. Nevertheless, under any rule, it has always been difficult for censorship boards, gossip columnists, and courts to determine whether content is obscene or whether it is artistic or literary. Obscenity laws have been used to ban everything from diving magazines to information about birth control. This issue promises to be a problem for years to come and will no doubt be interpreted in different lights depending on changing societal mores.

Keyconcept

Controlling Obscenity: Whether to protect obscene speech and how to define it have been enduring issues for the public, Congress, and the Supreme Court. The evolution of new technologies such as color photo printing and new media such as the Internet creates new issues that generate further discussions about the problems surrounding obscenity.

The issue of restraining obscene material distributed by electronic means remains a hotly contested issue in legislatures and courts. Sexually explicit material can be easily and cheaply sent directly to computers, and the buyers have more privacy than is found in video and book stores. This ease of delivery creates a problem. If adults can get the material easily, children can also.

Questions about which standards of obscenity should apply to electronic media and who should be responsible for children's access have led to technological efforts to protect children. Several programs for blocking Web material, such as SurfWatch and Net Nanny, became available to control access. But older children can figure out how to bypass them. ClarkNet offers KidzNet, which uses a central computer to filter objectionable content, so children could

364

not bypass access controls. Technology can help to censor material for individual computer users, but the debate about the types of material that should be available to censor will continue for years to come.

■ *Censorship during War.* Despite concerns about prior restraint, most journalists have accepted some censorship during times of war. The control of media during war dates to the Civil War, when President Lincoln shut down the *New York Journal of Commerce* for publishing a forged presidential proclamation announcing the draft of 400,000 men. But Lincoln was generally tolerant of the press and remanded an order by General A. E. Burnside to close the *Chicago Times,* arguing that such action would be more detrimental than criticism of the war effort.

Congress formalized war censorship of the press during World War I when it passed the Espionage Act in 1917 and the Sedition Act in 1918. These acts prohibited publishing "disloyal" information and bringing the U.S. government into "contempt, scorn or disrepute." The enforcement of these laws was the responsibility of the Postmaster General, who could prevent offending publications from being mailed. At least forty-four publications lost second-class mailing privileges as a result of the Espionage Act.[15]

In a classic World War I case, *Schenck* v. *United States,* Justice Oliver Wendell Holmes, Jr., evoked the standard for prior restraint of political material. For government to restrain publication, he said, the material must create "a clear and present danger." The potential harm from publication of any material must not be vague, merely possible, or in the distant future. Over the years, the test has become more strenuous, and prior restraint of political material has become difficult even in times of war.

During World War II, the 1917 Espionage Act was reactivated, and President Franklin Roosevelt declared a limited national emergency, which allowed him to control broadcasting. Hoping to avoid more stringent regulation, the National Association of Broadcasters asked its commentators not to editorialize. Because of widespread fear and public support of the war, the media cooperated in most censorship during that war. The Office of Censorship, created in 1941, administered a voluntary code of censorship and controlled communications coming into and leaving the country.

Because the United States never declared war on North Vietnam, wartime censorship was never imposed during that conflict. The media were free to report the war as they saw it, though military personnel often gave inaccurate information in news briefings. Although research indicates that public protest of the war coincided with official concern about the conduct of the war—and that negative media coverage followed, but did not precede, the official concern—many military officials believed that the media had helped to lose the war in Vietnam. Government efforts to prevent publication of the Pentagon Papers under the guise of national security created further mistrust between journalists and government.

After Vietnam the military tried to improve its management of the media. When the U.S. Congress does not officially declare war, the military tries to control information by controlling access rather than engaging in official restraint of content. This strategy was used when U.S. troops went into Grenada in 1983 and into Panama in 1989. It also proved fairly successful during the initial stages of the Gulf War in 1991. However, as the war moved from the air to land, some daring journalists were able to bypass military controls and pursue their own stories. At one point, television screens showed pictures of Iraqi soldiers surrendering to war correspondents who had arrived ahead of the military. Peter Arnett challenged this type of control by remaining in Baghdad and reporting from the enemy capitol throughout the conflict, despite censorship by the Iraqis.

Keyconcept

Control of Media Content During War: Techniques for controlling media content during wartime include censorship and restriction of access. The overriding question is whether the distribution of material will harm the war effort or endanger national security or whether censorship will restrict information the public has a legitimate right to know so as to make political decisions.

During military operations, government officials often try to limit public access to information, usually on the grounds that access would jeopardize the lives of those in combat. During the Gulf War, the military managed the news by providing attractive presentations that were designed to detract the media from initiating stories.

Arnett's reporting was controversial. Many journalists argued that he was just doing his best to get the story, but others claimed that broadcasting reports that were openly censored and possibly shaped by an enemy of the United States showed poor judgment.

During the Gulf War the military also actively provided the media with information and pictures—of the Pentagon's own design and choosing. By flooding the consumer market with carefully controlled content, the military was able to sustain public support of the war and to win the hearts of the public in spite of some media criticism. What television station could resist clear, exciting footage of smart bombs precisely striking military targets over enemy territory?

■ *Controlling Government Documents.* Prior restraint is not the only way in which government controls information. It can also control access to material that affects the decision-making process. Many federal agencies exist just to provide information to Congress and the administrative branch. At the federal level the President controls information because of the doctrine of **executive privilege,** which dates to the time of George Washington and James Madison. This doctrine states that the President may withhold information when disclosure might injure the public. During the twentieth century, Presidents have increasingly invoked the privilege in what might be seen as an abuse of the privilege.

During the 1960s, press associations and other citizens' groups lobbied extensively for open meetings and records acts, often called **sunshine laws.** As a result, all fifty states have some form of open records laws. However, just how information is released varies. Some states, such as Florida and New York, allow more access to computerized data than do others. The denial of access to databases reflects a desire to protect individual privacy. However, as more records are stored electronically, states will have to make such databases available as part of open records acts.

In an effort to make government information more available to the public, Congress passed the Freedom of Information Act (FOIA) in 1967. The act specified that a federal agency can withhold information in only nine areas: national security, agency interpersonal activities, statutory exemptions, trade secrets, some intraagency and interagency memos, issues involving personal privacy, police inves-

executive privilege: The President's right to withhold information if disclosure might harm the executive branch's functions and decision-making processes.

sunshine laws: Laws requiring that meetings of federal or state administrative agencies be open to the public.

tigations, protection of government-regulated financial institutions, and information about oil and gas wells.

A difficulty with the FOIA is that agencies have extensive leeway in following the act. Bureaucracies can make information access easier or harder to obtain, depending on what the particular administrator wants to do. For example, the person seeking information is expected to pay reasonable fees for search and copying. What is reasonable can vary from department to department and across time. The 1986 FOIA Reform Act tried to define the issues of national security and law enforcement exemptions, but it also gave departments more power to make some information less accessible. Even though the FOIA has limits, it does recognize that much government information should be available for public use.

Government can control information for justifiable public purposes, such as protection of troops. However, many times, information that is withheld ostensibly to protect the public is being suppressed to hide embarrassing or illegal acts. A classic example involves the thousand of hours of audiotapes that President Richard Nixon recorded during his presidency. President Nixon first released some tapes relating to the Watergate investigation in April 1974, but it was twenty more years before the public had access to many hours of tapes. Information was released gradually. In 1974 the Supreme Court ordered President Nixon to turn over sixty-four hours of tapes requested by a special prosecutor, but it recognized that a President has a constitutional right to withhold some information. In 1982 the Supreme Court allowed further access to portions of the tapes that were of public interest. The tapes continue to be a source of controversy. Trustees of the Nixon library are attempting to get personal portions of the tape moved from the National Archives to the library in California.

■ *Controlling News Events.* Not all information that reporters need can be found in documents. During breaking news stories, journalists want access to the people and locations involved in the news. Other important news events are governmental meetings at which ordinances and laws are decided. Because historically, many government bodies have sought to close meetings, all states and the federal government have enacted open meetings laws, known as *sunshine laws.* These laws require official government meetings to be open to the public, and thus the press, except under specific conditions.

The federal Government-in-Sunshine Act that took effect in 1977 applies to about fifty agencies, departments, and other types of groups. Their meetings can be closed if circumstances meet one of ten exemptions. State laws vary. Typical types of exemptions include meetings that include discussion of personnel matters, lawsuits, and land acquisition. Discussions about personnel could involve private material, considerations of lawsuits might involve confidential client-attorney information, and deliberating over land acquisitions could result in premature release of information that could affect the price of land.

In breaking news situations, such as the Branch Davidian confrontation near Waco, Texas, in 1994, journalists want total access. However, law enforcement officials can legally exclude journalists from crime scenes during and after the crime. This right exists to protect the public safety. Nevertheless, police sometimes restrict journalists when it is not necessary to do so, causing speculation that law enforcement personnel are simply trying to control information.

Another aspect of controlling information has to do with the conflict between the right of someone who has been charged with a crime to have a fair trial and the right of the news media to report on the trial. The Sixth Amendment to the Constitution guarantees the defendants right to a public trial, so journalists, as members of the public may attend trials. However, in some instances a judge may ban reporters from using information that they obtain in the courtroom, although more often a judge will instruct lawyers and jury members not to speak to the press. As the O. J. Simpson murder trial demonstrated, the impact of cameras in the courtrooms makes this conflict an even more difficult issue.

■ *Copyright Regulation.* Copyright law stems from a power granted by the Constitution to Congress. The purpose of copyright law is to promote the publication of information by protecting the property rights of authors. The first U.S. copyright law was passed in 1790. In 1976, Congress updated the 1909 law, providing increased protection for the creator of the work. Now the creator of a work has a copyright from the moment of creation until fifty years after his or her death.

Copyright law applies to newspapers, magazines, books, video, film, photographs, computer programs, speeches, and even professors' lecture notes. By providing the creator with control over the created materials, government hopes to encourage as much participation in the consumer market and marketplace of ideas as possible. People who make their living as writers, journalists, artists, and scholars cannot do so without legal control of the material they create.

Copyright covers the content but not the ideas in a publication. The words of this book are copyrighted, but the ideas are not. Often, it is impossible to determine who generated an idea. Individuals build on a set of ideas by adding or altering existing ideas. Allowing ideas to float freely in the marketplace fosters public debate.

Although the law has protected creators of information, it has not been proven perfect in its promotion of an active marketplace of ideas. For example, **fair use** is a problematic issue. Teachers, reporters, book reviewers, and researchers exercise fair use when they excerpt material for scholarly use or comment and criticism. However, it is often difficult to determine just exactly what is fair use. Therefore in lawsuits that involve fair use, the courts look at (1) the purpose of the use, (2) the nature of the work being used, (3) the amount used in relation to size of full work, and (4) the impact of use on market for the content.

New copyright infringement problems developed during the 1980s and 1990s. Increasing use of computers and the ability to download software via the Internet led to the **pirating** of computer programs. Copying a copyrighted program for one's own use is permissible under some conditions. Copying a program and selling it or giving it away is not. Many universities now have employees who check computer labs to see that the copyrights are in order.

The owners of copyrights also control, to a degree, the distribution of material. For example, in *Harper & Row Publishers, Inc.* v. *Nation Enterprises* the Supreme Court ruled that the *Nation* had violated Harper & Row's copyright by publishing stolen excerpts of former President Gerald R. Ford's memoirs. Harper & Row had an exclusive contract with *Time* magazine to publish excerpts before the hard-bound version of the book was to appear.

Copyright law affects a variety of "published" works, including music lyrics, television programs, and other types of performances. In *Solar Music* v. *Gap Stores,* the court ruled that Gap had infringed copyright by playing copyrighted radio music in 420 clothing stores. Gap was retransmitting music for commercial purposes, so the company had to pay royalties to the music artists.

REGULATING INFORMATION AFTER DISTRIBUTION Regulating content before the fact usually involves some conflict between news media and government. The government official wants to keep something secret. Regulating content after distribution, such as through libel and pri-

fair use: Use of a small portion of a copyrighted work by scholars, teachers, or reporters to further enlighten the public.

pirating: Using material without securing appropriate copyright authorization.

368

vacy law, usually involves an individual or nongovernmental organization and the media.

Regulating after publication or broadcast can take two forms. First, the media organization must pay the person or organization damages for the negative impact. These are *compensatory damages.* Second, the media organization might also be punished for its actions in an effort to discourage such actions in the future. These are *punitive damages.*

◾ *Libel and Slander.* Libel and slander are probably the best known types of regulation after distribution. *Libel* occurs when a person is defamed falsely in written form. *Slander* is spoken **defamation.** However, it is generally accepted that when a person is defamed through a broadcast, that defamation constitutes libel, not slander. Because broadcasting is not **limited speech,** as is interpersonal communication, it is considered to have the same impact as libel.[16] When libel or slander occurs, a person's reputation and character are damaged in some way. Comedian and actress Carol Burnett sued *The National Enquirer* in 1981 for running a story saying that she was drunk at a restaurant. She won. General William Westmoreland, the commander of U.S. troops in Vietnam, sued CBS for saying in 1982 that he deceived his superiors about enemy strength in the Vietnam War. The parties settled out of court after the trial started, with CBS paying Westmoreland's legal expenses and agreeing to apologize for errors in the report.

Keyconcept

Libel: Libel, or the defamation of a private individual, has always been considered beyond the bounds of free expression. A more complicated issue is the libel of a public official or figure. In 1964 the Supreme Court ruled in *New York Times* v. *Sullivan* that a reporter had to show disregard for the truth or falsify a report to be convicted of libeling a public official.

Libel cases often are perceived as the results of profit-hungry media organizations trying to build circulation or ratings by lying about someone. In reality, libel can result from mistakes, poor reporting skills, and arrogance when a news organization is asked to correct a mistake. The suits that get attention are not the average cases, and often the results of the trial are changed by higher courts. When libel suits go to trial, about seven of ten are won by the plaintiff (the person filing the suit), with average awards of $1 million for actual damages and $600,000 for punitive damages. In five of the seven cases won by the plaintiff, either the jury results are reversed or the damages are lowered to an average of $150,000.[17]

The difference between the initial jury awards and the eventual resolution during the appeal process reflects the complexity of libel laws. Just damaging a person's reputation is not enough to justify a judgment against a journalist. Several defenses can either absolve the journalist or lessen the impact of a judgment against the journalist.

Truth is a defense for libel. Reporting that someone is a convicted murderer constitutes defamation, but if that person was indeed convicted of murder, the report is not libellous. Even during the period of the Alien and Sedition Acts, truth was considered a defense for libel.

Qualified privilege is a second defense for libel. Privilege developed to make happenings in government proceedings available to citizens. Under qualified privilege a journalist is protected while reporting statements from a public meeting as long as the report is accurate. However, the definition of what is privileged information varies from state to state. Usually, remarks made in a trial are privileged, but informal remarks made by a police officer during an investigation are not.

Fair comment and criticism defenses allow a journalist to express opinion in the most offensive ways without committing libel. The statement must be presented as opinion and not fact. This allows a no-holds-barred criticism of anything from political ideas to artistic performances. Perhaps the most famous case of fair comment and criticism was the review of the Cherry Sisters' vaudeville act at the

defamation: To misconstrue facts or misrepresent a person in such a way as to lower the individual in the estimation of others.

limited speech: Speech that is not widely disseminated.

[profile]

Reed Hundt

Think of him as Jimmy Stewart in *Mr. Smith Goes to Washington*—except this time it's in the cyberspace age. That's how attorney Nicholas Allard described the emergence of his Latham & Watkins colleague Reed Hundt in November 1993 as the new Federal Communications Commission (FCC) chair. Hundt served as FCC chair until 1997.

Often at odds with the perceived philosophy of previous FCC chairs, Mark Fowler and Dennis Patrick, Hundt claimed that there is more to broadcasting than making money.

Ron Alridge of *Electronic Media* observed that Hundt believes that broadcasters must be responsible to the public in exchange for free use of the public's airwaves. Hundt has said that the public should be given the information it needs to make productive decisions because broadcasting is not just a business, but a vital component of the democratic process.

For two decades, Hundt was a general litigator in antitrust and communications. For more than ten years he worked on Al Gore's political campaigns. When Gore became Vice President, Hundt said the only job he would find interesting would be as head of the FCC. It was, he said, the future.

Under Hundt's chairmanship, the FCC completed its design of specifications for high-definition television. Hundt also updated communications technology within FCC offices, hired the first African Americans in FCC management positions, mandated another rollback in customers' cable prices, garnered $617 million by auctioning off portions of the electronic spectrum that were previously free, and convinced Congress to fund the FCC at considerably higher levels than it had during the last twenty years.

SOURCES: Ron Alridge, "In Speech, Hundt Thankfully Exceeds His Billing," *Electronic Media,* (October 31, 1994): 29; Karen Dillon, "Raw Power," *The American Lawyer* (September 1994): 69.

turn of the twentieth century. The sisters sued when this critique ran in the *Des Moines Leader*.[18]

> Billy Hamilton, of the *Odebolt Chronicle,* gives the Cherry Sisters the following graphic write-up on their late appearance in his town: "Effie is an old jade of 50 summers, Jessie a frisky filly of 40, and Addie, the flower of the family, a capering monstrosity of 35. Their long skinny arms, equipped with talons at the extremities, swung mechanically, and anon waved frantically at the suffering audience. The mouths of their rancid features opened like caverns, and sounds like the wailing of damned souls issued therefrom. They pranced around the stage with a motion that suggested a cross between the danse du ventre and fox trot—strange creatures with painted faces and hideous mien. Effie is spavined, Addie is stringhalt, and Jessie, the only one who showed her stockings, has legs with calves as classic in their outline as the curves of a broom handle."[19]

This review is cruel, but according to the Iowa Supreme Court, it is not libelous. The review is fair comment and criticism.

Absence of actual malice, perhaps the strongest libel defense for journalists other than truth, reflects the legal status of the subject being covered. People who find themselves in the public eye have less libel protection than a private person does, and they must prove actual malice on the part of a reporter to win a libel suit. There are two types of public persons: public officials and public figures. A *public official* is someone who holds a position in government that affects public policy. A *public figure* is someone who places herself or himself before the public through the media or someone who is swept involuntarily into public controversy. Published comments about the second type of public figure can be protected only if they concern the controversy.

In 1964 a Supreme Court decision in the *New York Times* v. *Sullivan* case assured reporters that as long as they followed careful reporting procedures, random errors would not result in large libel judgments. The Supreme Court ruled that public officials—elected officials and individuals appointed to high offices—had to carry a heavier burden than did private individuals in libel judgments. The case arose from a *New York Times* advertisement titled "Heed Their Rising Voices," which appeared in March 1960, shortly after whites used violence at Alabama State College in Montgomery against black demonstrators who were protesting the segregation of public facilities. Alabama police commissioner L. B. Sullivan filed suit against the *Times,* which was considered a Northern liberal newspaper, charging that he was libeled by the ad's general references to the police. The advertisement did contain errors. For example, it claimed that the students had sung "My Country, 'Tis of Thee," when in fact they had sung "The Star-Spangled Banner." Although the errors were minor, the implications of the suit were not. State libel laws were being used by Southern states to attempt to control news coverage of civil rights demonstrations. The *Times* alone was facing eleven other libel suits in Alabama courts. When the case reached the Supreme Court on appeal, Justice William Brennan wrote that something far more crucial than an individual seeking to protect a reputation was at stake: the right to be able to discuss and to criticize government and government officials. The Supreme Court enacted the *rule of actual malice,* requiring that public officials had to prove that statements were made with actual malice, or "knowledge that information is false or with reckless disregard of whether it was false or not." Brennan argued that the case had to be considered "against the background of a profound national commitment to the principle that debate on public issues should be uninhibited, robust, and wide-open."

Since 1964 and the *Sullivan* ruling, the court has extended the actual malice rule to public figures. Dennis Rodman (a basketball professional) and Madonna (a singer) are public figures because they have voluntarily placed themselves before the public through the media. Because they have sought public attention, they must tolerate the comments and criticism that come with it. A private person can demonstrate libel merely by showing that a journalist was negligent in carrying out his or her work or that a journalist showed a lack of care in collecting information and writing stories.

The difference between private and public people represents the concern Justice William Brennan voiced in the *Sullivan* case for a free and open marketplace of ideas. The need of a democratic society to explore as many ideas as possible, even despised ones, has led the courts to allow error on the side of open discussion. For this reason, people who are in the public spotlight are open for more criticism than those who are not. A sloppy journalist has some protection with public figures, though a malicious one does not.

■ *Privacy.* Privacy laws are similar to libel laws because they also involve protection of individuals from media abuse. Privacy laws address the right of a person to be left alone. People are entitled to keep parts of their lives away from public scrutiny. Although privacy is not written into the Constitution, it is derived from the Constitution's protection from unreasonable search and seizure and from self-incrimination. This area of law has become much more active as the number and type of national media outlets, both print and broadcast, have increased during the past thirty years.

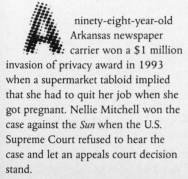

Nellie Mitchell Beats the Supermarket Tabloids

A ninety-eight-year-old Arkansas newspaper carrier won a $1 million invasion of privacy award in 1993 when a supermarket tabloid implied that she had to quit her job when she got pregnant. Nellie Mitchell won the case against the *Sun* when the U.S. Supreme Court refused to hear the case and let an appeals court decision stand.

In 1990, Mitchell's photograph ran next to a headline that read "World's Oldest Newspaper Carrier, 101, quits because she is pregnant!" The article concerned an Australian woman, but the photograph that ran was of the Arkansas woman. The photograph came from a 1980 story in *The Na-*tional Enquirer, which is owned by the same company as the *Sun*. The *Enquirer* had run a story about Mitchell because of her age in a job that usually was done by younger people.

The *Sun*'s editor explained that he assumed she was dead when he used her photograph to illustrate the story about someone else. Mitchell was not amused. She admitted that no one she knew believed the story, but she sued because it embarrassed her.

The newspaper's defense was that most of the stories in the *Sun* were fiction and no one believed them. If no one believed them, no harm was done to Nellie Mitchell. A jury in Arkansas awarded her $1.5 million, which was reduced to $1 million by the judge. Globe International Publishing, which publishes the *Sun,* appealed and argued First Amendment protection. The Supreme Court refused to hear the appeal without comment. Mitchell said she would use some of the award to help newspaper carriers attend college.

SOURCE: "Arkansas Woman Wins Libel Suit," Associated Press, October 28, 1993.

Invasion of privacy can take several forms. Physically invading a person's solitude is classified as *intrusion.* A radio journalist cannot hide a microphone or camera in someone's room to collect information. Putting someone in a commercial without getting permission—*commercial appropriation*—also is an invasion of privacy. *Disclosing embarrassing facts* can invade privacy through the release of information a person would consider awkward. A television program cannot broadcast details of a private person's sexual behavior without permission. A person cannot be portrayed in a *false light* by media. Journalists cannot infer something about someone that is not true. For example, a camera crew cannot record video of people on the street and use the tape while talking about sexually transmitted diseases. However, victims who claim that they have been portrayed in a false light must prove actual malice. The Hill family, who had been held hostage in their home for nineteen hours during a weekend in 1952, sued Time, Inc. for invasion of privacy when *Life* reported on a Broadway play that depicted the Hills as having heroically resisted brutish conduct by the invaders. In reality, the Hill's captors had treated them courteously. On appeal, the Supreme Court ruled that even private individuals must prove actual malice if they are involved in a newsworthy issue.

As with libel, laws regarding invasion of privacy are not equally applicable to all people. People who are part of newsworthy events can lose their right to privacy, but courts have differed in their interpretations of newsworthiness. Although the purpose of these laws is to protect people who are forced into embarrassing situations, sometimes media cover such situations as newsworthy events. In 1929, for example, Mrs. Lillian

Jones sued the *Louisville Herald-Post* for quoting her as saying she "would have killed" the people who stabbed her husband to death on a Louisville street. Mrs. Jones lost her case when the newspaper claimed it had simply covered a newsworthy event.

■ *Regulating Advertising Content.* Advertising falls under the heading of commercial speech, which is information aimed at promoting a commercial transaction. Until 1976, commercial speech was outside the protection of the First Amendment. That year, however, the Supreme Court ruled in the case of *Virginia State Board of Pharmacy v. Virginia Citizens Consumer Council*[20] that commercial speech that serves consumers with accurate and useful information deserves First Amendment protection. The Court did state that some forms of commercial speech should be subject to regulation.

The primary justification for advertising regulation is the protection of consumers from false claims that would mislead them. This justification dates to the late 1700s, when newspapers and other print media carried advertisements for patent medicines. Patent medicines were salves, ointments, and liquid concoctions that claimed to cure a wide range of illnesses and ailments. The following example ran in the *Pennsylvania Gazette* in 1777 for "Dr. RYAN'S incomparable WORM destroying SUGAR PLUMS, Necessary to be kept in all FAMILIES":[21]

> The plum is a great diuretic, cleaning the veins of slime; it expels wind, and is a sovereign medicine in the cholic and griping of the guts. It allays and carries off vapours which occasion many disorders of the head. It opens all obstructions in the stomach, lungs, liver, veins, and bladder; causes a good appetite, and helps digestion.

The effects of patent medicines never lived up to the advertising claims, and in some cases the contents of the patent medicine could kill. The *New York Evening Post* temporarily stopped taking patent medicine ads in 1805 after a young girl died from using a patent medicine.[22]

Concerns with patent medicine advertising and other forms of consumer abuse led to the passage of the Pure Food and Drug Act in 1906 and the creation of the Federal Trade Commission (FTC) in 1914. The Pure Food and Drug Act gave the federal government regulatory powers over foods and medicines, and the FTC Act gave the government power over false advertising. Until 1934 the FTC was concerned with consumer protection only in the context of antitrust actions. That year the Supreme Court extended the act to cover non-antitrust cases, and in 1938, Congress made unfair and deceptive acts and practice in commerce illegal by passing the Wheeler-Lea Act.[23] In addition to enforcement specified by the act, the FTC also enforces several other consumer protection laws.

Unfair advertisements and practices are ones that cause substantial injury without offsetting benefits to consumers and businesses. The FTC uses its power to regulate in this area against businesses that mistreat consumers, although unfairness can also apply to advertising. For example, Orkin Exterminating Company was forced to cancel a rate increase for treating houses against termites. The company had signed a contract with homeowners at a lower price.

For the FTC to decide that an advertisement is deceptive, the ad must be misleading *and* it must cause the reasonable consumer to act in a way that results in real injury to the consumer. The FTC does not pursue cases that involve obviously inflated claims, such as "The Greatest Soda Ever Invented," since only an "unreasonable" person would believe a claim such as this. A real injury occurs when something is bought; if the claim will not lead to a consumer's purchase, it is not likely to be regulated by the FTC.

If the FTC finds an advertisement to be deceptive, it can take a variety of actions. A consent agreement, for example, allows the company to stop the advertisement without admitting guilt. The FTC can also get a cease-and-desist order, which prohibits the practice in the future. It can even require corrective advertising, which attempts to correct false impressions created by past ads. For example, the Warner-Lambert Company, which produces Listerine mouthwash, had claimed that the product killed germs that caused colds and sore throats. In 1975 the company was required to include in Listerine ads a statement that the mouthwash does not prevent colds and sore throats. The corrective ads continued until $10 million was spent on Listerine ads.

The definition of regulatory power and the eagerness with which the power is used change across time. The changes often reflect court rulings, amendments to law, and even the political environment. For example, during the 1990s, in reaction to growing concerns among the population, both the FTC and the FCC have become more sensitive to advertising and television content aimed at children. They recognize that young children are not able to process information in the same way adults do. Three- and four-year-olds, for example, do not differentiate between television programs and advertising.

In 1991 the FTC ruled that Galoob Toys was misrepresenting the performance of its toys, since a doll could not twirl on one foot as shown in the advertisement. The same year, the FCC ordered broadcasters to air standard-length children's programs that are educational and informative and to limit the number and length of advertisements in children's programming. The long-term effect of these regulations remains to be seen, but the solution here reflects a growing trend of using media regulation to solve problems.

▣ *The Telecommunications Act and Content Regulation.* The passage of the Telecommunications Act of 1996 came at a time when control of content had been a serious topic of debate for several years. For example, during the early 1990s some members of Congress were concerned about violence on television and radio and about the content of children's television programming. The Children's Television Act of 1991 forced broadcast stations to program for children and to limit the number of commercial minutes in each hour of children's programming.

Although most of the TC Act concerns business activities, the most controversial portions cover content regulation. The act prohibits the transmission via computer of pornographic material to minors, requires television manufacturers to include a microchip (called a **V-chip**) in each set that will allow electronic blocking of programs on the basis of a ratings system, increases fines from $10,000 to $100,000 for television and radio obscenity, and requires cable to scramble programs for subscribers who think the programs are unfit for children.

Most of the business portion received slight attention in general circulation media because attention focused on the content regulation parts of the act. The regulation against indecent material on the Internet and the V-chip faced court challenges or threats of court challenges immediately after the act went into effect. These law suits involve arguments about the impact of these new regulations on First Amendment rights. In June 1997, the Supreme Court ruled that the Computer Decency Act was unconstitutional.

President Clinton visited a family in Alexandria, VA. after the Telecommunications Act of 1996 was passed. This revolutionary piece of legislation requires manufacturers of television sets to include a V-Chip, a device parents may use to control the television content their children may watch.

V-chip: An electronic device in a television set that can block certain television programs.

At issue in the Internet-related cases was whether online communications will enjoy the broad protection given print media or the more narrow rights traditionally given broadcasting. A former Texas Judge, Steve Russell, wrote an article in the *American Reporter,* a daily online publication, specifically aimed at violating the new law. He called Congress a variety of "obscene" names that have been protected in print but censored on broadcast television. He stated in the article: " . . . you (Congress) have sold the First Amendment, your birthright and that of your children. The Founders turn in their graves. You have spit on the grave of every warrior who fought under the Stars and Stripes."[24]

After the act was passed, hundreds of World Wide Web sites changed their backgrounds to black and issued protest statements about the new regulations that carry a fine of up to $250,000 and/or up to five years in prison. Many others added a picture of a blue ribbon with a slogan supporting free speech. Within a few weeks, a federal district judge in Philadelphia ruled that the part of the act concerning indecency was unconstitutionally vague and issued a temporary restraining order to stop enforcement. However, he ruled that the part of the act prohibiting "patently offense material" and information about abortion was legal. He argued that indecency is too vague, but the other material could be judged on a "community standard" basis. The American Civil Liberties Union and nineteen other organizations who originally filed the suit appealed.[25] Justice John Paul Stevens wrote the majority opinion for the Supreme Court, noting that the Computer Decency Act cast a "shadow over free speech" and "threatens to torch a large segment of the Internet community." Stevens argued that an attempt to protect children from harmful materials "does not justify an unnecessarily broad suppression of speech addressed to adults."

As various groups battled over Internet content, American broadcasters argued against the V-chip and threatened to go to court. The broadcasting industry cites five reasons it opposes the new regulation:

- "It infringes on their First Amendment right to free speech.

- It will be almost impossible to rate and code every hour of television.

- Television shows that are tagged with violent or adult-themed ratings may scare away advertisers.

- Implementation of the V-chip will force the networks to rely on sitcoms because adult-oriented dramatic fare will inevitably attract ratings for violent or sexual content.

- No one has ever adequately defined what constitutes a harmful violent act in television programming."[26]

Proponents of the V-chip respond that television has never been extended the same First Amendment rights that print enjoys. They also state that parents cannot watch every program before their children to evaluate its content and that the broadcasters are primarily concerned about making money.

Most Americans remain concerned about TV violence. A study paid for by the National Cable Television Association found that in 1995, 57% of all TV programs contained violence. The researchers concluded that the biggest problem was not the violence itself but how it was treated. In 73% of the violent scenes, the perpetrator went unpunished, often the negative consequences of violence were not presented in these programs, and only 4% of the programs presented an anti-violent theme.[27]

In March 1996 the top executives in the television industry met with President Clinton and agreed to pursue a voluntary rating system similar to the one used by the motion picture industry. The system adopted identifies six types of content with icons in the upper left corner of the TV set during the first fifteen seconds of the program. The levels are age based and start with TV-Y for programs suitable for all children and ends with TV-M, which is content not suitable for children under 17.

The industry's action reflected an awareness of viewers' concerns about TV and acknowledgment of increasing pressure from Washington. Because the federal government controls the airwaves, Congress can change broadcast television's distribution system or at least make the industry pay for the frequencies if it doesn't like what the networks are showing. The age-based system has been criticized by viewers and interest groups as being too vague. The FCC's position is that the ratings system should be given adequate time for evaluation before it is readdressed by the agency.

The threat of regulation

Regulations do not have to be enforced to change media content. The very threat of filing action under one of the regulatory laws affects what media organizations do. In some cases this benefits people. The knowledge that they could be sued for intrusion keeps most media organizations from sending a reporter to a person's house with a hidden camera and recording what happens. Not all such threats are beneficial, however. The threat of a costly libel suit can have a chilling effect on the work of journalists. This effect exists when journalists avoid covering a story or change their writing not because they doubt their information, but because they fear a lawsuit.

Litigation can be expensive even if the newspaper wins the case. In addition, the time the journalists spend on the case means time away from gathering news. People who appear in the news understand this and often file nuisance suits. Although the plaintiffs know that they will probably not win, they also know that the newspaper or other organization will have to spend money to defend itself. The plaintiff also may hope that the editors will be more reluctant to publish controversial articles in the future.

A small publication or broadcast station is more vulnerable to a chilling effect than are large media organizations. A weekly newspaper with a $500,000 budget is not likely to pursue stories that could cost $250,000 in legal fees even if the paper wins. Even large metropolitan dailies have limits to what they will spend to pursue controversial stories.

One of the dangers of legal punishments is a "chilling effect" that keeps publishers from pursuing difficult stories. Gossip newspapers such as the Star sometimes settle claims out of court to void legal consequences and publicity for questionable claims.

376

Measuring the impact of this chilling effect is difficult; it requires measuring what did not happen. Fear of adverse reactions leads to self-censorship. This process occurs in people's minds, often out of habit, and goes against the principles of open discussion of ideas and information in the marketplace of ideas.

Keyconcept

Chilling Effect: Advocates of absolute free expression argue that most regulations have a chilling effect on reporters; in other words, the regulations may cause reporters to avoid going after tough stories because they fear being sued. If lawsuits become too oppressive, they can affect how information gets disseminated and debated in the marketplace of ideas.

Media organizations are not the only groups that can be chilled by lawsuits. Libel suits can be filed against anyone. Lawsuits have been used against activist groups to discourage their activism. These suits are called Strategic Lawsuits Against Public Participation (SLAPPs). A public person who has been attacked can file such suits to discourage his critics. Such suits do not even need a chance of winning to be effective. The cost of litigation is often enough to keep the critics quiet.[28] Because the obvious purpose is the stifling of open discussion of matters that interest the public, SLAPP suits are being fought with countersuits. New York and California have passed laws against such lawsuits.[29]

Gaining access to journalists' information

Most media laws deal either with content or business operations. Another area of law that concerns media and focuses specifically on news gathering is called **evidentiary privilege.** Although this privilege is not universally granted to journalists, when it is, it means that a journalist who has promised a source anonymity does not have to identify that source in court. Such protection for confidentiality has long existed for lawyers and doctors; it has become an issue for journalists mostly in the second half of the twentieth century.

Shield laws are important regulations that protect reporters such as Patricia Mangan of the Boston Herald *and David Ropeik of Boston's WCVB-TV when district attorneys start searching for the names of sources.*

Privilege involves three types of litigation: (1) when the court seeks the identity of an anonymous source, (2) when the court demands materials such as notes and videotapes, and (3) when the court asks journalists who witnessed an event to testify. When a court seeks information, it issues a subpoena that orders the journalists to provide information or testify in court. The journalist and news organization can ask the court to quash, or dismiss, the subpoena.

The U.S. Supreme Court has not accepted the concept of journalists' privilege based on the First Amendment. But as of 1996, twenty-nine states had *shield laws* protecting journalists from being forced to disclose information. Another seventeen states and the District of Columbia have recognized privilege under common law or state constitutions.

Government officials argue that journalists should have no

evidentiary privilege: Rule of law that allows journalists to withhold identification of confidential sources.

more privilege than ordinary citizens because such privilege can hamper police and prosecutors' investigations. Journalists respond that the absence of such privilege would prevent sources from revealing information to them. They argue that privilege allows them to question people who are afraid to talk with police or other government officials. Many sources, such as government employees and crime witnesses, face retaliation if their identity is made public. As a result, a valuable source of information might dry up, and the public good would be harmed.

Trends and innovations

Trends affect regulatory efforts just as they do other types of social, political, and economic matters. After Newton Minow referred to television as a "vast wasteland," significant regulation was passed to try to make television more socially responsible. Requirements such as ascertainment encouraged broadcasters to program in the public interest.

Deregulation

During the early 1990s, two forces combined to promote deregulation. First, President Bush favored limiting government activity in the economic sector. Second, technology advanced to such a degree that many more channels were available to viewers. Because so many more channels were available, regulatory critics began to question whether scarcity, one of the fundamental tenets on which broadcast regulation was based, still existed.

The Telecommunications Act of 1996 deregulated broadcast, cable, and telephone companies by relaxing regulations on how the different companies interact and by lifting many restrictive ownership rules. Yet the act also represents a second trend: a growing nervousness about television content. The V-chip legislation and congressional debates about indecency reflect a political conservatism that is expressed in other political and social debates occurring in the late 1990s.

New forms of lawsuits

Libel suits are difficult to win because they require proving—not just knowing—the truth or falsity of a claim. Most businesses look for ways other than libel suits to gain redress, and in the 1990s a number of companies used alternative forms of lawsuits to attack reports about them. In 1992, ABC's *PrimeTime* sent producers into Food Lion stores with hidden cameras, and in a *PrimeTime* segment, Diane Sawyer narrated a tale of rat-gnawed cheese, spoiled meat, and unfair labor practices. The national supermarket chain's market value fell by $1.5 billion within a week. Food Lion sued ABC for fraud, deceptive trade practices, civil conspiracy, and breach of duty loyalty because the producers faked their employment applications and entered the meat and deli departments of the store under false pretenses. In 1997, a North Carolina jury awarded Food Lion $5.5 million in punitive damages and only $1,402 in actual damages. The jury delivered a clear message that it did not approve of ABC's reporting tactics. Some commentators claimed the high punitive damages would chill future investigations, but others, after viewing outtakes from the ABC film footage, declared that ABC's reporting practices clearly did not meet professional standards and that, indeed, selective editing created a story that wasn't there. ABC filed an appeal in early 1997.

378

These types of suits are easier to win than libel suits, and they can cost a news organization a great deal of money even if it wins. Some critics attributed CBS's response to the tobacco industry to this chilling effect.[30] In 1995, *60 Minutes* developed a segment about tobacco additives used by Brown & Williamson Tobacco Company. A producer worked with a former employee who had signed an agreement not to talk about his work when he left the company. CBS recorded an interview with the former employee and was preparing the segment when network lawyers suggested that the interview not run. The lawyers feared that the network would be sued for encouraging the former employee to break his nondisclosure agreement.

The ongoing conflict within CBS over the interview was reported in the press before the segment ran. CBS ran the report with a small piece of the interview that had been modified. The former employee's name and face were not revealed. The case became the center of extensive argument within the news media. Some legal experts said that the tobacco company would not have won such a lawsuit. Others criticized CBS for caving into a threat that was never made. This argument gained support when executives of the Liggett Tobacco Company admitted less than two years later that they had known cigarette smoking was addictive and harmful.

Whatever the ethics of the case, it demonstrated that even large news organizations can be intimidated by the mere threat of losing large sums of money. Once businesses and public figures know this, as they do now, little incentive exists for them not to pursue these tactics in the future. However, when networks willfully violate professional ethics and lose credibility, the argument for legal protection for reporting is diluted.

Summary

- Regulation exists to mediate conflicts between the rights of two individuals or between a government or corporation and an individual.

- The Bill of Rights was created to limit government control of private affairs and to preserve individual liberties.

- Government imposes regulations (1) when people or organizations interfere with the workings of the economic market system, (2) when the use of a product or an industry or company's behavior has a negative impact on society as a whole, (3) when a product or behavior has a negative impact on individuals that outweighs its contribution to society as a whole, (4) during times of war, and (5) to preserve its own security and power.

- The First Amendment was designed to protect robust intellectual exchange within a democratic society.

- Governments regulate (1) the economic behavior of media companies in the consumer and advertising markets, (2) certain internal business activities of media companies, and (3) some content and information.

- Media regulation evolved not only from federal and state legislation, but also from court decisions.

- Economic regulations include antitrust laws and direct regulation by government agencies, such as the FCC and FTC.

- Direct telecommunication regulation covers broader areas than print because in the early years, government sought to avoid chaos over the airwaves, to allocate scarce resources (airwaves), and to force licensees to act in the public interest.

- Levels of regulation vary with social conditions. During the 1960s and 1970s the FCC responded to activist requests to respond to the public; in the 1980s, political conservatism and technological advancements promoted deregulation; in 1996, Congress revamped the entire telecommunications regulatory apparatus.

- Media companies are also subject to regulations that affect most businesses, such as labor laws.

- Content can be regulated before or after distribution. Regulation before distribution includes prior restraint, controlling government documents, and copyright law. Prior restraint includes laws relating to obscenity and government regulation of the press during wartime. Regulation after distribution includes libel laws and privacy laws.

- Open meetings laws, such as the federal Government-in-Sunshine Act, increase access for the public and journalists to the decisions of government bodies.

- *New York Times* v. *Sullivan* was a landmark decision because it assured reporters that random errors in covering the conduct of a public official would not result in huge libel judgments against them. The Supreme Court decision further ruled that government entities could not use libel suits as a way of silencing the press.

- Advertising is subject to all regulations affecting regular content and to additional controls that are intended to protect the consumer from misleading and dangerous claims.

- Although the Telecommunications Act of 1996 primarily affected business practices, it also initiated new content regulation.

- Often, the threat of regulation can have a chilling effect that not only curbs the excesses of media, but also sometimes curbs their desire to address controversial issues.

- State shield laws protect journalists from being forced to reveal information to courts and government agencies.

Navigating the Web

Regulation on the web

Most Web sites that cover media regulation are maintained by either universities or governments. They provide access to material about regulation and law, including full texts of some legal documents.

| Communications Media Center at New York Law School | http://www.cmcnyls.edu |

This site has background about the Communications Media Center and a few other articles. Full use of the site requires registration.

The site provides several links to federal and state government records and sites. In addition, the user has access to the center's library.

This site provides links to extensive legal documents in the United States and throughout the world. Topics include access to government information, the Freedom of Information Act, and electronic privacy.

This site carries the full text of the 1996 Telecommunication Act. This Act was the first major overhaul of telecommunication regulations since 1934 and will have far-reaching effects on mass media in the United States and the world.

Questions for review

1. What are the five reasons why government regulates media in the United States?
2. Why are broadcast media regulated to a greater degree than are print media?
3. What are the three types of regulation of mass media in the United States?
4. How has antitrust law been applied to U.S. media?
5. What are the main elements of the 1996 Telecommunications Law?
6. Give two examples of how labor laws apply to media.
7. What are the major types of restrictions before publication?
8. What are the major types of restrictions after publication?

Issues to think about

1. Traditionally, broadcast media have been subject to more regulation than have print media. In the computer age, broadcast and print blend. How would you apply traditional laws, such as those protecting copyright and restrictions against pornography, in the on-line world?
2. Do you think the public is adequately protected from invasion of privacy? How do you reconcile the right to privacy with the public's right to know?
3. Do you think competition among telephone and cable companies and other media corporations will enhance our access to information?
4. Do you think the threat of regulation restricts reporters' desire to present full information about public behavior?

▪ Suggested readings

Dennis, Everette E., Donald M. Gillmor, and Theodore Glasser, eds., *Media Freedom and Accountability* (Westport, CT: Greenwood Press, 1989).

Dizard, Wilson *The Coming Information Age* (New York: Longman, 1993).

Gilmer, Donald M., Jerome A. Barron, Todd F. Simon, and Herbert A. Terry, *Fundamentals of Communication Law* (St. Paul, MN: West, 1996).

Head, Sydney, and Christopher Sterling, *Broadcasting in America,* 4th ed. (Boston: Houghton-Mifflin, 1994.)

Middleton, Kent, and Bill Chamberlin, *The Law of Public Communication* (New York: Longman, 1991).

Nelson, Harold, Dwight Teeter, and Don R. Leduc, *Law of Mass Communications* (Mineola, NY: Foundation Press, 1989).

Ethics

On November 17, 1992, the NBC television news magazine *Dateline* broadcast a fifteen-minute segment on General Motors (GM) pickup trucks. Entitled "Waiting to Explode," the story featured dramatic footage of a car crashing into a GM pickup, which then caught fire. The crash was taped during a demonstration by the Institute of Safety Analysis, a private Indiana firm hired by NBC. The story was aired against the backdrop of increasing trouble at GM, which faced more than one hundred injury lawsuits over pickups that were allegedly prone to explode because they were designed with gasoline tanks outside their frames.

Richard Jewell was first a suspect in the Atlanta Centennial Olympic Park bombing and as such became a media celebrity. Jewell sued the Atlanta Constitution, *and media personnel began to question whether they had rushed to judgment.*

Just after the story aired in November, GM strongly protested the *Dateline* claims and denied that its vehicles were unsafe. NBC just as strongly defended its story. However, on February 8, 1993, GM conducted a dramatic two-hour press conference, beamed by satellite to all GM employees and watched in horror by NBC executives in New York. GM had discovered that the *Dateline* team had faked the crash video by taping explosives to the pickups to ensure that they would explode. GM assembled a legal team and a public relations team, challenged the journalists' claims, and took its proof to the courts and to the public.

GM doubted the NBC story from the beginning. Officials had reviewed the tape in slow motion and detected some inconsistencies, but NBC refused access to

383

the crashed vehicles. Meanwhile, a California hot rod magazine editor also doubted the NBC tapes and criticized the network in a column. That prompted a call from an Indiana firefighter who was present when NBC's crash tapes were made. He told the editor that NBC had rigged the pickups with model rocket engines.

GM's crisis team, composed of legal and public relations experts, talked to the Indiana firefighter, then began combing the state's junkyards for the wrecked vehicles that NBC had refused to let them examine. At the twenty-second junkyard, they struck gold. A discharged toy rocket engine was found still taped to the pickups. On February 8, GM filed suit against NBC, alleging "outrageous misrepresentation and conscious deception."

On February 9, the day after the press conference, NBC and GM lawyers settled the lawsuit. *Dateline* anchors Jane Pauley and Stone Phillips read a full retraction and apologized to their viewers. They acknowledged that *Dateline* had not only taped rockets to the trucks, but also significantly understated the speed of the vehicles in the crash tests and falsely reported that a fuel tank erupted in one of the crashes. In March, NBC news president Michael Gartner resigned, and by the end of March, three senior producers on the program also had resigned. Throughout the media, Gartner was regarded as a scapegoat for the real problems plaguing NBC.[1]

What were the issues here? During the 1980s, increasingly concerned about financial survival, television networks cut costs in their news departments and focused more intensively on ratings and less on ensuring high news standards. NBC had tried repeatedly to compete in the news magazine format, particularly against CBS's long-running *60 Minutes*. *Dateline* was getting respectable ratings, and corporate pressure for the show to succeed was intense. Did the reporters get caught up in an **infotainment** mode, desiring to please General Electric, NBC's corporate owner, by producing high profits at the expense of accuracy and fairness? Did the economic stakes here influence news judgment? Did reporters follow reasonable standards of moral conduct? In this case, did GM's public relations and legal efforts act as a watchdog on journalism? Do corporations, when they believe they are treated unfairly, have recourse to challenge journalistic reports? Obviously, in this case, GM, with the help of knowledgeable citizens, successfully challenged *Dateline*'s accusations and created favorable publicity for itself. How does this affect the credibility of journalists and the credibility of corporations and the personnel who represent them?

Welcome to the world of media ethics. In this world, political and economic pressures can affect the media content that consumers receive.

"Ethics" is easily defined as standards of conduct and moral judgment. What is not so easily defined is "moral judgment." Defining *morality* requires judging the goodness or badness of human behavior and character. John N. Davenport, the originator and first anchor of the successful news program *Washington Week in Review*, once said that a book on media ethics would be the shortest book in the world simply because "there aren't any [media ethics]." Davenport's cynical view was that people in the news and entertainment industries would do almost anything to make a profit. They would stop at nothing to sell their product to consumers and to sell consumers to advertisers.

When people question whether mass media employees have ethics, they are really asking whether these influential professionals have standards to guide their decisions and conduct and whether they adhere to those standards. Ethical behavior is an issue for all types of people, both those who supply news to reporters and those who process news. News reporters and editors have long claimed that they adhere to standards of truth without obligation to any economic imperative,

Ethics *in your life*

Whom Do You Trust?

Do you trust that journalists behave in ethical ways? What about public relations practitioners? If you had a discussion with your friends, what would they say? Do you think credibility is an important issue for information gatherers? As you read this chapter, think about the various individuals who try to control the flow of information. To what extent does their credibility have an impact on your life?

WHOM DO YOU TRUST?	WHO IS MOST LIKELY TO ADHERE TO ETHICAL BEHAVIOR?	DO MOST PEOPLE AGREE WITH YOU?
Print journalists?		
Reporters and anchors for network television news?		
Reporters for special news programming, such as news magazines?		
Reporters and anchors for local news?		
Public relations practitioners who work for nonprofit companies?		
Public relations practitioners who work for profit-making companies?		
Advertisers?		
Sources for news: Politicians?		
Sources for news: People who hold high positions in the business world?		
Sources for news: Social and political activists?		

but research reveals that economics and politics have often dictated news content. Furthermore, although public relations personnel are often thought to be more loyal to the organization that employs them than to the truth, standards of professional conduct also are applied to decision making in public relations. Public relations professionals consider part of their job to be convincing upper management of the ethical position that a company should take with regard to public service and information.

Ethical decision making is not easy to understand or to do. But because mass media permeate our society and are our primary source of information, we need to address ethical issues. Some of those addressed in this chapter include the following:

- ■ Why is adherence to ethical behavior an important consideration for media workers?

  - ■ How is ethical behavior related to political and social issues?

    - ■ How is ethical behavior influenced by economic issues?

      - ■ What is the relationship of ethical behavior to the marketplace of ideas?

infotainment: Combination of information and entertainment. Some critics today believe entertainment is considered more important than the level of information. This leads to sensationalism and news programs that contain little hard news and many consumer- and entertainment-oriented features.

386 Ethics in American life

Media critics have long been concerned with ethical standards. That concern, reported as early as the eighteenth century, was part of a continuing dialogue about the role of a free press in a democratic society. If the media are to be protected—that is, if freedom of expression is to be paramount—then the public must be able to trust the media to adhere to well-understood standards. The political importance of ethical behavior is strongly connected to the concept of a free-flowing marketplace of ideas that is the foundation of a democratic society.

History of journalistic standards

Ethical standards are intrinsically related to the political and cultural milieu in which the media operate. In colonial days, newspapers were highly partisan, and ethical discussions focused on whether editors should print points of view of competing parties rather than just the views of the party they supported. As newspaper editors adopted an **information model** during the middle of the nineteenth century, they remained partisan but also began to include stories about common people. This focus on individuals gave rise to new discussions about ethics. Critics denounced editors for trivializing the news, claiming that giving public notice to ordinary people was harmful to the public and "misled most people . . . into thinking them[selves] important."[2] After 1850, however, critics began to focus on the relationship between press and society, and they increasingly addressed press issues. They attacked editors for publishing trivial gossip and argued that publishing details of people's lives, such as accounts of weddings, invaded individuals' privacy.

With the rise of sensational journalism at the end of the nineteenth century, critics began to focus on attributes of news. They argued that fact and opinion should be separated, that care "beyond the profit principle must be exercised in news selection," and that material that violated good taste and judgment should be avoided. Critics, of course, differed in their definitions of good taste. Some thought crime stories were not in good taste. Others thought editors should print only certain types of detail about crime stories. Critics also noted that business and editorial operations should be separated. These discussions paved the way for development of journalism education, ethics codes, and other means of monitoring journalistic conduct.[3]

Sensational stories, such as those about murder/love triangles, have always been standard fare for newspapers. Critics have argued whether the editor should decide what the reader needs to read, or whether the reader can make intelligent individual choices. After World War II, the idea of a socially responsible press gained credence, and critics viewed it as the press' obligation to report the news in full context of political and social events.

information model: Pattern of behavior for disseminating information as news; incorporates values such as objectivity over partisanship.

Global *Impact*

Global Media and Ethics

Just as press systems vary throughout the world, so do ethical standards. In the United States, most reporters are discouraged from taking gifts from people they write stories about, but in Korea this practice is common. In Italy, writing self-serving articles about media owners who are also politicians is generally accepted.

Press ethics reflect the society and the regulations that shape the press system. David Weaver, Klaus Schoenbach, and Beate Schneider used data from Germany and the United States during the 1990s to compare reporting methods and ethics. They found the following:

In the early 1980s, West German journalists were also slightly more likely to say that claiming to be somebody else might be justified (22 percent, compared to 20 percent of the U.S. journalists), but the West Germans were slightly less likely to approve of paying for confidential information (25 percent, compared to 27 percent of U.S. journalists).

By 1992, U.S. journalists had not changed much in their willingness to endorse these ethically questionable reporting methods, except for dramatic increases in the proportions willing to justify the use of confidential business or government documents (from 55 percent to 82 percent) and the use of personal documents without permission (from 28 percent to 48 percent). The proportion of West German journalists who were willing to say that these methods may be justified increased between 1980–1981 and 1992 for every method, however, except for badgering unwilling informants.

SOURCE: David Weaver, Klaus Schoenbach, and Beate Schneider, "West German and U.S. Journalists: Similarities and Differences in the 1990s." Paper presented to the Association for Education in Journalism and Mass Communication, Kansas City, August 1993.

Journalists' Opinions on Questionable Reporting Methods in 1992

MAY BE JUSTIFIED *ON OCCASION*	WEST GERMANY (N = 983)*	UNITED STATES (N = 1156)*
Using confidential business or government documents without authorization	75%	82%
Getting employed to gain inside information	46%	63%
Paying people for confidential information	28%	20%
Claiming to be somebody else	28%	22%
Using hidden microphones or cameras	22%	60%
Making use of personal documents such as letters and photographs without permission	10%	48%
Badgering unwilling informants to get a story	6%	49%
Agreeing to protect confidentiality and not doing so	3%	5%

*N indicates the number of respondents.

In a study of journalistic standards, Marion Marzolf wrote,

By the end of the [nineteenth] century, the lines of debate over the modern daily newspaper had been set. The newspaper was still seen as the people's educator and as such had a moral responsibility to serve the public. Its independence from advertising and political parties was, therefore, considered essential. But dominance by the commercial side was tipping the press toward the immoral, degrading vulgarity that threatened impressionable minds and put it on a runaway course toward irresponsibility and even higher profits.[4]

Marzolf's statement reflects a concern that dominates criticism of the media today: the controversy between commercial gain and the traditional democratic values that a free press was thought to foster.

Key concept

Ethical Decision-Making: Making ethical decisions has been a concern of journalists at least since the early twentieth century, when many reporters wanted to be considered to be among the emerging groups of professionals. However, attempts to determine exactly what standards of conduct and moral judgment constitute ethical behavior have resulted in a continuing debate rather than absolute standards.

By the end of World War I, extensive use of propaganda techniques during the war raised ethical issues for practitioners of public relations as well as for journalists. In 1923, Edward L. Bernays, who had developed campaigns for the War Department, published *Crystallizing Public Opinion,* which argued that the modern public demanded information and made up its own mind. However, because society was growing in complexity, Bernays said, someone was needed to bring specialized information to the public in an honest, ethical way. He and his colleague and wife, Doris Fleishman, coined the term "counsel on public relations" to describe the work of the public relations practitioner. In essence, Bernays argued that in the marketplace of ideas the job of the public relations counsel was to get a client the best possible hearing for a legitimate message.[5]

History of press responsibility

When the First Amendment was written, idealists adhered to the Enlightenment philosophy that all individuals are born equal to learn, improve, and make proper decisions from which to lead productive lives. The government exists only as an extension of the people. The media's role is to provide information to individuals, who are rational beings able to discern truth from falsehood. If the press exists within a free marketplace of ideas, then all voices can be heard and the truth will emerge. The Founders had faith in the individual to make the right decisions based on all the information presented. The ability of individuals to make the right decisions depended on many people contributing their ideas to the discussion. For the marketplace of ideas to succeed, the market needs to provide free access for those who would contribute.

Key concept

Press Responsibility: Changes in theories of press responsibility have evolved with changes in the role of government and the relationship between the individual and society. Initially, the press sought to provide information that individuals could use to make rational decisions. As government assumed increased social roles, the role of the media shifted from providing basic information to sorting information and presenting a balanced report in a context of meaning.

By the twentieth century the Industrial Revolution had changed society and the press. Individuals became more interdependent, and national media developed as radio and television expanded. During the Depression, Franklin Delano Roosevelt introduced federal programs that were based on the concept that government has the responsibility to make sure people live in acceptable conditions. In addition, with the implementation of compulsory education, people gave government the responsibility of educating their children. To some degree, Americans had exchanged individualism for protectionism and collectivism.

With that change came renewed calls for offering individuals information that would allow them to put events and issues into context. As the volume of information increased, individuals made choices about what news to include in the newspaper. Theodore Peterson, coauthor of *Four Theories of the Press,* argued that somewhere along the way, "faith diminished in the optimistic notion that virtually absolute freedom and the nature of [humans] carried built-in correctives for the press."[6] Peterson noted that **libertarianism** was based on access, but if people are given only limited sources of information, it is harder for them to discern truth from falsehood.

In 1947 a commission chaired by Robert Hutchins expressed the change in society's expectations of the press system. The Hutchins Commission, which was funded mostly by Henry Luce, founder of *Time* and *Life,* said that the great influence of media and the concentration of ownership required that media be socially responsible. The commission called for journalists to give a fair, balanced, and complete report of world happenings in a context that gave the events meaning.[7] In other words, journalists needed to sift, process, and package information in a way that has meaning for their audiences.

During the twentieth century, **social responsibility** has replaced libertarianism as the dominant standard for media. As Peterson said, "freedom carries concomitant obligations; and the press, which enjoys a privileged position under our government, is obliged to be responsible to society for carrying out certain essential functions of mass communications in contemporary society."[8] In addition, media should continue to be free from government so that they can watch over government.

Although most journalists and media critics accept social responsibility in some form, not all do. Communication scholars John Merrill and Jack Odell have written about the hazards of the social responsibility approach:

> We simply (1) cannot understand exactly what is meant by a *theory* of social responsibility, and (2) cannot help feeling that a growing emphasis on such a theory will lead a nation's press system away from freedom toward authoritarianism. In the eyes of individual persons in *any* society various media at times will perform what they see as irresponsible actions; for irresponsibility, like beauty, is in the eye of the beholder.[9]

Critics of social responsibility see it as **self-censorship** that could deprive the marketplace of ideas of information that could help society. They also fear that standards of responsibility will come from the powerful and not from ordinary citizens.

Classical ethics in a modern society

In their book *Media Ethics,* three prominent ethics scholars, Clifford G. Christians, Kim B. Rotzoll, and Mark Fackler, outline five classical principles for understanding modern ethical decisions. Remember that these are philosophical principles that underlie discussions—they are not prescriptions for solutions, as you can see in the following examples.

Keyconcept

Theoretical Approaches to Ethics: The wide variety of theoretical approaches to ethical decision making indicates how hard it is to create ethical standards that apply to all situations. Some theorists argue that this is impossible, that decisions must be made within a specific context. Others suggest that overarching rules can provide contexts within which specific circumstances can be evaluated.

1. *The Golden Mean.* This concept was advocated by Aristotle, who believed that moderation in life, as well as in eating habits, best serves the individual. Moderation as applied to ethics means operating somewhere between two extremes. For example, in the NBC case, using rockets to cause explosions is not a form of moderation. Moderation would have required NBC to broadcast a story that contained information, but was not over dramatized for ratings effect.

libertarianism: A philosophy that espouses absolute freedom of action and thought for the individual without the restrictions of society.

social responsibility: As applied to freedom of the press, a philosophy that states that with freedom comes responsibility to the social good.

self-censorship: A media company's or individual's decision not to publish or broadcast particular content.

2. *The Categorical Imperative.* Eighteenth century philosopher Immanuel Kant believed that ethical principles should be determined by analyzing what principles could be applied universally. This imperative is related to what some call **absolute ethics.** What is right for one is right for all, and what is right for one situation is right for all situations containing similar elements. In the case of NBC's report on General Motors, would you condone the withholding of information about the rockets used to ignite the gas tanks of the pickup trucks? If you did, under Kant's theory you would need to be able to say universally that it is acceptable for reporters to present an incomplete picture of a situation.

People who advocate absolutist positions believe that if lying, for example, is unethical, then all variations from the truth are wrong; it would be out of the question to utter a white lie or to lie to protect someone. If an editor decrees that names of suspects will not be published until they have been found guilty, then that rule covers all cases, with no exceptions.

3. *The Principle of Utility.* Nineteenth century philosopher John Stuart Mill advocated that ethical decisions be made on the basis of what provides the greatest good for the greatest number of human beings within society. Using this principle, NBC might argue that although *Dateline* did not present the details on taping the rockets to the truck, NBC was doing the greatest good by helping people to recognize that older-model GM trucks are dangerous. (The assumption here is that the trucks were indeed dangerous, a position that GM would still argue is an outright lie.)

4. *The Veil of Ignorance.* John Rawls espouses a decidedly twentieth century philosophical position, arguing that justice emerges when social differentiations are eliminated in the process of negotiation. Therefore information is treated outside of social context, and power, wealth, and other social factors do not enhance one position over another. This principle means that NBC, in considering its story about GM pickups, should have ignored the size of General Motors and General Motors should have ignored the power of NBC. Then both could have acted fairly without being influenced by economic or political power.

5. *Judeo-Christian Ethic.* The Golden Rule, "Do unto Others as You Would Have Them Do unto You," applies here. Individuals who adhere to this religious ethic are encouraged to "Love Thy Neighbor as Thyself" and to treat all individuals with respect.[10]

Other ethical approaches include **antinomian ethics,** which rejects all rules. (The word "antinomian" is associated with the Protestant break from the Catholic Church and is the doctrine that claims that salvation is attained through faith and divine grace rather than through rigid adherence to law.) There are no guiding principles; each decision is made case by case. An editor would have no standard rule on whether to publish names of suspects in crimes, and story styles within a single broadcast, magazine, or newspaper issue could be inconsistent.

Situational ethics recognizes a set of principles, but exceptional circumstances surrounding a particular instance might modify the guideline or prove to be an exception to the general rule. Suppose an editor said there would be no appearance of suspects' names until they have been proven guilty. Journalists adhered to this general guideline until police arrested the mayor for embezzling from the city. The editor published the mayor's name, arguing that the public had a right to know the actions of its community leaders.

absolute ethics: A code of ethics that allows no deviation from its rules.

antinomian ethics: The absence of an ethical code to guide decisions. Each case is evaluated on its own merits.

situational ethics: A code of ethics that allows for variation in actions, depending on the circumstances of a given situation.

Political and economic demand for ethical behavior

The evolution of journalistic standards and concern about the ethics of reporting information—from both journalistic and public relations standpoints—clearly reveal that the public, press, educators, and critics demand ethical behavior. The standards are not always clear, and they change as cultural norms within society change. The nineteenth century critics who thought that reporting on crime was distasteful would be laughed off the television screen that thrives on realistic reenactments of police investigations.

However, there are also economic demands for ethical behavior because of the enormous impact of information dissemination in a free market society. Economic demand involves several factors: (1) the **credibility** of the news organization and its ability to make a profit, (2) the economic concentration of media outlets, and (3) the impact on other industries affected by media coverage.

Credibility and profit

When the public believes that those who work in the mass media act without thinking ethically, then media credibility is at stake. People listen to the radio, watch television, and read newspapers and magazines to find out what is going on in the world around them. If the local newspaper is known for routinely publishing inaccurate information, then people will stop buying the paper and turn to local television or radio for news.

Key concept

Credibility as an Economic Reason for Ethics: Credibility, or a measurement of how trustworthy a journalist or media organization is considered to be, is not just an ethical issue, but also an economic one. Some critics believe that for a new organization to remain profitable over time, the public must view it as credible.

If people question the credibility of one network news department, as they did when NBC staged the explosion of a GM truck in 1993, then people may turn to a more credible network for national news. After the NBC *Dateline* disaster a Times Mirror Center for the People & the Press study found that CNN had replaced NBC as the most believable news operation since a similar survey done four years earlier.[11] As programs drop in the ratings and lose advertisers, the profits of networks and/or stations can be seriously damaged.

Declining credibility continues to be a problem for all news organizations. A 1987 survey by the Times Mirror Center for People and the Press found that 62 percent of the respondents said there was no **bias** in presidential election coverage. In 1996, that figure had slipped to 53 percent.[12]

Another 1996 survey sponsored by the New York public relations firm of Porter/Novelli said 46 percent of 1,100 people interviewed found television and newspaper news believable. This was a drop of about a third since 1991.[13]

Ethics and media concentration

With increased concentration of media organizations, critics and the public become more attuned to the possibilities and effects of unethical behavior. In both news and entertainment the number of companies controlling the flow of mass information has declined. Concentration through takeover and merger continues today. In 1996, Time Warner, a corporation that owns movies, cable systems, and

credibility: A measurement of how well a journalist or media organization is trusted. If a high percentage of the public perceives a journalist as truthful, that person has credibility.

bias: A subconscious or intentional slant in reporting on a subject because of one's beliefs or prejudice on the issue. Such bias may or may not be obvious to the viewer or reader, who may thus receive incomplete or incorrect information.

392 magazines, started the acquisition of Turner Broadcasting, which started Cable Network News. This was one of several big mergers in a year that included Disney's acquisition of Cap Cities/ABC, and Westinghouse buying CBS.

Increasing concentration of power over media presents more opportunities for unethical behavior and expands the impact if such behavior occurs. Will movie reviewers at CNN and Time Magazine **pan** or praise films produced by Times Warner? How will Disney use ABC to promote its movies and theme parks? If media conglomerates use their control over content, say promoting a film through network news programs, will viewers be aware this is happening? Concentration of power does not automatically result in unethical behavior by the powerful, but it certainly provides increased opportunity, and consumers should know about that potential.

Impact on other industries

News stories affect not only readers, but also the subjects covered. They can affect an industry's credibility or a company's profits, as well as affecting the amount of government attention paid to an industry. Such attention can result in a change in regulation, that also ultimately affects profit. Increasingly, company officials and their public relations practitioners are challenging media reports that they believe are not accurate or complete. The following example of the effects of a combined public relations and news campaign on the apple industry illustrates these factors.

News organizations constantly struggle to overcome a negative perception that reporters are likely to stop at nothing to get a story. In The Paper, *Glenn Close plays an unscrupulous character, typical of movie depictions of reporters.*

On February 26, 1989, reporter Ed Bradley of the CBS news magazine *60 Minutes* sternly looked American consumers in the eye and declared, "The most potent cancer-causing agent in our food supply is a substance sprayed on apples to keep them on the trees longer to make them look better." As a result, he said, one of every 4,000 preschoolers who eat these apples will develop cancer during the child's life. Televisions in millions of American homes then glowed with a red apple—ringed by a skull and crossbones. The substance was Alar, a trade name for daminozide that was registered to Uniroyal Chemical Company, and it had been widely used by apple growers for two decades. The *60 Minutes* report was entitled "A Is For Apple," and it struck at the softest part of parents' hearts: safety of their kids.

Alar was federally registered for use on food in 1968. In 1973, Bela Toth, a cancer researcher in Omaha, fed high doses to mice and reported development of tumors. By 1984 the Environmental Protection Agency had placed Alar under review. The Natural Resources Defense Council (NRDC), an activist environmental group, filed suit against Uniroyal and its Alar product in 1984. During the mid-1980s, amid the NRDC campaign and general public concern with environmental causes of cancer, many grocery chains announced that they would not sell apples that had been treated with Alar, and Tree Top Company, the world's largest producer of apple products, declared that it would not use Alar-treated apples. Within this context, however, there was general scientific agreement that the Toth research data were fatally flawed. In 1985 the Scientific Advisory Panel reported to the EPA that Alar presented no threat. Nevertheless, the

pan: To criticize heavily.

Economic Impact

Media, Ethics, and the Cigarette Industry

I n October 1994, *Weekly Reader,* a children's magazine, published an article about the negative economic impact and unfairness of recent antismoking ordinances. K-III Communications owns *Weekly Reader* and is a subdivision of Kohlberg Kravis Roberts & Company, which happens to be a controlling shareholder in RJR Nabisco. RJR produces more cigarettes than any other U.S. company.

Also in 1994 a group of African American newspapers in Southern California ran full-page ads and articles supporting a ballot initiative that had been organized by Philip Morris to limit state antismoking restrictions. The papers editorialized in favor of the initiative and failed to publicize the other side of the issue.

No one is born smoking cigarettes. At some point, usually when they are young, people must be convinced that smoking cigarettes is a good idea. For a long time, the mass media have played a big role in promoting smoking by glamorizing it and by withholding information about its dangers.

Media promotion of smoking before the 1950s can easily be explained and excused. The connection between smoking and heart and lung diseases was not well established. Since then, scientists have learned that smoking cigarettes greatly increases the likelihood of developing cancer and other life-threatening diseases. Yet many magazines and newspapers continue to advertise tobacco products. Some publishers argue that media personnel should not make decisions about whether products are good or bad and that the public has a right to see information and make a decision on their own. Readers of the *Weekly Reader,* however, are ten years old. They have not yet gained the knowledge and developed the cognitive skills that allow individuals to make informed, rational decisions.

Media's ethical dilemma about covering the tobacco industry became more difficult in 1997 when Liggett admitted that its executive knew cigarette smoking was both harmful and habit forming. The company's release of internal documents raises issues about the truth of the industry's public relations campaigns and just how fair media should be in covering those campaigns.

SOURCE: "Darts and Laurels," *Columbia Journalism Review* (January–February, 1995): 19–21.

EPA, confronted by NRDC activism and a public concern about chemical use, moved in early 1989 to phase Alar out by 1990.

The *60 Minutes* report was not a story individually generated by an enterprising reporter. It was a story that was placed by public relations specialist David Fenton, who specialized in environmental causes. NRDC hired Fenton to renew interest in NRDC's regulatory agenda, to raise money for the organization, and to punish the apple industry as a lesson to other users of pesticides. Fenton negotiated a deal with *60 Minutes* that allowed the news magazine to be the first to release the NRDC report "Intolerable Risk: Pesticides on Our Children's Food." He then arranged follow-up interviews, an NRDC press conference, and appearances on morning talk shows. He even enlisted Hollywood personalities such as Meryl Streep, who founded "Mothers and Others for Pesticide Limits."

Fenton summed up his strategy as follows:

> Usually public interest groups release similar reports by holding a news conference and the result is a few print stories. Television coverage is rarely sought or achieved. . . . Our goal was to create so many repetitions of NRDC's message that average American consumers (not just the policy elite) could not avoid hearing it—from many different media outlets within a short period of time.[14]

394

Because of the *60 Minutes* report, people quit buying apples, national grocery chains pulled apples off their shelves, school systems banned apples, apple production was down more than a million bushels the next year, and some growers were forced out of business. One mother chased down a school bus to retrieve an apple from her child's lunch. Uniroyal pulled Alar off the market, and in May 1989, Congress passed a $15 million apple buyout package to save the industry. The International Apple Institute (IAI), a Washington-based trade group that was responsible for worldwide promotion of apples and apple products, had no orchestrated public relations response ready. Although the signals through the 1980s should have given them cause for concern, they had enjoyed favorable publicity for such a long time that they did not respond wisely or creatively to the NRDC challenge. The IAI could not even provide basic facts about the industry to its critics. The lesson of the Alar scare was not lost, however, and in June 1993, when the National Academy of Science released a report on diet, pesticides, and American children, the IAI was ready with facts on the industry, safety of chemicals, and a strong message that food is safe for children and adults.

Clearly, the NRDC public relations campaign affected the apple industry economically, with ramifications so great that it also affected taxpayers, who contributed to the $15 million buyout. But was it ethically responsible? There is strong scientific evidence that Alar did not pose a cancer threat to children or adults. Furthermore, the EPA had already moved to phase out Alar. Yet, in an effort to increase attention to NRDC's regulatory agenda, Fenton created an atmosphere of fear so great that mothers were afraid to let their children consume apple products. Further, CBS participated in creating and perpetuating that fear. Was this activity justified? Was the NRDC public relations campaign based on accurate, complete, and fair material? Was the *60 Minutes* account accurate, complete, and fair? Was either report morally responsible? Was the emotional appeal of the story too great to resist? Were the dramatic visuals—an apple coupled with a skull and crossbones—good journalism or emotional hype? Was the promise of even higher ratings for *60 Minutes* too hard to ignore?

Basic ethical standards in American media

Professional communicators recognize the value of fundamental standards of ethical behavior. In addition, media audiences have come to expect certain standards. Among these are accuracy, fairness, balance, accurate representation, and truth. The Public Relations Society of America, for example, recognizes, in its code of professional standards, values such as truth, accuracy, fairness, responsibility to the public, and generally accepted standards of good taste.

Keyconcept

Fundamental Ethical Standards: Although the debate about ethical decision making may never be settled, most individuals and groups agree on a few fundamental standards. Among these are accuracy, fairness, balance, accurate representation, and truth.

ACCURACY The bedrock of ethics is **accuracy.** For public relations professionals, reporters, and editors, being accused of being inaccurate is one of the worst charges that can be leveled. However, accuracy is not simple truth, but the reporting of information in a context that allows people to discern the truth. Some inaccuracies can be damaging, such as the one revealed in this correction printed in the *Fulton County Expositor* in Wauseon, Ohio: "The Fulton County Expositor incorrectly reported in Tuesday's edition that recently deceased John T. Cline of Delta was a Nazi veteran of World War II. The obituary should have read he was a Navy war veteran."[15] And subjects do notice. Actress Sharon Stone sent reporter Sandra Sobieraj flowers because she was the only writer to accurately report the actress's speech at the National Press Club.[16]

accuracy: The reporting of information in context that allows people to understand and comprehend the truth.

[profile]

Heywood C. Broun

Decades ago, Heywood Campbell Broun gave journalists a motto to remember as they work in the marketplace of ideas: "For the truth, there is no deadline."

Broun, a prominent newspaper columnist during the 1920s and 1930s, showed perpetual concern for the underdog. Today, the Heywood Broun Award is given to select journalists who have helped right a wrong or correct an injustice.

Broun began writing for newspapers in 1908 and did not stop until his death in 1939. He wrote novels, political tracts, and pieces about sports and drama. He invented the newspaper column in which writers expressed opinions that could differ from those of the owners. His six columns a week rooted out injustices, and they were read by thousands of people who felt that he was their friend.

Broun was educated at Harvard University. From 1912 to 1920 he was a drama critic and then literary editor for the *New York Tribune*. He and his wife, Ruth Hale, whom he married in 1917, also spent time in Europe, he as a war correspondent and

she as editor of a Paris-based edition of the *Chicago Tribune*.

In 1921, he began a daily column, "It Seems to Me," for the *New York World*, but in 1928 he was fired from the *World* because of his support for Italian anarchists Nicolo Sacco and Bartolomeo Vanzetti, who were convicted of murder on slight evidence but in an atmosphere of fear of anarchists.

Ruth Hale was America's first female movie critic, a reporter for the *New York Times*, and a drama critic for *Vogue*. This professionally successful couple led a somewhat tortured private life and after seventeen years of marriage were divorced, although they maintained what their son called a "special intimacy." Ruth Hale battled the State Department for the right to carry a passport bearing her name rather than her husband's, and she founded the Lucy Stone League, a group of women who championed the right to retain their birth names.

Broun ran for Congress as a Socialist in 1930. A few years later, he became the founding president of the American Newspaper Guild. When he died in

1939, more than 10,000 people, some of them readers, attended his funeral. In 1941, two years after his death, the Guild established the Heywood Broun Award for outstanding journalistic achievement that reflects "the spirit of Heywood Broun."

SOURCES: William Hunter, "In Bed with Broun, Star of the Liveliest Sheets," *The Herald* (Glasgow), March 14, 1995, p. 14; Mary Anne Ramer, "A PR Practitioner's Memo to Journalists," *Editor and Publisher* (October 10, 1992): 64; Joseph McLellan, "His Mother, His Father, Himself; Whose Little Boy Are You?: *A Memoir of the Broun Family* by Heywood Hale Broun," *The Washington Post*, August 8, 1983, Style Section, Book World, p. C8.

Some issues of accuracy are more complex. In August 1995, Capital Cities/ABC, Inc. settled a lawsuit filed by Philip Morris Companies that charged ABC's *Day One* with libel for reporting that the tobacco company "spiked" cigarettes with nicotine to keep smokers hooked. This lawsuit and a later threat of a suit against CBS's *60 Minutes* raises many issues, including whether the suits are simply used to intimidate news programs from tackling other tough issues. Nevertheless, the fundamental question is which is relating accurate material in context: the tobacco company and its public relations personnel or *Day One*. *Day One* charged that tobacco companies, when making reconstituted tobacco, added nicotine, keeping it at levels that would sustain addiction. The industry developed reconstituted tobacco several decades ago to transform unusable parts of the tobacco plant—stems, stalks, and leftover bits of leaf—into a paper product that can be blended with the pure leaf. Tobacco officials argued that in this process, some nicotine was lost, and the company added it back in. They argued that while *Day One* implied that they spiked the tobacco with additional nicotine, they were only returning it. Who is being accurate here? The public relations personnel and other officials acting for Philip Morris or *Day One* reporters, editors, and producers? Although ABC settled the suit and ran an on-air apology, the apology focused specifically on the addition of nicotine from outside flavor houses. ABC stated in the apology that the major focus of the report was on how tobacco companies used reconstituted tobacco to control levels of nicotine and that while Philip Morris said that it did not, ABC thought the reports spoke for themselves and that the issue should be resolved "elsewhere," probably a reference to the Food and Drug Administration. Again, this example raises many issues; a fundamental one is the accuracy of those who are communicating information.[17]

OBJECTIVITY To be truly unbiased is an admirable but unattainable goal. From birth on, society and familial upbringing subtly influence a person's view of the world. However, journalists who accept objectivity as a goal need to be aware of their biases and then report and produce as objective a story as possible.

Objectivity means more than being aware of personal biases. How objective—simply relating what someone else has said—should a journalist be? Perhaps some interpretation is necessary to give people the complete story. For example, in the 1950s the media unwittingly helped Wisconsin Senator Joseph McCarthy to instill a fear of Communism in American society that caused serious harm to innocent people. Actors and others who had only attended a meeting of the Communist party decades earlier were blacklisted and could not get a job in their profession. McCarthy and his aides understood how the media operated, and they carefully timed speeches and press conferences close to deadlines, knowing that reporters would have to choose between checking facts and being scooped by another news organization. Often, reporters followed the dictates of objectivity, quoting McCarthy verbatim. However, some newspaper reporters questioned McCarthy's actions, and in his television program *See It Now,* Edward R. Murrow exposed the McCarthy witchhunt.

However, sometimes journalists can interpret too much and mislead readers. In 1993 the father of basketball star Michael Jordan was found dead in his car on the side of the road. Mass media professionals delved into the son's history of alleged drug use and gambling, intimating a connection between huge debts and his father's death. But after an investigation, police found that the criminals had had no idea that the man they killed was Jordan's father. Meanwhile, the public, mislead by the framing of the story, had formed a false impression about Michael Jordan and his father's death.

Objectivity is not a fundamental ethical attribute of public relations and advertising personnel, whose goal is to persuade as well as to inform. But it has been a fundamental aspect of twentieth century reporting, and it is one of the factors that distinguishes journalism from public relations and advertising communication.

FAIRNESS AND BALANCE Fairness and balance often go hand in hand with accuracy and objectivity. Reporters attempt to investigate the many sides of a story. For example, abortion is a much-debated issue in many state legislatures. If the mass media quote and run video only on active demonstrators on the pro-choice and pro-life sides, the complete story remains untold. Stories need to take into account a range of differing opinions. Often, complexity must be preserved for **journalistic balance** to be achieved.

journalistic balance: Providing equal or nearly equal coverage of various points of view in a controversy.

Diane Sawyer speaks to reporters outside the courthouse after testifying during the trial of Food Lion vs. ABC.

An attempt to get a big story and reducing complexity to "gotcha journalism" may have been the problem for ABC News in its November 5, 1992, *PrimeTime Live* segment that charged that Food Lion, Inc., a nonunion food chain based in North Carolina, was selling out-of-date meat and substandard deli products. The broadcast, anchored by Diane Sawyer, also charged that Food Lion forced its workers to work overtime without being paid in order to accomplish their tasks. Food Lion sued the network and four producers of *PrimeTime Live* for fraud, deceptive trade practices, breach of the duty of loyalty, and trespass. The jury found that the producers had lied on their applications for employment at Food Lion stores, where they subsequently wore tiny cameras in their wigs and shot footage of Food Lion employees in the meat and deli departments.

Although the legal issue here centered on the information gathering process, other issues emerged during the trial. ABC had received leads for the story from the United Food and Commercial Workers Union (UFCW), which also helped the producers obtain references so they would get hired in Food Lion stores. All their on-camera sources had suits pending against the union. And the UFCW had made it public knowledge that its strategy for increasing union influence was to use unpaid, overtime work as an issue to gain negative media coverage for nonunion organizations.

Food Lion, after obtaining the many hours of out-takes—videotape shot but not used in the broadcast—claimed that the account was grossly distorted. The company made the out-takes available to other journalists, but almost no one visited the law firm in Washington, D.C., where they were housed to determine whether they believed the report was true. Yet other reporters claimed that Food Lion had sued for fraud and breach of duty of loyalty because they could not challenge the truth of the broadcast. If one reviews the tapes, the court records, and the journalistic accounts that are available, he or she has to question the fairness and balance of the broadcast. One scene in the broadcast where a worker appears to be slipping on a greasy floor, when viewed in the context of the out-takes, becomes instead an employee slipping on a soapy floor. The consequences to Food Lion of this story were enormous—stock value dropped $1.5 billion in several days. Yet few journalists were willing to take the time to pursue the truth of the conflict between ABC and Food Lion. In fact, network officials severely criticized Fox for showing some of the out-takes.

ACCURATE REPRESENTATION AND ABSENCE OF FAKERY Can a program ever be believed once it stages an incident? Sometimes. NBC's *Dateline* was not the first network to fake a car crash when it used igniters in its dramatization of the hazards of some GM trucks—all three networks have done the same. Unfortunately, the public was not told that program personnel "helped" to ignite the fire. Why did the network do it? Because of competition for viewers. The line between entertainment and news was badly blurred. The reason for the media error? "Because one side of the line is an Emmy. The other, the abyss," said *Dateline* anchor Jane Pauley.[18]

Misrepresentation and fakery can be sinking quicksand for public relations firms as well. In 1990, after Iraq invaded Kuwait, public relations firm Hill and Knowlton received $11.5 million from the Kuwaiti government–financed Citizens for a Free Kuwait. Hill and Knowlton's task was to help stir Americans' anger at Iraqi treatment of the Kuwaitis. In the fall of 1990, a young hospital worker known as Nayirah testified before a congressional committee that she had seen Iraqi soldiers throw babies out of incubators, leaving

398

them to die on the floor. This atrocity story became an important part of the congressional debate on whether the United States should go to war. Later, it became public that Nayirah was not a hospital worker, but rather the daughter of Kuwait's ambassador to the United States. Kuwaiti hospital officials said the incidents had never happened. Nayirah's testimony had been prepared with the help of Hill and Knowlton.[19]

TRUTH Although journalists cannot always ensure that their stories are true, they can make an extra effort to be truthful and to avoid lying. In July 1996, *Newsweek* columnist Joe Klein admitted publicly that he had written the best-selling novel *Primary Colors.* The book, which had sold 1.2 million copies, carried the name "Anonymous" on its cover and title page. Klein's admission would seem unimportant except that he had denied on several occasions that he had written the unflattering book based on President Clinton's 1992 primary campaign. Journalists around the country attacked Klein for lying. He replied that he had a right to privacy in writing the novel, and he asked whom his denials had hurt. Critics noted that making an estimated $6 million from a book and movie rights is certainly a person's right, but they added that readers would not trust his journalism or that of others, knowing that influential journalists are willing to lie to make money.

As the journalists and critics roasted Klein, many recounted a prominent earlier case that also involved truthfulness of a journalist. In 1981, Janet Cooke, a twenty-six-year-old *Washington Post* reporter, won a Pulitzer Prize for a front-page article called "Jimmy's World." Jimmy was an eight-year-old heroin addict. Soon after receiving the award, Cooke confessed that she had concocted the story; Jimmy did not exist. She returned the prize and left the *Post.* She resurfaced in 1996 after working at a department store in Michigan. Her return received national attention following an assignment from *Playboy* to get an interview with Washington, D.C., Mayor Marion Barry. Barry had been the mayor of D.C. when "Jimmy's World" was written and had helped to reveal Cooke's fraud. Barry refused the interview, but Cooke appeared on *Nightline* and *Today.* She also reportedly received an initial payment of $700,000 for a movie based on her life.[20]

Cases involving Klein and Cooke seem to imply that being an unethical journalist has its rewards. Such a conclusion would be appropriate if becoming rich were a journalist's goal. But when an audience begins to question a journalist's personal ethics, the credibility of the profession, as well as of the person, is at stake.

INTEGRITY OF SOURCES A journalist's story is only as good as his or her sources. Reporters who become too loyal to sources risk the possibility of being blinded and missing important cues to stories. The *Washington Post*'s revelations about the Watergate scandal initially came not from reporters covering the White House who had access to top-level sources, but from young metropolitan desk staffers Carl Bernstein and Bob Woodward, who connected one of the burglars who broke into the Democratic Party headquarters in the Watergate complex to the Central Intelligence Agency.

Keyconcept

Conflict of Interest: Along with government officials and others in a position of responsibility, journalists are under pressure to avoid allowing personal activities or interests to conflict with their professional responsibilities. Journalists have an obligation to strive for unbiased coverage of an event.

AVOIDING CONFLICT OF INTEREST Mass media professionals' outside business, social, and personal activities and contacts can subtly influence their work. An animal rights activist might not comprehensively and fairly cover a story on animals and scientific experiments; a city council member might not effectively relate all sides of a housing bill; and the spouse of a political contender might not write **objectively** about the candidate's platform.

objectively: Reporting facts without bias or prejudice, including a deliberate attempt to avoid interpretation.

Stories of conflict of interest abound. For example, *Columbia Journalism Review* gave one of its "Darts" to David Brinkley, who produced an article during the fall of 1995 that focused on the "twisted" logic of a federal tax code aimed at "soaking the rich." Brinkley was paid for the article by *Rising Tide,* a four-color glossy magazine put out by the Republican National Committee. Brinkley's receiving money from a political party put his ability to be objective in jeopardy.[21]

Supplying ethical standards

Standards can be imposed through agreements among professionals to behave in certain ways and to punish certain behaviors and by educating professionals in moral reasoning processes that help individuals and organizations to make decisions about how to handle specific situations.

Industry's response: Codes of ethics

Media organizations establish codes of ethics to standardize media behavior in response to events and to safeguard themselves against increased government regulation. Although critics argue that many codes are shallow, guidelines still serve as reminders that ethical standards are considered important to credibility, profit, and the good of society.

Although industry associations such as the American Society of Newspaper Editors developed ethics codes early in the century, many news organizations did not adopt formal codes until the 1980s, when ethics became a hot topic for journalists. Many other news organizations have firmly established verbal policies or guidelines set by precedent. Because of the small number of employees in some organizations, verbally communicated policies may be sufficient.[22]

The American Society of Newspaper Editors in 1923 was the first national press association to draw up an official code of ethics. Since then the Society of Professional Journalists (SPJ) and the Radio-Television News Directors Association (RTNDA) have formulated policies. In addition, national advertising and public relations codes have been drawn up. All have been revised with the changing times.[23] Figure 13.1 is the Society of Professional Journalists Code of Ethics that was revised in 1996.

Several years ago, the television code for advertisers that the National Association of Broadcasters (NAB) had established was ruled unconstitutional by the Supreme Court because the code required all broadcast bodies to be answerable to the same uniform policies. The industry code was seen as a violation of antitrust rules because it required all media organizations to behave in the same way.

National advertisers, public relations practitioners, film makers, TV program producers, and even **infomercial** producers have codes of ethics. These national policies serve primarily as voluntary guidelines for local member organizations. Some organizations simply follow the national or state code, or they modify the standard to fit their own news objectives and geographic areas. However, many media chains have written lengthy ethics policies that they expect their local affiliates to follow.

An organization's codes can be enforced in the same way as any company policy. Adherence to the national codes is voluntary and cannot be enforced. Many professionals fear the adoption of mandatory codes, arguing that they would be used as the basis for lawsuits that would harm the media.

Keyconcept

Role of Ethics Codes: Many media organizations establish codes of ethics to standardize their employees' behavior in response to events and to safeguard themselves against increased government regulation. Guidelines remind employees that ethical standards are considered important to credibility, profit, and the good of society.

infomercial: A media message that offers consumer information.

FIGURE 13.1

Society of Professional Journalists: Code of Ethics

PREAMBLE

Members of the Society of Professional Journalists believe that public enlightenment is the forerunner of justice and the foundation of democracy. The duty of the journalist is to further those ends by seeking truth and providing a fair and comprehensive account of events and issues. Conscientious journalists from all media and specialties strive to serve the public with thoroughness and honesty. Professional integrity is the cornerstone of a journalist's credibility.

Members of the Society share a dedication to ethical behavior and adopt this code to declare the Society's principles and standards of practice.

SEEK TRUTH AND REPORT IT

Journalists should be honest, fair and courageous in gathering, reporting and interpreting information.

JOURNALISTS SHOULD:

- Test the accuracy of information from all sources and exercise care to avoid inadvertent error. Deliberate distortion is never permissible.
- Diligently seek out subjects of news stories to give them the opportunity to respond to allegations of wrongdoing.
- Identify sources whenever feasible. The public is entitled to as much information as possible on sources' reliability.
- Always question sources' motives before promising anonymity. Clarify conditions attached to any promise made in exchange for information. Keep promises.
- Make certain that headlines, news teases and promotional material, photos, video, audio, graphics, sound bites and quotations do not misrepresent. They should not oversimplify or highlight incidents out of context.
- Never distort the content of news photos or video. Image enhancement for technical clarity is always permissible. Label montages and photo illustrations.
- Avoid misleading re-enactments or staged news events. If re-enactment is necessary to tell a story, label it.
- Avoid undercover or other surreptitious methods of gathering information except when traditional open methods will not yield information vital to the public. Use of such methods should be explained as part of the story.
- Never plagiarize.
- Tell the story of the diversity and magnitude of the human experience boldly, even when it is unpopular to do so.
- Examine their own cultural values and avoid imposing those values on others.
- Avoid stereotyping by race, gender, age, religion, ethnicity, geography, sexual orientation, disability, physical appearance or social status.
- Support the open exchange of views, even views they find repugnant.
- Give voice to the voiceless; official and unofficial sources of information can be equally valid.
- Distinguish between advocacy and news reporting. Analysis and commentary should be labeled and not misrepresent fact or context.
- Distinguish news from advertising and shun hybrids that blur the lines between the two.

- Recognize a special obligation to ensure that the public's business is conducted in the open and that government records are open to inspection.

MINIMIZE HARM

Ethical journalists treat sources, subjects and colleagues as human beings deserving of respect.

JOURNALISTS SHOULD:

- Show compassion for those who may be affected adversely by news coverage. Use special sensitivity when dealing with children and inexperienced sources or subjects.
- Be sensitive when seeking or using interviews or photographs of those affected by tragedy or grief.
- Recognize that gathering and reporting information may cause harm or discomfort. Pursuit of the news is not a license for arrogance.
- Recognize that private people have a greater right to control information about themselves than do public officials and others who seek power, influence or attention. Only an overriding public need can justify intrusion into anyone's privacy.
- Show good taste. Avoid pandering to lurid curiosity.
- Be cautious about identifying juvenile suspects or victims of sex crimes.
- Be judicious about naming criminal suspects before the formal filing of charges.
- Balance a criminal suspect's fair trial rights with the public's right to be informed.

ACT INDEPENDENTLY

Journalists should be free of obligation to any interest other than the public's right to know.

JOURNALISTS SHOULD:

- Avoid conflicts of interest, real or perceived.
- Remain free of associations and activities that may compromise integrity or damage credibility.
- Refuse gifts, favors, fees, free travel and special treatment, and shun secondary employment, political involvement, public office and service in community organizations if they compromise journalistic integrity.
- Disclose unavoidable conflicts.
- Be vigilant and courageous about holding those with power accountable.
- Deny favored treatment to advertisers and special interests and resist their pressure to influence news coverage.
- Be wary of sources offering information for favors or money, avoid bidding for news.

BE ACCOUNTABLE

Journalists are accountable to their readers, listeners, viewers and each other.

JOURNALISTS SHOULD:

- Clarify and explain news coverage and invite dialogue with the public over journalistic conduct.
- Encourage the public to voice grievances against the news media.
- Admit mistakes and correct them promptly.
- Expose unethical practices of journalists and the news media.
- Abide by the same high standards to which they hold others.

Sigma Delta Chi's first Code of Ethics was borrowed from the American Society of Newspaper Editors in 1926. In 1973, Sigma Delta Chi wrote its own code, which was revised in 1984 and 1987. The present version of the Society of Professional Journalists' Code of Ethics was adopted in September 1996. Reprinted by permission.

■ Critics' response

Both regulations and ethics involve standards of behavior. Regulation, however, carries the force of law. If a newspaper libels someone, it must pay damages. If a news reporter acts unethically, the only way to punish the journalist is through social sanctions, such as damaging his or her reputation. Problems arise because some people who work in media don't care about social sanctions. Often, money becomes the only concern.

One way of enforcing ethics comes through criticism of a media organization by other media organizations. During the newspaper wars at the turn of the twentieth century, editors of one newspaper delighted in telling their readers that another newspaper was being dishonest. Even today, newspaper media critics often criticize television news and occasionally other newspapers for unethical actions.

NEWS COUNCILS By 1947, increased chain ownership of newspapers meant fewer independent newspapers. The Hutchins Commission feared that less independent media would not freely criticize themselves. The commission recommended the establishment of **news councils,** which would hear complaints against news media, investigate each complaint, pass judgment on the complaint, and publicize that judgment.

During the 1950s and 1960s, several European countries, including Germany, England, and Sweden, established press councils. In 1972, a consortium of foundations started the Council on Press Responsibility and Press Freedom in the United States. It later became the National News Council, and its role was to investigate public complaints about national news organizations. Newspaper owners reacted to the News Council with the same vehemence that they had shown the Hutchins Commission. The vast majority of newspapers did not support the News Council and criticized the very idea of an independent watchdog for news organizations. In 1984 the National News Council closed because of lack of money and of support from the news media.

Despite the demise of the National News Council, two regional news councils survived as of 1997. The Minnesota News Council continued into its twenty-seventh year, supported by corporations, media, foundations, and individual donations. The Northwest News Council, founded by two chapters of the Society of Professional Journalists to serve Oregon and Washington, continued at a diminished level because of funding problems.

News councils try to help people and news organizations work out their differences. When this cannot be done, the councils hold public hearings on complaints and issue reports about the council's findings.

Growing concerns about credibility of news organizations and the increasing number of large libel suits being lost by media have rekindled interest in news councils. Steve Geimann, president of the Society of Professional Journalists, suggested that a national news council might help reduce criticism of media.[24] Mike Wallace, long-time reporter on *60 Minutes,* expressed a similar viewpoint in late 1996. Wallace said in a December 1996 lecture, "All journalists are perfectly willing to call attention to profligate politicians and potentates, but we show little enthusiasm when similar attention is focused on us."[25]

OMBUDSMEN Another effort to enforce ethics originated at the *Louisville Courier-Journal and Times* in 1967, with the appointment of the first newspaper **ombudsman.** The role of ombudsman varies from newspaper to newspaper, but the primary function is to represent the readers and to criticize the actions of the newspaper when the ombudsman believes it has done something wrong.

news council: A committee that reviews potentially unethical activities of news organizations.

ombudsman: A person within an organization who represents customers and investigates potentially unethical conduct of the organization and people within it.

A key ingredient of the ombudsman's job is writing a column in the newspaper revealing the results of investigations into complaints. Sometimes complaints are supported, and sometimes they are not. An effective ombudsman will serve as the newspaper's conscience and help to ensure that readers and the community are served and ethical standards are observed. Although only a minority of newspapers employ ombudsmen, by 1996 this group had a national organization—the Organization of News Ombudsmen—with about fifty members.

JOURNALISM REVIEWS Only a small percentage of newspapers have ombudsmen, and news media have failed to support news councils, but another forum for exposing questionable media behavior exists: the journalism review. These publications report and analyze examples of ethical and unethical journalism. Three national reviews provide extensive criticism of the media: *Quill, American Journalism Review,* and *Columbia Journalism Review. Quill* is published by the Society of Professional Journalists; *American Journalism Review* is published by the University of Maryland College of Journalism; and *Columbia Journalism Review* is published by Columbia University.

Moral reasoning processes for ethical decisions

Codes of ethics are good for outlining standard practices and procedures, but they cannot take every situation into account. Media practitioners must go through a **moral reasoning process** to help them make decisions. Instead of simply saying that the decision "felt like the thing to do," professionals need to be able to articulate and justify why a decision was made. They must be accountable.

Several ethical decision-making procedures and models have been developed to help professionals make ethical decisions. Some that are presented within the next few pages include a framework advanced by philosopher Sissela Bok, a decision-making process designed by Peter Roy Clark of the Poynter Institute, a method advocated by media ethics expert H. Eugene Goodwin, and the Potter Box. Not every model or every item within each model will be equally pertinent to every situation; however, each item should at least be considered.

Sissela Bok devised three questions to help all types of professionals make ethical decisions. Each question is discussed in great detail in her book, *Lying: Moral Choice in Public and Private Life:*[26]

1. How do you feel about the action? (Look inside yourself and have a talk with your conscience.)

2. Is there any other way to achieve the same goal that will not raise ethical issues? (Talk to others to find out what they would do. Or think about what a trusted friend or ancient philosopher would suggest.)

3. How will my actions affect others? (Think about what readers, viewers, sources, and those affected by the story might feel or say.)

Roy Peter Clark of the Poynter Institute for Media Studies suggests that all types of journalists should have a moral reasoning process at hand for deadline decisions. He offers five questions that should be answered before a story is published or broadcast:[27]

1. Is the story, photo, or graphic complete and accurate to the best of my knowledge?

moral reasoning processes: Processes that help communication professionals make ethical decisions from a principled basis rather than reacting intuitively.

2. Am I missing an important point of view?

3. How would I feel if this story or photo were about me?

4. What good would publication do?

5. What does my reader or viewer need to know?

H. Eugene Goodwin, retired journalist and professor emeritus of journalism at Pennsylvania State University, wrote a book titled *Groping for Ethics in Journalism* after "becoming bothered by some of the things journalists and news media proprietors do. They do not always seem to have a strong sense of morality, of what is right and wrong." He recorded seven questions that he found to be successful in teaching journalism ethics and for working journalists:[28]

1. What do we usually do in cases like this? (Consider whether a policy for this situation has been established. Is it a good policy or does it need to be modified?)

2. Who will be hurt and who will be helped? (Recognize that most stories will hurt someone or some group. Weigh that hurt against benefits to the community. "Realizing who is apt to be hurt and whether the benefits can justify that hurt can help us make an intelligent decision.")

3. Are there better alternatives? (Think about all alternatives before making a decision. Harmful results often can be softened or eliminated by going a different route.)

4. Can I look myself in the mirror again? (You must think about how you feel personally. Can you live with yourself afterward? James D. Squires, formerly of the *Chicago Tribune,* advised media people not to "do anything that your momma would be ashamed of.")

5. Can I justify this to other people, the public? (If you know that you have to explain your decisions, in an editor's column or television newscast, for example, you are often more careful with your decisions.)

6. What principles or values can I apply? (Some established principles, such as not lying, justice, or fairness, will take priority over others.)

7. Does this decision fit the kind of journalism I believe in and how people should treat one another? (Your judgments should correspond with the way you believe that media ought to act and how "people in a civilized society ought to behave.")

The Potter Box, constructed by Harvard philosopher and theologian Ralph Potter, is a sequence of four steps designed to help people reason their way in an ethical situation.[29] Sometimes the initial reaction to a set of circumstances is not the final judgment one has after progressing through facts, values, principles, and loyalties as portrayed in the Potter Box, depicted in Figure 13.2.[30]

Ethical situations and dilemmas

Some situations are variations on common dilemmas. Because these dilemmas recur often, personnel in many news organizations have developed consistent ways of dealing with them.

404

FIGURE 13.2 Modified Potter Box

```
┌─────────────────┐              ┌─────────────────┐
│   Definition    │─────────────▶│     Values      │
└─────────────────┘              └─────────────────┘
 Examine the situation            Analyze how different
    and identify                   actions might affect
   who is involved.                 different parties.
   (What happened?)

┌─────────────────┐              ┌─────────────────┐
│   Principles    │◀─────────────│    Loyalties     │
└─────────────────┘              └─────────────────┘
 Look at the ethical              Identify to whom we
   issues involved.               have allegiance and why.
```

The original version is described in Ralph B. Potter, "The Structure of Certain American Christian Responses to the Nuclear Dilemma, 1958–1963" (Ph.D. Dissertation, Harvard University, 1965).

Business and media content

In 1994 a New Haven, Connecticut, *Register* editor gained national attention when he was given a two-week suspension without pay. He had committed the sin of running a story that explained how customers could buy cars at less than the sticker price. Automobile dealers, who spent considerable money for ads in the *Register,* complained to the newspaper's publisher.[31]

Most media outlets are businesses, and many depend heavily, if not entirely, on advertising revenue. This often creates ethical dilemmas for people who create media content. When the dilemmas are solved in favor of the advertiser, the public becomes more cynical about the media. Such situations give rise to charges by critics such as scholar Herbert Altschull that the person who pays the piper calls the tune.

Businesses can affect content in a variety of ways, but the most effective impact is created through advertising. Advertisers can withhold advertising in what is called an advertising boycott, or the fact that they buy advertising can result in favorable treatment.

Business content sometimes reflects advertisers' needs and wishes as much as it does the focus of the editor and reporter. Automotive and real estate sections often carry content that support advertisements.

In 1989, *Washington Post* reporter Kirstin Downey wrote a story about Harvard University research that predicted a decline in house prices for the next eighteen years. During the next year the *Post* lost $750,000 in advertising from builders who viewed the coverage as negative.[32]

In 1993, the California Department of Health Services asked *Essence* magazine to publish an antismoking ad that had pictures of three African American singers who had died of smoking-related diseases. The ad read, "Cigarettes Made Them History." It never appeared in *Essence,* which runs cigarette advertisements.[33]

Not all media organizations knuckle under to advertisers' pressures, nor do all news organizations ignore the negative side of local businesses. In 1992 the Greensboro, North Carolina, *News & Record* published a detailed record concerning what the cigarette industry knew about the dangers of smoking and did not reveal. The story ran despite the newspaper's location in the heart of tobacco-growing country.[34]

Just how advertising and business pressure affects content depends on the ethics of the individual journalists and media managers. Some managers give in to pressure more quickly than others, and some do not give in at all. Allowing advertisers to influence news and information has at least two dangers—one for consumers and one for the media companies. If consumers know that the information they receive represents a business's bias, they can take this into consideration when using that information. If they don't know, as may happen when media are influenced by advertisers, then they can be influenced to act in ways that may not be in their interest.

Being influenced by businesses has a cost to the media organizations as well. The price is a loss of credibility. Once readers, listeners, and viewers learn that the news and information they receive has been influenced by advertisers, the consumers may never trust the media organization again. Without trust, readers and viewers will not use information, and without an audience, the newspaper, magazine, or television program is of no use to advertisers.

Advertisers affect entertainment content as well as news. By the early 1990s, daytime talk shows had been given the name "trash talk." Topics such as love triangles, incest, and sex in a variety of forms dominated the programs. Backlash to the programs developed on a variety of fronts. Former U.S. education secretary William Bennett attacked the shows and asked advertisers not to support them. Some stations stopped carrying particularly offensive shows. Ratings began to decline, and finally, advertisers such as Procter & Gamble stopped advertising on some shows. As a result of these trends, some talk shows moved away from the more sensational topics.

■ Freebies and junkets

At different times in history, and up until the 1980s, at least some people who worked in mass media took for granted that their low pay would be supplemented by gifts, free trips, and meals. **Publicists** made freebies and junkets (gifts and trips) simply **perks** of the job. Freebies and junkets were among the first practices to be attacked as unethical. During the early 1900s, editors began to reject free railroad passes in return for advertising. But the practice persisted. In 1986 a *Houston Post* writer described the lack of American tourists in Monaco. Many tourists chose not to travel to Europe that summer because of terrorism. The writer explained that he had found Monaco safe during his recent visit, but he failed to tell the readers that his visit was paid for by the Monaco Government Tourist and Convention Bureau.[35]

Just as journalists have rejected this practice, so have professional public relations practitioners. One element of treating each other with

publicist: Person who seeks publicity for another person, a product, or an event.

perks: Short for perquisite, or payment for something in addition to salary.

Video News Releases

Media publicity special-ists, such as public re-lations practitioners and advertisers, produce video news releases (VNRs) to promote political candidates or supplement advertising campaigns.

VNRs are an extension of press releases. Initially, written press releases were sent to televi-sion stations (and are still sent to radio and print media) in hopes of meriting enough attention for the organization to follow up with a story. Now many press releases are VNRs. These professionally produced television packages, which run one to three minutes, can be sent by satellite and slipped into any national or local news program. The transition within the newscast between lo-cally produced news reports and the public-relations-produced VNR is invisible to the public.

Just like real news stories, the best VNRs contain human inter-est or feature angles. Some are complete corporate-sponsored packages. Others include profes-sional footage of their experts giving sound bites, into which the local stations can insert their reporters asking questions. Addi-tional options include highlights from events to which the stations can add its own comments. Members of Congress use video news releases to inform con-stituents about their roles in par-ticular legislative packages, for example.

A 1992 national survey of television news directors found that most used VNRs (often in their unedited, complete form) and relied on the information presented. In other words, many stations checked neither the facts nor the credibility of the sources. Furthermore, only a little more than half (58 percent) of sur-veyed news directors said that they had a policy regarding VNRs. More than 76 percent of these admitted that their policy was unwritten.

VNRs are good for advertisers, politicians, public relations practi-tioners, and corporations. The cost of production and dissemination is less than that of a commercial or advertisement. VNRs can also be helpful to stations that are ex-periencing budget cuts and staff reductions. Above all, the public relations objective is achieved—getting legitimate news exposure for a cause.

However, the seamless quality of public relations material inter-woven with news can deceive viewers, who trust the integrity of television news programs. When stations do not identify VNRs and run them without checking facts, they become agents of the public relations practitioners. Viewers look to news programs for objec-tive information with which to form opinions. Instead, they are receiving carefully designed VNRs that are used to further a corporation's profits or to pro-mote a particular candidate.

SOURCE: John Pavlik and Mark Thalhimer, "From Wausaw to Wi-chita: Covering the Campaign via Satellite," *Covering the Presidential Primaries,* Freedom Forum Media Studies Center, June 1992, pp. 36–46.

respect has been an acknowledgment that public relations is most effective when it is based on accurate and convincing information and that journalists can best act with in-tegrity when they are not indebted to specific organizations or people.

Anonymous attribution

Public relations professionals and advertisers often make use of the anonymous source, claiming that a product is "first in the nation," or "rated No. 1" without attributing the information or discussing the research behind the claim. It then falls to the consumer either to accept the claim or to doubt it and the credibility of related information.

In other instances it may be difficult to find someone who understands a situation and is willing to be quoted. Often, media professionals manage to get someone to talk only by agreeing not to use the source's name. Then, instead of investigating other sources who might be willing to be named, the professional simply goes with the unnamed source, noting in the story that the information came from a "government official," "knowledgeable source," or "expert." In 1977, about 70 percent of *Newsweek* magazine's stories and 75 percent of *Time*'s stories had anonymous attribution. In 1984 that rose to 84 percent in *Newsweek* and 77 percent in *Time*.[36] How would it look if all the stories in those magazines never named a source? Why is no one willing to be named? Why don't they want to be held accountable for the information? Is it not accurate? When there are no named sources, it is easy to imagine that someone fabricated the whole story.

Checkbook journalism

News organizations, both broadcast and print, sometimes pay sources for story ideas and information.[37] This **checkbook journalism** occurs mostly in entertainment, but it happens in news organizations as well. Television drama, special events, and news are especially notable areas. For example, producers of television dramas, often bidding large sums against each other, pay people for their real-life stories. Tabloid news and entertainment program producers buy amateur videos and electronic memoirs. Consultants are paid highly for their services. Ethical questions are often ignored in the interests of increasing program ratings. One important ethical question should be whether the person would have much to say if he or she were not being paid. Are participants exaggerating their involvement just for money?

Privacy versus people's need to know

When does information change from news to voyeurism? Is it necessary to watch a woman cry on television about the death of her spouse? Is it important to write that the man who rescued a drowning child was also gay? The question here is whether the account serves a public interest.

Many media professionals believe that there are times when the public's right to know takes precedence over the **right of privacy** of an individual. Journalists often report when a political candidate has been unfaithful to a spouse. Although some reporters believe that personal life has nothing to do with business or politics, others think that personal actions illuminate character. A candidate who breaks a solemn vow to someone as important as his or her spouse might also break promises to constituents. How much of a public person's private life do people need to know? What constitutes "the public's right to know" is an ethical question that media workers and the public share.

At times, a public event becomes a media circus. The trial of O. J. Simpson for murder is a ready example. From the summer of 1994 until the fall of 1995 the O. J. Simpson case was a topic or news segment on NBC's *Nightly News,* a regular topic on tabloid television, and the target of farcical skits on Jay Leno's late-night show and *Saturday Night Live.* Almost buried under discussions of prosecutor Marcia Clark's hairstyles and child support problems, defense attorney Robert Shapiro's tailored suits, and Judge Lance Ito's whimsical comments lay the real tragedy of two murdered people.

checkbook journalism: Paying subjects or witnesses for information or interviews.

right of privacy: An ethical and legal area of decision making. The right to be protected from unwarranted intrusion by the government, media, or other institutions or individuals.

408

Public figures are not given as much consideration as private citizens. Public figures, such as politicians or movie stars, deliberately place themselves in the limelight and know that their lives and movements will be constantly scrutinized by the press. Private citizens, however, usually have indirectly attracted publicity for some other reason. Therefore ethical journalists look at whether someone is a private citizen or a public figure when considering whether to include some types of information about that person.

Some debate surrounded the 1992 coverage of the late tennis star Arthur Ashe. Ashe qualified as a public figure because of his tennis success during the 1960s and 1970s. He contracted the HIV virus during surgery in 1983 and developed AIDS a few years later . When a *USA Today* reporter asked Ashe whether he had AIDS, Ashe felt compelled to hold a press conference before the story could appear. Ashe said that his privacy had been invaded. Some journalists considered it a legitimate story; others said it had no real news value. What public interest did this coverage serve?

In 1991, William Kennedy Smith, nephew of Senator Ted Kennedy and of assassinated President John F. Kennedy, was accused of rape. Immediately, months before the trial, reporters began to cover the story. They peeked into the alleged victim's windows to tell the public what books were on her shelves. Television and print professionals dug into her background and highlighted her high school drinking and dating habits.[38] The media also delved into Smith's background and discussed his personal and social habits.

The trial became a sensational soap opera. What public interest did this coverage serve?

Controversy also surrounded the coverage of the Olympic bombing incident in Atlanta in August, 1996. Richard Jewell, a part-time security guard, originally was lauded as a hero, then questioned as a suspect by the FBI. Atlanta media, which received a tip that Jewell was a suspect, printed and broadcast numerous stories about him. Jewell now has sued for libel and slander. However, he has benefitted in some ways from the publicity. For example, in early 1997 he signed a contract with Fox for the movie rights to his story, and he was profiled in the February, 1997 issue of *Vanity Fair.*

The issue of naming victims is an important question of privacy versus a reporter's belief that the public has a right to know what is happening in a community. Many local stations can describe a victim or the accused so completely that name identification is unnecessary. The amount of detail that will be given is an ethical decision.

The "media circus" effect of high-interest incidents has long been an ethical dilemma for news editors and a strain for judges. Tonya Harding's attempts to win an Olympic medal through unsavory means provided fodder for journalists seeking sensation.

Whether to make a victim's name public is also an ethical decision. Although most states have no legal constraint against publicizing a victim's name, Florida did at the time of the William Kennedy Smith's trial. The statute provided for criminal penalties for "identifying the victim of a sexual offense in any instrument of mass media." Florida brought criminal charges against *The Globe,* a national supermarket tabloid based in Boca Raton, Florida, for publishing the alleged victim's name and other identifying information. (*NBC News* also publicized the name of the alleged victim.) The paper challenged the Florida statute under both Florida and U.S. Constitutions. In 1995 the Florida Supreme Court held that the previous Florida statute was unconstitutional.[39]

■ Sensationalism, decency, and good taste

Some material, especially visual information, will always be more offensive to some viewers than others. Material that is used merely to shock, startle, or violate a person's sense of decency may attract attention, but it is not newsworthy.

Stanley Forman, a photojournalist for the Boston *Herald-American* took several photos of a young woman and little girl standing on the fire escape about to be rescued from a burning building. Suddenly, the fire escape collapsed, and Forman took dramatic pictures of the two falling. Although the woman died, newspapers all over the world published the photos, and Forman was awarded a Pulitzer Prize. As mass media educator Fred Fedler noted, readers "accused the newspapers of sensationalism: of poor taste, insensitivity, an invasion of the victims' privacy, and a tasteless display of human tragedy to sell newspapers."[40]

Keyconcept

Ethics and Sensationalism: In the 1980s, many media companies went public (offered sale of their stocks to the public), thus becoming vulnerable to stockholders' demands for continuous high profits. They found that talk shows featuring sensational topics could be produced inexpensively and garner high profits. Other sensational content also seems to attract viewers and readers. However, media companies are also under pressure to balance the need for profit against social responsibility and a high quality of journalistic performance.

The realism of images can create controversy, as it did when the Associated Press transmitted, and newspapers printed, a graphic and shocking photo of an identifiable American soldier being dragged by ropes through the streets of Mogadishu, Somalia, in October 1993. Is it the media's responsibility to protect and shield the public, or is it to educate the public? Does the publication of some photos result in a societal good?[41]

Images that are distributed electronically can cause as much controversy as printed images. During the 1980s and 1990s, viewers became more concerned with the high number of graphic depictions of violence and sex scenes on television and in movies. How advertisers and public relations firms portray women and minorities in selling products in ads or for product promotions has also concerned different segments of society. Critics are concerned that adults and children may adopt behavior patterns and attitudes that are based at least in part on media portrayals.

Many critics believe that the constant repetition of graphic violence and sex in all media sends the wrong message, especially to young viewers, about the world around them. These scenes grab viewers' attention but rarely show the consequences associated with violence and indiscriminate sexual acts. Are violent aggressors to be admired? What are the repercussions of casual sex? Although few scholars believe that watching a few indiscriminate sex acts on television will cause a teenager to be sexually active, many are concerned that a multiplicity of such shows helps to shape a child's view of norma-

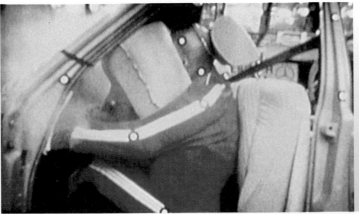

This image of a crash-test dummy reflects editors' dilemmas over whether to show mangled bodies along with stories of car accidents. Critics and viewers increasingly ask whether such pictures are within the bounds of good taste.

410

tive behavior. Do excessive violence and sexual behavior become accepted by the viewer as what "probably" goes on in most people's lives?

Direct quotations

Quotation marks signify the exact words of a source. However, research shows that media professionals do not agree on the practice of quoting bad grammar, cursing, ramblings, and accents.[42] Nor do they agree on when a quote should be edited. For example, cursing might be edited out of a quote from a student but left untouched in one from a ball player or politician (or the other way around, depending on the subject). Normally, if a quotation is to be changed, a media professional should paraphrase, using indirect or partial quotations. This should be done for all types of people and situations. Journalists almost universally denounce making up quotes, even if they are based on notes and represent a partial reconstruction of what the person might have said.

Awards

Hundreds of organizations present awards to journalists for coverage of specific topics. Over the years, awards have been given for such topics as travel stories about Las Vegas, medical stories about hypertension, and editorial coverage of men's fashion. The amounts of the awards vary from a few hundred dollars to several thousand dollars. The expressed purpose of awards given by business organizations and foundations is to increase coverage of their particular interests.

Such awards become an ethical issue when reporters begin to cover topics and issues mainly to win an award. Time that a reporter spends writing about one topic is time that cannot be spent on another. Awards can also alter news judgment such that less weight is given to what readers need and want and more weight is given to the possibility of getting outside income.

Correction of errors

Media sometimes publish or broadcast inaccurate information; yet often, the public is never notified of the inaccuracy. When was the last time a network news anchor admitted to a mistake made the previous night? While covering the Gulf War, the networks had live reports and inevitably broadcast a variety of mistakes while trying to be first with the news. Most of these mistakes were never identified or addressed. Instead, more accurate news was broadcast in a follow-up story.

Newspapers are usually better than magazines, television, and radio about rectifying errors. However, readers rarely know where to look for corrections because notifications are not a standard practice. When a correction is made, it is usually published on an inside page, not in a prominent position. Some newspapers, such as the *Chicago Tribune,* either place corrections at the same location as the original story or put the corrections in the same location every day.

docudramas: Films or television programs that blur fact and fiction. Part documentary, part drama, these programs often do not make clear what is factual and what has been added to make the story interesting and exciting.

Fiction and fact

When real-life events provide the basis for entertainment, professionals often are confronted with the issue of mixing fact and fiction. **Docudramas** make great viewing. But they often blur the lines between fact and fiction in a way that is so compelling that viewers remember the visual representation better than the facts. Historians are

Scaling Back on Crime Coverage

Sensationalism and gore abound on television, especially during ratings sweeps. In Florida there has been a backlash.

People in south Florida say they are "sick of graphic images of crime and concerned about the glorification of criminals," said Miami's WCIX-TV vice-president. In response, WCIX-TV began screening out graphic video and made newscasts appropriate for family viewing in 1994.

Other television stations, such as WCCO-TV in Minneapolis and KRQF-TV in Albuquerque, New Mexico, had made similar determinations just a few months earlier.

In addition to violence and graphic images increasing, the sheer amount of televised crime cover-age has increased. Murder coverage tripled and graphic crime news doubled from 1992 to 1993 on the three major networks. WCIX-TV is now striving for more balanced reporting, using less sensationalism and devoting a lower percentage of news time to crime coverage.

With local news becoming so violent and tabloidlike, the Miami station's decision was applauded by media critics, including Katherine Montgomery, president of the Washington-based Center for Media Education. Critics are concerned that as children and adults watch more and more graphic violence, they lose the ability to be shocked or outraged and instead become numbed. As they watch exaggerated coverage of crime, they are more likely to view the world as it is depicted by television, when in reality most people's chances of being affected by crime are much smaller than the TV version would indicate.

SOURCE: "Miami TV Station Slashes Crime Coverage," *AP Industry News,* The Associated Press, May 9–16, 1994.

therefore justifiably concerned about films such as *Mississippi Burning,* the story of the murder of three civil rights workers during the 1960s. *Mississippi Burning* gave Gene Hackman a starring role as a tough and decent FBI warrior and distorted the role of the FBI. In fact, many historical journals have introduced new sections to evaluate historical docudramas and films. Docudramas about recent crimes often obscure the details and sensationalize the characters, encouraging viewers to feel sorry not only for the victims, but often for the perpetrators of the crime.

Some of Oliver Stone's movies in the 1990s have created a great deal of controversy. Stone's *Platoon* won the best picture Oscar in 1986 for its realistic treatment of the Vietnam War. He ventured into politics in 1991 with *JFK* and in 1995 with *Nixon*. Both films received critical acclaim, but both were also attacked as revisionist history. *JFK* explored the possibility that a conspiracy lay behind the assassination of President John F. Kennedy in 1963. The film was criticized for its factual errors and questionable assumptions. *Nixon* portrayed the life of Richard M. Nixon, who resigned from the presidency in 1974 after the U.S. Congress began impeachment proceedings in the wake of the Watergate scandal. *Nixon* has fewer inaccuracies than *JFK,* but it did poorly at the box office. Film makers such as Stone say they use movie story-telling techniques to get their version of truth to viewers. As one writer put it, "Asked if he believed that art could arrive at the truth even faster than journalism, Stone replied, 'I know it.' "[43]

Altering fact to get one's version of the truth across to people requires ethical decision making. How much alteration is permissible? How much should the viewer or reader be told about the alteration? How can an artist be sure his or her version of the truth is really the truth? How can changing fact reveal truth? Again, these pose serious questions about whether the results contribute to society's understanding of its own history.

■ Visual depictions

Digitally manipulated photographs have been cause for ethical concern. People tend to believe that a photograph freezes a moment in time. Now photos create fiction. Publications have begun to use the term "illustration" instead of photo in describing these manipulated graphic images, but is the change in the photo explained to consumers? Are practitioners being honest with the public or simply portraying what they want the public to believe?

Trends

Increasing competition among media will cause conflicting trends in the future. As media companies compete for readers, viewers, and listeners, organizations will be more tempted to emphasize sensational content to get attention. This is how talk shows responded during the early 1990s. Because talk shows cost little to produce, they can be highly profitable, even with relatively small audiences. Such profitability guaranteed their expansion. In the fall of 1995, eleven different television talk shows in Chicago could be viewed during a two-hour period. The programs competed for viewers with increasingly sensational topics and guests. A public backlash toned down the content, but it is highly probable that sensationalism will continue, as it has throughout media history.

Sensationalism has always been part of competition, and it is likely to occur repeatedly with varied forms of media. A second force, the segmented audience, will also test the ethics of media managers. As media outlets proliferate, audiences have increased choices about what to read or watch. Specialization gives the advertisers more power over content because the media company becomes more dependent on a few advertisers. *Glamour* magazine, for example, has a much smaller pool of potential advertisers than *Newsweek* does because *Glamour* has a narrow reader appeal. If an article in *Glamour* upsets the large cosmetic advertisers, an advertiser boycott could reduce the magazine's revenue drastically.

A third factor affecting media ethics is the growing demand for high profits by publicly owned corporations. Media companies such as Gannett and Knight-Ridder must keep their profits high to keep their stock prices from falling. Declining stock prices can result in changes in management and takeovers by corporations that think the media company's stock is undervalued. Companies with high profit margin requirements might be

Television talk show hosts often skirt the boundaries of ethical behavior. Jenny Jones testifies here in a case filed by the family of a man who was shot to death after personal revelations on her television show.

less likely to write or broadcast negative information about their advertisers and more likely to give in to advertiser boycotts.

Although competition can often increase the possibility of unethical behavior, it can also help to expose that behavior. Media companies competing for audiences do not hesitate to expose the questionable behavior of their competitors. One network news department might eagerly expose that another network's news department is paying sources or staging events to create video.

Summary

- Ethics are important because citizens rely heavily on media to make informed decisions in a democratic framework and because media credibility is necessary to attract and keep an audience.

- Ethical behavior has political and economic implications.

- In the nineteenth century, editors were criticized for trivializing the news when they printed material about the details of people's lives.

- Standards for ethical behavior vary within and across cultures.

- The increasing volume and complexity of information in the early twentieth century led to the development of professional public relations practitioners whose task was to get a client the best possible hearing for a legitimate message.

- In 1947 the Hutchins Commission called for development of a socially responsible press that would put the news in context.

- If media organizations do not regulate themselves (with standards of good taste and decency), then government is more likely to impose regulations.

- Five classical positions for understanding modern ethical dilemmas include the principles of (1) the golden mean, (2) the categorical imperative, (3) utility, (4) the veil of ignorance, and (5) the Judeo-Christian ethic.

- Accuracy, fairness, balance, and accurate representation are fundamental ethical standards accepted by most professional communicators. Objectivity is a basic value of most journalists.

- Some media organizations joined together to support the National News Council, but it lacked support throughout the industry; other organizations have hired ombudsmen to act as internal critics.

- Industry ethics codes are used as guidelines for media professionals. Adherence is voluntary. Many local media operations have devised their own codes, enforcing adherence in the same way that other company policies are enforced.

- Although many media organizations have a code of ethics for their various staffs to follow, such codes are not enough. Individuals need to develop a process of moral reasoning and understand ethical issues at all levels to articulate and justify the reasons behind their decisions and actions.

- The reliance of media on advertising makes media vulnerable to business demands. However, advertisers also need media.

- Increasing competition, development of a segmented audience, and demands by corporations for high profits are among the trends that foster sensationalism.

414

Navigating the Web

Ethics on the web

Ethics-related World Wide Web sites provide information about ethics in the United States and in the world. These sites may include journalistic codes of ethics, reports from think tanks, and journalism magazine articles that discuss ethical issues.

| EthicNet | http://www.uta.fi/ethicnet |

This site was created by the Department of Journalism and Mass Communication at the University of Tampere in Finland. It has journalistic codes of ethics from all over the world.

| Fairness and Accuracy in Reporting (FAIR) | http://www.fair.org/fair |

FAIR is a liberal think tank that criticizes media for their biased coverage of areas such as minorities, women, and labor. FAIR's site provides reports and a variety of links.

| The Media Institute | http://www.mediainst.org |

This is a conservative think tank that criticizes media, lobbies Congress about media policy, and supports deregulating media. The institute's site provides articles and reports.

| Poynter Online | http://www.poynter.org |

The Poynter Institute for Media Studies is a nonpartisan, nonprofit organization that studies media ethics, management, and graphics. It conducts seminars on a variety of these topics.

| AJR NewsLink | http://www.ajr.org |

AJR NewsLink is the online version of the *American Journalism Review.* Maintained by the University of Maryland College of Journalism, this site provides articles and links about journalism performance.

Questions for review

1. Why did social responsibility replace the libertarian philosophy as the basis for the United States press system?
2. How do absolute and situational ethics differ?
3. Under what conditions can profit affect news credibility?
4. Why is accuracy a basic element of most communication ethics?
5. What types of impact can advertisers have on media content?

■ Issues to think about

1. How might questionable ethics, such as those shown in NBC's story about the GM pickup truck, affect the way people think about television news? What could TV news departments do about this?

2. How might media organizations be forced to behave ethically? What drawbacks would this method create?

3. What can companies and industries do if they think the news media are not being fair and balanced in their coverage?

4. In what ways do someone's personal ethics affect his or her professional ethics?

5. Do you use a moral reasoning process in making decisions? How would you describe that process?

6. If you were writing a code of ethics for a news organization, how would you go about that process? Who would you talk with for input about what should be in the code?

7. How are ethical and legal problems similar? How are they different?

■ Suggested readings

Altschull, J. Herbert *Agents of Power,* 2nd ed. (White Plains, NY: Longman, 1995).

Jaska, James A. and Michael S. Pritchard, *Communication Ethics: Methods of Analysis* (Belmont, CA: Wadsworth, 1988).

Lambeth, Edmund B., *Committed Journalism* (Bloomington, IN: Indiana University Press, 1986).

Merrill, John C., *The Dialectic in Journalism: Toward a Responsible Use of Press Freedom* (Baton Rouge, LA: Louisiana State University Press, 1989).

Rivers, William L. and Cleve Mathews, *Ethics for the Media* (Englewood Cliffs, NJ: Prentice Hall, 1988).

Public Relations

Keyconcepts

More than 300,000 people watched as 30 floats, 30 marching bands, and 300 clowns marched through the heart of Atlanta in May 1986. These people shared the 100th birthday of Coca-Cola with the 12,500 employees

Cigarette Smoking
Not Addictive

who came to Atlanta from 120 countries. The three-day celebration included a gigantic picnic in Georgia Tech's football stadium and satellite hookups to countries around the world. Coca-Cola spent more than $23 million on a birthday party designed to celebrate and gain the attention of the world.

Planning the centennial took years, and an important part of this planning was letting the world know about the party. This task fell into the hands of Coca-Cola's public relations staff. Publicizing of the events began five months before the celebration with a press conference. During the next five months, the public relations staff used press releases, video news releases, executive interviews, and a variety of other tools to tell the public about the upcoming events.

The party celebrated a birthday, but it also made a statement to the financial community. The Atlanta-based firm had made a major blunder about a year before when it tried to change the formula used in making Coke. Soda drinkers rejected the new Coca-Cola, and the company returned the old formula, renamed Classic Coke, to the stores. The aborted effort to reformulate Coke had hurt

Public relations as a discipline strives not only to provide information but to make corporate executives understand they must behave ethically to gain prestige in the public eye. No public relations activities could salvage the image of cigarette companies after executives testified that cigarettes were not addictive.

sales, but the company had rebounded by 1986. It wanted the world to know it was as financially strong as before—and what better way than to invite the world to its birthday party.

The plan worked. The twenty largest circulation newspapers covered the centennial, as did all three major television networks and publications throughout the world. Without skilled public relations practitioners the events might have occurred with little notice. Because of a strong communications staff, Coca-Cola employees celebrated the birthday of a piece of Americana with the world, and the company delivered a message of financial strength to competitors and stockholders.[1]

Generating media coverage for special events is only a part of the field called public relations (PR). PR also includes activities such as writing newsletters and magazines for a company's employees, influencing legislation, staging events to raise money for charities, and writing press releases about sports teams. The great variety of PR activities prevents any one definition from being inclusive. However, public relations can be defined adequately as *a planned and sustained unpaid communication between an organization and the publics that are essential to its success.*[2]

An examination of the terms in this definition will clarify it. First, public relations usually involves *organizations.* Some individuals, such as actors and musicians, might hire a PR firm to create and promote an image, but these are exceptions. Second, public relations differs from advertising in that companies pay for advertising messages. They do not pay for media content that is generated by public relations activity. Advertising and public relations both fall under the heading of promotion, which is a part of marketing, but PR is fundamentally different from advertising. Public relations practitioners hope that their materials will be used or will generate interest and news stories. Advertising practitioners simply buy time or space to advance the exact message they want to promote.

Some organizations define public relations as a consistently positive force. For example, in 1978 the International Public Relations Association adopted as a definition of public relations "the art and science of analyzing trends, predicting their consequences, counseling organization leaders, and implementing planned programs of action which will serve both the organization's and the public's interest." However, James Grunig, prominent public relations scholar, notes, "not all public relations is done responsibly; neither is all medicine or law or journalism." Public relations may be better defined as the "management of communication between an organization and its publics."[3]

Publics constitute the audience for public relations practitioners. Publics provide *feedback;* that is, their actions influence the success of an organization. If an organization's publics are small, the people who run the organization do not need someone to speak for them. The president or manager can talk to boards of directors, community groups, and the press. When the publics grow in size and become dispersed, the organizations that serve them grow too. The people who run such large organizations do not have the time or the expertise to communicate with these large publics, so they hire specialists.

A company's publics are all the people or organizations that the company deals with. Consumers are a public for a department store because their purchases determine whether a store will make a profit or not. Television station owners consider the government to be one of their publics because the Federal Communication Commission licenses stations. Good public relations involves knowledge of publics and monitoring of the messages that publics return to public relations and company personnel.

In addition to sending out messages and monitoring feedback from various publics, organizations *plan and sustain* their PR activities. Not all statements and activities that flow from an orga-

Public relations in your life

Do You Know It When You See It?

Sometimes it is difficult to decide what information comes from public relations sources and what constitutes news and entertainment. Think about some recent public events that you consider to be examples of PR and events you consider to be non PR-generated news or entertainment. Using these events, develop your own definition of public relations material.

PR-GENERATED EVENTS	NON-PR-GENERATED NEWS/ENTERTAINMENT
Local radio station's sponsorship of a charity walk-a-thon	Any natural disaster, such as a flood

nization represent PR efforts. Off-the-cuff remarks by a company's manager may affect the company's image, but the remarks qualify as PR only when statements are part of a planned, long-term policy.

Understanding public relations is essential to navigating through public life in modern American society. The pervasiveness of information generated through public relations efforts poses many issues:

- What is the role of public relations in a complex, postindustrial, democratic society?

- What are the inevitable tensions for public relations practitioners whose commitment is to an organization but also to ethical standards of fairness and accuracy?

- What role will the Internet play in the future of public relations?

- How does increased specialization affect public relations activities?

Public relations in American life

Although communication between organizations and publics has occurred for thousands of years, public relations was perfected as an art and practice in the United States. In ancient Athens, orators in public forums provided information and persuaded people about public policy. Some historians describe Samuel Adams as the first PR practitioner. Adams was a radical patriot in Massachusetts who helped to bring about the American Revolution. His goal was to whip up the fervor for rebellion and keep the public's ire sustained so that they would act, not just protest, against England. He used a variety of media, created an activist organization, employed symbols and slogans, created **pseudo-events** such as the Boston Tea Party, orchestrated conflict, and recognized the need for a sustained saturation campaign.[4] However, only in modern times have professional public relations people been paid to represent organizations through planned and sustained public relations activities.

pseudo-event: An event created solely for the purposes of public relations, to gain favorable notice.

420

Public relations history can be viewed from two perspectives. It can be understood as the evolution of professional public relations practice, but it can also be recognized as a type of communication that evolved to serve specific social needs.

■ Public relations in social context

The practice of public relations developed from people's desire to hold political power and to profit from entertainment and business. As the United States grew and diversified during the early 1800s, Andrew Jackson sponsored a Kentucky editor named Amos Kendall, who supported Jackson's candidacy. Kendall wrote speeches and advised Jackson, while "Old Hickory" capitalized on his military image to become President.[5] Although sponsored through government printing contracts rather than being paid directly, Kendall was an early political PR consultant.

Keyconcept

Public Relations and Society: Public relations—systematic, planned communication with an organization's publics—helps to explain complex information and to shape the news agenda. However, it can also be used to mislead if practitioners do not adhere to ethical standards.

Jackson's use of PR to gain political office suggests a social condition in the United States that generated a need for public relations: the dispersion of power. Voters in a democracy have the power to influence their government. Therefore Jackson, along with other government officials, needed to use the power of persuasion to influence the voters to choose him. Voters constitute a significant public in American society. Political advertising, news, entertainment, and public relations efforts all crowd the marketplace of ideas. Voters hold the power to choose from all the ideas available. Strong monarchies and dictatorships can coerce; governments that hold less power rely more on persuasion.

PRESS AGENTS AND ENTERTAINMENT Early press agents hawked their wares and worked doggedly with entertainment businesses to get publicity in newspapers. The first master of publicity was P. T. Barnum. In the late 1830s he toured the eastern United States with an African American woman, Joice Heth, who claimed to be the 160-year-old nurse of George Washington. With a combination of advertising and publicity in newspapers, Barnum drew large crowds. When attendance slumped in Boston, he wrote a letter to a local newspaper claiming that Heth was an early form of robot run by springs. Attendance grew as people checked out the story of fraud.[6] An autopsy of Heth after her death revealed that she was about half her announced age. Meanwhile, Barnum had been collecting about $1,500 a week from people who wanted a look at the pipe-smoking old woman.

P. T. Barnum, who provoked curiosity for a variety of circus side-shows, was a genius at using publicity techniques to arouse expectations.

When Barnum formed the Barnum and Bailey Circus with James A. Bailey, he hired his own press agent, Richard Hamilton. With the increased business responsibilities of a company of 800 employees, Barnum could no longer afford to do what he did best—get people into the tent. The world's greatest press agent had to hire a press agent.

PRESS AGENTRY AND BUSINESS In the mid-1800s, businesses began to experiment with similar press agentry techniques. However, in addition to publicity they used lobbying tactics, hiring press agents to persuade agents of government to serve their cause. During the 1850s, capitalizing on fears of a coming civil war, the Illinois Central Railroad organized a public relations campaign to get the government to construct a North-South railway that would bind the country together. This successful campaign for federal funds altered a historic pattern of local funding for railroad development. Other railroads used similar persuasion techniques. They argued that building railroads served the public, and Congress responded by giving forty grants to railroads between 1852 and 1857. Railroad companies continued to use lobbying and press relations throughout the nineteenth century, eventually influencing the Interstate Commerce Act of 1886 in their favor.[7]

> **Key**concept
>
> *The Evolution of Press Agentry:* Press agentry, which was one of the earliest forms of public relations, involves publicizing an event or person or promoting a campaign. As press agents and those who hired them became more sophisticated about audience response to messages, publicity evolved into a process of communication.

Railroad executives were vulnerable public targets because they were viewed as land grabbers with little regard for local communities. To create more positive public images, railroad officials became masters of early press relations. They offered editors appealing tours through various parts of the country in return for free advertising. At the turn of the century most editors carried free railway passes in their wallets.

EMERGING PROFESSIONALISM During the last half of the 1800s, big business became a target of citizen anger as the public began to perceive it as a greedy octopus that grabbed power and money and worried little about the common person. Efforts to break up large steel, oil, and railroad monopolies increased as the twentieth century began. The muckrakers from *McClure's Magazine* began to expose the excesses of wealthy industrialists such as J. P. Morgan, Cornelius Vanderbilt, and John D. Rockefeller. Recognizing that they needed a better public image, the captains of industry turned to public relations experts.

Ivy Ledbetter Lee emerged during this period as the model for public relations practitioners. Lee worked as a newspaper reporter for three years before becoming a PR counselor for a number of corporations. Lee advocated honest communication between his clients and their publics. John D. Rockefeller sought Lee's advice after two women and eleven children were killed during a strike at his Colorado coal mines, in an incident known as the Ludlow Massacre. Lee replied that "the first and most important feature of any plan of publicity should be its absolute frankness; that there should be no devious ways employed."[8] Rockefeller hired Lee to tell his side of the labor war that had developed.

Not everyone believed that Lee lived up to his own words. Poet Carl Sandburg attacked Lee for his role in publicity following the Ludlow Massacre. In his 1919 book on the press, *The Brass Check,* Upton Sinclair gave Lee the nickname "Poison Ivy."[9] Nevertheless, Lee's admonition to public relations practitioners to avoid deceit remains the basis of the professional approach to PR.

PUBLIC RELATIONS AND WAR About the time Lee gained prominence, the United States itself began a gigantic public relations effort. During the early part of the twentieth century, much of the American public did not believe that the country should take an active

422

part in European affairs. To promote U.S. participation in World War I, President Woodrow Wilson set up the Committee for Public Information, run by George Creel. Creel, a former newspaper editor, successfully ran a propaganda campaign that generated support for U.S. involvement and created hatred of Germans. The committee's efforts cost $4.5 million. It mailed 6,000 news releases that generated about 20,000 columns of newsprint each week. The committee developed cartoons, created posters, and issued war photographs to the schools. Many of those who worked for the Creel Committee took the techniques they learned with them and moved into the modern, postwar world of business and government public relations. Part of the appeal was based on fear, and Germans were depicted as the *HUNS* without morals.

Keyconcept

Propaganda and Public Relations: Some of the modern persuasive techniques of public relations were learned during World War I, when the federal government conducted a propaganda campaign to encourage Americans to support an unpopular war. However, this connection between propaganda and public relations led to a negative perception of PR that professional public relations practitioners had to overcome during the mid-twentieth century.

Edward Bernays, who worked on the committee, wrote the first book about public relations in 1923. *Crystallizing Public Opinion* received mixed reviews, but it introduced hundreds of thousands of people to the activities of public relations.[10]

Bernays's career in public relations lasted more than five decades. He argued that public relations should be a profession in which social science principles are applied and consideration for the public takes precedence over profit. He wrote,

> The standards of the public relations counsel are his own standards, and he will not accept a client whose standards do not come up to them. While he is not called upon to judge the merits of his case any more than a lawyer is called upon to judge his client's case, nevertheless he must judge the results which his work would accomplish from an ethical point of view.[11]

Public relations activities expanded during the 1930s, though most people in the United States were not very aware of PR techniques until after World War II. PR efforts similar to those in World War I occurred during World War II. The United States established the Office of War Information (OWI) to handle propaganda and public relations efforts. Elmer Davis, a former *New York Times* journalist, ran the OWI. The office proved adept at getting citizens to support the war effort. Hollywood joined in the PR efforts with movies and personal appearances by movie stars such as Douglas Fairbanks and Mary Pickford.

The Committee on Public Information helped develop a variety of public relations techniques during World War I. This Liberty Bond poster resembles many designed by the committee and those who supported its efforts.

[profile]

Edward L. Bernays

Edward Bernays wrote the first book on public relations and taught the first public relations class at a major university. In 1989 *Life* magazine named him one of the most important Americans in the twentieth century.

The nephew of Sigmund Freud, Bernays sold the public on everything from Presidents to Ivory soap. Clients whose images and products he promoted included singer Enrico Caruso, automobile manufacturer Henry Ford, inventor Thomas Edison, movie maker Sam Goldwyn, and first lady Eleanor Roosevelt. Bernays worked for every President from Calvin Coolidge in 1925 to Dwight D. Eisenhower in the late 1950s. He is said to have turned down Adolf Hitler and Generalissimo Francisco Franco of Spain.

Bernays was born in Vienna, Austria, in 1891 and was brought to New York a year later. He received his bachelor's degree from Cornell University in 1912. During World War I he worked for

the War Department as a government propagandist, learning how to mold public opinion. He used this experience as a foundation when he opened his public relations business with Doris Fleishman in 1919.

Three years later, he married Fleishman. She kept her maiden name and was the first American woman to maintain it on her passport. Bernays and Fleishman ran their business together until she died in 1980.

In 1923, Bernays wrote *Crystallizing Public Opinion,* the first book on public relations. In this book he moved from using mass communication to reach one large public to targeting specific audiences. He stressed that clients had different relations with different publics.

Bernays wrote fourteen books in all. In his 1965 autobiography, *Biography of an Idea,* he wrote that public relations had moved "from a one-way street of information and persuasion from client to public" to a two-way interaction between client and public. How-

ever, he was unsuccessful in his drive to have public relations practitioners licensed, an attempt to legitimize the field.

Bernays had about 350 clients, ranging from federal government departments to labor unions and from individuals to large corporations. He continued giving speeches until a few years before his death at age 103, on March 9, 1995, in his home in Cambridge, Massachusetts.

SOURCES: Harvey Smith, "The Original Persuader," *The Guardian,* March 24, 1995, Section: The Guardian Features Page, p. T21; "Edward Bernays," *The Boston Herald,* March 10, 1995, Section: Obituary, p. 61.

◾ Information and persuasion

The definition of public relations emphasizes PR activities as communication. Public relations specialists act as senders who encode messages and send them to receivers, the organization's publics. Because these messages are planned, they have purposes. The exact purpose may vary, but public relations messages usually aim either to inform or to persuade.

Informational messages make the receiver aware of some event or issue that the sending organization considers important. A public information director at a local community college sends course catalogues to residents of the community to remind them which classes are available. A sports information director mails pregame press releases to tell sportswriters about the importance of an upcoming basketball game. Publics cannot

424

make effective decisions without information, so organizations must inform their publics.

Persuasion causes people to change their beliefs or to act in certain ways. The environmental lobbyist who talks with a Senator over lunch tries to persuade the Senator to vote for a bill that will protect an endangered species. The press release about a new department store aims to get a newspaper to publish a story about the grand opening. Ultimately, whether they use an informational or persuasive model, public relations practitioners want to persuade their publics that the company's position is accurate, complete, and justified.

However, effective public relations relies on accurate information. Consumers who do not trust a company's communication or reporters who cannot trust a PR practitioner will not be persuaded by communication from those organizations and people. Publics may be fooled a few times, but sustained PR efforts will falter without accurate information.

Keyconcept

The Process of Public Relations: Public relations messages, which can be informational or persuasive, are created by interacting with the publics addressed. The continuous process involves surveying and monitoring publics, creating messages, and evaluating feedback.

Public relations activities constitute a process. An organization and its publics are *interdependent.* Because of differences in exposure, attention, perception, and retention, people experience the same events in many different ways. Public relations communicates the organization's perspective on the events, and, in doing so, tries to alter the results of people's selective processes. Hospital PR departments call patients after discharge to see how they feel about their stays. If the patients have a negative perception of the hospital, the PR specialists will talk with them or send them some printed material to change that perception. Perceptions of service, people, and products determine success.

Internal public relations

Unlike external PR, which has been around in some form for almost 200 years, internal public relations is relatively new. The study of communication in organizations progressed "from a footnote mention in pre–World War II days" to an entire area of study in the 1990s.[12] Before 1930, managers thought of employees as pieces of a big industrial machine. They did their work, got paid, and went home. However, in the process of studying the impact of lighting and environment on productivity, researchers at the Western Electric plants in Cicero, Illinois, discovered that relationships among employees were as important as technological working conditions. People who enjoyed their work performed better. Managers now began to think in terms of human relations, recognizing that employee well-being and effective communication increased productivity.

Keyconcept

The Human Dimension: In the late 1930s some corporate managers began to realize that employees who were satisfied with their workplace performed better than those who disliked their jobs. Public relations then took on an internal dimension, one goal being to inform employees and to make them feel part of the overall company effort.

In 1938, Chester Barnard, the former president of the New Jersey Bell Telephone Company, wrote in *Functions of the Executive* that three elements were essential to the existence of all organizations: a purpose, people willing to pursue that purpose, and communication to coordinate the pursuit.[13] As companies consolidated and increased in size, they also became more bureaucratic. Layers of management often acted as blocks to communication, spurring the development of departments of internal communication during the last half of the twentieth century. Internal public relations then developed as a process of planned and sustained communication between the organizational leadership and its employees.

Internal public relations remains a phenomenon of developed countries such as Japan and the United States. In most other parts of the world, the concept of human relations is still unheard of. Women in developing countries often receive less than subsistence wages for 60 to 100 hours of work per week.[14]

Social and cultural impact

Ethics and integrity within public relations practice have been continuing issues. Journalists often refer to PR practitioners as *flaks,* a name implying that PR people present only their employers' side of the story. However, public relations education is often housed within journalism schools, and many journalists eventually become PR professionals. Since the time of Ivy Lee, PR practitioners have argued that honesty and accuracy must be the ethical foundation of the profession. Another ethical value of journalism—objectivity—does not apply to professional public relations. No one, journalist or ordinary citizen, expects public relations experts to present multiple views. The public relations view is one piece of information within the marketplace of ideas. Often it is a powerful message generated by sophisticated communication techniques and backed with power and money.

Cultural Impact

The Greening of PR

The 1990s saw public relations turn green—but not green as in money. PR became green by promoting products that would not harm the environment.

The trend toward environmental concern by businesses reflects a remarkable change in American values; a change brought about in part by public relations by such groups as the Sierra Club, the National Wildlife Federation, and Greenpeace.

Between the first Earth Day celebration in 1970 and the twenty-first in 1990, most Americans adopted environmental concern as a basic value. Today, more than half of all households in the country recycle on a regular basis; in 1970, only a small percentage of Americans even knew what the word "recycling" meant.

The introduction in 1990 of Origins, a cosmetic line by Estee Lauder, shows how green PR works.

The cosmetic line includes skin care products and makeup made from plant extracts and packaged in recyclable material. Lauder introduced the cosmetics with public relations campaigns aimed at consumers, department stores, and media. The company had press conferences and sponsored events, such as a "Run for Earth," to gain attention. Lauder's product and the public relations worked. Within a month, sales were 70 percent higher than expected.

But the greening of business has not eliminated ethical problems for PR practitioners. Some companies claim that their products are environmentally safe even though they are not. The environmental business movement will face difficulties if consumers decide they cannot trust green claims. The ethics of individual practitioners will greatly affect that trust.

SOURCES: Josh Baran, "Every Day Is Earth Day," *Public Relations Journal* (April 1991): 22–23; "Public Relations, Store Tie-Ins Launch "Green" Cosmetic Line," *Public Relations Journal* (April 1991): 24–25.

Public relations in our lives

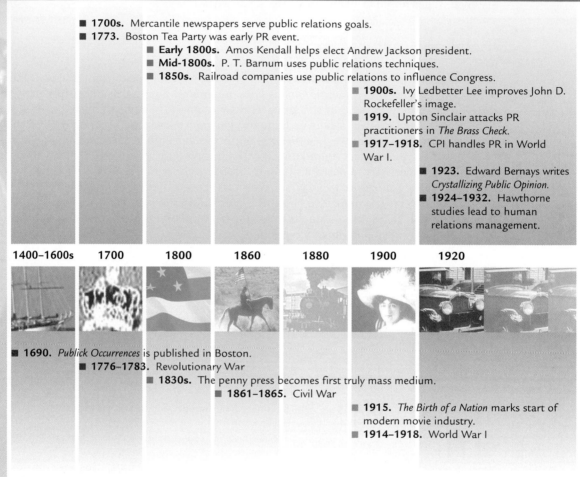

- **1700s.** Mercantile newspapers serve public relations goals.
- **1773.** Boston Tea Party was early PR event.
  - **Early 1800s.** Amos Kendall helps elect Andrew Jackson president.
  - **Mid-1800s.** P. T. Barnum uses public relations techniques.
  - **1850s.** Railroad companies use public relations to influence Congress.
    - **1900s.** Ivy Ledbetter Lee improves John D. Rockefeller's image.
    - **1919.** Upton Sinclair attacks PR practitioners in *The Brass Check*.
    - **1917–1918.** CPI handles PR in World War I.
      - **1923.** Edward Bernays writes *Crystallizing Public Opinion*.
      - **1924–1932.** Hawthorne studies lead to human relations management.

| 1400–1600s | 1700 | 1800 | 1860 | 1880 | 1900 | 1920 |

- **1690.** *Publick Occurrences* is published in Boston.
  - **1776–1783.** Revolutionary War
    - **1830s.** The penny press becomes first truly mass medium.
      - **1861–1865.** Civil War
        - **1915.** *The Birth of a Nation* marks start of modern movie industry.
        - **1914–1918.** World War I

The period after World War II saw a drive toward professionalism and a growth in public relations education. The Public Relations Society of America (PRSA) started in 1948. It merged in 1961 with the American Public Relations Association, which began in 1944. The number of universities and colleges offering public relations classes increased from a handful after World War II to 300 by 1970.[15]

The degree of professionalism found in public relations is higher now than it was fifty years ago, but ethical problems remain. The heart of the professional approach to PR concerns openness between the organization and its publics. Advocates of professional PR, such as Bernays, argue that public relations practitioners should advise their clients to be honest with those affected by their business.

Johnson & Johnson followed the ethics of professional PR when it reacted with concern for the public after someone placed cyanide in some Extra-Strength Tylenol capsules in 1982. Seven people died in and around Chicago. Johnson & Johnson immediately stopped production and recalled all of its Tylenol capsules. The company contacted the media and federal government. Johnson & Johnson did not try to hide

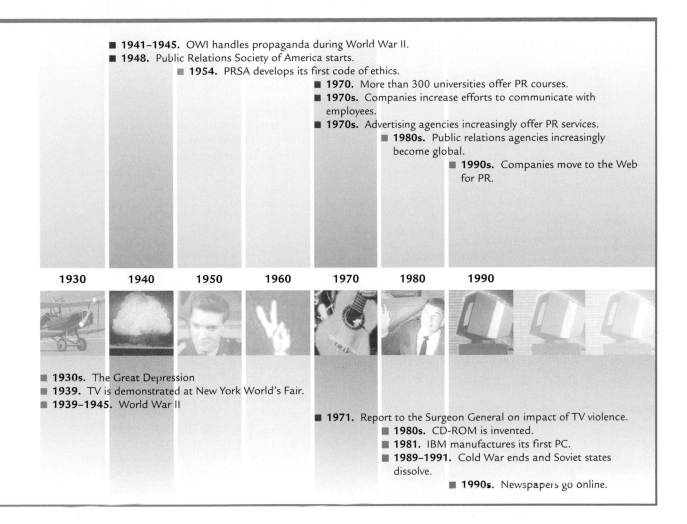

- **1941–1945.** OWI handles propaganda during World War II.
- **1948.** Public Relations Society of America starts.
  - **1954.** PRSA develops its first code of ethics.
    - **1970.** More than 300 universities offer PR courses.
    - **1970s.** Companies increase efforts to communicate with employees.
    - **1970s.** Advertising agencies increasingly offer PR services.
      - **1980s.** Public relations agencies increasingly become global.
        - **1990s.** Companies move to the Web for PR.

| 1930 | 1940 | 1950 | 1960 | 1970 | 1980 | 1990 |

- **1930s.** The Great Depression
- **1939.** TV is demonstrated at New York World's Fair.
- **1939–1945.** World War II

- **1971.** Report to the Surgeon General on impact of TV violence.
  - **1980s.** CD-ROM is invented.
  - **1981.** IBM manufactures its first PC.
  - **1989–1991.** Cold War ends and Soviet states dissolve.
    - **1990s.** Newspapers go online.

anything that had happened. Its first response involved protecting and warning the public. Instead of a knee-jerk reaction aimed at short-term results—keeping Tylenol on the shelves—Johnson & Johnson considered long-term goals and the importance of credibility to continuing business success. As a result, the company lived up to its business credo of public responsibility and regained its share of the market within a year.[16]

In contrast to Johnson & Johnson, Dow Corning created a public relations nightmare when it concealed research that questioned the safety of its silicone breast implants. In 1991 a jury in a California federal court awarded a woman $7.3 million for damages to her immune system that allegedly resulted from silicone implants. The trial revealed that Dow Corning scientists had warned managers that leaking silicone could create problems. The company never made the research public. As a result of the trial and its aftermath, new management was appointed at Dow Corning, the company got out of the silicone implant business, and it offered money for further research into health problems caused by implants.[17]

428

Today, industry and government recognize public relations as an important and legitimate part of their activities. In 1994, college majors in public relations made up the second largest percentage of students in mass communication programs, coming in just behind majors in advertising.[18] Efforts to promote professionalism among practitioners continue.

Demand for public relations

Public relations practitioners serve as a pipeline to move information from organizations to their publics. Demand for public relations activity can be viewed from both ends of the pipe. At one end, organizations demand PR services to get their information out; at the other end, various publics demand PR information from the organizations. Newspapers use PR releases as the basis of news stories; government agencies use PR information in policy decisions; and consumers use PR information as a basis for voting and buying products.

Demand for PR services

The demand for PR services depends on the types of publics that interact with the organization. In some cases, organizations depend on publics for revenue. Customers of J C Penney form a public for that company. In other cases the organizations depend on a public for resources. General Motors communicates with its employees, who form a public that supplies labor. Consumers demand certain actions of J C Penney, and laborers demand fair treatment by General Motors. Communication is part of the process that ensures that consumers and laborers get what they need.

National Transportation Safety Board Vice Chairman, Robert Francis held a news conference during the summer of 1996 to announce that the examination of a plane crash in the Florida everglades was finished. He was addressing several publics: Congress, the general public, and relatives and friends of those who were killed.

Most daily newspapers in the United States belong to the Newspaper Association of America (NAA). Through this membership, publishers constitute a public and express a demand for intelligent lobbying, that is, representing their interests to state and federal governments. The NAA tries to influence legislation that affects daily newspapers, such as laws that limit access to public meetings.

Public relations people deal with two types of publics: those inside their organization and those outside the organization. *Internal publics* include employees, managers, trustees, and stockholders. These inside publics have a much stronger commitment to the organization than do those outside. *External publics* include consumers and voters, government organizations, interest groups, business organizations, and media.

Although publics can be broadly defined as groups such as governments, consumers, and employees, each organization must be more geographically specific about its public. An oil company that sells gasoline throughout the world recognizes that automobile owners in various countries have different demands. A supermarket chain in the Midwest would include only shoppers who lived in its geographic markets as part of its public.

Demand for PR information

Just as organizations eagerly send information about themselves, individuals and other groups need information about those organizations. Press releases, electronic and print, and press conferences are prime ways in which journalists find out about activities of organizations. Figure 14.1 shows the topics of press releases available to newspapers over the PR News Wire, an electronic source of information. Of the eight topics, financial and new products make up more than 40 percent of the press releases. However, a variety of other topics are available. Figure 14.2 shows the percentage of the press releases used at nine large daily newspapers. More than 60 percent of the releases used were financial and new products, a figure that reflects the heavy use of press releases by business reporters.

Looking at the two figures, you can see that only 15 percent of the releases available were used by one of the nine dailies. Research indicates that small newspapers use more press releases, some times without editing, than do large newspapers. Up to 30 percent of the content in some smaller newspapers comes from press releases.

News media organizations' demand for information from organizations is much like automobile makers' demand for steel and plastic. PR information serves as a raw material for creating news content. Just as steel and plastic vary in quality, so does information. Inaccurate and misleading information, whether purposeful or accidental, does not adequately meet the general public's need for useful information.

Andrew Schneider, winner of two Pulitzer Prizes for investigative journalism, tells about a project in which he used government data concerning kidney transplants. The reporting team found that African Americans waited 200 percent longer than whites for transplants. They checked the data before running the story and found that the government had erroneously included all Native Americans, Hispanics, and Asian Americans

FIGURE 14.1 Press Releases Sent on PR News Wire During One Day

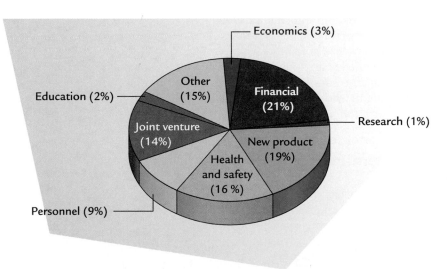

Source: Data from Linda P. Morton and Shirley Ramsey, "A Benchmark Study of the PR Newswire," *Public Relations Review* 20 (Summer 1994): 171–182.

FIGURE 14.2 Press Releases Used from PR News Wire by Nine Important Newspapers*

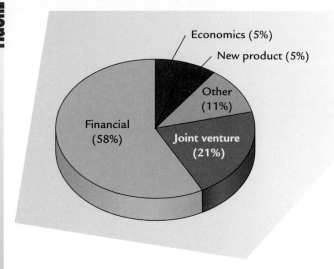

* These releases were used in one or more of nine daily newspapers: eight of the 100 largest circulation newspapers plus *The Christian Science Monitor.*

Source: Data from Linda P. Morton and Shirley Ramsey, "A Benchmark Study of the PR Newswire," *Public Relations Review* 20 (Summer 1994): 171–182.

in the listing of African Americans. The waiting period for African Americans was only 59 percent longer, which was significant but not as shocking. The story ran, and it was more accurate.[19]

Unfortunately, not all journalists have as much time or commitment as Schneider has. When a news organization is understaffed and has too much space or broadcast time to fill, unchecked public relation information can appear as news. If the information is wrong and the truth later emerges, the organization that released the information and the news organization both lose credibility.

Messages that are aimed at any public must be in a usable form. A department store that serves a large Hispanic population must have public relations people who understand and communicate in Spanish. A message that the public cannot comprehend will not persuade and inform them.

Supplying the demand for public relations

Almost every organization has public relations needs. The manager of a small retail store can usually conduct all the public relations the store requires. However, large organizations require public relations specialists. At least four groups use public relations to fulfill their goals: political and government groups, interest groups, profit-making companies, and nonprofit organizations.

Political and government groups inform citizens and advocate political candidates and positions. These groups include political parties, elected and appointed government officials, and candidates for public office. Information is supplied through videotapes, media interviews with politicians, press releases, newsletters, and advertisements. The Michigan Department of Natural Resources distributes information to residents about a variety of outdoor activities, such as hunting, fishing, and gardening. Most of the newsletters sent by members of Congress during an election year try to influence the voters to reelect them. Table 14.1 describes different public relations functions used by a variety of organizations. Although nearly all groups work to coordinate events, only some use direct lobbying.

Interest groups attempt to influence politicians to achieve public policy decisions that favor the groups' interests. The National Rifle Association is a powerful interest group that represents the interests of gun owners and manufacturers. For years, the NRA has been able to limit legislation to control guns even though a majority of American citizens support control of certain types of weapons.

Almost every cause and profession imaginable has an organized interest group to advocate its political position. Offices for most interest groups are located in Washington, D.C., and state capitals, where they are close to the legislative processes.

Profit-seeking organizations use public relations to create and maintain favorable attitudes toward their goods and services. Consumers who do not trust a company or a particular type of product will be less likely to purchase it. PR practitioners in profit-seeking organizations use advocacy and information to maintain a positive image in the public's minds.

Nonprofit organizations depend heavily on public relations because much of their support comes from public donations. Organizations such as the Red Cross, the United Way, and the Salvation Army receive a large portion of their funds from individual donations. It is important for those fund-raising efforts that the public recognize the community work they do. In addition, people who use nonprofit organizations' services must be aware of those services if they are going to use them.

TABLE 14.1 PR Functions Used by Different Types of Organizations

TYPE OF ORGANIZATION	PR FUNCTION
Government and political organization	Political PR Fund raising Crisis management Event coordination
Interest groups	Political PR Fund raising Lobbying Event coordination
For-profit organizations	Lobbying Crisis management Financial PR Event coordination
Nonprofit organization	Fund raising Event coordination Lobbying Crisis management

432

Often, public relations practitioners seem to do their jobs effortlessly. But PR works best when it is based on solid planning. Several models of the public relations process are available. In 1955, Edward Bernays listed eight steps in the public relations process:[20]

1. Define your objective.
2. Research your publics.
3. Modify your objectives to reach goals that research shows are attainable.
4. Decide on your strategy.
5. Set up your themes, symbols, and appeals.
6. Blueprint an effective organization to carry on activity.
7. Chart your plan for both timing and tactics.
8. Carry out your tactics.

The public relations process starts with an objective or goal. An automobile company might want to publicize its latest car. Its PR objective would be getting as much mass media publicity as possible. Researching the publics would involve checking the media outlets that are most likely to carry information about a new auto model. These would include automotive magazines, the business and automotive sections of newspapers, and business-oriented television shows. Part of this research would include the probability that these media outlets would write stories about the new model.

Keyconcept

Components of Public Relations: The public relations process starts with a goal, requires a plan, progresses through implementation, and then evaluates the plan for effectiveness. Successful public relations campaigns require careful planning and reliance on research.

A political party that seeks support for a candidate is in a similar situation. The party must identify the types of people who are likely to vote for that candidate and the particular issues that will convince them to vote for the person. Part of the research includes surveying the public about issues and reactions to a candidate's position. Without specific knowledge about these two topics, time and money will be wasted on people who will not be swayed or on issues that voters consider unimportant.

On the basis of the research, the automobile public relations practitioners would specify particular goals for publicity. For example, the PR department would aim for long articles in *The Wall Street Journal,* the *New York Times* business section, *Business Week,* and each of a dozen regional daily newspapers. With these goals set, the particular ways of approaching the various media outlets would be designed. These would include personal contact, press releases, videocassettes messages, electronic press releases, and press conferences.

In the political example, public relations personnel and political consultants would examine the research, advise the candidate to modify her position on certain issues, and select appropriate media outlets and schedule public appearances so that the candidate can advance her message.

The fifth step involves creating the types of messages that will be used. For the automobile company these messages would include special attributes of the car, such as safety features, sporty image, or mileage performance. A political candidate usually attempts to provide a cohesive and consistent message, often referred to as a campaign theme.

The sixth step requires specifying the way people and financial resources will be used to carry out the campaign. Who will write what? Where and when will press conferences be held? Who will get to test drive the new car? Who will promote the candi-

The T-shirts on these children not only identify them as Head Start youngsters, but they serve an identifying role for the importance of the program itself. Part of the public relations process requires keeping a message before the various publics that an organization or program serves.

date, raise funds, and plan public appearances? What is the budget for each type of activity?

As a seventh step, the PR practitioner plans the detailed tactics or processes that will be carried out. This includes the timing of the various activities. For example, the car might be announced at a press conference, which would be followed by interviews with company officials and test drives by journalists. Tactics include national announcement and efforts to provide public relations at regional levels. The political candidate might tour a factory, meet with spouses, and give a speech on the factory steps.

Finally, the tactics are carried out. After the process begins, the results must be evaluated. This evaluation will involve short-term and long-term evaluations. An effective plan will include ways of checking how the tactics are working as the plan is being executed. The practitioners will monitor stories run in magazines, newspapers, and on television. Evaluation will allow the PR practitioner to adjust the tactics as the plan unfolds. Finally, after the plan has been completed, the practitioner will evaluate the overall success of the plan so that future plans will work better.

The unifying activity of all steps in the planning process is decision making. At each step, decisions must be made. Effective decisions are based on two important activities: specifying goals and conducting research. All PR activities should take place with a goal in mind; otherwise, the effort may be wasted. The goal may be to improve a car manufacturer's image or to increase the donations at a university, but without goals, efforts cannot be focused and cannot be evaluated. Research is the second critical activity because all planning must be based on knowledge.

■ Conducting external PR

External communication deals with publics outside the organization. Common PR activities in this area include lobbying, political PR, financial PR, fund raising, crisis management, and event coordination. This list is far from exhaustive, and even these activities vary with the publics addressed, the goals pursued, and the communication methods employed.

External public relations activities can be handled in-house, that is, by organizational employees, or they can be handled by consultants who are hired from outside an organization. Each method has advantages and disadvantages. In some situations a combination of in-house practitioners and consultants might work best. For example, media training might best be handled by a combination of internal media relations practitioners advising corporate officials on how to stick to a corporate theme while consultants might provide on-camera training. In Table 14.2 you can see that decisions about external and internal assignment of tasks vary with the task itself.

In-house practitioners have more familiarity with the company's managers and operations than do consultants. This gives them more credibility with media and allows for

TABLE 14.2 How Organizations Perform PR Tasks

PR FUNCTIONS	PERCENT PERFORMED INSIDE THE ORGANIZATION	PERCENT PERFORMED OUTSIDE THE ORGANIZATION
Media relations	94	28
Official spokesperson	93	5
Employee communication	92	8
Community relations	89	13
Speech writing	85	23
Crisis management	82	23
Issues management/strategic planning	78	31
Industry trade press relations	70	20
General news bureau	62	13
Product/news service	62	16
Environmental issues	59	22
Legislative/regulatory	59	25
Speakers bureau	58	8
Sports/special events tie-ins	56	22
Media training	54	55
Fund raising	46	13
Financial/investor relations	38	19
International counseling	26	15

Note: These percentages are based on 285 organizations.

Source: Deborah Hauss, "The Purchasing Power of Public Relations Practitioners," *Public Relations Journal* (April 1993): 26–29. Percentages do not always add to 100 because some functions are performed both in-house and outside. Copyright April 1993. Reprinted by permission of *Public Relations Journal,* published by the Public Relations Society of America, New York, NY.

informal interaction with the press. This familiarity can make the PR practitioner a valuable member of the management team. In addition, an in-house public relations staff usually costs less than outside consultants unless PR activities are only periodic.

Despite in-house advantages, it is not the best approach in all situations. Some organizations do not need ongoing external PR activities. For example, a small firm that sells manufacturing equipment to furniture companies deals with a small identifiable public and does not require extensive public relations. In such a case, an in-house PR staff would be an unnecessary expense.

PR consultants also may be used in specialized situations even if a company has in-house public relations. If a cereal company plans to sell a new offering of public stock, a financial public relations firms will be hired. Most companies do not have in-house financial public relations.

Keyconcept

The Role of the Public Relations Agency: Businesses and political organizations often rely on agencies, rather than in-house public relations personnel, to plan and conduct external campaigns. This means that the emphasis is on strategy and technique, with goals and knowledge of the company supplied by organizational leaders.

TABLE 14.3 Top Ten PR Firms Based on 1995 Fees

AGENCY	NUMBER OF EMPLOYEES	NET FEES (IN MILLIONS)
Burson-Marsteller*	1,860	$212
Shandwick	1,856	$171
Hill and Knowlton*	1,250	$141
Fleishman-Hillard	829	$ 90
Edelman Public Relations Worldwide	987	$ 90
Ketchum Public Relations*	531	$ 64
Porter/Novelli*	451	$ 46
Manning, Selvage & Lee*	384	$ 44
Ogilvy Adams & Rinehart*	404	$ 41
GCI Group*	445	$ 40

*Related to an Advertising Agency.

Source: O'Dwyer's Directory of Public Relations Firms (New York: J. R. O'Dwyer Co., 1996), p. A7. Copyright, J.R. O'Dwyer Co., New York.

Public relations firms vary greatly in size. A few collect more than $100 million in fees annually; others have only a few employees. Small PR firms survive in a world of big companies because the heart of PR is mediated and interpersonal communication. From writing press releases to persuading a legislator to support a new bill, PR involves people with communication talent. Many of these people prefer to work for themselves and not larger companies.

Several of the larger PR firms work as subsidiaries of advertising agencies. Because PR and advertising are both in the business of promotion, it often makes sense to have both types of services available in the same organization. A client can have both the public relations and ad campaigns planned and executed by the same organization. Table 14.3 shows the top ten PR firms. Of these firms, seven are related to an advertising agency.

LOBBYING Lobbying is an effort to influence the legislative and administrative activities of government. Legislators need information when they are writing a law or considering whether to vote for it. They need to know who will be affected by a law, what will be the cost of administering it, and what effects, positive and negative, it is likely to have. A lobbyist provides the information that supports his or her organization's position.

For example, the Wisconsin state legislature might consider a law that would prohibit the injection of hormones into cows to increase milk production. Wisconsin's dairy council would provide state legislators with information explaining why such hormones are safe. An environmental special-interest group might suggest that the legislators examine whether the hormones alter the milk or have any effects on people who drink the milk. The dairy council's aim is to stop passage of a bill that might hurt the dairy industry in Wisconsin. The environmental group's aim is to make sure the milk from hormone-injected cows will be safe.

PR and New Media

The shabbily dressed thirteen-year-old girl puts out her hand and says, "Hey mister, my brother and me need some food. Ya got any extra change?" The five-year-old beside her stares up with dull eyes, as if his mind could not hold a thought for long.

"What would you do?" A soft but authoritative voice asks from the computer's speakers. A menu of choices appears in the upper corner of the screen beside the video of the children. The Association for Helping the Homeless is seeking your support with an interactive, online appeal.

This scenario illustrates how effective public relations communication can be in the interactive media world. In this example the association is raising funds for homeless shelters and other activities. The aims of public relations are to inform and to persuade; the active pictures and the words, right there on the screen, are more appealing than static, printed direct mail. The menu of choices allows the viewer to respond immediately and easily, while feeling that he or she has control of the response.

CD-ROMs are also providing new public relations tools. Many organizations now provide reporters with information on searchable CD-ROMs. Reporters can type in key words and search for passages of text on the disk that will help them to structure a story and fill in the details. By giving reporters such options, public relations personnel increase the likelihood that their view will be presented in the story—or even that the story will be written at all. They also give reporters the illusion that they are writing their own story. The catch is that the public relations experts controlled what content was put on the disk in the first place.

Lobbying is often accomplished through one-on-one encounters; although the use of mass media to sway public opinion can sometimes help lobbying efforts. Mediated communication may be used, such as reports and video, but the public that the mediated communication reaches is relatively small. Lobbyists work mostly with government officials on an interpersonal basis.

POLITICAL PR Political PR activities resemble lobbying efforts, but the voters form the public of interest. Political public relations tries to get a certain person elected or to influence public opinion about a political issue, such as abortion or tax reform. During an election campaign, PR practitioners write news releases; set up print, radio, and television interviews; prepare campaign literature that goes to voters through the mail; distribute yard signs and bumper stickers; answer questions from journalists; and plan advertising campaigns.

EVENTS COORDINATION Public relations also includes coordinating events. These range from concert tours to political campaigns. A concert tour by R. E. M. requires public relations activity to help organize the tour, buy advertising, and communicate with various music media organizations. The PR practitioner creates and distributes **media kits** about the tour, coordinates times for media interviews of the artists, writes press releases, and makes sure reporters cover the tour stops.

media kit: A package of video and print news releases and other information to make it easy for reporters to follow up on a public relations generated event or issue.

FINANCIAL PUBLIC RELATIONS Financial public relations, sometimes called investor relations, are efforts by corporations to communicate with their investors, potential investors, and other interested parties. The financial public relations practitioner communicates with three publics: investment analysts, financial journalists, and institutional investors.[21] Investment analysts advise the public about buying stocks and securities, and institutional investors represent investment organizations, such as mutual funds, that have large amounts of money to invest. Financial journalists from such publications as the *Wall Street Journal* provide information about businesses to a variety of audiences.

Financial PR people communicate about a corporation's performance and explain its underlying causes. They use financial media, investor newsletters, advertising, and government documents that are required by the Security Exchange Commission to circulate information about their clients' corporations. Such information becomes crucial when a new block of stock is sold.

Financial public relations tries to maintain the value of a corporation's stock. If a company performs well and investors do not know it, the stock value may fall. Undervalued stock leaves a company vulnerable to another company's buying the stock and absorbing the company in a hostile takeover.

FUND RAISING Some public relations practitioners participate in fund raising for nonprofit organizations. Public broadcasting stations exemplify this activity. Twice a year, PBS stations interrupt their regular programming to ask viewers to donate money to pay for the station's operations. Many stations also hold auctions, soliciting donated goods and services from the community and then selling them to raise money. Philanthropic organizations, such as United Way, and universities and colleges also raise funds. Immediately on graduation, if not sooner, college students receive solicitations for donations from their college's public relations department, which is usually called the development office.

CRISIS MANAGEMENT Public relations personnel develop long-range plans for managing issues so they can help companies avoid crises. Nevertheless, sometimes an unexpected catastrophe hits, and the public relations staff is called upon to manage the crisis. Typical crises include product tampering, product recalls, serious accidents, and even some labor disputes. In addition to the potential financial damage done to a company by the crisis, the organization's image can be damaged if the crisis is not handled well.

Companies usually design contingency plans for crisis management during periods of decline or unfavorable publicity. In answer to critics who have been predicting the death of Apple, the company touts its wares during this 1997 trade show with a message that is future oriented—symbolizing Apple's determination to continue to be a player in computer development.

438

Union Carbide Corporation had a dire need for crisis management in 1984 when a pesticide plant exploded in Bhopal, India. More than 3,800 people died, and 20,000 received injuries from escaping poison gas. Union Carbide Corporation, which owned about 51 percent of the plant, assumed moral responsibility, although not legal responsibility, even though the explosion was later blamed on a disgruntled employee. The company offered aid for the injured and eventually paid $425 million to settle lawsuits.[22]

Crisis management requires contingency plans that anticipate possible crises. These plans include who and what should be communicated to news media and what actions should be taken with products if they are involved. These plans play a crucial role in management actions. An unexpected crisis can cost an organization millions of dollars and even run a company out of business.

Keyconcept

Crisis Management: This increasingly important dimension of public relations requires that organizations develop a plan for dealing with crises such as oil spills, media attacks, or other events that could create antagonism between an organization and any of its publics. The emphasis is on determining what crises could occur and planning in advance of the event, so that reactions help to alleviate the crisis rather than enhance it.

EXTERNAL PR TOOLS Public relations uses a variety of tools; most either generate information or communicate that information. Information-generating tools include research methods, such as surveys, focus groups, and databases. PR specialists conduct *surveys* with telephones, mail, and personal interviews. In each situation the respondent answers questions about topics of interest to the PR practitioner. The questions may concern a company's image, use of a product, or opinion about an issue. The answers to the questions are analyzed by using computers, and the information can be used for planning and executing PR plans.

Focus groups are generally composed of eight to twelve people who are selected to meet in a group with a facilitator and answer specific questions. A focus group allows for follow-up questions and in-depth discussion that cannot be accomplished through a survey. However, the dynamics of being in a group can influence some people's responses. A person who does not like a political candidate, for example, might say so over the phone but might not say so when he thinks he is the only member of a focus group who dislikes the candidate. Also, the members of a focus group tend not to be representative of society at large.

Surveys, by contrast, contain more structure but may miss some opinions. For example, the people who conducted one survey of readers at a Michigan daily newspaper did not anticipate that readers would be angry over a price increase three years earlier. But 20 percent of the respondents mentioned their anger when allowed to say whatever they wanted. Including a question about the price increase would have generated better information about the anger.

Surveys and focus groups create new data, but *existing databases* can also be used for research. Databases contain research conducted by government agencies, such as the U.S. Census Bureau, and by private research organizations. Databases have the advantage of being cheaper than original research, but they are not as specific as original research. Most databases are accessible by computer and can be very useful in identifying publics of interest. The databases then help practitioners to design original research to gather more information.

The second set of tools includes communication methods, both mediated and interpersonal, to inform and persuade people. A record company faxes news releases about a new album to music critics at newspapers and magazines. The releases provide information about the group, the album title, and the release date, with the aim of getting the critic to listen to the album and review it. A day or two after the release arrives, a PR practitioner will call to remind the music critic about the album. Both of these efforts are part of a larger plan to create publicity for the album. Interpersonal communication tools for PR range from giving speeches to one-to-one discussions.

James Carville and Mary Matalin, spin doctors extraordinaire (as well as husband and wife), symbolize the growth of a business that uses public relations techniques to manage political campaigns and issues.

SPIN DOCTORS OFFER NEW TOOLS Spin doctors lobby journalists to influence coverage. Spin doctors became prevalent during the 1980s and earned their name from the term "spin," which means placing a certain interpretation on statements or data. Putting spin on a PR issue did not start in the 1980s; the practice goes back to the beginning of PR efforts. However, the practice gained attention during the 1988 presidential contest between George Bush and Michael Dukakis. Whenever an important issue gained attention, the spin doctors contacted the campaign press corps to put their candidate's spin on the coverage. Eventually, the spin doctors themselves became subjects of news stories.

Spin doctors do not operate just in politics; they often work with businesses as well. John Scanlon is an example of a successful spin doctor. His clients have included CBS, the *Dartmouth Review,* and tobacco companies Philip Morris, Lorillard, and the Liggett Group.[23] He worked for the tobacco companies when a New Jersey man sued them over his wife's death from cancer. Bruce Porter described Scanlon's work:

> Scanlon succeeded in badgering reporters into giving closer consideration to his clients' side of the issue than they might have otherwise been inclined to give, in view of the hoary nature of much of the defendants' evidence. On several occasions, for instance, AP reporter Dan Wakin would arrive at work to find yesterday's piece red-penciled to point out instances in which he might have done more justice to the companies' case. "There is no question the cigarette companies got their money's worth," says Amy Singer, a reporter for *American Lawyer* who covered the trial. "With all the constant pressure, the press paid much more attention to experts from the cigarette companies than they might have otherwise."[24]

Even though spin doctors communicate with journalists through writing, the greatest effect comes through interpersonal communication. Spin doctors provide information, but their real goal is to persuade journalists to at least look at an issue from their client's perspective. Understanding the process of the media and how reporters create news is a central requirement of being a spin doctor.

The phenomenon of the spin doctor received so much notice during the late 1980s and early 1990s that two scholars suggest it may be a new model for public relations.[25] They concluded, "The spin doctors seem to have found ways of circumnavigating the reporter's traditional wariness of the source who is an advocate, and they seem to be more skilled at this than the traditional public relations practitioner." This recent spurt in spin doctoring suggests that journalists and PR practitioners need to decide how best to deal with these intense efforts to manipulate the news toward particular angles.

PROBLEMS FACING THE PRACTITIONER The types of problems that an external PR practitioner faces vary with the person's position. Those who work for corporations face a different set of problems from those who work in PR agencies. But both must deal with two basic problems: *budgets* and *respect.*

Economic Impact

The millions of movie viewers sitting in theaters might not know it, but public relations affected their decision to see that particular film. Helping consumers to make decisions is the primary way in which PR contributes to the economy.

Consumers buy goods and services on the basis of their perception of quality and price. Four forms of information mold these perceptions: advertising, personal experience, comments from family and friends, and information in the mass media. For movies the mass media information consists of television, radio, and newspaper reviews.

Public relations can affect movie reviews in several ways. Film companies make sure journalists get to interview movie stars, they hold parties

PR as an Information Subsidy

and premieres for films, and they invite journalists to visit Hollywood at the movie company's expense. These PR practices do not guarantee that a bad film will get good reviews, but it might get a positive spin on an average film. Film companies also send press kits to reviewers and make sure they get to see a film shortly before it is released to theaters so that reviews of the film will appear at just the right time.

The movie industry is only one of many that try to influence people indirectly through mass media. Media scholar Oscar Gandy calls these efforts "information subsidies." Organizations that have something to gain

economically or politically subsidize the information gathering of journalists by providing information to them, providing trips to places of interest, or otherwise making it easy for a journalist to write a story. Sometimes these efforts create stories—journalists write about topics they otherwise would have ignored.

Companies provide this subsidy to promote their product or service, and news organizations accept it because it reduces the cost of creating information. It is difficult to measure the impact of such subsidies on the economy, but it is certain that they influence economic decisions by individuals and organizations.

When the economy takes a downturn, many companies cut budgets to preserve profit levels. Because PR does not contribute directly to the production of goods and services and PR people do not run machines or wait on customers, communication departments often face the sharpest edge of the downsizing ax. PR budgets are cut, and resources for outside consultants are reduced.

In addition, company managers do not always understand—or respect—the fact that PR practitioners have particular expertise in understanding the impact of communication. Managers assume that people in their organization who can write and speak well know as much about communication as the PR experts do. However, exercising the mechanical process of communicating is not the same as understanding how that communication will affect people.

PR practitioners also encounter respect problems because their contributions are difficult to measure. Managers can determine how many people hours it takes to produce a car, but they cannot tell how many practitioner hours it took to get the public to think well of those cars. As a result of these managerial assumptions, PR people can sometimes be like comedian Rodney Dangerfield: They get no respect.

In spite of the problems, external PR remains important to a company's success. A classic example occurred in November 1994 when a college professor discovered that the Intel Corporation's Pentium chip, which runs many computers, had a flaw that would cause minor calculation errors. Initially, Intel downplayed the problem. The company said it would replace chips when the computer owner could show a need for a replacement chip. This response created a consumer backlash against Intel. Faced with consumer anger, Intel apologized and offered to replace the flawed chip on request at no cost. An experienced external PR practitioner might have predicted the consumer response to the initial action and saved Intel some embarrassment.

Conducting internal PR

Internal public relations activities include all of the formal communications activities within an organization, except for interpersonal communication in the organization's daily activities. Broadcasting a company news program to Ford plants around the United States is internal PR; an assembly line foreperson telling a welder to speed up is not.

As with external PR activities, internal activities are planned and sustained. These activities include company publications about social activities, communication about policies and goals, and training activities. Such communication becomes crucial if a company wants its employees to cooperate effectively and efficiently in achieving the organization's goals.

Both managers and employees of a company must continually make decisions. These decisions affect the company's production and services and the lives of the people who work for the company. Employees deserve to know the truth about the company in which they work, and managers must know about their employees if they are to motivate them. Internal PR is a classic case of two-way communication, and much of the PR success is determined by how much employees are "listened to" rather than "told to."

WHO COMMUNICATES WITH WHOM? Internal communication involves four directions of information exchange: downward, upward, horizontal, and diagonal.[26] Figure 14.3 illustrates these four directions.

Downward communication involves managers communicating with employees that they supervise. The company's president announcing a new vacation policy qualifies as downward communication. *Upward communication* involves employees communicating with their supervisors. A task force of employees issuing a report for their supervisors is upward communication. *Horizontal communication* includes communication among employees at the same level of hierarchy in an organization. When the editor of a newspaper communicates with the director of circulation at a newspaper, horizontal communication occurs. *Diagonal communication* takes place between departments at different levels. If a reporter at a newspaper communicates with the advertising director, diagonal communication occurs.

FIGURE 14.3 Directions of Internal Communication

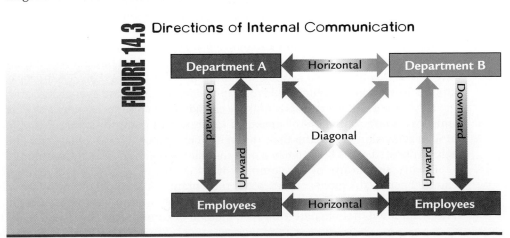

442

Downward communication has five main uses: (1) to explain the duties of a job and how to do them; (2) to provide a reason for doing a job and how the job fits with other jobs; (3) to communicate an organization's policies, procedures, and practices; (4) to give employees feedback about their performance; and (5) to provide employees with a sense of the organization's missions and goals.[27] All of these are essential for employees to perform well.

Upward communication can perform seven important functions: (1) providing feedback for managers about employees' attitudes; (2) providing suggestions for improving job procedures; (3) giving feedback about the effectiveness of downward communication; (4) providing information about whether employees are able to achieve company goals; (5) filling requests for assistance and supplies; (6) expressing employees' grievances before they become problems; and (7) increasing employees' involvement with their jobs.[28] All effective communication requires feedback. Upward and downward communication work as feedback for each other. Without both, organizations cannot perform to their potential.

Horizontal and diagonal communication are just as crucial to organization performance as upward and downward communication. However, horizontal and diagonal communication are more likely to involve direct communication among managers and employees without the intervention of a PR practitioner. Diagonal and horizontal communication typically involve small numbers of people, so interpersonal communication works best without someone intervening.

METHODS OF INTERNAL COMMUNICATION Communicating with employees inside a company involves three forms: *text, verbal,* and *visual.* Text includes letters, memos and reports, e-mail, faxes, newsletters, newspapers, teletext, and magazines. Verbal forms include telephone, radio, speeches, voice mail, and conferences. Visual includes video, broadcast television, posters, and photographs in printed material. The most effective form depends on the type of message, how many people are involved, the media with which the employees are most comfortable, the nature of the company, and the timing needed for the communication.

The more important the information is to the receiver, the more effective interpersonal communication will be. Information about layoffs and drastic changes in working conditions should be delivered face-to-face by the employees' supervisors. Under such conditions the employees will have questions that need to be answered, and a newsletter will not help. When a minor procedure or policy has been changed, a notice by e-mail or in the employee newsletter will work fine.

The type of communication also depends on the number of people involved. Interpersonal communication with 10,000 people is not feasible, but a television broadcast would work. Many large companies with multiple plants have daily TV broadcasts with satellite distribution to keep employees up-to-date on corporate events and concerns.

The employees' media habits must be considered if communication is to work. Companies with large numbers of unskilled laborers will communicate more effectively through television and audio than through a newspaper. White-collar companies with highly educated staffs tend to use e-mail, newsletters, and memos to communicate.

Finally, the nature of the company itself comes into play. Some companies are scattered across the globe; others locate their branches close together or have a single location. Because of current technology, distance should not hamper good communication, but it will help to determine the method of communication. Satellite and cable

Good "internal communication" has been a buzzword and selling point of Saturn automobiles. Public relations constituencies vary, but they sometimes overlap. Good internal communication is a selling point for customers as well as employees.

distribution communicate more quickly around the globe than do magazines and newspapers.

Type of technology also plays a role in the nature of the organization. Organizations that use extensive computer technology have more options for communication than those that do not. Communication companies, such as newspapers and TV stations, depend heavily on computers. Their employees are likely to feel comfortable with and use computers for communication with others.

Deciding which communication form works for which public under which circumstances is a big part of the practitioner's job. Just as any communicator must understand his or her audience, the practitioner needs an understanding of the employees' and managers' communication needs and abilities. In larger organizations, this means using research. Surveys and focus groups can be just as important for internal communications as for external communications.

PROBLEMS FACING INTERNAL PR PRACTITIONERS Internal PR is usually conducted by practitioners who are hired by the organization and work for a supervisor or executive who controls information. The practitioner cannot release more information than is authorized. This subordinate condition differs from consulting public relations. A PR consultant who disagrees with a client can usually sever the relationship and find other clients. Internal practitioners usually work only for the particular company and might have to leave the organization if they disagree with their manager or the company's policies too often.

One former PR person told of a manufacturing plant in which the internal communication department conducted a survey of employees to find out their attitudes toward management. The employees were told that they would remain anonymous, but managers used the returned questionnaires to identify "trouble makers." The trouble makers were eventually fired. Additional efforts to measure employee attitudes at the plant had no success.

Just as external PR practitioners suffer from lack of respect and budgets, so do internal communicators. This lack of respect comes from both above and below. Managers often don't appreciate the complexity of communication, and employees often do not trust the communicators because they represent management.

The public relations business as a profession

For well over 100 years, public relations specialists have debated whether public relations could be a profession with a code of ethics. PR practitioners cannot be professionals in the same sense as lawyers and doctors. The guarantee of freedom of speech in the First Amendment to the U.S. Constitution means that no one may license people to be com-

444

municators. However, the constraints of the First Amendment have not stopped arguments over whether practitioners should behave in a professional manner.

The Public Relations Society of America (PRSA) plays the most important role in promoting PR professionalism. PRSA has a code of ethics, a publication called *Public Relations Journal,* and an accrediting program. To become accredited, a PR practitioner must take an exam that tests knowledge of PR practices and ethics and communication law. Practitioners who pass the exam become accredited in public relations and can use the acronym APR after their names. Research indicates that accredited practitioners make about $20,000 more a year than do nonaccredited personnel. Accreditation is enforced through the code of ethics. Complaints can be filed against APR practitioners, and if they are found to have violated the PRSA Code of Ethics (see Figure 14.4), they can be stripped of their accreditation.

Keyconcept

Ethics in Public Relations: Ethical practice is most likely to exist within a society that values truth in communication and holds the people who have the most access to media to high ethical standards. Ethical practices are endorsed by professional public relations organizations, but good practice is ultimately the responsibility of the individual.

Despite efforts to promote professionalism, practitioners continue to debate the role of public relations. A 1993 article in *Public Relations Journal* about the role of PR concluded, "According to our results, the public relations profession is one very much in search of a definition. While most respondents feel their role fits into more than one category, many view the public relations function as one that incorporates many aspects of each classification."[29]

FIGURE 14.4 Public Relations Society of America

CODE OF PROFESSIONAL STANDARDS
FOR THE PRACTICE OF PUBLIC RELATIONS

Declaration of Principles

Members of the Public Relations Society of America base their professional principles on the fundamental value and dignity of the individual, holding that the free exercise of human rights, especially freedom of speech, freedom of assembly and freedom of the press, is essential to the practice of public relations.

In serving the interests of clients and employers, we dedicate ourselves to the goals of better communication, understanding and cooperation among the diverse individuals, groups and institutions in society.

We pledge:

■ To conduct ourselves professionally, with truth, accuracy, fairness and responsibility;

■ To improve our individual competence and advance the knowledge and proficiency of the profession through continuing research and education;

■ And to adhere to the articles of the Code of Professional Standards for the Practice of Public Relations as adopted by the governing Assembly of the Society.

Source: David A. Haberman and Harry A. Dolphin, *Public Relations: The Necessary Art* (Ames, IA: Iowa State University Press, 1988), pp. 413–414.

Eighty-four practitioners responded to the *Journal*'s call for comments. Of these, 21 percent said that practitioners are advocates on behalf of clients, 7 percent said that practitioners are consensus builders who try to bring competing sides together to find solutions, and 57 percent said that practitioners must be both advocates and consensus builders. The remaining 15 percent said that practitioners should perform other functions, such as those of information broker, strategist, and educator.

However, the dichotomy between advocate and consensus builder misses the key issue that has always defined PR professionalism. The question is not whether to advocate or not. The important question concerns the role of truth in PR practice. The question is: Should PR practitioners purposefully mislead any of their publics?

The professional practitioner, as defined by PRSA, would answer no to this question. The third article of the PRSA Code of Ethics says, "A member shall adhere to truth and accuracy and to generally accepted standards of good taste." However, most PR specialists are not members of PRSA.

Disagreement over PR professionalism within the ranks of public relations exploded into the media in 1986. The Securities and Exchange Commission (SEC) accused Anthony M. Franco of insider trading. The SEC said that he used information about a PR client's pending sale to another company to buy stock in the client's company. What made this newsworthy was Franco's position as president-elect of PRSA when the alleged insider trading took place.[30]

Franco signed a consent decree, which means that he settled the SEC lawsuit but neither admitted nor denied the allegations in the complaint. While all of this was happening, Franco became president of PRSA. After the SEC's announcement of the settlement of the case, Franco resigned as president, but letters announcing his resignation gave no details about the nature of the SEC's claims. *The Wall Street Journal* said of the situation, "The Franco affair is being dragged out, and Mr. Franco and the PRSA are being dragged through the mud, in one of the biggest and most embarrassing PR gaffes in years. In short, it is not a textbook case of effective public relations."[31]

Professionalism of public relations finally rests on the personal ethics of individual practitioners. In a real sense, public relations can be no more professional than society will allow. A society that values truth in communication will produce professionally oriented practitioners; a society that has a low regard for truth will produce a class of practitioners who use whatever methods suit their purposes.

Trends and innovations

As in all areas of society today, diversity is an issue for public relations. Firms are striving to expand the number of women and minorities on their PR staffs and in management, both out of a concern for fairness and out of a desire to be able to serve all publics in a professional manner. Another issue is innovation in the media. Firms serve publics in increasingly electronic ways. Companies and associations are creating extensive sites on the World Wide Web and are experimenting with electronic delivery of press releases. The complexity of issues in today's society is another concern. PR practitioners increasingly need to be specialists, so many firms are looking for individuals who are qualified in such areas as health care, rather than for PR generalists. In addition, companies and activities are going global. PR practitioners in large companies will most likely work in at least two countries during their careers.

Diversity

Public relations is like any form of communication that deals with a public: It requires an understanding of that public. As the publics in society become more culturally and ethnically diverse, PR staffs should reflect that diversity. Otherwise, their communication may be ineffective and misdirected. Like most communication fields, public relations remains unrepresentative of society's racial and ethnic diversity. In 1988, of 151,000 PR specialists, only 5.1 percent were African American and 2.4 percent were Hispanic.[32] This is roughly equivalent to the 8.2 percent of U.S. journalists who were members of a racial minority in 1992.[33] More women than men work in public relations, but white men continue to hold most of the senior management positions.

The unequal distribution of power in PR management reveals itself in various forms. A survey of minority PR practitioners found that 51 percent said they had been denied jobs, 43 percent said they had been denied clients, and 41 percent said they had been denied pay raises because of their race.[34] Patterns of gender-based discrimination also exist. A 1993 study of PR salaries found that women's median salary was $39,542, compared to $58,477 for men.[35] Men had higher salaries in all ranges of experience, but the difference was less among less experienced practitioners.

The early 1990s saw a growth in the number of minorities enrolled in university communication programs, while the percentage of women remained stable at about 60 percent. Social pressures to reduce and eliminate discrimination will continue in public relations. However, delays in equal treatment may make it more difficult to attract qualified PR practitioners in the future.

Electronic PR

Just as advertising grew greatly on the Internet in the mid-1990s, so did the presence of public relations. Often companies connect the two by using a home page for both advertising and the dispersion of information. Veronis, Suhler & Associates, Inc., for example, is an investment banking firm for media companies. Its home page offers information about media industries, complete with press releases, and it also includes advertising for the companies' publications.

The number of companies with Web sites has grown rapidly. In October 1996, Yahoo Net Directory listed more than 129,000 sites for companies. This had tripled from seven months earlier.

Companies tend to adopt one of three types of sites on the World Wide Web.[36] The single-page brochure style includes an illustration, the company logo, textual information and a link to another location. The information center has multiple pages with a variety of links, text, and images. The virtual storefront can include all that appears in an information center and a structure for ordering products over the Internet. General Motors set up a Web site in 1996 that had 16,000 pages and 98,000 links to other sites.

A number of nonprofit and lobby groups have also set up Web sites. The Association for Education in Journalism and Mass Communication has a home page that provides information about the association and its activities. In addition, it lists teaching jobs. Education institutions got on the Web early; thousands of colleges and universities present their information electronically.

As a result of the expanding opportunities presented by the Internet, electronic PR firms have developed. Some are general PR firms, as could be found anywhere; others specialize in electronic communications. Vancouver-based Communicopia, for example, started in 1993 on the Web and specializes in news media public relations, World Wide Web home page development, information distributions and databases, and corporate environmental communications (see *http://www.communicopia.bc.ca*).

It appears that companies will depend increasingly on electronic communication in some form. A survey of 750 newspaper and magazine editors in 1995 found that 56 percent said that within five years, they will want all media releases submitted electronically, compared to 18 percent who will want paper submissions.[37] The exact form of electronic communication might vary, but the use of the U.S. Postal Service for delivering PR information to journalists will decline as the twenty-first century approaches.

The World Wide Web is affecting public relations by allowing organizations to go directly to publics more easily. PR practitioners used to require mass media outlets to reach dispersed publics, such as automotive consumers. If GM announced a new car model, the media carried the message. They still do, but GM can now use the Web to go directly to potential customers. This gives companies more control of their message.

447

Some Web sites contain bundles of PR information. The PR Newswire, for instance, carries a collection of press releases from its member's organizations. Since 1954, when the association was formed to provide news releases to the media, it has provided journalists with information from a a large number of organizations. Now, the very same information that was once available primarily to journalists can be found on the Web (www.prnewswire.com). Web surfers can access information about a variety of companies in industries ranging from automotive to entertainment to health and biotechnology.

■ Specialization

In the Broadway musical *The Music Man* a salesman advises his colleagues that "you gotta know the territory" to be a successful salesperson. Similar advice seems to have crept into the PR profession, as practitioners have had to deal with increasingly complex issues. Communicating information to publics requires that the communicator have a knowledge of the topic being addressed.

The specialty can be a type of business, such as health care, or it can be a type of public relations, such as lobbying. Rossman, Martin & Associates of Lansing, Michigan, specialize in political public relations. They help interest groups to influence legislation and work with candidates who are running for office. Often, specialization exists within larger PR agencies. As Table 14.4 shows, in 1995, Burson-Marsteller received the highest fees in the specialty areas of environmental, financial, food and beverage, and health care.

TABLE 14.4 Top PR Firms within Specialty Areas Based on 1995 Fees

SPECIALTY	AGENCY	NET FEE (MILLIONS)
Agriculture	Gibbs & Soell	$ 4.7
Beauty/Fashion	Rowland Worldwide	$ 6.0
Entertainment/Cultural	Shandwick	$16.0
Environmental	Burson-Marsteller	$26.2
Financial PR/Investor Relations	Burson-Marsteller	$36.5
Foods & Beverages	Burson-Marsteller	$50.6
Health Care	Burson-Marsteller	$57.6
High-Tech	Shandwick	$41.7
Home Furnishings	Shandwick	$ 4.6
Sports	Cohn & Wolfe	$ 7.3
Travel	Shandwick	$12.7

Source: O'Dwyer's Directory of Public Relations Firms (New York: J. R. O'Dwyer Co., 1996), pp. A25 & A27. Copyright, J.R. O'Dwyer Co., New York.

The need for specialization reflects the growing role of PR practitioners as advisers and not just communicators. Carole Howard and Wilma Mathews advise future practitioners:

> We must demonstrate that we have a solid grasp of both our organization's objectives and the world in which we are operating, so that we can provide concrete assistance in articulating and dealing with the complex problems top management faces in relating to this ever-changing environment.[38]

Global public relations

An American public relations specialist in the 1950s would probably spend his or her entire career working somewhere in the United States. Today, a public relations practitioner will likely work in at least one other country. As corporations have become international and governments have lowered trade barriers, public relations publics have become international as well.

In an international economy, practitioners require additional skills. They must understand languages other than English, variations in culture and political processes, different media environments, and the role of communication technology in other countries. Each country has political variations that affect international relations. For example, the Canadian government is very sensitive to efforts by U.S. companies to sell services and goods in Canada. A certain percentage of television content, for example, must concern Canadian interests. France has similar laws. These regulations affect efforts by U.S. companies to sell television programs in Canada and France.

Keyconcept

Technology and Globalization: As business and political relations become increasingly international, public relations firms are increasingly called on to practice in a variety of cultures. Electronic PR via the Internet and satellite help to deliver messages globally and to communicate with a variety of publics, but an understanding of each public's culture is necessary to create a valuable message.

Media environments also vary from country to country, especially in the area of journalistic practices. For example, only 6 percent of German journalists support badgering sources, compared to 49 percent of U.S. journalists.[39] Such variations affect the interaction of PR specialists and journalists. Spin doctors will not influence British reporters by attacking their objectivity. Objectivity is not nearly as widely accepted as good journalistic practice in Britain as it is in the United States.

Technology also influences global PR. The dominant mass medium differs from one continent to another. Spreading information in Western Europe requires the use of television, but influencing residents of Africa requires using radio. Variations exist even within countries. The inhabitants of some metropolitan areas of China are avid readers, while some rural areas have low literacy rates.

International communication can create a nightmare for PR practitioners, as false information can travel as quickly as accurate information. For more than a decade, Nestlé S. A., an international corporation based in Switzerland, battled accusations about its international infant formula sales.[40] In 1973 an article in the *New Internationalist,* a small English publication, accused Nestlé and other infant formula manufacturers of reducing breast feeding of babies in Third World countries through the promotion of their formulas. The article said that many women did not understand the instructions for using infant formulas and the results were often malnutrition and even death.

The article was reprinted in various publications, and an international boycott of Nestlé's products began in summer 1977. From the beginning of the controversy, Nestlé offered to cooperate with international monitoring groups and international health organizations. The company's public relations activities helped to set up a commission to investigate ethics in infant formula promotion. Independently, the American Academy of Pediatrics said in 1981 that no substantial scientific evidence had been provided to support the claim that infant formula marketing practices had reduced breast feeding in developing countries. The boycotts were called off in the mid-1980s. However, many people still have an unfavorable perception of Nestlé, and the Internet has contributed to this

Nestlé faced a significant problem dealing with international criticism based on questionable support and journalistic practices. Language differences and variation in journalistic practices complicate international PR practitioners' jobs. These problems will become even more common as the world economic and political systems integrate more.

Summary

- Public relations concerns planned and sustained unpaid communication from organizations to publics.
- PR practitioners communicate with internal and external publics.
- Any of an organization's many publics can influence whether that organization achieves its goals.
- The aims of public relations are to inform, persuade, and seek information from the organization's publics.
- External public relations by specialists in the United States began during the first half of the 1800s.
- The size and complexity of America and limitations of human selectivity contribute to the need for public relations practitioners.
- Public relations did not become recognized by the general population until after World War II, although some corporations had used PR for almost 100 years.
- External PR activities include lobbying, political PR, financial PR, fund raising, crisis management, and events coordination.
- Many managers remain skeptical about the need for internal communications.
- Public relations specialists can work in-house for an organization or as a consultant for an organization.
- The public relations process includes setting goals, conducting research, creating a PR plan, and evaluating the success of the plan.
- The problems facing practitioners include low budgets and lack of respect from managers.
- Internal communication includes downward, upward, horizontal, and vertical communication.
- Ethnic, racial, and gender bias continues to plague the public relations field.
- A variety of technologies are available for PR communication, and the type that is used must fit the information needs and habits of the publics.
- PR practitioners debate whether public relations is a profession and what the PR practitioner's role is. The key question concerns whether PR practitioners should purposefully mislead members of their publics.
- The growth of the international economic system has created global public relations. This creates additional problems for practitioners.

Navigating the Web

Public relations on the web

The World Wide Web is an ideal public relations tool. In fact, many web sites are promotional sites for organizations or corporations. In addition, various public relations firms maintain sites. Also included are trade publications that give information about public relations.

PR Newswire	http://www.prnewswire.com

PR Newswire presents press releases and articles about the range of industries in the United States and around the world. It organizes companies by industry and provides a quick look at business and industry.

Public Relations Society of America	http://www.prsa.org

PRSA is a professional society that accredits PR practitioners. The site contains information about PRSA and its membership requirements, publications, and professional activities. This site also links to the PRSSA (Public Relations Student Society of America (site). The PRSSA promotes professional public relations on college campuses.

Burson-Marsteller Public Relations	http://www.bm.com

Burson-Marsteller is the largest public relations firm in the world. This site provides information about the services it offers.

PR Post	http://www.diamondpub.com

This site provides a location for posting press releases by companies that do not have a Web site. Each client has a page with a table of contents.

Questions for review

1. Define public relations in your own words.
2. Describe public relations as an interactive process between an organization and its publics.
3. What contributions did Ivy Lee and Edward Bernays make to public relations?
4. What four groups require public relations in order to reach their goals?
5. What are the eight steps in the public relations process? Describe each briefly.
6. Why is respect an issue for public relations personnel?

▇ Issues to think about

1. What is meant by the concept that public relations evolved to serve social needs?
2. What is the relationship between public relations and propaganda?
3. What is the significance of spin doctors in the world of politics and democracy?
4. Analyze the importance of directional communication in internal public relations.
5. What is the significance of global public relations?

▇ Suggested readings

Cutlip, Scott M. *Public Relations History: From the 17th to the 20th Century: The Antecedents* (Hillsdale, NJ: Lawrence Erlbaum Associates, 1995).

Public Relations Journal

Public Relations Review

Seib, Philip. *Public Relations* (Fort Worth, TX: Harcourt Brace College Publishers, 1995).

Advertising

Advertising

Key concepts

- Advertising and Emerging Newspapers
- The Penny Press and "Let the Buyer Beware"
- Product Responsibility and Advertising
- Advertising and Consumer Culture
- Advertising and Awareness
- The Economics of Advertising
- The Social Costs of Advertising
- Advertising versus Consumer Spending
- Commercial and Information Blending
- Online Advertising

Many young people felt a deep sense of shock on October 6, 1993. They heard the news from a press conference that three networks carried live. That afternoon, the stock price of Nike dropped 75 cents.

That tiny Nike symbol on Tiger Woods' sweater circulates a powerful message to an admiring crowd: Buy Nike. Commercial images are an integral part of American society, and athletes such as Woods and Michael Jordan often set the product pace.

It was not the death of an international dignitary that affected the country; it was Michael Jordan's retirement from the National Basketball Association. No one then suspected that Jordan would return.

Jordan was news that day, but not just because of his basketball skills. He had become America's hero because of advertising. His athletic ability made him special, but advertisements for Nike, Gatorade, Hanes, and Coca-Cola made him a household name. Millions of young people wanted to "Be like Mike." Because of Jordan's endorsement, Nike was able to sell basketball shoes for more than $100, and they were so sought after that some teenagers killed for them.

Not every great athlete becomes a household name because of advertising, although many try. But under the right circumstances, advertising can use an image as a powerful tool for influencing the way people, especially younger people, spend their money and view the world around them.

The same promotion machine that made Michael Jordan an international icon started work on Tiger Woods in 1996, when he signed a $40 million contract with Nike. In 1997, Woods became the first African American to win the Master's Tournament, and his value as a spokesman for golf, young people and, of course, Nike shoes zoomed. He was not just concerned with making money, however, as some Nike television ads spoke out against the racial segregation that still occurs at some private golf clubs.

Because advertising has permeated the social and cultural fabric of the nation, few types of media content draw such a strong reaction from people. Advertising clearly comes from a biased source. Some consumers see advertising as an effort to trick them into buying what they do not need. Some journalists see advertising as an unwanted influence on news coverage. Parents resist the brand-name appeals made to children and teenagers. Yet many consumers rely on advertising for information about products and to get a good deal. Each of these perspectives contains some truth.

Advertising is defined as *a paid mediated presentation of information about services, products, or ideas with the specific goal of influencing the consumers of the information.* Advertising differs from news coverage and public relations activities because the advertising message is created, produced, and paid for by the advertiser, and the source of the information is clearly identified. News sources and public relations experts must hope that a reporter will relay a message accurately; advertisers simply buy the message they want. Nike had to pay for its 1994 ads calling for an end to the major league baseball strike; the TV networks did not give them that time.

Advertising usually tries to sell products, such as soda, and services, such as real estate sales. However, some ads try to promote ideas. All ads share the goal of trying to influence people in some way.

The effort to influence is not a serious problem for consumers as long as they understand the purpose of advertisements. Many ads serve a basic media social function of coordinating economic activities. Advertising allows sellers to tell buyers what products and services are available at what prices and in what places. Without this exchange of information, consumers would waste time and money.

However, advertising has real and social costs. Some people argue that it raises the price of goods. Others fear that it alters social norms; affects the attitudes of children and adults; and undermines the influence of family, church, and schools. Commercialization through advertising, they argue, directs society away from serious issues and raises the art of acquisition to a new level.

For the service of connecting buyer and seller, U.S. media organizations receive large amounts of money. In 1996, media companies took in $172.8 billion in advertising. The bulk of the money went to newspapers, television, direct mail, and radio; newspapers received 22.1 percent, broadcast and cable television got 23.3 percent, direct mail got 20.2 percent, and radio received about 7 percent.[1]

Consumer households pay an average of $1,700, through the prices of goods, for the consumer information they receive through advertising. Put another way, if advertising disappeared, the average household would have to spend an additional $1,700 a year to keep existing media organizations in business. Now the consumer dollar is routed from products through business organizations and into media.

Advertising has been a controversial fact of American life. Because advertising has an economic and a social effect, the issues that it raises are complex:

■ Advertising is most prominent in a free market economy. As you read this chapter, try to analyze how and why advertising and the free market are related.

   ■ Advertising uses social images and appeals to people's psychological and physical needs. Its content may sell a product or persuade people to adopt a specific lifestyle. Given this type of impact, think about how advertising is related to the marketplace of ideas.

      ■ Some individuals think that certain types of advertising should be banned because well-produced messages have an enormous impact. After you read about

Advertising in your life

Advertising as a Political and Social Message

Advertising is a controversial subject in American life. Think about your own reactions to the ads you see, read, and hear. As you read this chapter, look for clues about the positive and negative aspects of advertising. Think about which forms of media you rely on for advertising and which forms of advertising you think are credible or effective.

WHICH MEDIA DO YOU MOST RELY ON FOR ADVERTISING? (Rank in Order of Importance to You)	WHICH MEDIA DO YOU MOST TRUST? (Rank in Order of Trustworthiness)	DO YOU THINK ADVERTISING FOR SOME TYPES OF PRODUCTS IS MORE CREDIBLE THAN FOR OTHERS? (Rank in Order of Credibility)	WHICH TYPES OF POLITICAL ADS ARE MOST EFFECTIVE? (Rank in Order of Effectiveness)	WHICH TYPES OF POLITICAL ADS CONTRIBUTE THE MOST TO DEMOCRACY? (Rank in Order of Contribution)
Magazines ____	Magazines ____	Cosmetics ____	Issue-oriented ____	Issue-oriented ____
Newspapers ____	Newspapers ____	Household goods ____	Attack ____	Attack ____
Television ____	Television ____	Clothing ____	Personal ____	Personal ____
Radio ____	Radio ____	Cars ____	Informative ____	Informative ____
Direct mail ____	Direct mail ____	Appliances ____	Mood creating ____	Mood creating ____
Internet/online ____	Internet/online ____	Services ____	Other ____	Other ____

the various types of influence advertising has on the society, try to decide whether advertising significantly changes our society.

▨ Politics has changed with advertising, particularly as political managers have learned to master television. After you learn about how political advertising has changed, think about its effect on a democratic society.

▨ Internet advertising is in its early stages. A major issue is how advertising will make use of the new electronic technologies. What are the implications here for the Internet, online services, and older media?

Advertising in American life

Advertising dates to the ancient Greek and Roman civilizations. In the cities, **criers** walked the street announcing commercial ventures, as well as providing information about religion, politics, and other public matters.[2] In a sense, these criers were verbal newspapers, with a mixture of news and advertising similar to that found today.

A more traditional definition of a medium would connect early advertising to printing. The earliest printed **broadside,** or handbill, in England was an advertisement for a religious book in 1477. Although some disagreement exists, the first English newspaper advertisement

crier: A person who walked around the streets and "cried out" news to the people. Preceded printed news.

broadside: Handbills, also called broadsheets, that were printed only on one side.

456 has been dated from August 1622. A weekly publication of "Newes" carried an advertisement for two earlier copies of the newspaper.[3] Almost eighty years later, the first advertisement appeared in an American newspaper, the *Boston News-Gazette*. The ad offered to sell advertising in the *News-Gazette*.

The mercantile press and advertising

As commerce grew in the American colonies, so did advertising in the **mercantile press.** The mercantile press was aimed at shopkeepers and other small business owners rather than at participants in political discussion. The first issue of the first American daily newspaper, the *Pennsylvania Packet and Daily* that began in 1784, contained 63 percent advertising. The next year, a daily was started in New York with similar success in advertising. These cases suggest that advertising demand, as well as the demand for news, promoted the creation of daily newspapers in the United States.[4]

While most of today's newspaper ads are aimed at consumers, many of the mercantile press ads tried to sell goods to other businesspeople, often for use in their businesses. A shipping company would advertise a shipment of clothing so that retailers would buy it for resale. Early advertisements also promoted real estate, services, and goods for sale, just as newspapers do today. However, advertisements often read like announcements. For example, a small ad in the November 18, 1771, *Pennsylvania Packet and General Advertiser* read: "A few barrels of Carolina Pork to be sold by John Murgatroyd, in Water-street, near Tun-Alley."[5]

Advertising in the mercantile press often targeted other businessmen. Today the tradition is carried forward at trade shows where businesses or companies try to attract product users through promotional favors.

Keyconcept

Advertising and Emerging Newspapers: Demand for news and for advertising created a demand for newspapers. Early newspaper ads were simple paragraphs of type, promoting real estate, services, and goods for sale to retailers and consumers.

By the 1820s, the mercantile newspapers had become important commercial bulletin boards with advertising and announcements for the business community.

Despite similarities in purpose, early advertisements looked nothing like the ads that are found in today's newspapers. Only a few crude illustrations were used, and printing technology limited the diversity of type. Ads were typically one column wide and rarely contained graphics.

The development of mass advertising

Because of their focus on business and trade, the mercantile newspapers were poor advertising vehicles for consumer goods. Their small targeted audience kept their circulations low. In 1816, seven New York dailies sold only about 9,400 copies in a city of 125,000.[6] Average people could not afford these papers, nor did they like the content.

mercantile press: Early American newspapers that served businesses, shopkeepers, and tradesmen. These newspapers also contained political news.

Just as the penny press revitalized the consumer market, it also revolutionized **mass advertising.** By 1842, New York circulation had grown to 92,700 daily; two-thirds of these issues cost two cents or less.[7] Now merchants could reach large numbers of customers with one newspaper.

Keyconcept

The Penny Press and "Let the Buyer Beware": As newspapers grew in circulation, they advertised a wide variety of products about which the editor did not have personal knowledge. Therefore editors adopted a "let the buyer beware" philosophy, assigning to the reader the responsibility of determining the truth of an ad and the worth of a product.

In addition to expanding the advertising market, the penny press changed the nature of advertising. Penny newspapers ran want ads similar to ones found in English newspapers. They charged advertisers by a unit of space rather than the flat price charged by the mercantile press, and they separated advertising and news content.

Not everyone praised the penny press for its changes. The mercantile papers, which charged six cents for a copy, attacked various penny newspapers for printing patent medicine ads. These advertisements sold liquids and salves that at their best did no harm, but at their worst could kill. The criticism of penny newspapers was justified, but the mercantile press ignored the fact that some of its newspapers had been carrying patent medicine ads for decades.

After the Civil War, advertising increased rapidly. The Industrial Revolution expanded the middle class and brought an influx of immigrants, both of which increased the demand for goods and services. Businesses met the increasing demand for goods by advertising in the thousands of newspapers that were springing up around the country. Between the Civil War and 1900, printing and graphic technology allowed for more visually appealing advertising. Ads with graphic illustrations became more common.

Although efforts were made to make advertisers more responsible for their products, nicotine ads flourished. Advertising for cigarettes, Hanes underwear, and appeals to a sense of adventure financed the development of the general interest magazine.

You may remember from Chapter 6 that the post–Civil War period also saw the maturation of magazine advertising. An expanding national economy and a consumer thirst for the information and entertainment that were found in magazines created a national advertising market. A few magazines had reached large circulations before this period, but printing technology and localized economies had limited their advertising. Advertising became the mainstay of the big, high-quality monthlies. The November 1899 edition of *Harper's* magazine, for example, had 135 pages of advertising and 163 pages of editorial material, an advertising percentage of 45 percent, only slightly lower than the percentage of advertising carried by many magazines today.[8]

Because of changes in the economy and mass media, advertising agents became more important in the late 1800s. They bought space in publications and resold it to advertisers. An agent could place an ad in a number of newspapers and magazines around the country for one price. This made advertising more efficient and easier for the advertiser, compared to buying an ad separately for each newspaper and magazine.

mass advertising: Advertisements that aim to reach the largest number of people possible.

458 Advertising in our lives

- **1477.** First handbill advertisement in England
- **1622.** First English newspaper advertisement
  - **1704.** First newspaper advertisement in America
  - **Late 1700s.** Commercial notices grow as proportion of newspapers.
    - **1830s.** Penny press gets heavy advertising support.
      - **1869.** Rowell & Ayers publish newspaper directories for advertising.
        - **Late 1800s.** Printing technology allows visually appealing ads.
        - **Late 1800s.** Magazines provide vehicle for mass national advertising.
        - **Late 1800s.** Advertising agencies grow in importance.
          - **1906.** First Pure Food and Drug Act passed.
          - **1914.** Federal Trade Commission created.
            - **1922.** First radio advertisement.

1400–1600s	1700	1800	1860	1880	1900	1920

- **1690.** *Publick Occurrences* is published in Boston.
  - **1741.** First magazine published in America.
  - **1776–1783.** Revolutionary War
    - **1861–1865.** Civil War
      - **1914–1918.** World War I
        - **1920.** KDKA in Pittsburgh gets first commercial radio license.

Key concept

Product Responsibility and Advertising: The government assumed some responsibility for accurate labeling of products. In 1906, Congress passed the Pure Food and Drug Act, and in 1914 it established the Federal Trade Commission. However, many businesses sidestepped the spirit of the law, and accurate labeling continues to be an issue today, particularly in the areas of harmful substances, such as cigarettes, and in claims about so-called health foods.

Although several agents were in business before the Civil War, agents had no accurate listings of publications, circulation levels, and advertising rates. These problems were reduced by the George P. Rowell and N. W. Ayers & Sons agencies when they began publishing newspaper directories in 1869. These directories provided some information about where an ad might be placed to achieve a desired effect.

Although the mercantile press had attacked the penny papers in the early part of the century for their reliance on patent medicine advertising, newspapers and magazines continued to carry ads for the popular medicines. Lydia E. Pinkham's Vegetable Compound, first marketed in 1876, was advertised as

A Sure Cure for Prolapsus Uteri, or Falling of the Womb . . . Pleasant to taste, efficacious and immediate in effect. It is a great help in pregnancy and relieves pain during

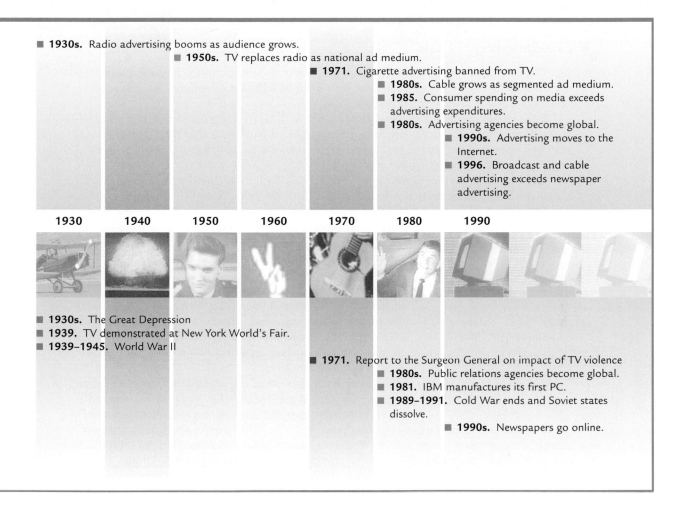

■ **1930s.** Radio advertising booms as audience grows.

■ **1950s.** TV replaces radio as national ad medium.

■ **1971.** Cigarette advertising banned from TV.

■ **1980s.** Cable grows as segmented ad medium.

■ **1985.** Consumer spending on media exceeds advertising expenditures.

■ **1980s.** Advertising agencies become global.

■ **1990s.** Advertising moves to the Internet.

■ **1996.** Broadcast and cable advertising exceeds newspaper advertising.

1930　1940　1950　1960　1970　1980　1990

■ **1930s.** The Great Depression

■ **1939.** TV demonstrated at New York World's Fair.

■ **1939–1945.** World War II

■ **1971.** Report to the Surgeon General on impact of TV violence

■ **1980s.** Public relations agencies become global.

■ **1981.** IBM manufactures its first PC.

■ **1989–1991.** Cold War ends and Soviet states dissolve.

■ **1990s.** Newspapers go online.

labor . . . For all weaknesses of the generative organs of either sex. It is second to no remedy that has ever been before the public and for all diseases of the kidneys it is the Greatest Remedy in the World.[9]

Patent medicines did not cure people, but the high alcohol content in many of them often made people feel better, at least temporarily. Unfortunately, some patent medicines contained addictive drugs and deadly poisons.

Patent medicine companies poured millions of dollars into advertising, especially into religious publications, but in the early 1900s, several newspapers and magazines refused to accept such advertising. The *Ladies Home Journal,* edited by Edward Bok, dealt the biggest blow when it exposed the medicines as frauds and refused to accept further advertising for these products.

The selling and advertising of patent medicines contributed to passage of the Pure Food and Drug Act in 1906, the establishment of the **Federal Trade Commission** in 1914, and the **Food and Drug**

Federal Trade Commission: Government agency that enforces truth in advertising laws and regulates trade of goods across state and national boundaries.

Administration of 1931. The FTC and FDA had the power to limit false advertising of patent medicines, but the agencies continued to fight some of these companies into the 1940s.[10]

Broadcasting arrives

The creators of radio did not envision it as a mass medium, much less an advertising mass medium. It was supposed to be a form of wireless telephone. As you read in Chapters 8 and 9, that idea did not last long.

Radio programming developed to sell radio sets, but as the cost of programming increased, more money was needed. In 1922, WEAF in New York sold five 10-minute advertising spots to Long Island real estate promoters. Radio advertising was born. Twenty years later, radio advertising was a $100 million business.[11]

Radio advertising prospered for several reasons. Radio was the first instantaneous national medium. Magazines circulated nationally, but they arrived in the mail and on newsstands days and weeks after they were printed. Radio was heard all across the country simultaneously. That's why General Motors spent $500,000 on radio advertising in 1928.[12] GM could announce the arrival of new car models to thousands of listeners at the same time.

Radio advertising also grew because the U.S. economy boomed through most of the 1920s. After World War I, industrial production and consumer buying expanded, and the middle class continued to grow. People had more discretionary income to spend on goods and services other than food and housing. Advertising helped them decide how to spend that money.

Broadcasting gave modern advertising agencies more choices to offer their clients. As agencies became full-service organizations, they bought advertising space, wrote copy, developed illustrations for ads, placed ads in newspapers and magazines, researched the wants and needs of the audience, and coordinated advertising in more than one publication. Now they could advise clients on where best to place their ads.

Until the early 1950s and the advent of television, radio was the prime broadcast advertising medium. But soon television eclipsed radio; consumers went wild for it, and advertisers capitalized on the fact that viewers could both see the product and hear the national message. In 1950, only 9 percent of American homes had television sets; by 1960, 87 percent had TV.[13] Advertisers could reach increasing numbers of people, and the ability to create positive images of a product on the new visual medium seemed limitless.

By the 1970s, most of the current mass advertising options had developed, advertising expenditures were growing rapidly, and various forms of mass media were competing for advertising dollars. Figure 15.1 shows two trends during the 30 years from 1940 to 1970. First, the amount of money spent on advertising grew enormously. In 1940, businesses spent about $2.1 billion on advertising. This grew to $19.6 billion in 1970, a 933 percent increase. When adjusted for the decline in a dollar's value due to inflation, advertising increased by 337 percent during this 30-year period.

The second trend concerns the distribution of advertising resources. While all media increased their advertising revenues from 1940 to 1970, some increased more than others. Television enjoyed the greatest growth, moving from 3 percent of all advertising expenditures in 1940 to 18 percent 20 years later. The increasing proportion

Keyconcept

Advertising and Consumer Culture: Advertising—paid information about services, products, and ideas—is designed to entice the audience to buy a product or an idea. Critics argue that in American society, advertising has become the dominant form of popular culture and that our values have become commercial, rather than emanating from traditional institutions such as the family, school, and church.

Food and Drug Administration: Government agency charged with regulating foods and drugs. Created in response to patent medicine manufacturers who included drugs such as cocaine in over-the-counter medicines.

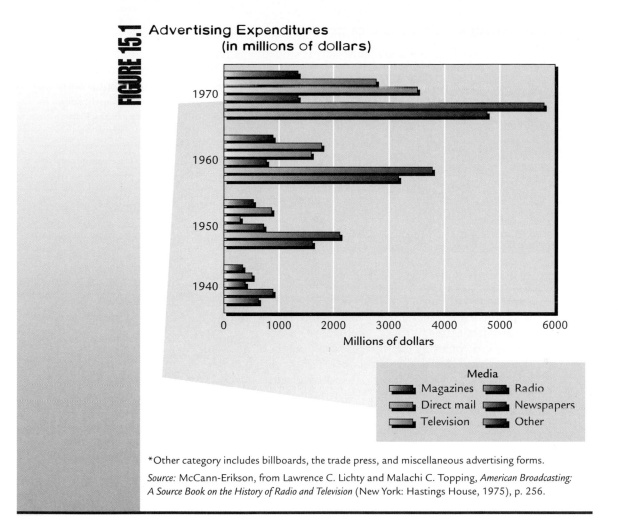

FIGURE 15.1 Advertising Expenditures (in millions of dollars)

Media
Magazines · Radio
Direct mail · Newspapers
Television · Other

*Other category includes billboards, the trade press, and miscellaneous advertising forms.

Source: McCann-Erikson, from Lawrence C. Lichty and Malachi C. Topping, *American Broadcasting: A Source Book on the History of Radio and Television* (New York: Hastings House, 1975), p. 256.

of ad dollars for television came mostly at the expense of newspapers and radio. Magazines and direct mail also experienced small declines as television boomed.

The growth of cable drew advertisers' attention during the 1980s. Cable, with its dozens of channels, provided segmented audiences for advertisers. Rather than advertising to mass audiences, advertisers could identify groups that watched specialized channels and might be more interested than the public at large in their products. Although cable offered more effective advertising than broadcast television could, it did not kill mass advertising. In 1994, *Seinfeld* sold 30-second commercial spots for $390,000 each.

Keyconcept

Advertising and Awareness: The simplest goal of advertising is to make people aware of a product. Advertising also gives people information about the quality, price, and availability of products and services.

Interest in online and Internet advertising grew during the mid-1990s. However, advertising expenditures were relatively modest because of concerns about how many people were viewing the ads, how viewers might use these ads, and how to reach particular groups of viewers. Total advertising revenue on the Internet in 1997 was estimated at $400 to $699 million, which was twelve times more than 1995, but it was still only a small portion of all advertising spending.[14]

■ Advertising and the price of products

Economists disagree about how advertising affects the prices consumers pay for goods. Some argue that advertising increases prices because the money companies spend on advertisements is tacked onto the price of the goods. Campbell's tomato soup costs more than the store brand, they argue, to pay for Campbell's national advertising budget. Typically, nationally advertised products cost more than generic and regional brands.

Keyconcept

The Economics of Advertising: Critics debate whether advertising raises or lowers the price of goods. In some instances, economies of scale allow producers, in response to demand created by advertising, to manufacture larger quantities at a lower price. However, many critics argue that advertising, particularly on television, is expensive and that the cost of such advertising is often added to the product price.

Other economists argue that advertising reduces the cost of goods by increasing production. The more cans of Campbell's tomato soup are produced, the less each can costs to make. The average cost of almost all goods will decrease as the number of units increases, up to the capacity of a production plant. Economists call the savings from producing large quantities *economies of scale.* The economies occur because a company has to invest a certain amount of money in a plant no matter how many units of the product are made. Producing the first 10,000 cans of tomato soup requires equipment to cook and can the soup. If a plant is already making 10,000 cans of tomato soup, producing another 1,000 will add only the cost of the ingredients, the cans, and some extra labor time.

Because advertising can increase the number of units people will buy, it decreases the average cost of making the product. The average cost per can of 11,000 cans of soup is less than the average cost per can of 10,000 cans. However, research is not conclusive on the impact of advertising on price. In some situations the lower cost of increased production will be passed on to the consumers as price breaks. In other cases the price of the product will be kept high, and the company will keep the difference as profit. Similarly, the advertising costs that companies pay may be added to the price of the product in some cases but not in others. The impact of advertising on price varies based on a variety of factors, but a key element is competition. If consumers can buy the same quality of goods at a lower price, companies will probably not pass on the cost of advertising to consumers.

Interestingly enough, whether a similar good is perceived to be of equal quality sometimes depends on advertising. For example, advertising convinces some people that

Campbell's tomato soup is better than the store brand. Much of television advertising aims to convince consumers that a product is better than other similar products. Nike spends millions of dollars to get people to believe that their athletic shoes are worth paying three times more than some other athletic shoes cost. Burger King has long advertised its hamburgers as flame broiled rather than fried, implying that its burgers are

Some critics argue that advertising increases the costs of products. Others note that through a demand that advertising helps create, the economics of large-scale production are realized. Generic products are sold at lower cost than those with nationally recognized names. What role does advertising play here?

better. This is called *differentiating the product,* that is, getting the consumer to perceive it as different in quality from other products.

463

Just how advertising affects price is a complicated process that varies from product to product. It depends on the level of demands, consumers' perceptions of quality, the scale of production, and a variety of other business factors. Consumers can make better choices if they understand how these factors work.

Cultural and political impact of advertising

Advertising serves society in positive and negative ways. It brings buyers and sellers together in economic markets that supply the goods and services that people need and want. It also distributes economic resources for society. Advertising contributes to these processes by giving consumers information.

On an individual level, advertising makes life easier. Without advertising, just getting the basics for living would be far more difficult and expensive. Imagine hunting for an apartment with no advertising except signs on apartment buildings. You would have to drive to each apartment to find out how much it cost. Without ads, you would not know which grocery store was offering the best specials each week. Price comparison would take enormous amounts of time.

Keyconcept

The Social Costs of Advertising: Advertising can be manipulative and can influence news and entertainment content. Television critics argue that the primary, if not the sole, criterion for media programming is to cater to advertisers' needs, not to perform social, cultural, or political functions.

However, the social contributions of advertising also have a social price. The price comes in the form of negative effects that advertising can have on society. Some of these effects are direct, such as manipulation of people's spending behavior; others are more indirect, such as the influence of advertising on news media and politics. Critics question the impact of advertising, especially in connection with television and radio, media on which children and young adults rely heavily. The concern is not only about short-term effects, but also about whether advertising actually changes expectations of normative behavior. For example, a short-term effect might be that teenage girls buy more lipstick. But a long-term effect of campaigns such as Benetton's and Calvin Klein's advertisements showing emaciated young people might be to persuade young people that they have to stay ultra-thin, no matter what the cost to their health.

Manipulation by advertising

Even though advertising serves legitimate functions of bringing buyers and sellers together, not all advertising is designed just to provide information. Many ads aim to manipulate people's behavior, sometimes influencing them to buy unneeded goods and services.

Of particular concern in this area is advertising aimed at children. Children develop **rational thinking abilities** at about the age of twelve. Before that, children have trouble understanding the nature and purpose of advertising. Research indicates that children under the age of four cannot tell programs from the commercials. Often the commercials, with quick camera cuts and lots of action, appeal even more to children than do the programs. The result is that parents hear their children say, "I want that" every time the children see a toy or cereal ad on television. Luckily for parents, advertisements have less influence over children as they grow older.

rational thinking abilities: The cognitive processing of information by considering options based on conscious comparison of influencing factors.

Because advertising provides all of the revenue for television news and 70 to 80 percent of the revenue for newspapers, media critics often raise the question of advertisers' influence over news content. The concern is justified. Advertisers do sometimes succeed in altering news coverage.

Advertisers often have an impact on what is covered as well as on what is not covered. For example, the Bellevue, Washington, *Journal American* ran stories for four days about the reopening of an enlarged Nordstrom's department store. These stories included front-page coverage and full-page "shoppers' guides" of the store. It seems unlikely that it was just coincidence that Nordstrom's is an advertiser in the *Journal American*.[15]

News departments sometimes respond to complaints by advertisers, but they also avoid pursuing stories that would create problems for big advertisers. A newspaper might downplay stories about union concerns at a local department store chain because of the advertising the department store buys. Class action suits against a company might not make the front page in a community with a plant owned by that company.

Because profit margins are smaller and advertisements more dramatic, magazines often have more difficulty with advertisers trying to influence or control content than do newspapers. According to an April, 1997 story in the *Wall Street Journal,* editors at *Esquire* killed a short story about a gay man because they feared Chrysler Corporation would withdraw its advertising if company officials considered the story offensive. Chrysler had asked to review material in magazines in which the company advertises.[16]

The basic conflict is that information that serves the advertiser may not serve the reader. For example, a story telling readers how to get the best deal for a car can lead to lower profits for auto dealers. This conflict comes from serving the consumer and advertising markets with the same media product. Just who wins depends on the size of the media organization and the beliefs of the managers. Big media companies, which have a large number of the advertisers, can withstand advertising boycotts better than smaller ones can. And managers who accept the social responsibility of news organizations will be more likely to side with readers, listeners, and viewers than with advertisers.

Structure of advertising and demand

Advertising is a form of promotion. *Promotion* involves all the ways of gaining attention for a company, product, or service. In addition to advertising, these include public relations, packaging, personal selling, and gifts. Marketing experts take four steps in marketing, which involve determining product, price, place, and promotion. To market a product well, you must start with a good product, price it correctly, place it well, and promote it. Advertising is interrelated with other aspects of marketing. Advertising cannot sell an inferior product for long, and advertising cannot get most adults to buy overpriced services and products.

The economics of advertising concerns the interaction of supply and demand in the advertising market and the connection between the advertising market and the consumer market. Media that serve both markets cannot disconnect the two. Advertisers buy ads in media because they want to reach the audience that is attracted by the information in the media. Some of the audience seeks the information in advertisements. Economists call serving two markets with the same production process a *joint product.*

To promote goods and services, a company enters the advertising market. Producers and sellers of goods and services pay media companies for space and time in their media products. When a company spends more than $300,000 for 30 seconds on *Monday Night Football,* this exchange takes place in the advertising market.

There is also a connection between the advertising market and what happens in the consumer market. In the consumer market, people spend their time and money for information. A person who watches *Monday Night Football* is in the consumer market. This person is exchanging his or her attention for the entertainment of the game. The viewer would have no game to watch if advertising did not pay for it, and the advertiser would have no one to see the ads if the game wasn't provided.

The difference between the two markets is more clear-cut with media that consumers buy. Readers buy newspapers for information, which comes in the form of news and advertising. Advertisers buy space and reader attention from the newspaper company. As a result, the newspaper serves two different but interconnected markets with the same production process. The nature of this joint product occurs because advertising is the primary support for some media. It also makes media companies' performances more difficult to predict.

The influence of advertising on consumer behavior

The study of how advertising affects people is called *consumer behavior.* Consumer behavior can be viewed from two perspectives. The *cognitive* view concerns the effects of mental processes, such as perception and knowledge, on people's behavior. The *behavioral* approach concentrates on how people's actions are reinforced by other people and media. Both of these terms include several theories about how people process information and act. Neither can fully explain the way advertising influences people. People's thoughts do affect their actions, but we also base our behavior on patterns of reinforcement.[17]

Keyconcept

Advertising versus Consumer Spending: Although many people perceive media in the United States to be available almost for free, customers are increasingly paying for media such as cable television, home video, recorded music, and Internet access. This causes concern about whether all Americans will have access to the information that is necessary for participation in the society.

The cognitive approach assumes that individuals are active decision makers who use information to make rational and effective decisions. Advertising provides information that helps people to select a product or service that meet their needs. Applying the cognitive approach to buying a house, people look for information about the quality and price of various houses and the desirability of living in a particular neighborhood. Some of this information comes from advertisements. After collecting this information about several houses, the buyers select the one that best suits their budget and lifestyle. They have acted rationally by collecting information and evaluating the information systematically.

Cognitive advertising gets people to buy through information about low prices and high quality. Behavioral advertising appeals directly to emotions and the images people have of themselves. It assumes that the environment plays a primary role in people's actions. Print ads work best for cognitive advertising, and television provides the best behavioral ads.

Some television ads affect behavior by connecting a product with a good time and by getting people to identify with appealing characters. These are called *identity advertisements.* In the mid-1990s, Coors beer ran advertisements showing young men and women playing a variety of sports superimposed over scenes from the Rocky Mountains. A seemingly giant man grabs a football as he falls on a mountain, just missing a miniature figure skiing below. The contrast between the giants and the Rockies helps people to remember the ad, but the smiles on the faces of young, healthy people were designed so that viewers associated drinking Coors with having a good time.

By identifying a product with good times, the enjoyment of using the product is reinforced. Over time, the ads and use of a product create a habit that the producer wants

Calvin Klein, Taste & Appeal

n a 1995 television ad, a young man stood before the camera in denim shorts. A male voice said, "You got a real nice look. How old are you? Are you strong? You think you could rip that shirt off? That's a real nice body. You work out. I can tell."

With this advertisement and billboards and bus signs featuring young teens in provocative positions, Calvin Klein, Inc. attracted a storm of negative criticism from media critics, the American Family Association, advertising and public relations executives, and even the U.S. Department of Justice. Critics charged that Klein had created an advertising campaign that bordered on child pornography. Klein withdrew the $6 million advertising campaign because, he said, people misunderstood it.

Richard Kirshenbaum, chief creative officer for a major New York advertising firm, told the *New York*

Times that Klein had "crossed a line in the allusions to children or teen-agers and sexuality." He said advertisers "should think twice if they do something that smacks of child pornography. At the end of the day, you do have a responsibility."

Klein has long been famous for sexually oriented advertisements aimed at teenagers. He made a splash in 1980 with Brooke Shields in jeans mouthing the words, "nothing comes between me and my Calvins." Some critics suggested that the 1995 campaign was attacked because of a change in the times. With increasing attention from Congress and citizen groups about violence and sex on television and the Internet, the public rebelled against this venture into teenage appeal. Others speculated that Klein had designed the campaign knowing that he risked having to withdraw it—but fully aware of the publicity that would be gained in the process.

SOURCE: Stuart Elliott, "Will Calvin Klein's Retreat Redraw the Lines of Good Taste?" *The New York Times,* August 29, 1995, pp. D1, D8; Kim Masters, "Rival Says Calvin Klein Ads 'Over the Line,'" *The Washington Post,* August 29, 1995, pp. B1, B2.

Key concept

Commercial and Information Blending: One advertising technique involves making ads appear to be editorial content to enhance their credibility. As such blending techniques become more common and consumers have difficulty distinguishing between messages designed to inform and those designed to persuade, the credibility of both advertising and news may be at stake.

people to have. Identity advertisements are behaviorally based and assume that consumers will be more likely to buy products that they associate with pleasant activities and people. Companies that produce goods that are similar to other products often use identity ads. Most best-selling beers and colas have similar recipes, which gives them similar tastes. As a result, the advertisements cannot feature the different tastes of the drinks. Instead, the companies use emotional appeals to create positive but different images of their product.

Identifying consumers as types

By using sophisticated social science methods, advertising agencies can identify the types of people who will likely buy a product. People are most often classified for advertising by demographics, geographics, and pyschographics. *Demographics* concerns characteristics of people and households, such as age, gender, income, marital status, and family size. *Geographics* concerns the physical location (state, region, or country) of potential buyers. *Pyschographics* concerns the lifestyles and activities of people, such as movie attendance, hobbies, and types of physical exercise.

467

▪ Effectiveness of advertising

Some critics describe advertising as manipulating people's behavior and getting them to buy things they don't need. Others see advertising as a useful sort of information that allows people to make better consumer decisions. The truth of advertising lies somewhere in between.[18]

People find value in some advertising. One study reported that 46 percent of readers look at the Sunday newspaper advertising inserts regularly. Another 26 percent looked at them occasionally.[19] A person may throw away one clothing catalogue that came through the mail and order a shirt from another.

Economic Impact

Whittle and Advertising-Based Media

Chris Whittle created a huge media company during the 1980s with advertising-based media. Magazine and newspaper articles during this period concluded that he had tapped into media's future with this approach. But a decade later, the company discontinued its most bally-hooed projects.

Whittle and his company, Whittle Communications, turned the traditional information-advertising relationship on its head. The company first sold the advertising space in magazines, books, and television programs. Then it created the information content to go with the ads.

Advertising-based media existed before Whittle in the form of weekly shoppers, newspapers containing ads, but little or no editorial copy. However, Whittle saw a profit to be made in placing advertising-based media in new locations, such as doctors' offices and schools. The content was developed after the advertising was sold and was written to support the advertising.

Whittle distributed *Special Reports* magazines free in doctors' waiting rooms. Later, a television version of *Special Reports* aired in the same places. Whittle also began a project called "Channel One," a 12-minute news program played in schools. Whittle Communications gave the schools the equipment needed to run the programs, which included commercials for jeans and candy.

Initially, Whittle succeeded, and he sold half his company to Time, Inc. for $185 million in 1988. But he also caused controversy. People criticized him for emphasizing advertising over information content and for putting ads into schools where the students could not escape them.

By 1994 the Whittle empire had shrunk. The books-with-advertising project and *Special Reports* were abandoned, and Whittle sold "Channel One." Some critics argued that doctors did not want to pitch products to patients in their waiting rooms. Whittle said that his company had simply tried to do too much.

Indeed, "Channel One" was profitable in 1994, and advertising-based media have made a profit in supermarkets. However, Whittle Communications' problems leave open the question: Just who will accept advertising-based media and under what circumstances?

SOURCES: Jack Lail, "What's a Whittle?" *Washington Journalism Review*, November 1990, pp. 24–28, 45; David Lieberman, "Whittling a Media Empire," *USA Today*, August 11, 1994, pp. 1B–2B.

468

The same people who find supermarket advertising useful may use their remote control to avoid looking at television advertisements for hemorrhoid medicine. Yet television can be very effective at telling people that something is available. McDonald's hasn't sold billions of burgers because it produces the best food in the world. The company produces fast food that has an acceptable taste for most people and advertises its products effectively, especially to children.

From society's perspective the best consumer of advertising is the one who understands the purpose of ads and how ads are made. Understanding allows people to use advertising information for their purposes, not the purposes of the advertiser.

■ Advertising's effects on consumers

Advertisements affect consumers in four ways: (1) They make people aware of a product or service; (2) they provide price information about a product or service; (3) they provide information about the quality of a product or service; and (4) they get people to identify a product or service with a particular person or activity.[20]

The simplest effect is *awareness.* Consumers must know that a product or service exists before they can decide to buy it. When General Motors planned to create a new car, the Saturn, it spent hundreds of millions of dollars to make the public aware of the car's existence. The advertisements began running before a single Saturn had been produced.

Focused advertising reaches demographic groups with local promotional materials often distributed by zip code as well as through cable television stations that cater to specific groups.

Price information also plays an important part in advertising. From a business perspective, advertising that features special prices can attract customers to a store. Supermarkets run grocery prices in the local newspaper to bring customers into the store. The supermarket won't make much, if any, money on the advertised specials, but the customer will buy other products that are not on sale. From the customer's perspective, price advertisements save them time. A person who wants to buy a car will not waste time looking at models that are out of his or her price range.

Quality advertising strives to influence the buyer's impression of how good a product or service is. Quality claims can be vague and unsupported, such as "the best burger in town." But quality claims can also have some authority behind them, such as "The *Motor Trend* Car of the Year Award." Quality claims can influence the decision to buy, but they will not get consumers to buy a second time if the product turns out not to have the quality that was claimed.

Identity advertising attempts to get a customer to associate a product with a particular person or enjoyable activity. People in beer commercials always enjoy themselves. Only young, healthy people smoke cigarettes in magazine ads. If consumers associate products with pleasant activities and people, they will be more likely to buy them.

A particular advertisement can include more than one of these effects. Often, ads that are aimed at creating awareness of a new product feature a celebrity. When Oral-B introduced toothpaste for kids in the mid-1980s, the company used the Muppets to promote its toothpaste.[21] These ads produced awareness and identity for children.

How effectively an advertisement achieves its purpose depends on several factors. Media type is among the most important. Price advertising seems to be most effective in print. Print is more permanent, and the listed prices can be cut out and kept. Prices that are broadcast over television and radio have to be remembered or written down, and both of these are inconvenient. Television works well with identity ads because of its visual nature. Connecting beer with fun at parties is much easier when the party is shown on TV than when it is described in print.

A second important factor in advertising effectiveness concerns the consumer. Not all people can be reached effectively by the same medium. As a result, most advertising campaigns, especially for large companies, use several media. McDonald's, for example, advertises on television, billboards, and on public transportation vehicles. Advertising agencies help to design plans that incorporate more than one medium to reach a variety of people with a variety of ads.

Supplying the demand for advertising

A business that wants to advertise its product or service faces an almost staggering number of advertising forms and advertising outlets. Since 1970, cable TV and yellow pages have grown as advertising outlets. Currently, businesses are experimenting with advertising over the World Wide Web and computer bulletin boards. A business can no longer depend on just one form of advertising. Companies need a mix of media to reach all of their potential customers. This multimedia advertising approach explains why old advertising forms continue to survive as new forms developed.

Table 15.1 shows advertising revenue and proportion of revenues by medium for 1996. In 1992, more than $132.2 billion was spent on advertising in the United States. In 1996, the figure was $172.8 billion, a 30 percent increase in four years.

The growth in advertising represents the movement of the U.S. economy away from manufacturing toward service and information. Service and information companies face much more competition, which requires more advertising. The stability of the distribution of revenues among different types of media over the years illustrates the use of multimedia advertising. Companies must spread their ad dollars around to reach an audience that uses a variety of media.

Advertising support for media

The growth of mass media during most of the twentieth century has been interwoven with the growth in advertising. As the U.S. economy became more consumer oriented, companies sought increasingly larger audiences. The result was an influence over media content, especially radio and television, that outweighed the influence of consumers. Media companies rightfully saw advertising as their biggest source of revenue.

Times have changed, however. More of the money spent on mass media comes from the consumer now than from the advertiser. Table 15.2 shows the distribution of advertising and consumer revenues for mass media from 1984 to 1992. In 1984, 50.4 percent of media revenue came from advertising. That dropped to 42 percent only eight years later. The main reason for the change is the growth in cable, home video, and recorded music. The increasing use of the electronic information highway and pay-per-view movies, concerts, and sports events on cable likely will continue to reduce the dependence of media on advertising.

TABLE 15.1 Advertising Revenues and Proportions, 1996

	REVENUE (BILLIONS OF DOLLARS)	PERCENTAGE OF REVENUE
Print		
Daily newspapers	38.2	22.1
Direct mail	34.8	20.2
Miscellaneous	21.8	12.6
Yellow pages	10.8	6.3
Magazines	9.2	5.3
Business and farm publications	4.1	2.4
Outdoor	1.4	0.8
Total print	120.3	69.7
Electronic		
Broadcast TV	36.0	20.8
Radio	12.1	7.0
Cable TV	4.4	2.5
Total electronic	52.5	30.3

Note: "Miscellaneous" includes weekly newspapers, various forms of shoppers, and bus and train signs. Internet advertising was not included because it was such a small percentage of advertising in 1996.

Source: Facts About Newspapers (Reston, VA: Newspaper Association of America, 1997), online version: *www.naa.org/info/facts/07.htm.* Original source of data: NAA and McCann Frickson, Inc.

TABLE 15.2 Distribution of Media Revenue Between Advertising and Consumers

YEAR	ADVERTISING SPENDING	CONSUMER SPENDING
1984	50.4%	49.6%
1985	49.8%	50.2%
1986	49.1%	50.9%
1987	47.7%	52.3%
1988	46.9%	53.1%
1989	45.8%	54.2%
1990	44.7%	55.3%
1991	42.5%	57.5%
1992	42.0%	58.0%

Source: Veronis, Suhler & Associates, *Communication Industry Forecast,* 1993.

TYPES OF ADVERTISEMENTS Advertisements can be classified in a number of ways, but two are most common: geographic coverage and purpose. *Geographic coverage* is defined as the market where the advertisements are placed and the advertised product is sold. The *purpose of the ad* reflects the type of influence the advertiser seeks to have over the customer.

■ *Geographic Coverage.* Traditionally, geographic coverage was divided into national and local. *National advertisements* are ads for products and services that are available throughout the country. *Local advertisements* are ads for companies that serve a much smaller market, such as a city or metropolitan area. Typically, national agencies or companies in New York, Chicago, or Los Angeles place national ads in media. Ads for Nintendo, McDonald's, and Coors beer are national. Local ads are placed by a company such as a supermarket that has a solely local market.

The two types of advertisements are sometimes combined. Burger King, for example, has national TV ads, but the local outlet might run ads in the student newspaper about special prices. Most nationally advertised companies do not own retail outlets; therefore both local and national ads sometime promote the same item. The local department store benefits from national Nike ads but also runs its own ads to tell customers when Nike shoes are on sale.

A hybrid form of geographic coverage grew during the 1980s. *Regional advertisements* are local and regional ads that are placed in national media. The USA cable network, for example, might carry ads for a local bookstore. These ads are inserted into predetermined time slots by the local cable company. Regional ads allow local companies the prestige of advertising in national media without the high prices for ads that reach the entire country. *Newsweek* magazine has carried advertisements for Detroit television stations, but only in magazine copies that are distributed in the Detroit area. Copies that are distributed in another area might contain ads aimed at that region. When the magazine goes to press, space is left for local ads, which are inserted in the regional printing plants.

The Nike symbol is so well-known that it doesn't need words to explain it, but tying it to a successful athlete gives it a world-class image.

Geographic coverage is important because some media serve local businesses better and some serve national businesses better. Newspapers excel as vehicles for local businesses, and television has traditionally been strong for national advertising because of its national audience. But as cable has fragmented the TV audience, many network programs have become less attractive for mass national advertising. As a result, businesses are increasingly using national advertisements targeted to narrower, demographically defined groups of consumers. For example, the Lifetime cable channel reached about 65 percent of all U.S. households in 1996, but its programs and ads were aimed mostly at women.

Geographic coverage also affects the price of advertising. The price that a business pays for an advertisement depends on the number of people who will be exposed to the ad. *Time* magazine charges more for an ad than *Crain's Chicago Business* does. The first

472

is a national publication; the other is a regional publication. A business that sells computers just in Chicago would be foolish to buy a national ad in *Time*. A regional ad in *Time* or an ad in *Crain's* would be more effective and efficient.

■ *Advertisement's Purpose.* Although most advertisements promote a product or service, not all do. Advertisements fall into three categories: business ads, public service ads, and political ads.

Business ads try to influence people's attitudes and behaviors toward the products and services a business sells, toward the business itself, or toward an idea that the business supports. Most of these ads try to get consumers to buy something, but sometimes a business tries to improve its image through advertising. This often occurs when a company has been involved in a highly publicized incident that can negatively affect its image. Exxon had to rebuild its image after the *Valdez* accident in 1989, in which an Exxon tank spilled millions of gallons of oil in Prince William Sound and damaged the Alaskan coast. Many people saw Exxon as having a callous attitude toward the environment, so the company used advertising to try to change this public perception.

Occasionally, businesses use advertisements to contribute to the marketplace of ideas. These **advertorials** promote a political position and try to influence people's attitudes toward public issues or policy. Mobil Oil created numerous advertorials during the 1980s, often criticizing media coverage as biased. Although advertorials can target the general public, they often aim to influence people who affect public policy, such as politicians and journalists. During 1993, 1994, and 1995, Blue Cross Blue Shield Plans of New York State, a health insurance company, ran a variety of advertisements in the *Columbia Journalism Review*. These ads praised managed health care as a way to lower medical costs and provide high-quality health care services. The purpose was to provide journalists with the health insurer's side of a national debate about health care.

Public service ads promote behaviors and attitudes that are beneficial to society and its members. These types of ads may be either national or local and usually are the product of donated labor and media time or space. The Advertising Council produces the best known of public service ads. The Council, which is supported by advertising agencies and the media, was formed during World War II to promote the war effort. It now runs about twenty-five campaigns a year. These campaigns must be in the public interest, timely, noncommercial, nonpartisan, nonsectarian, and nonpolitical.[22] The Ad Council has consistently run campaigns against illegal drug use and in support of such organizations as the United Negro College Fund.

Political ads aim to persuade voters to elect someone to political office or attempt to influence the public on legislative issues. These advertisements run at the local, state, and national levels. They incorporate most forms of media but use newspapers, radio, television, and direct mail most heavily. During a presidential election year, more than $1 billion is spent on political ads.

Political advertising receives a lot of attention because it provides a way of increasing voter identification of a candidate. It also gives candidates a way to define the issues during an election. During the 1988 presidential campaign, George Bush's organization ran an advertisement featuring a convicted murderer named Willie Horton. The ad claimed that an early release program sponsored by his opponent, Massachusetts Governor Michael Dukakis, had allowed Horton to get out of prison and kill again. Many people questioned the truth of the ad, but it was effective in helping to frame the issue of crime during the election campaign.

MASS VERSUS TARGETED ADS As part of advertising planning, companies must decide how large an audience they want to reach. Not every product or service is designed for mass consumption, nor is it avail-

advertorial: Combination of an advertisement and an editorial. Designed to look like an editorial but is actually a paid message.

able in every geographic location. Advertising the performances of the Dallas Symphony Orchestra during an episode of MTV's *Beavis and Butthead* would be inefficient and ineffective. Most viewers would be too far from Dallas to attend the symphony even if they wanted to, and the audience that watches *Beavis and Butthead* is probably not an audience that would be interested in attending symphonies.

473

Advertisements that aim at the largest audience possible constitute *mass advertising*. Advertisements that seek to reach a selected audience are classified as *targeted advertising*. Yellow pages serve as mass advertising because every household that has a telephone gets them. **Direct mail** catalogues from retailers such as Lands' End are targeted advertising because they are mailed to people who are likely to buy clothes through the mail. The most appropriate type of advertising depends on the nature and price of the product or service.

Classifying groups is not enough to produce effective target advertising. Media products have to be available to reach those targeted groups. Magazines, direct mail, and radio are traditional forms of delivering targeted advertising, but the 1980s and 1990s have seen a growth in possible advertising vehicles. Cable can now deliver audiences based on geography, demographics, and psychographics. Online computer services hold promise as ways of reaching certain types of groups.

Who produces advertisements?

The nature of jobs in advertising varies greatly. Some involve creative writing and art; others consist of selling and buying advertising space and time. Most advertising personnel work either in an advertising agency or in the advertising department of a company. Others work within media advertising departments. Ad agencies act to connect advertising buyers with media organizations. Table 15.3 illustrates the millions of dollars billed by the top ten advertising agencies. The advertising departments within companies may handle most of the same activities as an agency, or they may be small departments that rely heavily on agency services.

The most common services of advertising agencies include creative production, media buying, research services, merchandising, and advertising planning.[23] *Creative production* includes all the steps in creating advertisements for various media. *Media buyers* place the advertisements in media outlets. *Research* involves planning and conducting research about the effectiveness of advertising. *Merchandise experts* oversee other forms of promotion besides advertising. *Advertising planning* incorporates all of the above.

There are two types of advertising agencies. *Full-service* advertising agencies offer a client all of the five services just mentioned. A *boutique* agency often specializes in creative services and restricts its activities to a few specialties. A large company, such as a soup manufacturer, would probably use a full-service agency to plan and produce multimedia advertising campaigns. The company's advertising manager would work closely with the agency. A small mail-order company might do most of its work in-house and then contract the creation and production of a catalogue to a boutique agency.

Full-service agencies have teams that serve clients. These account teams provide the basic services mentioned above. Typically, the account teams are headed by an account executive, who is the agency's contact with the client. The team also includes a media planner, who buys ad space and time; a research director; and creative people, who produce the ads. The creative process involves writing copy and creating illustrations. The copy director oversees the copywriters, and the art director supervises the artists and layout people.

The positions that are found in an agency team also can be found within the advertising department of large companies. These departments have media buyers and planners as well as creative staff. Larger

direct mail: Print advertisement that is delivered, usually by the postal service, directly to consumers. This includes catalogues and coupon packages.

TABLE 15.3 1996 Top Ten Advertising Agencies
(in millions of dollars)

AGENCY	U.S. GROSS INCOME	NON-U.S. GROSS INCOME	WORLDWIDE GROSS INCOME
McCann-Erickson Worldwide	329.6	967.4	1,299.0
J. Walter Thompson	375.2	697.8	1,073.0
BBDO Worldwide	289.3	635.9	925.2
Leo Burnett Co.	393.7	472.6	866.3
DDB Needham Worldwide	271.9	576.4	848.3
Grey Advertising	352.2	489.6	841.8
Ogilvy & Mather Worldwide	233.3	559.7	793.0
Foote, Cone & Belding	299.9	468.0	767.9
Young & Rubicam	241.9	465.4	707.3
Saatchi & Saatchi Advertising	274.1	411.1	685.2

Sources: www.adage.com/dataplace/achieve/dp105.html
www.adage.com/dataplace/achieve/dp103.html

companies, such as department stores, often have an in-house ad department because it cuts their expenses and gives them greater control over their advertising.

Trends and innovations

The advertising business faced two important trends during the 1980s and early 1990s. The business saw a concentration of advertising agencies, and many businesses sought a more targeted approach to advertising. In the 1980s, larger agencies bought smaller ones to increase their business and to expand the services they offer. Large agencies merged with other large agencies as they expanded in the global markets. Global expansion reflected the rapidly growing markets outside the United States, especially in Asia.

The concentration trend slowed slightly during the 1990s as some of the creative people left larger agencies to form their own boutiques. When the creative people leave a large agency, they often carry accounts with them. Imaginative advertisements stand out in the clutter found in today's mass media, so creative people are crucial to an ad campaign's success. But creativity sometimes suffers in the bureaucratic structures of large agencies.

The 1980s and 1990s also saw a growth in the targeting of specific audiences with advertising. This had long been the trend with radio, and new technology now allowed other media

The trend toward global advertising is seen in this Pepsi sponsorship of a marathon in Vietnam.

Racing for Kid Consumers

Three giant media companies have entered a global race, and the prize is more than $100 billion. Fox Children Network, Turner's Cartoon Network, and Nickelodeon, owned by Viacom, joined the fight in the 1990s for the largely untapped global children's market. Each wants to expand its broadcasting and capture the children of the world.

Estimates are that the international market will generate up to $800 million in advertising revenue annually, but that's not the big prize. The real money will come from the sale of li-

censed children's toys. The international market may yield up to $100 billion in this area annually.

The imbalance between the advertising revenues and the money from selling toys illustrates the reality of children's programming in the United States, where Fox, Nickelodeon, and TBS dominate. The cartoons and live programming are often advertisements for the characters and products that appear in the show. The Slime that is used on Nickelodeon programs is sold in stores. The cartoon characters that are seen on Fox and the Cartoon Network are the basis for games, action

figures, and stuffed toys that are available for sale.

One possible problem that these sprinting conglomerates face is the reluctance of some countries to have their children turned into easily influenced consumers. The French government has not allowed the Cartoon Network to be broadcast in France, although some people can receive it by satellite. Korea and Canada use regulations aimed at cultural protection to control children's access to programs from other countries.

SOURCE: Laurie Mifflin, "Can the Flintstones Fly in Fiji?" *The New York Times*, November 27, 1995, p. D1.

to identify and produce content for targeted groups of people. A company selling Mercedes Benz automobiles would find a local newspaper advertisement to be inefficient. Most of the people reading the ad could not afford to buy a Mercedes. The company would do better to identify the census tracts where people who make more than $100,000 a year lived and mail advertising directly to these people.

This targeting approach means that some advertisers do not use mass media to reach their buyers. The segmentation of consumers could reduce the money available for newspapers and broadcast stations that supply news. The money spent on news could then decline, negatively affecting programming quality. Such a decline in quality could damage the effectiveness of the marketplace of ideas.

Blends and infomercials

Concern over ads aimed at children caused Congress to pass the 1990 Children's Television Act, limiting the amount of advertising time in children's television programs. An hour of children's programming may not have more than ten and a half minutes of commercials on weekends and twelve minutes during weekdays. The law did not outlaw programs based on toys and candy, such as *G.I. Joe* and *The Adventures of the Gummi Bears*. However, if these programs run commercials for the same products that are featured in the show, they become program-length commercials and violate the Children's Television Act.

Efforts to manipulate through advertising are not limited to children. Two trends that followed television deregulation during the 1980s have been program-length commercials

Leo Burnett

As the founder of one of the top advertising firms in the world, Leo Burnett influenced what Americans and others around the world buy.

Burnett was born in a small town in Michigan in 1891 and lived to be seventy-nine. He claimed that his name was supposed to be George, but because of his father's tendency to abbreviate, coupled with bad handwriting, the "Geo" turned out to be "Leo"—and the name stuck.

Burnett's parents owned a small store in Michigan, and his first remembrance of advertising was seeing the store's name and slogan on the umbrella of its delivery cart. While he was growing up in Michigan, he claimed, "you could hear the corn growing on hot nights." By the time he reached Chicago and opened his advertising agency in 1935, he was forty-four years old.

In contrast to the stereotype of the gregarious advertising man, Burnett was shy. He was also short and sloped-shouldered and had a paunch. The front of his head was bald and freckled, and his lapels were often sprinkled with Marlboro cigarette ash. His most prominent feature,

however, was his lower lip, which became the focal point of his writers' and art directors' attention. The more displeased Burnett was with an idea, the farther out his lip would jut.

To Burnett, the most powerful ideas were nonverbal. Their true meanings were too deep for words, like the large, playful (Tony the) tiger and the strong (Marlboro) man on top of a horse. A successful ad, he said, was one that made an audience respond not with "That is a great ad!" but with "That is a great product!"

For Burnett it was important to find the inherent drama of the product and present it. If no inherent drama could be found, it had to be created. Usually, the creation would be through *borrowed interest,* a concept that allows the drama to come from someone, such as the Lonely Repairman for Maytag washing machines or Morris the cat for 9 Lives cat food. Other successes for Burnett were animations: the Keebler Elves, Charlie the Tuna, and the Jolly Green Giant.

In his sixties, Burnett had an enviable vitality that would not quit. David Ogilvy once said that

he turned down Burnett's proposal to merge because Burnett was the only person he knew who worked harder than he did: "The thought of Leo ringing me in New York at 2 A.M. and asking me to meet him in Chicago for breakfast with some fresh campaign ideas was more than I could bear."

Burnett continued working hard into his seventies, and his loyalty to his clients was unwavering. When he grew faint from low blood sugar, someone ran for a candy bar. "Make sure it's a Nestle," he cried hoarsely.

SOURCES: Michael L. Rothschild, *Advertising* (Lexington, Mass: D.C. Heath, 1987), p. 217; Simon Broaddbent (ed.), *The Leo Burnett Book of Advertising* (London: Business Books, 1984), pp. ii and 1–8.

and the formatting of commercials to look like news shows. These long advertisements are often labeled *infomercials.* A quick glance at cable channels after midnight or during the weekend reveals the abundance of commercials that last for 30 minutes or an hour. A company buys the time from the stations or cable channels and controls the content.

These programs most often involve demonstrations of a product and testimonials from people who use, or supposedly use, the product. The Federal Trade Commission oversees the truth of claims made in these programs, but often these claims stop just short of deceptive practices. Even if claims are false, limited resources prevent the FTC from checking all of these commercials.

The format of program-length commercials can affect the credibility viewers give them. During the 1980s, some of the long ads started using a format that made them look like local television news programs. An older man and a younger woman sitting behind a newsroom-style desk might announce a remarkable discovery about how to reduce weight. The program that followed would have **stand-up shots** of people who looked like reporters and a continuation of the news anchor format. The format of these ads was problematic because it confused some people as to whether they were commercials or news programs. The practice did not become widespread because stations became concerned that selling products with the news format would reduce the credibility of their local news shows.

477

Political advertising

Joe McGinniss published a book in 1969 called *The Selling of the President, 1968.* McGinniss claimed that Richard Nixon had used television advertising techniques to win the presidency and that the 1968 election would forever change the nature of political advertising.[24] Most TV political advertising moved from a cognitive approach to a behavioral approach, and the cost of getting elected skyrocketed.

Every time there is a state or federal election, the candidates spend huge amounts of money on advertising. In high-profile elections, such as those of presidents and governors, most of the money goes to television. Critics are concerned more about the content of the ads than about the mere use of advertising. Many of these ads avoid providing information about the issues of a campaign and instead appeal to voters' emotions.

Images of crime and violence contribute little to the marketplace of ideas, but they do arouse concerns in voters. Such ads attempt to identify a candidate's opponent with a negative image and do not provide information for making a rational decision. Scholars and critics are concerned that such advertising emphasizes trivial problems and plays down the issues that are most urgent.[25] Even the heads of large advertising agencies question the usefulness of advertising in the political process.[26]

Campaign strategist Richard Morris was adept at raising funds to meet the ever-increasing costs of expensive television advertising. Although his political image was tarnished when he was caught in a sexual misdemeanor, he managed to make a small fortune for himself in the 1996 campaign that topped all records in spending for advertising.

As a reaction to concern about manipulative advertising, newspapers and television stations began running critiques of political ads during the 1990, 1992, and 1994 elections. These critiques discussed the truth and accuracy of the ads. However, it is not always easy to evaluate subtle forms of advertising. Checking the truth of statements is not the same as revealing the ways in which a commercial tries to manipulate a voter.[27]

Online advertising

Always eager to reach customers, businesses began moving cautiously online during the early 1990s. The caution came from not knowing much about this new medium for reaching customers. Companies had several questions: What types of people go online?

stand-up shot:
Photographs of active people who appear to be news sources or reporters.

The World Wide Web May Change Ad Agencies

Don't laugh at that computer nerd who sits next to you in class. He or she may become a millionaire through the Internet.

As major companies move advertising onto the World Wide Web, they are hiring small specialty boutiques instead of the massive traditional advertising agencies. Corporations such as AT&T and Coca-Cola are hiring companies with names such as On Ramp Inc., which was started by former MTV video jockey Adam Curry. These small companies specialize in computer advertising.

They build and maintain Web sites for companies that are trying to enter the fast lane of the information highway.

Reacting to these electronic entrepreneurs, the larger ad agencies have created teams with pop names such as "Blue Marble" aimed at advertising online. As would be expected, the giant agencies are telling companies that the boutiques may know computers but they don't know advertising. The new agencies respond that most of the large agencies' computer divisions don't understand the nature of the online world.

Whether companies such as Modem Media, which won the AT&T account over several larger firms, will grow into giants themselves remains uncertain. However, converging technologies have opened up competition among advertising agencies, and that is likely to help the buyers of advertising.

SOURCE: Harry Berkowitz, "Tiny Ad Firms Make Big Money Online," *Lansing State Journal*, May 30, 1995, p. 5B.

How can the number of people who are exposed to an ad be measured? Who will measure them? How do online users respond to ads?

Key concept

Online Advertising: Advertising online is in its infancy, and companies are experimenting with the effectiveness of different types of product services, advertising, and subscription fees. The evolution of how online material is paid for will determine, in large part, the tone and character of online content in the same way the commercial base of broadcast television has influenced the entertainment and news received through that medium.

Online advertising has taken off during the mid-1990s. In 1995, advertising spent on the Web was about $30 million, but half of the money was for computer- and Internet-related companies. Estimates for advertising expenditures during 1997 run from $400 to $699 million with estimates that online advertising will exceed $1 billion by the end of the decade.[28] Although much of the advertising continues to be related to electronics, the percentage continues to decline as other businesses move to the Web. Even though recent growth has been strong, the amount of money spent on online advertising remains relatively small, between 1 and 2 percent of the money spent just on newspaper advertising.

Advertising on the Web has grown because problems confronting Web advertisers are being solved. One issue facing new forms of media is how to verify exposure to advertising. Nielsen ratings provide TV advertisers with data about who and how many people use TV, and the Audit Bureau of Circulations verifies the circulation of daily and some weekly newspapers. Advertisers have more faith in these independent auditors than in figures provided by media organizations themselves.

The same organizations that monitor other media use have moved into **auditing** Web sites. For example, Internet Profiles Corp. (www.ipro.com) started research of online use in July 1995 and by mid-1997, it had more than 100 clients. The Audit Bureau of Circulations also audits Web sites. An audit of the National Geographic site, for example, showed an averaged 18,460 visits (a series of one or more impressions to a single user during an uninterrupted sequence) a day in March 1997. Auditors also report the type of domain (educational, organization, etc.) that visitors use to access sites and the country of origin.

A second problem, which seems to have been solved, concerns standardization of advertisement sizes. It costs time and money to make ads fit various sizes on different Web sites. In late 1996, more than 250 different sizes of advertising could be found on the Web.[29] However, the Internet Advertising Bureau and the Coalition for Advertising Supported Information & Entertainment set up a joint recommendation for nine sizes of Web advertisements. These include full horizontal banners, vertical banners, and various sizes of smaller ads called buttons. This standardization will reduce costs and help Web advertising grow.

Web advertising falls roughly into two types: banner ads and classified ads. Banner ads include graphics, sometimes moving, in ads that take up 10 percent or more of the display area in a computer window. The newspaper equivalent is a display ad. The classified Web ad is equivalent to the classifieds found in a newspaper and involves mostly textual information, although visuals can be used. Banner ads are usually bought by an organization, but classified ads are bought by individuals and organizations.

Internet advertising experienced a slow start because advertisers had little information about how consumers would use or react to the new medium. However, experimentation has proven that such advertising has vast potential when targeted to specific groups.

Direct marketing material might be classified as a third form of Web advertising, although it is closer to a mail catalogue than traditional ads. Direct marketing sites allow interaction between the site owner and a customer. Customers can order material directly from the company by using a credit card and interactive technology. Lands' End, which also sells clothing through the mail, has a direct marketing Web site.

A further problem confronting online advertisers is how people use advertisements on computers. Ads cannot force themselves on computer users because the user controls interaction online. Computer users can simply ignore ads.

Roland J. Sharette of J. Walter Thompson USA, a prominent ad agency, has said that online advertising will resemble total marketing. To be successful, it will have four characteristics:

- The information must be important to the consumer's understanding of the product.
- The ad must be entertaining enough to draw people into the ad.
- The consumer needs to be able to accomplish a transaction (buy something if she or he wants to).

audit: Checking the truthfulness of reader and viewer figures reported by a media company.

- The information needs to build a dialogue with the consumer (develop a continuing two-way communication).[30]

Online advertising will continue to expand, but it will probably target specialized audiences rather than a mass audience. In addition, it will allow for interaction. Customers will be able to ask questions about products and solicit additional information. Some analysts argue that it will become a more sophisticated form of target marketing that will benefit the consumer as well as the companies that advertise.

Worldwide advertising

During the late 1980s, advertising agencies accentuated the trend to become worldwide organizations through a series of mergers and joint agreements. Advertising agencies that served clients throughout the world had existed previously, but this period saw a boom that reflected the changing world economy. Two important trends pushed agencies more toward worldwide status. First, companies have increasingly become transnational corporations. Such a corporation "runs its business and makes its decisions based on all the possible choices in the world, not simply favoring domestic options because they are convenient."[31] American companies such as Coca-Cola, IBM, and Xerox are transnationals, as are companies that are headquartered in other countries, such as Shell Oil, a Dutch company. These transnational companies need advertising agencies that can prepare ad campaigns throughout the world. Using such an agency is more efficient than dealing with a different agency in every country.

Advertisers and marketers of products such as cigarettes think globally in promoting their lines throughout the world. Even if the demand for cigarettes shrinks in the United States, the worldwide market undoubtedly will remain competitive, and cigarette makers look to expand their markets.

A second trend promoting worldwide agencies is the opening of new consumer markets around the world. As Communist governments in Europe and Asia accepted more international trade during the 1980s, Western companies gained access to billions of potential customers. Many markets, such as China, have continued to expand during the 1990s. These new markets, combined with growing television markets around the world, presented transnational corporations with great opportunities to sell more products. To sell these products, consumers must know that they exist. This is the role that worldwide advertising agencies have come to fill. Today, people on every continent know the round red and white Coca-Cola symbol.

As a result of these trends, no top ten advertising agency gets the majority of its income from one particular country anymore. Of the ten largest American agencies, Leo Burnett receives the largest percentage of its gross income from the United States with 45 percent. Large worldwide agencies will continue to see the proportion of their revenues from outside the United States grow in the future.

Summary

- Advertising serves a basic economic function in the United States. It allows sellers and buyers of goods and services to find each other in the marketplace.
- Advertising sometimes aims at mass audiences and other times concentrates on segmented audiences.
- Segmented audiences can be classified by demographics, psychographics, and geography.
- Advertisements can be classified by the geographic area they cover, the purpose of the ads, and the effect the ads have on consumers of media.
- Most advertising plans incorporate more than one type of medium.
- Cable, home video, and other new technologies will compete for advertising that has in the past supported the traditional mass media.
- Not all of advertising's effects on society are positive. Some advertisers attempt to manipulate audiences to buy certain products and services. This is especially a problem with very young television viewers.
- Advertisers sometimes influence the news coverage of media organizations through advertising boycotts and informal pressure that affects the contents of stories that are run.
- Agencies provide a wide range of services from creating advertisements to placing them and testing the effectiveness of ads with research.
- Most advertising jobs are found in advertising agencies or in the advertising departments of large companies, including media organizations.
- Political advertising can become problematic when it emphasizes emotion and not useful information.
- Online advertising will likely include more marketing elements than traditional mass media.
- Online advertising, especially on the World Wide Web, is expected to increase greatly by 2000, but it will remain a targeted form of advertising.
- Advertising agencies have become both concentrated and global in nature.

Navigating the Web

Advertising on the web

More and more advertising is being seen on the World Wide Web. Many sites have advertising, but information about advertising is not plentiful. The following sites represent a range of sites related to advertising.

American Association of Advertising Agencies   http://www.commercepark.com/AAAA

This site is maintained by a national trade organization for ad agencies. The association promotes integrity and ethics in advertising. The site contains information about the organization and its goals.

Scarborough Research	http://www.scarborough.com

This is a market research organization that conducts research for media and advertisers. The site contains information about the services it offers.

Ad Age	http://www.AdAge.com

Advertising Age is the dominant trade magazine for advertising. It carries a wide range of information about media that carry advertising. This is an online version of the print magazine.

Yahoo Classified Ads	http://www.yahoo.com/business_and_economy/classifieds

This is an index of classified ads carried on the Web. It allows access to ads from all over the country and includes such things as used computers and used law books.

Lands' End	http://www.landsend.com

This is an example of direct marketing on the Web. Lands' End is a clothing company that has traditionally sold to people through direct mail catalogues. These types of businesses will adapt easily to the Web.

Questions for review

1. What is the difference between advertisements and news?
2. What kinds of advertising promote ideas?
3. What factors contributed to the development of mass advertising?
4. Why did some publications begin to refuse patent medicine advertising?
5. Why are advertisers concerned about geographic coverage?
6. What are the primary tasks of an advertising agency?

Issues to think about

1. What is the economic role of advertising in a free market society?
2. How does cultural change affect advertising?
3. What impact did the arrival of broadcasting have on advertising?
4. How does advertising have both a negative and a positive effect on journalism?
5. Does advertising coerce people into buying things they don't need?
6. What are the implications of heavy political advertising on television?
7. How will advertising find its place on the Internet?

■ Suggested readings

Ewen, Stuart, *Captains of Consciousness: Advertising and the Social Roots of the Consumer Culture* (New York: McGraw-Hill, 1976).

Marchand, Roland, *Advertising the American Dream* (Berkeley: University of California Press, 1989).

Ogilvy, David, *Confessions of an Advertising Man* (New York: Atheneum, 1963).

Pope, Daniel, *The Making of Modern Advertising* (New York: Basic Books, 1983).

Schudson, Michael, *Advertising: The Uneasy Persuasion* (New York: Basic Books, 1984).

Mass Communication Research: From Content to Effects

Some uses and effects of mass communication are obvious. Readers browse through newspapers for movie schedules. Television viewers enjoy their favorite programs. But mass communications affect people in less obvious ways—ways that develop slowly over time.

Almost everyone under 45 years of age grew up with television. Each identified with and imitated TV characters, from the Lone Ranger to Wonder Woman to the Teenage Mutant Ninja Turtles. These childhood behaviors are a simple example of how television and other media influence the way people act, beginning at a very early age. Mass communication research is a study of these behaviors and other influences of media content on people. Research also focuses on the forces that shape media content.

Research leads to technological advances. Here members of the Mars Pathfinder team give a briefing after the craft landed and successfully began transmitting data and images.

485

Such research becomes increasingly important as people spend more time with media. Media content can benefit consumers, but it can also create social and personal problems. Research provides understanding of mass communication and its impacts.

Issues in research can vary from how human subjects are treated in experiments to whether the researcher is measuring the effects she or he intends to measure. The issues that are treated in this chapter relate to how research has contributed to understanding media. Some of these are the following:

- How do media directly and indirectly affect individuals and groups?

- What forces shape media content?

- How do media affect individuals' knowledge of public issues and events?

- How do people use media?

- How do political and economic structures shape culture?

Defining mass communication research

Mass communication research begins with a *paradigm,* which is a set of assumptions about the nature of human behavior. A variety of paradigms are available for scholars to use.[1] Each is based on previous scholarship. However, two paradigms dominate mass communication research. One uses a social science approach, and the other uses a critical studies approach. Of course, each of these can be broken down into many subdivisions. Not all scholars who use a single paradigm, for example, agree on which questions are important to ask, how answers are sought, or how results are interpreted.

The social science approach emphasizes the use of quantitative measurement and statistical analysis to learn about human behavior. The basic unit that is studied is the individual or a small social group. The origins of this approach lie in an effort to adapt scientific methods to the study of human behavior. The social science approach involves studies such as experiments and surveys. Some experiments, for instance, have exposed college students to violent pornography and then measured their attitudes toward women. The purpose is to see if this type of pornography contributes to aggressiveness toward women.

The critical approach seeks an understanding of issues that are raised by the connections between media and society. Scholars studying these connections use a variety of techniques and have different economic and cultural perspectives. They may define themselves as qualitative studies scholars or as cultural or critical theorists. Here, we will use the terms interchangeably. *Cultural theorists* look at the symbolic meaning behind behavior. These connections can be made through a historical study of social and cultural theory, through an analysis of technology, through a study of media professionals, or through a variety of other approaches. *Critical scholars* are interested in the intersection of media and everyday life and often focus on the relationship of the media text to its audience. For example, critical scholars have analyzed the narrative texts of television programs such as *Hill Street Blues.* They also use the interview to investigate topics such as how the news media reinforce, or legitimate, the moral order. These topics indicate the broad focus of critical studies.[2]

Research in your life

What Do You Think? What Do You Know?

Often people think they know how mass media affects them. They make comments such as, "I never buy a product because it's advertised on television." Or "I already know who I'm going to vote for. I don't care how candidates advertise themselves on television." Use the following to decide what you think the media's effects are on you. Then, as you read this chapter, decide whether the research you read about makes you change your mind about these effects. What you thought about effects on you may be correct—or you may discover that the media have a more powerful effect on you than you thought.

POSSIBLE EFFECT	YES	NO
Advertising causes me to buy certain products.		
Advertising affects the brand of product that I buy.		
Media coverage of a political candidate affects what I think of him/her.		
How media cover issues causes me to think more about certain issues than about others.		
I try to act in ways similar to those I admire on television and in film.		

Each approach is limited by its paradigm. No single method of inquiry is sufficiently comprehensive and free of bias to explain all human behavior adequately. Recently, some scholars have begun to try to combine the two approaches into better theories of mass communication creation and effects.[3]

■ The importance of theory

The social scientific method uses several research techniques, including statistical procedures, reporting methods, and historical analysis. This method, which was adapted from physical science research, begins with *empirical research,* which is the systematic collection and analysis of data. From these data, researchers draw generalizations about social behavior and form these generalizations into theories. A *social science theory* is a set of related statements about people's behavior that (1) categorize phenomena, (2) predict the future, (3) explain past events, (4) give a sense of understanding of why the behaviors occur, and (5) provide the potential for influencing future behavior.[4]

The critical approach also is interested in developing theoretical frameworks, but the methods that are used to develop them vary. For example, ethnographic description may be a way to contextualize human experience in a given culture. Norman K. Denzin describes such interpretive research as "the studied commitment to actively enter the worlds of native people and to render those worlds understandable from the standpoint of a theory that is grounded in the behaviors, languages, definitions, attitudes, and feelings of those studied."[5]

The importance of developing theory is illustrated by considering how children could benefit if the public wanted to reduce the impact of television violence. If a social science approach were used, a formal theory would categorize the TV violence and predict which types would be most harmful to children. It would explain violent behavior of children in the past and future. More important, a useful theory would allow an in-

488

formed public to influence policy and influence TV programmers to reduce types of harmful violence. Cultural theorists might develop a theory aimed at explaining the relationship between violent content on television and the nature of the economic structure or production process.

Creating a theory from research is just part of the process. The theory must be tested with further research and modified when necessary. Theories are based on *hypotheses,* which are statements of relationships between people and things. For example, the statement, "the more violent television a child watches, the more aggressive acts the child will exhibit toward his or her playmates" is a hypothesis connecting violence on television with play behavior by children. Research tests these hypotheses. If the research results support the hypothesis, the theory that generated the hypothesis becomes stronger and more useful. If the research does not support the theory, the theory must be modified to make it more consistent with reality, or it may be discarded entirely.

Mass communication scholarship has produced few theories yet that fulfill all these functions because the field of study is young compared to more established fields such as economics and psychology. However, the research discussed below fulfills some of these goals of theory, and mass communication scholarship remains ripe for theory development.

Research and public policy

Scholarship on television violence and children has demonstrated the impact of research and theory on public policy. The Report to the Surgeon General on Television Violence and Children in 1972 concluded that TV violence could promote aggression in children. This report was followed four years later by *cultivation theory,* which was developed by George Gerbner and colleagues at the University of Pennsylvania. Cultivation theory states that heavy television viewing influences people to adopt values, roles, and world views that are based on television.[6] Much of the research involves violence on television. The Surgeon General's report, cultivation theory, and subsequent research indicate that violent television has the most impact on children. This conclusion played an important role in the mandate in the Telecommunications Act of 1996 for TV program ratings and a V-chip to help shield children from violent content. In addition, the FCC moved to require television stations to broadcast three hours of educational children's programming per week. Despite strong opposition from the television industry, policy was thus changed because research has convinced most of the public and public officials that children should be protected from violent TV content. Today, the issue is not whether violent television affects children's behavior but exactly how this effect occurs and what can be done to protect children. Currently, the television industry is experimenting with content ratings that will allow parents to select the programs their young children watch. The exact nature of these ratings and what they reveal about a program remains open to debate.

Modifying theory

Over time, most social science theory gets modified for several reasons: (1) Behavior changes as societies and humans evolve; (2) the ability to measure social behavior improves and allows for better tests; and (3) the accumulation of research over time allows for better theory.

Mass communication social science research falls into three categories: influences on content, effects, and uses.[7] *Influences on content* involve the many factors that affect the creation of media content. These include individual characteristics, such as ethics; organizational influences, such as news-gathering patterns; and market characteristics, such as economic competition. All these factors shape media content in a variety of ways. For example, the nature of communication between sources and reporters affects news-gathering patterns. Studies show that some reporters start to think like their sources after years of covering a beat. This assimilation of source values affects the way the reporter selects and writes about news. Research about this relationship contributes to our understanding of how content is shaped.

Effects research concentrates on the impact the content has on people, either individually or in groups. The effects can be social, cultural, political, and economic. Research on the ability of political advertisements to change people's attitudes toward a candidate is effects research.

Uses research concerns why and how people decide to use media content. Scholars use the term "uses and gratifications" to describe this research. It is similar to effects research, but it starts with a different assumption about people. Effects research assumes that people are passive users of media content, while uses research assumes media consumers are active users. Effects research looks at impacts on users who may be categorized by education or income level, but it does not study how the audience chooses content. Uses research studies audience decision making and use of media. Figure 16.1 shows that the relationship between theory and research is dynamic, with new hypotheses constantly leading to more research and theory modification.

Early social science research concentrated on effects, but all three types are important. Knowing that television carries violent programs for children because they attract large numbers of young viewers at a low cost means little if the impact of TV violence on children is unknown. Likewise, it serves little purpose to know that TV violence makes children more aggressive if people don't know how to limit the violent content.

Critical studies in the United States developed in at least two major schools. The Frankfurt School developed in Germany from work by philosophers Georg W. F. Hegel and Karl Marx. It views history as a series of conflicts between opposing forces—the thesis and the antithesis. Eventually, the conflict is resolved through a synthesis, and the conflict begins anew. The Chicago School saw communication as a foundation for community in a postindustrial world that had lost its reliance on personal ties.

FIGURE 16.1 Relationship Between Theory and Research

Research leads to a theory, which suggests a hypothesis. The hypothesis is tested with research, which either supports the theory or suggests a new theory. The cycle continues as social science develops more useful theory.

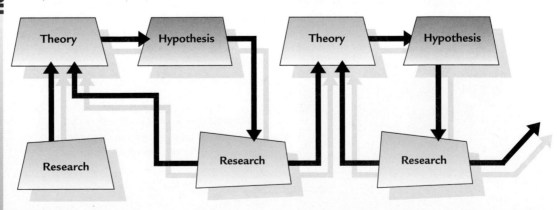

490

Mass communication research in American life

Mass communication research started two decades into the twentieth century. During the 1920s and 1930s, it was assumed that mass media had powerful effects on individual behavior. From the 1940s through the 1960s, researchers took the opposite tack and argued that the effects of mass media on people were limited. During this time, researchers also began to explore the influences on media content. After the 1970s, research into content influences grew enormously. Effects and uses research indicate that the impact of mass media on people and society is neither as powerful as was once thought nor as limited as researchers later claimed but depends on many factors. Critical studies scholars have pursued a variety of topics during recent years, with an emphasis on the commercialization of culture and the role of media in maintaining power structures.

Keyconcept

Media Research and Theory: Statements that help to explain the relationship of media to past experience and to the future and to give an understanding of why media-related behaviors occur.

■ Early critical studies research in the United States

Two strains of critical studies developed in the United States during the first third of the twentieth century. In Chicago, Charles Cooley, Robert Park, and John Dewey, three Midwesterners who had studied at Michigan and Minnesota, explored the positive possibilities of modern communication. They saw communication as the foundation for developing a sense of community in a postindustrial world. A second group of communication scholars came to the United States from Frankfurt, Germany. Theodor Adorno, Herbert Marcuse, and Max Horkheimer, theorists associated with the Institute for Social Research, which had been founded in Frankfurt in 1923, fled Hitler's fascist regime in 1933 and established themselves in New York with connections to Columbia University. In 1949, after World War II, some of the members returned to Germany; others stayed in the United States. The Frankfurt School's thought was more negative than that of the Chicago School. Frankfurt theorists did not believe that modern media had the potential to improve society. Their theoretical approach was based on the economics of media organizations and so they considered the specifics of professional practice to be irrelevant.

CAN
Vegetables
Fruit AND
the Kaiser too

Tomatoes   *Peas*

Kaiser Brand
Unsweetened

Write for Free Book to
NATIONAL WAR GARDEN COMMISSION
WASHINGTON, D.C.

Charles Lathrop Pack., President   P.S.Ridsdale, Secretary

Posters distributed during World War I such as this one encouraging people to grow vegetables to support the war effort were considered to be highly effective propaganda pieces. This belief led to a supposition that mass media effects were exceedingly powerful and resulted in the "magic bullet theory" of media effects.

The Frankfurt School's theories developed out of traditional Marxist thought. Principles of Marxist thought include a belief that the economic basis of a society determines its social structure as a whole as well as the psychology of the people within it. Historical change is thought to be a result of conflict between owners of property and workers, and class struggle is inevitable within a capitalist society. Marxist theorists believe that only revolution, not reform, can accomplish change; therefore, although labor unions might be useful training grounds for radicals, they only temporarily relieve the condition of workers. Because reform creates only temporary relief, conditions will worsen until workers' misery drive them to revolution. The government in capitalist societies is perceived to be the coercive instrument of property owners.

The young Marxist intellectual radicals who made up the Frankfurt School were disappointed that the revolution that occurred in Russia in 1917 had not spread throughout Europe. The dark years of fascism in Europe affected them deeply, and they were concerned that the postwar Western world appeared to be politically stable. Such stability, in their minds, meant the end of a conscious recognition of the need for radical change from within the working class. They saw workers as suppressed by the culture industries—by the mass media. They viewed the Western press as being organized through rules and institutions.[8] The Frankfurt School theorists believed that within a capitalist society art could not be a revolutionary force. They argued that the media made art part of the established order, and although it might have made certain forms of high culture more accessible to the middle class, it did so at the expense of robbing high culture of its critical substance. Art thus became intertwined with official function. Marcuse argued that language constantly imposed images, which worked against conceptual thinking.[9] One of the primary criticisms of the Frankfurt School was that as a group, they rejected the idea that theory could affect practice, and they retreated from allowing their research to lead them into a dialogue about modern media. Although there are now many strains within the cultural studies traditions, both in the United States and abroad, the traditions of the Frankfurt School had an enormous impact on the development of American cultural theory.

■ Powerful effects research

Early research into the impact of mass communication developed from World War I propaganda. Governments, including that of the United States, supported mass communication efforts to mobilize their citizens in support of the war and to discourage the populations in enemy countries. Although some political and social groups in the United States opposed America's entry into the war, the U.S. propaganda arm, the Committee on Public Information, flooded the country with leaflets, programs, and other materials that were designed to reduce media and citizen opposition to the war. Reflecting on these activities, Harold Lasswell published *Propaganda Techniques in the World War* in 1927.[10] The conclusions of Lasswell and others that media propaganda had been successful in generating support for the war led to the concept of universal, powerful media effects, which is known as the **magic bullet** theory. Scholars argued that the media worked like a bullet in their powerful persuasive impact on audiences.

Support for the *powerful effects theory* grew after the war with a series of studies between 1929 and 1932 that examined the impact of

Keyconcept

The Magic Bullet Theory: A media theory made popular by the propaganda efforts of World War I that suggested media were all powerful. Propagandists believed that you could simply hit individuals with information, as though it were a bullet, and it would have powerful and immediate effects.

magic bullet: Metaphor for powerful media effects. The presumption was that media content hit a person and had a definite effect upon impact, as with a bullet. Therefore media content became magic content.

492

movies on children. During the 1920s, millions of children under the age of fourteen were attending films that often contained sex and violence. In response to concern about the power of movies, the Payne Fund financed these studies of adolescents that concluded that media—in the form of movies—did indeed have powerful effects.[11]

Scholars who developed the powerful effects approach conducted research at a time when social science methods were just evolving. Often, such research failed to control for other influences that could have caused the effects that they found. Furthermore, these studies started with simplistic assumptions about humans. They assumed that genetics determined people's behavior and that all people are motivated in similar ways. Today, we know better.

■ Limited effects research

At the beginning of World War II, the U.S. government again used communication to develop support for the war effort. Carl Hovland and his colleagues used more sophisticated social science methods and found that although films and other forms of communication did motivate troops, their effects were specific and limited.[12] These results surprised communication scholars because they contradicted the powerful effects research during the previous two decades.

Keyconcept

Limited Effects Model: Concept that media have limited effects on individuals—that interpersonal impact is more important in influencing attitude and creating change. This approach recognizes that individuals interact with each other as well as respond to the media messages they receive.

However, the conclusion that mass media had limited effects on people found increasing support during the 1940s, particularly in studies of voting behavior. Researchers studied the voters in Erie County, Ohio, during the 1940 presidential election[13] and the voters in Elmira, New York, during the 1948 election.[14] They found that mass media converted only a small percentage of voters. Interpersonal communication played a greater role in influencing voting behavior than did media.

These projects and others that followed suggested a *two-step flow* of media information. Voters turned to other people—**opinion leaders**—for information. Researchers found that opinion leaders within a community are selected for their specific expertise. For example, the high school coach may be an opinion leader on sports, and the mayor may be a leader in politics.

Researchers soon discovered that media were not all-powerful, but rather that it had limited effects. These limited effects were often filtered through interpersonal discussion and derived not only from media directly, but from discussion about media-generated or media-covered issues.

Critics claim that the two-step flow theory is simplistic, but it introduced a revolutionary concept for the 1940s. It revealed that mass media affect individuals indirectly as well as directly. A person who reads a movie review, decides not to see a film, and explains the decision to a friend delivers a message from mass media. The friend who decides not to see the movie is reacting to interpersonal communication but is also being indirectly affected by mass media. Limited effects research suggested a complicated process by which media content affects individuals.

opinion leader: Person within a community who has areas of expertise and pays more attention to information derived from mass media than do most citizens.

FIGURE 16.2 — The Process of Creating Media Content

493

The creation of media content begins with observations and interviews with sources. Using these, the creator generates content that is edited by managers. This creation process is influenced by routines and social interaction within the media organization. In addition, economic, political, and social forces outside the organization help to shape the process. Ultimately, the content is used by media consumers, and it affects them in a variety of ways.

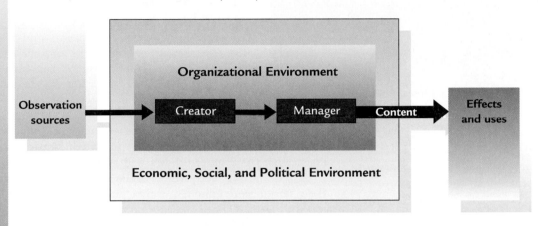

Early content studies

During the 1940s, people also began to study the forces that shape mass media content. Critics had always assumed that mass media content reflected the rational decisions of the people who created the content. If a story of government corruption appeared in a newspaper, it ran only because the editors wanted to achieve some specific goal, such as to punish crooked politicians. This approach seemed to explain media creation, but it failed to acknowledge that media workers face pressure as they create content. This pressure comes from advertisers, readers, sources of news, and even other journalists. Figure 16.2 indicates the complexity of creating media content and emphasizes that both external and internal forces are at work.

GATEKEEPING The earliest content influence research involved gatekeeping studies. David Manning White studied the decisions of a wire service editor as he selected material to put in the newspaper.[15] White asked the editor to explain why he excluded and included particular articles. The editor ran stories according to personal biases, his perceptions of what readers wanted, and the editorial policies of the newspaper. The editor was acting as a **gatekeeper** of information.

Since that time, numerous studies have found that a variety of factors influence the gatekeeper's decisions. For example, how often a particular type of article appears in the wire or other news services influences the gatekeepers' decisions more than do their shared news values.[16] If 25 percent of Associated Press stories are about other countries, about 25 percent of the newspaper's stories will be about other countries. Television gatekeepers are influenced by their biases, the visual impact of stories, and how attractive the stories will be to viewers.[17] One evening a house fire will get 30 seconds on the

gatekeeper: A person who controls the flow of information into and through the mass media.

494

Media professionals who decide what content will go into a newspaper or be included in an evening newscast become gatekeepers who decide which items—of all the range of news possibilities—will reach the public.

local TV news, and the next evening another house fire will get a one-minute story. The two stories are similar, but the station shot video of the second fire. Another factor influencing coverage is what other news stories are available on a given day.

SOCIAL INFLUENCES Soon after the first gatekeeping study, researchers began studying the role of news organizations as social influences on news selection. Warren Breed interviewed 120 newspaper journalists during the early 1950s to determine how editors enforce newsroom policy.[18] He found that a **socialization process** taught reporters news policy without the editors having to explicitly tell them. Journalists learn what the paper's editors will accept as news from what was and was not printed in the newspaper, the way their stories were edited, and their knowledge of the editors' interests.

Breed also discovered that factors other than newsroom policy influence news selection. A reporter who thought a story should be covered had ways of sidestepping informal policy constraints. Because the policies were vague and the editors did not actually cover news, the reporter had some autonomy in picking stories. Stories that were assigned by editors left the reporters little discretion, but reporter-initiated stories allowed them to control content. Breed's research indicated that not all reporters were equal. Star reporters, those with experience and public recognition, could avoid following policy more than general assignment reporters could.

REPORTING Another area of exploration involved the relationship between reporters and sources. In 1961, Walter Gieber and Walter Johnson published a study of reporters covering their local city hall and found that reporters often shared the values of their sources. The beat reporters and government officials depended on each other to do their jobs. Their informal relationships resulted in collaboration and cooperation in gathering and writing news.[19] Sometimes this meant that the journalists agreed with the government officials even when their agreement might not have been in the best interest of their readers.

In a public debate between a city council and homeowners about a new industry moving to town, a reporter plays an important role. A journalist who has covered city hall for ten years might be influenced by the mayor to emphasize the economic advantages of the new industry. Meanwhile, the negative impact on the surrounding homeowners might be downplayed or neglected all together. Fairness and balance can become difficult when sources become more like friends than sources.

This problem commonly occurs on the police beat. When reporters spend as much time with law enforcement officers as they do in the newsroom, it is often easy for them to identify with the officers. If reporters are not careful, their decisions about stories will reflect

socialization process: Process by which reporters learn patterns of behavior through observing others and by learning to recognize the systems of rewards and punishments in a newsroom.

the police view more than the readers' interests. News organizations sometimes rotate reporters among beats to keep journalists from acquiring their sources' values.

These early studies of gatekeepers and socialization showed that journalists were not autonomous individuals exercising their freedom of expression. Rather, journalists face a complex series of interactions with people who influence their actions in ways journalists don't even recognize.

Evolution of cultural studies in the United States

The work of Charles Horton Cooley, John Dewey, and Robert E. Park ushered in a new way of thinking about modern media. Theorizing from philosophical and sociological traditions, these **pluralist** social reformers believed that modern media could make possible a truly democratic community. Together, writes Daniel Czitrom in *Media and the American Mind,* they "construed modern communication essentially as an agent for restoring a broad moral and political consensus to America, a consensus they believed to have been threatened by the wrenching disruptions of the nineteenth century: industrialization, urbanization, and immigration."

Cooley tried to understand the interplay between modern media and social groups such as the family, friends, play group, and peer group. He laid the foundation for later empirical research into how media effects are moderated and changed by interaction with other individuals and groups. Dewey and Park addressed the form and content of journalism, occasionally lamenting that it too often lined the pockets of the businessman but also speculating about a newspaper that would carry no advertising and would appeal to the higher intellect. Unlike the Frankfurt theorists, these communication scholars of the **Progressive generation** had great hopes about the effect of media on modern society. Dewey wrote in 1915, in *Democracy and Education,* that

> Society not only continues to exist by transmission, by communication, but it may fairly be said to exist in transmission, in communication. There is more than a verbal tie between the words common, community, and communication. Men live in a community in virtue of the things they have in common; and communication is the way in which they come to possess things in common.[20]

As the Progressive era gave way to the Great Depression of the 1930s, the emphasis on empirical research and social science approaches gained ascendancy. The daring hopes of the Progressives for a new form of community were dashed as the economy plummeted. Scholars turned to empirical methods to document media effects, and empiricism and social science approaches dominated in media studies, just as they dominated in other emerging fields such as political science. Through the 1960s, empirical research focused primarily on individual effects.

Current research topics

During the early 1970s, government and university interest in media research grew, and **media sociology** gained favor as a research methodology. Researchers shifted direction and began to label effects as "moderate," rather than "limited."[21]

Moderate effects research found that media content had a greater impact on people's behavior than limited effects studies suggested, but

pluralist: A school of thought that espouses coexistence and cooperation among different elements of a power structure.

Progressive generation: Group of individuals in the early 1900s who championed political and social reform.

media sociology: Analysis of media as an institution of society and its relation to society as a whole.

esearch is not free. Someone has to pay for computers, supplies, research assistants, mailing and phone bills, and even the researchers' own salaries. The source of funding depends on whether the research is academic or practical. Academic research is designed to answer questions of importance to society and its members. Practical research addresses specific problems that media organizations face.

Research-oriented universities assume the role of producing new knowledge through research, in addition to teaching graduate and undergraduate students. These universities, government agencies, and foundations fund research that is designed to de-

Who Pays the Bills?

velop usable theory to explain media conduct and effects.

Practical research uses the same tools as academic research, but its goal is to solve business problems, not to develop theory. For example, radio and television ratings systems represent results of practical research. To set advertising prices, broadcast and cable network managers need to know how many viewers watch their programs. They set up or hire organizations to validate claims made by various media organizations. Nielsen Media Research, which conducts television ratings sur-

veys, works closely with the industry to make sure Nielsen research accurately represents the viewing audience. The Audit Bureau of Circulation checks newspapers' circulation figures to make sure the papers sell the numbers they claim.

Funding is always a potential source of bias. Academic researchers should be concerned about who is funding their research. If researchers become too dependent on a single source of income, they may be tempted to bias the outcome to make sure their funding will continue.

the impact was not as great as was found by the powerful effects researchers. As television became the dominant mass medium, moderate effects studies often reflected the impact of television on viewers.

TELEVISION VIOLENCE In 1972 the Report to the Surgeon General on TV Violence and Children concluded that a connection exists between TV violence and some children's antisocial behavior. Controversy followed the release of the forty research projects that were part of the report. The television industry argued that the research had not shown a causal relationship. On the other hand, some researchers argued that the report's conclusions were weaker than the research warranted.

Ten years later, in 1982, the National Institute for Mental Health (NIMH) issued a report analyzing the massive research effort that had followed the Surgeon General's report. The NIMH report covered a wider range of TV effects than violence, but violence got the bulk of media attention when the report was released. The report found a correlation between heavy viewing of violent television by children and aggressive behavior. It also found that television advertising affected children and that television could contribute to prosocial behavior as well as antisocial behavior.[22]

KNOWLEDGE GAP Other new ideas about media—especially about media and politics—emerged from massive research efforts during the 1970s. The *knowledge gap hypothesis* argued that people with more education and higher incomes would acquire knowledge

Knowledge gap research hypothesizes that those with the greatest amounts of information will more easily gather even more knowledge, increasing the gap between the information-poor and information-rich. This cyber cafe is an attempt to provide access to new forms of information to a wide variety of people.

of public issues more quickly than would those with less education and income.[23] Such a condition could dramatically affect democracy because it would mean that the poor and less educated would be disadvantaged when making political decisions. Knowledge gap research argued that a person who is uncomfortable reading or who cannot afford newspapers and magazines will be less likely than other people to participate politically and could be manipulated by politicians.

Research that followed the publication of the knowledge gap hypothesis supported its existence under some conditions.[24] However, the existence of the gap is influenced by more than socioeconomic background. The gap can narrow when people at lower socioeconomic levels have a strong interest in the topic and the information is accessible.

Keyconcept

Knowledge Gap Hypothesis: An argument that people with more education and higher incomes will acquire knowledge of public issues more quickly than those with less education and income.

NEWS GATHERING During the 1970s, many content influence studies concentrated on news gathering. In 1978, sociologist Gaye Tuchman published a book that created a whole new research language.[25] She described the routines that are used to gather news as a *news net.* The net catches some types of events, which become news, while allowing others to pass through. Events that are prescheduled, such as city council meetings, or nonscheduled, such as earthquakes, may qualify as news. Problems and issues that are not connected to public events, such as unequal pay for women, do not become news. According to Tuchman, journalists don't discover news; they create news on the basis of their routines for interacting with sources.

Keyconcept

News Net: The term, news net, indicates areas and sources that are normal places reporters go to gather news. Because reporters often go to the same places repeatedly, or develop routines for gathering news, the traditional news net sometimes leaves out certain types of news.

Tuchman's criticism of the media grew out of her feminism and the failure of news organizations to adequately cover the women's and civil rights movements of the 1960s and 1970s. It took some time, but many newspapers eventually discovered what she found: Using topical beats improves news coverage. Today, reporters cover the environment and civil rights beats as well as the city hall and school beats. However, this change did not represent editors' recognition of a good idea from researchers; rather, it was part of an effort to stop the decline in readership as people found newspapers increasingly irrelevant to their needs.

These areas of research continue today, with increased effort directed toward developing theory rather than conducting empirical research. The abundant data collected during the last twenty-five years need to be synthesized into theories that can predict behavior and provide understanding.

Mass communication research in our lives

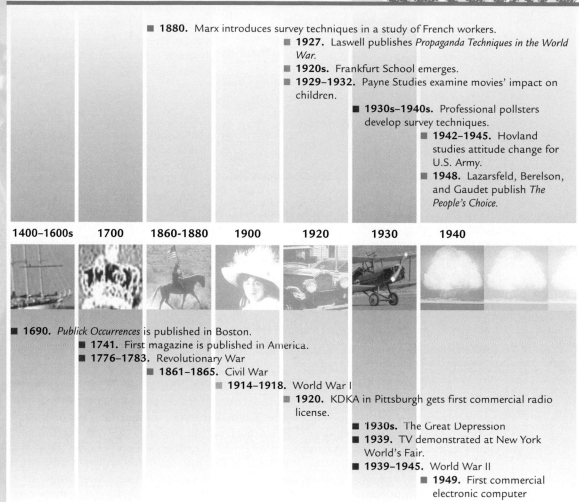

- **1880.** Marx introduces survey techniques in a study of French workers.
  - **1927.** Laswell publishes *Propaganda Techniques in the World War.*
  - **1920s.** Frankfurt School emerges.
  - **1929–1932.** Payne Studies examine movies' impact on children.
    - **1930s–1940s.** Professional pollsters develop survey techniques.
      - **1942–1945.** Hovland studies attitude change for U.S. Army.
      - **1948.** Lazarsfeld, Berelson, and Gaudet publish *The People's Choice.*

1400–1600s	1700	1860-1880	1900	1920	1930	1940

- **1690.** *Publick Occurrences* is published in Boston.
  - **1741.** First magazine is published in America.
  - **1776–1783.** Revolutionary War
    - **1861–1865.** Civil War
      - **1914–1918.** World War I
      - **1920.** KDKA in Pittsburgh gets first commercial radio license.
        - **1930s.** The Great Depression
        - **1939.** TV demonstrated at New York World's Fair.
        - **1939–1945.** World War II
          - **1949.** First commercial electronic computer

Mass media effects

Two of the most volatile social issues are the relationship between media and politics and the impact of media on individuals. Not surprisingly, these issues have been the focus of recent research. Scholars concern themselves not only with special types of effects, such as that of violence on children, but also with overall impact, which is explained theoretically through approaches such as dependency theory.

Political effects of mass media

Scholars and the public continue to be intrigued by the relationship between politics and mass media. The drafters of the Bill of Rights granted freedom of expression because

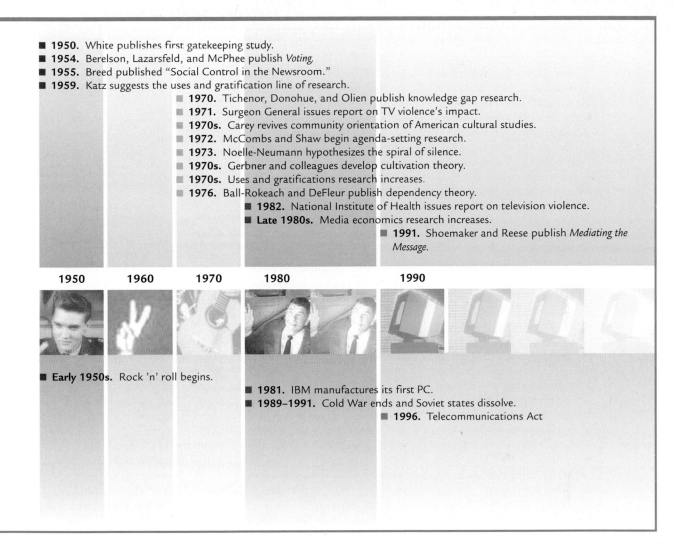

- **1950.** White publishes first gatekeeping study.
- **1954.** Berelson, Lazarsfeld, and McPhee publish *Voting*.
- **1955.** Breed published "Social Control in the Newsroom."
- **1959.** Katz suggests the uses and gratification line of research.
  - **1970.** Tichenor, Donohue, and Olien publish knowledge gap research.
  - **1971.** Surgeon General issues report on TV violence's impact.
  - **1970s.** Carey revives community orientation of American cultural studies.
  - **1972.** McCombs and Shaw begin agenda-setting research.
  - **1973.** Noelle-Neumann hypothesizes the spiral of silence.
  - **1970s.** Gerbner and colleagues develop cultivation theory.
  - **1970s.** Uses and gratifications research increases.
  - **1976.** Ball-Rokeach and DeFleur publish dependency theory.
    - **1982.** National Institute of Health issues report on television violence.
    - **Late 1980s.** Media economics research increases.
      - **1991.** Shoemaker and Reese publish *Mediating the Message*.

1950   1960   1970   1980   1990

- **Early 1950s.** Rock 'n' roll begins.
  - **1981.** IBM manufactures its first PC.
  - **1989–1991.** Cold War ends and Soviet states dissolve.
    - **1996.** Telecommunications Act

they believed that public debate would guard against the imposition of arbitrary power by a repressive government and would create an informed populace that would be capable of governing itself. Especially with the advent of television, critics have become increasingly concerned that in politics the image has come to outweigh consideration of the issues. The prevalence of image advertising, spin doctors, and manipulation of the media agenda by skilled politicians remains a critical area for study.

AGENDA SETTING Agenda-setting research contends that the media influence the importance individuals place on public issues. The agenda-setting process includes placing an issue and ranking it by importance on the public agenda. The original McCombs and Shaw study questioned 100 undecided voters in Chapel Hill, North Carolina, during the 1968 presidential election.[26] The researchers analyzed the media content that the voters used and ranked the importance of issues on the basis of the amount of time and space

[profile]

Wilbur Schramm

nternationally known communications researcher Wilbur Schramm wrote more than 100 journal articles and books, including *Mass Communication,* which was one of the world's most widely used textbooks on communication.

Schramm graduated Phi Beta Kappa from Marietta College in his hometown, Marietta, Ohio, in 1928. He obtained a master's degree from Harvard University in 1930 and a doctorate from the University of Iowa in 1932.

Schramm worked his way through school. He worked as a waiter, was a reporter and editor at the *Marietta Daily Herald* and the *Boston Herald,* wrote for the Associated Press, and played semi-pro baseball with a farm club of the Pittsburgh Pirates for five dollars a game. Later he played flute with the Boston Pops symphony before a Harvard professor told him he had to choose between playing the flute or his studies at Harvard.

From 1934 to 1947, Schramm taught at the University of Iowa, starting as a part-time teacher of honors English and eventually becoming an associate professor and the first director of the nationally known Writers Work-

shop. When World War II broke out, he took a two-year leave to become director of the Office of Facts and Figures for the U.S. Office of War Information. One of his jobs was writing speeches for Roosevelt's "fireside chats."

Schramm returned to the University of Iowa in 1943 as a communications scholar and the director of the Iowa Journalism School. Five years later, the department was granting the first doctorates of mass communication in the country. In 1947, Schramm moved to the University of Illinois to start the Institute of Communications Research. By the time he left in 1955 he had been also a research professor, director of the University Press, and dean of the division of communications. At Stanford he was the founder and director of the Institute for Communication Research, a research professor, a fellow at the Center for Advanced Study in the Behavioral Sciences, and the Janet M. Peck professor of communication.

Schramm retired in 1973, only to join the East West Center in Honolulu as director of its Communication Institute and then its Distinguished Center Researcher. He also taught for two years at

the Chinese University of Hong Kong as the Aw Boon Au professor in the Department of Communication. He conducted extensive research in many parts of the world, including Asia, Africa, El Salvador, Samoa, India, and Israel.

Schramm's last book, *The History of Communication,* was published a few days before he died at home in Honolulu on December 27, 1987, at 80 years of age.

SOURCES: "Stanford; Obit/ Wilbur Schramm, Internationally Known Communications Researcher," *Business Wire,* January 12, 1988; "Wilbur Schramm Wrote Many Works on Communications," *The New York Times,* January 1, 1988, Section 1, p. 64; Max MacElwain, "Meet Wilbur Schramm," *Saturday Evening Post,* 257 (April 1985): 49.

the issue received. The voters then ranked the importance of the same issues. The ranking of coverage in the media and the ranking of issues by the voters came close to being an exact match. The conclusion from the study was that media can affect politics by influencing what the public considers to be important.

Audience characteristics affect individual agendas. How important an issue is to individuals, or its *salience,* affects the placement of an issue on the public agenda. For example, if unemployment is higher in the automobile industry than in other industries, unemployment will be a more salient issue to automobile employees. Salience interacts with media coverage. In Detroit, where the automobile industry is a major employer, unemployment will have salience for many individuals. That salience will reinforce the media's agenda-setting role. If media do not cover salient issues, their agenda-setting role is reduced.

Related to salience is the idea of obtrusiveness. An issue is *obtrusive* if an individual can experience something about it directly. An issue that is beyond direct personal experience is *unobtrusive.* If the price of a pound of hamburger goes up every week, people have firsthand experience of inflation. Other issues, such as drought in Africa, are unobtrusive for most people in the United States because they have not experienced it directly. Media have more power when people do not have direct experience; this is why media play a big role in international policy.

Interpersonal communication also affects media agenda setting. Mass media provide a source of information, but so do friends and family. Sometimes interpersonal communication reinforces the media's agenda, and sometimes it competes with it. The impact depends on a variety of factors, such as the amount of media coverage[27] and the obtrusiveness of the topic.[28]

Research in agenda setting shows that mass media influence the public issues people discuss,

Proponents of agenda-setting theory argue that newscasters set the agenda—that is, they tell the public what to think about, not how to think about it.

and that, in turn, affects political behaviors. However, the importance of media in setting this agenda varies from person to person and from issue to issue. The goal of scholars in this area is to better explain these contingencies and to explore the relationship among media, government officials, and the public in setting the public policy agenda.

SPIRAL OF SILENCE Shortly after the original agenda-setting study, Elisabeth Noelle-Neumann published a theory called "the spiral of silence."[29] This theory concerns the impact of mass media on public opinion. It states that three characteristics of mass media produce powerful effects on people: (1) *cumulation,* or the increasing effect of media across time; (2) *ubiquity,* or the experiencing of media messages almost all of the time; and (3) *consonance,* or the presentation of a consistent unified picture of the political world.

According to the spiral of silence, the unified, constant, and consistent picture of the world that the mass media present shapes people's perceptions of dominant political ideas. The majority of people do not share the dominant ideas expressed in the media, the spiral of silence theory argues, but media consumers think they do because of the power of media coverage. People in the majority assume that they are in the minority, an assumption that makes them less likely to speak out about the issues. Over time, the "silent majority" remains quiet, and ideas that are held by a minority of people dominate the political discussion.

502

An example of the spiral of silence is media coverage of the National Rifle Association's support for allowing the sale of assault weapons. If news media provide extensive coverage of the NRA's position, people may assume that a majority of U.S. citizens support the sale of assault weapons. As a result, each media consumer thinks that he or she is in the minority and avoids speaking out against the sale of these weapons. However, public opinion polls show that the majority of people in the United States support a ban on assault weapons. In this case, media have provided an incorrect image of public opinion. This incorrect image was reinforced because people failed to express their opposition to this image.

Evidence indicates that perceptions of our political position in relationship to other people's positions can influence whether we make political statements. If fourteen of fifteen students in a classroom support abortion on demand, the one person who does not will tend not to speak. Nevertheless, there are many groups of people, and even individuals, who protest and express themselves loudly even when they hold a minority opinion.

A study of the spiral of silence in Austin, Texas, found that a person's perception of public opinion did influence outspokenness.[30] However, the person's perception was only one of several factors that had an influence. Gender, age, education, income, and political opinion also affected whether people would express their political opinions.

Individual effects

Research into media's effects on individuals examines what media do to people's cognitive processes, which determine how we learn and interact with others. Two notable areas, cultivation and dependency theory, are presented here as examples of this type of research. The two are related, cultivation addressing television and dependency theory covering a wider range of media.

Keyconcept

Effects Research: Research that traditionally concentrated on the impact the content has on people, either individually or in groups. Effects research assumes people are passive users. More recent media research accounts for individual reactions to media messages.

CULTIVATION Cultivation research concerns the effect of television viewing on how people perceive the world. It states that heavy television viewers are more likely than light viewers to think that the world is like what is presented on television.

Cultivation research started with studies of violent television content by George Gerbner and his associates at the University of Pennsylvania during the early 1970s. They found that heavier viewers tended to perceive the real world as more violent, similar to television's world, than it really was. A person who watched television 8 hours or more a day overestimated his or her chance of being a crime victim.

A steady viewing diet of *NYPD Blue, Homicide: Life on the Street,* and other police shows could easily create the impression of a scary, violent world. Just as important as what is watched is how much viewing takes place. Time spent watching television reduces exposure to reality. Without experience to counteract television, the TV world becomes reality. Dozens of studies have found a variety of limited cultivation effects in addition to violence. These include depression, changed political attitudes, sexism, and stereotyping.

Most scholars do not doubt that television affects people's perceptions of reality. However, just how much impact it has, and on how many people, remains in question. Cultivation research has found a consistent but weak relationship between television viewing and some people's view of the world. This finding is weakened further by the question of how other factors come into play. These factors might reduce the impact of cultivation.[31]

DEPENDENCY THEORY Sandra Ball-Rokeach and Melvin DeFleur tied together a variety of effects research with dependency theory.[32] Their theory explains why the impact of media varies from person to person and from situation to situation. It states that the system of media organizations controls information that people depend on to live. At the same time, people and groups in a society control scare resources, such as information and money, that media companies need to survive. This mutual dependency between media and individuals defines the effects that each group has on the other.

Keyconcept

Dependency Theory: Research exploring this theory identifies the dependency relationships among people, media, and social systems and explains how these affect people and groups.

The community newspaper illustrates this mutual dependency. Readers depend on the newspaper to help them know what has happened, and what will happen, in a community. People read the newspaper to learn the decisions of the city council, the results of the high school football game, who's getting married, who died, and when local events will take place. The newspaper journalists in turn depend on the local citizens to tell them what is happening in the community. The newspaper company depends on the community to support the newspaper with advertising and subscriptions.

In addition to dependency between media organizations and individuals, dependency theory also states that social systems are dependent. The political system depends on media to help inform the electorate, and the media system depends on the political system to define its freedoms and to maintain a stable economic environment. The mutual dependency among social systems, groups, and individuals means that all these types of units affect each other.

Dependency theory suggests that media affect individuals in six ways:

1. *Self-understanding:* People depend on media to learn about themselves and to grow as individuals.

2. *Social understanding:* People depend on media to learn about the world and their community.

3. *Action orientation:* People depend on media to decide what to buy and how to act.

4. *Interaction orientation:* People depend on media to decide how to behave toward other people.

5. *Solitary play:* People depend on media to divert and entertain them when they are alone.

6. *Social play:* People depend on media to entertain them when they are with friends and family.

The importance of media in these six activities varies from person to person, across time, and from activity to activity. An introverted person may use media more for solitary play; an extrovert may use media to interact with others. People create their own mix of media information, and some people depend more on one type of media than on another.

The overall impact of media on a person depends on availability of nonmediated information, the individual's goals and interest, and the individual's background. The famous American "couch potato," for instance, depends greatly on television for play and social orientation. The couch potato's images of society and how people act reflect what he or she sees on television. However, if that couch potato gets tired of watching reruns on cable and joins in church activities, his or her ideas about how other people behave will be shaped also by the church members. Media content alone does not shape people's images of their surroundings.

503

Research and Computers

Probably 90 percent of all the research ever conducted on mass communication has been produced during the past 35 years. Part of this explosion of productivity represents the growth in the number of mass communication scholars. However, a large part also reflects the contribution of the computer. Computers enable better statistical analysis and better writing, both of which save time and improve the quality of research.

Large mainframe computers first contributed to mass communication research. In the late 1950s and early 1960s these room-sized computers allowed researchers to conduct statistical calculations in seconds that once took months of work with mechanical calculators. In addition to the time savings, scholars could use even more sophisticated forms of statistics. A researcher who wanted to look at the impact of advertising on men could control for education and income and just examine gender. This ability to isolate factors leads to more accurate conclusions.

Researchers continue to use mainframes, although they are smaller than the monsters of the 1950s. But the memory capacity of personal computers allows PCs to process statistics almost as fast as mainframes can.

After the calculations are complete, scholars use their personal computers to write articles and reports based on the research. These articles can take several drafts and often have to be rewritten for different publications and conferences. The computers allow great flexibility because once an article is written, it can be altered easily for a different medium. PCs also allow quicker and more efficient editing.

The current trend is toward laptop and notebook PCs. Today, a researcher can analyze data and write reports while waiting for an airplane. This is quite a contrast to the days of slide rules and typewriters.

Dependency theory also discusses interaction between groups and social systems. The more dependent one social group is on another, the more power it loses. For example, mass media depend on businesses for the bulk of their revenue in the form of advertising. When a magazine receives a large amount of revenue from a few companies, those companies can influence the media content. Some consumer magazines must include stories that are favorable to large advertisers or risk losing their ad money.

Dependency theory is important because it unites several strains of effects research by incorporating elements of psychology, sociology, and economics. It explains the variation in media effects from person to person and from situation to situation.

■ Characterizing effects research

Ever since effects research began, the overriding question about media effects has been: How powerful an effect do mass media have on the public? Most answers to this question have concentrated on the numbers of people who are affected. Because of this focus, media effects have been characterized as powerful, moderate, or weak according to the numbers of people who exhibit the effects.[33]

However, effects research demonstrates that people are not all alike when it comes to media impact. The same content may have a strong influence on some but no impact at all on others. This suggests two dimensions in characterizing mass media effects: *extent* and *intensity*. The *extent* of media impact means the number of people affected. The *intensity* means how strong the impact is on the people who are affected. A particular media message could have a very intense impact on a small number of people, while another might have a slight impact on a large number of people.

Most children who watch the *Teenage Mutant Ninja Turtles* or the *Mighty Morphin Power Rangers* do not become violent. However, some do. In 1994 the Oslo, Norway, police investigated the connection between television and the death of a five-year-old girl. Three boys, aged five and six, stoned and kicked the girl and left her in the snow, where she froze to death. Early indications were that the boys were fans of the Ninja Turtles, who beat up their enemies with karate kicks.[34] Norwegian television banned the program after the death. However, later there was some doubt about whether the boys were influenced by the program.

Such examples are unusual because media usually affect people over a longer period of time—not quickly. However, children often imitate their favorite television characters. News stories also can have very extensive and intensive effects. When an earthquake strikes Southern California, media coverage creates an immediate sense of disaster throughout the country.

On the whole, research indicates that media do not have powerful or weak effects; they have **contingent effects.** Media content's impact is contingent on many factors. Some involve the content; some reflect the situation surrounding media use; and some involve the background of the media consumer.

Media scholars are concerned about the effects of television on individuals, particularly on children. Studies of violence and of heavy television watching indicate that media effects can be negative, as well as positive. The critical question is whether media contribute to the development of a good society. Such a statement involves many assumptions and unanswered questions.

The contingency approach makes predicting media effects more difficult, but this difficulty reflects the highly complex nature of how people select, use, and are affected by media content. Eventually, contingency research will make prediction more accurate, even if it is more difficult.

Cultural studies today

James Carey, writing from the mid-1970s onward, revived the community orientation of American cultural studies. Carey resisted the empiricists, who viewed communication as a transmission process. As you learned in Chapter 2, one model of communication includes a sender, a medium, and a receiver. Although interference of various kinds can affect the message, the task is to get the message intact from the sender to receiver. Carey argued that the transmission model did not adequately represent communication; instead, communication

contingent effects: Effects that are caused by contingent, or indirect variables, rather than by direct impact of media content.

should be viewed as a process through which a shared culture is created, modified, and transformed. Communication is not an extension of messages in space, but the maintenance of society across time. Carey further argued that communication was not the imparting of information or influence but the creation and transmission of shared beliefs. Carey has made an explicit effort to pursue cultural studies without reducing "culture to ideology, social conflict to class conflict, consent to compliance, action to reproduction, or communication to coercion." He writes convincingly that mass media should be viewed as a site, not as a discipline or subject, on "which to engage the general question of social theory." Communication, writes Carey, "is a symbolic process whereby reality is produced, maintained, repaired, and transformed."[35]

Keyconcept

Critical Studies: This broad category includes the study of power and ideology. It can take the form of historical analysis, textual analysis, or the study of news production, as well as of other investigations into media and society.

Carey's work built on that of Raymond Williams and Stuart Hall, both of whom were actively arguing the concept of culture and communications in the 1970s, during the period when empirical research was in ascendancy. Williams was then a fellow of Jesus College at Cambridge, and Stuart Hall was director of the Centre for the Study of Contemporary Culture at the University of Birmingham, which has become the center of Britain's cultural approach to communications. Williams and Hall both argued against using the term "mass communications research" because, expressed that way, it seemed to have little to do with culture. Also influential in the 1970s and beyond was Clifford Geertz, who, in his study of primitive cultures, attempted to explain the dilemma of describing the universality of human nature while acknowledging the importance of historical and cultural context.

During the 1980s and 1990s, Carey's optimistic views of community, communication, and culture were countered by scholars who are more oriented toward the study of the influence of power. *Political economy* scholars, for example, (1) look at "how capitalists use their economic power with a commercial market system to ensure that the flow of public information is consonant with their interests" and (2) "attempt to understand how meaning is made and remade through the concrete activities of producers and consumers." [36]

Hermeneutics (an ancient technique of analyzing scriptural and literary texts), semiotics (the study of culture as a formal system of signs and what they signify), and ethnography (the anthropological tracing of cultures), remain significant tools for investigating the connection between communication and culture.

Uses of media

Research about how consumers use media falls under the heading of uses and gratifications research, which tries to identify why and how people use various media and what types of rewards they get from media content. Effects research examines what media *do to people;* uses and gratifications research examined what people *do with* media.

Early uses and gratifications research classified the reasons people decide to view, read, or listen to media. A 1972 article stated that people use media to get information, to help them understand their personal identity, to interact and integrate socially, and to entertain themselves.[37] A more recent classification says that people use media for surveillance of the environment, for making decisions, for entertainment and diversion, and for social and cultural interaction.[38] This classification system also suggests that uses of media vary with the time. Some media content is used immediately and then forgotten; other content will be remembered for use later.

According to the second classification system, a person might read the comics for immediate entertainment but read the editorial page to form an opinion about a political

TABLE 16.1 Examples of Media Uses

These examples fit into the various categories of media uses. The same use of media can fit more than one category, as shown by including Shakespeare under both social/cultural interaction and diversion and entertainment.

	IMMEDIATE USE	DELAYED USE
SURVEILLANCE	Checking the cable weather channel in the morning	Following stock market trends
DECISION MAKING	Looking at the movie listings Friday afternoon	Reading about VCRs in *Consumer Reports*
SOCIAL/CULTURAL INTERACTION	Listening to Bush during a keg party	Reading Shakespeare
DIVERSION AND ENTERTAINMENT	Reading the comics page in the daily newspaper	Reading Shakespeare

candidate. The formation of such an opinion often occurs over time. Table 16.1 shows some of the specific uses of media that would fit within this classification system.

As the table illustrates, the same media content can be used in more than one way. Reading *Romeo and Juliet* by William Shakespeare contributes to social/cultural interaction because it is a classic play that has been made into several movies. It teaches about the pain caused by intolerance. At the same time the play can be excellent entertainment immediately and on a delayed basis. Art provides both immediate enjoyment and the delayed enjoyment that comes when we remember it.

Scholars have criticized uses and gratifications research for a variety of reasons.[39] One of the strongest critiques argues that the research is **atheoretical,** that it lists uses and gratifications but does not explain people's motivation for using media for these gratifications. Some research studies are exploring the relationship between motivation and uses, but much still needs to be learned.

Uses and gratifications research has also been criticized for its assumption of an active audience that makes decisions about media use. The critics contend that people use media in a passive way, out of habit. Both assumptions are true. People use media habitually, but they also purposely select some media content. Indeed, habit can be viewed as an active, purposeful behavior. People often watch television news while they eat dinner because it is convenient. This habit developed because making a decision every night about watching television news would take more time than is necessary. Future research will need to incorporate both active and passive media uses if they are to explain media behavior.

Influences on content

Just as a variety of factors determine the uses and effects of media, several types of influences shape media content. These influences can be classified as individual, organizational, economic, and ideological factors. *Individual influences* include the psychological makeup of the people creating the content. *Organizational influences* involve the work routines, social interaction, and ownership goals found in media organizations and in the organizations covered by media. *Economic influences* involve the demand for media content and competition for media consumers. *Ideological influences* include the shared values and beliefs that are found in a social system.

atheoretical: Lacking a theoretical basis.

These types of factors can work singly or together to influence media content. For example, a famous and successful novelist has more independence than does a beginning newspaper journalist. The famous novelist will be edited but ultimately has individual control over the book's content. The newspaper reporter depends on sources' statements to shape the story. This dependence reflects the organizational influence of work routines and professional ideology. Then an editor changes the story to fit available space, on the basis of the news value of the story. The available space depends on the amount of advertising sold by the newspaper, which reflects economic influence.

The nature of the medium affects content, as well. Television, for example, runs stories that have strong visual and emotional impact, such as stories about fires and accidents. Meetings do not make for riveting television unless people shout at each other. Newspapers, by contrast, can cover both fires and meetings effectively because print can be more abstract and still be effective.

Media garner national audiences for local human interest stories. Here, the Grand Forks Flood of 1997 became a national story, with a sympathetic audience that responded to the plight of staunch North Dakotans.

Individual factors

As was mentioned earlier, gatekeeping research examines the role of individual biases on the selection of news. As with all decisions, a journalist's perceptions will affect the decisions to include one source instead of another, to emphasize a particular idea, and to pick a particular quotation. During the past twenty years, scholars have examined the impact of individual characteristics, such as gender and professional beliefs, on content creation. Much of the research has concentrated on journalists, but the results have implications for a broader range of communicators.

Research about gender and content is inconclusive, but this reflects a limited number of studies. One study found that magazines with female publishers carried more favorable coverage of the Equal Rights Amendment than did those with male publishers.[40] Other scholars have argued that a journalist's gender has little effect because the definition of news is determined by the men who dominate journalism.[41] If this is the case, perhaps gender's influence is a socializing one, and when the number of women in power becomes large enough to overcome male definitions of news, coverage changes. Indeed, Robinson found that the amount of newspaper space given to news that is of interest to women increased as the percentage of editors who were women increased.[42]

Equally important in creating media content is the individual's perception of her or his journalistic role and acceptance of professional standards. Weaver and Wilhoit identified three roles journalists hold for themselves.[43] The *dissemination role* involves collecting information objectively and distributing it quickly to a large audience. The *interpretative role* requires journalists to investigate sources' claims and to analyze and explain complex issues to their audience. The *adversary role* assumes that journalists should act as antagonists to politicians and businesses. Adversarial journalists act as representatives for their audience to counterbalance powerful economic and political interests.

The interpretive role is supported by the highest percentage of journalists, followed by the disseminator and adversary roles. However, only a small fraction of journalists believe that journalists should be limited to a single role. All three serve news consumers in different ways at different times.

Also important in influencing content is the idea of professionalism. Media work is not professional in the ways that law and medicine are. Communicators cannot be licensed like doctors because this would violate the First Amendment guarantee of freedom of speech. Nor do journalists have a body of knowledge that they must learn, as lawyers do. But many communicators approach their work as if it were a profession. This includes accepting a code of ethics and treating the reader, listener, or viewer as a client. One study found that journalists who had motivations based on ethics were more likely to perform well in their jobs than were journalists who had other motivations.[44]

Shoemaker and Reese concluded that organizational factors have more influence than individual factors on media content, but individual background can affect what is produced.[45] Of particular importance are ethics and professional attitudes.

■ Organizational factors

Organizational factors take two forms. The first includes the socialization processes and work routines that are found within a media organization. The other involves the interaction between journalists and people from outside the organization. The study of organization factors dates from the beginning research on content influences. Warren Breed's 1955 study of socialization in news organizations continues to be applicable today. Media organizations tend to enforce policy more through social interaction than through formal policy.

Mark Fishman continued the work started by Breed and Tuchman. He found that journalists often face story quotas and overwork. This limits the time they can spend working on a story and makes them dependent on sources. When journalists do not have time to verify sources' statements, they often accept the statements at face value. Some journalists overcome these limits to pursue stories in more depth, but they usually do this on their own time.[46]

Research about the interaction of sources and journalists has continued along the lines started by Gieber and Johnson's work. A 1972 study of TV journalists found patterns of reporter-source relationships that were similar to those established by these two early researchers. The study concluded that journalists who do not assimilate the values of their sources are respected most by their sources.[47] A politician who can manipulate a journalist need not respect or fear that journalist.

Sources also influence story ideas. A study of six suburban dailies found that the ideas for 86 percent of the stories that were published during a week came from people associated with some form of organization. Fifty-two percent came from government sources, but more experienced reporters were less dependent on the government sources for story ideas.[48] Young reporters who lack knowledge about their beat have a hard time evaluating news on that beat. A city council that is about to raise taxes might give a reporter a lot of information about the city's recent designation as an "All-American City" and downplay the facts about the tax proposal. An inexperienced reporter might miss the significance of the tax issue.

One area that received extensive attention during the 1980s and 1990s involved the impact of company ownership on content. Scholars such as Ben Bagdikian[49] have argued that newspapers and television stations owned by a corporation that had many media outlets perform differently than those that were owned by an individual or family. It is fairly easy to find examples of situations in which corporate managers have interfered with local newspaper editors or have reduced news budgets. However, it also is fairly easy to find corporate managers who have invested heavily in newsrooms to improve coverage.

Research results have been mixed, but the bulk of research about newspapers indicates only minor variations in content when group and independent newspapers are compared.[50] Research about group ownership of television and radio also found no important differences in content.[51] The goals of a particular organization determine the impact of ownership on content. An independent newspaper company that wants a high profit will produce content that is similar to the content produced by a group-owned newspaper with high profit goals.

Group ownership appears to be less important than the type of the group. One study concluded that the more stock the public owns in a media corporation, the less profit the company reinvests into its media outlets.[52] This reflects the pressure of public stock ownership to distribute profits as dividends. Demand for a stock determines prices. The more profit that is given to stockholders, the higher the price people will pay for the stock. The result of giving profits to stockholders instead of reinvesting them will be smaller newsroom budgets. If a budget shrinks enough, news coverage will suffer.

■ Market factors

Market factors include forces outside the organization, such as government regulations, economic competition, and consumer demand. Government regulations establish acceptable types of market behavior. Governments regulate some media more than others, television being the most regulated, followed by cable and radio.

An important regulation involves cross-ownership of media outlets. *Cross-ownership* means that one company owns a newspaper and a broadcast station in the same city. Studies conducted during the 1970s found that markets with cross-ownership had less diverse news coverage, less total news available, and lower public knowledge about public affairs than did markets without cross-ownership.[53] The impact comes from news organizations sharing their news, which results in fewer reporters covering the market.

As a result, the Federal Communication Commission will not grant new broadcast licenses to newspapers. However, a few combinations continue to exist because they existed when the cross-ownership rules were put into effect. Debate over allowing cross-ownership reemerged during the mid-1990s. The argument for allowing cross-ownership states that the increased number of radio and television stations in a market reduces the negative impact of cross-ownership. The larger number of stations will now guarantee competition despite cross-ownership. The FCC was reexamining cross-ownership rules in 1997, as a result of the 1996 Telecommunications Act. However, the majority of markets do not have a large number of news voices (newspapers and electronic media newsrooms), and the impact on these smaller markets of removing cross-ownership rules remains uncertain.

Competition can have an impact on content, depending on the type of competition and the intensity. Competition between newspapers can affect the amount of money that is available to the newsrooms and the amount of space that is available to readers. This is called the *financial commitment model*.[54] As competition increases, the newspaper's managers spend more money to make the newspaper different from the competition's paper. This differentiation tries to attract readers from the competition, but the news product must also remain similar enough to its competition so it will be considered a substitute. The financial commitment model applies to local television news as well as to newspapers.

The exact impact of financial commitment varies from market to market, but the key to its effect has to do with the intensity of competition. Competition grows as the percentages of media consumers who use competing media outlets get close to being equal. If two television newscasts have equal shares, say 25, each will try to gain a larger share by taking viewers from the competition. The station that has the larger share can charge higher prices for the advertising spots. Increased newsroom spending becomes an investment in getting more viewers, with the goal of making higher profits.

Even though competition can improve news coverage, it also has a darker side. Some news organizations differentiate their newspapers and newscasts by using sensationalism. Two newscasts that have similar audience shares may hire more reporters, but those

Using Research

Professional communicators sometimes criticize academic mass communication research as too theoretical. The criticism stems from two sources. First, academic scholars often explore abstract questions. The editor of the *Grand Prairie Gazette* wants to know how she can keep readers from dropping their subscriptions to her newspaper. The academic scholar wants to know why readers decide to read newspapers. The two questions are related, but the first requires a quick answer that is specific to one newspaper. The academic scholar's research involves a long series of projects. The academic research results can be a useful guide for newspaper editors, but it will be too general to apply to the *Gazette.* without more specific research.

The second reason for criticism concerns the use of statistics. Statistical analysis allows researchers to find patterns of behavior among large numbers of people or organizations. Sometimes these patterns are difficult to discover using reporting methods but are easy to find with statistics. To someone who has no training in statistical analysis, the terms seem like gobbledygook. But statistics are part of a language that can be useful.

Communication professionals can learn from statistical analysis if they understand the language or have a competent person translate the results.

Mass communication research affects society in many ways. It provides educators with a better understanding of why and how mass media operate and how their content affects people. Writers use research as a basis for texts, and professors use research for lectures. As research refines what people know about mass communication, it replaces the old knowledge and becomes the basis for future education.

Researchers provided information in the 1990s as Congress prepared to pass the Telecommunications Act in 1996. Research also provides ideas that professionals can use. Public relations practitioners study research about sources and reporters to understand how they can and should communicate with journalists. Research about dependence on government explained why news media covered the civil rights movement so poorly during the 1960s. As a result, many newspapers now have topical beats, such as the environment.

Mass communication research can provide enlightenment or confusion. As with all information, the person who uses it must evaluate it. However, research is central to a society that seeks answers in an open marketplace of ideas.

---

reporters might end up covering more accidents and murders. Viewers may see more crime scenes than public affairs reporting. Just how competition translates into news content rests on the professionalism of the managers and the manager's perception of what the viewers want to see.

The competition between entertainment channels is also based on attracting the largest audience, but these channels focus on attracting groups that exhibit the demographic characteristics that advertisers want. Entertainment creators design content to appeal to groups that are defined by advertisers. Top 40 radio stations play songs that attract teenagers and young adults. Radio then sells advertising time to businesses that want to reach these groups. Disney films target young children and their parents. Action films attract young adult film viewers.

Characterizing content influence research

Social science characterizes content influences by classifying them into various types. This approach proves useful because it allows each type of factor to be isolated and studied. However, this approach makes a very complicated process seem too simple. It

512

is not easy to determine whether individual factors affect content creation more than organizational factors do. Just as with effects research, content influences involve contingencies.

Organization influences will affect content more when the media organization has little competition. When competition is intense, media companies respond more directly to consumers' wants. If a cable viewer can choose between MTV and VH-1, the managers of the two music video channels will have a good idea what content their particular viewers want, and they will give the viewers that content.

Large organizations reduce the influence an individual has on the final content. One of the concerns of scholars and critics has been the loss of individual autonomy within larger and larger media organizations. This concern may be lessened as new computer technologies allow individuals more power to communicate personally with others. But the exact impact of these factors on content remains undetermined. The next step in content research involves developing theories that explain these contingencies.

rends

Mass communication research remains a young field of scholarly inquiry compared to other social sciences. As a result, many questions remain unanswered. In the eighty years since the end of World War I, the field has changed from focusing almost entirely on individual and societal effects to include a study of factors that influence content creation. During this period, better forms of empirical investigation have also developed. As a result of these developments, three trends suggest the direction that future scholarship will take: contingency research, more theory, and integrated theory.

■ Contingency research

Increasingly, research into mass communication has demonstrated the complexity of studying communication's effects and content. In addition to the content, other factors, such as age, socioeconomic status, and motivation, play a role in the ways that media messages affect people and society. Content in media can be changed by competition, public ownership, background of creators, ideology, and information-gathering routines.

The impact of any one factor on content or effects is dependent upon a variety of other factors, which can be called "contingent" factors. For example, the impact of competition on television news is contingent upon the intensity of that competition, the way individual reporters respond to competition, and the resources of the newsrooms. The impact of TV violence on children may be contingent upon how much time is spent watching the violence, the graphic nature of video, comments about the violence from parents, and the actions of playmates.

Mass communication will continue to explore these contingent conditions. The issue for future research will be under what conditions do media contribute to certain behaviors, and under what conditions do certain factors affect media content.

■ More theory

Much of mass communication research has been aimed at developing empirical evidence. Studies identify relationships among factors, such as how news routines affect issues and how events become news. Less effort has been made to work these results into formal theories. Such formal theories specify the relationships among the factors far more exactingly than summaries of empirical results. Formal theories explain how factors should be measured and which types of empirical results support theories.

For a variety of reasons, mass communication researchers lag behind other social science fields in having formal theory. A major contributing element to this lag is the youth of the field. As a field that can be separated from other social sciences, such as economics and psychology, mass communication scholarship is only about fifty years old. A movement within the field is pushing scholarship in the direction of creating more formal theory.

Integrated theory

As a result of empirical studies and syntheses of research, mass communication scholars have a good handle on what types of factors contribute to mass communication content and what types of effects that content has. This will help build theory, but the field needs to include integrated theory as part of this process. Integrated theory combines the two main subdivisions of mass communication research: the study of what factors affect content and the effects of that content on people.

If society is concerned about the impact of violent TV and movies on children, it can follow the traditional approach. This means that some scholars will study the impact of violent video on children, while others will study the factors that lead to the media companies creating these violent programs. However, it would be useful to have these two groups connect the entire process into theory that would be helpful in solving problems as well as identifying them.

In the United States, the First Amendment protects content and therefore makes it difficult to alter media impact through content control. Society is willing to allow some negative effects of media content to preserve the positive effects. If people want to change content that has been found to have negative effects, they can do so by understanding the forces that contribute to the creation of the content.

For example, violent television programs make some children more aggressive. However, this impact is contingent upon many factors. Because of research into these contingencies and because of research about why the content is created, people have options for taking action to contract the negative effects. If parents and schools discuss the violence and what is and is not acceptable behavior, TV loses some of its power to influence. If parents prevent their children from watching unacceptable programs and write letters about why, the networks and cable channels will alter the content as ratings decline.

Tying the research together with integrated theory will allow people to connect the creation process with the effects of mass communication. These types of theories will go a long way toward allowing people not only to understand the nature and impact of media, but to have some control over that impact as well.

Summary

- Mass communication research plays an important role in teaching and public policy. This research produces knowledge about the impact of mass media and allows for some control over it.

- Mass communication research takes two approaches. The social science approach examines the behavior of individuals and groups associated with mass communication, and the cultural approach (also called the critical approach) emphasizes the connections between media and society.

- Early social science communication research concentrated on media effects.

514

- Critical studies developed from two major schools: the Frankfurt School in Germany and the Chicago School.

- World War I propaganda led researchers to believe that media had an all-powerful (magic bullet) effect.

- By 1940, researchers began to shift their thinking to a limited effects model, which suggested that interpersonal influences were as great as were media influences.

- Social science researchers now adhere to moderate effects models and are interested in the factors that contribute to media effects.

- An active area of political effects research is agenda setting, which deals with the impact of media on the political issues that are discussed by the public and addressed by government.

- Dependency theory holds great promise for individual effects research. It identifies the dependency relationships among people, media, and social systems and explains how these affect people and groups.

- Media uses research is an offshoot of effects studies. Uses research explores why and how people select media content.

- Research about factors that determine media content concentrates on several types of influences. Important among these are individual, organizational, economic, and ideological influences.

- Critical studies research involves the study of power and ideology. It can take the form of historical analysis, textual analysis, or the study of news production as well as other investigations into media and society.

- The Chicago School explored communication as a foundation for community in a postindustrial world.

- Supporters of the Chicago School took a more positive approach toward the impact of communication in society than did scholars in the Frankfurt School.

- Recent cultural studies scholars have emphasized the role of media in creating social reality and in maintaining political power.

Navigating the Web

Mass communication research on the web

Research resources are rich on the World Wide Web. As you saw in Chapter 3, archival materials for historical research are becoming increasingly accessible. In the other chapters you read that material about media, as well as forms of media, are also being designed into the Internet. Here are some sites that specialize in mass communication research.

The Media and Communication Studies Site   http://www.aber.ac.uk/~dgc/media.html

This site at the University of Wales, Aberystwyth, has large numbers of links to communication studies and research sites throughout the world.

This site lists most of the mass media research articles published in the United States between 1984 and the present.

This page is maintained by the Freedom Forum Media Studies Center. It provides articles about a variety of media and issues, including survey results and a daily news summary compiled from several publications.

The site contains bibliographies of academic research in a variety of media, lists of texts, and a few syllabi from courses. It also has links to several extensive lists of other useful links.

Questions for review

1. What is empirical research?
2. What were the major schools of cultural studies in the United States?
3. What is a social science theory? What is it used for?
4. What is the difference between effects and uses research?
5. What is the two-step flow theory?
6. What is the spiral of silence?

Issues to think about

1. What are the possible effects of the gatekeeping process on mass media content?
2. Pick a current topic in the news and discuss the implications of the agenda-setting concept on how this issue might be dealt with.
3. Discuss dependency theory and its connection to media effects.
4. Explain the different theoretical perspectives in social science research and cultural studies approaches. What separate contribution does each approach make in understanding mass communication?
5. Discuss some possible organizational influences on content.
6. Discuss some possible individual influences on content.

Suggested readings

DeFleur, M. L., and Sandra Ball-Rokeach, *Theories of Mass Communication,* 2nd ed. (New York: David McKay, 1982).

Lazarsfeld, P., B. Berelson, and H. Gaudet, *The People's Choice* (New York: Columbia University Press, 1948).

Wartella, Ellen, "Children and Television: The Development of the Child's Understanding of the Medium," in G. Wilhoit & H. deBock, eds., *Mass Communication Review Yearbook* (Beverly Hills: Sage Publications, 1980).

Wimmer, Roger D., and Joseph R. Dominick, *Mass Media Research: An Introduction* (Belmont, Calif: Wadsworth, 1994).

Glossary

A & B pictures: Studios commission or produce two types of films. A films are usually high budget films that studios expect to be box office hits. B films are low budget films that are basic money-makers. Studios invest little money in their production and marketing.

Absence of actual malice: A libel defense that means that a person must prove actual malice on the part of a reporter to win a libel suit.

Absolute ethics: A code of ethics that allows no deviation from its rules.

Accuracy: The reporting of information in context that allows people to understand and comprehend the truth.

Action film: A type of movie that emphasizes physical activities, such as car chases, fighting and explosions. Such films usually have simple plots and only limited development of the characters.

Action orientation: People depend on media to decide what to buy and how to act.

Adoptions: The decision of a school system to use a particular textbook.

Adversary role: Journalists should act as antagonists to politicians and businesses. They are representatives for their audience to counterbalance powerful economic and political interests.

Advertising market: This market involves selling the attention of readers, viewers, and listeners to advertisers. Business and other groups buy time or space in this market to influence what people buy or believe.

Advertising planning: All forms of advertising agency services including creative production, media buying, research services, and merchandising.

Advertorial: Combination of an advertisement and an editorial. Designed to look like an editorial but is actually a paid message.

Alien and Sedition Acts: Federalist laws passed in 1798 to restrict freedom of information.

Allocative control: Control over how money is spent by an organization.

AM: Stands for amplitude modulation, which is a way of attaching sound to radio waves. See modulators.

America Online (AOL): The online information service with the most subscribers in 1997.

Anthology: In the 1950s, a favorite television format, which consisted of stage plays remade for TV.

Antinomian ethics: The absence of an ethical code to guide decisions. Each case is evaluated on its own merits.

Apartheid: Strict racial segregation. Usually associated with South Africa's political system that was overthrown in the early 1990s.

Areas of dominant influence (ADI): Areas defined by the ratings company Arbitron for purposes of reporting listener data.

Art theater: Theater that shows films designed for their artistic quality rather than for their block-buster audience appeal. These films usually are produced by independent companies rather than by the big studios.

Association magazines: Magazines published by various associations to publicize their activities and communicate with their members.

Atex system: A centralized computer system used for word processing.

Atheoretical: Lacking a theoretical basis.

Audimeters: A meter for measuring audience demand for programs. Audimeters installed in homes record when a set is turned on, which channels it is tuned to, and for how long.

Audion: A three-electrode vacuum tube amplifier that was the basis of the electronic revolution that permitted the development of radio.

Audit: Checking the truthfulness of reader and viewer figures reported by a media company.

Awareness: In advertising, consumers must know that a product or service exists before they can decide to buy it.

Bias: A subconscious or intentional slant in reporting on a subject because of one's beliefs or prejudice on the issue. Such bias may or may not be obvious to the viewer or reader, who may have received incomplete or incorrect information.

Blacklist: A list of individuals compiled with the express purpose of forcing them out of their jobs. Used during the 1950s to label certain individuals as Communists and to force them out of the information and entertainment industries.

Blind booking: Marketing strategy common in the 1930s and 1940s that required theaters to book movies before they were produced.

Block booking: Declared illegal in the 1940s. The practice by movie studios of forcing a theater to book several movies as a package, rather than being able to choose them individually.

Bop: Jazz that developed during the 1940s as a reaction to big band swing music. Usually performed by small groups with fast tempos and conflicting rhythms. Also called be-bop.

Boutique agency: An advertising agency that specializes in creative services and restricts its activities to a few specialties.

Breaking stories: News stories that are continuing to develop as they are covered.

Breakout boxes: Shorter pieces of information, often direct quotes, that are connected to the larger story being covered. They are used to emphasize specific points and for design relief.

Broadside: Handbills, also called broadsheets, that were printed only on one side.

Broadside ballads: Songs and poems printed on single sheets of newsprint.

Brokering: The practice of buying space at a discount from publishers and selling it at a higher rate to advertisers.

Business ads: Ads designed to influence people's attitudes and behaviors toward the products and services a business sells, toward the business itself, or toward an idea that the business supports.

Camera obscura: Photography that dates to classic Greece. A completely dark room had a tiny hole in one wall that focused an upside-down, reversed left-to-right image on the opposite wall or a white screen.

Camera-ready copy: Collection of stories (copy), photographs and headlines that have been edited and placed on a large page. Ready to be photographed and made into a plate for printing.

Capital intensive: A production process that requires a large investment of money.

Capital investment: Start-up money. Funds spent for acquisition or improvement of equipment of technology.

Categorical imperative: In ethics this means that principles should be analyzed to see what principles could be applied universally—what is right for one is right for all.

CD-ROM: Compact diskette with read only memory. An electronic storage diskette with enough memory to support multi-media applications.

Censorship: Restricting access to information, deleting information from a story, or refusing to let a correspondent mail, broadcast, or otherwise transmit a story.

Channel: A way of transmitting a message from a person or group of people to a person or group of people, e.g., a telephone line or newspaper.

Channel noise: Interference in a communication channel, e.g., static on a radio.

Chapbooks: Cheaply printed paperback books produced during the 1700s.

Chartoon: A combination of a cartoon and a chart.

Chat groups: People who discuss a specific topic using computers for two-way communication at a specific time.

Checkbook journalism: Paying subjects or witnesses for information or interviews.

Chicano: A U.S. citizen of Mexican descent.

Cinerama: Trade name for process that produces wide-screen images.

Circulation: The number of copies sold by a newspaper during its production cycle (week or day).

City editor: An editor who manages the "city desk," which is the group of journalists who report and write about the city in which the newspaper is located.

Clear and present danger rule: Created by Justice Oliver Wendell Holmes at the close of the Schenck case in World War I. Holmes argued that to suppress material one must be able to argue that such material presented a clear and present danger to the country that the government had a right to prevent.

Coaxial cable: Cable that contains two conductors: a solid central core surrounded by a tubelike hollow one. Air or solid insulation separates the two. Electromagnetic energy, such as television transmission signals, travels between the two conductors.

Comics: Drawings that are provided primarily as entertainment for readers.

Commercial application: Viewing of prerecorded tapes and disks and the use of video by companies for training and communications.

Commercial appropriation: An invasion of privacy that involves putting someone in a commercial without getting permission.

Commercial stations: Stations in business primarily to make a profit.

Communication: Gathering, organizing, presenting, and disseminating information.

Communication software: Provides connections from one computer to another.

Compositor: The person who sets type and composes the plates from which a newspaper is printed.

Computer operating systems: These are the programs that tell the computer how to behave. DOS and Windows, produced by Microsoft, dominate the world market for operating systems. The MacIntosh operating system is second; it is used by about one tenth as many machines as the Microsoft systems.

Computer language: An intermediate programming language designed for programmers' convenience that is converted into machine language.

Conflict: A disagreement among people, i.e., difference in ideas or physical as in crime or war.

Conglomerate: A corporation formed by merging separate and diverse businesses under one ownership. The term usually means a media company is owned by a corporation with nonmedia businesses.

Consonance: The presentation of a consistent unified picture of the political world.

Consumer market: This market involves delivering information to readers, viewers, and listeners and the purpose varies from entertainment to persuasion to education.

Contingent effects: Effects that are influenced by contingent, or indirect variables, rather than just by direct impact of media contact.

Contracted services: These occur when an organization hires someone outside the organization to perform services instead of putting an employee on the payroll.

Controlled circulation: Technique of sending magazines free to individuals within an industry to increase identification with an organization.

Convergence: Coming together.

Coping information: Information that will help readers to live more efficiently and easily.

Copy-cat programming: When a network's new show pulls good ratings, other networks will quickly produce shows with similar plots or casts of characters. The process has three stages: invention, when new types of shows are developed; imitation, when similar shows are produced; and decline, when these types of programs decline in popularity.

Copyright: A law that protects authors, playwrights, composers, and others who construct original works and keeps others from reproducing work without permission.

Corporate downsizing: A term popularized during the 1990s used when a company laid off employees to lower their business costs.

CPM: Cost-per-thousand. A shortcut reference to how much it costs an advertiser to reach one thousand readers. M is the roman Numeral for 1000.

Creative production: All the steps in creating advertisements for various media.

Credibility: A measurement of how well a journalist or media organization is trusted. If a high percentage of the public perceives a journalist as truthful, that person has credibility.

Crier: A person who walked around the streets and "cried out" the news to the people. Preceded printed news.

Critical scholars: Those interested in the intersection of media and everyday life and often focus on the relationship of the media text to its audience.

Cultivation theory: Heavy television viewing influences people to adopt values, roles, and world views that are based on television.

Cultural theorists: Those that look at the symbolic meaning behind behavior.

Cumulation: The increasing effect of media across time.

Cumulative weekly audience: The total number of people who listen to radio during a given week in a given market.

Cyberspace: The concept of psychological space behind the computer screen.

Cybersurfing: Browsing through the Internet, the World Wide Web, or any online service

Databases: Software for recording statistics. Data can be sorted in categories and reports printed in various forms. Used by businesses who need to sort customers by zip code, for example.

Decision making: Collecting information to be able to select among options.

Dedicated technology: Piece of equipment dedicated to one purpose; early videotex equipment could be used only for receiving the videotex service, not to retrieve other information or for entertainment. Requirements for dedicated technology hamper development of services.

Defamation: To misconstrue facts or misrepresent a person in such a way as to lower the individual in the estimation of others.

Demand structure: This determines the nature of the aggregate demand for a product or service and involves three characteristics: audience similarity, the geographic nature of the market, and the available technology.

Democratic policy making: Regular users, not just telecommunications experts, should be involved with the design and policies of the new information infrastructure.

Demographics: The study of the characteristics of human populations and population segments. Also, characteristics of an audience for mass media based on age, gender, ethnic background, education, and income.

Desktop publishing: Writing, illustrating, and designing publications with a personal computer.

Diagonal communication: Communication between an organization's departments at different levels.

Diaries: A method of measuring audience viewing of a program that requires viewers to keep journals detailing what they are watching.

Differentiating the product: Getting the consumer to perceive a product as different in quality from other products.

Digital switching system: System that is computer operated and based on quantities represented electronically as digits.

Dime novel: Cheap, paperback fiction produced in the mid-nineteenth century.

Dime magazines: Magazines that cost 10 cents and appealed to a broad class of readers. These magazines were less expensive than the quality monthlies that preceded them.

Direct Internet provider: A company that provides access to the Internet.

Direct mail: Print advertisement that is delivered, usually by the postal service, directly to consumers. This includes catalogues and coupon packages.

Direct recording: All the parts of music are recorded together at the same time. The process has six steps: session preplanning; creating sound quality; consulting with musicians, recording session, selection of takes, and compiling the master tape.

Disaster: Natural calamities such as earthquakes or human-caused catastrophes such as an oil spill in the ocean.

Disclosing embarrassing facts: An invasion of privacy through the release of information a person would consider awkward.

Dissemination: Collecting information objectively and distributing it quickly to a large audience.

Distributors: Companies that help to get media content to viewers, readers, and listeners. In the movie, magazine, and recording industries, the term means getting the content from producers to wholesalers.

Diverse and competitive marketplace: An open and competitive marketplace among ideas, products, and information providers.

Diversion: Using information for entertainment and enjoyment, for example, reading a short story may make a person feel sad and/or happy.

Docudramas: Films or television programs that blur fact and fiction. Part documentary, part drama, theses programs often do not make clear what is factual and what has been added to make the store interesting and exciting.

Downlink: Transmitting an electronic signal from a satellite to a ground facility.

Downward communication: Managers communicating with employees that they supervise.

Dummy sheet: A sheet of paper that is used to design a page for the newspaper.

Economic actions: The exchange of goods, services, and money.

Economies of scale: The savings that result from large quantity production.

Editing: The joining of two pieces of film; this technique allows for moving images into different time sequences.

Effects research: This social science research concentrates on the impact the content has on people, either individually or in groups. The effects can be social, cultural, political, and economic.

Eight-track tape: A plastic cartridge that holds a continuous recording tape. Invented primarily for automobile play during the 1960s, its eight tracts allowed high quality stereo reproduction in an easy to handle cartridge.

Electronic mail: Written communication sent to one or more people with computers. Receivers of mail read it at their leisure.

Electrotyping: A metal plate used in letterpress printing, made by electroplating a lead or plastic mold of the page to be printed.

Empirical research: The systematic collection and analysis of data.

Entertainment software: Software that allows consumers access to a variety of media and activities online and from diskettes and CD-ROMS.

Entrepreneur: A person who assumes the risk of starting a business.

Equal time rule: In political elections, all candidates get equal time to air viewpoints.

Equitable workplaces: Training and guidance should be available for workers who have to upgrade their skills to deal with computers or who must find different work because computers replace some tasks.

Evidentiary privilege: Rule of law that allows journalists to withhold identification of confidential sources.

Executive privilege: The President's right to withhold information if disclosure might harm the executive branch's functions and decision-making processes.

External publics: In public relations, these people include consumers and voters, government organizations, interest groups, business organizations, and media.

Fair comment and criticism: A journalist is allowed to express opinion in the most offensive ways without committing libel. The statement must be presented as opinion and not fact.

Fair use: Use of a small portion of a copyrighted work by scholars, teachers, or reporters to further enlighten the public.

Fairness doctrine: A collection of rules that required stations to air opposing viewpoints concerning controversial issues.

False light: Invasion of privacy involving portraying or inferring something about someone that is not true.

Fast film: Generic term for film photographers use to stop "fast" action. Does not need long exposure to light to capture the photographic image.

Fax newspapers: Information delivered to readers by newspapers using fax machines.

Features: Stories that emphasize activities of people and do not involve "hard news events," such as crime and disasters.

Federal Communications Act of 1934: Provided the basis for federal telecommunication and television regulation until the 1996 Telecommunications Act.

Federal Trade Commission: Government agency that enforces truth in advertising laws and regulates trade of goods across state and national borders.

Fiber optic cable system : A cable company that uses fiber optic cable to transmit programs. Fiber optic cable uses glass fibers and light to carry electronic information.

Fiction factory: Late nineteenth-century publishing of formulaic books, in which publishers dictated story lines.

File transfer protocol (FTP): A system of code procedures that enables transfer of text and other files across the Internet.

Film editing: The joining of two pieces of film; this technique allows for moving images into different time sequences.

Financial commitment model: Competition between newspapers and local TV news can affect the amount of money that is available to the newsrooms and the amount of space or time that is available to readers and viewers.

FM: Stands for frequency modulation, which is a way of attaching sound to radio waves. *See* modulators.

Focus groups: Groups of individuals representing different interests who are assembled to discuss a topic. A form of research used to get in-depth information, but not information that is representative of an entire audience.

Food and Drug Administration: Government agency charged with regulating foods and drugs. Created in response to patent medicine manufacturers who included drugs such as cocaine in over-the-counter medicines.

Frame: A term used to describe the mental image formed by a message. Television frames events when it shows violent action when the only violent action was among a few of 50,000 individuals attending an event.

Freedom to communicate: People must have the right to exchange ideas and contribute to discussion.

520

Full power: A station that reaches a large percentage of houses in its market and that must broadcast a schedule of programs.

Full service: Advertising agency that offers a client all of the five services needed by advertisers.

Functional integrity: The national information system must be reliable under all conditions. The system cannot become antiquated nor experience national failure because of heavy workloads, natural disasters, or other national economic priorities.

Gatekeeper: A person who controls the flow of information into and through the mass media.

Genre A category of fiction distinguished by a definite form or style. The term is also used to categorize other forms of artistic endeavor such as film.

Gentlemen's club: Magazines produced in offices occupied by middle-aged white males. The atmosphere was similar to that of a gentleman's club.

Geographics: The physical location—state, region, or country—of potential buyers.

Geographic coverage: The market where the advertisements are placed and the advertised product is sold.

Golden Mean: This concept means moderation in life, and applied to ethics means operating somewhere between two extremes.

Halftone: A photographic process in which light and dark are represented by the number and density of dots. Halftones were first printed in newspapers in the 1880s.

Hard disk: Storage capacity built into a personal computer, in contrast to external drives for "soft" storage disks.

High fidelity: Reproduction of sound with minimal distortion.

High-definition television (HDTV): This technology produces a much sharper image than current TV sets by increasing the number of lines of electrons that hit the screen.

Hoax: An act or story intended to deceive; a tall tale; a practical joke or serious fraud.

Home page: The opening screen, or page, of a location on the World Wide Web.

Horatio Alger story: Began as a real story of how Horatio Alger worked his way up the social and economic ladder, but soon developed into a term to represent the glorification of individualism in American life.

Horizontal communication: Communication among employees at the same level of hierarchy in an organization.

Hot buttons: Timely topics that elicit an emotional reaction from the audience.

Household penetration: Term used to describe the percentage of houses in a market that a newspaper, cable channel, or other media form reaches. Newspaper personnel are concerned about declining household penetration.

Human interest: A news value that emphasizes personal details that intrigue readers, for example, a story about an 80-year-old bus driver called "Grandma" by the students.

Identity advertisements: Ads that affect behavior by connecting product with a good time or by getting people to identify with appealing characters.

Ideological influences: The shared values and beliefs that are found in a social system.

Illustrations: Pictures of people, things, or mental images.

Impact: A news value based on the number of people affected by an event or issue, or the degree of intensity to which individuals are affected by an event or issue.

Individual influences: The psychological makeup of the people creating the content of the media.

Industrial Revolution: The period during the late 1700s and 1800s when America and Europe moved from an agriculture-based economy to a manufacturing economy.

Influences on content: Social science research that involves the many factors that affect the creation of media content.

Infomercial: A media message that offers consumer information, usually an extended advertisement.

Information graphics: Devices that are used to illustrate numerical information, including tables, graphs, and charts.

Information services: Services that provide entertainment and information via telephone lines or through other technologies. Before 1996, telephone companies were prohibited from entering the information business. They now compete with cable companies and other service providers.

Information highway: The international network of cables and computers that support electronic communication through computers.

Information model: Pattern of behavior for disseminating information as news; incorporates values such as objectivity over partisanship.

Informational messages: Making the receiver aware of some event or issue that the sending organization considers important.

Infotainment: Combination of information and entertainment. Some critics today believe entertainment is considered more important than the level of information. This leads to sensationalism and news programs that contain little hard news and many consumer- and entertainment-oriented features.

Infotainment shows: Television programs that aim to inform and entertain viewers, but often the entertainment element is emphasized at the expense of the information.

Integrated: Combinations of media, for example, the incorporation of music into movies, television programming, and advertisements.

Interaction orientation: The influence on people of media in deciding how to behave toward other people.

Interactive: Interactive systems involve two-way communication. The information receivers act as senders and vice versa.

Interactive information sharing : Use of computers or broadcast technology to transmit information back and forth between individuals or between professional communicators and members of an audience.

Interactive video: A form of communication that integrated video and computers making it possible for viewers to influence the content of what they watch.

Interactivity: Mental and sensory participation. Used as a media term, it means actually having a physical interaction with a medium—ordering a movie via computer or typing in a response to a question.

Interest groups: Groups that attempt to influence politicians to achieve public policy decisions that favor the groups' interests.

Internal publics: In public relations the internal publics include employees, managers, trustees, and stockholders.

Internet: A linkage of hundreds of academic, government, and commercial computer sites created when the U.S. government saw the need for the framework for an emergency communication system. Computers are tied together through special high-speed telephone lines.

Interpretative role: Journalists investigate sources' claims and analyze and explain complex issues to their audience.

Interviews: A method of measuring audience demand for programs that involves personal or telephone interviews designed to inquire about watching habits.

Issue candidacies: Campaigns for political office that emphasize public issues rather than the candidates' images.

Joint operating agreement (JOA): An agreement that allows two newspapers in the same city to operate the business and production sides of a newspaper together in a fashion that would normally violate antitrust law.

Joint product: Serving two markets with the same production process.

Journalistic balance: Providing equal or nearly equal coverage of various points of view in a controversy.

Judeo-Christian ethic: The Golden Rule, "Do unto Others as You Would Have Them Do unto You".

Jump music: Small band music that merged swing and electric blues during the late 1940s. Jump developed into rhythm and blues music.

Kilobyte: A measure of memory size equal to 1024 bytes.

Kinetoscope: A box-like mechanism used to view short films during the late 1800s. The viewer looked into an opening and watched film move past a light bulb.

Knowledge gap hypothesis: An argument that people with more education and higher incomes would acquire knowledge of public issues more quickly than would those with less education and income.

Laptop computer: A portable computer about the size of a thick notebook and weighing from five to seven pounds.

Legal standing: Right to sue.

Libel: Unjustified defamation of a person. Defamation, identification, publication, and negligence are the elements of libel.

Libertarianism: A philosophy that espouses absolute freedom of action and thought for the individual without the restrictions of society.

Limited speech: Speech that is not widely disseminated.

Linotype: A machine invented in the nineteenth century that allowed an entire line of type to be set on a single piece of metal; this made for ease of newspaper composition. Prior to this each letter had to be set separately.

Local advertisements: Ads for companies that serve a much smaller market, such as a city or metropolitan area.

Low-power broadcast stations: Stations that serve limited areas because the station's signal cannot reach long distances.

Magazine programming: Selling time to several advertisers to share the support of a single show.

Magic bullet: Metaphor for powerful media effects. The presumption was that media content hit a person and had a definite effect upon impact, as with a bullet. Therefore media content became magic content.

Market economy: An economy in which the interaction of supply and demand determines the prices of goods and services and the levels of production. In a nonmarket economy, government determines prices and production.

Market niche: Portion of the audience a particular magazine gains as subscribers or buyers.

Market segments: The target audience. The group of individuals a magazine selects to target as a readership group.

Marketplace of ideas: In this market, ideas compete for acceptance by society and its subgroups. The accepted ideas determine policy and societal norms.

Mass medium: A form of communication (radio, newspapers, television, etc.) used to reach a large number of people.

Mass advertising: Advertisements that aim to reach the largest number of people possible.

Mass communication: Communicating with a high proportion of the designated audience for a message.

Mechanical rights: The copyright holder is paid when the song is recorded.

Media buyers: Those that place the advertisements in media outlets.

Media markets: Major markets are markets defined by a metropolitan area and many media choices; outstate markets are those with some diversity that are removed from metropolitan areas, but are not rural; isolated markets include rural areas in which traditional media choices are exceedingly limited.

Media mix: Consumers use of a variety of types of media by individuals or advertisers, such as newspapers, television, and World Wide Web.

Media kit: A collection of information about a particular event or person, such as a recording release. The kit can include text, photographs, audiotapes, and even computer diskettes and CD-ROMs. A package of video and print news releases and other information to make it easy for reporters to follow up on a public relations generated event or issue.

Media sociology: Analysis of media as an institution of society and its relation to society as a whole.

522

Mediated communication: Communication that uses a channel to carry the message; not face-to-face communication.

Mercantile press: Early American newspapers that served businesses, shopkeepers, and tradesmen. These newspapers also contained political news.

Merchandise expert: Someone who oversees other forms of promotion besides advertising.

Microcomputer: A small computer using a microprocessor as its central processor.

Microprocessor: The chip that contains all the components in a CPU. The best known chip in the 1990s was the Intel.

Minicam: A small, light-weight electronic camera. It comes in a variety of formats, such as VHS, disc, and eight millimeter.

Minstrel: An entertainer, with blackened face, performing songs and music of African American origin.

Model: A diagram or picture that represents how something works. In communication, models are used to explain what happens in the creation, sending, and receiving of a message.

Modem: A device that allows a computer to receive data over telephone lines or cable.

Modulator: Device that modulates, or processes, the carrier wave so that its amplitude or frequency varies. Amplitude modulation (AM), is constant in frequency and varies the intensity, or amplitude, of the carrier wave. Frequency modulation (FM) is constant in amplitude and varies the frequency of the carrier wave.

Moral reasoning process: Processes that help communication professionals make ethical decisions from a principled basis rather than reacting intuitively.

Morality: The consistency of an action with a given code of ethics.

Muckraking magazines: Magazines that emerged in the 1890s and exposed corruption while trying to educate the public about reform.

Multimedia packaging: The production and release of recordings with other media products, which could include a video, movie, and concert tour.

Multitrack recording: Recording the various elements of the music—singer, rhythm, and lead instruments—at different times and combining them through an electronic process.

National advertisements: Ads for products and services that are available throughout the country.

Network: Computers that are connected by communication lines. The computers may be connected within a restricted geographic area, such as a laboratory in a mass communication program. This network is a local area network (LAN). The Internet networks millions of computers worldwide through telephone and fiber optic lines.

Network compensation: Money paid by the networks to the local stations for running network programming.

News council: A committee that reviews potentially unethical activities of news organizations.

News judgment: The application of news value to particular stories.

News magazines: Fifteen-to-twenty minute news segments put together to form hour-long electronic magazines such as *60 Minutes* or *Dateline*. These programs combine soft features with hard-hitting investigative reporting.

Newsreel: Film depiction's of news events. Some were composed of real footage, others of dramatized events.

News service: Organizations that collect and distribute news and information to media outlets. Some professionals still use the term "wire services," even though the telegraph as a means of transmitting information to media organizations has not been used for decades.

News values: The standards that staff and news service reporters share for selecting what events and issues become news.

Niche publishers: These are smaller publishing houses that serve very narrowly defined markets.

Nickelodeon: Small store front functioning as a theater; popular about 1910. These preceded the grand movie palaces.

Noncommercial stations: Stations that are not operated for profit, for example, educational or public television.

Nonprofit organizations: Organizations that depend heavily on public relations because much of their support comes from public donations.

Novelty: A news value applied to stories that reflect the public's interest in the unusual and bizarre.

Objectively: Reporting facts without bias or prejudice, including a deliberate attempt to avoid interpretation.

Obscenity: Anything with a tendency to corrupt people whose minds might be open to immoral influences.

Obtrusive: An issue that an individual can experience directly, such as inflation.

Oligopoly: A business situation in which a few dominant companies control enough of the business that each one's actions will have a significant impact on actions of the others.

Ombudsman: A person within an organization who represents customers and investigates potentially unethical conduct of the organization and people within it.

On-air personalities: One of the attractions of radio and television has been the ability of listeners to identify with a personality who comes to them regularly. Whether a person who reads the news, announces music, or hosts a quiz show, the on-air personality gives a station a singular identity.

Online information services: Companies that provide searchable data bases via telephone line and modems for a fee.

Online newspapers: Newspaper content delivered via the Internet or other online services.

Open video system: A system that rents entire channels or time on channels to unaffiliated programmers without discrimination. Designed to provide access for those who don't own their own channels.

Opinion leader: Person within a community who has areas of expertise and pays more attention to information derived from mass media than do most citizens.

Organizational influences: The work routines, social interaction, and ownership goals found in media organizations and in the organizations covered by media.

Package deals: A series of media tie-ins.

Packaging: Selling of content in a bundle. For example, cable systems sell channel packages; newspapers bundle sections targeted to certain socio-economic groups through zip code sorting.

Packet switching: Small envelopes, or packets, of information are sent along the Internet. This allows the Internet to send information without actually establishing an extended connection between two computers.

Pamphlet books: Books printed in the 1800s without hard covers to look like magazines. Publishers wanted to get cheaper mail rates given magazines.

Pan: To criticize heavily.

Panavision: System of lenses used in filming. It enables a film shot in one wide screen version (Cinemascope, for example) to be shown in a theater without the lenses for that type of projection.

Papyrus: A Mediterranean plant whose stem was used to make paper and other products, such as twine.

Paradigm: A set of assumptions about the nature of human behavior.

Pass-along rate: The total number of readers who read a magazine regularly, including those who read copies that were given, or passed along, to them.

Patent medicines: Packaged drugs that can be obtained without a prescription. Before the Food and Drug Administration was created, these drugs often contained large amounts of alcohol and sometimes opium.

Payola: Paying disc jockeys and radio stations to play certain songs so recording sales will increase.

Peoplemeter: A method of measuring audience demand for programs that involves having each member of a household being assigned a different number to press on a control when watching or changing shows.

Performing rights: The copyright holder is paid every time a song is performed.

Perks: Short for perquisite, or payment for something in addition to salary.

Persuasion: Causing people to change their beliefs or to act in certain ways.

Photo opportunity: A controlled appearance designed to present a person in their best light.

Pictographs: Also known as chartoon, a combination of a chart and a cartoon.

Pirating: Using material without securing appropriate copyright authorization.

Pluralist: A school of thought that espouses coexistence and cooperation among different elements of a power structure.

Political actions: Mass media provide information about politicians and the political process.

Political ads: Ads used to persuade voters to elect someone to political office or attempt to influence the public on legislative issues.

Political cartoons: Drawings that comment on political, social, and cultural events and the people who influence those events.

Political economy: The study of how political and economic systems influence each other.

Powerful effects theory: A theory that grew after World War II with a series of studies that examined the impact of propaganda and movies on children. The theory says media have strong impacts on individuals.

Powertrains: Microprocessors—the power behind computers.

Precedent: A legal decision that sets a standard for how subsequent cases are decided.

Premium two-page spread: An advertisements that spreads across two pages in the center of the issue.

Press pool: A small group of reporters who are selected to gather information and pass it on the larger group of press people. Used when the number of reporters gathering in one spot is problematic.

Press release: An announcement of some event, such as a recording release, sent to various news media outlets.

Price advertising: Advertising featuring special prices to attract customers to a store.

Principle of Utility: The belief that ethical decisions should be made on the basis of what provides the greatest good for the greatest number of human beings within society.

Prior restraint: Traditionally, the requirement that printers obtain permission from government to print material, and subject that material to possible censorship before printing. Also, government's prevention of publication.

Privacy: Individuals' privacy must be protected, and this is an increasing problem when vast amounts of personal information are gathered and transferred via computer networks.

Privacy laws: Laws that protect individuals from media abuse based on the belief that people are entitled to keep parts of their lives away from public scrutiny.

Prodigy: An online information service.

Product placement: Showing products in movies as a way of advertising the product without viewers thinking of the presentation as advertising.

Profit margin: The cost of goods sold, minus that of goods that are returned, yield net sales. The net sales, minus the cost of the goods sold, is the gross profit. Gross profit is divided by net sales to get the profit margin, expressed as a ratio or percentage.

Profit-seeking organizations: Organizations whose goal it is to make a profit.

Progressive generation: Group of individuals in the early 1900s who championed political and social reform.

Prominence: A news value based on how notable or famous a person is.

524

Promotion: All the ways of gaining attention for a company, product, or service.

Propaganda: Efforts to influence and persuade the receivers of a mediated message.

Proximity: A news value based on the geographic location of an event. The more local the event, the more news value it has.

Psuedo-event: An event created solely for the purposes of public relations, to gain favorable notice.

Psychographics: The study of life styles, attitudes, and values.

Public figure: Someone who places herself or himself before the public through the media, or someone who is swept involuntarily into public controversy.

Public investment: The buying of stock in a company by the general public.

Public journalism: A distinctive and controversial effort to find ways to reconnect newspapers to their communities.

Public official: Someone who holds a position in government that affects public policy.

Public performance rights: The copyright holder is paid when an actual recording is played.

Public service ads: Ads that promote behaviors and attitudes that are beneficial to society and its members.

Publicist: Person who seeks publicity for another person, a product, or an event.

Pundit: An expert about a particular topic, a person consulted because of his or her wisdom.

Purpose of the ad: The type of influence the advertiser seeks to have over the customer.

Qualified privilege: Privilege developed to make happenings in government proceedings available to citizens.

Quality advertising: Advertising that strives to influence the buyer's impression of how good a product or service is.

Quality monthlies: Name given to staid political and literary monthly magazines popular in the mid-nineteenth century that set the tone for prestigious cultural values.

Quiz show: Show on which contestants appear to answer questions that show their knowledge of selected material.

Rack jobbers: A rack jobber handles sales of recordings in department and discount stores.

Radio Act of 1927: Law that governed the regulation of radio by government until the 1934 Communications Act.

Radio frequency: An electromagnetic wave frequency used in radio transmission.

Rap music: African American music with a rhythmic, repetitive beat and spoken lyrics. Gangsta rap reflects urban conditions and incorporates references to drugs, violence, and sex.

Rating: Percentage of all people in a market who listened to or watched a particular station during a time segment.

Rational thinking abilities: The cognitive processing of information by considering options based on conscious comparison of influencing factors.

Research: Collecting and analyzing data to answer specific questions. In advertising it means planning and conducting research about the effectiveness of advertising.

Right of privacy: An ethical and legal area of decision making. The right to be protected from unwarranted intrusion by the government, media, or other institutions or individuals.

Salience: How important an issue is to individuals.

Satire: Wit used to expose corruption of wickedness. Basis for political cartoons and comics.

Scarcity of the airwaves: Concept that because there are only limited airwaves, they must belong to the people and therefore be regulated by government, not owned by broadcasters.

Schema: Mental structures for explaining an individual's experiences and observations.

Scoop: Publishing the story of a new event before another news organization does.

Search engine: A software designed to search computer networks, such as the World Wide Web, for specific information.

Sedition: Inciting people to rebel against their government.

Seditious libel: Criticism of the government. In colonial times, criticism was considered libelous even if true.

Self-censorship: A media company's or individual's decision not to publish or broadcast particular content.

Self-understanding: People depend on media to learn about themselves and to grow as individuals.

Semantic noise: An interference with communication because of misunderstandings about the meaning of words or symbols.

Serialized: A book printed in parts in a magazine or newspaper over a certain period of time.

Share: Percentage of people with their radio or TV sets turned on who are listening to a particular station during a particular time period.

Situational ethics: A code of ethics that allows for variation in action, depending on the circumstances of a given situation.

Slander: Spoken defamation.

Social and cultural interaction: When people use or share information that defines, identifies, and maintains membership in a group. For example, sometimes people get information formally, through classes, other times information passes informally through conversations in discussions such as those held during fraternity and sorority rushes.

Social responsibility: As applied to freedom of the press, a philosophy that states that with freedom comes responsibility to the social good.

Social realism: Films that are critical of the social structure.

Social play: People depend on media to entertain them when they are with friends and family.

Social science theory: A set of related statements about people's behavior that have five uses; categorizing phenomena, predicting the future, explaining past events, sense of understanding of why behaviors occur, and providing the potential for influencing future behavior.

Social understanding: People depend on media to learn about the world and their community.

Socialization process: Process by which people learn acceptable behavior in a group. Applied to news organizations, it is the process by which reporters learn patterns of behavior through observing others and by learning to recognize the systems of rewards and punishments in a newsroom.

Solitary play: People depend on media to divert and entertain them when they are alone.

Sound bite: A short quotation used on radio or television to express an idea.

Specialized publishers: Publishing houses that produce a particular type of book, such as religious and children's books.

Spin doctor: A public relations specialist employed to put the most favorable interpretation on a politician's comments or activities or to minimize damage caused by charges against the politician.

Spot news: News that must be gotten "on the spot." News based on one-time events, such as an accident or crime.

Spots: Advertising time slots for a show that are sold by networks or stations to sponsors.

Spreadsheets: Software that allows for organization and tabulation of financial data. Commonly used in planning budgets.

Stand-up shot: Photographs of active people who appear to be news sources or reporters.

Stereotype: Process of creating metal plates with raised letters; used for printing before offset printing was developed.

Stereotyping: The use of a paper mat to make cylindrical molds for printing.

Stock: A term used to refer to types of paper. Also, shares of ownership in a company.

Stringer: A part-time or contract employee who works as a reporter on a story-by-story basis or on the basis of column inches.

Studio film rentals: Studios rent films they produce to distributors and/or theaters.

Sunshine laws: Laws requiring that meetings of federal or state administrative agencies be open to the public.

Superstation: Station that reaches hundreds of markets throughout the country by means of satellite distribution of a signal to cable systems.

Surveillance: Identifying important events and issues that affect a person's life.

Surveys: A form of research that asks people to respond to a collection of questions. Surveys are taken by phone, mail, and personal interviews.

Swing: Big band music played with a jazz rhythm that was popular during the 1930s and early 1940s.

Syncopated beat: In syncopated rhythm, the regular metrical accent shifts temporarily to stress a beat that is normally weak. Syncopation is important in African and African American musical traditions and is considered the root of most modern popular music.

Syndicates: Companies that contracts with a writer, cartoonist, or columnist to produce a certain number of products, such as stories, cartoons, and photographs, that the syndicate then sells to a number of media outlets.

Syndicated programming: Nationally produced programming that is supplied to stations through telephone lines and by satellite.

Take: One effort to record a piece of music, or video.

Talking head: Use of a person on television, usually as an expert. The visual consists of the individual's head and shoulders as he or she talks.

Targeted advertising: Advertisements that seek to reach a selected audience.

Targeted marketing: Trying to sell a product or service to a particular group of people, such as women between the ages of 25 and 39.

Task-oriented software: The programs that allow people to create text and images and to organize data.

Technological convergence: To blend technologies to deliver a message.

Telecommunications industry: Organizations that are involved in electronic media such as broadcast television, cable, radio, telephone, or the transmission of information over wires and with the use of satellites.

Television anthology: A favorite television format of the 1950s, which consisted of stage plays that were remade for TV.

Textbooks: Books used for elementary school, high school, and college classroom work.

Three Chinas: The term refers to China, Taiwan, and Hong Kong. Before the twentieth century, all three were classified by Europeans as China.

3-D: Film technique that produces 3-D images; required viewers to wear special glasses.

35 millimeter: Photographic film that has a frame exposure 35 millimeters in length. It is used for both still and moving pictures.

Tie-ins: The connection made when a magazine runs a story about a product that is being advertised in the magazine.

Timeliness: A news value based on how recent an event or issue is.

Toll broadcasting: The selling of time or advertising in radio.

Trade book: Most mass marketed books sold at bookstores or through book clubs. Excludes textbooks.

Trade press: Periodicals that target a specific industry. Broadcasting & Cable magazine, for example, targets the broadcast and cable industry and is an example of a trade magazine.

Traffic: Department that controls movement of programming through the day, logs what goes on the air, and supplies information for billing advertisers.

526

Transistor: A small electronic device containing a semiconductor. A key component of an integrated circuit. Paved the way for radio portability.

Two-step flow: A theory that suggested that mass media affects individuals indirectly as well as directly.

Ubiquity: The experiencing of media messages almost all of the time.

Universal access: Internet technology and training, and therefore information, should be affordable for all.

Unobtrusive: An issue that is beyond direct personal experience.

Uplink: Transmitting an electronic signal to a satellite for storage or further distribution.

Upward communication: Employees communicating with their supervisors.

Uses research: Social science research that concerns why and how people decide to use media content. Uses research studies audience decision making and use of media.

User groups: Groups of people who share their interests by communicating through computers.

User-friendly: Software that is designed for use by individuals who are not familiar with complex computer languages.

V-chip: An electronic device in a television set that can block certain television programs.

Veil of ignorance: In ethical situations, this means that information is treated outside of social context, and power, wealth, and other social factors do not enhance one position over another. Justice emerges when social differentiation's are eliminated in the process of negotiation.

Vertical integration: The control of production from obtaining the raw materials to the distribution of the product. A system in which a single corporation controls production, distribution, and exhibition of movies. Declared illegal in the 1940s.

Videotex: Online services that provide words and graphics and sometimes allow for interactive capability.

Vital civic sectors: All individuals should have the ability to participate, not merely vote, in government by designing legislation and formulating policy.

Wave band: A section of the electromagnetic spectrum. Some bands are used for communication.

Wholesalers: Companies that deliver products from a warehouse to dealers.

Wire editor: An editor assigned to edit the material that comes from wire services and news services.

World Wide Web: A network of computers that allows people to move easily from material stored on one computer to material stored on another.

World music: Generally used to refer to non-English speaking musicians singing in their native language. Usually applied to music originating in developing countries, including songs of protest.

WYSIWYG: Text on a computer monitor that corresponds exactly to the printout.

Zines: Inexpensive magazines produced with desktop publishing and usually distributed over the Internet.

Zoned sections: Sections of a newspaper, usually of a metropolitan daily, that are targeted to specific zones, usually zip-code areas. These sections provide news specific to the area and advertising targeted to the economic level of the particular audiences.

Zoning: Printing an edition of a newspaper for a specific geographic area (or zone) that has content aimed at that area, usually in a specific section of the paper.

References

CHAPTER 1

1. Christopher Georges, "Mock the Vote: What's Wrong with MTV's Hot New Political Coverage," *The Washington Monthly,* 25:5 (May 1993), pp. 30–35.

2. Frazier Moore, "This Election Year, the Boys are on MTV's Bus," *Chicago Tribune,* February 1, 1996, Sec. 2, p. 7.

3. "Media Wars," *Media Studies Journal* 6:2 (Spring 1992), Preface.

4. Mark A. Thalhimer, "A National Information Service Background Paper," published by the Freedom Forum Media Studies Center, December 1991; see also http://www.cnn.com/wires/US/02-01/telecom_glance/index.ap.html, February 1, 1996.

5. Philip Moeller, "The High-Tech Trib," *American Journalism Review* (April 1994): 14–21.

6. "Internet: The Undiscovered Country," *PC Magazine* (March 15, 1994): 116–118.

7. John Markoff, "I Wonder What's on the PC Tonight," *The New York Times,* May 8, 1994, Sec. 3, pp. 1, 8.

8. "The Emerging InfoStructure," *Bloomberg Business News* (February 22, 1994) See Ben Bagdikian, *The Media Monopoly,* 1983.

9. Jeff Cohen and Norman Solomon, "High-Tech Media Mergers: Good Business, Bad Policy," *Seattle Times,* October 23, 1993, pp. A11; Ben Bagdikian, *The Media Monopoly,* 1993.

10. Norm Alster, "Premature Obituary," *Forbes* (January 17, 1994): 79–80.

11. Michael Kelly, "David Gergen, Master of the Game," *New York Times Magazine* (October 31, 1993): 62–71, 94, 97, 103.

12. *1791–1991: The Bill of Rights and Beyond* (Washington, DC: Library of Congress), 1991, p. 18.

13. Norman Katzman, "Impact of Communication Technology," *Journal of Communication,* 24:4 (1974): 47–58.

14. P. J. Tichenor, G. A. Donohue, and C. N. Olien, "Mass Media Flow and Differential Growth in Knowledge," *Public Opinion Quarterly,* 34 (1970): 159–170.

15. *Letters of Thomas Jefferson* cited in Saul K. Padover, *Thomas Jefferson on Democracy* (New York: Penguin, 1939), pp. 92–93.

16. Marshall McLuhan, *The Gutenberg Galaxy: The Making of Typographic Man* (Toronto: University of Toronto Press, 1962), pp. 272–273.

17. John Merrill and Everett Dennis, "Global Communication Dominance," in *Media Debates: Issues in Mass Communication* (New York: Longman, 1991), pp. 212–222.

18. Richard W. Stevenson, "Russia Seeks Help to Fix Its Phones," *The New York Times,* May 10, 1994, p. D1.

CHAPTER 2

1. C. Shannon and W. Weaver, *The Mathematical Theory of Communication* (Urbana, IL., University of Illinois Press, 1949), p. 98.

2. "The Lower Case," *Columbia Journalism Review* (July/August 1986): 65.

3. Michael Norman, "Dole and Bennett Pop-Culture Slams Are Just A Cop-Out," *Cleveland Plain Dealer,* June 11, 1995, p. 1J.

4. Bruce H. Westley and Malcolm S. MacLean, Jr., "A Conceptual Model for Communication Research," *Journalism Quarterly* 34 (1957), pp. 31–38.

5. Stephen Lacy and Todd F. Simon, *The Economics and Regulation of United States Newspapers* (Norwood, NJ: Ablex, 1993), pp. 26–30.

6. Self-understanding as a use is taken from dependency theory. See Melvin DeFleur and Sandra Ball-Rokeach, *Theories of Mass Communication,* 5th ed. (New York: Longman, 1989), pp. 305–310.

7. Harold Lasswell, "The Structure and Function of Communication in Society," in *The Communication of Ideas,* Lyman Byron ed. (New York: Institute for Religious and Social Studies, 1948), pp. 37–51; Charles R. Wright, *Mass Communication: A Sociological Perspective,* 3rd ed. (New York: Random House, 1959), pp. 4–6. Together these scholars listed four functions of mass communication for society. Two of these, surveillance and entertainment, take place at the individual level and are considered individual uses here.

8. William B. Blankenburg and Gary W. Ozanich, "The Effects of Public Ownership on the Financial Performance of Newspaper Corporations," *Journalism Quarterly* 70 (1993): 68–75.

CHAPTER 3

1. S. H. Steinberg, *Five Hundred Years of Printing* (New York: Criterion Books, 1959), pp. 21–22.

2. For a detailed discussion of the impact of the printing revolution on Western society, see Elizabeth L. Eisenstein, *The Printing Revolution in Early Modern Europe* (Cambridge, England: Cambridge University Press, 1983). See also David Hall, "The World of Print and Collective Mentality," in John Higham and Paul K. Conkin, eds., *New Directions in American Intellectual History* (Baltimore: Johns Hopkins University Press,

528

1980), pp. 166–180. Eisenstein and Hall demonstrate the impact of technological change on society.

3. Ian K. Steele, *The English Atlantic, 1675–1740: An Exploration of Communication and Community* (New York: Oxford University Press, 1986), pp. 133–134; Richard D. Brown, *Knowledge Is Power: The Diffusion of Information in Early America, 1700–1865* (New York: Oxford University Press, 1989). Steele explores the transfer of information across the Atlantic and establishes the colony-to-mother-country connection as primary over colony-to-colony exchanges. Brown looks at letters, novels, and other forms of communication, and examines their importance in the development of colonial culture.

4. Paul Finkelman, "The Zenger Case: Prototype of a Political Trial," in Michael R. Belknap, ed., *American Political Trials* (Westport, CT: Greenwood Press, 1981); David Paul Nord, "The Authority of Truth: Religion and the John Peter Zenger Case," *Journalism Quarterly* 62 (Summer 1985), pp. 227–235; James Alexander, *A Brief Narrative of the Case and Trial of John Peter Zenger,* 2nd ed. (Cambridge: Harvard University Press, 1971), p. 13. *A Narrative* relates the text of the trial.

5. Jeffery A. Smith, *Franklin and Bache: Envisioning the Enlightened Republic* (New York: Oxford University Press, 1990), pp. 147–148. Jeffery Smith, also the author of *Printers and Press Freedom,* explains the intellectual dimensions of press in the early republic.

6. For a description of the times, see William E. Ames, *A History of the National Intelligencer* (Chapel Hill: University of North Carolina Press, 1972). The *National Intelligencer* was the prime political newspaper in early Washington, DC. See also Richard B. Kielbowicz, "The Press, Post Office, and Flow of News in the Early Republic," *Journal of the Early Republic* (Fall 1983), pp. 269–280. Kielbowicz connects the flow of news to congressional debates over postal policy.

7. James Morton Smith, *Freedom's Fetters: The Alien and Sedition Laws and American Civil Liberties* (Ithaca, NY: Cornell University Press, 1956). This is a classic study of civil liberties.

8. Richard Schwarzlose, *The Nation's Newsbrokers: The Formative Years from Pretelegraph to 1865* (Evanston, IL: Northwestern University Press, 1989), vol. 1. Schwarzlose's volumes are the first complete history of the wire services.

9. Cited in Moira Davison Reynolds, *Uncle Tom's Cabin and Mid-Nineteenth Century United States* (Jefferson, NC: McFarland & Company, 1985), p. 12. Reynolds puts Stowe's novel into a societal context.

10. Jean Folkerts and Dwight Teeter, *Voices of a Nation,* 2nd ed. (Columbus, OH: Merrill/Macmillan, 1994). This is a comprehensive, interpretative study of American media.

11. For works on the muckrakers, see Arthur and Lila Weinberg, eds., *The Muckrakers* (New York: Simon and Schuster, 1961), p. xiii, and David M. Chalmers, "The Muckrakers and the Growth of Corporate Power: A

Study in Constructive Journalism," *American Journal of Economics and Sociology* 18 (April 1959): 295–311.

12. See James R. Mock and Cedric Larson, *Words That Won the War: The Story of the Committee on Public Information, 1917–1919* (Princeton, NJ: Princeton University Press, 1939), and Stephen Vaughn, *Holding Fast the Inner Lines* (Chapel Hill: University of North Carolina Press, 1980). These two studies thoroughly explore the use of propaganda in World War I.

13. Christopher Sterling and John Kittross, *Stay Tuned,* 2nd ed. (Belmont, CA: Wadsworth, 1990), pp. 52–55. A complete history of broadcast media.

14. Robert McChesney, *Telecommunications, Mass Media, and Democracy* (New York: Oxford University Press, 1993). McChesney chronicles the development of television as a commercial medium and outlines the efforts of nonprofit broadcasters to try to preserve nonprofit channels.

15. See Erik Barnou's classic three-volume work, *A History of Broadcasting in the United States* (New York: Oxford University Press, 1966-1970). See also Philip T. Rosen, *The Modern Stentors: Radio Broadcasters and the Federal Government, 1920–1934* (Westport, CT: Greenwood Press, 1980).

16. Tino Balio, ed., *The American Film Industry* (Madison: University of Wisconsin Press, 1985). A collection of essays depicting the various aspects of film history.

17. Stephen Fox, *The Mirror Makers* (New York: William Morrow, 1984); David Ogilvy, *Ogilvy on Advertising* (New York: Crown Publishers, 1983); Roland Marchand, *Advertising the American Dream: Making Way for Modernity, 1920–1940* (Berkeley: University of California Press, 1985). Fox and Ogilvy chronicle the history of advertising agencies. Marchand describes advertising in the context of consumer culture.

18. Commission on Freedom of the Press, *A Free and Responsible Press* (Chicago: University of Chicago Press, 1947); Margaret Blanchard, "The Hutchins Commission, the Press and the Responsibility Concept," *Journalism Monographs* 49 (May 1977); and Jerilyn McIntyre, "Repositioning a Landmark: The Hutchins Commission and Freedom of the Press," *Critical Studies in Mass Communication* 4 (June 1987).

19. A. M. Sperber, *Murrow: His Life and Times* (New York: Freundlich Books, 1986); Edward R. Murrow, "See It Now" for March 9, 1954, in Edward W. Bliss, Jr., *In Search of Light: The Broadcasts of Edward R. Murrow 1938–1961* (New York: Knopf, 1967).

20. Margaret A. Blanchard, *Exporting the First Amendment: The Press-Government Crusade of 1945–52* (New York: Longman, 1952). Well-documented story of efforts to internationalize freedom of the press after World War II.

21. Daniel Hallin, *The Uncensored War* (New York: Oxford University Press, 1986). Study of the relationship of media coverage of the Vietnam War and public opinion.

CHAPTER 4

1. Jonathan Karp, "Decline? What Decline?" *Media Studies Journal* 6:3 (Summer 1992): 45–53.

2. Elizabeth L. Eisenstein, *The Printing Revolution in Early Modern Europe* (Cambridge: Cambridge University Press, 1983); David Hall, "The World of Print and Collective Mentality," in John Higham and Paul K. Conkin, eds., *New Directions in American Intellectual History* (Baltimore: Johns Hopkins University Press, 1980); Jeffery A. Smith, *Printers and Press Freedom: The Ideology of Early American Journalism* (New York: Oxford University Press, 1988).

3. Moira Davison Reynolds, *Uncle Tom's Cabin and Mid-Nineteenth Century United States: Pen and Conscience* (Jefferson, NC: McFarland & Company, 1985); and Thomas F. Gossett, *Uncle Tom's Cabin and American Culture* (Dallas: Southern Methodist University Press, 1985).

4. J. Preston Dickson, *Young Frederick Douglass: The Maryland Years* (Baltimore and London: Johns Hopkins University Press, 1980).

5. Lewis A. Coser, Charles Kadushin, and Walter W. Powell, *Books: The Culture and Commerce of Publishing* (New York: Basic Books, 1982). This comprehensive volume thoroughly explores the relationship between economics and culture in book publishing.

6. Christine Bold, "Popular Forms I," in the *Columbia History of the American Novel,* Emory Elliott, ed. (New York: Columbia University Press, 1991), p. 298. The *Columbia History* is particularly useful for studying genres historically and for understanding content in the context of history.

7. "Industry Report, Book Publishing," The Roper Organization, June 1992.

8. Daisy Maryles, "The Sky's the Limit," *Publishers Weekly* (March 7, 1994): S3.

9. John F. Baker, "Reinventing the Book Business," *Publishers Weekly* (March 14, 1994): 36.

10. Don R. LeDuc, *Law of Mass Communications,* 7th ed. (Westbury, NY: Foundation Press, 1992), p. 695; see also John F. Baker, "Reinventing the Book Business."

11. "Paramount's Last Chapter—Not Quite," *U.S. News and World Report,* February 28, 1994; "Business Notes," *Maclean's,* February 28, 1994, p. 40; Mark Landler and Gail DeGeorge, "Sumner at the Summit," *Business Week,* February 28, 1994, p. 32; John Greenwald, "The Deal That Forced Diller to Fold," *Time,* February 28, 1994, p. 50; Don Jeffrey, "Industry Awaits Fallout of Paramount Deal; Victors in Takeover Battle Now Must Pay Down Debt," *Billboard,* February 26, 1994, p. 6.

12. See Dan Lacy, "From Family Enterprise to Global Conglomerate," *Media Studies Journal* 6:3 (Summer 1992): 1–13, for discussion of the economics of book publishing.

13. Daisy Maryles, "How the Winners Made It To The Top," *Publishers Weekly* (January 6, 1997): 46–49.

14. Maryles, "Embraced by the List: Best Sellers 94," *Publishers Weekly* (January 2, 1995): 50+.

15. John F. Baker, "Reinventing the Book Business," *Publishers Weekly* (March 14, 1994): 36.

16. Elizabeth Gleick and Bill Shaw, "Mr. Bridge," *People* (November 8, 1993): 50.

17. "The Book Marketplace II," in *Reading in America: Literature and Social History,* Cathy Davidson, ed. (Baltimore: Johns Hopkins University Press, 1989), pp. 687–688.

18. Joseph L. Dionne, "Symposium: Twelve Visions," *Media Studies Journal,* 6:3 (Summer 1992), p. 37.

19. Trudi M. Rosenblum, "Audio at the Crossroads," *Publishers Weekly* (June 10, 1996): 53–56.

20. Daisy Maryles, "Embraced by the List: Bestsellers 94," *Publishers Weekly* (January 2, 1995): 50+.

21. R. Michelle Breyer, "Book Superstores Help Drive $19 Billion in U.S. Sales," *Austin American-Statesman,* October 15, 1995, p. A1.

22. Jim Milliot, "K-Mart To Sell Minority Stake in Borders-Walden; Future Plans Center on Expanding Borders, Improving Walden's Profits," *Publishers Weekly* (May 9, 1994): 12.

23. John Mutter, "One Size Doesn't Fit All," *Publishers Weekly* (January 6, 1997): 40–42.

24. Jim Milliot, "It's All About Content," *Publishers Weekly* (June 24, 1996): 28–30.

CHAPTER 5

1. Cheryl Gibbs, "Big Help for Small Papers," *Quill,* March 1995, pp. 32–35.

2. Kristin McGrath, "Women and Newspapers," *Newspaper Research Journal* 14:1 (Spring 1993): 95–109.

3. U.S. Senate (May 1832), Postage on Newspapers. Report 147, 22, 1, cited in Richard Kielbowicz, "Modernization, Communication Policy, and the Geopolitics of News, 1820–1860," in *Media Voices: An Historical Perspective,* Jean Folkerts, ed. (New York: Macmillan, 1992), p. 130.

4. Richard Kielbowicz, *News in the Mail: The Press, Post Office and Public Information, 1700–1860* (Westport, CT: Greenwood Press, 1989).

5. Thomas C. Leonard, *The Power of the Press* (Oxford, England: Oxford University Press, 1986), p. 4.

6. *New York Sun,* September 3, 1833, p. 1.

7. Dan Schiller, *Objectivity and the News: The Public and the Rise of Commercial Journalism* (Philadelphia: University of Pennsylvania Press, 1981).

8. Jean Folkerts and Dwight Teeter, *Voices of a Nation,* 2nd ed. (New York: Macmillan, 1994), pp. 119–139.

9. Gerald Baldasty, *The Commercialization of News in the Nineteenth Century* (Madison: University of Wisconsin Press, 1992).

10. Stephen Lacy, "Understanding and Serving Newspaper Readers: The Problem of Fuzzy Market Structure," *Newspaper Research Journal* 14:2 (Spring, 1993): 55–67.

530

11. Vernois, Suhler & Associates, *Communications Industry Forecast*, Investment Considerations, New York, 1996, p. 47.

12. Max King, speech at American Journalism Historians Association, Fall 1992, Philadelphia.

13. Adam Clymer, speech, George Washington University Graduate School of Political Management class, "Politics and the Media," 1994.

14. William Blankenburg and Gary W. Ozanich, "The Effects of Public Ownership on the Financial Performance of Newspaper Coporations," *Journalism Quarterly* 70 (Spring 1993): 68–75.

15. Barbara K. Henritze, *Bibliographic Checklist of African-American Newspapers* (Baltimore: Genealogical Publishing, 1994).

16. Stephen Lacy, James M. Stephens, and Stan Soffin, "The Future of the African-American Press: A Survey of African-American Newspaper Managers," *Newspaper Research Journal,* 12:3 (Summer 1991): 8–19.

17. Carolyn Foreman, *Oklahoma Imprints, 1835–1907: Printing before Statehood* (Norman: University of Oklahoma Press, 1936), cited in Sharon Murphy, "Neglected Pioneers: 19th Century Native American Newspapers, *Journalism History* 4:3 (Autumn 1977): 79.

18. James P. Danky and Maureen E. Hady, *Native American Periodicals and Newspapers, 1828–1982* (Westport, CT: Greenwood Press, 1984).

19. Carlos E. Cortes, "The Mexican-American Press," in *The Ethnic Press in the United States: A Historical Analysis and Handbook,* Sally M. Miller, ed. (Westport, CT: Greenwood Press, 1987), pp. 247–260.

20. Herminio Rios and Guadalupe Castillo, "Toward a True Chicano Bibliography: Mexican-American Newspapers: 1848–1942," *El Grito: A Journal of Contemporary Mexican-American Thought* 3 (Summer 1970): 17–24.

21. Felix Gutierrez, "Spanish Language Media in the U.S.," *Caminos* 5 (January 1984): 38–41, 65–66, cited in Cortes, "The Mexican-American Press."

22. Leo Bogart, *Press and Public,* 2nd ed. (Hillsdale, NJ: Lawrence Erlbaum Associates, 1989), p. 196.

23. Bogart, *Press and Public,* p. 322.

24. Frank P. Hoy, *Photojournalism: The Visual Approach* (Englewood Cliffs, NJ: Prentice-Hall, 1986), pp. 181–182.

25. For a thorough description of these projects developed by the three chains and for other information about innovation and trends, see "The Future of News/Visionary Projects," *Quill* (September 1992): 16–46.

26. Howard Kurtz, "Slicing, Dicing News to Attract the Young," *The Washington Post,* January 6, 1991, pp. A-1, 8.

27. Michael P. Smith, "Think Globally, Edit Locally," *Quill* (September 1992): 34.

28. Smith, p. 35.

29. Alan Deutschman, "Stop the Presses," *Wired* (June 1995): 116, 118–122.

30. Russell Shaw, "Cox Newspapers Teams with Prodigy," *Editor & Publisher* (July 24, 1993): 16.

31. Steve Outing, "Hold On (Line) Tight," *Editor & Publisher* (February 17, 1996): 41–61.

32. Gil Thelen, "The State," Case Study Series, The Poynter Institute, St. Petersburg, FL, 1995.

33. "Newsroom Circles: *The State* Rearranges Its Newsroom—and News Coverage," *Quill* (March 1993): 28–30.

34. Alicia C. Shepard, "The Gospel of Public Journalism," *American Journalism Review* (September 1994): 29–30.

35. Shepard, pp. 33–34.

36. The material on the Charlotte Project came from Edward D. Miller, *The Charlotte Project: Helping Citizens Take Back Democracy* (St. Petersberg, FL: The Poynter Institute for Media Studies, 1994).

37. "Minorities in the Newsroom," *ASNE Bulletin* (September 1993): 26–29.

CHAPTER 6

1. Comments by J. Henry Fenwick, editor (1995) of *Modern Maturity,* in Lorraine Calvacca, "This Is Not Your Father's Magazine," *Folio* (December 15, 1995): 28–29.

2. Richard Kielbowicz, *News in the Mail: The Press, Post Office, and Public Information, 1700–1860s* (New York: Greenwood Press, 1989), pp. 130–132.

3. Theodore Peterson, *Magazines in the Twentieth Century* (Urbana: University of Illinois Press, 1972), p. 60.

4. Magazine Publishers of America Fact Sheet, New York, 1996; and Samir A. Husni, *Guide To New Consumer Magazines* (New York: Hearst Magazine Enterprises, 1995).

5. Most of the following information about geographic publishing regions is from Kathleen Endres, "A 1990s Look at Changing Realities in Periodical Publishing." Paper presented to the magazine division, Association for Education in Journalism and Mass Communication National Convention, 1993.

6. Veronis, Suhler & Associates, *Communications Industry Forecast*, Magazine Publishing, 1995, p. 275.

7. Veronis & Suhler, pp. 276–278.

8. Lorraine Calvacca, "Shared Approach: Similarities Between Association and Commercial Publications," *Folio* (March 15, 1994): 5.

9. Samir Husni, "How Magazines are Born," *Folio* (October 1, 1991): 54–55.

10. Bruce Sheiman, "From Start-up Idea to Magazine," *Folio* (January 15, 1994): 118.

11. Some examples are from Gloria Steinem, "Sex, Lies & Advertising," *Ms.,* (July/August 1990), pp. 18–28; Michael Hoyt, "When the Walls Come Tumbling Down," *Columbia Journalism Review* (March/April 1990): 35–41.

12. Deirdre Carmody, *New York Times,* as it appeared in "*Lear's* Lived and Died on a Whim," *Houston Chronicle,* March 15, 1994, Sec. Houston, p. 1.

13. Valerie Seckler, "Who's Making Money?" *Women's Wear Daily,* October 28, 1994, p. 518.

14. Reed Phillips, "What We Learned from the Recession: Or Should Have," *Folio* (February 1, 1993): 61.

15. Leonard Mogel, *The Magazine,* 3rd ed. (Old Saybrook, CT: The Globe Pequot Press, 1992), p. 102.

16. For details organized by job categories such as ad sales, circulation, editorial, and art, see *Folio* (April 1, 1996): 50–57.

17. Bruce Sheiman, "Back to the Future of Magazines," *Folio* (October 15, 1995): 71–72.

18. Jan Jaben, "Are You Ready for the Year 2000?" *Folio* (January, 1991): 32.

19. Eve Asbury, "Give Your Readers What They Want," *Folio* (December 15, 1995): 57–59, 70.

20. Loudon Wainwright, *Great American Magazines* (New York: Alfred A. Knopf, 1986).

21. "SLACKERzines," *Folio* (May 1, 1995): 50.

22. "CD-ROMs Showcase Strength," *Folio* (January 1, 1996): 38.

CHAPTER 7

1. Douglas Gomery, "Hollywood's Business," in *American Media* (Washington, DC: Wilson Center Press, 1989), p. 94.

2. Bruno Bettelheim, Patricia Wise Lecture at the American Film Institute, Washington, DC, February 3, 1981, cited in *Hollywood: Legend and Reality,* Michael Webb, ed. (Boston: Little, Brown and Company, in association with the Smithsonian Institution Traveling Exhibition Service, 1986), p. 17.

3. Louis Giannetti and Scott Eyman, *Flashback: A Brief History of Film* (Englewood Cliffs, NJ: Prentice-Hall, 1986), p. 15.

4. From an original transcript in the collection of Gordon Hendricks, New York, cited in *The American Film Industry,* rev. ed., Tino Balio, ed. (Madison: The University of Wisconsin Press, 1985), p. 45.

5. Russell Merritt, "Nickelodeon Theatres, 1905–1914: Building an Audience for the Movies," in *The American Film Industry,* p. 86.

6. Robert Anderson, "The Motion Picture Patents Company: A Reevaluation," in *The American Film Industry,* p. 134.

7. Douglas Gomery, "The Coming of Sound: Technological Change in the American Film Industry," in *The American Film Industry,* p. 230.

8. Giannetti and Eyman, *Flashback,* p. 372.

9. Stephen Amidon, "Whatever Happened to Our Heroes?" *Sunday Times,* October 1, 1995, Features Section, p. 1.

10. Clayton R. Koppes and Gregory D. Black, *Hollywood Goes to War: How Politics, Profits and Propaganda Shaped World War II Movies* (New York: The Free Press, 1987).

11. Koppes and Black, "Blacks, Loyalty, and Motion-Picture Propaganda in World War II," *Journal of American History* (September, 1986): 394.

12. Sheila Benson, "Despite Oscar's 93 Salute to Women, Actresses Face the Same Old Obstacles," *Variety,* January 1, 1996, pp. 53–54.

13. Daniel J. Leab, *From Sambo to Superspade: The Black Experience in Motion Pictures* (Boston: Houghton Mifflin, 1975), pp. 70–72.

14. Leab, *From Sambo to Superspade,* pp. 173–174.

15. Mark A. Reid, *Redefining Black Film* (Berkeley: University of California Press, 1993).

16. Jacquie Jones, "The New Ghetto Aesthetic," in *Mediated Messages and African-American Culture: Contemporary Issues,* Venise T. Berry and Carmen L. Manning-Miller, eds. (Thousand Oaks, CA: Sage, 1996), pp. 40–51.

17. Gomery, "Hollywood's Business," p. 98.

18. Fred Pampel, Dan Fost, and Sharon O'Malley, "Marketing the Movies," *American Demographics, Inc.* (March 1994): 48.

19. Pampel, Fost, and O'Malley, "Marketing the Movies," p. 48.

20. J. D. Reed, "Plugging Away in Hollywood," *Time,* January 2, 1989, p. 103, as cited in *International Journal of Advertising* (January, 1993): 1–3.

21. Reed, "Plugging Away in Hollywood."

22. D. C. McGill, "Questions Raised on 'Product Placements'," *New York Times,* April 13, 1989, p. D18.

23. J. Schlosberg, "Film Flam Men" *Inside Media* (June 13, 1990): 34.

24. Gomery, "Hollywood's Business," p. 107.

25. Daniel Cerone, "'Jafar': New Journeys to Profitland?," *Los Angeles Times,* May 20, 1994, Home Edition, p. F-1.

26. Richard Natale, "Forget Peoria: Will It Play in Paris and Peru?," *Los Angeles Times,* October 7, 1995, p. F-1.

27. Bernard Weinraub, "Islamic Nations Move to Keep Out *Schindler's List,*" *New York Times,* April 7, 1994, p. C-15.

28. Patrick Robertson, *The Guinness Book of Movie Facts & Feats* (New York: Abbeville Press, 1993), p. 7.

29. Robert Sklar, *Film: An International History of the Medium* (New York: Harry N. Abrams, 1993), pp. 502–506; and David A. Cook, *A History of Narrative Film,* 2nd ed. (New York: W. W. Norton, 1990), pp. 816–820.

30. Sklar, *Film: An International History of the Medium,* pp. 508–517.

31. "Hollywood's Heart Throbs," *The Economist* (December 11, 1993): 97.

32. Bernard Weinraub, "Hollywood Shines Spotlite on Female Audiences," *Chicago Tribune,* February 23, 1997, p. 13.

CHAPTER 8

1. Susan Fraker, "The Chinese Take English Lessons," *Newsweek* (July 9, 1979): 44.

2. David Weaver and G. Cleveland Wilhoit, *Preliminary Report: The American Journalists in the 1990s* (Washington, DC: Freedom Forum, 1992), p. 3.

3. Thomas W. Hoffer, "Nathan B. Stubblefield and His Wireless Telephone," *Journal of Broadcasting* 15 (Summer 1971): 317–329.

4. Elliot N. Sivowitch, "A Technological Survey of Broadcasting's Prehistory, 1876–1920," *Journal of Broadcasting* 15 (Winter 1970-71): 1–20.

5. George H. Gibson, *Public Broadcasting: The Role of the Federal Government, 1912–76* (New York: Praeger Publishers, 1977), pp. 2–3.

6. Federal Communication Commission, "Early History of Network Broadcasting (1923–1926) and the National Broadcasting Company," *Report on Chain Broadcasting* (Commission Order No. 37, Docket 5060, May 1941), pp. 5–20.

7. Lawrence W. Lichty and Malachi C. Topping, "Audiences," in *American Broadcasting: A Source Book on the History of Radio and Television*, Lawrence W. Lichty and Malachi C. Topping, eds. (New York: Hastings House, 1975), pp. 445–457.

8. John W. Spalding, "1928: Radio Becomes a Mass Advertising Medium," *Journal of Broadcasting* 8 (Winter 1963-1964): 31–44.

9. Gibson, *Public Broadcasting: The Role of the Federal Government, 1912–76*, p. 21.

10. David H. Hosley, *As Good as Any: Foreign Correspondence on American Radio, 1930–1940* (Westport, CT: Greenwood Press, 1984), pp. 8–9. See also Jean Folkerts and Dwight Teeter, *Voices of a Nation,* 2nd ed. (New York: Macmillan, 1994), pp. 382–385.

11. Sammy R. Danna, "The Press-Radio War," Freedom of Information Center Report No. 213 (Columbia, MO: School of Journalism, University of Missouri, December 1968), pp. 1–7.

12. George A. Wiley, "The Soap Operas and the War," *Journal of Broadcasting* 7 (Fall 1963): 339–352.

13. Edwin Emery and Michael Emery, *The Press and America,* 4th ed. (Englewood Cliffs, NJ: Prentice-Hall 1978), p. 400.

14. Veronis & Suhler Industry Forecast, as reported by *IAC Database* (August 20, 1996).

15. Compiled from *Broadcasting & Cable Yearbook* (New Providence, NJ: RR. Bowker, 1995).

16. Glen T. Cameron, Glen J. Nowak, and Dean M. Krugman, "The Competitive Position of Newspapers in the Local Retail Market," *Newspaper Research Journal* 14 (Summer–Fall 1993): 70–81.

17. Bruce Girard, "Introduction," in *A Passion for Radio,* Bruce Girard, ed. (Montreal: Black Rose Books, 1992), p. 6.

18. Bruce Porter, "Has Success Spoiled NPR?," *Columbia Journalism Review* (September–October 1990): 26–32.

19. Eric Boehlert, "Fund Cuts Could Hurt Artists, Labels: Public Radio under Attack in Congress," *Billboard* (March 18, 1995), pp. 1, 85.

20. "American Broadcasting: Muggings on Sesame Street," *The Economist* (March 11, 1995): 84.

21. Michael McKean and Vernon A. Stone, "Deregulation and Competition: Explaining the Absence of Local Broadcast News Operations," *Journalism Quarterly* 69 (1992): 713–723.

22. David Bartlett, "News Radio—More Than Master of Disaster," *Media Studies Journal* 7 (Summer 1993): 46.

23. Lou Prato, "War Showed That Radio Listeners Want News," *Washington Journalism Review* (May 1991): 54.

24. Lou Prato, "A Major Expansion of Radio News," *American Journalism Review* (June 1994): 48.

25. Michael Oneal, Linda Himelstein, Judy Temes, Eric Schine, et al., "Everybody's Talkin' at Us," *Business Week* (May 22, 1995): 104.

26. Richard Corliss, "Look Who's Talking," *Time* (January 23, 1995) p. 22.

27. Steve Emmons, "Just What Do Talk Shows Listen For?," *Los Angeles Times,* Orange County Edition, May 10, 1995, p. E1.

28. Emmons, "Talk Shows," *Los Angeles Times.*

29. Peter Laufer, *Inside Talk Radio: America's Voice or Just Hot Air?* (Secaucus, NJ: Carol Publishing Group, 1995).

30. Donald R. Browne, *International Broadcasting: The Limits of a Limitless Medium* (New York: Praeger, 1982), p. 48.

31. George Wedell and Philip Crookes, *Radio 2000* (Manchester, England: The European Institute for the Media, 1991), p. 52.

32. *Australian Commercial Radio—A Study of Listener Attitudes* (Sydney: Federation of Australian Radio Broadcasters, 1979).

33. Donna Petrozzello, "Alternative Rock in the Mainstream," *Broadcasting & Cable* (May 20, 1996) pp. 51–52.

CHAPTER 9

1. The reference to "pictures in our heads" comes from a suggestion by Walter Lippman that a person learns to see with his or her mind "vast portions of the world that he could never see, touch, smell, hear, or remember. Gradually he makes for himself a trustworthy picture inside his head of the world beyond his reach." See Lippman, *Public Opinion* (New York: Harcourt, Brace and Company, 1922), p. 29.

2. Christopher H. Sterling and John M. Kittross, *Stay Tuned: A Concise History of American Broadcasting,* 2nd ed. (Belmont, CA: Wadsworth, 1990), p. 576.

3. Lynn Spigel, *Make Room for TV* (Chicago: University of Chicago Press, 1992).

4. For a discussion of the early debate over technical standards, see Sterling and Kittross, *Stay Tuned,* pp. 526–527.

5. Sterling and Kittross, *Stay Tuned,* pp. 265, 267.

6. *Broadcasting-Telecasting,* December 21, 1953, p. 29, cited in James Scofield O'Rourke IV, "The Development of Color Television: A Study in the Freemarket Process," *Journalism History* 9:3–4 (Autumn-Winter 1982): 78–85, 106.

7. For a thorough discussion of legal issues from 1945 to 1952, see Chapter 7, "Era of Great Change," in Sterling and Kittross, *Stay Tuned.*

8. James L. Baughman, *The Republic of Mass Culture: Journalism, Filmmaking, and Broadcasting in America since 1941* (Baltimore: Johns Hopkins University Press, 1992), p. 54.

9. Sterling and Kittross, *Stay Tuned,* p. 278.

10. Melvin Patrick Ely, *The Adventures of Amos 'n' Andy* (New York: The Free Press, 1991), pp. 1–10. The quote is cited in Ely from a resolution in Herbert L. Wright, letter to NAACP Youth Councils, College Chapters and State Youth Conferences, July 19, 1951, in National Association for the Advancement of Colored People Papers, II, A, 479, Manuscript Division, Library of Congress.

11. Stephen Fox, *The Mirror Makers* (New York: Random House, 1984), p. 212.

12. Walter Karp, "The Quiz-Show Scandal," *American Heritage* (May-June 1989): 77–88.

13. Fox, *The Mirror Makers,* p. 215.

14. Kristine Brunovska Kamick, "NBC and the Innovation of Television News, 1945–1953," *Journalism History* 15:1 (Spring 1988): 27.

15. Morrie Gelman, "75 Years of Pioneers," *Broadcasting & Cable* (November 6, 1995): 80. See also Sterling and Kittross, *Stay Tuned,* p. 110.

16. Michael D. Murray, "The End of an Era at CBS: A Conversation with Bill Leonard," *American Journalism* 8:1 (Winter 1991): 51.

17. Head and Sterling, *Broadcasting in America,* p. 321.

18. For transition in television, see Robert J. Donovan and Ray Scherer, *Unsilent Revolution: Television News and American Public Life* (Cambridge: Woodrow Wilson International Center for Scholars and Cambridge University Press, 1992). See also Todd Gitlin, *Sixties: Years of Hope, Days of Rage* (New York: Bantam Books, 1987).

19. Agnew text, *New York Times,* November 14, 1969, p. 24, cited in Donovan and Scherer, *Unsilent Revolution,* pp. ix, x.

20. Edward A. Hinck, *Enacting the Presidency* (Westport, CT: Praeger, 1993), pp. 17–24.

21. Joe McGinnis, *The Selling of the President 1968* (New York: Trident Press, 1969).

22. Stuart Taylor, Jr., "Witch-Hunt or Whitewash?" *The American Lawyer* (April 1995): 60.

23. "Fox and Murdoch Win a Big One," *U.S. News & World Report* (May 15, 1995): 17+.

24. Head and Sterling, *Broadcasting in America,* pp. 82–85.

25. Rebecca Piirto, "New Markets for Cable TV," *American Demographics* (June 1995): 40.

26. Jeannine Aversa, "Networks Vie for a Home on Cable TV," *Lansing State Journal,* March 19, 1997, p. 5B.

27. "Ugly NYC Cable Feud Gets Uglier," *Media Daily,* October 7, 1996.

28. Stephanie McKinnon, "Looking Ahead for PBS," *Lansing State Journal,* January 19, 1995, pp. B1, B5.

29. The Opinion Research Corp. of Princeton, New Jersey, surveyed 1,005 adults from January 5 to 8, 1995. Reported by Stephanie McKinnon, "Study Supports Public TV's Role," *Lansing State Journal,* January 19, 1995, p. B5.

30. Piirto, "New Markets for Cable TV."

31. "People's Choice," *Broadcasting & Cable* (July 8, 1996): 26.

32. Steve McClellan, "Broadcasters Lash Out at Nielsen," *Broadcasting & Cable* (October 16, 1995): 18.

33. Steve McClellan, "Combined Nets Take Aim at Nielsen," *Broadcasting & Cable* (December 30, 1996): 17–18.

34. Veronis, Suhler & Associates, *Communications Industry Forecast,* 1995, pp. 76–77.

35. Herbert Howard et al., pp. 16–19.

36. William B. Johnson, "The Coming Glut of Phone Lines," *Fortune* (January 7, 1988): 96–97.

37. Steve McClellan, "Current Affair Overhauled," *Broadcasting & Cable* (June 19, 1995): 25–26.

38. New York Times News Service, "Poll Says Parents Tuning out TV Ratings," *Chicago Tribune,* February 23, 1997, p. 1:7.

39. Ted Kulfan, "Marlboro Is Ordered to Butt Out," *The Detroit News,* June 7, 1995, p. 1B.

40. Veronis, Suhler & Associates, *Forecast, 1995,* pp. 25–26.

41. Richard Christiansen, "Digital video discs message is loud and clear, but not without problems," *Chicago Tribune,* April 3, 1997, Sec. 2, pp. 1, 4.

CHAPTER 10

1. H. Wiley Hitchcock, *Music in the United States: A Historical Introduction,* 3rd ed. (Englewood Cliffs, NJ: Prentice-Hall, 1988), p. 96.

2. David Ewen, *Panorama of American Popular Music* (Englewood Cliffs, NJ: Prentice-Hall, 1957), p. 58.

3. Ewen, *Panorama of American Popular Music,* p. 145.

4. John Rublowsky, *Popular Music* (New York: Basic Books, 1967), pp. 63–80.

5. Hitchcock, *Music in the United States,* p. 141.

6. Ronald L. Davis, *A History of Music in American Life: The Gilded Years, 1865–1920,* Vol. 2 (Huntington, NY: Robert Krieger, 1980), p. 63.

534

7. Hitchcock, *Music in the United States,* p. 276.

8. Hitchcock, *Music in the United States,* pp. 276–277.

9. Bob Dylan, *The Bob Dylan Song Book* (New York: M. Whitmark & Sons), p. 118.

10. Eric Berman, "The Godfathers of Rap," *Rolling Stone* (December 23, 1993), pp. 137–142, 180.

11. Gale Research, Inc., "Paul Simon," *Newsmakers,* October 1992.

12. James Henke and Anthony DeCurtis, eds., *Rolling Stone History of Rock and Roll* (New York: Random House, 1992).

13. Hitchcock, *Music in the United States,* pp. 286–291.

14. John von Rhein, "It's not over, Beethoven," *Chicago Tribune* (January 10, 1997), Sec. 7, pp. 1–13.

15. von Rhein, "It's not over, Beethoven," *Chicago Tribune* (January 19, 1997), p. 14.

16. Veronis, Suhler & Associates *Communication Industry Forecast,* 7th ed. (New York: Veronis & Suhler & Associates, 1993), pp. 23–24.

17. Russell Sanjek, *From Print to Plastic: Publishing and Promoting America's Popular Music (1900–1980)* (New York: Brooklyn College of the City University of New York, 1983), p. 53.

18. Keith Negus, *Producing Pop: Culture and Conflict in the Popular Music Industry* (London: Edward Arnold, 1992), p. 1.

19. William Moylan, *The Art of Recording* (New York: Van Nostrand Reinhold, 1992), pp. 136–139.

20. Sanjek, *From Print to Plastic,* p. 54.

21. Negus, *Producing Pop,* p. 13.

22. "Rock and Roll Forever," *Newsweek* (July 5, 1994): 48.

23. Glen Dickson, "Smart Radio Targets PC Users," *Broadcasting & Cable* (November 27, 1995): 98.

24. Sanjek, *From Print to Plastic,* p. 52.

25. Kerry Segrave, *Payola in the Music Business: A History from 1880–1991* (Jefferson, NC: McFarland, 1994), pp. 92–93.

26. Fredric Dannen, *Hit Men: Power Brokers and Fast Money inside the Music Business* (New York: Times Books, 1990).

CHAPTER 11

1. Milt Rockmore, "Newspapers: Are They Bull or Bear," *Editor & Publisher* (July 15, 1995):12–13.

2. Vannevar Bush, "As We May Think," *Atlantic Monthly* (July 1945), via *America Online.*

3. Larry Press, "Before the Altair: The History of Personal Computing," *Communications of the ACM* (September 1993):27+, via Lexis-Nexis.

4. Press, "Before the Altair." See also D. C. Engelbart and W. K. English, "A Research Center for Augmenting Human Intellect," *Proceedings of the 1968 Fall Joint Computer Conference* (Washington, DC: Thompson Book Co.), pp. 395–410.

5. Eugene Marlow, "The Electrovisual Manager: Media and American Corporate Management," *Business Horizons* (March 1994):61+, via Lexis-Nexis.

6. James Flanigan, "Look to Thomas Watson's Past for IBM's Future," *Los Angeles Times,* January 5, 1994, p. D1, via Lexis-Nexis.

7. Cited in Denise W. Gurer, "Pioneering Women in Computer Science," *Communications of the Association for Computing Machinery* (January 1995): 58.

8. Gurer, "Pioneering Women," p. 50.

9. Michael Swaine, "The Programmer Paradigm," *Dr. Dobbs' Journal of Software Tools,* p. 109+, via Lexis-Nexis.

10. Brent Schlender, "What Bill Gates Really Wants," *Fortune* (January 16, 1995):34+, via Lexis-Nexis.

11. Schlender, "What Bill Gates Really Wants."

12. Evan Ramstad, "Computing PC's Future," *Lansing State Journal,* September 26, 1996, p. D1.

13. For a full discussion of the network, see "What Is the Internet?" in Ed Krol, *The Whole Internet User's Guide and Catalog* (Sebastopol, CA: O'Reilly & Associates, 1992).

14. *Gale Directory of Databases,* Vol. 1: *Online Databases* (Detroit: Gale Research, 1994), p. x.

15. P. J. Tichenor, G. A. Donohue, and C. N. Olien, "Mass Media and Differential Growth in Knowledge," *Public Opinion Quarterly* 34 (1970):159–170.

16. Much of this section is from Lucinda D. Davenport, "The First Amendment Won't Save a Widening Knowledge Gap." Paper presented to AEJMC National Convention, Boston, August 8, 1991.

17. Werner J. Severin and James W. Tankard, Jr., *Communication Theories: Origins, Methods, and Uses in the Mass Media,* 3rd ed. (NY: Longman, 1992), pp. 232–242.

18. Jack Kitchner, "When No News Is Good News," *PC Magazine* (March 25, 1997):30.

19. Arbitron's *Pathways* study, 1995.

20. "Poll: More People Access Internet Through IPSs Than Online Services," *Media Daily* (September 24, 1996) [www.mediacentral.com/magazines/mediadaily].

21. Victoria Shannon, "Inquiring Minds Want to Know the Secrets of Your On-Line Life," *Washington Post,* December 4, 1995, p. F20. This story relied on studies by the Times Mirror Center for the People and the Press, Nielsen Reports, and Odyssey Research for Compuserve. This story was accessed online.

22. Walter Brooks, "U.S. Population of Online Adults Up 34%," *Editor & Publisher Interactive* (February 21, 1997) [http://www.mediainfo.com].

23. "Journalists Go Online to Get the Job Done," *Media Daily* (February 27, 1991) [www.mediacentral.com/magazines/mediadaily].

24. More listings of CD-ROMs and their holdings can be found in *CD-ROM Handbook,* 8th ed. (Peabody, MA: EBSCO Publishing, 1993).

25. Bob Kemper, "GI's Bosnia Weapons Seem Like a 'Star Wars' Takeoff," *Chicago Tribune,* December 13, 1995, p. 1.

26. Bill Gates, *The Road Ahead* (New York: Viking, 1995), p. 130.

27. David Astor, "Electronic Delivery of Comics Coming," *Editor & Publisher* (October 16, 1993):36–37.

28. Allen Weiner, "Newspapers Eye Fax as New Profit Center," *Interactive World* (February 1993):19–22.

29. James Fallows, "Tantalizing as the Internet May Seem, for Now the Practical Frustrations Outweigh the Cosmopolitan Rewards," *Atlantic Monthly,* via America On-Line.

30. In M. L. Stein, "Audiotex Success at Newspapers," *Editor & Publisher* (February 20, 1993):11, 44.

31. "Serving the Community: A Public-Interest Vision of the National Information Infrastructure," a paper written by Computer Professionals for Social Responsibility, Palo Alto, CA, 1994.

32. "Serving the Community."

33. Scott Shepard, "Information Superhighway Needs Design and Rules of the Highway," Cox News Service, July 4, 1993.

34. Mark Fitzgerald, "Still a Mystery to Most," *Editor & Publisher* (November 19, 1994):9. The survey was commissioned by the Audit Bureau of Circulations and conducted by the Charleston, S.C.–based America's Research Group. This was a national survey of 2,000 adults.

35. "Serving the Community."

36. Elizabeth Weise, "Bold Internet Plan in Works," *Lansing State Journal,* March 17, 1997, p. B-5.

37. Joseph Kahn, Kathy Chen, and Marcus W. Brauchli, "Beijing Seeks to Build Version of the Internet That Can Be Censored," *The Wall Street Journal,* January 31, 1996, p. A-1.

38. For more information dealing with electronic privacy and copyright, see Beth Haller, "Quoting in Cyberspace: Privacy and Copyright Issues in Journalistic Use of Computer Networks." Paper presented to the Communications Technology and Policy Division, Association for Education in Journalism and Mass Communication, National Convention, August 1994.

CHAPTER 12

1. Karen Miller, "Smoking Up a Storm: Public Relations and Advertising in the Construction of the Cigarette Problem, 1953–1954," *Journalism Monographs,* No. 136, December 1992.

2. Harold L. Nelson and Dwight L. Teeter, Jr., *Law of Mass Communications: Freedom and Control of Print and Broadcast Media,* 4th ed. (Mineola, NY: Foundation Press, 1982), pp. 189–190.

3. Harold L. Nelson and Dwight L. Teeter, *Law of Mass Communications: Freedom and Control of Print and Broadcast Media,* 2nd ed. (Mineola, NY: Foundation Press, 1973), pp. 26–27.

4. William Boot, "The Pool," *Columbia Journalism Review* (May–June 1991): 24–27; Chris Hedges, "The Unilater-

als," *Columbia Journalism Review* (May–June 1991): 27–28.

5. Bruce M. Owen, *Economics and Freedom of Expression* (Cambridge, MA: Ballinger, 1975); Stephen Lacy and Todd F. Simon, *The Economics and Regulation of United States Newspapers* (Norwood, NJ: Ablex, 1993).

6. James W. Tankard, Jr. and Kate Pierce, "Alcohol Advertising and Magazine Editorial Content," *Journalism Quarterly* 59 (Summer 1982): 302–305.

7. Lauren Kessler, "Women's Magazines' Coverage of Smoking Related Health Hazards," *Journalism Quarterly* 66 (Summer 1989): 316–322, 445.

8. Donna Petrozzello and Elizabeth Rathbun, "Radio's Mega-Week," *Broadcasting & Cable* (March 11, 1996): 5–6.

9. Elizabeth A. Rathbun, "Clear Channel Tops 100," *Broadcasting & Cable* (June 10, 1996): 27.

10. Jim McConville, "TCI Boosts Rates 15%–20%," *Broadcasting & Cable* (March 11, 1996): 12–13.

11. Alicia C. Shepard, "High Anxiety," *American Journalism Review* (November 1993): 20.

12. Ted Pease, "Race, Gender and Job Satisfaction in Newspaper Newsrooms," in *Readings in Media Management,* Stephen Lacy, Ardyth B. Sohn, and Robert H. Giles, ed. (Columbia, SC: Association for Education in Journalism and Mass Communication, 1992), pp. 97–122.

13. Bob Worthington, "Personnel Management Concerns for Media Managers," in *Readings in Media Management,* Stephen Lacy, Ardyth B. Sohn, and Robert H. Giles, ed. (Columbia, SC: Association for Education in Journalism and Mass Communication, 1992), pp. 201–217.

14. *Near* v. *Minnesota,* 283 U.S. 697, 51 S.CT. 625, 75 L.ED. 1357 (1931).

15. Jean Folkerts and Dwight L. Teeter, Jr., *Voices of a Nation: A History of Media in the United States,* 2nd ed. (New York: Macmillan, 1994), p. 319.

16. Donald M. Gillmor, Jerome A. Barron, Todd F. Simon, and Herbert A. Terry, *Mass Communication Law: Cases and Comment,* 5th ed. (St. Paul, MN: West Publishing, 1990), p. 172.

17. Gillmore et al., *Mass Communication Law,* p. 173.

18. *Cherry* v. *Des Moines Leader,* 86 N.W. 323 (Iowa 1910).

19. Martin L. Gibson, *Editing in the Electronic Era,* 2nd ed. (Ames, IA: Iowa State University Press, 1984), p. 225.

20. *Virginia State Board of Pharmacy* v. *Virginia Citizens Consumer Council, Inc.,* 425 U.S. 748, 96 S.CT. 1817, 48 L.ED.2D. 346 (1976).

21. Nelson and Teeter, *Law of Mass Communications,* 2nd ed., p. 517.

22. Alfred McClung Lee, *The Daily Newspaper in America* (New York: Macmillan, 1937), pp. 314–316.

23. Gillmor, Barron, Simon, and Terry, *Mass Communication Law: Cases and Comment,* pp. 525–526.

24. Debra Gersh Hernandez, "A Wave of Protests," *Editor & Publisher* (February 17, 1996): 15.

25. Debra Gersh Hernandez, "Unconstitutionally Vague," *Editor & Publisher* (February 24, 1996): 38.

26. "Top Five Reasons Broadcasters Say They Don't Like the V-Chip," *Broadcasting & Cable* (February 12, 1996): 21.

27. Michael Katz, "Pay Cable Tops Violence Ranking," *Broadcasting & Cable* (February 12, 1996): 22.

28. Kent R. Middleton and Bill F. Chamberlin, *The Law of Public Communication,* 3rd ed. (New York: Longman, 1994), p. 128.

29. Donald M. Gillmor, Jerome A. Barron, Todd F. Simon, and Herbert A. Terry, *Fundamentals of Mass Communication Law* (Minneapolis/St. Paul, MN: West Publishing, 1996), p. 121.

30. Lawrence K. Grossman, "CBS, 60 Minutes and the Unseen Interview," *Columbia Journalism Review* (January–February 1996): 39–51; Alicia C. Shepard, "Fighting Back," *American Journalism Review* (January–February 1996): 34–39.

CHAPTER 13

1. Leroy Towns, "NBC on Fire." Unpublished paper submitted as partial completion for degree requirements in the Graduate School of Political Management, George Washington University, Washington, DC, 1995; Benjamin Weiser, "Does TV News Go Too Far?" *The Washington Post,* February 28, 1993, p. A1; Walter Goodman, "Critics Notebook," *The New York Times,* February 11, 1993 p. C30; Elizabeth Jensen, Douglas Lavin, and Neal Templin, "How GM One-Upped an Embarrassed NBC on Staged News Event," *Wall Street Journal,* February 11, 1993.

2. Hazel Dicken-Garcia, *Journalistic Standards in Nineteenth-Century America* (Madison: University of Wisconsin Press, 1989), p. 229.

3. See Jean Folkerts's review of Hazel Dicken-Garcia, *Journalistic Standards in Nineteenth-Century America* (Madison: University of Wisconsin Press, 1989). Dicken-Garcia's book outlines the development of ethics within the context of the press as a social institution.

4. Marion Marzolf, *Civilizing Voices: American Press Criticism, 1880–1950* (New York: Longman, 1991), pp. 16–17.

5. Marzolf, *Civilizing Voices,* p. 106.

6. Fred S. Siebert, Theodore Peterson, and Wilbur Schramm, *Four Theories of the Press* (Urbana: University of Illinois Press, 1956), p. 77.

7. Commission on Freedom of the Press, *A Free and Responsible Press* (Chicago: University of Chicago Press, 1947).

8. Siebert, Peterson, and Schramm, *Four Theories of the Press,* pp. 74–78.

9. John C. Merrill and S. Jack Odell, *Philosophy and Journalism* (New York: Longman, 1983), pp. 162–163.

10. Clifford G. Christians, Kim B. Rotzoll, and Mark Fackler, *Media Ethics,* 2nd ed. (New York: Longman, 1987), pp. 9–17.

11. W. Dale Nelson, "Competition Casualty," *Quill* (May 1993): 38.

12. Alexandra Marks, "News Media Credibility Problem Goes Beyond Charges of Political Bias," *The Christian Science Monitor* (June 27, 1987):1.

13. "Media Credibility Sinking," *Editor & Publisher* (October 26, 1996):19.

14. This case study was provided by Leroy Towns, "Science and Fear: The Apple Industry and the Alar Crisis of 1989." Unpublished paper, 1995. For Fenton quote, see "Alar's Real Victims," *Washington Times,* February 26, 1990.

15. "Take 2," *American Journalism Review* (January–February 1996): 15.

16. "Take 2," p. 15.

17. Benjamin Weiser, "ABC and Tobacco: The Anatomy of a Network News Mistake," *The Washington Post,* January 7, 1996, pp. A1, 16–18.

18. Jane Pauley, "Defending *Dateline,*" *Quill* (November–December 1994): 63–69.

19. Arthur E. Rowse, "How to Build Support for War," *Columbia Journalism Review* (September–October 1992): 28–29; see also Alicia Mundy, "Is the Press Any Match for Powerhouse PR," *Columbia Journalism Review* (September–October 1992): 27–34.

20. James Warren, "Paths of Janet Cooke and Marion Barry Cross," *Chicago Tribune,* July 4, 1996, *Perspectives,* p. 2.

21. *Columbia Journalism Review* (January–February 1996): 19.

22. Lucinda D. Davenport and Ralph S. Izard, "Restrictive Policies of the Mass Media," *Journal of Mass Media Ethics* 1:1 (Fall–Winter 1985–1986): 4–9.

23. Updated versions of these and other industry codes can be found in Conrad C. Fink, *Media Ethics* (Needham Heights, MA: Allyn & Bacon, 1995), or upon request from the organizations themselves.

24. M. L. Stein, "Revive the News Council," *Editor & Publisher* (March 29, 1997): 8–9.

25. Alicia C. Shepard, "Going Public," *AJR NewsLink* (April 8, 1997, www.ajr.org.).

26. Sissela Bok, *Lying: Moral Choice in Public and Private Life* (New York: Random House, 1989), pp. 111–112.

27. Jay Black and Deni Elliott, "Justification Models for Journalists Facing Ethical Dilemmas." Unpublished materials presented at a teaching ethics seminar by Jay Black, Philip Patterson, and Lee Wilkins, AEJMC annual meeting, Kansas City, MO, 1993.

28. Eugene Goodwin, *Groping for Ethics in Journalism,* 2nd ed. (Ames: Iowa State University Press, 1987), pp. 24–25. For additional suggestions on what an ethical journalist should do in various situations, refer to the last sections in each chapter in Gene Goodwin and Ron F. Smith, *Groping for Ethics in Journalism,* 3rd ed. (Ames: Iowa State University Press, 1994).

29. Clifford G. Christians, Mark Fackler, and Kim B. Rotzoll, *Media Ethics: Cases and Moral Reasoning,* 4th ed. (White Plains, NY: Longman, 1995), pp. 3–10.

30. The Potter Box has been adapted and edited many times since Ralph Potter presented it in his 1965 dissertation. This version appears in Black and Elliott, "Justification Models for Journalists Facing Ethical Dilemmas."

31. "Darts and Laurels," *Columbia Journalism Review* (May–June 1994): 24.

32. Elizabeth Lesly, "Realtors and Builders Demand Happy News . . . and Often Get It," *Washington Journalism Review* (November 1991): 21.

33. Jan Ferris, "Butt Out: Publishers and Their Habits," *Columbia Journalism Review* (January–February 1994): 17.

34. "Darts and Laurels," *Columbia Journalism Review* (January–February 1993): 24.

35. "Darts and Laurels," *Columbia Journalism Review* (November–December 1986): 24.

36. For 1977, Hugh M. Culbertson, "Veiled Attribution—An Element of Style," *Journalism Quarterly,* 55 (Autumn 1978): 456; for 1985, K. Tim Wulfemeyer, "How and Why Anonymous Attribution Is Used by *Time* and *Newsweek,*" *Journalism Quarterly,* 62 (Spring 1985): 81–86, 126.

37. Mike Meeske and Fred Fedler, "Checkbook Journalism in the Electronic Media: Alive and Flourishing." Paper presented to the Radio-Television Division at the Association for Education in Journalism and Mass Communication annual meeting, Kansas City, MO, August 11–14, 1993.

38. See, for example, articles by Fox Butterfield, "Increasing Questions Impede Case of Kennedy Nephew," *New York Times,* April 15, 1991, p. A11; Roberto Suro, "Police Strategy in Kennedy Inquiry May Make It Harder to Win Justice," *New York Times,* April 18, 1991, p. A22; and Fox Butterfield, "Woman in Florida Rape Inquiry Fought Adversity and Sought Acceptance," *New York Times,* April 17, 1991, p. A17.

39. "Naming Victims," *Quill* (June 1995): 19.

40. Fred Fedler, *Reporting for the Print Media,* 5th ed. (Fort Worth, TX: Harcourt Brace Jovanovich, 1993), p. 477.

41. For more on photographs, see Richard Cunningham, "Photographs (Again) Worth Several Words as Readers Complain," *Quill* (June 1995): 16–17.

42. Lucinda D. Davenport, "News Quotes: Verbatim?" Paper presented to Association for Education in Journalism and Mass Communication, annual meeting, Portland, OR, 1988.

43. Tamar Vital, "Who Killed JFK?" *The Jerusalem Post,* January 31, 1992, Arts Section, p. 1.

CHAPTER 14

1. The discussion of the Coca-Cola centennial is based on Carlton L. Curtis, "Special Events: How They're Planned and Organized," in *Experts in Action: Inside Public Relations,* Bill Cantor and Chester Burger, eds., 2nd ed. (New York: Longman), pp. 246–257. Mr. Curtis was vice president of corporate communications when the Coca-Cola centennial took place.

2. This is a modified version of the definition from the United Kingdom Institute of Public Relations; see David W. Wragg, *The Public Relations Handbook* (Oxford, England: Blackwell Publishers, 1992), p. 3.

3. James E. Grunig and Todd Hunt, *Managing Public Relations* (New York: Holt, Rinehart and Winston, 1984), p. 8.

4. Scott Cutlip, "Public Relations and the American Revolution," *Public Relations Review* 2 (Winter 1976): 11–24.

5. David A. Haberman and Harry A. Dolphin, *Public Relations: The Necessary Art* (Ames, IA: Iowa State University Press, 1988), pp. 14–15.

6. Neil Harris, *Humbug: The Art of P. T. Barnum* (Boston: Little, Brown, 1973), pp. 21–25.

7. Marvin N. Olasky, "The Development of Corporate Public Relations," *Journalism Monographs,* No. 102 (April 1987): 2–15.

8. Ray Eldon Hiebert, *Courtier to the Crowd: The Story of Ivy Lee and the Development of Public Relations* (Ames, IA: Iowa State University Press), pp. 99–100.

9. Hiebert, *Courtier to the Crowd,* pp. 298–299.

10. Edward L. Bernays, *Biography of an Idea: Memoirs of Public Relations Counsel Edward L. Bernays* (New York: Simon and Schuster, 1965), pp. 291–292.

11. Edward L. Bernays, *Crystallizing Public Opinion* (New York: Boni and Liveright, 1923), p. 215.

12. William V. Ruch, *Corporate Communications: A Comparison of Japanese and American Practices* (Westport, CT: Quorum Books, 1984), p. 107.

13. Chester Barnard, *Functions of the Executive* (Cambridge, MA: Harvard University Press, 1938).

14. Jane Whitney Gibson and Richard M. Hodgetts, *Organizational Communication: A Managerial Perspective* (New York: HarperCollins, 1991), pp. 219–220.

15. Haberman and Dolphin, *Public Relations: The Necessary Art,* pp. 19–20.

16. Lee W. Baker, *The Credibility Factor: Putting Ethics to Work in Public Relations* (Homewood, IL: Business One Irwin, 1993), pp. 54–59.

17. Baker, *The Credibility Factor,* pp. 34–38.

18. Lee B. Becker and Gerald M. Kosicki, "Undergrad Enrollment Decline; Programs Feel Budget Squeeze," *Journalism Educator* 50(3) (1995): 66.

19. Andrew Schneider, "The Downside of Wonderland," *Columbia Journalism Review* (March/April 1993): 55–56.

20. Edward Bernays, "The Theory and Practice of Public Relations: A Resume," in Edward Bernays, ed., *The Engineering of Consent* (Norman, OK: University of Oklahoma Press, 1955), pp. 9–10.

21. Wragg, *The Public Relations Handbook,* pp. 87–89.

22. Baker, *The Credibility Factor,* pp. 45–53.

538

23. Bruce Porter, "The Scanlon Spin," *Columbia Journalism Review* (September–October 1989): 49–54.

24. Porter, "The Scanlon Spin," p. 50.

25. Randy Sumpter and James W. Tankard, Jr., "The Spin Doctor: An Alternative Model for Public Relations," *Public Relation Review,* 20(1) (1994): 19–27.

26. Gibson and Hodgetts, *Organizational Communication,* pp. 212–230.

27. Daniel Katz and Robert Kahn, *The Social Psychology of Organizations* (New York: John Wiley & Sons, 1966), p. 239.

28. Gibson and Hodgetts, *Organizational Communication,* pp. 219–220.

29. Jodi B. Katzman, "What's the Role of Public Relations?," *Public Relations Journal* (April 1993): 11.

30. Baker, *The Credibility Factor,* pp. 19–30.

31. Joanne Lipman, "PR Society Receives Some Very Bad PR—From Its Ex-Chief," *The Wall Street Journal,* September 26, 1986, p. 1.

32. Eugenia Zerbinos and Gail Alice Clanton, "Minority Practitioners: Career Influences, Job Satisfaction, and Discrimination," *Public Relations Review,* 19(1) (1991): 75–91.

33. David Weaver and G. Cleveland Wilhoit, *The American Journalists in the 1990s* (Arlington, VA: The Freedom Forum, November 1992).

34. Zerbinos and Clanton, "Minority Practitioners," p. 85.

35. Nicholas J. Totorello and Elizabeth Wilhelm, "Salary Survey," *Public Relations Journal* (July 1993): 10–19.

36. David Angell and Brent Heslop, *The Internet Business Companion: Growing Your Business in the Electronic Age* (Reading, MA: Addison-Wesley, 1995).

37. "Media Notes: Survey Finds Journalists' Cyberspace Use on Rise," Cowles/SIMBA Media Daily, *http://www.iworld.com,* January 29, 1996.

38. Carole Howard and Wilma Mathews, *On Deadline: Managing Media Relations* (Prospect Heights, IL: Waveland Press, 1988), p. 191.

39. David Weaver, Klaus Schoenbach, and Beate Schneider, "West German and U.S. Journalists: Similarities and Differences in the 1990s." Paper presented to the Association for Education in Journalism and Mass Communication, Kansas City, August 1993.

40. Baker, *The Credibility Factor,* pp. 78–88.

CHAPTER 15

1. Newspaper Association of America, *Facts About Newspapers,*1996, www.naa.org/info/Facts/facts0.html

2. Philippe Schuwer, *History of Advertising* (London: Leisure Arts Ltd., 1966), pp. 9–10.

3. Blanche Elliot, *A History of English Advertising* (London: Business Publications Ltd., 1962), pp. 20–21.

4. Frank Presbrey, *The History and Development of Advertising* (Garden City, NY: Doubleday, Doran & Co., 1929), p. 161.

5. Presbrey, *The History and Development of Advertising,* p. 160.

6. Presbrey, *The History and Development of Advertising,* pp. 180–181.

7. Presbrey, *The History and Development of Advertising,* p. 201.

8. James Playsted Wood, *The Story of Advertising* (New York: The Ronald Press Co., 1958), p. 200.

9. Wood, *The Story of Advertising,* p. 327.

10. G. Allen Foster, *Advertising: Ancient Market Place to Television* (New York: Criterion Books, 1967), pp. 120–121.

11. Foster, *Advertising: Ancient Market Place to Television,* pp. 156–157.

12. Presbrey, *The History and Development of Advertising,* p. 579.

13. Lawrence W. Lichty and Malachi C. Topping, *American Broadcasting: A Source Book on the History of Radio and Television* (New York: Hastings House, 1975), p. 522.

14. e-service Business Publications, www.e-land-com/e-stat_pages/ad_rev_today.html.

15. "Darts and Laurels," *Columbia Journalism Review* (March–April 1995): 22.

16. Walter Brooks, "Press Briefs," www.mediainfo.com/ephome/news/newshtm/nuggets/briefs.htm. May 2, 1997.

17. J. Paul Peter and Jerry C. Olson, *Consumer Behavior in Marketing Strategy,* 3rd ed. (Homewood, IL: Irwin, 1993), pp. 266–286.

18. Michael Shudson, *Advertising, The Uneasy Persuasion: Its Dubious Impact on American Society* (New York: Basic Books, 1984).

19. Leo Bogart, *Press and Public* (Hillsdale, NJ: Lawrence Erlbaum Associates, 1989), p. 166.

20. Stephen Lacy and Todd F. Simon, *The Economics and Regulation of United States Newspapers* (Norwood, NJ: Ablex, 1993), pp. 41–42.

21. David W. Nylen, *Advertising: Planning, Implementation & Control,* 4th ed. (Cincinnati, OH: South-Western Publishing, 1993), p. 238.

22. Michael L. Rothschild, *Advertising: From Fundamentals to Strategies* (Lexington, MA: D. C. Heath and Co., 1987), p. 729.

23. Nylen, *Advertising: Planning, Implementation & Control,* pp. 72–74.

24. Joe McGinniss, *The Selling of the President, 1968* (New York: Trident Press, 1969).

25. Ralph L. Lowenstein and John C. Merrill, *Macromedia: Mission, Message and Morality* (New York: Longman, 1990), p. 80.

26. Rothschild, *Advertising: From Fundamentals to Strategies,* p. 755.

27. Mark Crispin Miller, "Political Ads: Decoding Hidden Messages, *Columbia Journalism Review* (January–February 1992): 36–39.

28. Bob Woods, "Newsbytes," March 25, 1997, Lexis-Nexis.

29. Steve Outing, "At Last, Some Ad Banner Size Guidance," E & P Interactive, www.mediainfo.com/ephome/news/newshtml/stop/st 121397.

30. Mark Fitzgerald, "Advertising on the Internet," *Editor & Publisher* (March 4, 1995): 31

31. Eric N. Berkowitz, Roger A. Kerin, and William Rudelius, *Marketing,* 2nd ed. (Homewood, IL: Irwin, 1989), pp. 579–580.

CHAPTER 16

1. See Melvin L. DeFleur and Sandra Ball-Rokeach, *Theories of Mass Communication,* 5th ed. (New York: Longman, 1989), pp. 29–43.

2. Robert K. Avery and David Eason, *Critical Perspectives on Media and Society* (New York: The Guilford Press, 1991), pp. 3–6.

3. Pamela J. Shoemaker and Stephen D. Reese, *Mediating the Message,* 2nd ed. (New York: Longman, 1996).

4. Earl Babbie, *The Practice of Social Research,* 6th ed. (Belmont, CA: Wadsworth, 1992), pp. 27–48; and Paul Davidson Reynolds, *A Primer in Theory Construction* (Indianapolis, IN: ITT Bobbs-Merrill Educational Publishing, 1971), pp. 3–11.

5. Norman K. Denzin, "The Logic of Naturalistic Inquiry," *Social Forces* 50 (December 1971): 166–182.

6. George Gerbner and L. P. Gross, "The Scary World of TV's Heavy Viewer," *Psychology Today* (April 1976): 41–45, 89; and Werner J. Severin and James W. Tankard, Jr., *Communication Theories: Origins, Methods, and Uses in the Mass Media,* 3rd ed. (New York: Longman, 1992), pp. 249–250.

7. Shoemaker and Reese, *Mediating the Message,* pp. 1–8.

8. James Curran, Michael Gurevitch, and Janet Woollacott, eds., "The Study of the Media: Theoretical Approaches," in Michael Gurevitch, Tony Bennett, James Curran, and Janet Woollacott, eds., *Culture, Society and the Media* (London: Methuen, 1982), pp. 11–29.

9. Tony Bennett, "Theories of the Media, Theories of Society," in Gurevitch et al., eds., *Culture, Society and the Media,* pp. 30–55.

10. Harold D. Lasswell, *Propaganda Technique in the World War* (New York: Peter Smith, 1927).

11. Shearon A. Lowery and Melvin L. DeFleur, *Milestones in Mass Communication Research: Media Effects,* 5th ed. (New York: Longman, 1989), pp. 31–54.

12. Carl I. Hovland, Arthur A. Lumsdaine, and Fred D. Sheffield, *Experiments on Mass Communication* (Princeton, NJ: Princeton University Press, 1949).

13. Paul F. Lazarsfeld, Bernard Berelson, and Hazel Gaudet, *The People's Choice* (New York: Columbia University Press, 1948).

14. Bernard Berelson, Paul F. Lazarsfeld, and William McPhee, *Voting: A Study of Opinion Formation in a Presidential Campaign* (Chicago: University of Chicago Press, 1954).

15. David Manning White, "The 'Gatekeeper': A Study in the Selection of News," *Journalism Quarterly* 27 (Winter 1950): 383–390.

16. D. Charles Whitney and Lee B. Becker, "'Keeping the Gates' for Gatekeepers: The Effects of Wire News," *Journalism Quarterly* 59 (Spring 1982): 60–65.

17. Dan Berkowitz, "Refining the Gatekeeping Metaphor for Local Television News," *Journal of Broadcasting & Electronic Media* 34 (1990): 55–68; and John H. McManus, *Market-Driven Journalism: Let the Citizen Beware?* (Thousand Oaks, CA: Sage, 1994).

18. Warren Breed, "Social Control in the Newsroom: A Functional Analysis," *Social Forces* 33 (May 1955): 326–335.

19. Walter Gieber and Walter Johnson, "The City Hall 'Beat': A Study of Reporter and Source Roles," *Journalism Quarterly* 38 (Summer 1961): 289–297.

20. *Democracy and Education* (New York: Macmillan, 1915), p. 4, cited in Daniel Czitrom, *Media and the American Mind* (Chapel Hill: University of North Carolina, 1982).

21. Werner J. Severin and James W. Tankard, Jr., *Communication Theories: Origins, Methods and Uses in the Mass Media,* 3rd ed. (New York: Longman, 1992), p. 260.

22. National Institute of Mental Health, *Television and Behavior: Ten Years of Scientific Progress and Implications for the Eighties* (Rockville, MD: National Institute of Mental Health, 1982).

23. Philip J. Tichenor, George A. Donohue, and Clarice N. Olien, "Mass Media Flow and Differential Growth in Knowledge," *Public Opinion Quarterly* 34 (1970): 159–170.

24. Severin and Tankard, *Communication Theories,* pp. 230–246.

25. Gaye Tuchman, *Making News: A Study in the Construction of Reality* (New York: The Free Press, 1978).

26. Maxwell E. McCombs and Donald L. Shaw, "The Agenda Setting Function of Mass Media," *Public Opinion Quarterly* 36 (1972): 176–187.

27. Wayne Wanta and Yi-Chen Wu, "Interpersonal Communication and the Agenda-Setting Process," *Journalism Quarterly* 69 (Winter 1992): 847–855.

28. David H. Weaver, Jian-Hua Zhu, and Lars Wilhoit, "The Bridging Function of Interpersonal Communication in Agenda Setting," *Journalism Quarterly* 69 (Winter 1992): 856–867.

29. Elisabeth Noelle-Neumann, "Return to the Concept of Powerful Mass Media," in H. Eguchi and K. Sata, eds., *Studies of Broadcasting: An International Annual of Broadcasting Science* (Tokyo: Nippon Hoso Kyokai, 1973), pp. 67–112.

30. Dominic L. Lasorsa, "Political Outspokenness: Factors Working against the Spiral of Silence," *Journalism Quarterly* 68 (Spring–Summer 1991): 131–140.

540

31. W. James Potter, "Cultivation Theory and Research," *Journalism Monographs,* No. 147, October 1994.

32. Sandra J. Ball-Rokeach and Melvin L. DeFleur, "A Dependency Model of Mass Media Effects," *Communication Research* 3 (1976): 3–21.

33. Severin and Tankard, *Communication Theories,* pp. 247–268.

34. Doug Meligren, "Norway TV Pulls Shows over Deaths," *Lansing State Journal,* October 16, 1994, p. 3A.

35. James Carey, *Communication as Culture: Essays on Media and Society* (Boston: Unwin- Hyman, 1989), Chap. 1.

36. Peter Golding and Graham Murdock, "Culture, Communications, and Political Economy," in James Curran and Michael Gurevitch, eds., *Mass Media and Society* (London: Edward Arnold, 1991), pp. 15–32.

37. Dennis McQuail, J. G. Blumler, and J. R. Brown, "The Television Audience: A Revised Perspective," in D. McQuail, ed., *Sociology of Mass Communications* (Harmondsworth, England: Penguin, 1972).

38. Stephen Lacy and Todd F. Simon, *The Economics and Regulation of United States Newspapers* (Norwood, NJ: Ablex, 1993), p. 28.

39. Severin and Tankard, *Communication Theories,* pp. 274–276.

40. J. Farley, "Women's Magazines and the Equal Rights Amendment: Friend or Foe?," *Journal of Communication* 28 (1978): 187–192.

41. Tuchman, *Making News.*

42. Kay Robinson, "Women Newspaper Managers and Coverage of Women." Unpublished master's thesis, Michigan State University, 1991.

43. David H. Weaver and G. Cleveland Wilhoit, *The American Journalist* (Bloomington, IN: University of Indiana Press, 1986), pp. 115–120.

44. H. Allen White and Michael W. Singletary, "Internal Work Motivation: Predictor of Using Ethical Heuristics and Motivations," *Journalism Quarterly* 70 (1993): 381–392.

45. Shoemaker and Reese, *Mediating the Message,* pp. 53–81.

46. Mark Fishman, *Manufacturing the News* (Austin: University of Texas Press, 1980).

47. Dan Drew, "Roles and Decisions of Three Television Beat Reporters," *Journal of Broadcasting* 16 (1972): 165–173.

48. Stephen Lacy and David Matustik, "Dependence on Organization and Beat Sources for Story Ideas: A Case Study of Four Newspapers," *Newspaper Research Journal* 5 (Winter 1983): 9–16.

49. Ben Bagdikian, *The Media Monopoly,* 4th ed. (Boston: Beacon Press, 1992).

50. Lacy and Simon, *The Economics and Regulation of United States Newspapers,* pp. 131–157.

51. John C. Busterna, "Television Station Ownership Effects on Programming and Idea Diversity: Baseline Data," *Journal of Media Economics* 1 (Fall 1988): 63–73; and Stephen Lacy and Daniel Riffe, "The Impact of Competition and Group Ownership on All-News Radio," *Journalism Quarterly* 71 (1994): 583–593.

52. William B. Blankenburg and Gary W. Ozanich, "The Effects of Public Ownership on the Financial Performance of Newspaper Corporations," *Journalism Quarterly* 70 (Spring 1993): 68–75.

53. Guido H. Stempel, III, "Effects on Performance of Cross-Media Monopoly," *Journalism Monographs,* No. 29, June 1973; and William T. Gromley, *The Effects of Newspaper-Television Cross-Ownership on News Homogeneity* (Chapel Hill: University of North Carolina Press, 1976).

54. Barry R. Litman and Janet Bridges, "An Economic Analysis of Daily Newspaper Performance," *Newspaper Research Journal* (Spring 1986): 9–26.

Index